Lewis and Stempel's Ultimate TV Guide

Lewis and Stempel's **Ultimate TV Guide**

Jon E. Lewis and
Penny Stempel

First published in 1999 by Orion Media
An imprint of Orion Books Ltd
Orion House, 5 Upper St Martin's Lane, London
WC2H 9EA

All illustrations in this book reproduced courtesy of Scope Features.

A CIP catalogue for this book is available from the British Library.

ISBN 0-75281-805-8

Printed in Great Britain by
Butler & Tanner Ltd, Frome

Contents

Introduction

It's a TV jungle out there. Five terrestrial channels, twenty on satellite/cable, more if you have the technology. A thousand programmes a day.

What you need is a guide through the tangling, forbidding forest of multi-channel, non-stop TV.

And here it is. At the flick of a page, look up the programme, read a critical overview, peruse the cast. You can, for greater safety of viewing, cross-reference artists and behind-camera crew (credits include producers, directors, writers) and check-out their back catalogue. Then amaze the rest of the sofa with your erudition, before dazzling them with your grasp of totally useless trivia. This book is what your other, non-remote-control-holding hand was made for.

What's included and what's not? Chronologically, *The Ultimate TV Guide* spans from 1946 – the oldest programme is *Muffin the Mule* – the age of black-and-white nostalgia to the hi-tec, high definition present. There's no news, no documentaries (there's no space), but all forms of TV fiction are covered – crime, westerns, sci-fi, soaps, comedy, adventure, horror – along with children's TV and light entertainment (quizzes, game shows). Of these, we have selected the classics, the innovators, the lost treasures, the hits – the shows, in short, of screen note and desire. Even if it's only because, like the BBC's ferryboat melodrama, *Triangle*, they were such utter turkeys. All have been broadcast in the UK. Usually more than once.

Nostalgia stalks everywhere. Videos of *Watch with Mother* top the charts, Hollywood returns endlessly to the small screen in the search for product, and even *Captain Pugwash* gets updated. It is easy for nostalgia TV to trap the unwary: the mind has an uncanny tendency to play golden-glow-of-the-past tricks. Not every show from the sixties was a classic: if you doubt it, watch an episode of *Compact* sometime. And yet ... the fashion for screening timewarp TV addresses a real (or at least a perceived) problem. Contemporary TV seems dull and directionless by comparison, with the kidvid sector apparently led by toy merchandizing. More channels only mean more choice if the programmes are different. Thirty low-cost game shows introduced by a man in a suit with a tandoori tan is no choice at all.

Perhaps we ask too much from John Logie Baird's box. It's only television. But 99 per cent of British homes have it, and you'll spend as much as a sixth of your life watching it.

As we said, you need a guide. Select viewing.

And now, let's see what's out there...

How to Use This Book

All entries appear in this book in alphabetical order.

KEY

1 genre
2 channel
3 year(s) of transmission in UK
4 ➢appears elsewhere in the book
5 CAST Actors and characters
6 *cr* creator(s)
7 *exec pr* executive producer(s)
8 *pr* producer
9 *dr* director (s)
10 *wr* writer(s)
11 *mus* composer(s)
12 production company/companies
13 number and length of episodes
14 transmission dates in US

1 2 3

Ally McBeal

Comedy. C4 1998–

4

Hot-hit US romantic sitcom. The eponymous heroine (played by stick-like Calista Flockhart) was a bright young lawyer working in a bright young law firm – so hip that it had a unisex lavatory – alongside ex-boyfriend Billy, now married to Georgia (Courtney Thorne-Smith, late of ➢*Melrose Place*). Plagued by post-feminist neuroses and lingering lurve for Billy, and dazed by office politics, the ditzy short-skirted Ally McBeal skipped flakily from one comic dilemma to the next, with some wacky fantasy scenes (visualizations of McBeal's innermost thoughts: frolicking with Billy in a giant latte, bra-bursting breast growth, dancing embryos) along the way. Variously the best thing since the last best thing ('Button-pushing storylines hot off the cultural Zeitgeist', *Entertainment Weekly*) or cringe-making politically incorrect male fantasy, the show was dreamed up by David E. Kelley, previously a Steven Bochco sidekick and the creator of *Chicago Hope*, ➢*Doogie Howser, MD* and ➢*Picket Fences.* (Kelley, allegedly, modelled McBeal on his wife, Michelle Pfeiffer.) Stylistically, at least, the show was a treat with innovative – even unique – sound design that used mood music subjectively to show the emotional state of only one of the characters on screen.

5 6 7 8 9 10 11

CAST *Ally McBeal* Calista Flockhart *Billy Thomas* Gil Bellows *Richard Fish* Greg Germann *Renee Radick* Lisa Nicole Carson *Georgia Thomas* Courtney Thorne-Smith *Elaine Vassal* Jane Krakowski *John 'The Biscuit' Cage* Peter MacNicol *Judge Jennifer 'Whipper' Cone* Dyan Cannon /*cr* David E. Kelley /*exec pr* David E. Kelley /*pr* Mike Listo, Jonathan Pontell /*dr* inc Thomas Schlamme, James Frawley, Daniel Attias, Allan Arkush, Tom Moore, Jonathan Pontell, Arlene Sanford, Elodie Keene, Peter MacNicol /*wr* inc David E. Kelley /*mus* Danny Lux, Vonda Shepard /*20th Century Fox: David E. Kelley Productions* (USA) /28 x 50m col /US tx Fox TV 1997–.

12 13 14

A for Andromeda
Sci-fi. BBC 1961

An early classic of British sci-fi TV, based on a storyline by astronomer Professor Fred Hoyle. When strange radio signals from the remote constellation of Andromeda are decoded by brilliant young scientist John Fleming (to the ire of his ambitious colleague, Bridger, played by Frank Windsor, later ➢*Z Cars*), they reveal instructions for the construction of a super-computer. Duly built by the naive earthlings, the machine quickly reveals its true purpose: Domination of Earth. To this end it creates a beautiful blonde android, Andromeda, but she – under the human influence of the admiring Fleming – eventually rejects and wrecks her machine master. Intended by Hoyle as a populistic parable – the need for humanity to contain science in the nuclear age – with a dash of H.G. Wells for good scary-narrative measure, the series, under the pen of scriptwriter John Elliot (➢*The Troubleshooters*), also exploited Cold War espionage fears through a running subplot in which foreign powers and Swiss big business cartel Intel intrigued to seize the terror-computer. This artful plucking of the mood-chord of the times garnered huge audience figures (which grew by a million per week) and established the tenability of telefantasy on UK TV. The show's other enduring legacy was to launch Julie Christie, discovered by producer Michael Hayes at a drama school exercise, to international stardom. A sequel, *The Andromeda Breakthrough* (BBC, 6 x 45m), followed in 1962, with Fleming and co-worker Dawnay tracking Andromeda (now played by the less lustrous Susan Hampshire, ➢*The Forsyte Saga*) to the Middle East, where the threesome battle the computer's legacy, including a poison enzyme set to slowly suffocate Earth.

CAST *John Fleming* Peter Halliday *Prof. Reinhart* Esmond Knight *Madeleine Dawnay* Mary Morris *Dennis Bridger* Frank Windsor *Christine/Andromeda* Julie Christie /*cr* Norman James, Fred Hoyle /*pr* Michael Hayes, Norman James /*dr* Michel Hayes /*wr* Fred Hoyle, John Elliot /*BBC TV* (UK) /7 x 45m bw.

Absolutely
Comedy. C4 1989–93

Anarchic and surreal sketch show, the ➢*Monty Python* of latter televisual times, derived from the Scottish school of alternative comedy. Although it ran the gamut of skit-show possibilities, from animation (*pace Python*) to spoofed-up songs, its particular pleasure was its regular gallery of invented characters: Little Girl, rabid nationalist McGlashen, the Stoneybridge town council, melodious Mr Muzak, anorak Calum Gilhooley, disaster-prone DIY expert Denzil and scatological Frank Hovis (these two characters performed by Welsh team-member John Sparkes), Hovis coming complete with tips on how to cure a chapped anus. The creations Donald McDiarmid and George McDiarmid (Jack Docherty and Moray Hunter, ➢*Friday Night Live*) even enjoyed their own spin-off show, *mr don and mr george*. Since *Absolutely*, Gordon Kennedy has progressed to such lesser things as co-hosting *The National Lottery Live*.

CAST Morwenna Banks, Jack Docherty, Moray Hunter, Gordon Kennedy, John Sparkes /*pr* David Tyler, Alan Nixon /*dr* inc Graham C. Williams /*wr* Morwenna Banks, Jack Docherty, Moray Hunter, Gordon Kennedy, John Sparkes /*Absolutely Productions* (UK) /24 x 30m col.

Absolutely Fabulous
Comedy. BBC2/BBC1 1989–93/1996

'Oh sweetie…'

Cult early 90s sitcom, set in the trendy world of the fashion biz, developed from a ➢*French and Saunders* sketch in which Saunders portrayed a baseball-capped parent berated by her staid daughter (French) for playing hip hop. In translation to a series, Saunders played Edina Monsoon – rumoured to be based on Saunders' sometime PR, Lynne Franks – a late 30-something unreconstructed flower child with her own London PR business, who behaved badly (drugs, Bollinger, cigarettes, Bollinger, men, Bollinger) with bouffanted pal, Patsy (Joanna Lumley), a *Cosmo*-type fashion writer. Looking on aghast was Edina's daughter, sensible Saffron (Julia Sawalha from ➢*Press Gang*) and her mother (played by veteran comic actress June Whitfield). Also seen occasionally was restaurant critic Hamish (played by Adrian *Young Ones* Edmondson, Saunders' real life husband). The show was Saunders' first solo project and its politically incorrect, slay-every-sacred-90s-cow (crystals, cosmetic surgery) humour made the show an immediate hit, securing two BAFTAS for its first season (Best Comedy, Best Light Entertainment Performer for Lumley as the dipso, nymphomaniacal Patsy). A second season saw the plot lost and an over-reliance on guest stars (Lulu, even) before a return to form in the third season. By then, '*AbFab*' had sold around the world, and a rapturous response in the USA led to Roseanne Barr buying the rights for a state-side version. This floundered when ABC wanted the characters' drunkenness and swearing removed.

A one-off *AbFab* special was released in 1996, in which Edina and Patsy contemplated the setting up of a cable TV station, but got distracted by a chance to go on the piste at Val d'Isere.

CAST *Edina Monsoon* Jennifer Saunders *Patsy Stone* Joanna Lumley *Saffron Monsoon* Julia Sawalha *Mother* June Whitfield /*cr* Jennifer Saunders /*pr* Jon Plowman, Janice Thomas /*dr* Bob Spiers /*wr* Jennifer Saunders /*mus* Julie Driscoll and Adrian Edmondson ('This Wheels on Fire' theme vocals), Bob Dylan and Rick Danko (lyrics) /*BBC TV* (UK) /Comedy Central 1994 /18 x 30m, 2 x 45m col.

Ace of Wands
Children's. ITV 1970–2

Telefantasy for the junior set, in which a youthful stage conjurer, Tarot, used his magical skills to solve bizarre crimes, these perpetrated by *Dick Tracy*-like supercriminals. Hailed as a '20th-century Robin Hood, with a pinch of Merlin and a dash of Houdini', Tarot was assisted in his detective endeavours by ex-convict Sam (Tony Selby, ➢*Get Some In*), telepathic stage partner Lulli and tweedy antiquarian bookseller Mr Sweet. For the last season, Sam and Lulli were replaced by journalist Mikki and her photographer brother Chas. Unafraid to push the boundary of kidvid TV towards the adult shiver genre – one episode, 'Nightmare Gas', featured a substance which caused its sleeping victims to scare themselves to death – the series enjoyed stratospheric ratings. It also gave early (if minor) screen roles to Tim Curry and David Prowse. Presdigitorial advice was by Ali Bongo.

CAST *Tarot* Michael MacKenzie *Sam Maxsted* Tony Selby *Lillian 'Lulli' Palmer* Judy Loe *Mr Sweet* Donald Layne-Smith *Mikki* Petra Markham *Chas* Roy Holder *Ozymandias* Fred the Owl /*cr* Trevor Preston /*pr* Pamela Lonsdale, John Russell /*dr* inc John Russell, Michael Currer-Briggs, Pamela Lonsdale, Darrol Blake /*wr* Trevor Preston, Don Houghton, P.J. Hammond, Victor Pemberton, Maggie Allen, Michael Winder, William Emms /*mus* Andrew Brown /*Thames TV* (UK) /46 x 30m col.

Adam Adamant Lives!
Adventure. BBC1 1966–7

Suave Gerald Harper played an even suaver Edwardian hero, Adam Llewellyn De Vere Adamant, in this quirky meld of swashbuckler and ➢*The Avengers*, in which the said dashing toff, frozen in 1902 by arch-enemy The Face, was thawed out in the (bemusing) London of the Swinging 60s. Acquiring two companions, with-it girl Georgie and valet William E. Simms, Adamant threw down the gauntlet to modern villains and foreign foes, none of whom proved a match for his gallant, gentlemanly style. Inspired in concept, the series was executed with script-writing wit (by, amongst others, ➢*The Avengers* old hands Tony Williamson and Brian Clemens), televisual verve and a commercial shade of experimental photography; those at the helm included tyro director Ridley Scott, later to direct Hollywood features *Alien* and *Blade Runner*.

CAST *Adam Adamant* Gerald Harper *Georgina Jones* Juliet Harmer *William E. Simms* Jack May /*pr* Verity Lambert, Tony Williamson /*dr* inc Ridley Scott, Philip Dudley, Paul Ciappessoni, Moira Armstrong, Laurence Bourne /*wr* inc Tony Williamson, Robert Banks Stewart, Brian Clemens, Vince Powell & Harry Driver, Ian Stuart Black /*mus* David Lee (theme), Kathy Kirby (theme song) /*BBC TV* (UK) /29 x 50m bw.

The Addams Family

Comedy. ITV 1966–8

'They're creepy and they're kooky, mysterious and spooky…'

Spoof horror show, developed from Charles Addams' famous *New Yorker* cartoon strip. Head of the eponymous and altogether 'kookie family' was Latino lawyer Gomez Addams (hobbies: blowing up toy trains and decapitating dolls), seldom seen without a Castro-sized cigar and gangster suit, and his tantalising, black-haired wife, Morticia. Their ramshackle mansion at 000 North Cemetery Ridge was filled with strange *objets d'art* and *de mort* (including a stuffed fish with a protruding human leg), as well as the ghoulish, bald-headed Uncle Fester, who lit light bulbs by placing them in his mouth, haggish Grandmama, and gaunt family retainer Lurch. The perfectly perverse spawn of Morticia and Gomez were daughter Wednesday and fat son Pugsley, who kept an electric chair in his room. Household tasks were performed by a disembodied hand-in-a-box, Thing. Making up the distended Addams clan was hirsute cousin Itt. Much of the appeal of *The Addams Family* lay in its blackly comic inversion of normalcy (an extended joke shared with contemporary, if less sophisticated, rival ➢*The Munsters*), catchy finger-clicking theme tune, plus the simmering sexual attraction between Gomez and Morticia, the latter only having to speak a word of French for her husband to lose all control ('Tish! That's French'). The outlandishness of *The Addams Family* made them the virtual TV definition of 60s counterculture.

To ensure broad couch viewing, however, ABC insisted that the part of Morticia went to a named Hollywood actress. Accordingly, Carolyn Jones (sometime wife of TV mega-producer Aaron Spelling), winner of an Oscar nomination for a role as a beatnik in the 1956 feature *Bachelor Party*, was cast in the role. The part of Fester went to former 20s child star Jackie Coogan, while John Astin auditioned for the part of Lurch but was cast instead as Gomez. Since *Addams Family* days, Astin has enjoyed a career as a TV director of note (➢*CHiPS*, ➢*McMillan and Wife*, ➢*Murder, She Wrote*).

An animated version of *The Addams Family* appeared in 1973, to be followed eighteen years later by a Hollywood movie version, *The Addams Family* (*dr* Barry Sonnenfield), with Anjelica Huston as Morticia, which became a monster box office hit. A second feature, *Addams Family Values*, appeared in 1993.

CAST *Morticia Frump Addams* Carolyn Jones *Gomez Addams* John Astin *Uncle Fester Frump* Jackie Coogan *Lurch/Thing* Ted Cassidy *Grandmama Addams* Blossom Rock *Pugsley Addams* Ken Weatherwax *Wednesday Thursday Addams* Lisa Loring *Cousin Itt* Felix Silla (voice: Tony Magro) /*cr* Charles Addams, David Levy /*exec pr* David Levy /*pr* David Levy, Nat Perrin /*dr* inc Nat Perrin, Stanley Z. Cherry, Sidney Solkon, Jerry Hopper, Arthur Hiller /*wr* inc Carol Henning, Hanibal Coons, Preston Ward /*mus* Vic Mizzy /*Filmways* (USA) /64 x 30m bw /US tx ABC 1964–6.

The Adventures of Black Beauty

Children's. ITV 1972–4

A dashing thoroughbred horse (rescued from neglect) and a young girl share escapades on a Victorian country estate. Pleasantly diverting show for the juvenile market, but with no discernible relation to Anna Sewell's 1877 equestrian classic book. Charles Crichton (later *A Fish Called Wanda*) was among the directors. A sequel, *The New Adventures of Black Beauty*, cast Amber McWilliams as Black Beauty's mistress, Vicky, with William Lucas and Stacy Dorning reprising their original roles as her father and sister.

CAST *Vicky Gordon* Judi Bowker *Dr James Gordon* William Lucas *Jenny Gordon* Stacy Dorning *Kevin Gordon* Roderick Shaw *Amy Wintrop* (*housekeeper*) Charlotte Mitchell /*exec pr* Paul Knight /*pr* Sidney Cole /*dr* inc Charles Crichton, Alan Gibson, Freddie Francis /*wr* inc Richard Carpenter /*LWT: Talbot TV: Freemantle TV* (UK) /50 x 30m col.

The Adventures of Champion

Children's. BBC1 1956–7

The talented exploits of Champion, a wild stallion who befriends twelve-year-old Ricky North in the Texas of the 1880s. Although Ricky, who lived on his Uncle Sandy's ranch, had a peculiar penchant for trouble, he was always rescued by the white-faced Wonder Horse (which only he could ride), aided by the boy's other constant companion, German shepherd dog Rebel. Light relief was provided by cowpoke Will Calhoun.

The series was created by singing cowboy star Gene Autry as a means of promoting his famed mount. Frankie Laine sang the popular theme song.

CAST *Ricky North* Barry Curtis *Sandy North* Jim Bannon *Will Calhoun* Francis McDonald /*cr* Gene Autry /*pr* Gene Autry /*dr* George Archainbaud /*wr* Various /*mus* Frankie Laine (theme vocal) /*Flying A Productions* (USA) /26 x 26m bw /US tx 1955–6.

The Adventures of Don Quick

Sci-fi. ITV 1970

Space-age version of Cervantes' classic literary satire, *Don Quixote*, with the picaresque anti-hero tilting at alien civilisations instead of windmills. Astronaut Don Quick (Ian Hendry, formerly *Police Surgeon*), a member of the Intergalactic Maintenance Squad, was accompanied in his unwelcome know-best meddling by his faithful companion, Sergeant Sam Czopanzer ('Sancho Panza'). The sfx, for a British 70s space opera, were laudably done, but a deficiency of laughs resulted in most ITV regions demoting it from its prime-time slot.

CAST *Capt. Don Quick* Ian Hendry *Sgt Sam Czopanzer* Ronald Lacey /*exec pr* Peter Wildeblood /*dr* Mike Newell, Quentin Lawrence, Cliff Owen, Cyril Coke, Bob Hird, Bill Turner /*wr* Peter Wildeblood, Kenneth Hill, Keith Miles, Charlotte & Dennis Plimmer /*London Weekend TV* (UK) /6 x 30m col.

The Adventures of Long John Silver

Adventure. ITV 1957

Pleasingly rollicksome skull-and-crossbones series, based on Robert Louis Stevenson's novel *Treasure Island*, chiefly notable for the theatrical performance of Robert Newton (who died shortly afterwards) in the grog-swilling, shiver-me-timbers title role. In this version, Silver and his cabin-boy friend, Jim Hawkins, were located on the island of Portobello on the Spanish Main, where they worked for British Governor Strong to thwart the 1700s advance of the perfidious Spaniards. Treasure hunting was thus reduced to an occasional pastime. Off duty, Silver was to be found in the pub of Mrs Purity Pinker. Although filmed in colour, the Australian-made series was given its UK transmission in black and white.

Other actors to play Silver on the small screen were Peter Vaughan (*Treasure Island*, BBC1, 1968) and Brian Blessed (*John Silver's Return to Treasure Island*, HTV, 1986).

CAST *Long John Silver* Robert Newton *Jim Hawkins* Kit Taylor *Purity Pinker* Connie Gilchrist *Governor Strong* Harvey Adams /*pr* Joseph Kaufman, Mark Evans /*dr* inc Lee Sholem /*wr* inc Martin Rackin, Kay Keavney /*mus* Sydney John Kay /*Isola del'Oro Productions* (Australia) /26 x 30m bw.

The Adventures of Rin Tin Tin

Children's. ITV 1954–9

One boy and his dog show. The sole survivors of an 1880s Indian attack on an Arizona wagon train, 11-year-old Rusty and his German shepherd dog, Rin Tin Tin ('Yo ho, Rinty!'), are rescued by 'B' Company of the 101st Cavalry and taken back to Fort Apache. There they are unofficially adopted by Lieutenant Rip Masters, made honorary troopers and henceforth courageously assist the 'Fighting Blue Devils' in their rugged action campaign against the Redskins. Three dogs played the title role, two of them bloodline descendants of the dog who starred in the *Rin Tin Tin* movies and famously rescued Warners from bankruptcy in the 1920s.

Debuting on TV only a month later than great canine rival ➢*Lassie*, *Rin Tin Tin* was popular enough to merit a rerun in the USA immediately after the final episode of the series; it was then rerun on CBS. New colour wraparounds and a sepia tint were added in 1976 for the syndication market. A completely new show, *Rin Tin Tin K-9 Cop*, in which the infinitely resourceful shepherd dog was recruited to the Toronto Police Department, was made by The Family Channel in 1987.

CAST *'Corporal' Rusty* Lee Aaker *Lt Rip Masters* James L. Brown *Sgt Aloysius 'Biff' O'Hara* Joe Sawyer *Cpl Randy Boone* Rand Brooks /*pr* Herbert B. Leonard, Fred Briskin /*dr* inc William Beaudine, Douglas Heyes, Ida Lupino, Charles S. Gould, Earl Bellamy /*wr* inc Douglas Heyes, Roy Erwin, Frank Moss /*mus* Hal Hopper /*Screen Gems: Herbert B. Leonard Production* (USA) /165 x 26m bw /US tx ABC 1954–9.

The Adventures of Robin Hood

Adventure. ITV 1955–9

If not quite up to the swashbuckling standards of Hollywood's 1938 cinematic *The Adventures of Robin Hood* – which starred Errol Flynn – Lew Grade's wholesome version of the noble exploits of England's legendary 12th-century outlaw kept a young TV nation glued to its sofa. Throughout,

Robin Hood was played by Richard Greene; his merry men included the yet-to-be-famous Paul Eddington (as Will Scarlet). Shot at Nettlefold Studios – where art director Peter Proud ingeniously placed most of the props (trees, baronial fireplaces, entrance halls) on wheels to facilitate the quick set changes that the factory-like production schedule (a 26-minute episode every four and a half days) demanded – the series enjoyed notably high standards of scriptwriting. This was due mainly to executive producer Hannah Weinstein's importation of blacklisted Hollywood writers (such as Ring Lardner Jr), who wrote under various aliases; this 'secret history' of *TARH* later became the basis of the 1989 theatrical feature *Fellow Traveller*. Lindsay Anderson, Terence Fisher and Don Chaffey were among the directors. Successful on both sides of the Atlantic, the show spawned a hit theme – ITV's first – and a host of costume-actioner imitations, among them ➢*The Buccaneers*, ➢*The Adventures of William Tell*, and ➢*Sword of Freedom* which starred Edmund Purdom as a 15th-century Italianate version of the man in Lincoln green.

British TV returned to Sherwood Forest with the BBC's 1977 *The Legend of Robin Hood* (starring Martin Potter), HTV/Goldcrest's ➢*Robin of Sherwood* (starring Michael Praed, ➢*Dynasty*, ➢*Riders*, then Jason, son of Sean, Connery) and the award-winning ➢*Maid Marian and Her Merry Men*.

CAST *Robin Hood* Richard Greene *Maid Marian* Bernadette O'Farrell/Patricia Driscoll *Little John* Archie Duncan/Rufus Cruikshank *Friar Tuck* Alexander Gauge *Will Scarlet* Ronald Howard/Paul Eddington *Prince John* Hubert Gregg/Brian Haines/Donald Pleasance *Sheriff* Alan Wheatley *Prince Arthur* Peter Asher/Richard O'Sullivan/Jonathan Bailey / *exec pr* Hannah Weinstein / *dr* inc Ralph Smart, Lindsay Anderson, Don Chaffey, Terry Bishop / *wr* inc Ralph Smart, Ernest Borneman, Ring Lardner Jr, Alan Hackney, Leon Griffiths, Louis Marks / *mus* Dick James / *A Sapphire Films Production for ITC* (UK) / 143 x 30m bw / US tx CBS 1955–8.

The Adventures of Sherlock Holmes

Crime & Mystery. ITV 1984–5

'Elementary, my dear Watson.' Modelled closely on the mood and style of the original Victorian *Strand Magazine* stories (illustrated by Sidney Paget), old Etonian Jeremy Brett's interpretation of Conan Doyle's famous creation is generally accepted as definitive: Holmes as a man of awesome genius, but also prone to something akin to melancholia and madness under the influences of his cocaine habit. Handsomely mounted, with a specially created Baker Street set at Granada's Manchester studios (next to that of ➢*Coronation Street*), the show inaugurated a trend for historical detective series as evidenced by, *inter alia*, ➢*Miss Marple* and ➢*Agatha Christie's Poirot*. Scriptwriters included Alan Plater and John Hawkesworth (➢*Upstairs, Downstairs*, ➢*Duchess of Duke Street*). Holmes' *Adventures* came to a finale in 1985, with the pipe-smoking sleuth plunging to his death at the Reichenbach Falls ('The Final Problem'); however, Brett's Holmes was resurrected from the dead in *The Return of Sherlock Holmes* (1986, 11 x 60m), in which the role of Dr Watson was now played by Edward Hardwicke (son of thespian Sir Cedric). Hardwicke kept the part of Holmes' companion for a 120-minute Brettian *The Hound of the Baskervilles* and a valedictory series *The Casebook of Sherlock Holmes* (1991, 6 x 60m).

CAST *Sherlock Holmes* Jeremy Brett *Dr Watson* David Burke / *pr* Michael Cox / *dr* inc Paul Annett, John Bruce, Alan Grint, David Carson / *wr* inc Alexander Baron, Anthony Skene, Derek Marlowe, John Hawkesworth, Alan Plater / *mus* Patrick Gowers / *A Granada Television Network Production* (UK) / 13 x 60m col / US tx WGBH 1985–6.

The Adventures of Sir Lancelot

Adventure. ITV 1956–7

Costume actioner relating the glorious exploits of King Arthur's bravest knight and Guinevere's champion, Sir Lancelot du Lac (brilliantined William Russell, later ➢*Dr Who*, ➢*Coronation Street*). Lavishly photographed, the series used specially commissioned research from Oxford University to ensure the accuracy of its 14th-century settings. As with ➢*The Adventures of Robin Hood*, also executive-produced by Hannah Weinstein, series writers included expatriate Americans blacklisted by McCarthy. One of the series' greatest legacies was that it provided actor

Patrick McGoohan with an early role in the segment 'The Outcast'; here he met director-writer Ralph Smart, who would later devise ➢*Danger Man*, the series that would propel McGoohan to stardom and ➢*The Prisoner*.

CAST *Sir Lancelot du Lac* William Russell *Queen Guinevere* Jane Hylton *Merlin* Cyril Smith *Brian* Robert Scroggins *King Arthur* Bruce Seton/Ronald Leigh-Hunt /*exec pr* Hannah Weinstein /*pr* Sidney Cole, Dallas Bower, Bernard Knowles /*dr* inc Ralph Smart, Bernard Knowles, Peter Maxwell /*wr* inc Ralph Smart, Ian McLellan Hunter, Ring Lardner Jnr /*mus* Edwin Astley /*Sapphire Films* (UK) /30 x 25m bw / US tx NBC 1956–7.

The Adventures of Superman

Sci-fi. ITV 1956–7

'Look! In the sky ... it's a bird ... it's a plane ... it's Superman!'

Originally invented as an *Action* comic character by Ohio duo Jerry Siegel and Joe Shuster in 1938, *Superman* was transferred to US syndicated (non network) TV in 1952, becoming one of the fledgling medium's first hits. Episode one, 'Superman on Earth', provided a helpful genealogy. Born on Krypton, the baby Kar-El was rocketed to Earth by his father, Jor-El, and mother, Lara, moments before the planet exploded. Landing outside Smallville, USA, the baby was adopted by the Kent family, christened Clark, gradually discovered his amazing powers (x-ray eyes, the strength of a locomotive, the ability to fly like a bird), and moved to Metropolis at the age of 25. There he worked as a reporter for *The Daily Planet* under blustering editor Perry White ('Great Caesar's ghost!') and alongside scoop-hungry hackette Lois Lane. At the merest hint of trouble in Metropolis, bespectacled Clark changed into his caped, blue-and-red Superman costume and flew off to fight for 'truth, justice and the American way'. He did, however, have an alien Achilles heel – he was vulnerable to Kryptonite, green fragments of his home planet, a commodity much prized by the show's bad guys (generally Mafia-type villains). Initially, Superman's *Adventures* were jaw-socking actioners, but at the behest of copyright owners, National Comics, and sponsors, Kellogg, the show became suitable family fare, verging on pantomime comedy. (Thus Noel Neill's soft-centred Lois replaced Phyllis Coates' hard-boiled version of the *Planet* reporter). Production was strictly low-budget, and special effects limited. The sequences of Superman 'flying' were achieved by use of invisible wires or by actor George Reeves lying outstretched on a glass table, the scene then matted over an aerial view of Metropolis (in fact, Hollywood). George Reeves – who had made his acting debut in *Gone with the Wind* – eventually felt typecast by the Superman role and this was a factor in his suicide by gun in June 1959.

The fictional Man of Steel, however, has proved immortal. Aside from a tranche of movies starring Christopher Reeve, TV itself has seen CBS cartoons *Superman* and *New Adventures of Superman*, together with the 90s live romantic makeover ➢*The New Adventures of Superman* featuring Dean Cain as the hero in tights.

CAST *Superman/Clark Kent* George Reeves *Lois Lane* Phyllis Coates/Noel Neill *Jimmy Olsen* Jack Larson *Perry White* John Hamilton *Insp. Henderson* Robert Shayne /*pr* Robert Maxwell, Bernard Luber, Whitney Ellsworth /*dr* inc Thomas Carr, Lee Sholem, George Reeves /*wr* inc Whitney Ellsworth, David Chantler, Ben Peter Freeman, Richard Fielding, Jackson Gillis /*sfx* Thol 'Si' Simonson /*Lippert: National Perodical Publications* (USA) /104 x 30m bw; col /US tx Syndicated 1953–4.

The Adventures of Tugboat Annie

Comedy. ITV 1958

Much-publicised but short-lived TV exercise in screwball comedy. Widow Annie Brennan was the fog-horn-voiced skipper of the *Narcissus*, a tug based in the Pacific Northwest of America. Her main preoccupation was one-up-womanship over rival skipper Horatio Bullwinkle but, although the two of them constantly exchanged 'a-pox-on-you'-type insults and stole each other's business, they also shared adventures together.

The character of Tugboat Annie first appeared in short stories by Norman Reilly Raine, before progressing to cinema in 1933, where she was played by Marie Dressler (against Wallace Beery's drunken Bullwinkle). A Canadian TV company bought the rights in 1954, but became quagmired by casting and production problems. As a result, the series was not aired until 1957 (it debuted in the USA), and then only for a single run of 39 episodes.

CAST *'Tugboat' Annie Brennan* Minerva Urecal *Capt. Horatio Bullwinkle* Walter Sande /*pr* Anthony Veiller_/ *Normandie* (Canada) /39 x 30m bw /US tx Syndicated 1957.

The Adventures of Twizzle

Children's. ITV 1957–60

Puppet show for poppets. A boy doll, who can 'twizzle' his arms and legs longer, escapes from a toy shop. Together with befriended cat, Footso, he sets up a sanctuary for mistreated toys. Created by Roberta Leigh, the series marked the TV advent of former Gainsborough film unit director Gerry Anderson (later ➢*Thunderbirds* et al), whose AP Films – standing for Gerry Anderson and Arthur Provis – made the show, rescuing it from imminent bankruptcy. A series by AP Films – featuring another Leigh creation, ➢*Torchy*, in the same innocent ➢*Andy Pandy*-ish vein – shortly followed.

CAST (voice) Denise Bryer /*cr* Roberta Leigh /*pr* Gerry Anderson, Arthur Provis /*dr* inc Gerry Anderson / *wr* Roberta Leigh /*An AP Films Production for Associated Rediffusion Network* (UK) /52 x 15m bw.

The Adventures of William Tell

Adventure. ITV 1958–9

Or, Robin Hood in the Alps. A costume actioner from ITV's 50s adventure factory, loosely based on Johann von Schiller's tale about the legendary 14th-century Swiss freedom fighter's struggle against Austrian occupation. The opening episode saw Tell (Conrad Phillips, later to resurface as estate manager Christopher Meadows in ➢*Emmerdale Farm*) perform his celebrated act of archery, shooting an apple off his son's head, before fleeing for the peaks, from where he led his outlaw band against the despicable deeds of corpulent Austrian Governor, Gessler (a superbly hammy Willoughby Goddard). Aside from its stirring sword and arrow play, the series was also an allegory on Nazism and World War II, concerning as it did a hegemonic German power which organises slave labour camps; one episode, 'The Magic Power', was a retelling of the Albert Einstein–Atom bomb story. Filmed partly on location in Snowdonia (a surprisingly good stand-in for the Alps), *William Tell* contained a quiver-full of aspiring actors, notably Michael Caine and Frazer Hines. An Anglo-French-American remake of the Tell saga, *William Tell* was produced in 1989 with Will Lyman as Tell and Jeremy Clyde as Gessler. Conrad Phillips appeared as a guest star, playing the hero's avuncular, aged mentor.

CAST *William Tell* Conrad Phillips *Hedda Tell* Jennifer Jayne *Walter Tell* Richard Rogers *Gessler* Willoughby Goddard *Fertog (The Bear)* Nigel Greene / *cr* Leslie Arliss /*pr* Leslie Arliss, Ralph Smart /*dr* inc Ralph Smart, Quentin Maxwell, Terry Bishop /*wr* inc Leslie Arliss, John Kruse, Ralph Smart, Ian Stuart Black, Roger Marshall /*mus* Harold Durrell (theme song) /*ITC* (UK) /39 x 25m bw /US tx Syndicated 1958.

Aeon Flux

Crime & Mystery. MTV 1995–

Ultra-violent spy v. spy animation. Created by Peter Chung of Colossal Pictures for MTV's ground-breaking 'Liquid Television' show (which also debuted ➢*Beavis and Butt-Head*), the cartoon follows the fantasy adventures of volatile female secret agent/assassin Aeon and her arch rival/soul mate Trevor, invariably compressing scores of deaths into each episode's duration. (*AF* may boast the highest body count ever seen on the small screen). More than once the nearly nude heroine herself has been bizarrely terminated, only to rise again. Although Chung eschews narrative in favour of visual form (viz. relentless screen movement and image manipulation), a continuing storyline is discernible: Aeon is on a search-and-destroy mission for a man carrying a deadly virus. First aired on 'Liquid Television' in 1991, *AF* was given its own separate MTV show in 1995, the year which also saw the launch of an *AF* video game. Peter Chung's follow-up series, *Phantom 2040*, was a futuristic adaptation of the Marvel comic-book hero of that name.

CAST (voices) *Aeon Flux* Denise Poirier *Trevor Goodchild* John Rafter Lee /*exec pr* Japhet Asher, Abby Terkuhle /*pr* Catherine May Winder, John Andrews /*dr* Peter Chung, Howard Baker /*wr* Peter Chung /*Colossal Pictures: MTV Networks* (USA) /20 x 10m, 10 x 30m col /US tx MTV 1991–5.

Agatha Christie's Poirot

Crime. ITV 1989

Agatha Christie's fastidious Belgian sleuth with the 'leetle grey cells', who first appeared in the 1920 novel *The Mysterious Affair at Styles*, had been depicted in cinema by, among others, Albert Finney and Peter Ustinov before David Suchet (brother of newscaster John) brought the character to TV in the definitive screen interpretation. The confines of the 'box' suited well the detective's meticulous pernickety *modus operandi*, while his boiled-egg demeanour and withering put-downs of nice-but-dim assistant, Hastings, were perfectly captured by Suchet. Scrupulous in its period 30s settings (usually British upper class, with the occasional foray to the Med.) and handsomely produced, the series sold to over 40 countries around the world.

CAST *Hercule Poirot* David Suchet *Capt. Hastings* Hugh Fraser *Insp. Japp* Philip Jackson *Miss Lemon* Pauline Moran /*exec pr* Nick Elliott, Linda Agran /*pr* Brian Eastman /*dr* inc Edward Bennett, Renny Rye, Andrew Grieve /*wr* inc Clive Exton, Anthony Horowitz /*mus* Christopher Gunning /*London Weekend Production* (UK) /2 x 90m, 34 x 60m col / US tx WGBH Boston 1990.

Airwolf

Adventure. ITV 1984–6

Techno actioner in which the hero, ace US pilot Stringfellow Hawke (recreations: cello-playing, solitude), used a super helicopter to battle evil. To the disadvantage of the latter, the said Airwolf was capable of supersonic flight and had a weapons capability exceeding that of most Third World nations. In return for flying the dangerous missions of the US government's secret agency, The Firm, Hawke insisted that the White House find his brother, a Vietnam MIA. Hawke's co-pilot was the less than svelte Dominic Santini, played by Hollywood character actor Ernest Borgnine; in later episodes, Hawke was joined by female top gun Caitlin O'Shannessy. The series, which made a virtue of stunning aerial photography, was co-executive-produced by Donald Bellisario (*Black Sheep Squadron*, ➢*Magnum PI*, ➢*Quantum Leap*), and premiered almost simultaneously with another dramatic series built around a hi-tech helicopter, *Blue Thunder*.

Airwolf left the American CBS network in 1986 and moved to cable, where it appeared with more economical production values and a new cast. On the supposed death of Santini and serious injury of Hawke, their places in the Airwolf cabin were taken by Hawke's now rescued brother, St John, and Santini's niece Jo (Michele Scarabelli, ➢*Alien Nation*, ➢*Dallas*). In 1996, in a curious case of life imitating art, *Airwolf* star Jan-Michael Vincent broke his neck in an automobile accident.

CAST *Stringfellow Hawke* Jan-Michael Vincent *Dominic Santini* Ernest Borgnine *Michael Archangel* Alex Cord *Caitlin O'Shannessy* Jean Bruce Scott /*cr* Donald Bellisario /*exec pr* Bernard Kowalski, Donald Bellisario /*pr* Calvin Clements Jr, Lester William Berke, Carol Gillson /*dr* inc Donald Bellisario, Alan Cooke, Alan J. Levi, Ray Austin, Don Baer, Tom Blank / *wr* inc Donald Bellisario, Steve Hayes, Phil Combest, Calvin Clements Jr, Alfonse Ruggiero Jr, T.S. Cook / *Universal TV: Bellisarius Prods* (USA) /60 x 30m col / US tx CBS: cable 1984–8.

AJ Wentworth, BA

Comedy. ITV 1982

The last screen work of narcoleptic actor Arthur Lowe (➢*Dad's Army*, ➢*Pardon the Expression*), in which he played a pompous but benign maths master at a 1940s prep school. Though obsessed with the honour of the school, Wentworth was frequently preoccupied by such diverting details as the rising cost of pen nibs, the tactics of arch-enemy Matron and the antics of his arch-tormentor, Mason of 3A. Adapted by Basil Boothroyd from the short stories of Punch writer H.F. Ellis.

CAST *A.J. Wentworth, B.A.* Arthur Lowe *Matron* Marion Mathie *Rev. R.G. Saunders (Headmaster)* Harry Andrews *Rawlinson* Ronnie Stevens *Mason* Marcus Evans /*cr* Basil Boothroyd /*pr* Michael Mills / *wr* Basil Boothroyd /*Thames TV* (UK) /6 x 30m col.

Alas Smith and Jones

Comedy. BBC2/BBC1 1982–7/1998

Originally the half of ➢*Not the Nine O'Clock News* that none could name, Mel Smith (son of a betting shop owner) and Griff Rhys Jones (son of a doctor) spun their friendship into a double-act comedy show of skits and sketches that became a mainstay of BBC comedy in the 1980s, as familiar as the sitting-room wallpaper. Their head-to-head sketches, between a continually bemused Jones and a know-all Smith, were minimalist classics (if lifted outrageously from Peter Cook and Dudley Moore) and their sperm donor routine is almost as often rehearsed by TV-comedy aficionados as ➢*Monty Python's* dead parrot skit. As a sign of their gold-standard status, the BBC switched them from cult channel BBC2 to primetime on BBC1, eventually shortening the show title to *Smith and Jones*. Yet their material was always uneven, and as Smith and Jones' other commitments grew at exponential rate, the writing of *Morons from Outer Space*, the adaptation of *Wilt* for the big screen, the show leaned more towards traditional comedy's usual suspects: the police, politicians and TV ads (this despite the fact that Smith and Jones' own production company made many of them). Rob Grant and Doug Naylor (➢*Red Dwarf*), Graeme Garden (➢*The Goodies*) and Clive Anderson – a Cambridge friend of Rhys Jones – were amongst the writers. A one-off Christmas special, *Alas Sage and Onion*, was released in 1988, and Smith and Jones followed *Alas* with a spate of lookalikes (*The World According to Smith and Jones*, etc.) before reviving *Alas* itself in 1998.

CAST Griff Rhys Jones, Mel Smith /*cr* Mel Smith, Griff Rhys Jones /*pr* Martin Shardlow, John Kilby, Jimmy Mulville, John Plowman, Jamie Rix /*dr* inc Robin Carr, John Kilby /*wr* inc Mel Smith, Griff Rhys Jones, Clive Anderson, Jimmy Mulville, Rory McGrath, Rob Grant, Doug Naylor, Colin Bostock-Smith /*A Talkback Production* (UK) /43 x 30m, 1 x 60m col.

Albion Market

Melodrama. ITV 1985–6

Twice weekly (Fridays and Sundays) soap, intended as a supporting sister to ➢*Coronation Street*, set in a Manchester covered market. Although lavished with a £3-million budget, it was poorly scheduled and its ethnically mixed crowd of characters (white Mancunians, Vietnamese, Ugandans, West Indians, Jews) failed to light viewer interest, even when the cast list grew by the addition of minor TV legend Tony Booth (➢*Till Death Us Do Part*) and 60s popster Helen Shapiro (who played a hairdresser). *Albion Market* was duly dismantled after 100 episodes.

CAST *Derek Owen* David Hargreaves *Tony Fraser* John Michie *Morris Ransome* Bernard Spear *Miriam Ransome* Carol Kaye *Phil Smith* Burt Ceasar *Jaz Sharma* Paul Bhattacharjee *Raju Sharma* Dev Sagoo *Lam Quoc Hoa* Philip Tan *Ly Nhu Chan* Pik-Sen Lim *Lynne Harrison* Noreen Kershaw *Ted Pilkington* Anthony Booth *Viv Harker* Helen Shapiro /*pr* Bill Podmore, Gareth Jones /*dr* inc John Michael Phillips, Gareth Jones, Jonathan Wright Miller, Jeremy Summers, Sue Butterworth, Patrick Lau /*wr* inc Peter Whalley, Ron Rose, Trevor Cooper /*Granada TV* (UK) / 100 x 30m col.

Alexei Sayle's Stuff

Comedy. BBC2 1988-91

After an ill-conceived sojourn (alongside Chris Tarrant and Lenny Henry) on *OTT*, Central TV's lamentably crude adult version of ➢*Tiswas*, bulbous Jewish Liverpudlian comic Alexei Sayle found his alternative legs with guest appearances on ➢*The Young Ones* and ➢*The Comic Strip Presents...*, the latter's episode 'Didn't You Kill My Brother' acting as something of a taster for Sayle's first solo series. This was the eclectic *Stuff*, mixing mock-reflective monologues and (like so many other 80s and 90s sketch shows) parodies of TV itself. But it also had an experimental edge of wry absurdist observation, which won the show numerous awards, prime among them a 1989 Emmy Award for Best Foreign Comedy Show. It was followed by the *All-New Alexei Sayle Show* (BBC 2), which, its title aside, relied on the same format, generating such bizarre comic concepts as a nationwide film critics' strike, with the army brought in to run all columns, including an emergency Barry Norman. Yet for all the shaven-headed, tight-suited Sayle's surrealism, it was the precision of his one-line gags (recalling the neighbourhood Catholic girls' school as the 'virgin megastore', claiming that Churchill's real place in history was as 'the last white man to be called Winston') and proletarian putting-downs of the middle-class, *Observer*-reading milieu which adored him ('anyone who uses the word "workshop" outside of the context of light engineering is a prat') that truly hit home.

CAST (presenter) Alexei Sayle /*cr* Alexei Sayle /*pr* Marcus Mortimer, Jon Plowman /*dr* inc Marcus Mortimer, Bob Spiers /*wr* inc Alexei Sayle, Andrew Marshall, David Renwick /*BBC TV* (UK) /18 x 30m col.

Alf

Sci-fi. ITV 1987–91

In which a small, hirsute, 229-year-old Alien Life Form (hence the title) called Gordon Shumway, from planet Melmac, crashes his spaceship through the garage roof of archetypal suburban American family, the Tanners. Unlike fellow alien acronym ET, ALF stayed, moving in with the Tanners, whom he proceeded to satirise mercilessly. (The conceit of employing an extra-terrestrial lodger to demonstrate human foibles dates back to ➢*My Favourite Martian*, via ➢*Mork and Mindy*). Episodes also related ALF's evasion of the government's Alien Task Force and his various disruptive hobbies which, to a standard fast exit from the Tanners' pet feline, included cat-snacking. Paul Fusco, the show's creator, provided puppet ALF with his voice, while three-foot midget Michu Meszaros donned fur for walkabout scenes. An *ALF* cartoon (1987) prequeled Shumway's life on Melmac. For the big screen *ALF: The Movie* was developed.

CAST *Willie Tanner* Max Wright *Kate Tanner* Anne Schedeen *Lynn Tanner* Andrea Elson *Brian Tanner* Benji Gregory *Trevor Ochmonek* John LaMotta *Raquel Ochmonek* Liz Sheridan *ALF* (voice) Paul Fusco /*cr* Paul Fusco, Tom Patchett /*pr* Tom Patchett /*dr* inc Paul Bonerz, Nancy Heydorn, Tom Patchett, Paul Fusco, Tony Csiki /*wr* inc Paul Fusco, Tom Patchett /*Lorimar TV* (USA) /102 x 30m; 2 x 60m col /US tx NBC 1986–96.

Alfred Hitchcock Presents

Drama. ITV 1957–62

Anthology of murder mysteries, usually of macabre bent and with a sting in the tale (thus reflecting the Hitchcockian mode of storytelling). Although only 20 of the 300 episodes were directed by the 'Master of Suspense', he presented every episode (usually from some eerily weird setting, such as an electric chair), signing off with a sardonic, deadpan explanation of the small but fatal slip that had proved to be the criminal's undoing. One of the first anthologies to have a personality of its own, *Alfred Hitchcock Presents* (aka *The Alfred Hitchcock Hour*) raided the shelves of the suspense classics for its narratives, these translated for the screen by such renowned inkslingers as Ray Bradbury, Nicholas Monsarrat and Sterling Silliphant. The show was produced by Norman Lloyd, later to appear before the camera as Dr Daniel Auschlander in ➢*St Elsewhere.* In 1987 *AHP* was revived, with a mix of new scripts and remakes (directed by, amongst others, Tim 'Batman' Burton), with Hitchcock's original to-camera introductions receiving the dubious benefit of computer colour enhancement.

PRESENTER Alfred Hitchcock /*cr* Alfred Hitchcock /*pr* Norman Lloyd /*dr* inc Alfred Hitchcock, Robert Altman, Sydney Pollack, Don Medford, Paul Henreid, Ida Lupino /*wr* inc Ira Levin, Roald Dahl, Ray Bradbury, Sterling Silliphant, William Link, Richard Levinson /*mus* Gounod ('Funeral March of a Marionette' theme) /*Shamley Productions* (USA) /US tx CBS 1955–9: NBC 1960–2: USA Network 1987–8.

Alias Smith & Jones

Western. BBC2 1971–73

Tongue-in-cheek, end-of-the-West oater in which Hannibal Heyes and Kid Curry, under their respective aliases, were likeable outlaws trying to stay out of trouble in order to earn a secret amnesty from the governor of Kansas ('Only you, me and the governor'll know'). They never did. The series starred Ben Murphy as Jed Curry (based on the real-life 'Wild Bunch' robber, Kid Curry) and Peter Duel (aka Peter Deuel) as Heyes. On 30 December 1971, the 31-year-old Duel mortally shot himself in the head after watching the show on TV, leaving his role to be speedily recast. It was taken by Roger Davis, the former narrator. Intended as a TV cash-in on the cinematic bonanza *Butch Cassidy and the Sundance Kid* (but also inspired by wunderkind producer Glen Larson's own reading of the Pinkerton Detective Agency's files), the series sometimes showed too much influence of that movie. Good-looking exterior photography and ebullient humour, however, made it one of the few Western hits of the 70s.

CAST *Hannibal Heyes (Joshua Smith)* Peter Duel/Roger Davis (1972–3) *Jed 'Kid' Curry (Thaddeus Jones)* Ben Murphy *Clementine Hale* Sally Field *Narrator* Roger Davis/Ralph Story (1972–3) /*cr* Glen A. Larson /*exec pr* Roy Huggins /*pr* Glen A. Larson /*dr* inc Roy Huggins, Mel Ferrer, David Moessinger, Arnold Laven, Jeannot Szwarc /*wr* inc Glen A. Larson, Roy Huggins /*mus* Billy Goldenburg /*Universal TV: Public Arts* (USA) /1 x 90m, 49 x 52m col /US tx ABC 1971–3.

Alien Nation

Sci-fi. BSkyB 1990–1

After *V*, producer Kenneth Johnson continued the aliens-have-landed theme with science fiction cop show *Alien Nation.* A spin-off from the 1988 movie of the same title (which starred Mandy Pantinkin, later *Chicago Hope*, and James Caan), the TV series was markedly different in its concerns, being an extended liberal allegory of racism. Set in Los Angeles in 1995, it featured impulsive *homo sapiens* police detective Matt Sikes and his mottle-headed partner, George Francisco, one of 250,000 Tenctonese whose slave spaceship had crashed in the Mojave desert. The *policier* element of *AN* was traditional stuff (Sikes and Francisco were as different as chalk and cheese but male-bonded like super glue); where the show luminesced was in its careful creation of an alien culture (complete with an invented language, subtitled on screen) and biology. Soured milk made the Tenctonese – humanoid in appearance save for their bald craniums and vestigial ears – drunk, whereas salt water killed them. One long-running storyline dealt with the pregnancy of the Franciscos: George's wife, Susan (Michele Scarabelli, ➢*Airwolf*, ➢*Dallas*), was first 'prepared' by a Binnaum, a religious proxy husband, and only carried the foetus for the first half of pregnancy; thereafter it was carried by George, who eventually gave birth to their baby (an emergency delivery by Sikes), later ceremonially named Vesna.

It was through the eyes of the Francisco family that the problems of racial integration were viewed. George's salary as the first Newcomer – or, pejoratively, 'Slag' – detective enabled the Franciscos to move to an all human neighbourhood. In a memorably poignant episode, daughter Emily's first day at school was greeted with an hysterical anti-alien protest. Meanwhile, the Francisco's attitudinous teenage son, the appositely named Buck, joined a Newcomer gang and refused to adapt to Earthling ways.

Though the show lasted for only a single season, fandom pressure was instrumental in the production of five TV movie sequels: *Alien Nation: Dark Horizon* (1994), in which the Tenctonese's former slave masters attempted to re-subjugate them; *Alien Nation: Body and Soul* (1995); *Alien Nation: Millennium* (1996); *Alien Nation: The Enemy Within* (1996) and *Alien Nation: The Udara Legacy* (1997).

CAST *Det. Matt Sikes* Gary Graham *Det. George Francisco* Eric Pierpoint *Susan Francisco* Michele Scarabelli *Emily Francisco* Lauren Woodland *Buck Francisco* Sean Six *Cathi Frankel* Terri Treas *Albert Einstein* Jeff Marcus /*cr* Kenneth Johnson, Rockne O'Bannon /*exec pr* Kenneth Johnson /*pr* Andrew Schneider, Arthur Seidel, Tom Chehak /*dr* inc Kenneth Johnson, Gwen Arner, Rob Bowman, Steve Dubin /*wr* inc Kenneth Johnson, Craig Van Sickel, Diane Frolov, Tom Chehak, Andrew Schneider /*mus* Steve Dorff, Larry Herbstritt, Kenneth Johnson, David Kurtz (theme) /*Kenneth Johnson Productions: 20th Century Fox* (USA) /1 x 120m, 21 x 60m col /US tx Fox 1989–90.

All Creatures Great and Small

Drama. BBC1 1978–90

James Herriot's craftedly charming tales of a country vet first appeared on screen as a 1974 cinema feature starring Simon Ward, and then in a 1976 sequel, *It Shouldn't Happen to a Vet,* with John Alderton. For the TV series, Christopher Timothy was cast as Herriot, a tyro vet who joined the practice of volatile Siegfried Farnon and feckless younger brother Tristan in the Yorkshire Dales town of Darrowby (a fictionalisation of Thirsk) in the 1930s. The first seasons stuck fairly closely to the books, with Herriot dealing with all manner of animal ailments and meeting his soon-to-be-wife, Helen, while Siegfried developed ever more fanciful schemes for the advancement of the practice, and Tristan wooed the local girls, occasionally interrupting the chase for drinking sessions with the church bell-ringers. The humour was infinitely gentle – impotent bulls, Mrs Pumphrey's hypochondriacal Pekinese, Tricky-Woo – and the period nostalgia redolent. Like the Scottish country medical drama of a generation before, ➢*Dr Finlay's Casebook, All Creatures Great and Small* evoked a kinder, gentler Britain of rural tranquillity and stability. The popularity of the series, which spawned a lucrative James Herriot industry around Thirsk ('Herriot Country'), was undiminished by reports of a torrid off-screen affair between Timothy and Carol Drinkwater.

In 1980 the series ended with Herriot and Tristan Farnon heading off to World War II. (Herriot's original tales had nearly run dry). There were two Christmas specials, in 1983 and 1985, before public pressure succeeded in bringing about a return of the series in 1988. Events in Darrowby had moved on to the post-war period, and saw Siegfried married and a new vet, the Glaswegian badger-keeping idealist Calum Buchanan, joining the practice. There was also a major cast change in the replacement of Carol Drinkwater by Oxo-advertising Lynda Bellingham as Helen Herriot. Though the writers were given a freer hand – seen most obviously in an unlikely action-man episode in which Herriot skied across the Dales to rescue some piglets – the series continued to be a pleasing Sunday evening mellow-out. It bowed out with another Christmas special, with Tristan in high dudgeon about the composition of the campanologist's contingent. *Plus ça change.*

CAST *James Herriot* Christopher Timothy *Siegfried Farnon* Robert Hardy *Tristan Farnon* Peter Davison *Helen Alderson/Herriot* Carol Drinkwater/Lynda Bellingham *Calum Buchanan* John McGlynn *Mrs Hall* Mary Hignett *Mrs Pumphrey* Margaretta Scott /*pr* Bill Sellars /*dr* inc Terence Dudley, Christopher Barry, Peter Moffat, Robert Tronson /*wr* inc Brian Finch, Johnny Byrne, Anthony Steven, James Herriot / *BBC TV* (UK) /88 x 50m, 3 x 90m col.

All Gas and Gaiters

Comedy. BBC1 1967–71

Much-loved 60s charactercom which trespassed on previously hallowed ground by poking (affectionate) fun at the clergy. Derived from a *Comedy Playhouse* presentation ('The Bishop Rides Again'), it centred around a trio of incompetent incumbents – the Bishop, Archdeacon and Chaplain – at St. Oggs Cathedral, who were the bane of the severely unamused Dean. Derek Nimmo took his verbose, bumbling, be-cassocked character on to ➢*Oh Brother!* and its sequel *Oh Father!* The series was created and written by the husband-and-wife writing team of Edwin Apps and Pauline Devaney.

CAST *Rev. Mervyn Noote* Derek Nimmo *Bishop* William Mervyn *Archdeacon* Robertson Hare *Dean* Ernest Clark/John Barron /*cr* Edwin Apps, Pauline Devaney /*pr* Stuart Allen, John Howard Davies /*wr* Edwin Apps, Pauline Devaney /*BBC TV* (UK) / 32 x 30m bw.

All in the Family

Comedy. BBC1/BBC2 1971–5

Transplantation of British sitcom ➢*Till Death Us Do Part* from London's East End to downtown New York that changed the face of American TV comedy. Initially developed for ABC (who rejected two pilots), the show was eventually launched on the airwaves of CBS, the president of which, Robert Wood, was consciously searching for small screen packages which reflected the controversies of contemporary society. *Family* had them in abundance; along with an abrasive style totally at odds with the cosy 'Hi honey, I'm home' TV mores of the time. Like its British model, it was built upon the clashes of a working class bigot with his daughter and son-in-law, here dock foreman Archie Bunker, determined offspring Gloria and her Polish-American sociology student spouse, Mike Stivic ('Meathead'). Other targets of Bunker's armchair ire were his ethnic neighbours in Houser Street, the Lorenzos (Italian) and the Jeffersons (Black). And throughout all Bunker's dimwitted wife, Edith ('Dingbat') long-suffered.

For five consecutive years *Family* was the highest rated series on US TV, garnering audiences of around 50 million. It also spun off two other successful series, *The Jeffersons* and *Maude*, the latter based around Edith's cousin, Maude Findlay (played by pre- ➢*The Golden Girls* Bea Arthur). When the parent show began to fade, it was dramatically restructured, with Archie (implausibly) taking shares in a bar, Edith dying of a stroke (actress Jean Stapleton had tired of the part), and Gloria and Mike moving to California. It opened the 1979–80 season with a new title, *Archie Bunker's Place* and continued in such vein until 1991, by which time 'Bunker' had entered the US lexicon as a term for a blue-collar reactionary and Archie's chair – along with the leather jacket of the Fonz from ➢*Happy Days*, another of the TV icons of the 70s – had been gifted to the Smithsonian. Actor Rob Reiner (son of comedian Carl Reiner, ➢*The Dick Van Dyke Show*, *Caesar's Hour*), meanwhile, had left behind his 'meathead' persona to direct such Hollywood movies as *This is Spinal Tap* (of which he was also the scriptwriter), *When Harry Met Sally*, *Stand By Me*, and *A Few Good Men*.

CAST *Archie Bunker* Carroll O'Connor *Edith Bunker* Jean Stapleton *Gloria Stivic* Sally Struthers *Mike Stivic* Rob Reiner *Joey Stivic* Jason and Justin Draeger *Lionel Jefferson* Mike Evans *Louise Jefferson* Isabel Sanford *Henry Jefferson* Mel Stewart *George Jefferson* Sherman Hemsley *Irene Lorenzo* Betty Garrett *Frank Lorenzo* Vincent Gadenia /*cr* Norman Lear, Bud Yorkin /*pr* Norman Lear /*dr* inc John Rich, Michael Ross, Paul Bogart /*wr* inc Norman Lear /*mus* Strouse and Adams ('Those Were The Days' theme, sung by O'Connor and Stapleton) /*Tandem Productions: Yorkin-Lear* (USA) /160 x 30m col /US tx CBS 1971–91.

'Allo, 'Allo

Comedy. BBC1 1982–4

'Leesten very carefoolly, veel say this ernly wernce…'

Spoof version of the stiff-upper-lip WWII Resistance drama, ➢*Secret Army*, and loaded – like Croft and Perry's ➢*Are You Being Served?* and ➢*Hi-De-Hi* – with innuendo. Almost every episode of the show, which was set in the Occupied French town of Nouvion had a scene in which Rene, the cafe owner and reluctant Resistance member, was caught *in flagrante* with a waitress by hatchet-faced wife Edith, or a development in the convoluted saga of the stolen masterpiece 'The Fallen Madonna with the Big Boobies'. ('Boobies' were a favourite *'Allo, 'Allo* subject, evidenced most celebratedly in the scene where Yvette sought to sell ice cream in a vibrating truck.) Another running gag was the fumbling attempt to use the secret radio hidden beneath Rene's mother-in-law's chamber pot, and the preposterous French of the British secret agent Crabtree ('Good moaning').

It wasn't politically correct, but accusations of racism missed the mark; in the small world of Nouvion absolutely *everybody* – French, German, British – was a pantomime joke. The series ended with the war drawing to a close and Germans, Von Strohm and Gruber (a homosexual) heading for the Spanish border dressed as flamenco dancers. Tasteless, but as with the very best of *'Allo, 'Allo* done to farce perfection. Appropriately, given the show's obvious debt to *Carry On*, its cast contained one of the last of the living *Carry On* stars, Kenneth Connor as M Alfonse.

CAST *Rene Artois* Gordon Kaye *Edith* Carmen Silver *Yvette* Vicki Michelle *Maria* Francesca Gonshaw *Lieutenant Gruber* Guy Siner *Mme Fanny* Rose Hill *Flying Officer Fairfax* John D. Collins *Flying Officer Carstairs* Nicholas Frankau *Colonel Von Strohm* Richard Marner *General Von Klinkerhoffen* Hilary Minster *Captain Hans Geering* Sam Kelly *Helga* Kim Hartman *M Leclerc* Jack Haig/Derek Royle/Robin Parkinson *Herr Otto Flick* Richard Gibson/David Janson *Von Smallhausen* John Louis Mansi *Alfonse* Kenneth Connor *Crabtree* Arthur Bostrom *Bertorelli* Gavin Richards/Roger Kitter /*cr* David Croft, Jeremy Lloyd /*pr* David Croft, Mike Stephens, John B Hobbs / *dr* inc David Croft, Mike Stephens /*wr* inc David Croft, Jeremy Lloyd, Paul Adams /*BBC TV* (UK) / 86 x 30m col.

Ally McBeal

Comedy. C4 1998–

Hot-hit US romantic sitcom. The eponymous heroine (played by stick-like Calista Flockhart) was a bright young lawyer working in a bright young law firm – so hip that it had a unisex lavatory – alongside ex-boyfriend Billy, now married to Georgia (Courtney Thorne-Smith, late of ➢*Melrose Place*). Plagued by post-feminist neuroses and lingering lurve for Billy, and dazed by office politics, the ditzy short-skirted Ally McBeal skipped flakily from one comic dilemma to the next, with some wacky fantasy scenes (visualizations of McBeal's innermost thoughts: frolicking with Billy in a giant latte, bra-bursting breast growth, dancing embryos) along the way. Variously the best thing since the last best thing ('Button-pushing storylines hot off the cultural Zeitgeist', *Entertainment Weekly*) or cringe-making politically incorrect male fantasy, the show was dreamed up by David E. Kelley, previously a Steven Bochco sidekick and the creator of *Chicago Hope*, ➢*Doogie Howser, MD* and ➢*Picket Fences*. (Kelley, allegedly, modelled McBeal on his wife, Michelle Pfeiffer.) Stylistically, at least, the show was a treat with innovative – even unique – sound design that used mood music subjectively to show the emotional state of only one of the characters on screen.

CAST *Ally McBeal* Calista Flockhart *Billy Thomas* Gil Bellows *Richard Fish* Greg Germann *Renee Radick* Lisa Nicole Carson *Georgia Thomas* Courtney Thorne-Smith *Elaine Vassal* Jane Krakowski *John 'The Biscuit' Cage* Peter MacNicol *Judge Jennifer 'Whipper' Cone* Dyan Cannon /*cr* David E. Kelley /*exec pr* David E. Kelley /*pr* Mike Listo, Jonathan Pontell /*dr* inc Thomas Schlamme, James Frawley, Daniel Attias, Allan Arkush, Tom Moore, Jonathan Pontell, Arlene Sanford, Elodie Keene, Peter MacNicol /*wr* inc David E. Kelley /*mus* Danny Lux, Vonda Shepard /*20th Century Fox: David E. Kelley Productions* (USA) /28 x 50m col /US tx Fox TV 1997–.

Alvin and the Chipmunks

Children's. BBC1 1990–3

Reversing the usual TV-pop music course, *Alvin and the Chipmunks* began life with a 1958 novelty record by David Saville (aka Ross Bagdasarian Sr), 'The Chipmunk Song'. It sold 4.5 million copies in seven weeks, 'Chipmunk fever' prompting Saville to create an animated *The Alvin Show* (CBS 1961, 26 x 30m bw), featuring three singing Chipmunks – impulsive Alvin and his sensible siblings, Simon and Theodore – in which the characters spoke in the same high-pitched, sped-up voice he had used on vinyl. The setting for Alvin's antics was the home of Saville, who acted as the Chipmunks' manager. While furry, fat-cheeked mischief took up most of the cartoon's 30 minutes, there were also a number of other segments, including 'The

Adventures of Clyde Crashcup' (a nutty inventor) and 'Sinbad Jr' (a brawny matelot). Hugely popular, *The Alvin Show* enjoyed reruns on US network CBS during 1962–5, but the greater part of Chipmunk fame was still to come. Over a decade later, a US DJ invented a sound he called 'Chipmunk Punk', an album of that title going platinum by 1981. Once again keen to cash in on Chipmunk mania, an American station (this time NBC) commissioned a Chipmunk cartoon. Voiced by Ross Bagdasarian Jr, the son of the by-now-deceased Saville, *Alvin and the Chipmunks* became the no. 1 ranked Saturday morning series in America, and spun off a full-length animated feature movie, *The Chipmunk Adventure* (1987). Bagdasarian Jr's principal collaborator on the show – which was later retitled *The Chipmunks Go to the Movies*, to reflect its mainstay parodying of Hollywood products (e.g. 'Robomunk', 'Batmunk') – was Janice Karman, later his wife.

CAST (voice) *David Saville/The Chipmunks* Ross Bagdasarian Jr /*cr* Ross Bagdasarian /*pr* Joe Ruby, Ken Spears /*wr* Ross Bagdasarian Jr, Janice Karman / *Bagdasarian Productions* (USA) /50 x 30m, 3 x 60m col / US tx NCB 1983–91.

American Gothic

Crime & Mystery. C4 1996

Cult American horror soap, with obvious influences (➢*Twin Peaks*, ➢*Eerie, Indiana*, ➢*The X-Files*) but executed with an unnerving atmosphere and a dramatic, bone-chilling panache all of its own. Created and written by Shaun Cassidy (brother of David and star of *The Hardy Boys*), it starred Gary Cole (from *Midnight Caller*) as demonic Sheriff Lucas Buck, *de facto* ruler of the small and apparently normal South Carolina town of Trinity. The story, an epic tale of good v. evil, revolved around teenager Caleb Temple, effectively an orphan after the bloody death of his sister and the ensuing arrest of his seemingly deranged father. Buck sought to have himself appointed the boy's guardian. Most of the townsfolk were weak and venal, but there were would-be saviours in the shape of newcomer doctor Matt Crower and journalist Gail Emory. Directed by Sam Raimi, whose flair for frightening was evidenced previously by the *Evil Dead* film trilogy.

CAST *Sheriff Lucas Buck* Gary Cole *Caleb Temple* Lucas Black *Selena* Brenda Bakke *Deputy Ben Healy* Nick Searcy *Dr Matt Crower* Jake Weber *Gail Emory* Paige Turco /*cr* Shaun Cassidy /*exec pr* Sam Raimi, Robert Tapert /*dr* inc Lou Antonio, Mike Binder /*wr* Shaun Cassidy /*Renaissance Pictures* (USA) /22 x 60m col /US tx CBS 1995–6.

Amos 'n' Andy

Comedy. BBC 1954

TV version of the enormously popular radio series about a black Harlem conman, George 'Kingfish' Stevens, and his endlessly gullible prey, Andy Brown. Both were members of The Mystic Knights of the Sea Lodge, and any qualms on Andy's part were always soothed by Kingfish's appeal to lodge fraternity, 'We's all got to stick togethah in dis heah ting…'. The Amos of the title was actually a minor character, a hardworking, philosophical cabbie who also narrated. The series ceased production not for lack of viewers, but because African-American pressure groups such as the NAACP objected to its racist stereotyping of black people (viz. 'inferior, lazy, dumb and dishonest'). When Blatz Beer withdrew its sponsorship and Kenya banned the show, CBS responded to the protests by withdrawing it from domestic and foreign sale. Produced by Freeman Gosden and Charles Correll, the white actors who had created and starred in the radio version, the series had the technical distinction of being one of the first to be broadcast with a canned-laughter soundtrack, and the cultural distinction of being the first with an all-black cast.

CAST *Andrew Hogg Brown* Spencer Williams Jr *George 'Kingfish' Stevens* Tim Moore *Amos Jones* Alvin Childress *Sapphire Stevens* Ernestine Wade *Mama* Amanda Randolph /*cr* Freeman Gosden, Charles Correll /*pr* Freeman Gosden, Charles Correll, James Fonda /*dr* inc Charles Barton /*wr* inc Freeman Gosden, Charles Correll /*mus* Gaetano Braga (theme song) /*CBS* (USA) /78 x 30m bw /US tx CBS 1951–5.

Andy Pandy

Children's. BBC 1950–70

The visibly-stringed puppet, dressed in a blue-and-white striped suit and floppy hat, was the creation of schoolteacher Maria Bird and made at the behest of the BBC's Head of Children's Programmes, Freda Lingstrom. The first four episodes were screened as an experiment, with the Corporation inviting mothers' views before producing a full series. For the big time, Andy

Pandy was joined in his picnic-basket home by Teddy and Looby Loo, a rag doll, who had her own special song, 'Here we go Looby Loo'. Stories were as simple (and innocent) as the means by which Andy was manipulated – a ride on the swing, a turn on the see-saw – accompanied by commentary from Vera McKechnie and songs by Janet Ferber, later replaced by Gladys Whitred.

Andy Pandy, which filled the Tuesday slot of ➢*Watch with Mother*, was repeated up to 1969, by which time the original, oft used 26 black-and-white prints had become too poor to use. Thirteen new episodes, shot in colour at the Abbey Road Studios, were made in 1970, and repeated to 1976.

The immortal closing refrain: 'Time to go home, time to go home, Andy is waving goodbye, goodbye.'

CAST (narrator) Vera McKechnie /*cr* Maria Bird, Freda Lingstrom, Mary Adams /*wr* Maria Bird, Freda Lingstrom /*sfx* (puppeteers) Audrey Atterbury, Molly Gibson /*mus* Maria Bird /*BBC TV* (UK) /26 x 15m bw; 13 x 15m col.

The Andy Williams Show

Light Entertainment. BBC 1963–8

The longest-running and most-loved of smooth-voiced crooner Andy Williams' music–variety shows of the 50s and 60s. Initially, the main support act was the New Christy Minstrels, but these were later replaced by – to quote the introductory billing – a 'youthful barbershop harmony group from Ogden, Utah'. Williams had discovered The Osmond Brothers. Among the other regulars were Dick Van Dyke, comedian Jonathan Winters (➢*Mork and Mindy*), and the Mike Post Orchestra. In an attempt to keep abreast of the swinging times, the hitherto straight show was zanily updated in the late 60s, complete with psychedelic sets and a talking bear. Other programme fixtures included Big Bird, and 'The Williams Weirdos' slot. The theme tune was 'Moon River', performed by Henry Mancini and Johnny Mercer.

CAST (presenter) Andy Williams /*pr* Alan Bernard, Bob Finkel, Andy Williams /*dr* inc Walter Miller /*wr* inc Jonathan Winters /mus Henry Mancini & Johnny Mercer ('Moon River' theme) /*Barnaby Productions* (USA) /100 x 60m bw /col /US tx NBC 1962–71.

Angels

Melodrama. BBC1 1975–83

Medicated soap opera, set in London's (fictitious) St Angela's Hospital, following the fortunes of six student nurses. Notable for its quasi-documentary style (it was dubbed the '➢*Z Cars* of nursing'), it also proved a training ground for young actresses: Pauline Quirke (➢*Birds of a Feather*), Fiona Fullerton, Kathryn Apanowicz (➢*EastEnders*), Shirley Cheriton (also *EastEnders*), and Lesley Dunlop (➢*May to December*) were among those who donned capes and latex gloves. Creator Paula Milne's later work included a return to medical theatre with *An Affair of the Heart*.

CAST *Patricia Rutherford* Fiona Fullerton *Maureen Morahan* Erin Geraghty *Shirley Brent* Clare Clifford *Jo Longhurst* Julie Dawn Cole *Sita Patel* Karan David *Kathy Betts* Shirley Cheriton *Rose Butchins* Kathryn Apanowicz *Vicky Smith* Pauline Quirke *Ruth Fullman* Lesley Dunlop /*cr* Paula Milne /*pr* Ron Craddock, Julia Smith, Ben Rea /*dr* inc Julia Smith, Tristan de Vere Cole, Derek Martinus /*wr* inc Paula Milne, Anne Valery, Deborah Mortimer /*BBC TV* (UK) /57 x 50m; 97 x 25m col.

Animal Magic

Children's. BBC/BBC1 1962–84

A former presenter of *The Hot Chestnut Man*, Johnny Morris became the man who could talk to the animals after a BBC executive suggested the idea of a whimsical zoology show. *Animal Magic* became a mainstay of the Corporation's junior-time output for 21 years, with Morris observing animals in the studio, Bristol Zoo (a favourite habitat) and, later, such faraway places as Miami Seaquarium. Dubbed over the visuals were Morris' animal voices, which put humorous words into the various faunas' mouths and beaks. Also seen in the early years were wildlife film-maker Tony Soper and naturalist Gerald Durrell. Towards the end of its lifespan the show was co-presented by Terry Nutkins.

CAST (presenter) Johnny Morris /*pr* inc Winwood Reade /*BBC West* (UK) /approx. 440 x 30m bw:col.

Animals of Farthing Wood

Children's. BBC1 1994–

Mega-ECU animation, funded by 19 countries, which sought to create a specifically European style of cartoon-making. Based on the books by Colin Dann, it told – the frequently lachrymose – tale of how the animals of Farthing Wood, their homes threatened with destruction, made the long trek to the 'safety' of White Deer Park. At the heart of the anthropomorphic, fable-like stories was the oath of Farthing Wood, by which the animals sought to live in harmony.

CAST (voices) Ron Moody, Sally Grace, Jon Glover, Pamela Keevil Kral, Rupert Farley, Jeremy Barrett, Stacey Jefferson /*exec pr* Theresa Plummer Andrews, Siegmund Grewenig /*pr* John M. Mills /*dr* Elphin Lloyd-Jones /*wr* Steve Walker /*mus* Detlev Kuhne / *Telemagination: La Fabrique* (UK/Fr) /29 x 25m col.

Animaniacs

Children's. ITV 1995–

After decades of imprisonment in the water tower at Warner Bros studio lot (so the premise went), three cartoon characters – Yakko, Wakko and Dot – escaped to wreak madcap mayhem and drop sight-gags galore, often to musical accompaniment. Each episode consisted of either one 30-minute adventure (occasionally 60 minutes) or two to three shorts. The 'Warner brothers (and sister)' were joined in their 'zany to the max' antics by a crayon-case of comic creature creations, among them: Slappy Squirrel, the Goodfeathers (three pigeons who were clever take-offs of the mafiosa in the 1990 film *Goodfellas*), the Hip Hippos, Mr Skullhead, Pinky and the Brain, Mindy and Buttons, and Viennese psychiatrist Dr Scratchensniff. Intended as a successor to Warner Bros' *Tiny Toon Adventures*, the show combined classic Warner Bros animation with rapid-fire pop culture references (Gorbachev walking the streets with a board proclaiming 'Will Sell Secrets for Food', countless Jack Nicholson jokes) to enjoy crossover success. *Animaniacs* was executive produced by Steven Spielberg – indeed, its full title was *Steven Spielberg Presents Animaniacs* – who personally supervised each script.

CAST (voices) *Yakko/Pinky* Rob Paulsen *Wakko* Jess Harnell *Dot* Tress MacNeille *The Brain* Maurice Le Marche /*exec pr* Steven Spielberg /*pr* Tom Ruegger, Rich Arons, Sherri Stoner /*dr* inc Rusty Mills, Dave Marshall, Barry Caldwell, Rich Arons, Bob Kline /*wr* inc Tom Ruegger, Sherri Stoner, Paul Rugg, Randy Rogel /*mus* (theme) Richard Stone, Tom Ruegger / *Amblin Entertainment: Warner Bros* (USA) /98+ x 30, 60m col /US tx Fox: Kid's WB 1993–8.

The Appleyards

Children's. BBC 1952–7

A suburban, Home Counties family experience domestic ups and downs every fortnight. Transmitted as part of the *Children's Television* slot of 50s golden short-trousered memory, *The Appleyards* was the first British soap-opera for children, its tales of serial ordinariness making it the junior version of the BBC's own ➢*The Grove Family*, which ran for the same period. The title was not to the liking of the Controller of Programmes, Cecil McGivern, who famously suggested that it sounded like 'suet pudding with a dash of cement'. A reunion special, *Christmas with the Appleyards*, was screened in 1960.

CAST *Mr Appleyard* Frederick Piper/Douglas Muir *Mrs Appleyard* Constance Fraser *John Appleyard* David Edwards *Janet Appleyard* Tessa Clarke *Tommy Appleyard* Derek Rowe *Margaret Appleyard* Pat Fryer / *cr* Philip Burton /*pr* Kevin Sheldon /*wr* Philip Burton, Kevin Sheldon /*BBC TV* (UK) /160 x 20m bw.

Are You Being Served?

Comedy. BBC1 1972–84

The shutters of Grace Brothers department store first opened for business as part of BBC's ➢*Comedy Playhouse*, launching the sales staff of Ladies' and Gentlemen's Ready-to-Wear on an 11-year career of cut-price double entendres ('We'd like to complain about the state of our drawers – they're disgusting') and off-the-peg visual gags. John Inman's portrayal of mincing, limp-wristed menswear assistant Mr Humphries, who volunteered to measure an inside leg with a cry of 'I'm free!', made him a household name. (Initially the target of gay protest in the USA, Inman, a former Austin Reed window-dresser, eventually became a homosexual icon.) It fell, though, to the lilac-eyeshadowed Mrs Slocombe to deliver the show's most risqué lines, which involved the activities of her 'pussy'. Making up the rest of the stereotyped staff were pompous floor-walker Captain Peacock, crotchety menswear head Mr Grainger, libidinous assistant Mr Lucas (later replaced by Mr Spooner), bosomy Miss Brahms (Wendy Richard, ➢*EastEnders*), ineffectual departmental manager Mr Rumbold, uppity caretaker Harman and geriatric dolly-bird-chasing owner Young Mr Grace ('You've all done very well'). A film version was released in 1977 by Anglo-EMI. Although *Are You Being Served?* shut up shop in 1984, most of its characters were revived by writers Jeremy Lloyd and David Croft a decade later for a spin-off, *Grace and Favour* (BBC1, 1992–3), which set them in a rundown country hotel, Millstone Manor, bought by Young Mr Grace with the store's pension fund. The humour, however, remained unchanged, a latter-day TV version of seaside-postcard vulgarity.

Are You Being Served? enjoyed a successful run on America's PBS, but a US version of the show, *Beane's of Boston,* singularly failed to attract customers.

CAST *Mr Humphries* John Inman *Mrs Betty Slocombe* Mollie Sugden *Miss Brahms* Wendy Richard *Captain Stephen Peacock* Frank Thornton *Mr Granger* Arthur Brough *Mr Lucas* Trevor Bannister *Mr Cuthbert Rumbold* Nicholas Smith *Mr Harman* Arthur English *Young Mr Grace* Harold Bennett *Mr Spooner* Mike Berry /*cr* Jeremy Lloyd, David Croft /*exec pr* David Croft /*pr* David Croft, Bob Spiers /*dr* Bob Spiers, Bernard Thompson, Ray Butt, David Croft, Jeremy Lloyd /*wr* Jeremy Lloyd, David Croft /*BBC TV* (UK) / 69 x 30m col /US tx PBS 1984–5.

Armchair Theatre
Drama. ITV 1956–74

Launched by ABC Television (UK) as a heavy-weight player in a quality-drama Sunday schedule dominated by the BBC, *Armchair Theatre* translated a number of classics to the small screen (among them Scott Fitzgerald's *The Last Tycoon* and Wilde's *The Picture of Dorian Gray*) but specialised in contemporary 'kitchen sink' dramas. Typical of these grimy proletarian pieces, which flourished particularly under the auspices of Canadian producer Sydney Newman (➢*Dr Who*), was Alun Owen's 1960 'Lena, O My Lena', about a Liverpool student who falls in love with a woman factory worker (played by Billie Whitelaw). Of the same type and vintage was Harold Pinter's 'A Night Out'. Directors working for 'Armpit Theatre' – as it was soon nicknamed – in this period included John Moxey (later to work a berth in Hollywood), Philip Saville and George More O'Ferrall, all of whom helmed movie-like work despite the constraints of live broadcast. This *AT* Golden Age also produced two major spin-off series: John Wyndham's 1962 'Dumb Martian' play acted as a trailer for the sci-fi anthology ➢*Out of This World,* while James Mitchell's 'Magnum for Schneider' eventually became ➢*Callan.* During the ITV franchise changeover of 1968, *AT* became the property of Thames TV, who let it dwindle before reviving it in the early 70s as *Armchair Cinema.* While this resurrection proved short-lived, its influence lasted beyond the televisual grave. The 1974 *AC* film 'Regan' served as the pilot for ➢*The Sweeney,* the most influential British *policier* series of the 70s.

CAST *pr* inc Sydney Newman, Leonard White /*dr* Sydney Newman, Ted Kotcheff, John Moxey, Philip Saville, Charles Jarrott, David Greene /*wr* inc Alun Owen, Mordecai Richler, Harold Pinter, Ted Willis, Robert Muller /*ABC: Thames TV* (UK) /100 x 60:90m bw:col.

The Army Game
Comedy. ITV 1957–61

Phenomenally popular Granada TV series, modelled on the 1956 film, *Private's Progress.* Set in Hut 29 of Nether Hopping transit camp and surplus ordnance depot in remotest Staffordshire, the initial *Army Game* recruits consisted of Private 'Excused Boots' Bisley (so-called because he was allowed to wear plimsolls instead of regulation soldierly footwear), Private 'Cupcake' Cook, moronic Private 'Popeye' Popplewell (whose standard refrain 'I only arsked' became a national catch-phrase – and the title for a 1958 movie spin-off), and their Bilkoesque ringleader, Corporal Springer. Bellowing Sergeant Major Bullimore was charged with the maintenance of their discipline, whilst upper class Major Upshot-Bagley was camp commandant. Initially broad-cast fortnightly (live), then weekly, its theme song (sung by Leslie Fyson, with cast members Michael Medwin, Alfie Bass and Bernard Bresslaw) became a top five hit in 1958. That same year, however, saw the haemorrhaging of actorly talent which would ultimately prove the show's demise. Among the first to go were Charles Hawtrey, Bernard Bresslaw, William Hartnell (later ➢*Dr Who*), and Michael Medwin (➢*Shoestring*). Despite new thespian blood in the form of Bill Fraser as CSM Claude Snudge ('I'll be leaving you now, sah!') and Dick Emery's Private 'Chubby'

Catchpole (Emery's later catch-phrase, 'Hello, honky tonks', was born as a *TAG* line) and such scriptwriters as Barry Took and Marty Feldman, the show slid slowly down the ratings. When, in 1960, producer Peter Eton decided to transfer the characters Bootsie and Snudge into another series, *Bootsie and Snudge in Civvy Street, The Army Game* was quietly terminated. Although its innocent, unsophisticated humour dated quickly, it launched a whole generation of British actors and remains, alongside ➢*Get Some In* and ➢*Blackadder Goes Forth*, one of the few indigenous military sitcoms to be set outside World War II.

CAST *Cpl Springer* Michael Medwin *Pte 'Excused Boots' Bisley* Alfie Bass *Pte 'Cupcake' Cook* Norman Rossington/Keith Banks *Pte 'Popeye' Popplewell* Bernard Bresslaw *Pte 'Professor' Hatchett* Charles Hawtrey/Keith Smith *Sgt Major Bullimore* William Hartnell *Major Upshot-Bagley* Geoffrey Sumner/Jack Allen *CSM Claude Snudge* Bill Fraser *Major Geoffrey Duckworth* C.B. Poultney *Pte Bone* Ted Lune *Cpl 'Flogger' Hoskins* Harry Fowler *L/Cpl Ernest 'Moosh' Merryweather* Mario Fabrizi *Pte 'Chubby' Catchpole* Dick Emery */cr* Sid Colin */pr* Peter Eton, Graeme McDonald */dr* Milo Lewis, Max Morgan-Witts, Gordon Flemyng, Graeme McDonald */wr* inc Sid Colin, Lew Schwarz, Barry Took, Marty Feldman, John Antrobus, Larry Stephens */mus* (theme lyric) Pat Napper */Granada TV* (UK) /157 x 30m bw.

Arrest and Trial

Crime. BBC1 1964

Innovative but short-lived crime show: the first 45 minutes depicted the efforts of LAPD Detective Sergeant Nick Anderson (Ben Gazzara) to catch the episode's villain, the second 45 minutes the attempts of lawyer John Egan (Chuck Norris in an early screen part) to get him or her found not guilty. Its joining of crime caper and courtroom melodrama has been widely imitated since, not least by ➢*Law and Order.*

CAST *Det. Sgt Nick Anderson* Ben Gazzara *Attorney John Egan* Chuck Norris */pr* Frank P. Rosenberg */dr* inc Lewis Milestone, Jack Smight */A Revue Production for Universal* (USA) /30 x 90m bw /US tx ABC 1963–4.

Arthur of the Britons

Adventure. ITV 1972–3

Hyper-realistic version of the life and times of King Arthur, Merlin, Camelot, Guinevere and even the Round Table, sans myth. Instead, Patrick Dromgoole's (➢*Children of the Stones*) production depicted a brutish and barbaric 6th-century Britain, with Arthur as a wildly rugged (if also handsomely youthful) Welsh chieftain attempting to fend off the Saxon hoards. The sets were dirtily authentic and the set-piece battle sequences juiced with scenes of bloody swordplay. This, plus clean-limbed direction, and a charismatic lead in Oliver Tobias, made the serial a high point in 70s adventure programming for the just-home-from-school crowd.

CAST *Arthur* Oliver Tobias *Llud* Jack Watson *Kai* Michael Gothard *Mark of Cornwall* Brian Blessed *Cerdig* Rupert Davies */exec pr* Patrick Dromgoole / *pr* Peter Miller */dr* inc Pat Jackson, Sidney Hayers / *wr* inc Robert Banks Stewart, Terence Feely */HTV* (UK) /24 x 30m col.

Astroboy

Children's. ITV 1964

The first Japanese cartoon to become a hit in the UK was an imaginative sci-fi fantasy relating the adventures of a robot boy. Built by Dr Boynton in the year 2003 as a 'duplicate' of his own son (Toby, who had perished in a car crash), Astroboy used his formidable powers (computer brain and rocket-powered feet) to combat a relentless parade of outer-space monsters and super-villains. Clever storylines and engaging characterisation offset fairly unsophisticated animation. *Astroboy* was revived in 1982, under Noboru Ishiguro's direction for Tezuka of Japan.

CAST (voices) *Astroboy* Billie Lou Watt *Dr Elefun* Ray Owens */cr* Fumiro Suzuki */pr* Fumiro Suzuki, Osamu Tekuka */Mushi Productions* (Jap) /26 x 30m bw.

The A-Team

Adventure. ITV 1984–8

Popular actioner with a cartoon-strip tendency towards explosive violence with little or no injury to the protagonists (even the baddies). It featured cigar-chomping Colonel John 'Hannibal' Smith (George Peppard, ➢*Banacek, Night of the Fox*) as the leader of an ex-Vietnam War special forces outfit (an A-Team), who had gone AWOL in the USA after the authorities deemed their last military action – robbing the Bank of Hanoi – unauthorised. Underground, they used their crack military skills to help anyone in need. Handsome 'Faceman' Peck (Dirk Benedict, ➢*Battlestar Galactica*) was the No. 2, air-travel-phobic giant black sergeant Bosco BA ('Bad Attitude') Barracus provided muscle power and engineering skills and drove the team's heavily armed transit van, while HM ('Howlin' Mad') Murdock was the wingsman, sprung from a psychiatric hospital for missions. For their first season the ragtag soldiers of fortune were joined by a journalist, Amy Amanda Allen ('Triple A'); for their last, they recruited 'Dishpan' Sanchez. Many of the show's devotees (14.6 million at its British height) were children who idolised the grunting ('Watch it, sucker!'), gold-swathed BA, played by actor Mr T (aka Lawrence Tero, born Lawrence Tureaud). This, perhaps, was not surprising, since the show had been essentially created for Mr T, after NBC programme chief Brandon Tartikoff had seen him as Clubber Lang in the movie *Rocky III*. Complaints about the *A-Team*'s violence quotient eventually caused it to be withdrawn from transmission in Britain.

CAST *Col John 'Hannibal' Smith* George Peppard *Lt Templeton 'Faceman' Peck* Dirk Benedict (Tim Dunnigan in pilot) *Bosco BA Barracus* Mr T *HM 'Howlin' Mad' Murdock* Dwight Schultz *Amy 'Triple A' Allen* Melinda Culea *Frankie 'Dishpan' Santana* Eddie Velez *Gen. Hunt Stockwell* Robert Vaughn /*cr* Brandon Tarikoff, Frank Lupo, Stephen J. Cannell /*exec pr* inc Stephen J. Cannell, Frank Lupo, John Ashley /*pr* Gary Winter /*dr* inc Bruce Kessler, Bernard McEveety, Christian I. Nyby, Ron Satloff, Arnold Laven, Michael O'Herlihy /*wr* inc Stephen J. Cannell, Frank Lupo, Stephen Katz, Mark Jones, Bill Nuss /*mus* Mike Post / *Stephen J Cannell Production: Universal TV* (USA) / 98 x 60m col /US tx NBC 1983–7.

At Last the 1948 Show

Comedy. ITV 1967

A frenetically-paced sketch and gag show, derived from executive producer David Frost's own *Frost Report*. Notably, it brought together the madcap scribing and performing talents of John Cleese, Graham Chapman, Marty Feldman and Tim Brooke-Taylor. The result was a product that was anarchic, surreal and highly visual. The only link between the skits was the baby-voiced commentary of Aimi Macdonald. Thus *At Last* prefigured both ➢*Monty Python's Flying Circus* and ➢*The Goodies*, and along with ➢*Do Not Adjust Your Set* was one of the decisive moments in the rise of the new generation of 60s TV comedians.

CAST Marty Feldman, Aimi Macdonald, Graham Chapman, Tim Brooke-Taylor, John Cleese /*cr* David Frost /*exec pr* David Frost /*dr* Ian Fordyce /*wr* Marty Feldman, John Cleese, Graham Chapman, Tim Brooke-Taylor /*Rediffusion* (UK) /13 x 30m col.

Auf Wiedersehen, Pet

Comedy. ITV 1983–6

Or ➢*The Likely Lads* go to Germany. Created by Dick Clement and Ian La Frenais (from an idea by expatriate bricklayer Franc Roddam), *AWP* related the misadventures of three Geordies philosophical Denis, anxious Neville and slobbish Oz – persuaded by local unemployment to seek work on a Dusseldorf building site. En route, they were joined by cockney lothario Wayne, Bristolian ex-boxer Bomber, boring Brummie Barry, and pock-faced Liverpudlian arsonist Moxey. Like the contemporaneous ➢*The Boys from the Blackstuff*, the series acutely reflected societal concern about 'dole queues', but was written with an altogether broader scope: above all, *AWP* was a wry analysis of human nature in its British manifestation, with the close confines of the Düsseldorf accommodation hut (where much of the action took place) acting as a comic-dramatic intensifier. By the end of the first season, the popular success of *AWP* (13.4 million viewers in February 1984) had ingrained its characters in the national consciousness, with the bigoted, dirty-underpants-wearing Oz (played by former nightclub singer and ex-convict Jimmy Nail) elevated to the pantheon of television immortals. A second season found 'The Magnificent Seven' obliged to work for Tyneside gangster Ally Frazer on his tasteless piles, first in Derbyshire, then on Spain's Costa Del Crime. There were many fine moments, none more memorable than Oz, beneath the Tyne bridge, saying goodbye to a son lost through his own carelessness, displaying the emotional side viewers had always hoped existed. (The best gag line of the season also fell to Oz: asked by a pressman who thought him an armed robber, whether he was 'tooled up on his last job', the bricklayer replied: 'Oh aye, with a spirit-level and trowel'.) However, the tragic drink-and-drug induced death of actor Gary Holton during filming removed a vital presence, and the show was visibly diminished, despite use of a 'double' so that the character of Wayne appeared in every episode. In recognition of Holton's contribution, the remainder of the cast refused to make a third series, provisionally set in Moscow. Most, however, have since progressed to other things, with Spall (➢*Frank Stubbs Promotes*, ➢*Outside Edge*), Whately (➢*Inspector Morse*, ➢*Peak Practice*), Healy (*Boys from the Bush*, ➢*Common as Muck*) and Nail (➢*Spender*, *Crocodile Shoes*) becoming staples of the British box of delights.

CAST *Denis* Tim Healy *Neville* Kevin Whately *Oz* Jimmy Nail *Wayne* Gary Holton *Bomber* Pat Roach *Barry* Timothy Spall *Moxey* Christopher Fairbank *Dagmar* Brigitte Khan *Ulrich* Peter Birch *Magowan* Michael Elphick *Ally Fraser* Bill Paterson /*cr* Ian La Frenais, Dick Clement, Franc Roddam /*exec pr* Allan McKeown /*dr* Roger Bamford, Baz Taylor, Anthony Garner /*wr* Dick Clement, Ian La Frenais, Francis Megahy, Bernie Cooper /*mus* Ian La Frenais, Joe Fagin ('That's Livin' Alright' theme) /*Witzend; Central TV* (UK) /26 x 60m col.

Automan

Crime. BBC1 1984

Futuristic cop show featuring a 3D-hologram detective, inadvertently created by wimpish desk-bound LAPD computer operator Walter Nebicher. Essentially Nebicher's macho alter ego, Automan also possessed such distinctly useful – and meta-human – qualities as being able to walk through walls. With the Automan by his side and the Cursor – a freewheeling computer-screen dot able to materialise anything on command – in attendance, Nebicher became an ace crime-buster. A significant blip, however, in Nebicher's sleuthing was that peak-time LA electrical consumption would cause the volt-hungry Automan to fade, even disappear. The character of Nebicher was played by Desi Arnaz Jr, son of ➢*I Love Lucy* stars Desi Arnaz and Lucille Ball.

CAST *Automan* Chuck Wagner *Walter Nebicher* Desi Arnaz Jr *Lt Jack Curtis* Robert Lansing *Capt. E.G. Boyd* Gerald S. O'Loughlin /*cr* Glen A. Larson /*pr* Glen A. Larson /*dr* inc Rick Kolbe, Allen Baron, Lee H. Katzin, Gil Bettman, Kim Manners /*wr* inc Glen A. Larson, Doug Heyes Jr /*mus* J.A.C. Radford, Morton Stevens / *Kushner-Locke* (USA) /3 x 60m, 12 x 50m col / US tx ABC 1983–4.

The Avengers

Crime & Mystery. ITV 1961–9

Cultish espionage series which began as an orthodox crime vehicle for Ian Hendry (*Police Surgeon*), who departed in 1962 to be replaced as top billing by Old Etonian Patrick Mcnee. If Mcnee's perfect portrayal of smilingly insolent, bowler-hatted MI5 undercover agent John Steed hinted at escapism, the show's trend towards fantasy truly began with the introduction of ex-World War II dispatch rider Honor Blackman as leather-clad female sidekick Cathy Gale, who judo-threw her way to TV immortality – and a role as Pussy Galore in the 007 film *Goldfinger* (1964). Her vacant fetishistic series clothes were later filled by Elizabeth Shepherd, who was quickly forsaken for Diana Rigg as Emma Peel (the name being a pun on 'M[an]-Appeal). Recalled Rigg of the series some years later: 'It really was quite kinky. I always seemed to be strapped to a dentist's chair with my feet in the air, and the camera always seemed to linger a lot on my high-heeled boots.' One scene featuring Rigg in a Miss Whiplash costume was cut for the sake of public decency. This notwithstanding, Peel's wardrobe, which was designed principally by couturier John Bates, was marketed successfully in Britain and abroad as 'The Avengers Collection'.

The Peel period was the *Avengers*' apogee. An increase in location filming enabled the series to break out of its studio-bound look, while plots became ever more baroque, and villains ever more diabolical (Peter Cushing and Christopher Lee were among those playing MI5's enemies). Above all, there was the faultlessly maintained illusion of a picture-postcard Britain devoid of factories and poverty; as key writer-producer Brian Clemens (later ➢*The Professionals*) expressed it: 'We admitted to only one class ... and that was the upper.'

When Rigg left the series (after a dispute over wages), the distaff side of the partnership passed to Linda Thorson as Tara King. Alas, the previous chemistry was missing, and to fill the charisma vacuum, Mother, a portly, wheelchair-bound (male) controller was introduced. More fundamentally, the cultural moment for the *Avengers* – which was suffused with the swinging self-confidence of the 60s – had passed. The show was cancelled in 1969.

Six years later the uninspired *New Avengers* reached the screen (1976–7), with Macnee – now 54 – once again twirling his brolly as Steed, but with the action falling to the younger limbs of ex-ballerina Joanna Lumley as Purdey (named after the exclusive shotgun firm) and Gareth Hunt as ex-SAS major Mike Gambit. Lumley, at least, was destined for greater things (➢*Sapphire and Steel*, ➢*Absolutely Fabulous*), but the series left little impression beyond her much copied page-boy style haircut.

CAST *John Steed* Patrick Macnee *Dr David Keel* Ian Hendry *Catherine Gale* Honor Blackman *Emma Peel* Diana Rigg *Tara King* Linda Thorson *Mother* Patrick Newell /*cr* Sydney Newman, Leonard White /*exec pr* Albert Fennel, Julian Wintle, Gordon L.T. Scott /*pr* Leonard White, John Bryce, Albert Fennell, Brian Clemens /*dr* inc Charles Crichton, Bill Bain, Jonathan Alwyn, John Moxey, Cyril Frankel, Don Chaffey, Peter Hammond /*wr* inc Brian Clemens, Malcolm Hulke & Terence Dicks, John Lucarotti, Roger Marshall, Dennis Spooner, Berkley Mather, Peter Ling, John Kruse, Robert Banks Stewart, Terry Nation /*mus* Johnny Dankworth, Laurie Johnson /*An ABC Television Production* (UK) /161 x 50m bw:col / US tx ABC 1966–9.

B

Babylon 5

Sci-fi. C4 1994–

It is the year 2258 AD. After decades of interplanetary conflict between the five major solar systems – the Earth Alliance, Minbari Federation, Narn Regime, Vorlon Empire and Centauri Republic – a fragile peace is overseen by a council of humans and aliens which sits aboard lone space station *Babylon 5*. This five-mile long, 2.5 million tons of metal is commanded by Jeffrey Sinclair (later replaced by Captain John Sheridan), who is also the Earth Alliance representative on the Council, the other chief members of which are: Ambassador G'Kar of the Narn; fan-haired Ambassador Londo Mollari of the once-great Centauri ('We have become a tourist attraction'); mysterious Ambassador Kosh Naranek of the Vorlon Empire, eventually revealed to be an angel-type being beneath his protective encounter suit; and bald female Ambassador Delenn of the Minbari, who forms romantic attachments with both Sinclair and Sheridan.

Conceived by J(oseph) Michael Straczynski as a televisual novel, complete with beginning, middle and end, *B5* was the thinking person's sci-fi drama of the 90s, replete with allegory (including of the civil wars in Yugoslavia), plot and deeply-drawn characters. Those with their brains switched off found much to mesmerize them in Ron Thornton's computer-generated special effects.

In accordance with the promise from Straczynski (who retained auteur-like control over the programme) to provide constant narrative surprise, season two culminated in a star war between the Narn Regime and the Centauri, the latter triumphing after allying themselves with the evil shadows, a species amassing predatorily at the edge of the Universe. Henceforth the role of *Babylon 5*, under the guiding hand of Captain John Sheridan (Bruce Boxleitner, ➢*Scarecrow and Mrs King, I Married Wyatt Earp*) changed from the 'last, best hope for peace' to 'our last, best hope for victory'. Among the show's suitably stellar guest cast were David McCallum, Walter ➢'*Star Trek*' Koenig and Bill Mumy, formerly Will Robinson of ➢*Lost in Space*, who appeared as semi-regular Minbari attache, Lennier.

CAST *Cmdr Jeffrey Sinclair* Michael O'Hare *Capt John Sheridan* Bruce Boxleitner *Ambassador Delenn* Mira Furlan *Ambassador Londo Mollari* Peter Jurasik *Security Chief Garbaldi* Jerry Doyle *Ambassador G'Kar* Andreas Katsulas *Lt Cmdr Susan Ivanova* Claudia Christian *Talia Winters* Andrea Thompson *Dr Stephen Franklin* Richard Biggs *Carn Mollari* Peter Trencher *Lyta Alexander* Patricia Tallman *Marcus Cole* Jason Carter *Lennier* Bill Mumy *Na'Toth* June Caitlin Brown/Mary K. Adams *Vir Cotto* Stephen Furst /*cr* J. Michael Straczynski /*exec pr* J. Michael Straczynski /*pr* Robert Latham Brown, John Copeland, Richard Compton /*dr* inc David J. Eagle, Jim Johnston, Bruce Seth Green, Janet Greek, Michael Vejar, John C. Flinn III /*wr* inc J. Michael Straczynski, Scott Frost, D.C. Fontana, Lawrence G. Ditillo, David Gerrold, Mark Scott Zicree, Kathryn M. Drennan /*mus* Stewart Copeland (pilot), Christopher Franke /*sfx* Ron Thornton (visual effects design) /*Babylonian Productions* (USA) / 1 x 90m, 110 x 60m col /US tx TNT 1993–8.

BAD Cats

Crime & Mystery. ITV 1980

American police show out of the ➢*Starsky and Hutch* squealing-tyres school, so lamentable that it was cancelled after a mere six episodes. This early death caused the producer to complain that $40,000-worth of cars, bought for pyrotechnical screen smash-ups, were left unused. The contrived title stood for 'Burglary Auto Detail, Commercial Auto Thefts', whose ace, fast-driving, rule-bending cops, Ocee James and Nick Donovan, provided the main thrills'n'spills. The show's sole interest was its misused cast; Michelle Pfeiffer, in one of her earliest roles, played beautiful cop Samantha Jensen, while the part of schlerotic Captain Nathan, the detail commander, was taken by the veteran star of ➢*Combat*, Vic Morrow.

CAST *Ocee James* Steven Hanks *Nick Donovan* Asher Brauner *Samantha Jensen* Michelle Pfeiffer *Capt. Skip Nathan* Vic Morrow *Rodney Washington* Jimmie Walker /*exec pr* Aaron Spelling, Douglas S. Cramer / *pr* Everett Chambers /*dr* inc Bernard Kowalski /*mus* Barry De Vorzon, Mundell Lowe, Andrew Kulberg / *A Spelling–Cramer Production* (USA) /6 x 60m col / US tx ABC 1980.

Bagdad Cafe

Comedy. C4 1991

Percy Adlon's 1988 German art-house movie, transmogrified into an American sitcom. Ex-mortuary beautician Whoopi Goldberg took the part of Brenda, the cynical, long-suffering boss of a rundown diner in the middle of California's Mojave Desert. Husband Sal (Cleavon Little from *Blazing Saddles*) was an absent philanderer, single-parent son Junie an aspiring pianist, and daughter Debbie (Monica Calhoun reprising her movie role) the consort of a local biker, Snake. Her customers were looney tunes. Just when matters could only get better, there entered into the diner warm-hearted, fiftysomething tourist, Jasmine (Jean Stapleton, Mrs Archie Bunker in ➢*All in the Family*), who had abandoned her husband after an argument. Virtually destitute, Jasmine began work as the Bagdad Cafe's maid. The two women's subsequent roller-coaster friendship – engagingly acted by a high-octane Goldberg and a reflective Stapleton – proved the bedrock of the series.

CAST *Brenda* Whoopi Goldberg *Jasmine Zweibel* Jean Stapleton *Junie* Scott Lawrence *Debbie* Monica Calhoun *Sal* Cleavon Little /*cr* Percy Adlon /*exec pr* Zev Braun, Mort Lachman /*dr* inc Paul Bogart /*wr* Mort Lachman, Sy Rosen /*mus* Bob Telson ('Calling You' theme), Jevetta Steele (theme vocal) /*Mort Lachman and Associates: Zev Braun Productions: New World Television* (USA) /15 x 30m col /US tx CBS 1990–1.

Bagpuss

Children's. BBC 1974

An animation from the celebrated partnership of Oliver Postgate and Peter Firmin (➢*The Clangers*, ➢*Ivor the Engine*, ➢*Pingwings*) about a Victorian girl, Emily, the owner of a magic shop. There she left *objets trouvés* for repair by her beloved eponymous cloth cat – roused to action (and colour) by Emily's voice – and his friends, all of whom also habituated the Bagpuss & Co. emporium. Down from the shelf came wooden woodpecker-bookend Professor Yaffle, the mice started up the Marvellous Mechanical Mouse Organ, Madeleine the rag doll sat up, and Gabriel the toad strummed the banjo. As they mended, so they sang invented work songs ('We will mend it, we will bend it, we will fix it with glue…'). When the item was duly restored to its original glory, it was displayed in the window for collection by its rightful owners. After this, the pink and white striped Bagpuss ('baggy and a bit loose at the seams') would give a big yawn and go to sleep until the following week's adventure. Since its original transmission, the series has frequently been repeated.

CAST (narrator) Oliver Postgate /*cr* Peter Firmin, Oliver Postgate /*dr* Peter Firmin /wr Oliver Postgate / *mus* John Faulkner, Sandra Kerr /*Smallfilms* (UK) / 13 x 20m col.

Ballykissangel

Comedy. BBC1 1996–

Devised by Kieran Prendiville (also the oil rig drama *Roughnecks* and a former presenter of *That's Life*, *Tomorrow's World* and *The Holiday Programme*), *Ballykissangel* took a front pew with ➢*Father Ted* and ➢*The Vicar of Dibley* in the 90s TV resurrection of clerical comedy. Set in the gloriously pretty country of Ireland's County Wicklow (specifically the village of Avoca), it followed the comic reversals and occasional small triumphs of a newly arrived priest, Englishman Peter Clifford (played by Stephen Tompkinson, ➢*Drop the Dead Donkey*). Many of his secular travails were caused by superbly obnoxious landlady, Assumpta Fitzgerald (Dervla Kirwan, ➢*Goodnight Sweetheart*), and local fixer and businessman Brian Quigley (Tony Doyle, ➢*Between the Lines*) whose great gift to the church was a deluxe confessional, complete with fax and electronic doors, made by an Italian firm with Mob connections. Quaintly amusing, *Ballykissangel* (it means 'town of the banished angel') was the first-ever popular drama production of BBC Northern Ireland. Although executive produced by Tony Garnett (*Up the Junction*, *Cathy Come Home*, ➢*Days of Hope*, ➢*Between the Lines*) it was conspicously free of politics.

CAST *Father Peter Clifford* Stephen Tompkinson *Assumpta Fitzgerald* Dervla Kirwan *Brian Quigley* Tony Doyle *Father MacAnally* Niall Toibin *Orla O'Connell* Victoria Smurfit /*cr* Kieran Prendiville /*exec pr* Tony Garnett /*pr* Joy Lale, Chris Clough /*dr* inc Richard Standeven /*wr* Kieran Prendiville /*BBC Northern Ireland* (UK) /30+ x 30m, col.

Banacek

Crime & Mystery. ITV 1975–7

The profusion of American private eyes who walked the mean TV screen of the 70s required each to have a defining gimmick: Thomas Banacek's was his Polish ethnicity plus a high-society lifestyle. For a 10 per cent commission Banacek (George Peppard, later ➢*The A-Team*) tracked down stolen goods – though never anything worth less than a cool US$10 million – for the Boston Insurance Company. To convey him around town he had a chauffeur-driven limo and he rested his immense brain at his exclusive Beacon Hill abode. Among the several providential gifts bestowed on Banacek was an effortless ability to solve apparently insoluble cases (viz. the vanishing of an airliner, the disappearance of a footballer before a packed stadium). A regular romantic interest was provided by Boston Insurance op Carlie Kirkland, but Banacek was irresistably attractive to any passing beautiful woman. Felix Mulholland, proprietor of Mulholland's Rare Book and Print Shop, was the well-heeled gumshoe's chief confidant. To no great surprise, Polish–Americans (pejoratively 'Polacks'), long a disadvantaged group in the USA, awarded *Banacek* a postive-image prize. (Creators Richard Levinson and William Link had tackled racism via the medium of TV as early as 1959, with scripts for oater ➢*Johnny Ringo.*) The series began life as part of *The Wednesday Mystery Movies* rotating anthology.

CAST *Thomas Banacek* George Peppard *Jay Drury (chauffeur)* Ralph Manza *Felix Mullholland* Murray Matheson *Charlie Kirkland* Christine Belford *Penniman* Linden Chiles /*cr* Richard Levinson, William Link /*exec pr* George Eckstein /*pr* Howie Horowitz /*dr* inc Lou Antonio, Herschel Daugherty, Richard T. Heffron, Bernard L. Kowalski, Bernard McEveety, Andrew McLaglen, Jack Smight /*wr* inc Richard Levinson, William Link, Stephen Kandel, Paul Playdon /*mus* Billy Goldenburg /*A Universal TV Production* (USA) /1 x 98m, 16 x 90m col /US tx NBC 1972–4.

The Banana Splits

Children's. BBC 1969–71

'One banana, two banana...'

The Banana Splits – Snorky the baby elephant, Bingo the gorilla, Drooper the lion and Fleegle the dog – were a madcap animal pop group, played by men in outsize, LSD-vision costumes. At hyper speed, they cavorted around the Banana Pad (complete with a bin which refused trash), raced Buggie cars on a track, played wacky games on a football pitch and performed soft rock songs. They also told jokes which were surreally nonsensical ('What's yellow, delicious and coaches a baseball team?' 'Yogi Banana!'). During the 'Dear Drooper' spot, the wiseacre lion answered viewers' queries; this was often succeeded by the leonine one being beaten up by teenyboppers from rival pop band, The Sour Grapes. Such shenanigans (which owed a debt to both ➢*The Monkees* and ➢*Rowan and Martin's Laugh-In*, in the latter case concretized by the hiring of *RMLI* dancer, Byron Gillian, as Splits choreographer) acted as the buffers between an assortment of live-action and animated shorts: 'Danger Island', 'The Arabian Knights' (cartoon legends, with Shari Lewis providing the voice of Princess Nidor), 'The Three Musketeers' (animated version of Dumas' novel), 'The Hillbilly Bears', and 'The Micro Adventure'. In its parent USA, the series was broadcast as *The Banana Splits Adventure Hour* (sponsors: Kelloggs).

And how the mighty have risen. Richard Donner, director of movies *Superman* and *Lethal Weapon* et al, was the prime helmsman of the *Splits* 'Danger Island' segments, while soul crooner Barry White began his career penning lyrics for Drooper, Bingo, Snorky and Fleegle. Legend even has it that his immenseness was the man inside Snorky's suit.

'Hold the bus!'

CAST (voices) *Bingo* Daws Butler *Fleegle* Paul Winchell *Snorky* Don Messick *Drooper* Allan Melvin /*cr* William Hanna, Joseph Barbera /*exec pr* William Hanna, Joseph Barbera /*pr* Edward J. Rosen /*dr* inc Charles A. Nichols, Richard Donner, Tom Boutross /*wr* inc Neal Barbera, Joe Ruby, Jack Hanrahan /*mus* Ritchie Adams & Mark Barkan ('Tra La La Song') /*Hanna-Barbera* (USA) /125 x 60m col /US tx NBC 1968–70.

Band of Gold

Melodrama. ITV 1995–6

Tacky drama about a group of prostitutes who try to escape northern streets by setting up a cleaning cooperative (Scrubbitt), only to relapse into their old money-making ways. The cast, most of whom had done better things, included sometime chanteuse Barbara Dickinson, Geraldine James (➢*The History Man*, ➢*Jewel In the Crown*) and Cathy Tyson, ex-wife of Craig ➢'*Red Dwarf*' Charles, who made her screen name playing the prostitute who beguiled Bob Hoskins in the 1986 film *Mona Lisa*. Despite a broadcast slot after the 9 p.m. watershed, the characters were encumbered by such unlikely expressions as 'Blimey' and unrealistically low levels of sex and violence. The show's enormous popularity took on a sinister aspect when the police complained that it had encouraged an increase in kerb crawling in the Bradford area where the characters allegedly worked. A third series was transmitted simply as *Gold*. Created by Kay Mellor, also the adapter of *Jane Eyre* (ITV, 1997).

CAST *Rose* Geraldine James *Carol* Cathy Tyson *Anita* Barbara Dickinson *Tracy* Samantha Morton *Colette* Lena Headey *George Ferguson* Tony Doyle /*cr* Kay Mellor /*pr* Elizabeth Bradley, Tony Dennis /*dr* David Evans, Richard Standeven /*wr* Kay Mellor /*Granada TV* (UK) /12 x 60m col.

Baretta

Crime & Mystery. ITV 1978–9

Tony Baretta was a maverick undercover cop (lowlife disguises, illegal methods of apprehension) of 'Eyetalian' descent who worked out of LA's 53rd Precinct. A continuing storyline was provided by his desire to avenge his murdered girlfriend, but much the most memorable aspect of the show was the sartorially-challenged detective's habit of monologuing to his cockatoo, Fred, in their shared room in the rundown King Edward Hotel. As graphically violent as the TV conventions of the time would allow, *Baretta* grew out of another master-of-disguise police drama, ABC's ➢*Toma* (1973–4). When actor Tony Musante left that show, the vacancy was filled by former child-star Robert Blake (aka Michael Gubitosi) and the programme's title changed. For his work on *Baretta*, Blake was awarded a 1975 Best Actor Emmy.

CAST *Det. Tony Baretta* Robert Blake *Insp. Shiller* Dana Elcar *Lt Hal Brubaker* Edward Grover *Rooster* Michael D. Roberts /*cr* Stephen J. Cannell /*exec pr* Bernard L. Kowalski, Anthony Spinner /*pr* inc Robert Harris, Howie Horwitz, Robert Lewis /*dr* inc Robert Blake, Reza S. Badiyi, Jeannot Swarc, Douglas Heyes, Don Medford, Russ Mayberry, Burt Brinckerhoff /*wr* inc Richard Bluel, Stephen J. Cannell, Robert Crais, John Thomas James, Roy Huggins, Edward J. Lasko / *mus* Dave Grusin, Tom Scot ('Keep Your Eyes on the Sparrow' theme), Sammy Davis Jr (theme vocal) /*Roy Huggins: Public Arts Productions: Universal TV* (USA) / US tx ABC 1975–8 /80 x 60m col.

Barnaby Jones

Crime & Mystery. ITV 1974–80

Buddy Ebsen overcame the typecasting of backwoodsman roles in ➢*Davy Crockett* and ➢*The Beverly Hillbillies* to play retired Los Angeles PI Barnaby Jones, who retakes the reins of family firm Jones Investigative Agency on the murder of his son (also a gumshoe). Though Jones went everywhere armed with a gun, he relied on ratiocination, psychology and the forensic tests of his own home crime laboratory to solve cases; a deceptively slow and vague manner, meanwhile, helped lull the errant into a fatal and false sense of security. His daughter in law Betty (Lee Meriwether from ➢*The Time Tunnel*) assisted in the enquiries, and they were joined in the fifth season by Jones' young cousin, J.R., a student lawyer.

The show was something of a gentle sister to another Quinn Martin caper, ➢*Cannon*. To give *Barnaby Jones* an initial boost, the popular fatman sleuth occasionally appeared in *Jones* episodes.

CAST *Barnaby Jones* Buddy Ebsen *Betty Jones* Lee Meriwether *Jebediah Roman ('J.R.') Jones* Mark Shera / *exec pr* Quinn Martin /*pr* Gene Levitt, Philip Saltzman, Robert Sherman /*dr* inc Corey Allen, Marc Daniels, Robert Douglas, Leslie H. Martinson, Michael Caffey, Walter Grauman, Lawrence Dobkin, Russ Mayberry, Winrich Kolbe, Virgil W. Vogel /*wr* inc Larry Brody, Mort Fine, Robert Hamner, Shirl Hendryx, Stephen Kandel, Robert Pirosh, B.W. Sandefur /*mus* Jerry Goldsmith /*Quinn Martin Productions* (USA) /174 x 60m col /US tx CBS 1973–80.

Barney Miller

Comedy. ITV 1979–83

Eventually to be awarded the 1981 Emmy for Best Comedy, *Barney Miller* almost never got made. It had two strikes against it: it featured a Jewish policeman, which US network bosses considered 'too ethnic'; worse, its humour was wryly sophisticated and tilted at such prime-time taboos as homosexuality, teenage pregnancy and arson. Pestered by co-creators Danny Arnold (➢*Bewitched*) and Theodore Flicker into a pilot, 'The Life and Times of Barney Miller', ABC then binned the project to near audible sighs of corporate relief. The network only resurrected it to please hot director John Rich of ➢*All in the Family*, whom they were desperate to recruit. Rich's price was the commissioning of a season of comedy-cop shows written by his friend Danny Arnold: *Barney Miller*. Shot on videotape (a parsimony insisted on by ABC), the series achieved its celebrated moody look by altering the lighting for each scene as is done in movie-making. Unusually, almost all the action was confined to a single set, that of a chaotic squad-room of New York's 12th Precinct (Greenwich Village). To bring his curious and varied police characters to life, Arnold hired a troupe of thespians. These were headed by Hal Linden (aka big band sax player Harold Lipschitz) as the compassionately moral Miller, and Abe Vigoda (Tessio in *The Godfather*) as the crotchety, weak-bladdered Phil Fish, who was eventually spun-off to his own (short-lived) show, *Fish*. Frequently, however *Barney Miller* rested on the talents of the guest stars and bit players who acted the assorted human flotsam and jetsam parading through the squadroom: mad bombers, gay purse snatchers, prostitutes, teenage burglers, sex fetishists, even a werewolf. All, no matter what their deviation or disadvantage, were treated with respect. *Barney Miller*, like ➢*M*A*S*H*, was one of TV's great exercises in humanity. After eight seasons, the cast and crew decided to bow out while they were still artistically on top. The jail cell door and duty roster board used on the show were presented to the Smithsonian Institute, the director of which declared the artefacts to be 'part of American culture'.

And so they were.

CAST *Capt. Barney Miller* Hal Linden *Det. Sgt Phil Fish* Abe Vigoda *Det. Sgt Chano Amenguale* Gregory Sierra *Det. Stan Wojciehowicz* Maxwell Gail *Det. Sgt Nick Yemena* Jack Soo *Det. Sgt Ron Harris* Ron Glass *Insp. Frank Luger* James Gregory *Det. Sgt Arthur Dietrich* Steve Landesburg *Off. Carl Levitt* Ron Carey *Elizabeth Miller* Abby Dalton/Barbara Barrie /*cr* Danny Arnold, Theodore J. Flicker /*pr* Danny Arnold, Theodore J. Flicker /*dr* inc Danny Arnold, Theodore J. Flicker, Noam Pitlik, Lee Bernhardi /*wr* Danny Arnold, Theodore J. Flicker, Richard Baer, Tony Sheehan, Bob Colleary, Chris Hayward, Reinhold Weege, Frank Dungan, Jeff Stein /*mus* Jack Elliot, Allyn Ferguson / *MTM* (USA) /168 x 30m col /US tx ABC 1975–82.

The Baron

Crime & Mystery. ITV 1966–7

Quintessential 60s crime adventure serial for the transatalantic market, from the same ITC stable as ➢*The Saint* and ➢*The Persuaders!* John Mannering, aka 'The Baron', was a muscular Texan rancher (purveyor of the Baron brand) turned fine arts dealer, with exclusive establishments in London, Paris and Washington. Mannering – played by Steve Forrest, later ➢*S.W.A.T.* – also worked unofficially for Britain's Special Diplomatic Service on a slew of global action-packed capers against the forces of crime and espionage. Most of the missions had some antique or art world connection: in 'Diplomatic Immunity' a functionary from the Communist country of Pamaranea was privately masterminding the theft of Western treasures; in 'Epitaph for a Hero' Mannering was forced to participate in the robbery of priceless jewels (before foiling the dastardly deed). Other plots involved such crime stand-bys as drug-smuggling. Agent Cordelia Winfield, whose glamour was attested to by the beauty spot on her cheek, was an occasional helpmate, while pin-striped John Templeton-Green was Mannering's main contact at SBDS. Two TV features were made from recut episodes: *Mystery Island* (1966) and *The Man in the Looking Glass* (1968).

Ostensibly based on the character created by John Creasey (under the pseudonym Anthony Morton), the TV Baron had little if any connection with Creasey's thoroughly British, Raffles-like figure.

CAST *John Mannering, 'The Baron'* Steve Forrest *John Templeton-Green* Colin Gordon *Cordelia Winfield* Sue Lloyd *David Marlowe* Paul Ferris /*cr* Robert Baker, Monty Berman /*pr* Monty Berman /*dr* inc Leslie Norman, John Moxey, Cyril Frankel, Don Chaffey /*wr* inc Dennis Spooner, Harry H. Junkin, Terry Nation, Tony O'Grady (aka Brian Clemens) /*mus* Edwin Astley / *ITC* (UK) /30 x 50m col /US tx ABC 1966.

The Basil Brush Show

Children's. BBC1 1968–80

The aristocratic, tweed-coated puppet fox first appeared in Rediffusion's *The Three Scampis* in April 1964 (sharing the limelight with a Scottish hedgehog called Spike McPike), before securing a regular slot on magician David Nixon's children's show, *Now for Nixon*, and his adult offering, *Nixon at 9.5*. Here Basil perfected such jokes as: (Nixon) 'How do you work, Basil?'/(BB) 'As little as possible'. Therafter the character starred in his own half-hour series, where a succession of straight men of improbable lustre – Rodney Bewes (➢*The Likely Lads*), Derek Fowlds (later ➢*Yes, Minister*), Roy North, Howard Williams and Billy Boyle – read him stories and bore the brunt of his gags. After eventually being dispensed with by the BBC, Basil resurfaced in series for ITV's Border and Granada regions. The man with his hand up the fox's bottom was Ivan Owen (➢*Five O'Clock Club*) who also provided the upper-class voice. Boom-Boom!

CAST (voice) *Basil Brush* Ivan Owens /*cr* Ivan Owens / *pr* Johnny Downes, Ernest Maxin, Robin Nash, Brian Penders, Jim Franklin, Paul Ciani /*dr* inc Brian Penders /*wr* inc Ivan Owens, George Martin /*mus* inc Bert Hayes Sextet /*BBC TV* (UK) /60 x 30m col.

Batman

Children's. ITV 1966–8

Robin. 'Holy Inferno! Is this the end, Batman?'
Batman: 'If it is, let us not lose our dignity.'

ZAP! BAM! Launched at a Manhattan disco party attended by such luminaries as Andy Warhol, *Batman* sought to sell an essentially kiddietime product – a *Detective Comics* character – to an early evening crossover audience. The means executive producer William Dozier (later ➢*The Green Hornet)* hit upon was to camp up Bob Kane's 1939 crusader to the top of his masked visage: 'What we had on *Batman*,' Dozier later recalled, 'was an exaggerated seriousness that became amusing to adults and provided high adventure for the youngsters.' The casting of virtual unknown, Adam West, as Bruce Wayne/Batman caused criticism – *Newsweek* complained that he was 'a flabby travesty of muscle beach' – but in hindsight it proved a shrewd move, for much of the show's humour stemmed from his unlikeliness as a superhero, plus his preternaturally regular-Joe manner and voice. Burt Ward as sidekick Robin was more suited to action frolics; he was a brown belt in karate. If the leads were newcomers, Dozier insisted on screen stalwarts for the show's other regular characters, Commissioner Gordon (Neil Hamilton), Chief O'Hara (Stafford Repp) and Alfred the Butler (gentlemanly Alan Napier).

Episodes followed a formula that scarely deviated. Whenever some villainous oddity threatened Gotham City, Commissioner Gordon and excitable Chief O'Hara would rush to their red phone. 'I don't know who he is behind that mask of his,' Gordon would declare as he dialled Batman, 'but I know we need him and we need him now!' At the manor house of millionaire Bruce Wayne, the Batphone would bleep, to be answered by retainer Alfred, who would coyly deliver the message to his master under the nose of unsuspecting Aunt Harriet (introduced to the series solely to offset fears that three men home alone might be suggestive of homosexuality). Wayne and ward Dick Grayson would then disappear down the Batpoles hidden behind the drawing room bookcase, to emerge seconds later in the Batcave as Batman and Robin. From the Batcave they would speed to the scene of crime in the Batmobile (a converted Lincoln Continental), only to follow absurdly improbable clues – which would then lead them straight into the villain's dastardly trap. Just as Batman and Robin seemed doomed to a diabolical death (grilled alive, served up to carnivorous plants, frozen into ice lollies) the episode would end, leaving the announcer to urge viewers to tune in for the conclusion 'same bat time, same bat channel'. In part two, luck or ingenuity would see the heroes escape and vanquish their 'arch enemies'. These included the Riddler (Frank Gorshin, John ➢*'Addams Family'* Astin), the Joker (Cesar Romero), the leather-clad Catwoman (Julie Newmar, Lee ➢*'Time Tunnel'* Meriwether, Eartha Kitt) and the Penguin, that 'pompous, waddling perpetrator of foul play' (Burgess Meredith).

The episodes might have been as formulaic as Noh plays, but they were executed with considerable visual verve. Fight scenes were synched with animated title effects – BAM! LOK! – and filmed with much tilting of the camera. To create a comic-strip ambience, scenes were bathed in coloured lights: amber for Catwoman appearances, green for the Riddler and purple for the Joker.

An overnight sensation, the show spawned a dance craze (the 'batusi'), a chart hit for Neil Hefti's theme, a film, and bat-merchandize

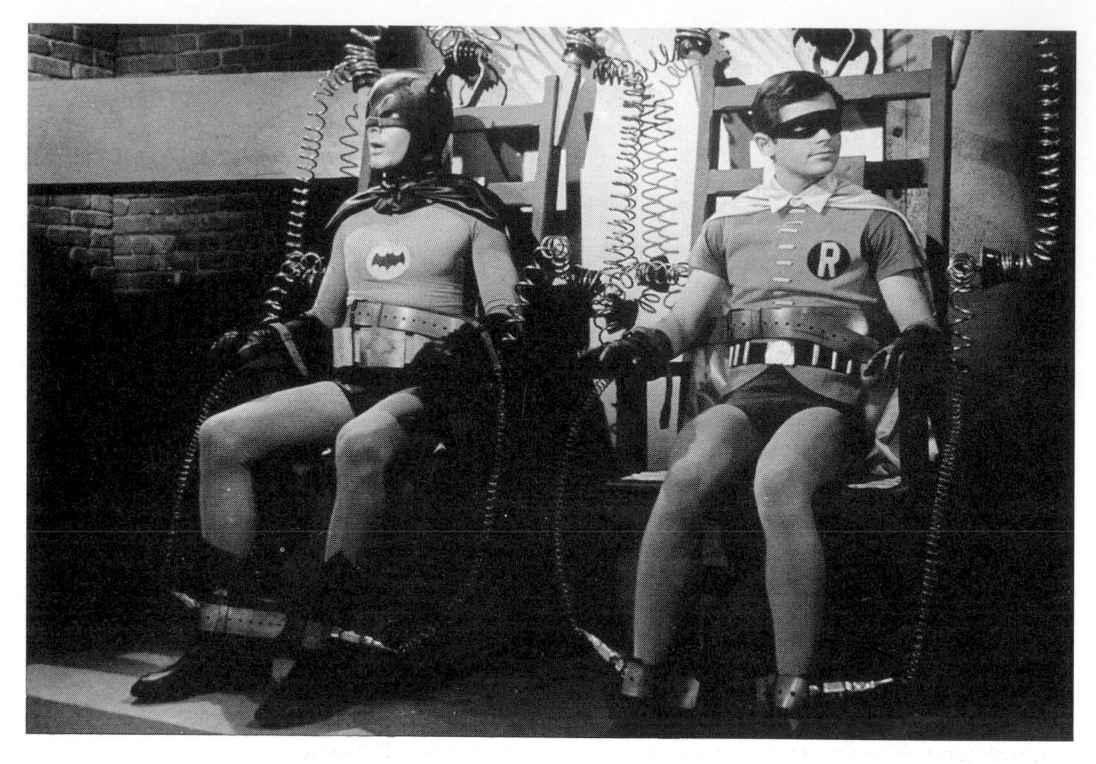

'Holy Mackerel!' Another case for Gotham City's caped crusaders in *Batman*. Burt Ward secured the part of Robin by cracking a brick with his bare hand at audition. ZAP!

galore. Hollywood stars queued for the opportunity to menace the Caped Crusader: Tallulah Bankhead, Milton Berle, Joan Collins, Ethel Merman, Zsa Zsa Gabor, Liberace, George Raft. Safety campaigners praised the show for its sense of social responsibility: Batman and Robin always wore seat belts, while a run to the Batmobile was interrupted in the episode 'Fine Finny Friends/ Batman Makes the Scenes' for Batman to tell Robin, 'Always look both ways before crossing the road.'

All good TV things, however, must come to an end. By mid 1967 the show was beginning to slide in the ratings. To stop the drift, producer Howie Horwitz introduced former ballerina Yvonne Craig (➢*77 Sunset Strip*) as the slinky Batgirl. The reprieve was only temporary and in February 1968 the show was axed. KERPOW! Numerous repeats, however, plus a cycle of big budget movies, have ensured Batman's immortality.

CAST *Batman/Bruce Wayne* Adam West *Robin/Dick Grayson* Burt Ward *Alfred* Alan Napier *Aunt Harriet* Madge Blake *Commissioner Gordon* Neil Hamilton *Chief O'Hara* Stafford Repp *Batgirl* Yvonne Craig *Narrator* William Dozier /*cr* Bob Kane, William Dozier / *exec pr* William Dozier /*pr* Howie Horwitz /*dr* inc Robert Butler, Tom Gries, Richard Sarafian, Don Weiss, Oscar Rudolph, George Waggner /*wr* Lorenzo Semple Jr, Stephen Kandel, Sheldon Stark, Rik Vollaerts, Stanley Ralph Ross, Charles Hoffman, Stanford Sherman /*sfx* L.B. Abbott /*mus* Neil Hefti (theme), Nelson Riddle /*A Greenway Production: 20th Century-Fox Television* (USA) /120 x 30m col /US tx ABC 1966–8.

Bat Masterson

Western. ITV 1959–61

The adventures of dapper, gambler-lawman William Barclay Masterson, 'the fastest cane in the West'. Immensely popular Western from the Ziv-TV conveyor belt, whose off-beat humour was heavily plundered from James Garner's ➢*Maverick*. Multiple episodes were directed by William Conrad, later the before-camera star of ➢*Cannon*.

Gene Barry (born Eugene Klass) made something of a speciality of dandyish parts, also showing sartorial elegance in ➢*Burke's Law*, *The Name of the Game* and *The Adventurer*. The actor reprised his Masterson role in a 1989 episode of ➢*Paradise*.

CAST *Bat Masterson* Gene Barry /*pr* Andy White, Frank Pitman /*dr* inc Alan Crosland Jr, William Conrad /*wr* inc John Tucker Battle /*Ziv-TV: UA-TV* (USA) /107 x 30m bw /US tx NBC 1958–61.

Battlestar Galactica

Sci-fi. ITV 1980–1

Overblown space opera which cited Moses' leading of the Israelites to the Promised Land as its inspiration, but which was actually sourced from *Star Wars* to the extent that the movie's producers issued a plagiarism suit. Another clear influence was venerable oater show ➢*Wagon Train*.

In the seventh millenium AD a tribe of space humans, the last survivors of an ambush by Cyclon robots, search for a 'lost' colony, Earth. Leading the battered caravan of 220 vessels is the *Battlestar Galatica*, commanded by silver-haired Adama (Lorne Greene, ➢*Bonanza*). Prominent among the crew are Viper fighter-pilots Captain Apollo (Adama's son) and womanizing Lieutenant Starbuck (Dirk Benedict in a virtual try-out for his 'Faceman' role in ➢*The A-Team*). A traitor in their midst, Count Baltar, is in league with the Cyclons, who continue to pursue the humans across the heavens.

Spectacular special effects (courtesy of *Star Wars*'s John Dykstra), however, failed to hide the show's lack of plot or real characaterization. It was cancelled at the end of its debut season, having cost over 1.5 million dollars for each hour of screen time. A revival, *Galactica 80*, was also ignominiously torpedoed. In Britain, to maximize profits, Universal Studios insisted on releasing the *Battlestar Galactica* pilot as a theatrical feature before the serial was shown on TV.

CAST *Commander Adama* Lorne Greene *Lt Starbuck* Dirk Benedict *Captain Apollo* Richard Hatch *Athena* Maren Jensen *Boxey* Noah Hathaway *Cassiopea* Laurette Spang *Count Baltar* John Colicos /*cr* Glen A. Larson /*exec pr* Glen A. Larson /*pr* inc Don Bellisario, John Dykstra, Paul Playdon /*dr* inc Alan Levi, Christian Nyby, Winrich Kolbe /*wr* inc Glen A. Larson, Don Bellisario, Jim Carlson, Terence McDonnell /*mus* Stu Phillips /*sfx* John Dykstra / *A Glen Larson Production: Universal TV* /1 x 180m, 1 x 120m, 19 x 60m col /US tx ABC 1978–9.

Baywatch

Melodrama/Adventure. ITV 1990–

The story behind the world's most popular TV series might make an uplifting Hollywood film. It was conceived one summer by 17-year-old Californian Gregory J. Bonann, who was working as a lifeguard in order to pay his way through business school (winning a Medal of Valor for a rescue from the sea en route). For ten years Bonann harboured his dream of a sun-kissed TV lifeguard melodrama, but could find no takers. Then, as luck would have it, his sister married a TV producer, Douglas Schwartz. In 1987 Bonann, Schwartz and Schwartz's cousin, Michael Berk, collaborated on a script for a TVM, *Baywatch: Panic at Malibu Pier*, which was sold to NBC. The network decided to commission a season of prime time episodes. They flopped. Only after star David Hasselhoff (➢*Knight Rider*, ➢*The Young and the Restless*, and a major pop chanteur in Germany) gave the show a financial kiss of life did it live again. Aired on off-network syndication it eventually rose to a global viewing figure estimated at 150 billion.

As Lieutenant Mitch Buchannon, Hasselhoff presided over a corps of LA County Lifeguards (based at the Will Rogers station) of statuesque physique but dubious acting ability. Fortuitously, the frictionless plots these himbos and bimbos were required to hold up were vacuous and usually moralistic, filled with hokey emotions, padded with footage of beach scenery, and interrupted only by some overly dramatic air-sea rescue. (The most memorable of these, in a steal from *Jaws*, saw lifeguard Jill Riley become a shark's breakfast.) Although Haselhoff – whose wife, Pamela Bach, appeared in early episodes as Buchannon's date, reporter Kate Morgan – was the show's nominal star, the real celebrity of later seasons was Canadian Pamela Anderson, who played C.J. Parker. A former Labatt's Blue Zone girl, *Playboy* model (as was fellow cast member Erika Eleniak), and 'Tool Time' girl of the series ➢*Home Improvement*, the pneumatic Anderson became immortalized as 'Baywatch Barbie', complete with plunge-line bikini.

After five years the seemingly invincible *Baywatch* began to show signs of fatigue. A spin-off detective series, *Baywatch Nights*, was only a modest success, and in 1996 it was revealed that Hasselhoff – by now an executive producer – had ordered a *Baywatch* paycut in response to falling ratings and spiralling costs.

CAST *Lt Mitch Buchannon* David Hasselhoff *Shauni McLain* Erika Eleniak *Eddie Kramer* Billy Warlock *Lt Stephanie Holden* Alexander Paul *C.J. Parker* Pamela Anderson *Matt Brody* David Charvet *Police Sgt Garner Ellerbee* Greg Alan-Williams *Hobie Buchannon* Brandon Call/Jeremy Jackson *Caroline Holden* Yasmine Bleeth *Logan Fowler* Jaason Simmons *Capt. Ben Edwards* Richard Jaeckel /*cr* Gregory Bonann /*exec pr* Douglas Schwartz, Michael Berk, Gregory Bonann, David Hasselhoff /*dr* inc Tommy Lee Wallace, Doug Schwartz, Gus Trikonis, Bruce Seth Green, Reza Badiyi, Scott Brazil /*wr* inc Gregory Bonann, Doug Schwartz, Michael Berk /*All American TV: The Baywatch Production Company* (USA) / 176+ x 30m col /US tx NBC: Syndicated 1989–.

Beauty and the Beast

Crime/Drama. ITV 1988–9

Pretty telefantasy which transferred the classic fairy tale of *B&B* from medieval France to contemporary New York. When beautiful attorney Catherine Chandler is attacked and left for dead in Central Park, her life is saved by the deformed, leonine Vincent who takes her to the city's secret catacombs ('Tunnel World'). There, under the guidance of subterranean guru, Father (Roy Dotrice), she is nursed back to health. On Chandler's return to 'civilization', telepathic bonds enable soulmate Vincent to rescue her in times of distress. As with the fable, platonic friendship gives way to love, but the series took an unexpected turn when Catherine was murdered by Gabriel, a criminal boss (though not before she had borne Vincent a son). In the American manner, *B&B* overloaded sentimentality and splattered inappropriate cultural references ('Only Van Gogh could paint sunflowers that make your heart beat faster'), but remains one of the more unusual pieces of late 80s mainstream programming.

CAST *Asst DA Catherine Chandler* Linda Hamilton *Vincent* Ron Perlman *Father* Roy Dotrice *Kipper* Cory Danziger *Mouse* David Greenlee *Gabriel* Stephen McHattie *Pascal* Armin Shimerman /*cr* Ron Koslow /*exec pr* Ron Koslow, Paul Junger Witt, Tony Thomas, Stephen Kurzfeld /*dr* inc Thomas J. Wright, Gus Trikonis, Christopher Leitch, Victor Lobl, Daniel Attias /*wr* inc Alex Ganza, Howard Gordon, David Peckinpah, Don Balluck, Mark & Michael Cassutt, George R.R. Martin /*Repubica Pictures TV* (USA) /56 x 60m col /US tx CBS 1987–90.

Beavis and Butt-Head

Comedy. MTV 1993–7

Beavis and Butt-Head, a blonde guy in a Metallica T-shirt and a dark-haired guy in an AC/DC T-shirt, a pair of snickering rock fans with one hand ever on the TV remote control in an all-consuming search for music and babes: these two putrid pubescents were the inner voice first of American, then worldwide, teenagerdom. Initially styled as Bobby and Billy, stars of a one-off cartoon entitled 'Frog Baseball', they were created by 30-year-old Mike Judge – a former physics major and bass player in Dallas blues-rock bands – who dreamed them up as a parody of the MTV generation. Scrawled on a $300 animation kit in 1990, they became in turn an Animation Festival sensation, a feature on MTV's 'Liquid Television', a separate half-hour series and an international phenomenon spawning millions in merchandizing: T-shirts, toys, an all-star CD album (including the boys' rendition of 'I Got You Babe' together with Cher), a book, and two feature films. Not bad for two moronic, vicious geeks (they killed a grasshopper with a chainsaw, put a poodle in a washing machine) whose time was spent sneering at suggestive words ('He said "come", huh-huh, huh-huh, huh-huh.'), playing air guitar, torturing living animals and dividing the world into things that were 'cool' (naked chicks, chicks with big thingees, loud music that kicks ass, music that's like really LOUD!! LOUD!!) or things that 'sucked' (authority figures and everything else).

Not everyone loved this pair (Americans for Responsible Television orchestrated a campaign that peaked in 1993 when the activities of a five-year-old pyromaniac were blamed on Beavis and Butt-Head's pronouncement 'Fire is cool! Huhuhuhuh!') and the audience demographics skewed male, but it kicked hard at just the right time against the prevailing tide of political correctness and hit a chord with every young (and older) male. As creator Mike Judge said: 'It's just this funny, awkward moment in life when you want to be supermacho and show everyone you're not a kid any more. You wear serious, badass death-rock T-shirts, but you've got to put the rubber bands on your braces.' As Beavis and Butt-Head would say 'That guy's an asswipe, huh huh, huh huh, huhuh!'

CAST (voice) *Beavis/Butt-Head* Mike Judge *Daria* Tracy Grandstaff /*cr* Mike Judge /*exec pr* Abby Terkuhle /*pr* inc John Andrews /*wr* inc Mike Judge, Joe

Stilman, Glenn Eichler, Chris Marcil, David Felton, Tracy Grandstaff, Geoff Whelan /*An MTV Networks Production* (USA) /approx 186 x 10/30m, 1 x 60m col /US tx MTV 1993–7.

The Beiderbecke Affair

Crime. ITV 1985

Alan Plater's comedy-thriller in which teacher and jazz buff Trevor Chaplin (James Bolam, ➢*The Likely Lads*) buys a set of dud Bix Beiderbecke records from a platinum blonde only to land himself and teacher-girlfriend Jill (Barbara Flynn, *Chandler & Co*) in the midst of a sinister local government conspiracy. Finely-tuned writing and an ensemble of bizzare supporting characters (such as a wannabe super-grass), ensured the series hit status and led to a sequel, *The Beiderbecke Tapes* (ITV, 1987), in which the reluctant amateur sleuths investigated the illegal dumping of nuclear waste in the Dales. A triquel, *The Beiderbecke Connection* (ITV, 1988), found Chaplin ill-advisedly giving sanctuary to a Russian refugee. All this was played out to the sound of the music of trumpeter Bix Beiderbecke, re-played for the series by Kenny Baker. The *Beiderbecke* trilogy had its roots in an earlier Plater serial, *Get Lost!* (ITV, 1981), in which two teachers investigated missing person cases.

CAST *Trevor Chaplin* James Bolam *Jill Swinburne* Barbara Glynn *Mr Carter* Dudley Sutton *Mr Wheeler* Keith Smith *DS Hobson* Dominic Jephcott /*cr* Alan Plater /*exec pr* David Cunliffe /*pr* Anne W. Gibbons / *dr* inc David Reynolds /*wr* Alan Plater /*mus* Bix Beiderbecke, Frank Ricotti /*Yorkshire TV* (UK) / 6 x 60m col.

Belle and Sebastian

Children's. BBC1 1967

Gallic live-action series about a young French boy and his canine pal, a white Pyrenean mountain dog called Belle, and the enchanting, morally wholesome adventures they have together in their beautiful, air-clear-as-a-crystal village home. Dubbed.

CAST *Sebastian* Pierre Mehdi /*RTLF* (Fr) /30 x 25m bw.

Ben Casey

Melodrama. ITV 1961–5

Doctors emerged as the TV heroes par excellence in the early 60s, in such shows as ➢*Dr Kildare* and ➢*Emergency – Ward 10*, most of which depicted them as saints in surgical garb. Not so *Ben Casey*, which portrayed its central character as a tough-guy rebel. A neurosurgeon at County General Hospital, Ben Casey – his shirt always open to reveal a macho mat of chest hair – refused to bow to the medical establishment, routinely risking dismissal to save his patients. Only wise oldster mentor Dr Zorba (who spoke the show's famous 'Man, woman, birth, death, infinity', opening line) gave a stablizing influence. Immensely realistic, taut with tension (occasioned, partly, by pioneering use of close-up shots in surgical scenes), *Ben Casey* caught the feeling of the urgent intensity of a big hospital like no other drama before it. Actor Vince Edwards was propelled to stardom by the series, but proved curiously unable to translate his success and sex-symbol status into other major screen work. Made by Bing Crosby Productions, *Ben Casey* was created by former novice priest James Moser (also *Medic*), while the *BC* directors list included tyro director Sydney Pollack, eventually to work his way out of the TV mill to oversee such features as *They Shoot Horses, Don't They?* and *Out of Africa*.

CAST *Dr Ben Casey* Vince Edwards *Dr David Zorba* Sam Jaffe *Dr Maggie Graham* Bettye Ackerman *Nurse Wills* Jeanne Bates /*cr* James E. Moser /*pr* James E. Moser /*dr* inc Sydney Pollack, Fielder Cook, James E. Moser /*wr* inc James E. Moser /*Bing Crosby Productions* (USA) /153 x 50m bw /US tx ABC 1960–5.

The Benny Hill Show

Comedy. ITV 1969–89

The first British comedian to be made by the medium of TV, Alfred Hawthorne 'Benny' Hill (born 1925, the son of a surgical appliance fitter) enjoyed years of fortune with the BBC before transferring *The Benny Hill Show* to ITV in 1969, where it enjoyed even greater success. Steeped in the revue tradition, combining visual gags, slapstick sketches and corny jokes, Hill's 18 series (plus numerous specials) brought accusations of sexism for the arrays of scantily-clad women he lecherously leered on screen. For the defence, Hill maintained that his humour was in the mould of seaside postcardist, Donald McGill. This was disingenuous, since McGill's saucy pictures showed men to be red-faced losers whereas Hill's infamous chases frequently had women ('Hill's Angels') pursuing him. Eventually the criticism mounted and Thames cancelled the show in 1989, though it continued to make millions from *Benny Hill* sales around the world, including the USA where Hill was one of the few British comedians to hit the payola.

Stock Hill characters included Captain Fred Scuttle, the Fireman's Choir, and Prof. Marvel, while the pudgy comedian was aided and abetted by a number of stooges over the years, Henry McGee (the straight-man announcer, and star of breakfast cereals ads), Jack Wright (the small, bald 'slap head') and Nicholas Parsons being the most prominent of them. Though she might now wish to forget it, ➢*Frasier* star Jane Leeves was one of those who bared almost all as a Hill's Angel.

Hill died on 20 April 1992.

CAST Benny Hill, Henry McGee, Bob Todd, Felicity Buirski, Patricia Hayes, Nicholas Parsons, Bella Emberg /*cr* Benny Hill /*pr* inc John Robbins, Mark Stuart, Dennis Kirkland, Keith Beckett, John Street /*dr* inc John Robbins /*wr* inc Benny Hill /*mus* Ronnie Aldrich Orchestra, The Ladybirds (vocals) /*Thames TV* (UK) /99 x 30m bw:col /US tx Syndicated 1979–82.

Benson

Comedy. ITV 1981–4

A spin-off from ➢*Soap* in which the black, back-talking butler Benson DuBois was sent to take charge of the household of widowed, incompetent State Governor Gatling. This was almost as lunatic an establishment as *chez* Tate; prominent residents included the Governor's precocious daughter Katie, secretary Marcy, formidable – and incomprehensible – German housekeeper Gretchen and aide Taylor (later replaced as bag-carrier by Clayton Endicott III, played by Rene Auberjonois, ➢*Star Trek: DS9*). Over the course of the 150-plus episodes, Benson rose inexorably from his lowly buttling post to Lieutenant Governor, in the last episode even challenging Gatlin for the governorship itself and becoming, in the process, something of a role model for Afro-Americans. Actor Robert Guillaume first achieved screen fame as a star of cult blaxploitation pic *Superfly TNT*; post-Benson he returned to the wackier edges of sitcom in Californian police spoof *Pacific Station.*

CAST *Benson DuBois* Robert Guillaume *Governor James Gatling* James Noble *Katie Gatling* Missy Gold *Gretchen Kraus* Inga Swenson *Marcy Hill* Caroline McWilliams *James Taylor* Lewis J. Stadlen *Clayton Endicott III* Rene Auberjonois /*cr* Susan Harris, Paul Junger Witt, Tony Thomas /*dr* inc John Rich, Peter Baldwin, Jay Sandrich, Bob Fraser, Hilton Smack /*wr* inc Susan Harris, Ron Silver / *Witt Thomas Harris Productions* (USA) /60 x 30m col /US tx ABC 1979–86.

Begerac

Crime. BBC1 1981–91

Britain's ➢*Hawaii Five-0.* Only created by Robert Banks Stewart because Trevor Eve refused to do another season of ➢*Shoestring*, this *policier* set on the sparkling-sea'd island resort of Jersey became one of the BBC's prime crime hits of the 80s, with ratings approaching 15 million. John Nettles (previously ➢*A Family at War* and Sandra's boyfriend in ➢*The Liver Birds*) played divorced, ex-alcoholic, gammy-legged Detective Sergeant Jim Bergerac of the Bureau des Etrangers, a police unit which dealt exclusively with crimes involving visitors to the isle. By improbable but enjoyable coincidence, all Bergerac's cases entangled his ex-father-in-law, Charlie Hungerford, a millionaire cigar-smoking businessman of flyboy, roguish bent. To convey himself around the island Bergerac conspiciously avoided the plodding regulation police vehicle in favour of a 1947 Triumph TR1 sports car. With his loner mode of investigation looked on with disapproval by superior Barney Crozier, a tendency to hanker for the bottle, a troubled personal life (tourist guide Francine, lawyer Marianne and estate agent Susan Young were among the main squeezes), and a mumble-mouthed manner of speaking bordering on inarticulacy, Bergerac was a notably human creation (*cf.* Eddie Shoestring), a conscious reaction to the 70s tough-guy school of police show. On several occasions Bergerac, devilishly putting duty aside, dallied with beautiful jewel thief Philippa Vale (Liza Goddard). And it was for the love of a woman, Danielle Aubry, that 'Je-e-em' finally quit the Bureau and moved to Provence, where he became a private eye. As with Steve McGarrett and Hawaii, so Bergerac and Jersey have become indisolubly linked, the show dramatically boosting the island's tourist industry. Appropriately, then, John Nettles, on completing *Bergerac*, made Jersey his home.

CAST *DS Jim Bergerac* John Nettles *Charlie Hungerford* Terence Alexander *Chief Insp. Barney Crozier* Sean Arnold *Deborah Hungerford* Deborah Grant *Francine* Cecile Paoli *Marianne Bellshade* Celia Imrie *Susan Young* Louise Jameson *Philippa Vale* Liza Goddard *Danielle Aubry* Therese Liotard *Diamante Lil* Mela White /*cr* Robert Banks Stewart /*pr* Robert Banks Stewart, Jonathan Alwyn, George Gallaccio /*dr* inc Paul Ciappessoni, Graeme Harper, Baz Taylor, Tristan de Vere Cole, Ben Bolt /*wr* inc Robert Banks Stewart, Terence Feely, John Collee, Chris Boucher, John Milne, Brian Clemens, Robert Holmes, Rod Beacham /*mus* George Fenton (theme) /*BBC TV: Seven Network* (UK:Aus) /87 x 50m, 6 x 90m col.

Best of the West

Western. ITV 1983

Spoof Western. After service in the Civil War, Sam Best heads West to the frontier town of Copper Creek, accompanied by refined Southern belle wife, Elvira, and city raised kid Daniel ('I want you to understand, Dad, I'm never going outside.'). When Best accidentally trounces local gunfighter, the Calico Kid (Christopher Lloyd, ➢*Taxi*, the *Back to the Future* movies), he is elected marshal and duly charged with keepin' law'n'order amongst the ultra-caricatured townsfolk: alcoholic Doc Kullens, no-good saloon owner Parker Tillman, raucous mountain woman Laney Gibbs and all.

CAST *Marshal Sam Best* Joel Higgins *Elvira Best* Carlene Watkins *Daniel Best* Meeno Peluce *Parker Tillman* Leonard Frey /*cr* Earl Pomerantz /*pr* Earl Pomerantz, David Lloyd, James Burrows, Ronald E. Frazier /*dr* inc Howard Storm, Stan Daniels, James Burrows /*wr* inc David Lloyd, Earl Pomerantz /*mus* Roger Steinman /*Weinberger-Daniels: PAR-TV* (USA) / 22 x 25m col /US tx ABC 1981–2.

Between the Lines

Crime. BBC1 1992–4

British state-of-the-90s cop show, much influenced by such gritty (and beautifully produced) American *policiers* as ➢*Homicide – Life on the Street* and ➢*NYPD Blue*. Seamlessly watchable, it followed the internal investigations into police corruption of hard-drinking Detective Superintendent Tony Clark (Neil Pearson, ➢*Drop the Dead Donkey*), as well as his seamy, complicated external affairs with a small parade of women (hence the series being dubbed 'Between the Sheets'). Clark was assisted in the Metropolitan Complaints Investigation Bureau by Harry Naylor and Mo Connell, the latter one of the few sympathetically-portrayed lesbians in the annals of UK TV. For the third series, Clark, Naylor and Connell found themselves outside the force, working for a private security company run, ironically enough, by their corrupt former police boss, John Deakin. The executive producer was Tony Garnett (*Cathy Come Home*, ➢*Days of Hope*, ➢*Law and Order*, ➢*Ballykissangel*).

CAST *Det. Supt Tony Clark* Neil Pearson *DI Harry Naylor* Tom Georgeson *DS Maureen Connell* Siobhan Redmond *Chief Supt John Deakin* Tony Doyle *Com. Huxtable* David Lyon *Angela Berridge* Francesca Annis / *cr* J.C. Wilsher /*exec pr* Tony Garnett /*pr* Peter Norris, Joy Lale /*dr* inc Roy Battersby, Charles McDargall / *wr* inc J.C. Wilsher, Dusty Hughes /*mus* Hal Lindes (theme), Colin Towns /*BBC: Island World* (UK) / 35 x 50m col.

The Beverly Hillbillies

Comedy. ITV 1964–70

Classic US sitcom charting the adventures of the crazy Clampett family, who found oil on their backwoods Ozark ranch and decamped to Beverly Hills in their boneshaker car to live the high life. Alas, their attempt to do so was doomed; although they bought every mod con that $25 million could buy, they were not always sure what to with them. Granny Clampett, notably, had difficulty differentiating the washer from the TV. The other members of the Clampett clan were level-headed patriarch, Jed (ex-thirties song-and-dance man, Buddy Ebsen, also ➢*Davy Crockett*, ➢*Barnaby Jones*), dim-witted Cousin Jethro (played by Max Baer Jr, son of the former World Heavyweight Boxing Champion Max Baer), and animal-loving daughter Elly May, wearer of famously tight blue jeans. Elderly cousin Pearl Bodine also featured for the first season, before being spun-off to *Petticoat Junction*. Actress Sharon Tate, later murdered by the Charles Manson gang, appeared as bank secretary Janet Treago, one of her first professional roles. At the show's best, when scripts matched performance, *The Beverly Hillbillies* could be seen as an attack on materialism; at its worst it simply ridiculed rural people. This notwithstanding, it was the fastest hit in US small-screen history, succeeding to the top of the US ratings poll, Nielsen, within four months, and staying there for nearly two years. Along with *The Andy Griffith Show*, *BH* was responsible for inventing a new sub-genre of TV humour, the 'rural sitcom' (see also ➢*Green Acres*). In 1994 the series was adapted for the cinema, without the benefit of the original cast.

CAST *Jed Clampett* Buddy Ebsen *Granny (Daisy Moses)* Irene Ryan *Elly May Clampett* Donna Douglas *Jethro Bodine* Max Baer Jr *Milburn Drysdale* Raymond Bailey *Margaret Drysdale* Harriet MacGibbon *Jane Hathaway* Nancy Kulp *Pearl Bodine* Bea Benaderet / *cr* Paul Henning / *exec pr* Martin Ransohoff / *pr* inc Paul Henning, Jospeh DePew / *dr* inc Joseph DePew, Richard Thorpe, Richard Whorf / *wr* inc Paul Henning / *mus* Jerry Scoggins (theme vocal), Lester Flatt, Earl Scruggs / *Filmways* (USA) /216 x 25m bw:col /US tx CBS 1962–71.

Beverly Hills 90210

Melodrama. Sky1/ITV 1991–

Nothing sells like teen spirit. Originally titled *Class of Beverly Hills* but altered to incorporate the zip code of the elite LA area in which it was set, Fox TV's pubescent high-school soap was the top rated network drama amongst the 18–34 age group in the USA. It also netted more than $450 million per annum in merchandising. In Britain, where it was a Sunday evening flagship for Sky1, it garnered a relatively small audience share (300,000 per episode) but was the subject of veritable media mania. Much of the show's success – whether measured by audience figures or newspaper column inches – was due to its beautiful, perma-tanned cast (many way too old to be teenagers), but also to its celebrated tackling of 'issues', such as AIDS, rape and gun control. For American teenagers in particular, *BH 90210* was a TV agony column, a place where their concerns were addressed. Yet the show's real pull was its ability to develop romantic entanglement storylines (notably that between Brenda Walsh and Dylan McKay, consummated in the episode 'Spring Dance'), plus its voyeuristic look at the lives of the young super wealthy, bedecked with Mercedes, Rolex watches, Armani clothes – and chronic angst. The rich might have all the possessions, *90210* reassured, but they also had more problems. Ultimately *90210* was a glossy, small-screen version of a teen photo-love magazine. It was the creation of 22-year-old Darren Star, who followed up its success with spin-off ➢*Melrose Place* and the NY smart-set publishing melodrama, *Central Park West*. *Beverly Hills 90210* was produced by veteran US glitz-maker Aaron Spelling (➢*Charlie's Angels*, ➢*Dynasty*, ➢*Savannah*, etc) who, in an admirable piece of nepotism, cast his daughter Tori as the unfeasibly chaste Donna Martin.

CAST *Brenda Walsh* Shannen Doherty *Brandon Walsh* Jason Priestly *Jim Walsh* James Eckhouse *Cindy Walsh* Carol Potter *Kelly Taylor* Jennie Garth *Steve Sanders* Ian Zierling *Dylan McKay* Luke Perry *Andrea Zuckerman* Gabrielle Carteris *Donna Martin* Tori Spelling *Scott Scanlon* Douglas Emerson *David Silver* Brian Austin Green / *cr* Darren Star / *exec pr* Charles Rosin / *pr* Aaron Spelling, Darren Star, Jeffrey White, Sigurjon Sighvatsson, Paul Waigner / *dr* inc Charles Braverman, David Carson, Burt Brinckerhoff, D. Attias, Paul Schneider, Darren Star, Michael Katleman, Corey Allen, Eric Laneuville, Jason Priestly / *wr* inc Charles Rosin, Darren Star, Amy Spies, Steve Wasserman, Jessica Klein / *mus* John E. Davis / *Propaganda Films Production: Torand Productions Inc* (USA) /246+ x 50m col /US tx Fox TV 1990–.

Bewitched

Comedy. BBC1 1964–72

Long-running sitcom starring Elizabeth Montgomery (daughter of Robert Montgomery) as Samantha Stephens, the housewife who only had to twitch her nose cutely to get the washing up done, thanks to beguiling white magic. Dick York and later Dick Sargent played her hapless, merely mortal husband, Darrin, an accountant at NY advertising agency McMann and Tate. Oscar-nominee Agnes Moorhead took the role of Samantha's interfering mother, Endora. Perhaps the real star of the show, however, was special effects man Dick Albain, who invented Samantha's 'magic' self-operating vacuum-cleaner and used a network of wires to make objects float through the air. To make things 'disappear' Albain required Montgomery to freeze, whereupon he would remove the object, his appearance on film then being edited out. Segments followed a standard format whereby Darrin begged his witchly wife not to use her supernatural powers but temptation proved too great, resulting in big trouble for Darrin (or some other mortal), before happy order was restored. (Rival supernatural sitcom ➢*I Dream of Jeannie* used exactly the same structure.) *Bewitched*'s population of magicians increased by two when

Samantha gave birth to Tabitha and Adam, the former achieving the distinction of being the only offspring born to a sitcom mother to be given a show of her own – *Tabitha* (1977–8), in which she featured as a young adult working at TV station KXLA. One of American network ABC's biggest hits, *Bewitched* was produced by William Asher, Montgomery's husband.

CAST *Samantha Stephens/Serena* Elizabeth Montgomery *Darrin Stephens* Dick York/Dick Sargent *Endora* Agnes Moorehead *Maurice* Maurice Evans *Larry Tate* David White *Louise Tate* Irene Vernon/Kasey Rogers *Tabitha Stephens* Heide and Laura Gentry/Erin and Diane Murphy *Adam Stephens* David and Greg Lawrence *Abner Kravitz* George Tobias *Gladys Kravitz* Alice Pearce/Sandra Gould *Aunt Clara* Marion Lorne / *cr* Sol Saks /*pr* William Asher, Harry Ackerman /*dr* inc William Asher, Richard Michaels, Richard Kinon, R. Robert Rosenbaum, E.W. Swackhamer /*wr* inc Sol Saks, Danny Arnold, Richard Baer, Ed Jurist, Barbara Avedon /*Screen Gems* (USA) /254 x 30m col /US tx ABC 1964–72.

Big Deal

Drama. BBC1 1984–6

Drama-cum-comedy about a dishevelled West London card-sharp, Robby Box, who, aged 40, begins to have a notion that respectable clean-shaven, semi-detached society might be attractive. In this he is encouraged by his patience-of-a-saint girlfriend, Jan. With a charisma-loaded performance by Ray Brooks (*Cathy Come Home*, ➢*Mr Benn*) as the likeable, anxious Box, the series proved a respectable ratings deal for the BBC, earning a second season. Brooks and co-star Duce later returned to BBC TV together in *Growing Pains*, a drama by Steve Wetton about a foster family.

CAST *Robby Box* Ray Brooks *Jan Oliver* Sharon Duce *Debby Oliver* Lisa Geoghan /*cr* Geoff McQueen / *pr* Terence Williams /*dr* Jeremy Summers, Carol Wiseman /*wr* Geoff McQueen /*BBC TV* (UK) / 20 x 50m col.

Biggles

Children's. ITV 1960

Aerial adventure series featuring Captain W.E. John's famous derring-do pilot, Bigglesworth ('Biggles'), here demobbed from the RAF to chase skyborne crooks on behalf of Scotland Yard. He was accompanied on his high-octane stories by war chums Bertie and Ginger. (The latter was played by aspiring popster John Leyton, who later topped the charts with 'Johnny Remember Me'.) Series writers included tyro playright Tony Warren, soon to devise ➢*Coronation Street.*

CAST *Det. Air Insp. 'Biggles' Bigglesworth* Neville Whiting *Bertie* David Drummond *Ginger* John Leyton /*cr* W.E. Johns /pr Harry Elton, Kitty Black /*wr* inc Tony Warren /*Granada TV* (UK) /28 x 30m bw.

The Big Valley

Western. ITV 1965–8

Matriarchal Western starring Barbara Stanwyck (previously the heroine of 50s proto-feminist big-screen oaters *Cattle Queen of Montana* and *The Maverick Queen*) as Victoria Barkley, an iron-willed cattle rancher in California's San Joaquin Valley in the 1870s. Aside from the usual suspects who threaten cattle empire-building (rustlers and Mexicans) in TV horse operas, Barkley had soapish difficulties with her assorted progeny: lawyer Jarrod (Richard Long, ➢*Maverick*, ➢*77 Sunset Strip*), ranch foreman Nick, feisty Heath (Lee Majors, later ➢*The Six Million Dollar Man*, in his premier TV outing), introspective Eugene and beautiful daughter Audra (a youthful Linda Evans, ➢*Dynasty*). Intended to rival contemporary ranch sagas ➢*Bonanza* and ➢*The Virginian*, it never lit the same flames of affection, despite the Hollywood likes of Joseph H. 'Gun Crazy' Lewis sharing the directing chores.

CAST *Victoria Barkley* Barbara Stanwyck *Jarrod Barkley* Richard Long *Nick Barkley* Peter Breck *Heath Barkley* Lee Majors *Eugene Barkley* Charles Briles *Audra Barkley* Linda Evans *Silas* Napoleon Whiting / *cr* A.I. Bezzerides, Louis F. Edleman /*pr* inc Louis F. Edelman, Arnold Laven, Jules Levy /*dr* inc Joseph H. Lewis, Ida Lupino, Virgil W. Vogel, Paul Henreid, Richard Sarafian /*wr* inc Harry Kronman, Peter Packer, Christopher Knopf /*mus* Lalo Schifrin (theme), George Duning /*Four Star Productions* (USA) / 112 x 52m col /US tx ABC 1965–9.

The Bill

Crime. ITV 1984–

Modern tales of everyday coppers in London's East End. *The Bill* first patrolled the screen in 1983 as a one-off play, 'Woodentop', in Thames TV's *Storyboard* before being launched as a one-hour weekly series, transforming into a twice-weekly half-hour series (with an earlier evening slot of 8 p.m.), and finally a thrice-weekly 30-minute show. The changes in format were at the cost of plot and it ended up something like soap opera, though the characters' personal problems were always conspiciously worked out within the confines of the station house (a show rule forbade scenes of the officers' homes). Throughout all, realism was maintained by a free-wheeling, fly-on-the-wall camera style (borrowed by director/producer Peter Cregeen from Roger Graef's documentary *The Police*), and believably mundane storylines. In the first 500 episodes there were only two deaths among the regulars of Sun Hill station, those of PC Ken Melvin and WDC Viv Martell (Nula Conwell, the barmaid in ➢*Only Fools and Horses*). That said, it earned several condemnations from police bodies – notably for a 1988 episode in which a teenager was hit in the face by a Sun Hill officer, the event followed by DI Frank Burnside drinking away the afternoon in a strip club – but rose through the TV ranks to become Britain's most popular police drama of its age. An ensemble cast of characters was cornerstoned by uniformed Sergeant Bob Cryer, whose old-fashioned honesty was highly reminiscent of ➢*Dixon of Dock Green.* The show was created by Geoff McQueen (➢*Big Deal*).

CAST *Sgt Bob Cryer* Eric Richard *DI Roy Galloway* John Salthouse *WPC June Ackland* Trudie Godwin *PC Francis 'Taffy' Edwards* Colin Blumenau *PC Reg Hollis* Jeff Stewart *PC/DC Jim Carver* Mark Wingett *Chief Supt Charles Brownlow* Peter Ellis *PC Ken Melvin* Mark Powley *WPC/WDC Viv Martell* Nula Conwell *Det. Chief Frank Burnside* Christopher Ellison *PC Dave Litten* Gary Olsen *DC Mike Dashwood* Jon Iles *DC Alfred 'Tosh' Lines* Kevin Lloyd *PC Tony Sharp* Graham Cole, *DS Alistair Greig* Andrew Mackintosh /*cr* Geoff McQueen /*exec pr* inc Lloyd Shirley, Peter Cregeen, Michael Chapman /*pr* inc Geraint Moris, Tony Virgo, Richard Handford, Mike Dormer, Michael Simpson / *dr* inc Peter Cregeen, A.J. Quinn, Morag Fullarton, John Woods, James Hawes /*wr* inc Geoff McQueen, Mike Holloway, Simon Moss, Julian Jones, J.C. Wilsher, Margaret Phelan /*mus* Andy Pask, Charles Morgan (theme) /*Thames TV* (UK) /100 x 50m, 1 x 90m, 600+ x 30m col.

Billy Bunter of Greyfriars School

Comedy. BBC 1952–61

The 'Oh, Crikey!' schoolboy misadventures of ever-hungry William George Bunter, the Owl of the Remove, translated for the small screen from *Magnet* comic by creator Frank Richards. Cast as Greyfriars' fattest was 29-year-old(!) Gerald Campion, while Bunter's beastly schoolboy tormentors were played by such aspiring thespians as Michael Crawford (➢*Some Mothers Do 'Ave 'Em*), Anthony Valentine (➢*Colditz*) and Melvyn Hayes (➢*It Ain't Half Hot, Mum*). Initially, Knyaston Reeves performed the role of fearsome form-master Mr Quelch, foiler of all Bunter's best-laid plans for the liberation of sticky buns from the tuckshop, before passing the cane on to Raf de la Torre and Jack Melford. Made in the days before videotape, the show was performed live twice (5.25 p.m. for juniors, 8 p.m. for adults) on Tuesday nights. Yaroo.

CAST *Billy Bunter* Gerald Campion /*cr* Frank Richards /*pr* Joy Harington, David Goddard, Pharic Maclaren, Shaun Sutton, Clive Parkhurst /*wr* Frank Richards /*BBC TV* (UK) /approx 120 x 30m bw.

The Bionic Woman

Sci-fi. ITV 1976–9

Successful spin-off from ➢*The Six Million Dollar Man* (courtesy of the first ever script by budding sci-fi maestro Kenneth Johnson), in which Steve Austin's sometime fiancée, Jaime Sommers, an ex-tennis pro, was refurbished after a sky-diving accident with atomic-electronic legs, arm and ear. This latter 'bionic' device enabled Sommers to hear conversations a mile or more away. Like Austin, she worked on behalf of Oscar Goldman's OSI agency, fighting – sometimes with the assistance of Max, the bionic dog – the assorted terrorists, aliens, spies and criminal masterminds who habitually threaten the US of A on videotape. Probably the most memorable of these was the army of deadly female robots who appeared in 'Fembots in Las Vegas'. Such arch touches (the series ended with a spoof of the final episode of ➢*The Prisoner,* entitled 'On the Run') saved the series from being a pale imitation of its master, as did the sensitive, emotionally deep acting of Lindsay Wagner, who won a 1976 Emmy for her endeavour. In Britain the series topped the ratings on its debut, running for several years in the ITV regions.

CAST *Jaime Sommers* Lindsay Wagner *Oscar Goldman* Richard Anderson *Dr Rudy Wells* Martin E. Brooks /*cr* Kenneth Johnson /*exec pr* Harve Bennett /*pr* Kenneth Johnson /*dr* inc Alan Levi, Gwen Arner, Jack Arnold /*wr* inc Kenneth Johnson /*mus* Jerry Fielding /*MCA TV* (USA) /57 x 60m col /US tx ABC:NBC 1976–8.

Bird of Prey

Drama. BBC1 1982–

One of TV's first credible forays into the complex world of computer fraud, this 'thriller for the electronic age' starred Richard Griffiths (fresh from playing GP Hooper opposite Elaine Stritch in *Nobody's Perfect*, LWT 1980–82) as portly, conscientious civil servant Henry Jay. A gripping four-parter, its premise was thus: while investigating a bog standard case of computer malpractice, Henry stumbled upon a massive international financial conspiracy and determined to uncover the facts, despite threats from agents of shadowy organization 'Le Pouvoir' and attempts by powerful bureaucrats to silence him. A sequel (*Bird of Prey 2*, BBC1) which had Henry on the run with his wife, was made in 1984. In 1982 Griffiths also starred as Soviet premier Dubienkin in ➢*Whoops! Apocalypse*, LWT's off-the-wall series chronicling events leading up to the Third World War. The following year he made the mistake of playing Potbelly in ➢*The Cleopatras*, a move which did little for his career, which only picked up with ➢*Pie in the Sky*.

CAST *Henry Jay* Richard Griffiths *Anne Jay* Carole Nimmons /*pr* Michael Wearing /dr Michael Rolfe /*wr* Ron Hutchinson /*BBC TV* /1 x 55m, 3 x 50m col.

Birds of a Feather

Comedy. BBC1 1989–

Girls behaving badly sitcom, in which sisters Sharon (plump, pudding-basin hairdo) and Tracey (blonde highlights) shared the latter's neo-Georgian pile in Chigwell, the back door of which had a habit of being persistently opened by scene-stealing, man-eating, socially aspirant Jewish neighbour Dorien. Sharon and Tracey's husbands were banged up in Maidstone prison for a spot of armed robbery, which left the Essex girls to pine, dream up business schemes, lark about (Tracey taking charge of a boys football team), and fancy a bit of the other; Dorien's accountant husband Marcus was almost permanently detained on business, allowing her to prey on any hapless and, preferably, young man to come her way. Sex and money were uppermost in the minds of all three but family concerns also raised their dramatic head in storylines which centred on Tracey's son Garth (away at boarding school) and the sisters' discovery that they were adopted. Much of the love-hate screen chemistry between Tracey and Sharon was attributable to actresses Pauline Quirke and Linda Robson being long-time friends (though the sepia, opening cine-film shots of two girls playing was not them), who had trained together at Anna Shear's East End drama school. They first appeared together on the TV in children's sketch show ➢*You Must Be Joking!* From the well-practised pens of Laurence Marks and Maurice Gran (➢*Shine on Harvey Moon*, ➢*The New Statesman*), *Birds of a Feather*'s scriptwriters also included Peter Tilbury (inventor of ➢*Shelley*) and Alun Lewis, who played Tracey's husband Darryl in the show.

Airline chief Richard Branson and perma-tanned Hollywood actor George Hamilton topped the guest cast list.

CAST *Sharon Theodopolopoudos* Pauline Quirke *Tracey Stubbs* Linda Robson *Dorien Green* Lesley Joseph *Chris Theodopolopoudos* David Cardy/Peter Polycarpou *Darryl Stubbs* Alun Lewis *Garth Stubbs* Simon Nash/Matthew Savage *Marcus Green* Nickolas Grace/Stephen Greif /*cr* Laurence Marks, Maurice Gran /*pr* Esta Charkham, Nic Phillips, Candida Julian-Jones, Charlie Hanson /*dr* inc Nic Phillips, Charlie Hanson /*wr* Laurence Marks, Maurice Gran, Alun Lewis, Geoff Rowley, Gary Lawson, Peter Tilbury, John Phelps /*Alomo Productions* (UK) /95 x 30m col.

The Black Adder

Comedy. BBC1 1983–9

A cycle of sitcoms which began with the crude *The Black Adder*, concerning the medieval exploits of venomous young aristocrat Edmund Blackadder, and rose through *Black Adder II* (set in Elizabethan times) and *Blackadder the Third* (the Regency period), to finish with the sublime *Blackadder Goes Forth* (the Great War). Accompanying Blackadder on his ophidian odyssey was foul-smelling retainer Baldrick (Tony Robinson, after Timothy Spall turned down the part), seemingly possessed of 'dung for brains'. When the first series almost emptied the BBC coffers, new headman Michael Grade reached for the axe, but writer Richard Curtis (➢*Not the Nine*

O'Clock News, ➢*The Vicar of Dibley*, the movie *Four Weddings and a Funeral*) and new partner Ben Elton produced, in veritable Blackadder professor-of-cunning fashion, scripts for a second series with all the expensive bits removed. Curtis and Elton also decided to trim back the gurning and slapstick on which the premier season had relied, and instead nursed a wondrous mix of schoolboy jokes ('The enemy is thinner on the ground precisely opposite your trenches, Blackadder.' 'Could be my batman's socks, sir.'), convoluted wordplay, historical parody and lampooning of exactly the sort of costume dramas the Corporation itself likes to make. Yet to make it all work, it needed performances of scintillating skill. These were provided by rubber-faced Rowan Atkinson (➢*Not the Nine O'Clock News*, ➢*Mr Bean*, ➢*The Thin Blue Line*), the said Robinson and a regular supporting cast of Tim McInnerny (Lord Percy in *The Black Adder* and *Black Adder II*, Captain Darling in *Blackadder Goes Forth*), Hugh Laurie (Prince Regent in *Black Adder the Third*, Lt George in *Blackadder Goes Forth*), and Stephen Fry (Lord Melchett in *Black Adder II*, the General in *Blackadder Goes Forth*). Others who provided sterling thesping included Patsy Byrne (Nursie in *Black Adder II*) and Miranda Richardson (Queenie in *Black Adder II*). The series took its curtain bow in 1989 with an uncompromisingly bleak scene in which Blackadder, by now a thoroughly subtle and sympathetic character, and his pals went 'over the top' to assault German trenches on the Western Front. The eighties were not a great era for the sitcom – proved, not least, by declining viewing figures – but *Blackadder* was a shining peak of achievement.

CAST *Edmund Blackadder* Rowan Atkinson *Baldrick* Tony Robinson /*cr* Richard Curtis, Rowan Atkinson /*pr* John Lloyd /*dr* Martin Shardlow, Mandie Fletcher, Richard Boden / *wr* Richard Curtis, Rowan Atkinson, Ben Elton /*mus* Howard Goodall /*BBC TV* (UK) / 24 x 30m, 1 x 45m, 1 x 15m, col.

The Black and White Minstrel Show

Light Entertainment. BBC1 1958–78

Undemanding Saturday night variety show which quick-waltzed from one medley of sing-something croons to the next, these sung by white men blacked up as nigger minstrels and white women left virginally untouched by sooty make-up. The background glamour to the vocal performances of the George Mitchell Minstrels was provided by the Television Topper dancers; light relief came from the turns of such comedians as Leslie Crowther. Derived from a one-off special, *The 1957 Television Minstrels*, the show – which made stars of solo vocalists Dai Francis, Tony Mercer and John Boulter – lasted for 21 seasons, before finally dying from public realization that it was an incongruous piece of racism.

CAST The George Mitchell Minstrels, Television Toppers /*cr* George Inns /*pr* George Inns, Ernest Maxin, Brian Whitehouse /*dr* George Mitchell, George Inns /*BBC TV* (UK) /200+ x 45m bw.

Blackeyes

Drama. BBC2 1989

Playwright Dennis Potter (➢*Pennies from Heaven*, *Blue Remembered Hills*, ➢*The Singing Detective*, ➢*Lipstick on Your Collar*) moved behind the camera for the first time to direct the television version of his own novel, with dubious results. The glossy production told the tale of an ageing author who manipulated his doe-eyed niece Jessica's experiences as a model into a novel entitled *Blackeyes*, which became a titillating and overnight success.

Potter's tale, sophisticated and multi-layered in form, purported to be an exposé and critique of the workings of pornography. However, even his most loyal supporters strained to view it this way and most saw it instead as the self-indulgent out-pourings of an elderly playwright's fantasies of younger women.

CAST *Jessica* Carol Royle *Blackeyes* Gina Bellman *Detective Blake* John Shrapnel /*cr* Dennis Potter /*pr* Rick McCallum /*dr* Dennis Potter, Michael Gough /*wr* Dennis Potter /*BBC TV*: ABC-TV (AUS): Television NZ (NZ) (UK) /4 x 55m col.

Black Forest Clinic

Melodrama. C4 1988

Euro-soap of the medical sort. A major success in its native Germany (drawing 60 per cent of available audience share), *Die Schwarzwaldklinik* failed to travel to Britain, where audiences were bemused by bad dubbing, atrocious lip-sync and long panning shots of pine forests, suggestive of a Bavarian tourism promo. Actor Sascha Hehn had previously been a teenage star of porn movies.

CAST *Prof. Klaus Brinkmann* Klausjurgen Wussow *Dr Udo Brinkmann* Sascha Hehn /*dr* Alfred Vohrer, Hans Jurgen Togel /*wr* inc Herbert Lichentenfeld /*Polyphon Film* (Ger) /1 x 90m, 11 x 45m col (UK tx).

Blake's 7

Sci-fi. BBC1 1978–81

'Liberty became a crime punishable by death...'

Cult British sci-fi serial. Penned by Terry Nation (inventor of the Daleks and ➢*The Survivors*), *B7* followed the tribulations and adventures of a motley band of freedom fighters led by Roj Blake in the second century of the third calendar. Although its sources were obvious – ➢*Star Trek*, the legend of Robin Hood, *Star Wars* (whose Imperial Empire was the model for *B7*s evil Terran Federation) – Nation suffused the serial with an intense personal and political vision, which turned it into a parable of the duty of an individual and honourable man in an immoral society. (The Federation against which Blake battled had associations of Nazism, a subject Nation had also artistically tackled in his Dalek contributions to ➢*Doctor Who*.) This said, *B7* was not a one-man show. Others added vital elements, particularly script editor Chris Boucher (creator of ➢*Star Cops*), who developed its exemplary human characterization – the 7 were an engagingly complex lot, whose private feuds were as interesting as their public war – and made Blake a study in revolutionary leadership. The magnificent 7 from the frontier of future space who fought the Terran Federation were: Blake (Gareth Thomas, ➢*Children of the Stones*); Jenna Stannis, a smuggler; Kerr Avon, a supercilious computer expert; Vila Restal, a thief; Cally, a telepathic alien warrior from planet Auron; Gan, a gentle giant; and Zen, master computer of Blake's ship, *Liberator*. However, going against accepted drama serial practice, *Blake's 7* killed off several leading characters – Gan, Zen, Cally – with Blake himself going MIA in the season two episode 'Star One'. To make up this loss of personnel, the band – now under the command of the devious and paranoid Avon – recruited mercenary Del Tarrant, black gunwoman Dayna Melanby, avenger Soolin (Glynis Barber, ➢*Dempsey and Makepeace*) and Orac, a super-super computer. A new ship, *Scorpio*, was also introduced. Fittingly, given its eschewing of accepted TV sci-fi norms, the serial signed off with an episode in which Avon killed the reappeared Blake with a smile on his lips – arguably the most enigmatic conclusion to a show since McGoohan's ➢*The Prisoner*.

CAST *Blake* Gareth Thomas *Avon* Paul Darrow *Vila* Michael Keating *Gan* David Jackson *Cally* Jan Chappell *Zen/Slave Orac* (voice) Peter Tuddenham *Jenna Stannis* Sally Knyvette *Servalan, Federation Supreme Commander* Jacqueline Pearce *Travis, Federation Space Commander* Stephen Greif/Brian Croucher *Dayna* Josette Simon *Tarrant* Steven Pacey *Soolin* Glynis Barber /*cr* Terry Nation /*pr* David Maloney /*dr* inc Vere Lorimer, Pennant Roberts, Michael E. Briant, David Maloney, Viktors Ritelis, Mary Ridge /*wr* inc Terry Nation, Chris Boucher, Roger Parkes, James Follett, Trevor Hoyle, Robert Holmes /*mus* Dudley Simpson /*BBC TV* (UK) / 52 x 50m col /US tx PBS 1986.

Blankety Blank

Light Entertainment. BBC1 1977–89

Banal Saturday evening game show, responsible for making a TV star of charming 'Oirish' Radio 2 DJ Terry Wogan. Members of the public ('MOTPs' in industry parlance) had to guess the missing word – the blank of the title – in a given sentence and hope that the six celebrity panellists had written down the same. Prizes were infamously inexpensive, while losers walked away with 'a Blankety Blank cheque book and pen'. Wogan found a useful gimmick in a wand-like mike and bantered effectively with the assorted celebs, at least one of whom (usually Sandra Dickinson, ➢*The Hitchhiker's Guide to the Galaxy*) had no discernible brain, and most of whom were clearly in need of the exposure. When Wogan left for more illustrious TV work with *The Terry Wogan Show*, comic Les Dawson amply filled the presenter's gap with a diametrically opposed style – a fitting world-weary sarcasm.

CAST (presenters) Terry Wogan, Les Dawson /*pr* Alan Boyd, Marcus Plantin, Stanley Appel /*BBC TV* (UK) / 300 x 30m col.

Bless This House

Comedy. ITV 1971–6

Independent TV's contribution to the 70s middle-class domestic sitcom. Sid Abott was a sales rep for a stationery firm, a fiftysomething who alphabetically listed his pleasures as 'Ale,

Birds and Chelsea'. He shared his Birch Avenue, Putney, home with wife Jean and troublesome teenage children Mike (unemployed, ex-art-college student) and Sally (grammar schoolgirl; played by Sally Geeson, sister of Judy). As signalled by the title of the opening episode, 'The Generation Gap', the main theme of the series (along with the proverbial battle of the sexes) was Sid and Jean's exasperation at the permissive manners and mores of their offspring. Trevor was the meddlesome next-door neighbour, Betty his caricature nagging wife.

A popular hit, the series marked alcoholic veteran actor Sid James' (➢*George and the Dragon*, ➢*Hancock's Half Hour*, *Citizen James*, ➢*Carry On Laughing*) last starring venture on the small screen. He died of a heart attack on 26 April 1976, allegedly caused in part by unrequited love for *Carry On* co-star Barbara Windsor. Created by Vince Powell and Harry Driver, produced by the future host of ➢*Fifteen To One* William G. Stewart, with occasional scripts by Carla ➢*'The Liver Birds'* Lane. Peter Rogers Productions made a 1972 spin-off film featuring most of the TV line up.

CAST *Sid Abbott* Sid James *Jean Abbott* Diana Coupland *Mike Abbott* Robin Stewart *Sally Abbott* Sally Geeson *Trevor* Anthony Jackson *Betty* Patsy Rowlands /*cr* Harry Driver, Vince Powell /*pr* William G. Stewart /*dr* William G. Stewart /*wr* Vince Powell & Harry Driver, Carla Lane, Myra Taylor /*mus* Geoff Love (theme) /*Thames TV* /65 x 30m col.

Blind Date

Light Entertainment. ITV 1985–

British variant of the US show *The Dating Game*, here hosted by Cilla Black (born Priscilla White, *Surprise, Surprise*), in which young men with gelled hair, and Essex girls in white shoes, gave scripted answers to an unseen questioner (of the opposite sex) in the hope that they would be chosen for his or her 'blind date'. This could be anything from parascending in the North Weald to a luxury sojourn in the Bahamas. On returning from the date, the couple revealed their real opinions of each other (via separately filmed interviews), with Cilla playing them alternately for a 'lorra, lorra' laughs, fake pathos or sexual prurience. Did they or did they not have sex was always the question engineered to linger over the proceedings. A disproportionate number of the contestants were the wannabe famous (one or two did actually turn their appearance into a short-lived media career), while some, starting with Sue Middleton and Alex Tatham in 1991, found 'true love' on their date and married.

CAST (host) Cilla Black /exec *pr* Marcus Plantin /*pr* inc Gill Stribling-Wright, Sean Murphy, Robert Randell, Philip Livingstone, Kevin Roast, Michael Longmire, Chris O'Dell, Thelma McGough /*dr* inc Terry Kinane, John Gorman, Martin Scott /*London Weekend TV* (UK) /200+ x 30m col.

Blockbusters

Light Entertainment. ITV/Sky1/Family Channel 1983–

Unlikely cult quiz show, hosted by inoffensive ex-Radio 2 DJ Bob Holness (also the heavyweight *World in Action*, *What the Papers Say*), in which two sixth-formers pitched their wits and general knowledge against another adolescent in a jumper. Correct answers lit up hexagonal blocks on a screen. Since each block contained the letter of an alphabet, there was much studio tittering when contestants asked, 'Can I have a T, Bob?' or even, 'Can I have a P?' The rewards were fiscal, the big prize won by a 60-second 'hot spot' in which the winning side had to light up a path across the board. Britain's first daily TV quiz, it began on ITV, to continue its run on Sky1 and, from 1996, on the Family Channel. The format was taken up in the USA, where it was broadcast on NBC with Bill Raferty as host.

CAST (presenter) Bob Holness /*pr* Graham C. Williams, Tony Wolfe, Terry Steel, Bob Cousins /*dr* inc Graham C. Williams /*Talbot TV: Freemantle Prods* (UK) /400+ x 30m col.

Blossom

Comedy. C4 1991–

Touted as the American sitcom successor to 80s hits ➢*Cheers* and ➢*The Cosby Show*, *Blossom* – which related the misadventures of a teenage girl growing up in an all-male (and totally dysfunctional) household – never quite made the mega-grade, but was amiable enough. In the standard manner of American TV programmes with a big pre-adult audience, it tackled 'issues', such as sex, drugs and first periods, with alacrity. One of the best storylines found Blossom's ambulance-driving, substance-abusing brother

Anthony waking up after a drinking spree in Las Vegas to find himself married to a black girl he had no memory of ever meeting. Guest celebrities, among them TV sitcom legends Estelle Getty and Rhea Perlman, and musicians Little Richard and Sonny Bono, regularly appeared in Blossom's fantasies to proffer comedic advice on her current problem. A junior version of Bette Midler, Mayim Bialik was cast as Blossom after coming to studio notice with her performance in the movie *Beaches*. Among the show's directors was Bill Bixby, better known for his before-the-camera appearance as ➢*The Incredible Hulk*.

CAST *Blossom Russo* Mayim Bialik *Nick Russo* Ted Wass *Joseph* Joey Lawrence *Anthony* Michael Stoyanov *Vinnie* David Lascher *Six* Jenna Van Oy /*cr* Don Reo / *exec pr* inc Paul Junger Witt, Tony Thomas, Don Reo, Judith D. Allison, Allan Katz /*dr* inc Gil Junger, Bill Bixby, John Whitesell, Ted Wass /*wr* inc Don Reo / *Witt-Thomas Production: Touchstone TV* (USA) / 90+ x 30m col /US tx NBC 1991–.

Blue Peter

Children's. BBC/BBC1 1958–

The magazine show which taught generations of children how to make a fully operational jet fighter out of detergent bottles and 'sticky-backed plastic' began on 16 October 1958 as a 15-minute experiment in the *Children's Television* slot. From the outset, *Blue Peter* was reassuringly middle class, presented by a former army officer, Christopher Trace, and a former Miss Great Britain, Leila Williams. Its golden age, however, came in the early to mid 60s with the recruitment of Valerie Singleton, Peter Purves and hyperactive daredevil John Noakes (later in *Go With Noakes*) as presenters, and expansion to two 30-minute episodes per week (Mondays and Thursdays). Since that halcyon era there have been 20 presenters, among them: Lesley Judd, Simon Groom, Sarah Greene (*Going Live*), Peter Duncan (later in *Duncan Dares*), Caron Keating (daughter of Gloria Hunniford), and Anthea Turner.

Stiffly conscious of the BBC's Reithian duty to educate and inform, *Blue Peter* – under the guiding eye of producer Biddy Baxter – has long stressed foreign culture (learned about on jaunts to Sri Lanka and such other exotic locales), the building of social conscience through charity appeals (which never involved the raising of anything as tawdry as money, but the collection of bottle tops and silver paper), and the fostering of DIY entertainment through the construction of toys and decorations out of discarded household objects ('Here's one I made earlier.'). To compensate urban children, who could not keep a pet of their own, the show foregrounded a series of studio pets, beginning with Petra in 1962. (Alas, the first Petra promptly died of distemper and had to be replaced by a look-alike from a Lewisham petshop.) Among the most famous of the *Blue Peter* pets have been Patch, Jason the Siamese cat, Shep ('Get down, Shep!'), Bonny, and Honey the guide dog. It was, however, Lulu, a guest Sri Lankan elephant visitor to the studio, who provided the show with its folkloric moment, the depositing of a steaming turd on the floor (Noakes: 'Whoops, I've trodden right in it!').

More a national institution than a mere TV show, *Blue Peter* added a third weekly programme in April 1995.

CAST (presenters) Leila Williams, Christopher Trace, Valerie Singleton, John Noakes, Peter Purves, Lesley Judd, Simon Groom, Christopher Wenner, Tina Heath, Sarah Greene, Peter Duncan, Janet Ellis, Michael Sundin, Mark Curry, Caron Keating, Yvette Fielding, John Leslie, Diane-Louise Jordan, Anthea Turner, Tim Vincent, Stuart Miles, Katy Hill, Romana D'Annunzio, Richard Baron, Konnie Huq /*cr* John Hunter Blair /*ed* Biddy Baxter, Lewis Bronze, Oliver MacFarlane /*BBC TV* (UK) /3000+ x 30m bw:col.

The Boat (Das Boot)

Adventure. BBC2 1974

Epic and extraordinary TV war mini-drama, recording the lupine patrols of German submarine U-46 through the Atlantic and Mediterranean in 1941. Made simultaneously with the abridged (and inferior) movie version, the adrenaline-propelled serial gave a candid, German sailor's eye-view of WWII and the intense claustrophobic nature of life aboard a U-boat. Directed with brio by Wolfgang Pedersen, the £8 million budget *Das Boot* (which necessitated the building of a lifesize, 70-metre model submarine, accurate down to the last bolt) secured him a mooring in Hollywood. Also sent Hollywoodwards was Jurgen Prochnow, who played the old-before-his-time Kapitan. Based on *Das Boot*, the autobiographical novel of German war correspondent Lothar Gunther-Bucheim, the programme was released in Britain afore its native Germany.

CAST *Der Kapitan* Jurgen Prochnow *Lt Werner* Herbert Grunemeyer *Chief Engineer* Klaus Wennermann *First Lt* Hubertus Bengsch *Second Lt* Martin Semmelrogge *Bridge Officer* Bernd Tauber / *pr* Gunther Rohrbach / *dr* Wolfgang Petersen / *wr* Wolfgang Petersen / *mus* Klaus Doldinger / *Bavaria Atelier* (Ger) / 1 x 90m, 4 x 55m col.

Bonanza

Western. ITV 1960–73

'What we want is Western action and Western adventure, concerning a worthy and dramatic problem for the Cartwrights… We want human drama…' Writer guidelines for *Bonanza.*

A Western family saga ('saddle-soap') of prodigious longevity, running on its native NBC network for 14 years. Set on a vast timber and cattle spread called 'The Ponderosa' in 1860s Nevada, it featured thrice-widowed Ben Cartwright ('Pa') as the head of an upright clan which consisted of eldest son Adam, middle son Hoss, and youngest son Little Joe (Michael Landon, star of the 1957 film *I Was a Teenage Werewolf*). There was also a Chinese cook and other regulars were drifter cowboy 'Candy' Canaday, orphan Jamie Hunter and Sheriff Roy Coffee of nearby Virginia City. Stories usually revolved around (misfit/luck-challenged/persecuted) guest characters, enabling the series to explore serious human themes. Consequently the Cartwright boys were endlessly tortured by ethical conflicts that required a fireside chat with Pa. Robert Altman (later the movies *M*A*S*H* and *The Player*) and Jacques Tourneur were among the directors. The first Western to be made in colour (location filming was in the stunning Lake Tahoe area), *Bonanza* spawned a posse of frontier-sudster imitators, notably ➢*The High Chaparral* (also by David Dotort), ➢*The Big Valley* and ➢*Lancer.* A hit for most of its run (not only in the USA but in Britain, where it helped establish the fledgling ITV network, plus 58 other countries), *Bonanza* was eventually brought low by the untimely death of Dan Blocker, whose 'gentle giant' Hoss character had become the show's most loved creation, an archetype of an earlier, more decent America. He left a void impossible to fill. To exacerbate matters, the producers then screened a segment (written and directed by Michael Landon) which saw the death of Little Joe's bride, Anne. Another *Bonanza* loss, even a fictional one, was too much for fans to bear. This, in the general context of the decline of the Westerner as a TV hero, meant that *Bonanza*'s 430th episode (screened on 23 January 1973) was its last. A year later Michael Landon premiered his ➢*Little House on the Prairie,* and later achieved another hit with ➢*Highway to Heaven.* Lorne Greene, meanwhile, went to the final frontier of space in ➢*Battlestar Galactica* and Pernell Roberts starred as *Trapper John, MD.*

Stars Lorne Greene (centre), Michael Landon (right) and Dan Blocker on the set of *Bonanza.* Shown in Britain from 1960, the oater show helped establish fledgling ITV as the most popular network.

In March 1988 the Cartwright saga hit the TV trail once more with a TVM, *Bonanza: The Next Generation,* starring an entirely new cast which included the now-deceased Michael Landon's son, Michael Landon Jr, as Little Joe's son, Benji. Another made-for-TV movie and a short series followed.

CAST *Ben Cartwright* Lorne Greene *Little Joe Cartwright* Michael Landon *Eric 'Hoss' Cartwright* Dan Blocker *Adam Cartwright* Pernell Roberts *Hop Sing* Victor Sen Yung *Sheriff Roy Coffee* Ray Teal *Candy* David Canary *Jamie Hunter* Mitch Vogel *Griff King* Tim Matheson / *cr* David Dotort / *exec pr* David Dotort / *pr* inc David Dotort, Richard Collins, Robert Blees / *dr* inc Joseph Sargent, William F. Claxton, Paul Henreid,

Tay Garnett, Jacques Tourneur, Robert Altman, R.G. Springsteen, Virgil W. Vogel /*wr* inc Michael Landon, Joseph Bonaduce, William R. Cox, D.C. Fontana, John T. Kelley /*mus* Jay Livingston & Ray Evans (theme), David Rose /*NBC Productions* (USA) /430 x 52m col / US tx NBC 1959–73.

Boney

Crime. ITV 1975–6

Languid murder cases in the Oz outback, investigated by aboriginal Detective Inspector Napoleon Bonaparte (played incongruously by blacked-up white New Zealand actor James Laurenson), who used bushman skills to track his quarry. Based on the novels of Arthur W. Upfield.

CAST *DI Napoleon 'Boney' Bonaparte* James Laurenson /*exec pr* Bon Austin, Lee Robinson /*pr* John McCallum /*Norfolk International* (Aus) /26 x 50m col.

Boon

Comedy. ITV 1986–92/1995

'Ex-fireman seeks interesting work – anything legal considered.'

Thus did lugubrious Ken Boon (Michael Elphick, ➢*Private Schulz*, ➢*Auf Wiedersehn, Pet* and *Three Up, Two Down*) begin his ill-starred career as a Birmingham troubleshooter, since the replies to Box 13 inevitably resulted in Boon riding his 650cc BSA motorbike into police-type trouble, or being pursued by enormous heavies. The self-styled 'urban cowboy' then founded a courier agency, The Texas Rangers, in which he was unably assisted by intellectually-challenged biker Rocky (Neil Morrisey, ➢*Men Behaving Badly*) and teenager Debbie Yates as secretary. When the courier business began to fail to amuse Boon – actually more Peter Pan than Wyatt Earp – he opened up shop as a private eye, eventually joined by his best friend, the eternally optimistic Harry Crawford (David Draker, ➢*Coronation Street*), whose country hotel business had taken its last reservation. The secretary at Crawford Boon Security was Alex Wilton (Saskia Wickham, *Clarissa* and ➢*Peak Practice*). To freshen jaded audience taste buds, the fourth series was relocated to Nottingham. Middlebrow fare, with so-so plots, it was frequently carried by the performances of Elphick and Draker.

CAST *Ken Boon* Michael Elphick *Harry Crawford* David Draker *Rocky Cassidy* Neil Morrissey *Debbie Yates* Lesley-Anne Sharpe *Laura Marsh* Elizabeth Carling *Alex Wilton* Saskia Wickham /*cr* Jim Hill, Bill Stair /*exec pr* Ted Childs, William Smethurst /*pr* inc Michelle Buck, Esta Charkham, Simon Lewis /*dr* inc Laurence Moody, Nick Laughland, Matthew Evans, Robert Tronson /*wr* inc Jim Hill, Bill Stair, Bernard Dempsey, Anthony Horowitz, Anthony Minghella, Geoff McQueen /*mus* Jim Diamond & Chris Parren ('Hi Ho Silver' theme) /*Central TV* (UK) /93 x 50m col.

Boots and Saddles

Western. BBC 1958–60

The adventures of the Fifth Cavalry fighting Injuns and bad whitemen in the Wild West of the 1870s. Captain Shank Adams was leader of the troop, Lieutenants Kelly and Binning his right-hand men, Luke Cummings the obligatory buck-skinned scout. Moderate oater, improved by fine location filming (Utah) and stirring action scenes.

CAST *Capt. Shank Adams* Jack Picard *Lt Col. Hays* Patrick McVey *Lt Binning* David Willock *Lt Kelly* Gardner McKay *Sgt Bullock* John Alderson *Luke Cummings* Michael Hinn /*pr* George Cahan, Robert Stillman /*California National Productions* (USA) / 39 x 26m bw /US tx Syndicated 1957–9.

Bootsie and Snudge

Comedy. ITV 1960–3/1974

Initially transmitted as *Bootsie and Snudge in Civvy Street*, this ➢*The Army Game* spin-off transplanted diminutive Pte 'Boots Excused' Bisley (Alfie Bass) and pompous CSM Snudge (Bill Fraser) into a decrepeit London gentleman's club, The Imperial, run by the Right Honourable Secretary, Hesketh Pendleton. Bootsie became the shoeshine, his old army antagonist the major-domo. The establishment's 84-year-old waiter, Johnson, was played by a pre-➢*Dad's Army* Clive Dunn. The show topped the ratings in 1960 and 1961. Unwilling to let a successful sitcom partnership go, the Bass-Fraser duo were then placed in the diplomatic service in the sitcom *Foreign Affairs* (1964, 8 x 30m), where they served in the British Embassy in Bosnik. Ten years later Bass and Fraser were hauled out for another *Bootsie and Snudge* (this time under the producership of Bill Podmore) but with the power relationship reversed: the whining, devious Bootsie had become the world's first £1 million pools winner, the pop-eyed Snudge the humble man from the pools company.

CAST *Bootsie Bisley* Alfie Bass *Claude Snudge* Bill Fraser *Hesketh Pendleton* Robert Dorning *Henry Beerbohm 'Old' Johnson* Clive Dunn /*cr* Peter Eton, Milo Lewis /*pr* Peter Eton, Bill Podmore /*dr* Milo Lewis, Eric Fawcett, Bill Podmore /*wr* inc Barry Took, Marty Feldman, John Antrobus, David Climie, Ronnie Cass /*Granada TV* (UK) /100 x 30m bw, 6 x 30m col.

The Borgias

Melodrama. BBC2 1981

Unintentionally amusing costume drama which serialized the story of 15th-century Rodrigo Borgia's climb to the papal throne. Famously impious, Rodrigo – aka Pope Alexander VI – was the sire of seven bastard offspring, the most infamous of whom were Cesare Borgia (the model for Machiavelli's *The Prince*) and Lucrezia (the toxicologist). Clearly intended by the BBC to follow in the classic sandals of ➢*I, Claudius*, *The Borgias* was reduced to ➢*Up Pompeii!* levels of ludicrousness by theatrical overacting, Sicilian Adolfo Celi's fractured command of English, and long-winded explantory dialogue ('As Vice-Chancellor of the Holy Church, should you not be here to welcome the King of France?'). There were also several gratuitous orgy scenes, one of which required the cast to crawl half-naked on the floor picking up chestnuts with their mouths. When screened in Italy, the show earned the distinction of a formal censure from the Vatican.

CAST *Rodrigo Borgia* Adolfo Celi *Cesare Borgia* Oliver Cotton *Giuliano della Rovere* Alfred Burke *Lucrezia Borgia* Anne Louise Lambert *Juan Borgia* George Camiller /*cr* Mark Shivas /*pr* Mark Shivas /*dr* Brian Farnham /*wr* John Prebble, Ken Taylor /*mus* Georges Delerue /*BBC TV* (UK) /7 x 55m, 3 x 50m col.

Boss Cat

Children's. BBC1 1963

Prohibited from using its US title of *Top Cat* in Britain (where this was a branded pet food), Hanna-Barbera's show about the indisputable leader of a gang of NY alley cats was a feline cartoon take on Nat Hiken's *Bilko* (➢*The Phil Silvers Show*). Always on the look-out for new money-making scams, TC lived in a customized dustbin, used the police telephone of long-suffering Officer Dibble for his private calls, and stole milk from doorsteps. The full line-up of his multi-coloured entourage, all of whom were based loosely on *Bilko* characters, was: corpulent blue Benny the Ball (voiced by Maurice Gosfield, the actor who played his Fort Baxter model, Pte Doberman); Choo Choo; Spook; dim-witted Brain; and ladies tom, Fancy-Fancy – Cary Grant with fur. Since the conclusion of the show's original transmission, TC has been a running character on *The Funtastic World of Hanna-Barbera*, and in 1987 was accorded a TV special entitled *Top Cat and the Beverly Hills Cats*. For the record, the theme song was:

Top Cat
The most effectual Top Cat
Whose intellectual close friends get to call him TC
Providing it's with dignity.
Top Cat
The indisputable leader of the gang
He's the boss
He's the VIP
He's a championship
He's the most tip top Top Cat... Yes – he's the boss
He's the king
But above everything
He's the most tip top... Top Cat!

CAST (voices) *Top Cat* Arnold Stang *Benny the Ball* Maurice Gosfield *Choo Choo* Marvin Kaplan *Spook / The Brain* Leo DeLyon *Fancy-Fancy Pierre* John Stephenson *Officer Dibble* Allen Jenkins *Goldie* Jean Vander Pyl /*cr* Joseph Barbera /*exec pr* William Hanna, Joseph Barbera /*pr* Berny Wolf, Jeff Hall /*dr* Ray Patterson /*wr* inc Barry Blitzer, Harvey Bullock, Ray Allen /*Hanna-Barbera:Screen Gems* (USA) /30 x 22m col /US tx ABC 1961–2.

Bottle Boys

Comedy. ITV 1984–5

Lowbrow, high-innuendo escapades of an amorous milkman, Dave Deacon of Dawson's Dairy, who risked all to deliver his daily round. Somewhat inevitably, the part of Deacon was taken by *Confessions Of...* actor, Robin Asquith.

CAST *Dave Deacon* Robin Asquith *Stan Evans* Richard Davies *Sharon Armstrong* Eve Ferret /*cr* Vince Powell /*pr* Stuart Allen /*dr* Stuart Allen /*wr* Vince Powell /*LWT* (UK) /13 x 30m col.

Bottom

Comedy. BBC2 1991–2

Originally to be called *Your Bottom* (as in 'I saw your bottom on TV last night'), this flatcom heavily reprised Rik Mayall and Adrian Edmondson's ➢*The Young Ones* characters. Richie Rich was snivelling and virginal, while Eddie Hitler was headbangingly violent, the two spending their fetid days in a Hammersmith gaff farting, vomiting, battering (each other), and daydreaming about sex. Scatologically crude, the series had its humorous moments, especially with Richie's woefully crass attempts at wooing, and belongs, like ➢*Men Behaving Badly* and ➢*Wayne's World*, to the TV backlash against the politically correct 80s. *Bottom*'s BBC2 slot was later home to ➢*Absolutely Fabulous*, the girls behaving badly show co-created by Edmondson's wife, Jennifer Saunders.

CAST *Richie Rich* Rik Mayall *Eddie Hitler* Adrian Edmondson /*cr* Rik Mayall, Adrian Edmondson /*pr* Ed Bye /*dr* Ed Bye /*wr* Rik Mayall, Adrian Edmondson /*BBC TV* (UK) /18 x 30m col.

Bouquet of Barbed Wire

Melodrama. ITV 1976

A tangled and tormented tale set in deepest suburban Surrey whose (mostly female) viewers craved each anguished episode. Adapted by Andrea Newman from her own steamy novel, it told the tale of suave, silver-haired publisher Peter Manson, his wife Cassie and their daughter Prue – a model middle-class family until the arrival of young American Gavin Sorenson in their midst unleashed a torrent of lust, incest and infidelity. Gavin married Prue but desired her mother, while Peter's dark obsession with his full-lipped daughter finally tore the family apart. The series climaxed with Prue's death after childbirth but a sequel, *Another Bouquet* (LWT, 7 x 60 mins, *dr*/*pr* John Frankau), saw Peter, Cassie and Gavin continuing their dark trysts. Although scripted once again by Newman, with the original cast resuming their roles, it lacked the punch of the first series.

CAST *Peter Manson* Frank Finlay *Prue Manson* Susan Penhaligon *Gavin Sorenson* James Aubrey *Cassie Manson* Sheila Allen /*cr* Andrea Newman /*exec pr* Rex Firkin /*pr* Tony Wharmby /*dr* Tony Wharmby /*wr* Andrea Newman /*LWT* (UK) /7 x 60m col.

'Gis a job…' Yosser (Bernard Hill, right) and gang in Alan Bleasdale's BAFTA-winning black comedy, *The Boys from the Black Stuff*.

The Boys From the Black Stuff

Drama. BBC2 1982

'Gis a job.'

Together with *Cathy Come Home*, one of the few British dramas to alter public attitudes, in this case towards unemployment. Originating in writer Alan Bleasdale's 1980 single drama *The Black Stuff*, the darkly comic serial depicted the lives of a gang of unemployed tarmac layers in a wasteland Liverpool. Undoubtedly Yosser Hughes (a BAFTA-winning performance by Bernard Hill), pathetically trailed by his children as he begged 'Gis a job', 'Ah can do that' and drove himself into a psychotic state, was the most memorable of the characters. But the more subtly penned trials of Chrissy (Michael Angelis, ➢*The Liver Birds*) also left poignant images: searching down the back of the sofa for money mislaid in better days, being nagged by his wife and, finally, cracking up and slaughtering his pet geese. The series also provided career-enhancing roles for Julie Walters, Jean Boht (later ➢*Bread*) and veteran James Ellis (➢*Z Cars*). Bleasdale's subsequent work includes the Liverpool-based ➢*GBH*, which viewed the city (and thus the nation) through notably more jaundiced lenses.

CAST *Yosser Hughes* Bernard Hill *Chrissy Todd* Michael Angelis *Angie Todd* Julie Walters *Dixie Dean* Tom Georgeson *George Malone* Peter Kerrigan *Loggo Logmond* Alan Igbon *Kevin Dean* Gary Bleasdale *Miss Sutcliffe* Jean Boht *The Wino* James Ellis /*cr* Alan Bleasdale /*pr* Michael Wearing /*dr* Philip Saville /*wr* Alan Bleasdale /*BBC TV* (UK) /5 x 50m col.

The Brady Bunch

Comedy. ITV 1970–3

A young widow and widower amalgamate their families in a second marriage.

The last of the great domestic 'Hi honey, I'm home' sitcoms, *TBB* was full of smiling, white-teethed children in artificial battles for the bathroom/phone, with spotless suburban Mr and Mrs Brady good-naturedly attempting to control the mayhem. Of course, it had a dog too, a shaggy beast called Tiger. With a feelgood factor of 10 out of 10 (at a time of growing family break-ups *TBB* promised future hope), it enjoyed a long run. And, like Russian monk Rasputin, was almost impossible to kill. It first spun off the animated *The Brady Kids*, then a sequel, *The Brady Bunch Hour* (1977, in which the Bradys became a TV variety act), then a triquel, *The Brady Girls Get Married* (1981), a quadrel, *The Brady Brides* (1981), and finally *The Bradys* (1990). By the time of the latter, a collective madness had descended on the producers, for *The Bradys* was a grotesque soap opera with, just for openers, Bobby Brady paralyzed in a car crash. Even the Bradys were unable to smile at that one.

CAST *Mike Brady* Robert Reed *Carol Brady* Florence Henderson *Alice Nelson* Ann B. Davis *Marcia Brady* Maureen McCormick *Jan Brady* Eve Plumb *Cindy Brady* Susan Olsen *Peter Brady* Christopher Knight *Bobby Brady* Mike Lookinland *Greg Brady* Barry Williams /*cr* Sherwood Schwartz /*pr* Sherwood Schwartz, Howard Leeds, Elroy Schwartz /*dr* inc John Rich, Russ Mayberry /*wr* inc Sherwood Schwartz, Lloyd J. Schwartz /*mus* Frank de Vol /*Paramount TV* (USA) /117 x 25m col /US tx ABC 1969–74.

Branded

Western. ITV 1965–6

During the 1880s Indian Wars, Westpoint graduate Captain Jason McCord (grim-faced Kevin 'Chuck' Connors, ➢*The Rifleman*) was unjustly cashiered for cowardice at the Battle of Bitter Creek, Wyoming. *Branded* told the story of McCord's subsequent Western wanderings as he sought to prove his innocence, carrying with him everywhere a broken sabre, the symbol of his shame. To subsist he hired out his skills as a mapmaker and engineer. Cadaverous Hollywood actor John Carradine (*Stagecoach*, father of ➢*Kung Fu* star David Carradine) featured as General Joshua McCord. The series was created by Larry ➢'*The Invaders*' Cohen and intended as an allegory of the McCarthyite political blacklisting of the 1950s. As the theme libretto – sung over the title sequence, in which McCord was stripped of his epaulettes to the sound of a drum roll – had it: 'What do you do when you're branded? Well, you fight for your name!' A three-part episode of *Branded*, 'The Mission', formed the 1965 cinema feature, *Broken Sabre.*

CAST *Jason McCord* Chuck Connors *Joshua McCord* John Carradine /*cr* Larry Cohen /*pr* Andrew J. Fenady, Cecil Baker /*dr* inc Joseph H. Lewis, Lee H. Katzin, William Whitney, Bernard McEveety /*wr* inc Larry Cohen /*mus* A. Alch & Dominic Frontiere (theme) / *Goodson–Todman Productions* (USA) /48 x 26m bw:col /US tx NBC 1965–6.

Brass

Comedy. ITV 1983–4/C4 1990

Fairly amusing parody of the 'Grim up North' school of TV drama (e.g. ➢*When the Boat Comes In*), which related the 1930s class war between the rich mill-owning Hardacre family and their ever-so-proletarian employees, the Fairchilds. Paterfamilias of the Hardacre clan was ruthless, self-made millionare Bradley (Timothy West), whose wife, Patience, was a paraplegic dipsomaniac and whose offspring were variously immoral or innocently naive. Head of the Fairchilds was George (Geoff Hinsliff, ➢*Coronation Street*), grovellingly grateful for his work in Hardacre's factory, and whose spouse, Agnes, was sleeping with the class enemy in the corpulent shape of Bradley Hardacre himself (this despite a loathing of 'the bosses' which earned her the moniker 'Red Agnes'). Their sons were made of stern Marxist stuff. The setting was the town of Utterley.

After being closed down in 1984, the series was revived for a short-lived, six-episode season by Channel 4 in 1990, with most of the original cast.

CAST *Bradley Hardacre* Timothy West *Patience Hardacre* Caroline Blakiston *George Fairchild* Geoffrey Hinsliff/Geoffrey Hutchings *Agnes Fairchild* Barbara Ewing *Austin Hardacre* Robert Reynolds/Patrick Pearson *Morris Hardacre* James Saxon *Charlotte Hardacre* Emily Morgan *Isobel Hardacre* Gail Harrison *Jack Fairchild* Shaun Scott *Matthew Fairchild* Gary Cady *Dr Macduff* David Ashton /*cr* John Stevenson, Julian Roach /*pr* Bill Podmore, Mark Robson (1990) /*dr* Gareth Jones, Les Chatfield /*wr* John Stevenson, Julian Roach /*Granada TV* (UK) /32 x 30m col.

Bread
Comedy. BBC1 1986–91

The saga of the Boswells – matriarch Nellie, philandering Freddie and their five grown-up children, Joey, Jack, Aveline, Adrian and Billy – a teeming Catholic working-class family residing in the cramped terraced premises of 30 Kelsall Street, Liverpool. In common with many on Merseyside, the Boswells shared a predicament; they were all (save, initially, for one) unemployed. They were also united in their response, accepting state handouts with a pride that befitted their expert working of the system. The hub of the series was the table on which Nellie Boswell laid food for her family and around which she insisted they gathered. Here they squabbled or joked and provided at least some of the blend of pathos–humour that was creator Carla Lane's (➢*The Liver Birds*, *Luv*, ➢*Solo*, ➢*Butterflies*) trademark. Meanwhile, intolerant and intolerable Grandad in the house next door hollered continually for his dinner. Also featured were DHSS clerk Martina, Freddie's allotment-shed peccadillo Lilo Lil, Irish cousin Shifty, pet dog Mongy, Oswald the vicar (Aveline's eventual spouse), and Billy's wife Julie. While some thought *Bread* mirthless and unpalatable fare, most apparently found it more succulent. For much of its run it was comfortably rated within the top ten programmes. At its peak at the end of 1988 it was second only to ➢*EastEnders* and achieved an audience of 21 million.

CAST *Nellie Boswell* Jean Boht *Freddie Boswell* Ronald Forfar *Joey Boswell* Peter Howitt/Graham Bickley *Jack Boswell* Victor McGuire *Aveline Boswell* Gilly Coman/Melanie Hill *Adrian Boswell* Jonathon Morris *Billy Boswell* Nick Conway *Grandad* Kenneth Waller *Lilo Lil* Eileen Pollock *Shifty* Bryan Murray *Martina* Pamela Power *Julie* Caroline Milmoe/Hilary Crowson *Oswald* Giles Watling *Celia Higgins* Rita Tushingham /*cr* Carla Lane /*pr* Robin Nash, John B. Hobbs /*dr* Susan Belbin, Robin Nash, John B. Hobbs /*wr* Carla Lane /*BBC TV* (UK) /68 x 30m col.

The Bretts
Drama. ITV 1987

Expensive drama series about a 1920s acting dynasty, the ratings of which were so catastrophically low that it was shoved unceremoniously into a graveyard slot. One of the few who survived the debacle was Belinda Lang (➢*Dear John*), later to resurface in ➢*2 Point 4 Children*.

CAST *Charles Brett* Norman Rodway *Lydia Brett* Barbara Murray *Edwin Brett* David Yelland *Martha Brett* Belinda Lang /*pr* Tony Charles /*dr* inc Ronald Wilson /*wr* inc Rosemary Anne Sisson /*Central TV* (UK) /12 x 50m col.

Brideshead Revisited
Drama. ITV 1981

Lavish adaptation (by John Mortimer) of Evelyn Waugh's novel concerning a young Oxford student, Charles Ryder, who is drawn like a moth to the bright and dangerous flame of the British aristocracy between the wars. After years of torment, and the descent of teddy-bear-carrying friend Sebastian Flyte into alcoholism, Ryder eventually finds Catholic absolution in the chapel of Brideshead Castle (actually Castle Howard, Yorkshire). With its heavy air of nostalgia, it caught a national mood and gained nine million viewers. Few complained that Mortimer's slavish adherence to the original text made for long-windedness; the photography was gorgeous, the acting immaculate. Laurence Olivier and John Gielgud gave performances to be counted amongst their greatest, while Anthony Andrews won a BAFTA (though his career since has been overshadowed by that of Irons). Despite concerns about its homo-eroticism, it was taken by TV networks around the world, the consequent sales more than offsetting the series' £5 million overspend. The teddy bear's name was Aloysius.

CAST *Charles Ryder* Jeremy Irons *Lord Sebastian Flyte* Anthony Andrews *Lord Marchmain* Laurence Olivier *Edward Ryder* John Gielgud *Lady Julia Flyte* Diana Quick *Lady Marchmain* Claire Bloom *Celia Mulcaster* Jane Asher *Lord Brideshead* Simon Jones *Anthony Blanche* Nickolas Grace *Cara* Stephane Audran /*pr* Derek Granger /*dr* Michael Lindsay-Hogg, Charles Sturridge /*wr* John Mortimer /*BBC TV* (UK) / 11 x 50m col.

The Brittas Empire
Comedy. BBC1 1991–7

After playing the nerdish Rimmer in sci-fi spoof ➢*Red Dwarf*, Chris Barrie (formerly of the sports department at Harrods, and providing voices for ➢*Spitting Image*) chose not to stretch his thespian abilities by starring in this sitcom about the antics of Gordon Brittas, the nerdish manager of Whitbury Newtown Leisure Centre. Possessed of the jinx-touch, every improvement the insufferable Brittas planned for his personal fiefdom ended in disaster, with assistant manager Laura obliged to save the day. Despite this, bumbling, whiney-voiced Brittas was appointed a European Commissioner. At its core, *The Brittas Empire* was a traditional 'Britcom', its positing of an incompetent in charge of others already seen in ➢*Dad's Army* and ➢*Are You Being Served?*; however, it also locked on elements of absurdism (receptionist Carole keeping her children in a cupboard behind her desk, Brittas' quasi-bionic indestructibility) designed to appeal to the younger end of the audience on the couch. It was even possible to see *Brittas* as a satire on the shiny-suited managers who sprang up in the Thatcherite 80s.

CAST *Gordon Brittas* Chris Barrie *Helen Brittas* Pippa Heywood *Laura Lancing* Julia St John *Carole* Harriet Thorpe *Colin Wetherby* Michael Burns *Tim Whistler* Russell Porter *Linda* Jill Greenacre *Julie* Judy Flynn / *cr* Richard Fegen, Andrew Norris / *pr* Mike Stephens / *dr* inc Mike Stephens / *wr* Richard Fegen, Andrew Norris, Terry Kyan, Paul Smith / *BBC TV* (UK) /52 x 30m col.

Bronco

Western. BBC 1959–62

The picaresque adventures of a former Confederate Army captain Bronco Layne, which began as a rotating segment of ➢*Cheyenne*, only spinning off into a solo series when *Cheyenne*'s Clint Walker walked out the Warners' studio door in a wages dispute. Ty Hardin (aka Orton Hungerford) rose without trace to take the part of Layne, a template loner do-gooder who habitually bumped into such historical westerners as Wild Bill Hickok, Billy the Kid and Jesse James (played by James Coburn). Hardin later appeared in the Australian series *Riptide*.

CAST *Bronco Layne* Ty Hardin / *exec pr* William T. Orr / *dr* inc Alan Crosland Jr / *WB-TV* /68 x 50m bw /US tx ABC 1958–62.

Brookside

Melodrama. C4 1982–

C4's flagship soap, sent onto the airwaves on the network's opening night. Created by Phil Redmond (a former writer for ➢*The Squirrels*), and set in a suburban close on the outskirts of Liverpool, *Brookside*'s avowed policy of addressing social issues in a realistic manner (complete with proletarian Merseyside vernacular and expletives) immediately generated public critcism; it also required its main characters to enjoy notably busy lives. Not only did Sheila Grant, for instance, suffer rape, middle-age pregnancy and the death of a son, but also trade-unionist husband Bobby's financially crippling months on strike. (This was a prime case of art imitating life; the actor who played Bobby Grant, Ricky Tomlinson, had himself played a leading role in the national building workers' strike of the 1970s, which had resulted in his imprisonment as one of the 'Shrewsbury Three'.) However, *Brookside*'s latter-day kitchen sink-ism did little for audience figures, resulting in a change of course towards sensationalism. This was especially manifest under the reign of former *Brookside* props boy, Mal Young, who took over as producer in 1991 (that year saw the set expanded to include the Brookside Shopping Parade). It was Young who gave *Brookside* its most infamous moments: the lesbian kiss in a doorway between Beth Jordache and Margaret; the discovery of the body of wife-beater and incestuous rapist Trevor Jordache (Bryan Murray, ➢*Bread*, ➢*The Irish RM*) under the patio; the conflagration at No. 5 when the religious cult, the Church of Simon, incinerated itself; and the explosive culmination of the Dixon/Corkhill feud. Yet there was more to Young's captaincy than a desire to shock and titillate; many of the most outrageous plotlines coincided with (even preceeded) similar real-life events, such as the self-immolation of the followers of guru David Koresh at Waco. The genius of Young's *Brookside* was the accuracy with which it caught the Zeitgeist. More prosaically, Young populated the soap – in a manner reminiscent of ➢*Neighbours* – with the youthful and the good-looking; actress Anna Friel even ascended to something like rock-star celebrity. Originally to be called *Meadowcroft*, *Brookside* was expanded to three weekly episodes in 1990 (from twice a week with a Saturday omnibus). There have been several spin-offs: *Damon and Debbie*, *South* and *Brookside: the Jordache Story*. 'Mr Grit' Redmond himself went on to create another series of celebrated realism, ➢*Grange Hill*, although his work of later years (➢*Hollyoaks* and *And the Beat Goes On*) shows an increasing lightness of touch.

CAST *Sheila Grant/Corkhill* Sue Johnston *Bobby Grant* Ricky Tomlinson *Barry Grant* Paul Usher *Damon Grant* Simon O'Brien *Karen Grant* Shelagh O'Hara *Roger Huntington* Rob Spendlove *Heather*

Huntington/Haversham/Black Amanda Burton *Paul Collins* Jim Wiggins *Anabelle Collins* Doreen Sloane *Lucy Collins* Katrin Cartlidge/Maggie Saunders *Gordon Collins* Nigel Crowley/Mark Burgess *Gavin Taylor* Daniel Webb *Petra Taylor* Alexandra Pigg *Harry Cross* Bill Dean *Edna Cross* Betty Alberge *Billy Corkhill* John McArdle *Doreen Corkhill* Kate Fitzgerald *Rod Corkhill* Jason Hope *Tracy Corkhill* Justine Kerrigan *Jimmy Corkhill* Dean Sullivan *Jackie Corkhill* Sue Jenkins *George Jackson* Cliff Howells *Thomas 'Sinbad' Sweeney* Michael Starke *D-D Dixon* Irene Marot *Ron Dixon* Vince Earl *Cyril Dixon* Allan Surtes *Jacqui Dixon* Alexandra Fletcher *Mike Dixon* Paul Byatt *Tony Dixon* Gerard Bostock/Mark Lennock *Margaret Clemence* Nicola Stephenson *Max Farnham* Steven Pinder *Patricia Farnham* Gabrielle Glaister *Michael Choi* David Yip *Trevor Jordache* Bryan Murray *Mandy Jordache* Sandra Maitland *Beth Jordache* Anna Friel *Rachel Jordache* Tiffany Chapman *Nat Simpson* John Sandford *Georgia Simpson* Helen Grace /*cr* Phil Redmond /*exec pr* Phil Redmond /*pr* Phil Redmond, Nicholas Prosser, Mal Young /*dr* inc Jeremy Woolf, Claire Winyward, Rupert Such, Cameron McAllister, Sue Butterworth, Jo Johnson, Jeff Naylor, Johnathan Young /*wr* inc Phil Redmond, Shaun Duggan, Julie Rutterford, Chris Webb, Barry Woodward, Kathleen Potter, Joe Ainsworth / *Brookside Productions: Mersey Television* (UK) /1600+ x 30m col.

The Brothers

Melodrama. BBC1 1972–6

Soapish Sunday evening saga about the ups and downs of a family-run road-haulage firm, the Midlands-based Hammond Transport Services. By the terms of his will, founder Robert Hammond accorded a sizeable shareholding in the business to mistress Jennifer. This proved irksome to wife Mary and three squabbling scions, brutal Edward, accountant Brian and immature David. The producers, astutely, kept the intricacies of the haulage business in the background, concentrating instead on operations in the boardroom and bedroom. Playing the baddie was Hilary Tindall, who scene-stole as Brian's ambitious wife, Ann. Later additions to the cast list were Kate O'Mara (airfreight boss Jane Maxwell), Gabrielle Drake, Liza Goddard and future ➢*Dr Who,* Colin Baker (financial whizz-kid Paul Merroney, voted 'The Nastiest Man on TV'). The characters played by Baker and Goddard got hitched on the screen; the thespian pair married in real life, too.

CAST *Mary Hammond* Jean Anderson *Edward Hammond* Glyn Owen/Patrick O'Connell *Brian Hammond* Richard Easton *David Hammond* Robin Chadwick *Jennifer Kingsley* Jennifer Wilson *Ann Hammond* Hilary Tindall *Bill Riley* Derek Benfield *Carol Hammond* Nicola Maloney *Jill Hammond* Gabrielle Drake *Paul Merroney* Colin Baker *April Merroney* Liza Goddard *Jane Maxwell* Kate O'Mara / *cr* Gerard Glaister, N.J. Crisp /*pr* Gerard Glaister, N.J. Crisp, Bill Podmore, Ken Riddington, Bill Sellars / *dr* inc Ronald Wilson, Quentin Lawrence /*wr* inc N.J. Crisp /*BBC TV* (UK) /92 x 45m col.

Brush Strokes

Comedy. BBC1 1986–91

Already versed in cockney Jack-the-laddism from service in ➢*Get Some In*, actor Karl Howman effortlessly chirped his way through this gentle Esmonde and Larbey sitcom about Jacko, a naughty-but-nice painter and decorator from Motspur Park. He loved and left most of the women upon whom his charm fell, before walking down the aisle with Sandra, secretary to his boss Lionel (Gary Waldhorn, ➢*The Vicar of Dibley*) after a cliffhanger in which he groaned: 'I think I've made a terrible mistake.' Most of the laffs came courtesy of the semi-surreal Elmo, the gross and gormless landlord of the White Hart who, after discovering a fortune in Australian opals (thanks to a pet dingo), opened a shocking pink wine bar. The theme song, by Kevin Rowlands of Dexy's Midnight Runners, reached No. 5 in the music charts.

Esmonde and Larbey later created a tailor made sitcom for Howman, *Mulberry* (BBC1, 1992–3), in which he starred as a mysterious (even ghostly) but lovable manservant hired to run the household of a cantankerous spinster, Miss Rose Farnaby (Geraldine McEwan).

CAST *Jacko* Karl Howman *Eric* Mike Walling *Jean* Nicky Croydon *Sandra* Jackie Lye *Lionel Bainbridge* Gary Waldhorn *Veronica Bainbridge* Elizabeth Counsell *Elmo Putney* Howard Lew Lewis *Lesley Bainbridge* Kim Thomson/Erika Hoffman /*cr* John Esmonde, Bob Larbey /*pr* Sydney Lotterby, Mandie Fletcher, Harold Snoad, John B. Hobbs /*dr* inc Mandie Fletcher /*wr* John Esmonde, Bob Larbey /*mus* Dexy's Midnight Runners ('Because of You' theme) /*BBC TV* (UK) /40 x 30m col.

The Buccaneers
Adventure. ITV 1956–7

Early swashbuckler from the ITV adventure-mill, concerning the exploits of reformed pirate Dan Tempest as he roved the Caribbean high seas in the 1720s on the good ship *The Sultana*, routing Spaniards and baddie buccaneers alike. The swordplay was generous, the cannon shot plentiful. Filmed entirely at the Nettlefold Studios, Walton-on-Thames, the series provided US actor Robert Shaw (*A Man for All Seasons, Jaws*) with his small-screen debut.

CAST *Capt. Dan Tempest* Robert Shaw *Governor Woodes Rogers* Alec Clunes *Lt Beamish* Peter Hammond /*pr* Sidney Cole, Ralph Smart, Pennington Richards /*dr* inc Robert Day, Pennington Richards, Ralph Smart, Leslie Arliss, Peter Hammond /*wr* inc Ring Lardner Jr, Ian McLellan Hunter /*mus* inc Edwin Astley /*Sapphire Films Productions: ITC* (UK) / 39 x 30m bw /US tx CBS 1956–7.

Buck Rogers in the 25th Century
Sci-fi. ITV 1980–2

Square-jawed space spoof in which US atronaut William 'Buck' Rogers is blown off course, spends 504 years in suspended animation, then returns to (a gently fried, post-nuclear) Earth to lead the good fight agains the dreaded Draconians. These are led by the beautiful but bad Princess Ardala. Buck's main helpers are the beautiful but good Earth Defense officer Wilma Deering (apparently shoe-horned into her jump suits), boffin Dr Huer, and a midget robot, Twiki. In the second season, Buck, Wilma and Twiki take to the heavens in the spaceship *The Searcher* in a desperate hunt for A-bomb survivors.

Pure, unadulterated pop corn. Zero per cent brain fibre, but providing 60 per cent of the Recommended Daily Allowance of humour.

Heading the guest cast was Buster Crabbe – who played Rogers in the 30s film serial – Roddy McDowall, Jamie Lee Curtis and Jack Palance, with William Conrad (➢*Cannon*) narrating. Glen A. Larson and John 'Gunsmoke' Mantley executive produced. The pilot episode was released theatrically as *Buck Rogers in the 25th Century* in 1979.

CAST *Capt. Buck Rogers* Gil Gerard *Col. Wilma Deering* Erin Gray *Dr Huer* Tim O'Connor *Twiki* Felix Silla, Mel Blanc (voice) *Princess Ardala* Pamela Hensley *Dr Goodfellow* Wilfred Hyde-White *Kana* Michael Ansara *Hawk* Thom Christopher *Dr Theopolis* Eric Server *Crichton* Jeff David /*exec pr* Glen A. Larson, John Mantley /*dr* inc Sig Neufeld, Bernard McEveety, Vincent McEveety, Jack Arnold, Larry Stewart /*wr* inc Glen A. Larson, Leslie Stevens, D.C. Fontana, Allan Brennert /*A Glen A. Larson Production: Universal TV* (USA) /1 x 120m, 34 x 60m col /US tx NBC 1979–81.

Budgie
Comedy. ITV 1971–2

Sixties pop star Adam Faith made a career change to play Budgie Bird, cheeky cockney chappie and lovable rogue-at-large in early 70s Soho. A small-time criminal, Budgie dreamed of getting rich but was a born loser. His wife Jean had left him for his best mate, his girlfriend Hazel had had a baby, and the gangsters of Soho could see him coming a mile off (not surprising given his long hair and wide lapels) with the result that he was the fall guy in all their scams. Most of his waking time was spent 'running' for tough Glaswegian gangster Charlie Endell (Iain Cuthbertson), proprietor of a dodgy bookshop and the manor's Mr Big. In return for his troubles, Budgie received a(nother) spell in jail. Created and written by Keith Waterhouse and Willis Hall, produced by Verity Lambert (➢*Dr Who*, later ➢*The Sweeney*, ➢*Eldorado*) and Rex Firkin (➢*New Scotland Yard*), the irrepressibly chirpy Budgie was the first TV criminal with the audience on his side. Scottish TV's attempt to create a spin-off series, *Charlie Endell Esquire*, seven years later, without Adam Faith but featuring the Scottish gangster returning to his old Glaswegian haunts, was short-lived (only two episodes were shown), due to an industrial strike taking ITV off air. Faith himself returned to the small screen as a cockney (naturally) millionaire in ➢*Love Hurts*.

CAST *Budgie Bird* Adam Faith *Charlie Endell* Iain Cuthbertson *Hazel* Lynn Dalby *Jean* Georgina Hale *Grogan* Rio Fanning /*cr* Keith Waterhouse, Willis Hall /*exec pr* Rex Firkin /*pr* Verity Lambert /*wr* Keith Waterhouse, Willis Hall /*LWT* (UK) /26 x 60m bw.

Buffy the Vampire Slayer
Horror. Sky1 1998–

'In every generation there is a chosen one. She will stand against the vampires, the demons and the forces of darkness. She is the chosen one...'

After dying at the cinema (where it was intended as a vehicle for ➢*Beverly Hills 90210*'s Luke Perry), screenwriter Joss Whedon's *Buffy the Vampire Slayer* was resurrected to become a mini-series for Warner Bros' fledging US TV network, WB. In its resurrected form, *BTVS* roled scream queen Sarah Michelle Gellar as the new Buffy, a teen relocated from LA to Sunnydale, where she was unimpressed to find that her high school was Hell – literally – and she was 'chosen' to be The Slayer. So, inbetween homework and dating, Buffy had to wrangle with bloodsuckers, giant praying mantis, Inca mummies and the like. Her coach in immortal combat was the Watcher, aka Giles the school librarian (played by Tony Head from the Gold Blend TV commercials), while Willow and Xander were Buffy's geekish sidekicks. Whereas the movie version played *BTVS* for popcorn comedy-horror (leaving the audience to laugh at the fright-time bits, and scream at the funny bits), the TV make-over upped the teen horror and demonic mytho-logizing, lacing the whole with *Heathers*-style smart-arse dialogue. ('Slayerspeak' – e.g. 'carbon dated' for *passé*, 'Scully' to explain away the paranormal with scientific skepticism – even enjoyed a brief vogue.) Classic episodes included: 'Own Nightmares', in which the principal characters got their bad dreams made flesh, and 'Invisible Girl', in which an overlooked classmate simply faded away to nothing, only to return to reap supernatural revenge. The show garnered WB its highest early season ratings. A 1999 spin-off, *Angel*, followed the travails of the eponymous 200-year-old vampire who had renounced evil to become Buffy's main crush. Fortuitously enough for teen TV, the vampire was trapped in the body of a brooding teen stud.

CAST *Buffy Summers* Sarah Michelle Gellar *Alexander 'Xander' Harris* Nicholas Brendon *Willow Rosenberg* Alyson Hannigan *Cordelia Chase* Charisma Carpenter *Angel* David Boreanaz *Rupert Giles* Anthony Stewart Head *Drusilla* Juliet Landau *The Master* Mark Metcalf *Joyce Summers (mother)* Kristine Sutherland *Oz* Seth Green *Spike* James Marsters *Principal Snyder* Armin Shimerman /*cr* Joss Wheadon /*exec pr* Gail Berman, Sandy Gallin, Fran Rubel Kuzui, Joss Whedon /*pr* Gareth Davies /*dr* inc Joss Whedon, Reza Badiyi, Bruce Seth Green, Ellen S. Pressman, David Semel /*wr* inc Joss Whedon /*mus* inc Nerf Herder, Christophe Beck, Shawn K. Clement /*Sandollar Television: 20th Century Fox-Television: Mutant Enemy: Kuzui Enterprises* (USA) /36+ x 60m col /US tx Fox TV 1997–.

Bugs

Sci-fi. BBC1 1995–

Smart, stylishly-dressed nonsense about three electronics whizz-kid crimebusters set in a near-future of Big Brother surveillance and miniaturized everything. Plot lines included such technological chillers as deadly crop-exterminating viroids, lethal 'nano-surges' of electricity, 'isotopic implosions' and electronic mosquitoes carrying 'pheromone specific' poisons. Any similarity to such classic 60s tongue-in-cheek, derring-do shows as ➢*The Avengers* was purely intentional; show consultants included Brian Clemens, Mr Avengers himself. Former plumbers mate from Tumbi Umbi in New South Wales, Craig McLachlan, having fled ➢*Neighbours* and ➢*Home and Away*, played brawny Ed (to whom fell the delivery of most of *Bugs*'s appalling quips), while another soap refugee, Jesse Birdsall (➢*Eldorado*) overcame type-casting to take the role of team-leader Beckett.

CAST *Ed* Craig McLachlan *Ros* Jaye Griffiths *Beckett* Jesse Birdsall *Alex Jordan* Paula Hunt *Jan* Jan Harvey /*pr* Brian Eastman, Caroline Oulton, Stuart Doughty, Rupert Ryle-Hodges /*dr* Brian Farnham, Andrew Grieve, Sandy Johnson /*wr* Colin Blake, Stephen Gallagher, Miles Millar & Alfred Gough, Frank De Palma & Terry Borst /*Carnival Films* (UK) /40+ x 50m col.

Bullseye

Light entertainment. ITV 1981–94

With its welding together of darts and the lounge bar's quiz night, this long-running ATV series offered something akin to a virtual reality visit to the local public house. Former deputy headmaster Jim Bowen (aka James Whittaker, *The Comedians*, ➢*El C.I.D.*) hosted with the six contestants playing in pairs (one throwing the darts, the other answer-ing Bowen's questions) in an eliminator which left the final pair aiming for consumer goodies and a weekly star prize. Not that anyone left empty-handed; a model rubber bovine mascot ('bendy Bully') was the consolation prize. To milk in-sincerity, a regular fixture saw a guest professional darts player throwing nine 'arrows' for charity. Aimed at the lowest brow, the programme became a cult hit amongst the college crowd for Bowen's amateurish clangers and mechanical handling of the contestants. Reputedly the quality of some shows was so poor that they were not even broad-cast. The creator was comedian Norman Vaughan. Super.

CAST (presenter) Jim Bowen, (darts commentator) Tony Green /*cr* Norman Vaughan /*pr* inc Peter Holmans, Bob Cousins /*ATV:Central TV* (UK) /approx 300 x 30m col.

Burke's Law

Crime. ITV 1963–5

The glossy murder cases of an urbane LA police chief, who oozed to the scene of crime in the back of a chauffeur-driven Rolls Royce. Originally intended as a TV outing for Dick Powell – who played the character in a presentation ('Who Killed Julia Greer?') for the *Dick Powell Theatre* – it fell eventually to Gene Barry (➢*Bat Masterson*) to fill the elegant series shoes of Captain Amos Burke. Every episode was trade-marked by 'Who Killed –?', and filled to the frames with guests stars – 63 in the first eight episodes alone – most of them hardly employed to dramatic purpose. Eventually Burke quit law enforcement to move into the glamorous end of the spy business, a change of occupation prompted solely by the producer's desire to ride the success of the Bond films and ➢*The Man from UNCLE*. Accordingly, the show was retitled *Amos Burke – Secret Agent*. It was altered back to *Burke's Law* 30 years later, when the series was revived, with Barry once again playing the dandy Burke, if in somewhat wrinklier form.

CAST *Capt. Amos Burke* Gene Barry *Det. Tim Tilson* Gary Conway *DS Lester Hart* Regis Toomey *Henry* Leon Lontoc *'The Man'* Carl Benton Reid /*cr* Ivan Goff, Ben Roberts, Ernest Kinoy /*pr* Arnold Spelling /*dr* inc Don Weis, Walter Grauman, Don Taylor, Jerry Hopper /*wr* inc Edith Sommer, John Meredyth Lucas, Harlan Ellison, William Link, Richard Levinson /*Four Star* (USA) /94 x 50m bw /US tx ABC 1963–5.

Butterflies

Comedy. BBC2 1978–82

Carla Lane (➢*The Liver Birds*) sitcom in which bored middle-class, mid-life Ria Parkinson begins to tire of her 19-year marriage to dentist Ben, and the lack of appreciation shown by teenage offspring Russell and Adam. A platonic but guilt-laden affair with smooth businessman Leonard followed. The eternally depressing Ben ('I don't like singing. I don't do a lot of it because there isn't much to sing about.'), meanwhile, added to his butterfly collection and tried to instil in the girl-crazy Parkinson *fils* a sense of conformist duty. (The junior Parkinsons, with their 'groovys' and Mini emblazoned with a rooftoop Union Jack were curious, anachronistic 60s leftovers.) If *Butterflies* was whimsical, it was also unusually bleak, and even pushed at the boundaries of the domestic sitcom with experimental dream sequences and voice-overs. BBC2's highest-rated show for much of its run, *Butterflies* was helped to fly to such heights by the faultless performances of the lugubrious Geoffrey Palmer (later in ➢*The Fall and Rise of Reginald Perrin, Executive Stress, As Time Goes By*) and an uncharacteristically soulful Wendy Craig (➢*Solo*). Even before *Butterflies* had finished its life, Nicholas Lyndhurst, the former child presenter of *Our Show* (with Susan Tully), had parlayed his role as Adam into that of Rodney in ➢*Only Fools and Horses*. Further down the cast list, Milton Johns and Wendy Williams were memorably timid as the Parkinson's unfortunate neighbours, several times trapped on their drive by the frantic vehicular comings and goings on the other side of the road. The title theme was a rejigging of Dolly Parton's, 'Love is Like a Butterfly'.

CAST *Ria Parkinson* Wendy Craig *Ben Parkinson* Geoffrey Palmer *Adam Parkinson* Nicholas Lyndhurst *Russell Parkinson* Andrew Hall *Leonard Dunn* Bruce Montague *Ruby* Joyce Windsor *Thomas* Michael Ripper /*cr* Carla Lane /*pr* Gareth Gwenlan, Sydney Lotterby /*dr* inc Mandie Fletcher, Gareth Gwenlan, John B. Hobbs /*wr* Carla Lane /*BBC TV* (UK) /36 x 30m col.

Byker Grove

Children's. BBC1 1991–

Teen soap of phenomenal popularity, closer to the socially aware ➢*Grange Hill* than the himbo-bimbo ➢*Neighbours*. Set in the fictional Tyneside youth centre of the title (in real life a former bishop's palace), it had storylines of puppy love, anguished bereavement, 'fanblinkintastic' raves, drug taking, demands for 'girl only nights', fire and, in 1995, to tabloid outrage, a gay kiss between Noddy and Gary. It also spawned pop duo PJ and Duncan (aka actors Ant McPartlin and Declan Donnelly), who later returned to the box with a children's sketch and chat series, *The Ant and Dec Show* (BBC1 1995–). Created by ➢*Coronation Street* writer Adele Rose.

CAST *Geoff Keegan* Phil Dawson *PJ* Ant McPartlin *Duncan* Declan Donnelly *Gary* George Trotter *Noddy* Brett Adams *Barney* Stephen Carr *Frew* Luke Dale *Flora* Kerry Ann Christiansen /*cr* Adele Rose /*wr* inc Adele Rose, Carrie Rose, Roy Apps, Brian B. Thompson /*Zenith* (UK) /210 x 25m col.

Cade's County

Western. ITV 1972

Low-key, modern-day Western set in Madrid County, California, with reflective Sheriff Sam Cade (Hollywood's Glenn Ford in a rare TV venture) policing a rural beat of prodigious underworld activity. Those assisting Cade on his crusade included aged J.J. Jackson (Edgar Buchanan from ➢*Hopalong Cassidy*) and young deputy Pete (played by Ford's own son). Aside from nepotism and stunning desertscapes, the show was notable for its positive portrayal of Native Americans, with American Indian actresses Sandra Ego and Betty Ann Carr sharing the regular roles of dispatcher. Executive producer David Gerber later rose to become head of TV at MGM-UA.

CAST *Sam Cade* Glenn Ford *J.J. Jackson* Edgar Buchanan *Arlo* Taylor Lacher *Rudy* Victor Campos *Pete* Peter Ford *Joanie Little Bird* Sandra Ego *Betty Ann Sundown* Betty Ann Carr /*cr* Rick Husky, Tony Wilson / *exec pr* David Gerber /*pr* Charles Lawson /*dr* Marvin Chomsky, Robert Day, George Marshall /*mus* Henry Mancini /*David Gerber Productions: Fox TV* (USA) / 24 x 60m col /US tx CBS 1971–2.

Cadfael

Crime & Mystery. ITV 1994–

Medieval monkish murder mysteries, based on the novels of Ellis Peters. Sir Derek Jacobi's performance as the sleuthing Brother Cadfael of Shrewsbury trailed disconcerting echoes (hesitancy of manner, intellectual sharpness) of his ➢*I, Claudius* in its wake, the cast's tonsures raised latent schoolboy humour, the sets were made of styrofoam hastily erected in the Hungarian countryside and the writing was often anachronistic; but the quaint whodunnit plots were shrewdly pitched Sunday evening viewing. They were stimulating enough to hold popular attention without being so demanding that they actually required effort.

CAST *Cadfael* Derek Jacobi *Abbot Herribert* Peter Copley *Prior Robert* Michael Culver /*exec pr* Ted Childs /*dr* inc Ken Grieves /*wr* inc Christopher Russell, Simon Burke /*Carlton Television* (UK) /12 x 90m col.

The Caesars

Drama. ITV 1968

Eclipsed by the later ➢*I, Claudius*, this Granada TV version of the decline and fall of the Roman Empire was almost its equal in illustriousness of script and staging. Its only lack was a charismatic central performer of the Jacobi stature. Penned and produced by Granada's Head of Drama, Philip Mackie, the six episodes of *The Caesars* each centred on an individual emperor or general, namely Augustus, Germanicus, Tiberius (played by Andre Morell, ➢*Quatermass*), Sejanus, Caligula (former Hammer-horror actor Ralph Bates, ➢*Poldark*, ➢*Dear John*), and Claudius (character actor Freddie Jones, later in ➢*The Ghosts of Motley Hall*). That Mackie's pen also scribed the ridiculous ➢*The Cleopatras* is probably best overlooked.

CAST *Augustus* Roland Culver *Germanicus* Eric Flynn *Tiberius* Andre Morell *Sejanus* Barrie Ingham *Caligula* Ralph Bates *Claudius* Freddie Jones *Livia* Sonia Desdel / *cr* Philip Mackie /*pr* Philip Mackie /*wr* Philip Mackie / *Granada TV* (UK) /6 x 55m bw.

Cagney and Lacey

Crime & Mystery. BBC1 1982–8

Acclaimed buddy-buddy cop show, its twist being that the eponymous couple were female detectives. Created by Barbara Corday (later president of Columbia Pictures Television) and longtime writing partner Barbara Avedon, it took ten years to reach the small screen, premiering in 1981 as a TVM, starring Tyne Daly and Loretta Swit. A series followed, but with the part of Christine Cagney going to Meg Foster, since Swit was committed to ➢*M*A*S*H*. The series was cancelled after indifferent ratings, a CBS executive explaining that the public 'perceived the characters as dykes'. An unprecedented mail campaign by fans, however, persuaded CBS to bring the show back, although with glamour-woman Sharon Gless (➢*McCloud*, ➢*Marcus Welby MD*) in the Cagney role. Thus rekindled, it ran until 1988.

In contradistinction to the typical police show, *C&L* explored the lives and relationships of its lead characters beyond the squad room, touching on alcoholism, date rape and other social evils. The result was a shelf of Emmys for its stars and executive producer Barney Rosenzweig (the then husband of Corday), including: Outstanding Drama Series, 1985 and 1986; Outstanding Lead Actress: Tyne Daly, 1983, 1984, 1985, 1988; Sharon Gless, 1986, 1987; Outstanding Supporting Actor: John Karlen, 1986. Rosenzweig went on to produce the *The Trials of Rosie O'Neill*, also starring Gless, whom he later married.

CAST *Det. Mary Beth Lacey* Tyne Daly *Det. Christine Cagney* Meg Foster/Sharon Gless *Harvey Lacey* John Karlen *Lt Samuels* Al Waxman *Det. Petrie* Carl Lumbly *Det. Isbecki* Martin Cove /*cr* Barbara Corday, Barbara Avedon, Barney Rosenzweig /*exec pr* Barney Rosenzweig /*pr* inc Terry Louise Fisher, Steve Brown, Peter Lefcourt /*dr* inc Georg Stanford Brown, Bill Dukes, Arthur Karen /*wr* inc Terry Louise Fisher, Ronie Wenker-Konner /*mus* Ron Ramin, Bill Conti (theme) /*Mace Neufeld: Barney Rosenzweig: Orion TV* (USA) /1 x 96m, 125 x 60m col /US tx CBS 1981–8.

Callan

Adventure. ITV 1967–72

Downbeat spy serial which made a star of Edward Woodward as the title character, a clinically efficient yet morally anguished British secret agent/assassin. First seen in a segment ('Magnum for Schneider') of ➢*Armchair Theatre*, Callan was assisted by snivelling petty thief, Lonely, and occasionally partnered by resentful fellow spook, Toby Meres (Peter Bowles in the *Armchair* play, Anthony Valentine in the series), later Cross (Patrick Mower). As if to underline the show's paranoic similarity with ➢*The Prisoner*, Callan's departmental heads went under a codename ('Hunter') and were changed, like No. 2, with unnerving frequency. Created by former ➢*The Avengers* writer James Mitchell (later ➢*When the Boat Comes In*), the show, with its memorable 'swinging light bulb' opening sequence, spun off a 1974 feature film, *Callan*, and was revived for a one-off 90 minute ATV drama, *Wet Job*, in 1981. Thereafter, Woodward departed for America and the CBS detective caper, ➢*The Equalizer*.

CAST *David Callan* Edward Woodward *Lonely* Russell Hunter *Hunter* Ronald Radd/Michael Goodliffe /Derek Bond/William Squire *Toby Meres* Anthony Valentine *Cross* Patrick Mower /*cr* James Mitchell /*exec pr* Lloyd Shirley /*pr inc* Reginald Collin, Leonard Lewis, Lloyd Shirley /*dr* inc Bill Bain, Piers Haggard, Peter Duguid /*wr* inc James Mitchell, Robert Banks Stewart, Michael Winder, George Markstein /*mus* Jack Trombey /*ABC TV/Thames TV* (UK) 44 x 60m bw:col.

Call My Bluff

Light Entertainment. BBC2 1965–

Erudite, long-running, pleasantly tweedy game show in which three celebrity panellists gave a definition of an obscure word, plucked from the depths of the *Oxford English Dictionary*, and the opposing panel of three celebs had to guess who the truth-sayer was. The original captains were Frank Muir and Robert Morley, with Robin Ray presiding. When Morley left, he was succeeded as panel captain by Patrick Campbell, then Arthur Marshall. Meanwhile, Joe Melia and Peter Wheeler played chairman's chairs, before Robert Robinson settled down for a lengthy tenure. After several years hiatus, the show was revived as lunchtime entertainment in 1994 with Nicholas Parsons (➢*Sale of the Century*, ➢*Four Feather Falls*) in the quiz-master's chair.

The show was based on a format devised by Americans Bill Todman and Mark Goodson for NBC in 1965, where it lasted but a single year.

CAST (presenters) Robin Ray, Joe Melia, Peter Wheeler, Robert Robinson, Nicholas Parsons /*cr* Mark Goodson, Bill Todman /*pr* T. Leslie Jackson, Bryan Sears, Johnny Downes /*BBC TV* (UK) /approx 400 x 30m bw: col.

Camberwick Green

Children's. BBC1 1966

Filling the Monday ➢*Watch with Mother* slot, Gordon Murray's rural puppet soap-opera opened with a musical box ('wound up and ready to play') which then revealed the lead character for that episode. The most famous inhabitant of Camberwick Green village was Windy Miller who made the flour, but local gossip Mrs Honeyman, baker Mickey Murphy, Dr Mopp, Peter the postman, Mrs Dingle the postmistress, Packet the post office puppy, Mr Carraway the fishmonger, Mr Crockett the garage owner, Thomas Tripp the milkman, Paddy and Mary Murphy, PC McGarry (No. 452), and Mr Dagenham the salesman all had their day. Whatever the particular minor crisis that made up the drama, it inevitably involved an SOS call to Captain Snort at Pippin Fort. The nicely whimsical narration was by Brian Cant (➢*Play School*). Such was *CG*'s success that it sired no less than two descendants, ➢*Trumpton* and ➢*Chigley*.

CAST (narrator) Brian Cant /*cr* Gordon Murray /*pr* Gordon Murray /*wr* Gordon Murray /*mus* Freddie Phillips /*BBC TV* (UK) /13 x 15m col.

Campion

Crime. BBC1 1980

Snobbery with violence. A quintessential gentleman amateur sleuth from the 30s 'Golden Age' of the English whodunnit, Margery Allingham's Albert Campion made his screen appearance in two BBC serials, *Dancers in Mourning* (1959) and *Death of a Ghost* (1960), starring Bernard Horsfall. For his 1980 resurrection Campion was played by Peter Davison, the actor playing the part in the daffy-diffident manner he had perfected on ➢*All Creatures Great and Small* (and would later employ on ➢*Dr Who*). A vintage Lagonda was Campion's means of tootling to the scene of the dastardly deed; his sidekick was faithful cockney manservant Magersfontein Lugg (ex-professional wrestler Brian Glover), a reformed burglar. CI Stanislaus Oates was the obligatory oikish contact at the Yard. Toodlepip.

CAST *Albert Campion* Peter Davison *Magersfontein Lugg* Brian Glover *Chief Insp. Stanislaus Oates* Andrew Burt /*pr* Ken Riddington, Jonathan Alwyn /*mus* Nigel Hess /*BBC TV: WGBH Boston, Consolidated Productions* (UK:USA) /16 x 55m col /US tx Syndicated 1989–91.

Candid Camera

Light Entertainment. ITV 1960–7

A hidden camera filmed the reactions of gullible members of the public to staged impossibilities (e.g. a man selling £5 notes for £4.10s, cars which moved without engines). Devised in America by Allen Funt – originally as a 1947 radio programme *Candid Microphone* – it was at its British best under the presentership of Bob Monkhouse (➢*The Golden Shot*), with Jonathan Routh has our man on the spot, who eventually informed the bewildered punters, 'Smile, you're on *Candid Camera*.' The show was resurrected by LWT in 1974, with Peter Dulay as host, and was the partial inspiration for ➢*Game for a Laugh*.

CAST (presenters) Bob Monkhouse, Jonathan Routh, Arthur Atkins /*cr* Allen Funt /*dr* inc Geoffrey Ramsay, Ronnie Taylor /*ABC* (UK) /150+ x 30m bw.

The Fatman cometh. William Conrad as private investigator *Cannon*, a show tailor-made for Conrad who had previously failed to get starring roles because of his corpulence.

Cannon

Crime. BBC1 1972–8

Rising to prominence as the radio voice of *Gunsmoke* marshal Matt Dillon, William Conrad found his 19-stone morphology virtually forbade screen parts – until producer Quinn Martin (➢*The Fugitive*) tailor-made a crime show featuring a fat PI. Looking, in Conrad's own words, like 'an overfed walrus', bald, moustachioed LA gumshoe Frank Cannon relied on smarts rather than fists and legwork to solve his cases. (One of the most enjoyable aspects of *Cannon* episodes was the staple scene in which the bad guy ran ... leaving California's most corpulent PI wheezing and sweating behind.) Possessed of a demonstrable taste for the good life – which included owning a Lincoln Continental, cooking up *haute cuisine* in his kitchen – Cannon, a former PD lieutenant, charged top-of-the-scale fees, although these were always waived for a deserving case. There were no sidekicks or secretaries, or even family, making Cannon the ultimate screen-sleuth loner. If the cases were sometimes slow and obvious, Cannon himself was a classic creation.

Cannon developed from a 100 minute CBS TVM, aired in 1970. The series had a close relationship with another Quinn Martin crime show, ➢*Barnaby Jones*, with Cannon occasionally appearing in the latter's stories.

Most of Conrad's before-the-screen work since *Cannon* (he is also an eminent TV director and producer) have been, small surprise, as a fat character. In 1981 he played Rex Stout's *Nero Wolfe* and was more recently seen in ➢*Jake and the Fatman.*

CAST *Frank Cannon* William Conrad /*cr* Quinn Martin /*exec pr* Quinn Martin /*pr* Alan A. Armer, Anthony Spinner, Harold Gast /*dr* inc John Badham, Don Meford, Jimmy Sangster, Virgil W. Vogel, Michael Caffey, Corey Allen, Richard Donner, Leo Penn, Alan Reisner /*wr* inc Robert Collins, Harold Gast, Michael Gleason, Stephen Kandel, David Moessinger, Ken Pettus, Paul Playdon, Ken Trevey, Carey Wilber / *mus* John Parker, John Cannon /*A Quinn Martin Production* (USA) /120 x 60m col /US tx CBS 1971–6.

Capital City
Drama. ITV 1989–90

Designer serial about the £100K per annum high fliers of the Shane Longman merchant bank in the City of London. A British equivalent of ➢*LA Law*, it mixed 'yuppie' professional pressures and personal problems to a serviceable degree, but the characters – perhaps because of their mania for money – evinced little sympathy. The most obviously likeable, the strong-but-sensitive Declan McConnochie (Douglas Hodge, ➢*Middlemarch*), was a mere contrivance. Arguably the TV series most imprinted with the mood of the Thatcher boom years, it also merits a footnote for boosting the Hollywood career of British bratpacker Julia Ormond (*Legends of the Fall, First Knight, Sabrina*).

CAST *Declan McConnochie* Douglas Hodge *Sirkka Nieminen* Joanna Kanska *Hudson J. Talbot III* Rolf Saxon *Jimmy Destry* Dorian Healy *Max Lubin* William Armstrong *Hannah Burgess* Anna Nygh *Chas Ewell* Jason Issacs *Sylvia Roux Teng* Emily Bolton /*cr* Andrew Maclear /*exec pr* Andrew Brown, John Hambly /*pr* Irving Teitelbaum /*dr* Mike Vardy, Clive Fleury, Diarmuid Lawrence, Paul Seed /*wr* inc Andrew Maclear /*mus* Colin Towns /*Euston Films* (UK) / 30 x 30m col.

Captain Pugwash
Children's. BBC 1957–75

A blustering pirate captain (leaky tub: the *Black Pig*) and his work-shy crew prove no match for the other rogues of the sea – especially cackling Cut-Throat Jake – and are repeatedly rescued by their cabin boy, Tom.

Classic but rudimentary animation, in which the characters' speech was simulated by moving a piece of card behind their open mouths. Unusually, for tiny tots TV, the storylines were stretched over several or more episodes. Voices were by Peter Hawkins (also the Daleks, ➢*The Flowerpot Men*). Derived from a comic strip in a boy's newspaper, *CP* was later rumoured to contain deliberate sexual innuendoes. This was strenuously denied by creator John Ryan, who also secured a berth on the BBC airwaves for another cartoon caper, the mock-knightly epic *The Adventures of Sir Prancelot* (1970). In 1999 *Captain Pugwash* was revived in a new series of 26 episodes, produced at the cost of a cool £1.5 million. Plundering porpoises!

CAST (voices) Peter Hawkins /*cr* John Ryan /*wr* Peter Hawkins /*mus* 'The Hornblower' (theme), performed by accordionist Tommy Edmondson /*BBC TV* (UK) / 86 x 5m bw:col.

Captain Scarlet and the Mysterons
Children's. ITV 1968

In 2065 AD Earth's Spectrum police force landed on Mars. Fearing an invasion, the planet's Mysteron inhabitants declared war, killing top Spectrum agents, Captains Black and Scarlet, with the intention of 'retrometabolizing' (resurrecting) them as Mysteron agents. This, indeed, was the fate of Black, but Scarlet recovered his humanity to become the Martians only immortal adversary.

Superlative 'supermarionation' from Gerry Anderson, which overcame the 'big-headed' look of his previous puppet shows by placing the machinery that worked the limbs, eyes and lips inside the body. As with ➢*Thunderbirds*, there was model hardware aplenty: *Cloudbase*, a flying aircraft carrier; ten-wheeled Spectrum Pursuit Vehicles (SPV); and 300 m.p.h. Angel Aircraft (these flown by a quintet of beautiful female pilots, Melody, Symphony, Rhapsody, Destiny and Harmony). Voice cast included Charles Tingwell, formerly ➢*Emergency – Ward 10.*

'Spectrum is Green.'

CAST (voices) *Capt. Scarlet* Francis Matthews *Col. White/Capt. Black/The Mysterons* Donald Gray *Capt. Grey/World President* Paul Maxwell *Capt. Blue* Ed Bishop *Capt. Ochre* Jeremy Wilkin *Capt. Magenta* Gary Files *Lt Green* Cy Grant *Dr Fawn* Charles Tingwell *Melody Angel* Sylvia Anderson *Symphony Angel* Janna Hill *Rhapsody/Destiny Angel* Liz Morgan *Harmony Angel* Lian-Shin /*cr* Gerry & Sylvia Anderson /*exec pr* Gerry & Sylvia Anderson /*pr* Reg Hill /*dr* inc Desmond Saunders, David Lane, Leo Eaton /*wr* inc Gerry Anderson, Tony Barwick, Shane Rimmer, Alan Pattillo, David Lee /*mus* Barry Gray /*sfx* Derek Meddings /*A Century 21 Production: ATV: ITC* (UK) /32 x 25m col.

Cardiac Arrest

Melodrama. BBC1 1994–6

Tales of everyday life of young doctors in a big city hospital. Scripted by real-life hospital physician, John MacUre, *CA* was touted as 'the most realistic medical drama yet'; certainly it caught the sleepless, adrenalin-pumped pressure of the junior doctor's lot, spicing this with trysts in the supplies cupboard and gory medical dilemmas. Only in the emergency department scenes did it suffer from budget comparison with the freewheeling cameras of US contemporary, ➢*ER*.

CAST *Dr Claire Maitland* Helen Baxendale *Dr Rajah* Ahsen Bhatti *Dr Andrew Collin* Andrew Lancel *Mr Cyril 'Scissors' Smedley* Peter O'Brien *Sister Julie Novac* Jacquetta May *Mr Ernest Docherty* Tom Watson /*cr* John MacUre /*pr* Tony Garnett /*dr* inc Jo Johnson, David Garnett /*wr* John MacUre /*Island World* (UK) / 36 x 35m col.

Car 54, Where Are You?

Comedy. ITV 1964–5

Nat Hiken's follow up to ➢*The Phil Silvers Show* (aka *Bilko*) was a lunatic comedy about a pair of inept police officers who shared the patrol vehicle of the title. Set in a NY remarkably free of major felonies, it starred Fred Gwynne (an occasional guest actor on *Bilko*) as the tall-but-dim Francis Muldoon and Joe E. Ross (Mess Sergeant Ritzik in *Bilko*) as his short and even-more-dim partner, Gunther Toody. The close comedic connection between *Bilko* and *54* was only emphasized by the presence of actress Beatrice Pons, who was Ross' nagging-wife foil in both. Superb characterizations and gold-standard scripts aside, the series lasted but two seasons. It did, however, give Gwynne the exposure which secured his casting as the immortal Herman in ➢*The Munsters*, where he was joined by fellow *54* member Al Lewis.

CAST *Off. Gunther Toody* Joe E. Ross *Off. Francis Muldoon* Fred Gwynne *Lucille Toody* Beatrice Pons *Capt. Martin Block* Paul Reed *Off. Leo Schnauser* Al Lewis /*cr* Nat Hiken /*pr* Nat Hiken /*wr* inc Nat Hiken / *Eupolis* (USA) /60 x 25m bw /US tx NBC 1961–3.

Caroline in the City

Comedy. C4 1995–

Nothing less – or more – than ➢*The Mary Tyler Moore Show* for the 90s. Lea Thompson (star of the first three *Back to the Future* movies) played Caroline Duffy, a well-groomed working girl adrift in the metropolis with humorous romantic problems. The main suitors were buffoonish ex-boyfriend Del, and eccentric cartoon colourist Richard. Incontinent advice on the Manhattan dating scene was provided by trampy next-door-neighbour Annie. Squeaky-clean, effortlessly written, difficult to dislike. To the unrestrained glee of US network CBS, it knocked ➢*Friends* off the top of the Nielsen ratings. Given the show's debt to *MTM*, it was appropriate that Lea Thompson – who began her career as a ballet dancer – and Mary Tyler Moore had once acted together, in the Emmy Award-winning TV movie *Stolen Babes*.

CAST *Caroline Duffy* Lea Thompson *Del Cassidy* Eric Lutes *Richard Karinsky* Malcolm Gets *Annie* Amy Pietz /*cr* Fred Barron /*exec pr* Fred Barron, Marco Pennette, David Nichols /*dr* inc James Burrows, Will MacKenzie /*CBS Entertainment Productions: Barron Pennette Productions* (USA) /50+ x 30m col /US tx NCB 1995–.

Carrott's Lib

Comedy. BBC1 1982–4

After a desultory TV career, Birmingham comic/ folk singer Robert Davies – aka Jasper Carrott – noticed that the comedic times were a-changing and used the opportunity to reinvent himself as an alternative humorist with *Carrott's Lib*. While it included Carrott's stock-in-trade, observational humour about everyday life, it also introduced bug-eyed diatribes (*Sun*-reading Robin Reliant drivers receiving a particular drubbing) and a sharp political satirizing, exemplified by the famous opening: 'Tony Benn is responsible for all evil in the world. He was in Denmark last week leading the English soccer hooligans...' Interspersing Carrott's stand-up (actually more sit-down) routines were sketches featuring, among others, showbiz novices Emma Thompson and Chris Barrie (later ➢*Red Dwarf*, ➢*The Brittas Empire*). Most of the material was self-penned, although occasional contributors included Ian Hislop, Rob Grant and Doug Naylor (the latter pair soon to create *Red Dwarf*). A follow-up series, *Carrott Confidential*, 1987), marked a failure of nerve (relying on material from such gagmen of yesteryear as Barry Cryer), before Carrott continued in liberated vein with *Canned Carrott* (1990). With Carrott up on his high stool ranting happily, most of the *Confidential* sketches fell to Steve Punt and bishop's son Hugh Dennis (both of the ➢*The Mary Whitehouse Experience*), though it was a Carrott–Robert Powell spoof slot which endeared most, even becoming a series in its own right: ➢*The Detectives*.

CAST Jasper Carrott, Emma Thompson, Chris Barrie, Debby Bishop, Steve Frost, Nick Wilton, Kay Stonham, Nick Maloney /*pr* Paul Jackson, Geoff Posner /*wr* inc Jasper Carrott, Rob Grant & Doug Naylor, Duncan Campbell, Ian Hislop /*BBC TV* (UK) /17 x 30m col.

Carry on Laughing

Comedy. ITV 1975

Soporific attempt to transfer the *Carry On* film series to TV, with a series of specially written half-hour pieces. Variously spoofs of TV shows ('And in My Lady's Chamber' sent up ➢*Upstairs, Downstairs*) or historical romps ('Under the Round Table'), the latitude of the small screen encouraged laziness where it might have produced exploration. The jokes numbered such past-their-sell-by-date offerings as 'Anyone for a little crumpet?' and (even), 'Hampton Court?'/ 'No, I always walk like this.' Simon Callow, in an early venture onto the airwaves, was to be glimpsed as a sailor in the segment 'Orgy and Bess'.

CAST inc Barbara Windsor, Sid James, Jack Douglas, Bernard Bresslaw, Peter Butterworth, Joan Sims, Kenneth Connor /*cr* Gerald Thomas /*exec pr* Peter Rogers /*pr* Gerald Thomas /*dr* Alan Tarrant /*wr* inc Lew Schwarz, Barry Cryer, Dick Vosburgh /*ATV* (UK) / 6 x 30m col.

Casey Jones

Children's. BBC 1958

Popular kid's Western, set in the 1890s, featuring Alan Hale Jr (later in ➢*Gilligan's Island*) as John Luther 'Casey' Jones, driver for the Illinois Central Railroad. Episodes invariably involved attempts by the elements or outlaws to prevent Casey Jones ('a-steamin' and a-rollin'') from bringing the Cannonball Express in on time – but he always did. Loyally supporting him in his wholesome endeavours were wife Alice, son Casey Jr, dog Cinders, fireman Wallie Simms and conductor Red Rock.

CAST *John Luther 'Casey' Jones* Alan Hale Jr *Casey Jones Jr* Bobby Clark *Alice Jones* Mary Lawrence *Wallie Simms* Dub Taylor *Red Rock* Eddy Waller /*pr* Harold Green /*Columbia: Birskin* (USA) /32 x 30m bw /US tx Syndicated 1957–8.

Casualty

Melodrama. BBC1 1986–

Top-rated medical drama, set in the A&E department of Holby City Hospital. Created by Jeremy Brock and Paul Unwin, it followed the fashion of imported 80s American dramas, notably ➢*St Elsewhere*, in presenting a lead narrative and two or more sub-plots (often of a humorous bent). However, it eschewed the glamour of its US counterparts; a tendency to mark scene changes by a spartan swishing of cubicle curtains was thus easily burlesqued, as was the stock manner in which episodes opened with some innocent member of the public about to suffer a hospitalizing tragedy. A move to film in 1994 was curtailed when viewers complained that they preferred the cheaper look of videotape. To the ire of Conservative governments, the series injected large amounts of politics, regularly criticizing NHS cuts. Cast changes have been frequent, but Derek Thompson (who came to screen notice playing an IRA terrorist in the 1979 movie *The Long Good Friday*) as caring charge nurse, Charlie Fairhead, endured. Among the early major characters was mother-figure Megan Roach, played by Brenda Fricker, who won an Oscar for her performance in *My Left Foot*. Over the seasons, the list of those admitted to *Casualty* in guest cameos reads like a *Who's Who* of British thespians – Peggy Mount, Hywel Bennett, Susan Penhaligon, Alfred Molina, Rula Lenska, Polly James and Frank Windsor, to name but a few.

CAST *Charlie Fairhead* Derek Thompson *Lisa 'Duffy' Duffin* Catherine Shipton *Megan Roach* Brenda Fricker *Dr Barbara 'Baz' Samuels/Hayes/Fairhead* Julia Watson *Kuba Trzcinski* Christopher Rozycki *Dr Ewart Plimmer* Bernard Gallagher *Jimmy Powell* Robson Green *Dr Julian Chapman* Nigel Le Vaillant *Martin Ashford* Patrick Robinson *Peter Hayes* Robert Duncan *Dr Mike Barratt* Clive Mantle *Josh Griffiths* Ian Bleasdale *Kate Wilson* Sorcha Cusack *Rachel Longworth* Jane Gurnett /*cr* Jeremy Brock, Paul Unwin /*pr* inc Geraint Morris, Peter Norris, Michael Ferguson, Corinne Hollingworth, Rosalind Anderson /*dr* inc Christopher Menaul, Keith Washington, Andrew Morgan, Steve Goldie, David Innes Edwards, Tony McHale, Catherine Morshead, Renny Rye /*wr* inc Jeremy Brock, Paul Unwin, Wally K. Daly, Lise Meyer, Christopher Penfold, Andrew Holden, Tony McHale, Barbara Machin /*BBC TV* (UK) /250+ x 50m col.

C.A.T.S. Eyes

Crime. ITV 1985–7

A dowdy British take on ➢*Charlie's Angels.* Pru Standfast, Maggie Forbes – a character who had previously featured in her own series, ➢*The Gentle Touch* – and fast-driving Frederica 'Fred' Smith (Leslie Ash, ➢*Men Behaving Badly*) formed the Eyes Enquiry Agency, a cover for the contrivedly titled security squad CATS (Covert Activities Thames Section) of the Home Office. Overseeing their investigations was 'the man from the ministry', Nigel Beaumont (Don Warrington, ➢*Rising Damp*). Such dangerous prey as the Mafia, the Triads and Russian spies were routine work for the all-women, all-action team; however, any tendency towards glamourous danger was offset by the Thames estuary locations (Gillingham, Rochester, Chatham) insisted on by production company TVS so as to make maximum use of their Maidstone studios. Season two saw the promotion of Forbes to team leader, replacing the departed Oxford-educated Standfast; Tessa Robinson (played by Tracy-Louise Ward, sister of ➢*The Thorn Birds*' Rachel Ward, and also the Marchioness of Worcester) was recruited to maintain the numbers.

CAST *Pru Standfast* Rosalyn Landor *Maggie Forbes* Jill Gascoine *Frederica 'Fred' Smith* Leslie Ash *Nigel Beaumont* Don Warrington *Tessa Robinson* Tracy-Louise Ward /*cr* Terence Feely /*exec pr* Rex Firkin /*pr* Dickie Bamber, Frank Cox, Raymond Menmuir /*dr* inc William Brayne, Carol Wiseman, Raymond Menmuir / *wr* inc Terence Feely, Don Houghton, Andy De La Tour, Anthony Skene /*mus* John Kongos, Barbara Thompson /*A TVS Network Production* (UK) / 1 x 90m, 30 x 60m col.

Catweazle

Children's. ITV 1970–1

A ragged magician (Geoffrey Blaydon) from the Middle Ages is accidentally thrown forwards in time to the present, where he befriends a young farmer's boy named Carrot Bennett. Tailor-made for Blaydon by writer Richard Carpenter (who took the name Catweazle from a farmyard gate), the comedy-fantasy series prompted a sequel, in which the eponymous wizard again visited the 20th century, this time to be aided by Cedric, scion of Lord and Lady Collingford.

CAST *Catweazle* Geoffrey Blaydon *Carrot* Robin Davies *Groome* Peter Butterworth *Cedric* Gary Warren /*cr* Richard Carpenter /*exec pr* Joy Whitby /*pr* Quentin Lawrence, Carl Mannin /*dr* Quentin Lawrence, David Reed, David Lane /*wr* Richard Carpenter /*London Weekend TV* (UK) /26 x 25m col.

Celebrity Squares

Light Entertainment. ITV 1975–

Dire British version of popular US game show *Hollywood Squares.* Two contestants played noughts and crosses on a giant board of squares populated by B list showbiz personalities (the Arthur Mullard, Pat Coombs type of rent-a-face). The ubiquitous Bob Monkhouse asked the celebs questions – the contestants having to gauge if the starry ones' answers were correct or not, winning X or O for that space if so – and Kenny Everett provided the 'zany' voice-over instructions. Cancelled in 1979, the show was inexplicably awakened from the dead in 1993.

CAST (presenter) Bob Monkhouse /*pr* Paul Stewart Laing, Glyn Edwards, Peter Harris /*ATV* (UK) / 120+ x 30m col.

The Champions

Sci-fi. ITV 1968–9

Superlative 60s sci-thriller featuring a trio of secret agents – Craig Stirling, Sharron Macready, Richard Barrett, 'the champions of law, order and justice' – who worked for a UN-like organization, Nemesis. After a fatal plane crash in the Himalayas in the opening episode, the three were resurrected from

Endowed with superhuman qualities, courtesy of a lost Tibetan tribe, spies Craig Stirling, Sharron Macready and Richard Barrett were *The Champions*.

the dead by a God-like Tibetan monk who kindly endowed them with 'unbelievable strength, a sharpening of ... reason' – not to mention ESP. Their boss at Nemesis, Tremayne (who remained ignorant of their new enhancements), habitually assigned them missions impossible on which nothing less than world stability depended. Those sharing the directing honours included US actor Sam Wanamaker (father of Zoe), veteran Hammer-horror flicksman Freddie Francis, and Roy Ward Baker. Despite the show's success, the cast notably failed to progress to other significant things: American heart-throb Stuart Damon appeared in espionage caper *The Adventurer* (1972–3), a rare ITC flop, and later co-hosted US magazine programme *America*; the rare screen appearances of polylingual blonde bombshell Alexandra Bastedo included a guest spot in 90s sitcom ➢*Absolutely Fabulous*; baby-faced William Gaunt, meanwhile, sank to the couch-fodder domestic comedies *No Place Like Home* (BBC1 1983–7) and *Next of Kin* (BBC 1 1994).

CAST *Craig Stirling* Stuart Damon *Richard Barrett* William Gaunt *Sharron Macready* Alexandra Bastedo *Tremayne* Anthony Nicholls /*cr* Monty Berman & Dennis Spooner /*pr* Monty Berman /*dr* inc Cyril Frankel, Sam Wanamaker, John Moxey, Roy Ward Baker, Freddie Francis /*wr* inc Dennis Spooner, Philip Broadley, Ralph Smart, Tony Williamson, Terry Nation, Brian Clemens, Gerald Kelsey, Ian Stuart Black /*mus* Ewin Astley, Tony Hatch (theme) /*ATV Midlands* (UK) /30 x 60m col /US tx NBC 1968–9.

Chancer
Melodrama. ITV 1990–1

By ➢*The Brothers* out of *Connie*, with a dash of DeLorean. Chancer told the story of on-the-make Stephen Crane (Clive Owen), a working-class entrepreneur who takes over an ailing family handmade sports-car firm, with the aim of making loadsamoney. Formula foolish (Crane's ruthlessness drove away his nice girlfriend, yawn) but plot wise, the show gripped Tuesday audiences with its brand of business chicanery, even outright villainy (by the end of the first season, Crane was in jail for fraud) and occasional flippant wit. For no reason other than pretentiousness, the producers insisted on calling each part an 'Act'. The music was by Jan ➢'*Miami Vice*' Hammer.

CAST *Stephen Crane* Clive Owen *Jo* Susannah Harker *Jimmy Blake* Leslie Philipps *Robert Douglas* Benjamin Whitrow /*pr* Sarah D. Wilson /*mus* Jan Hammer / *Central TV* (UK) /12 x 60m col.

Charlie's Angels
Crime. ITV 1977–82

'When the show was No. 3, I figured it was our acting. When it got to be No. 1, I decided it could only be because none of us wears a bra.' Farrah Fawcett-Majors.

Girlie private-eye show, derided – even by its principals – for its blatant sexism. Sabrina Duncan, Kelly Garrett and Jill Monroe (played by Farrah Fawcett, who changed her surname to Fawcett-Majors on her marriage to Lee Majors of ➢*The Six Million Dollar Man*) were three LAPD officers, taken away from humdrum meter-maiding by Charlie Townsend, wealthy head of Townsend Investigations, and sent out to do some serious crime-busting. Alas, the gossamer-thin plots endlessly contrived instead to place the bimbo trio in undercover cases where they were required to pose seductively as strippers, cheer-leaders or health-spa attendants. The assignments, notably, were always delivered telephonically by the never-seen Townsend (voiced by John Forsythe, later in ➢*Dynasty*); also jumping to the master's commands was John Bosley, who provided logistical backup to the Angels. After a single season, lion-maned Fawcett-Majors left the show, to be replaced by Cheryl Ladd (daughter-in-law of diminutive

Kate Jackson (left), Jaclyn Smith (centre) and Farah Fawcett were the rarely clad stars of *Charlie's Angels*. Produced by hitmeister Aaron Spelling, the show pioneered 'jiggle TV'.

Hollywood lead Alan), who played Kris Monroe, Jill's sister. Actresses Shelley Hack (a former Charlie perfume girl) and Tanya Roberts (later in the dire *Sheena: Queen of the Jungle* movie and a Bond girl in *A View to a Kill*) both took Buggins turns as Angels in subsequent seasons. When the show ended in 1981 Jaclyn Smith (married to British film director Tony Richardson) was the only survivor of the original heavenly threesome. An attempt to revive the show as *Angels 88* failed to fly. The pioneer of 'jiggle' broadcasting (its influence can be seen on shows as diverse as ➢*The Dukes of Hazzard* and ➢*Baywatch*), ➢*Charlie's Angels* earned the appropriate accolade of a soft-porn movie hommage, *Bobbie's Boobies*.

CAST *Sabrina Duncan* Kate Jackson *Jill Monroe* Farrah Fawcett-Majors *Kelly Garrett* Jaclyn Smith *Kris Monroe* Cheryl Ladd *Tiffany Welles* Shelley Hack *Julie Rogers* Tanya Roberts *John Bosley* David Doyle *Charlie Townsend* (voice) John Forsythe /*exec pr* Aaron Spelling, Leonard Goldberg /*pr* Rick Husky, David Levinson, Edward J. Lasko, Barney Rosenzweig /*dr* inc Richard Benedict, Don Chaffey, John Moxey, Bernard McEveety /*wr* inc John D.F. Black, Jeff Myrow, Kathryn Powers, Lee Sheldon /*mus* Jack Elliott, Allyn Ferguson, Henry Mancini (theme) /*Spelling: Goldberg Productions* (USA) /109 x 60m col /US tx ABC 1976–81.

Cheers

Comedy. C4 1983–93

'How would we know we were winners if we didn't have you guys?' Conman Harry the Hat to the staff and patrons of Cheers.

Sublime US charactercom set in a Boston bar ('Where everybody knows your name'), modelled on the city's real-life tavern, the Bull & Finch. The show's regulars were: intellectually-challenged, womanizing owner Sam 'Mayday' Malone, a former relief pitcher for the Red Sox; dense barman Ernie 'Coach' Pantusso; fecund, razor-tongued waitress Carla Tortelli (Rhea Perlman, ➢*Taxi* and sister of *Cheer*'s producer Heide Perlman); barfly Norm Petersen (who always entered to a holler of 'NORM!' from the bar's other patrons); know-it-all mailman Cliff Clavin; and the prim and proper Diane, an Eng. Lit. graduate. The storylines of the first seasons were dominated by Sam and Diane's love-hate relationship, with Diane eventually leaving him to marry neurotic psychiatrist Dr Frasier Crane. However, unable to forget Sam, she left Frasier at the altar and returned to bus tables at Cheers. Then Coach died (an exit caused by the death of actor Nicholas Colasanto, who was also one of US television's mainstay directors), to be replaced by hick-and-thick bartender Woody Boyd from Hanover, Indiana. Frasier, meanwhile, became a more or less permanent fixture, and eventually married ice-queen psychiatrist Dr Lilith Sternin. In 1987 Diane left the bar (to write a novel), and a lovesick Sam sold Cheers to a large corporation and set off to sail the world. Alas, his yacht sank and he washed up back at Cheers, where he had to beg a job off the new manager, gold-digging Rebecca Howe. Their mutual attraction-loathing mirrored Sam's earlier relationship with Diane; eventually, Rebecca fell instead for corporate raider Robin Colcord – who ended up in jail – and Sam won back control of the bar, making the snotty Rebecca *his* underling. Although the one-liners and gags were polished to shining brilliance, the fundamental wit of *Cheers* came from its characters, who were flawlessly, fleshfully realized and from whom plots and humour sprouted organically. To see them once was to know them to the point of intimacy. When Sam Malone removed his hairpiece to reveal a semi-bald pate it was more than a sight-gag – it was the punch line to a joke that had been eight years in the making. Such jokes were all the better for the fact that the regulars of Cheers were portrayed without the cloying sentimentality of most American comedy; on the contrary, they were losers with illusions (shades of writers Burrows' and Charles' earlier ➢*Taxi*), while their preoccupations – sex, dating, relationships – were those of their audience in an increasingly fragmented and alienated society. It was a tribute to the quality of the show that, of the principal players, only Shelley Long decided there was more to actorly life than pulling beers in a fictitious bar (although Danson, Alley and Harrelson combined *Cheers* with active film careers), while guest stars often gave performances of a lifetime. John Cleese, most notably, won an Emmy for his spot as a marriage guidance counsellor.

The final episode, transmitted in the USA in May 1993, saw Diane return to *Cheers* as a successful novelist and garnered an audience of 130 million, making it the most watched TV show in history. By that time, *Cheers* had won 26 Emmys, just three fewer than ➢*The Mary Tyler Moore Show*; it had also, at $65 million dollars for 26 episodes, become the most expensive comedy in television history to that date, largely due to cast salaries (Ted Danson alone earned a reported $450,000 per episode). Miraculously, a spin-off, ➢*Frasier*, was hardly less successful.

CAST *Sam Malone* Ted Danson *Diane Chambers* Shelley Long *Ernie Pantuso* Nicholas Colasanto *Norm Petersen* George Wendt *Cliff Clavin* John Ratzenberger *Carla Tortelli/LeBec* Rhea Perlman *Frasier Crane* Kelsey Grammer *Woody Boyd* Woody Harrelson *Rebecca Howe* Kirstie Alley *Lilith Sternin Crane* Bebe Neuwirth *Eddie LeBec* Jay Thomas *Robin Colcord* Roger Rees *Kelly Gaines/Boyd* Jackie Swanson *Harry* Harry Anderson *John Allen Hill* Keene Curtis /*cr* Les Charles, James Burrows, Glen Charles /*exec pr* inc James Burrows, Les Charles, Glen Charles /*pr* inc Ken Levine, Heide Perlman /*dr* inc James Burrows /*wr* inc James Burrows, Les Charles, Glen Charles, Heide Perlman, Sam Simon, David Lee /*mus* Judy Hart Angelo & Gary Portnoy ('Where everybody knows your name' theme song) /*A Charles Burrows Charles Production: Paramount TV* (USA) /273 x 25m, 1 x 90m col / US tx NBC 1982–93.

Chef!

Comedy. BBC1 1993–6

After his rise and rise on the British small screen, Lenny Henry (➢*New Faces*, ➢*The Fosters*, ➢*Tiswas*, ➢*The Lenny Henry Show*, ➢*Three of a Kind*) was tempted to America, the only result of which was the damp-squib Disney movie *True Identity* and, indirectly, this sitcom about the fearsome *chef de cuisine*, Gareth Blackstock, of the Le Château Anglais restaurant in the English Home Counties. *Chef!*, conceived during a 'rest period' in Hollywood, drew heavily on US sitcom ➢*The Cosby Show*, centring as it did on a black professional whose colour was unremarkable, and largely unremarked on. Additionally, *Chef*'s shooting on film – a first for a British sitcom – was inspired by the quality and realism of ➢*Cheers*. Important though these influences were, however, the ultimate success of *Chef!* lay in Henry's maturing as an actor; his restrained portrait of the obsessive Blackstock was a full-course meal away from such zaniness as *The Delbert Wilkins Show*. There was also fine supporting cast work (another US sitcom influence), notably from Caroline Lee Johnson as Blackstock's wife and Roger Griffiths (*The Posse*) as commis chef, Everton. When Blackstock's perfectionism eventually drove his Michelin two-starred restaurant over the financial brink, the *Chef!* players were joined by Dave Hill as profit-hungry businessman Cyril Bryson. The series was co-produced by Henry's own company, Crucial Films.

CAST *Gareth Blackstock* Lenny Henry *Janice Blackstock* Caroline Lee Johnson *Everton* Roger Griffiths *Lucinda* Claire Skinner *Cyril Bryson* Dave Hill /*cr* Lenny Henry /*pr* Charlie Hanson /*dr* inc Dewi Humphries /*wr* Peter Tilbury, Geoff Deane, Paul Makin /*APC: Crucial Films* (UK) /20 x 30m col.

Cheyenne

Western. BBC1 1958–61

Loosely based on the 1947 movie of the same title and, alongside ➢*Gunsmoke* and ➢*Davy Crockett*, the show most responsible for the 50s stampede into adult TV Westerns. Eugene 'Clint' Walker starred as Cheyenne Bodie, a half-breed who wandered the American West of the 1870s with an implacable sense of justice. Typically, episodes involved the barrel-chested Bodie standing alone against a lynch-mob crowd on behalf of an unpopular cause. While the series eschewed gunplay and saloon brawls, it tempered action with psychology. It also possessed a sometimes lavish look for a TV oater, due to Warner's habit of packing stories with surplus footage from their movies. Offscreen, the show had a famously turbulent history. It first appeared as one of the rotating elements (with *Casablanca* and *King's Row*) of *Warner Bros Presents.* At this stage, Cheyenne was accompanied on his adventures by mapmaker Smitty (played by L.Q. Jones, one of Sam Peckinpah's stock company and later the director of the low-budget sci-fi film, *A Man and a Dog*), but soon the sidekick was dropped to allow Cheyenne to become TV's first pardnerless Western hero. Then, during the 1958–9 season, Walker entered a contract dispute with the studio and the lead character was changed to Bronco Layne, an ex-Confederate officer played by Ty Hardin. Eventually, however, Walker was tempted back to the *Cheyenne* stage (by an increase in salary), and Hardin's character was given a show of his own, ➢*Bronco.* A year later, 1960, *Cheyenne* reverted to being part of an anthology series, *The Cheyenne Show*, where it rotated with *Bronco* and another Warners horse-opera, *Sugarfoot,* before going solo once more in the fall of 1962. After the show finally rode off into the sunset, Walker moved on to play the lead in the Alaskan police drama *Kodiak.*

CAST *Cheyenne Bodie* Clint Walker *Smitty* L.Q. Jones / *exec pr* William T. Orr /*pr* Roy Huggins, Arthur Silver / *dr* inc Lee Sholem, Richard Sarafian, Douglas Heyes, Thomas Carr, Paul Henreid, Jerry Hopper /*mus* William Lara (theme), Stan Jones, Paul Sawtell / *Warner Bros TV* (USA) /107 x 60m bw /US tx ABC 1956–63.

Chigley

Children's. BBC1 1969

The third of Gordon Murray's Trumptonshire puppet trilogy, markedly less bucolic than ➢*Camberwick Green* and ➢*Trumpton,* dominated as it was by Mr Cresswell's biscuit factory and Treadles (canal) Wharf, run by Mr Swallow. Also featured was Lord Belborough, a philanthropic aristocrat who, with imposing butler Mr Brackett, ran a steam train called Bessie for the benefit of the local hoi polloi. If *Chigley* had an air of modernity about it, continuity with Murray's earlier creations was maintained by the same hearty characterisation as, and regular appearances by folk from, *Camberwick.*

CAST (narrator) Brian Cant /*cr* Gordon Murray /*pr* Gordon Murray /*wr* Gordon Murray /*sfx* (puppet animation) Bob Bura, John Hardwick /*mus* Freddie Phillips (songs) /*Gordon Murray Puppets* (UK) /13 x 15m col.

Children of the Stones

Children's. ITV 1977

'Happy Day'.

Filmed amidst the Neolithic stone circles of Avebury, Jeremy Burnham and Trevor Ray's sci-fi show mixed a fascination for the paranormal with an apocalyptic 'They're taking us over!' plot to create a classic children's chiller. Arriving in the seemingly ordinary village of Milbury, scientist Adam Brake and his son quickly notice that the inhabitants are mindless, smiling drones. Trying to escape the secret power that holds the village in its thrall, Brake and son inexplicably crash their car, only to wake up in the house of local squire and astronomy professor, Hendrick. Convalescing, they realize that Hendrick has discovered a secret alignment between a black hole in space and the local standing stones which gives him totalitarian psychic control... A magnificent cast was headed by Iain Cuthertson and a pre-➢*Blake's 7* Gareth Thomas.

CAST *Hendrick* Iain Cuthertson *Adam Brake* Gareth Thomas *Matthew Brake* Peter Denin *Dai* Freddie Jones /*cr* Jeremy Burnham, Trevor Ray /*exec pr* Patrick Dromgoole /*pr* Peter Graham Scott /*dr* Peter Graham Scott /*wr* Jeremy Burnham, Trevor Ray /*An HTV Production* (UK) /7 x 30m col.

The Chinese Detective

Crime. BBC1 1981–2

The first British police show to feature a non-Caucasian hero. Liverpudlian–Chinese actor David Yip played scruffy Detective Sergeant John Ho of East London's Limehouse manor, attracted to carrying a warrant card in a bid to clear his father's name. Stories veered between 'Your nicked!' actioners (it was penned by ➢*The Sweeney* creator, Ian Kennedy Martin) and the personal life of loner Ho, an outsider not only to his own community but also to that of the racist Metropolitan Police. After some years of resting post-*Chinese Detective* Yip returned to the screen in the Merseyside sudster ➢*Brookside.*

CAST *DS John Ho* David Yip *DCI Berwick* Derek Martin *DS Donald Chegwyn* Arthur Kelly /*cr* Ian Kennedy Martin /*pr* Terence Williams /*wr* inc Ian Kennedy Martin /*BBC TV* (UK) /14 x 50m col.

CHiPs

Crime. ITV 1979–87

Two himbo motocycle cops with orthodontically perfect smiles, Jon Baker and 'Ponch' Poncherello, give high-speed chase to vehicular baddies around the freeways of LA. This, whilst keeping one eye open for 'foxy ladies', contrivedly inserted into the plot in improbable states of undress (such as the episode in which the buddies stop a speeding van to find it full of nude female volleyball players).

The non-stop cavalcade of auto-crashes and good-looking girls proved popular enough among boy viewers to give *CHiPs* – standing for Californian Highway Patrol – six years of TV life. In the final season Larry Wilcox, a Vietnam vet and former star of *The Adventures of Lassie*, refused to work alongside Hispanic co-star Erik Estrada (previously in the Christian morality movie, *The Cross and the Switchblade*) and quit the show, to be replaced by Tom Reilly. Among the other actors who drifted through CHiP HQ were former Olympic decathalon champion Bruce Jenner, Michael Dorn (later Worf in ➢*Star Trek: TNG*), while Robert Englund (➢*V*, the horror-flick *Nightmare on Elm Street*) received an early screen outing in the 1981 episode 'Forty Tons of Trouble'.

CAST *Off. Frank 'Ponch' Poncherello* Erik Estrada *Off. Jon Baker* Larry Wilcox *Sgt Getraer* Robert Pine *Off. Bobby 'Hot Dog' Nelson* Tom Reilly *Off. Bonnie Clark* Randie Oakes *Off. Turner* Michael Dorn *Off. Steve McLeish* Bruce Jenner /*cr* Rick Rosner /*exec pr* Cy Cermak /*pr* Rick Rosner, Ric Rondell /*dr* inc Michael Caffey, Larry Wilcox, Don Weis, Nicholas Colasanto, John Astin, John Florea /*wr* inc Marshall Herskowitz, Stephen Kandel /*mus* Mike Post, Pete Carpenter, John Parker (theme) /*Rosner TV: MGM TV* (USA) / 132 x 60m, 3 x 90m col /US tx NBC 1977–83.

Chronicles of Narnia

Children's. BBC1 1988–90

Hi-tech version of C.S. Lewis's literary fantasy for children, produced by Paul Stone, who had pioneered the same mix of electric gadgetry-animation-video in his 1984 adaptation of John Masefield's *The Box of Delights*. Unfortunately, the state-of-the-art sfx sat ill with Lewis's delicate imaginings and few were satisfied. As a result, only four of the *Chronicles – The Lion, the Witch and the Wardrobe*; *Prince Caspian*; *Voyage of the Dawn Treader*; and *The Silver Chair* – were filmed. An earlier, simpler, better version of *The Lion, the Witch and the Wardrobe* was made by Pamela Lonsdale for ATV in 1963.

CAST *Peter Pevensie* Richard Dempsey *Edmund Pevensie* Jonathan R. Scott *Lucy Pevensie* Sophie Wilcox *Susan Pevensie* Sophie Cook *The White Witch* Barbara Kellerman *Aslan* (voice) Ronald Pickup /*pr* Paul Stone /*dr* Marilyn Fox, Alex Kirby /*wr* Alan Seymour /*BBC TV* (UK) /17 x approx 30m col.

Circus Boy

Children's. BBC1 1957–8

When his circus parents are killed performing their highwire act, cute 12-year-old Corky is adopted by circus owner Big Tim Champion and becomes water boy to Bimbo the baby elephant and friend to Joey the Clown (Noah Beery Jr, later Rockford Sr in ➢*The Rockford Files*), Little Tom the Midget, Nuba the Lion and all. Episodes related Corky's adventures as the circus moved from town to town across the US of A. Child actor Mickey Braddock later resurfaced under his real name of Dolenz in the ➢*The Monkees*.

CAST *Corky* Mickey Braddock *Joey the Clown* Noah Beery Jr *Little Tom* Billy Barty *Big Tim Champion* Robert Lowery *Hank Miller* Lee Gordon *Swifty* Olin Howlin /*pr* Herbert B. Leonard, Norman Blackburn /*dr* inc Douglas Heyes /*wr* inc Douglas Heyes /*Columbia: Herbert B. Leonard* /49 x 25m bw /US tx NBC 1957–8.

The Cisco Kid

Children's. BBC 1954–6

Light-hearted Western for the moppet market. Duncan Renaldo played the dude-ish Mexican Robin Hood of the title, Leo Carillo – already in his 70s – his portly sidekick, Pancho, speaker of comically fractured Spanglish ('Pl-ee-s-e Ceesco! Let's went!'). The twosome saw action galore as they galloped around the American southwest of the 1890s, dispensing justice to brigands but riding clear (on horses Diablo and Loco) of sheriffs, who erroneously considered them outlaws. The violence quotient was low, with the Kid usually satisfying himself with shooting guns out of baddies' hands, or commanding Pancho to disarm them with his 'whe-ee-p'. The first Western to be filmed in colour, *The Cisco Kid* was based on the 1904 short story 'The Caballero's Way' by O. Henry.

CAST *The Cisco Kid* Duncan Renaldo *Pancho* Leo Carillo /*pr* Walter Schwimmer /*dr* inc Lambert Hillyer /*wr* inc Walter A. Thomkins /*Ziv-TV* (USA) /152 x 26m col /US tx Syndicated 1951–6.

Citizen Smith

Comedy. BBC1 1977–80

John Sullivan-scripted sitcom which parodied the Marxist Left in the shambolic fictional form of the Tooting Popular Front. Afghan-coated busker Wolfie Smith (Robert Lindsay) was the TPF's Che Guevara wannabee; weedy Buddhist sidekick Ken, fecund Tucker, and greaser Speed filled out the guerrilla army's ranks. Shirley was Wolfie's long-suffering girlfriend (the part was taken by Lindsay's wife, Cheryl Hall), whose parents – scowling conservative Mr Johnson (the evilly brilliant Peter Vaughn, ➢*Our Friends in the North*) and dim Mrs J. (who malapropped 'Wolfie' into 'Foxie') – eventually became the urban guerrilla's landlords. Wolfie's sheer *joie de vivre* and pleasing victories over narrow-minded adulthood made him one of the most engaging creations of British TV, while his tendency to con-artistry became the inspiration for Sullivan's greatest invention, Del Boy Trotter of ➢*Only Fools and Horses* (the title of a *Citizen Smith* episode). Probably the comic futility of the British revolutionary left – which became more sharply expressed as the series progressed – was best seen in the finale to season 3, 'The Glorious Day', when Wolfie and comrades found an abandoned tank and decided to invade Parliament. Their long-dreamed desire, alas, to stand the class enemy 'up against the wall ... bop-bop-bop' failed to fruit.

Robert Lindsay was cast as Wolfie Smith on the recommendation of Sullivan, who had noticed him as cockney sharp, Jakey Smith, in the National Service sitcom ➢*Get Some In*. (That both characters shared the surname Smith was not an accident; Wolfie was partly modelled on the boy in airforce blue.) While Lindsay would later express unease at *Citizen Smith*, it brought him household fame and paved the way to the serious, heavyweight roles of ➢*GBH* and *Jake's Progress*.

'Power to the People!'

CAST *Walter 'Wolfie' Smith* Robert Lindsay *Ken* Mike Grady *Shirley* Cheryl Hall *Mrs Johnson* Hilda Braid *Charlie Johnson* Peter Vaughn/Tony Steedman/Artro Morris *Tucker* Tony Millan *Speed* George Sweeney *Harry Fenning* Stephen Greif /*cr* John Sullivan /*pr* Dennis Main Wilson /*dr* Ray Butt /*wr* John Sullivan /*BBC TV* (UK) /30 x 30m col.

The Clangers

Children's. BBC1 1969–74

Charming, counter-culture puppet show from the roach end of the 60s. The Clangers were a clan of pink knitted, mouse-like creatures who lived on a small blue moon, which they shared with the Soup Dragon and the Froglets. They wore small suits of gold armour and communicated by musical whistles; their name derived from the sound the metal dustbin-lid entrances to their burrows made when the animals dived inside to avoid meteorites. Favourite pastimes of the Clangers included eating Blue String Pudding and conversing with Iron Chicken (who lived in a nest a little way off in space). Made by the Smallfilms Company of Oliver Postgate and Peter Firmin (➢*Pingwings*, ➢*Pogle's Wood*, ➢*Ivor the Engine*, ➢*Bagpuss*, ➢*Noggin the Nog*), the series most clearly expressed the duo's anti-materialistic ideals. This was particularly observed in the episode 'Treasure', when a supply of gold coins landed on the blue planet, causing the Clanger family to become avaricious and mutually resentful. Only when Tiny discovered that the coins were made of chocolate did the Clangers resume their previous idyllic lifestyle.

cr Oliver Postgate /*pr* Oliver Postgate /*wr* Oliver Postgate /*mus* Vernon Elliott /*sfx* Peter Firmin (set and puppet design) /*Smallfilms* (UK) /27 x 9m col.

The Cleopatras

Drama. BBC2 1983

After the sublime ➢*I, Claudius*, via the preposterous ➢*The Borgias*, BBC2 finally achieved a transition to the ridiculous with *The Cleopatras*, its third ancient-historical drama series. Although it had worthy antecedents (writer Philip Mackie was the man behind ITV's ➢*The Caesars*, 1968), this saga of the legendary Greek Queens who ruled Egypt from 145 BC to 35 BC was orgiastic excess posing as culture. Billed as 'horror–comic' and recounted in flashback by the last of the Cleos (played by Michelle Newell, who also played the character's great-grandmother), it related a litany of incestuous and murderous tales. Actress Amanda Boxer shaved her head for the role of Cleopatra Tryphenae whilst her handmaidens bravely went topless and wore little more than gold paint. Richard Griffiths (➢*Bird of Prey* in the same year), in ludicrous garb, played the evil, appositely named Potbelly, among whose catalogue of misdeeds were the murder of his sister's son, marriage to the same sister, and the dismemberment of their subsequent son. Griffiths was not first choice for the part (Roy Kinnear had been approached before him) and he may well have wished that he too had declined this unfortunate opportunity.

CAST *Cleopatra* Michelle Newell *Potbelly* Richard Griffiths *Cleopatra II* Elizabeth Shepherd *Cleopatra Thea* Caroline Mortimer *Cleopatra IV* Sue Holderness *Cleopatra Tryphenae* Amanda Boxer *Cleopatra Selene* Prue Clark *Cleopatra Berenike* Pauline Moran *Mark Antony* Robert Hardy *Arinsoe* Francesca Gonshaw /*pr* Guy Slater /*dr* John Frankau /*wr* Philip Mackie *BBC TV*(UK) /8 x 50m col.

Clochmerle

Comedy. BBC2 1972

Scatological but gentle farce, adapted by Ray Galton and Alan Simpson from Gabriel Chevallier's classic 1934 novel, in which a *pissoir* is installed in a French village to unrest from the primmer natives. Evocatively filmed in the Beaujolais village of Marchampt, with a weighty cast, headed by Cyril Cusack. *Un peu objet d'art de TV.*

CAST *Mayor Barthelemy Piechut* Cyril Cusack *Curé Ponosse* Roy Dotrice *Ernest Tafardel* Kenneth Griffith *Adele Torbayon* Cyd Hayman *The Baroness Courtebiche* Micheline Presle *Justine Putet* Wendy Hiller *Alexandre Bourdillat* Hugh Griffith *Hortense Girodot* Madeline Smith *Narrator* Peter Ustinov /*pr* Michael Mills /*dr* Michael Mills /*wr* Ray Galton & Alan Simpson /*BBC TV: Bavaria Atelier GMBH* (UK:Ger) / 9 x 30m col.

Colbys

Melodrama. BBC1 1986–7

Spin-off from ➢*Dynasty* relating the sudster intrigues and traumas of the Californian Colbys, headed by oil-magnate patriarch, Jason Colby. Like its televisual parent, its storylines demanded not so much the suspension of disbelief as its hanging, drawing and quartering: one plot involved Fallon Colby (née Carrington) being whisked away to galaxies far by a UFO. The lure of easy soap money persuaded several of Hollywood's greatest to slum it, among them Charlton Heston, Katharine '*The Graduate*' Ross and Barbara Stanwyck (➢*The Big Valley*). The arch bitch, meanwhile was (*cf. Dynasty*'s Joan Collins) played by a sultry English vamp, Stephanie Beacham (*Connie*). High production costs and low ratings resulted in quick cancellation.

CAST *Jason Colby* Charlton Heston *Sable Scott Colby* Stephanie Beacham *Jeff Colby* John James *Francesca Scott Colby/Langdon* Katharine Ross *Fallon Carrington /Colby* Emma Samms *Monica Colby* Tracy Scoggins *Miles Colby* Maxwell Caulfield *Zachary Powers* Ricardo Montalban *Constance Colby* Barbara Stanwyck *Lord Roger Langdon* David Hedison /*cr* Aaron Spelling /*pr* Esther & Richard Shapiro /*dr* inc Curtis Harrington /*wr* inc Esther & Richard Shapiro, Doris Silverton, Robert Pollock, Eileen Pollock /*Aaron Spelling Productions: Fox TV* (USA) /40 x 60m col /US tx ABC 1985–7.

Colditz

Adventure. BBC1 1972–4

WWII drama in which Allied officers attempted to escape the allegedly impregnable German POW camp, Oflag IVC, more sinisterly known as Castle Colditz. Though it had its share of plucky British derring-do, it was also moodily realistic, paying due attention to the intricate psychological relationship between inmates and guards, especially the growing respect between British Lieutenant Colonel Preston and the soldierly *Kommandant* (a virtuoso performance by Bernard Hepton). After the introduction of the cooly cruel Major Mohn (Anthony Valentine with an ersatz duelling scar) and threats of an SS takeover, the series ended with the inmates' liberation by advancing Allies in May 1945. Based on the 1955 film *The Colditz Story*, itself derived from the memoirs of real-life Colditz escapee

Major Pat Reid MC. Despite being co-produced with Universal TV, it has never screened in the USA.

CAST *Lt Col. John Preston* Jack Hedley *Flt Lt Phil Carrington* Robert Wagner *Flt Lt Simon Carter* David McCallum *Capt. Pat Grant* Edward Hardwicke *Kommandant* Bernard Hepton *Lt Dick Player* Christopher Neame *Major Horst Mohn* Anthony Valentine *Capt. Tim Downing* Richard Heffer /*cr* Brian Degas, Gerard Glaister /*pr* Gerard Glaister /*dr* inc Viktors Ritelis, Phil Cregeen /*wr* inc Ian Kennedy Martin, N.J. Crisp, Troy Kennedy Martin, Bryan Forbes, Robert Muller /*BBC TV: Universal TV* (UK:USA) /28 x 50m col.

Columbo

Crime. ITV 1972–

Cases of a dishevelled detective from the LAPD. Modelled on no less than Petrovitch in Dostoevski's literary masterpiece *Crime and Punishment*, Lieutenant Columbo was possessed by an indefatigable desire for the truth and a *modus operandi* of pretended naive puzzlement ('One more thing…') which led the *haute bourgeoisie* killers whom he sleuthed to underestimate him fatally. He worked alone, although a pet basset-hound, Dog, was to be found ensconsed in his beaten-up Peugeot and his unseen wife, Kate, was later used to populate cash-in spin-off, *Mrs Columbo/Kate Loves a Mystery* (the part of the sleuthette was taken by Kate Mulgrew, later ➢*Star Trek: Voyager*). Almost uniquely for a TV cop caper, *Columbo* was a howdunnit: Columbo instinctively guessed the murderer (the viewer was anyway witness to the crime, committed at the episode's opening), only leaving the cigar-smoking, wall-eyed one to puzzle out the means and find the evidence. Those cutting their directorial teeth on the show included Steven Spielberg and Jonathan Demme. Among the show's shelf of eight Emmys, two went to Patrick McGoohan (➢*The Prisoner*) and four to Peter Falk as lead actor. Though retrospectively Falk seemed born to be Columbo, the character was first played on screen by Bert Freed in a 1961 segment of *Sunday Mystery Hour*, and Bing Crosby and Lee J. Cobb were both offered the part for a sequence of belated TVMs, but were pressed by other engagements. Thus, in shambled Falk for the 1967 TVM *Prescription: Murder*, having previously meandered through an acting career of stage, oddball movies (with

'Oh, and one last thing…' Peter Falk as shambolic Californian detective Columbo, a character modelled on Petrovitch in Dostoevski's classic novel *Crime and Punishment*.

John Cassavetes), and TV bit parts (as gangsters). Preceeding this, Falk had applied to the CIA for a job as a spook. He was turned down because of leftish sympathies. Such was the actor's charm as *Columbo* that he was accorded the part of an angel in Wim Wenders 1987 feature film *Wings of Desire*. In the early 90s, at public and industry demand, Falk once again donned a shabby raincoat to pursue the big guilty of the small screen in a new series of 120 minute files.

CAST *Lt Philip Columbo* Peter Falk /*cr* Richard Levinson, William Link /*exec pr* inc Richard Levinson, William Link, Roland Kibbee /*pr* Douglas Benton, Everett Chambers, Dean Hargrove, Richard Alan Simmons, Edward K. Dobbs, Roland Kibbee, Robert F. O'Neill /*dr* inc Steven Spielberg, Jonathan Demme, Leo Penn, Peter Falk, Patrick McGoohan, Jeannot Szwarc, Sam Wanamaker, Edward M. Abroms, Alf Kjellin /*wr* inc Steven Bochco, Larry Cohen, Roland Kibbee, Richard Levinson, William Link, Barney Slater / *Universal TV* (USA) /27 x 90m, approx 42 x 120m col /US tx NBC 1971–7, 1991–.

Combat

Drama. ITV 1967

Stark cinematic war serial which chronicled the progress of a US Army platoon, led by Lieutenant Gil Hanley and Sergeant Chip Saunders (Vic Morrow), across Europe in the wake of D-Day 1944. Filmed at MGM's Lot Two, mostly in grainy black and white, the resolutely realistic, anti-war *Combat* benefitted much from the influence of Robert Altman (a WWII veteran himself) who used the opportunity to hone his directorial skills – later evidenced in such movies as *M*A*S*H* and *The Player* – in segments he regarded as 'mini movies'. Star Vic Morrow, after the closure of the show, acted only sporadically (including the risible ➢*BAD Cats*); he died in 1982 in an accident on the set of *The Twilight Zone* movie.

CAST *Sgt Chip Saunders* Vic Morrow *Lt Gil Hanley* Rick Jason *PFC Paul 'Caje' Lemay* Pierre Jalbert *Pte William G. Kirby* Jack Hogan *Littlejohn* Dick Peabody *Doc Walton* Steven Rogers *Doc* Conlan Carter *Pte Braddock* Shecky Greene *Pte Billy Nelson* Tom Lowell / *exec pr* Selig Seligman / *pr* Gene Levitt, Robert Blees, Burt Kennedy / *dr* inc Robert Altmann, Vic Morrow, Burt Kennedy, Dick Caffey / *wr* inc Robert Altman, John D.F. Black, Vic Morrow / *mus* Leonard Rosenman / *Selmur Productions* (USA) /152 x 60m bw:col /US tx ABC 1962–7.

Come Dancing

Light Entertainment. BBC 1949–

'From the Assembly Rooms in Derby...'

The world's longest-running TV music programme was begat in 1949 by Eric 'Miss World' Morley. Initially a dance showcase and home tuition programme (Syd Perkins and Edna Duffield did the steps for viewers to copy around the sitting room), the show assumed its famed amateur dance competition form in 1959. Encased in shiny sequins and with faces set in permanent grimace, lookalike regional teams have, over the decades, glided out the foxtrot, the waltz, the cha-cha-cha and the *paso doble*, but also the less than strictly ballroom style of rock'n'roll. Brian 'Johnners' Johnston, Michael Aspel OBE, Noel Edmonds, Terry Wogan and Angela Rippon topped a long line of surprisingly illustrious compères, some of whom have not been blind to the show's increasingly camp appeal.

CAST (presenters) inc McDonald Hobley, Sylvia Peters, Peter Dimmock, Peter West, Brian Johnston, Pete Murray, Keith Fordyce, Stuart Hall, Michael Aspel, Judith Chalmers, Terry Wogan, Noel Edmonds, Peter Marshall, Angela Rippon, David Jacobs, Rosemarie Ford / *cr* Eric Morley / *pr* inc Barrie Edgar, Ray Lakeland, Philip Lewis, Ken Griffin, Simon Betts / *dr* inc Reg Perrin, Simon Betts, David Pickthall / *mus* (performers) inc Phil Moss and His Orchestra, The Ken Mackintosh Orchestra, Andy Ross and His Orchestra / *BBC TV* (UK) /500+ x 35m bw:col.

Comedy Playhouse

Comedy. BBC1 1961–74/ITV 1993

BBC showcase for 'comedy playlets' with the process of natural selection – i.e. audience reaction – determining which would fall into extinction and which would evolve into series. Originally, all scripts were written by Alan Simpson and Ray Galton but, over time, other writers were invited to cast their creations onto the airwaves, among them Johnny Speight and Richard Waring. The numerous influential sitcoms which began their life on *Comedy Playhouse* included ➢*Steptoe and Son*, ➢*Till Death Us Do Part*, ➢*The Liver Birds*, ➢*All Gas and Gaiters*, ➢*Last of the Summer Wine* and, horror of TV horrors, ➢*Happy Ever After*, the forerunner of ➢*Terry and June*. The concept was revived in 1993 by Carlton, giving life to two (meritricious) series, *The 10%ers* and *Brighton Belles*, the British take on ➢*The Golden Girls*.

cr Tom Sloan / *wr* inc Alan Simpson & Ray Galton, Johnny Speight, Richard Waring, Roy Clarke, Carla Lane, Edwin Apps & Pauline Devaney, John Chapman & Eric Merriman, Hugh Leonard / *BBC TV: Carlton TV* (UK) /40 x 30m bw:col.

The Comic Strip Presents...

Comedy. C4 1983–9/BBC2 1990–2/1998

This was the progress to TV of Peter Richardson's Soho-based The Comic Strip club, the veritable crucible of 80s alternative humour, the change of medium overseen by impressario Michael White. The first small-screen offering, 'Five Go Mad in Dorset', transmitted on C4's opening night in 1982, ruthlessly spoofed Enid Blyton and was finished to perfection with a cameo by ➢*Crossroads*' Ronald Allen as dubious Uncle Quentin ('I'm a screaming homosexual, you little prigs.'). Post-modernist parody proved the mainstay of the ensuing *The Comic Strip* series, the pop-culture targets ranging from the music industry ('The Bad News Tour') to TV ('The Bullshitters', a send-up of the ultra-macho ➢*The Professionals* with Keith Allen and Richardson as Bonehead and Foyle), via – especially – film genres galore ('Slags', 'A Fist Full of Travellers Cheques', 'The Yob'). Richardson's preoccupation with cinema led to what was *The Comic Strip* apogee, the 1988 'Strike', a Hollywood socialist epic version of the British 1984–5 miners' dispute, with Richardson as Al Pacino playing Arthur Scargill, Jennifer Saunders as Meryl Streep playing Scargill's spouse, and Alexei Sayle as the committed leftist writer whose work is distorted for profit. The Hollywood treatment continued in 'GLC', which saw Robbie Coltrane as Charles Bronson playing Ken Livingstone, by which time (1990) *The Comic Strip* had decamped from C4 to BBC2. Although Richardson and team would produce 15 'films' for the Corporation, these tended to be reheats of previous themes and few lodged in folkloric memory, save for 'The Crying Game', the story of gay footballer Roy Brush and his hounding by *The Scum* newspaper. Yet, as *The Comic Strip*'s own star waned, those of its members who pursued individual TV careers waxed large (the two developments were not entirely unconnected) in ➢*The Young Ones*, ➢*Alexei Sayle's Stuff*, ➢*French and Saunders*, ➢*Bottom* and a score more. There was also a brace of *Comic Strip* cinema movies, *The Supergrass* (1985) and *Eat the Rich* (1987), both directed by Richardson, who also helmed many of the TV episodes. Also on the *Strip*'s director's list were Stephen Frears (the movies *My Beautiful Laundrette*, *Dangerous Liaisons*, *The Grifters*) and quick-flick specialist Paul Bartel (*Death Race 2000*, *Eating Raoul*). A *Comic Strip* reunion special, *Four Men in a Car*, was screened in 1998.

CAST Peter Richardson, Adrian Edmondson, Rik Mayall, Nigel Planer, Jennifer Saunders, Dawn French, Alexei Sayle, Daniel Peacock, Robbie Coltrane, Keith Allen; also inc Pauline Melville, Kathy Burke, Julie T. Wallace, Josie Lawrence, Miranda Richardson, Sara Stockridge /*cr* Peter Richardson /*exec pr* Michael White, Peter Richardson /*pr* Michael White (C4), Lolli Kimpton (BBC2) /*dr* inc Peter Richardson, Keith Allen, Paul Bartel, Robbie Coltrane, Stephen Frears, Bob Spiers, Adrian Edmondson /*wr* inc Peter Richardson, Peter Richens, Adrian Edmondson, Rik Mayall, Dawn French, Jennifer Saunders, Nigel Planer, Alexei Sayle, Keith Allen, Pauline Melville, Roland Rivron, David Stafford, Barry Dennen, Robbie Coltrane, Morag Fullerton /*Filmworks: Comic Strip* (UK) /21 x 45–60m col, 15 x 30m col.

Common as Muck

Comedy. BBC1 1995–7

Binmen drama scripted by former ➢*Coronation Street* actor William ('Billy') Ivory. Set in Hepworth, it touched emotional poignancy as well as comedy, particularly when tracing the struggling-but-dignified fortunes of the crew on their dismissal from the dustcart service. Thus it was frequently held up as a ➢*The Boys from the Black Stuff* for the mid-90s (and not only because of the subject matter; Ivory had something of Bleasdale's ability with eye-catching working-class scenes, e.g. Nev's retirement drive-past of veteran dustcarts). Too many half-baked plots (usually involving apostasy and redemption) in series 2, however.

CAST *Nev* Edward Woodward *Ken* Neil Dudgeon *Foxy* Tim Healy *Bernard* Richard Ridings *Jonno* Stephen Lord *Sunil* Anthony Barclay *John Parry* Roy Hudd *Marie* Michelle Holmes *Irene* June Whitfield /*cr* William Ivory /*pr* John Chapman, Catherine Wearing / dr Metin Huseyin /*wr* William Ivory /*BBC TV* (UK) / 11 x 60m, 1 x 75m col.

Compact

Melodrama. BBC1 1962–5

Twice-weekly (Tuesdays and Thursdays) serial set in the editorial offices of a woman's magazine, where the 'temperamental and talented staff' politicked and dallied romantically. Invented by writers Hazel Adair and Peter Ling, the sudster show attracted mild controversy for its daring-for-the-time storylines, such as youthful reefer madness and unmarried motherhood. The cast, meanwhile, were frequently encumbered by such leaden lines of script as: 'It can only mean one thing. Trouble.' Those suffering from trouble at the office included bouffanted female editor Joanne Minster (male prejudice), who left to have her swivel chair filled by the suave Ian Harmon (Ronald Allen), son of Sir Charles, the owner of controlling company Harmon Enterprises Incorporated, Ltd. Though the show achieved respectable ratings, it lagged behind ITV rival, ➢*Emergency – Ward 10*, and the BBC closed the page on *Compact*, its second-only venture – after

➢*The Grove Family* – into soap opera. Unabashed, Adair and Ling went on to create ➢*Crossroads*, in which Ronald Allen would also appear.

CAST *Joanne Minster* Jean Harvey *Mark* Gareth Davies *Gussie* Frances Bennett *Ian* Ronald Allen *Richard* Moray Watson *Mike* Clinton Green *Jimmy* Nicholas Selby *Camilla* Carmen Silvera /*cr* Hazel Adair & Peter Ling /*pr* inc Chris Barry, Alan Bromly, Morris Barry, Bernard Hepton, Douglas Allen /*dr* inc Vere Lorrimer, Chris Barry, Joan Craft, Michael Hart /*wr* inc Hazel Adair & Peter Ling /*BBC TV* (UK) /373 x 30m bw.

Cop Rock

Crime. BBC1 1991

A bizarre curio from the otherwise sane hit-meister, Steven Bochco (➢*Hill Street Blues*, ➢*LA Law*, ➢*NYPD Blue*), developed as part of his $50 million contract with ABC, which handcuffed musical fantasy to downtown Los Angeles police drama. Whenever anyone had a problem – be they police officer, criminal, judge or jury – they broke into song about it; a BMW-owner, for instance, on watching his car impounded, wailed a soulful 'I want my Beemer back!' Bafflement, then boredom, caused viewers to switch off and the show was cancelled after a mere 11 episodes. Bochco's actress wife Barabara Bosson (also a regular on ➢*Hill Street* and *Hooperman*) played Louise Plank, the city's 'iron lady' mayor.

CAST *Mayor Louise Plank* Barbara Bosson *Chief Roger Kendrick* Ronny Cox *Det. Vincent LaRusso* Peter Onorati *Capt. John Hollander* Larry Joshua *Off. Franklin Rose* James McDaniel *Off. Andy Campo* David Gianopoulos *Det. Ralph Ruskin* Ron McLarty /*cr* Steven Bochco, William Finkelstein /*exec pr* Steven Bochco, William Finkelstein /*mus* Randy Newman ('Under the Gun' theme) /*Fox TV* (USA) /11 x 60m col /US tx ABC 1990.

Coronation Street

Melodrama. ITV 1960–

Originally to be titled *Florizel Street* until a tea-lady at Granada pointed out that Florizel sounded like a lavatory cleaner, this nostlagic soap set in a terraced backstreet of the fictional Manchester district of Weatherfield is the world's longest-running drama show. It is also, with 18 million plus viewers per episode, Britain's most popular programme. Created by former child actor and ➢*Biggles* writer Tony Warren, '*Corrie*' has changed much since its early episodes, which were 'Grim up North' dramas, populated by ever-so proletarian characters, epitomized by hairnet harridan Ena Sharples, who supped stout in the snug of the Rovers Return. The issues of the real world occasionally intruded in these initial years (Sharples' house knocked down by ideological 60s planners, troublesome teenager Lucille Hewitt – who wore a skirt up to there – running away from home), but gradually the show was given a lighter tone which has continued to this day, despite a brief, bruising brush with social realism under the producership of Susi Hush (later ➢*Grange Hill*). Of the British soaps, it is the least interested in 'issues'; indeed, its time-warped 50s cobblestone morality virtually precludes them, hence the near-absence of blacks, AIDs victims, crack addicts and homosexuals in the street or the Rovers Return. To the competition offered by upstart 80s soaps ➢*Brookside* and ➢*EastEnders*, the response of *Corrie* was to slip subtly into outright comedy. The demise of Mavis 'Oh, Rita!' Wilton's budgie has even been held to rival ➢*Monty Python*'s dead parrot sketch.

Aside from humour and its reassuring proletarian folksiness, *Coronation Street* provides the TV equivalent of over-the-fence neighbourhood gossip, telling 'everyday' tales of petty scandals and adulteries (most celebratedly that between Mike Baldwin and Deidre Barlow in 1983, which was even reported in *The Times*). Although *Corrie*'s highest viewing figure of 27 million was for the 1987 episode in which Alan Bradley attempted the murder of Kabin owner Rita Fairclough, such high drama is doled out like rare gems. Character-driven instead of issue-led, the show, in a shrewd pitch at the main sudster-viewing base, has made something of a speciality of strong women characters: cut-glass publican Annie Walker, curlered char Hilda Ogden, home-maker Gail Platt, gossip Martha Longhurst, brassy barmaid Bet Lynch (Julie Goodyear OBE), and the longtime queen of the street, flashing-eyed Elsie Tanner (Pat Phoenix, wife of Tony Booth from ➢*Till Death Us Do Part*). The *Street*'s women have, however, become softened over the years. Rita Fairclough's dubious past as exotic dancer working with a trombone act has been shrugged off, while man-eaters Audrey Roberts (Sue Nicholls, ➢*Crossroads*) and Amanda Barrie (aka Shirley Ann Broadbent, previously Cleopatra in *Carry On Cleo*) have become tamed.

Even semi-prostitute Elsie Tanner ended up being almost respectable, while such a daffy modern creation as Raquel Wolstenhulme (Sarah Lancashire, daughter of *Corrie* scriptwriter Geoffrey Lancashire) would not have lasted a day with the ladies of the old *Street*. *Corrie* men, by contrast, have tended to be reduced to one of three stereotypes: the lothario hardman (Len Fairclough, Mike Baldwin), the irascible pensioner (Albert Tatlock, Percy Sugden) and the comic foil (Eddie Yates, Stan Ogden, Jack Duckworth). The most obvious exception is the bourgoisified Ken Barlow (Captain William Roache, ex-Royal Fusiliers), now the only survivor of the original *Street* residents.

Despite its resolutely northern setting, *Coronation Street* has sold around the world. Only the USA proved immune to its charms, although the ABC network sought to emulate its success by creating a neighbourhood soap of its own – ➢*Peyton Place.*

While they may now be embarrassed by the fact, many famous thespian faces started their careers with roles in Weatherfield. They number among them: Joanna Lumley (a Barlow girlfriend), Martin Shaw (hippie squatter), Michael 'Boon' Elphick, Paula Wilcox, Oscar-winner Ben Kingsley (a silver-tongued seducer), popster Peter Noone of Herman's Hermits (as a son of Len Fairclough), ➢*The Monkees*' Davy Jones (Ena Sharples' grandson), Prunella Scales, Arthur Lowe (whose portrait of draper Leonard Swindley was spun off in *Pardon the Expression*), Gordon Kaye, Joanne Whalley-Kilmer, Richard Beckinsale, Mollie Sugden (landlady of 'The Laughing Donkey'), Ray Brooks, Michael Ball and Peter Dean.

Originally screened live twice a week, the show went thrice-weekly in 1989. Since 1996 the show has been sponsored by chocolate makers, Cadbury.

CAST *Ena Sharples* Violet Carson *Annie Walker* Doris Speed *Jack Walker* Arthur Leslie *Elsie Tanner* Pat Phoenix *Hilda Ogden* Jean Alexander *Stan Ogden* Bernard Youens *Minnie Caldwell* Margot Bryant *Bet Gilroy (née Lynch)* Julie Goodyear *Len Fairclough* Peter Adamson *Albert Tatlock* Jack Howarth *Ken Barlow* William Roache *Ray Langton* Neville Buswell *Martha Longhurst* Lynne Carol *Leonard Swindley* Arthur Lowe *Deirdre Barlow (née Hunt)* Anne Kirkbride *Rita Sullivan (Fairclough)* Barbara Knox *Emily Nugent (Bishop)* Eileen Derbyshire *Ernie Bishop* Stephen Hancock *Billy Walker* Kenneth Farrington *Betty Turpin* Betty Driver *Maggie Clegg* Irene Sutcliff *Mike Baldwin* Johnny Briggs *Eddie Yates* Geoffrey Hughes *Mavis Wilton* Thelma Barlow *Derek Wilton* Peter Baldwin *Alf Roberts* Bryan Mosley *Audrey Roberts* Sue Nicholls *Gail Tilsley (née Platt)* Helen Worth *Brian Tilsley* Christopher Quentin *Ivy Brennan (née Tilsley)* Lynn Perrie *Don Brennan* Geoff Hinsliff *Alma Sedgewick* Amanda Barrie *Suzie Birchall* Cheryl Murray *Vera Duckworth* Elizabeth Dawn *Jack Duckworth* William Tarmey *Alec Gilroy* Roy Barraclough *Curly Watts* Kevin Kennedy *Raquel Watts (Wolstenhulme)* Sarah Lancashire *Percy Sugden* Bill Waddington *Phyllis Pearce* Jill Summers *Reg Holdsworth* Ken Morley *Des Barnes* Philip Middlemass *Steph Barnes* Amelia Bullmore *Jim McDonald* Charles Lawson *Liz McDonald* Beverly Callard *Kevin Webster* Michael Le Vell *Sally Webster* Sally Whitaker /*cr* Tony Warren /*pr* inc H.V. Kershaw, Bill Podmore, Tim Aspinall, Stuart Latham, Susi Hush, Eric Pryterch, Mervyn Watson, Jack Rosenthal, David Liddiment /*dr* inc Quentin Lawrence, Lawrence Moody, June Wyndham-Davies, Richard Argent / *wr* inc Tony Warren, H.V. Kershaw, Vince Powell, Harry Driver, Jack Rosenthal, John Finch, Adele Rose, Geoffrey Lancashire, Julian Roach, Kay Mellor /*mus* Eric Spear /*Granada TV* (UK) /4500+ x 30m bw:col, 2 x 60m col.

The Corridor People

Crime. ITV 1966

Self-consciously absurd, ➢*The Avengers*-influenced thriller series featuring an international villainess, Syrie Van Epp (Elizabeth Shepherd) and her various outlandish schemes – e.g. kidnapping the inventor of a perfume which caused amnesia. Those on her trail were private eye, Scrotty, and Kronk, Blood and Hound of the Yard. Short-lived, but stylish.

CAST *Phil Scrotty* Gary Cockrell *Kronk* John Sharp *Insp. Blood* Alan Curtis *Sgt Hound* William Maxwell *Syrie Van Epp* Elizabeth Shepherd /*cr* Edward Boyd /*pr* Richard Everitt /*dr* David Boisseau /*Granada TV* (UK) / 4 x 60m bw.

The Cosby Show

Comedy. C4 1986–94

Although Bill Cosby (➢*I Spy*, *The Bill Cosby Show*, *Captain Kangaroo*, *Fat Albert and the Cosby Kids*) had been a TV item for nearly two decades, few gave this comedy of domestic drolleries much hope of success; it was a sitcom at a time when the genre was held to be in decline and, worse, it was about a black family. Whites, it was feared, would turn off. This wisdom did not last *The Cosby Show*'s first season; by 1985 it had risen to No. 1 in the Nielsens, staying there for five years running, a record only ever surpassed by ➢*All in the Family*. What audiences watched were poignant and gently amusing moments (episodes were frequently plotless) in the life of the middle-class Huxtables, headed by caring Cliff (Cosby's most sensitive performance to date), an obstetrician, and wife, Clair, a lawyer (Phylicia Ayers-Allen, sister of ➢*Fame*'s Debbie Allen). Sharing their NY home at 10 Stigwood Avenue, Brooklyn Heights, were offspring Denise, Theo, Vanessa, Rudy and Sondra, all of whom were high achievers. The show was a conscious crusade by Cosby to enlighten: it was a role-model parade for blacks, a lesson in anti-racism for Caucasians and, above all, instruction for everybody on how to bring up children (i.e. with tolerance and love). Significantly, Cosby styled himself William H. Cosby Jr, Doctor of Education, in early episodes. *The Cosby Show* won four Emmys (Outstanding Comedy Series, 1985; Outstanding Writing in a Comedy Series, 1985; Outstanding Guest Performer in a Comedy Series – Roscoe Lee Browne, 1986; Outstanding Directing in a Comedy series – Jay Sandrich, 1986) and also made 'the Cos' one of the richest men in showbiz. A 1987 spin-off, entitled *A Different World*, related Denise Huxtable's experiences on leaving the family brownstone for Hillman College. Even with the benefit of an extended last *Cosby* episode, Cliff was unable to fix the hall chimes.

CAST *Dr Heathcliff 'Cliff' Huxtable* Bill Cosby *Clair Huxtable* Phylicia Rashad (née Ayers-Allen) *Denise Huxtable* Lisa Bonet *Sondra Huxtable* Sabrina LeBeauf *Vanessa Huxtable* Tempestt Bledsoe *Theodore Huxtable* Malcolm Jamal-Warner *Rudy Huxtable* Keshia Knight Pulliam *Pam Turner* Erika Alexander *Russell Huxtable* Earle Hyman *Anna Huxtable* Clarice Taylor /*cr* Ed Weinberger, Michael Leeson, William H. Cosby Jr, EdD /*exec pr* Marcy Carsey, Tom Werner /*pr* inc John Markus, Terri Guarnieri, Matt Williams /*dr* inc Jay Sandrich /*wr* inc Ed Weinberger, Michael Leeson, John Markus, Chris Auer, Gary Knott, Bill Cosby /*mus* Stu Gardner & Bill Cosby (theme) /*A Carsey-Werner Production in Association with Bill Cosby* (USA) / 196 x 25m, 4 x 60m col /US tx NBC 1984–93.

Countdown

Light Entertainment. C4 1982–

Deriving its format from the French quiz show *Des Chiffres et des Lettres*, *Countdown* became the highest-rated UK daytime programme; it was also a Junior Common Room cult, famous for the bumbling patter of patronizing presenter, Richard Whiteley, and mental arithmetic of numbers and letters dispenser, Carol Vorderman (the 'thinking person's crumpet' of the 80s, what Joan Bakewell had been to the previous generation). Part of the show's charm was its distinct lack of hi-tech – contestants had nothing more than pen and paper – and the opportunity it offered viewers to compete on an equal footing from the safety of the home sofa. Two contestants were required to construct, in 30 seconds, the longest word they could from nine randomly-drawn letters. A numbers round was also included in which contestants had to manipulate numbers, again randomly selected ('one from the top please, Carol'), to arrive at a specified total. The ultimate round was the 'Countdown conundrum', a ten-letter anagram to be solved a.s.a.p. Contestants' answers were verified by a guest celebrity. Those occupying 'Dictionary Corner' included Ted Moult, Kenneth Williams, Richard Stilgoe and be-jumpered Giles Brandreth, a Conservative MP-in-waiting. Former World Scrabble Champion Mark Nyman co-produced.

To doubly ensure its place in the TV book of records, *Countdown* was also the first ever programme broadcast on Channel 4 (4.45 p.m. on Tuesday 2 November 1982).

CAST (presenters) Richard Whiteley, Carol Vorderman, plus hostesses Beverley Isherwood, Kathy Hynter /*cr* Armand Jammot /*exec pr* John Meades, Frank Smith /*pr* Mark Nyman, Michael Whylie /*dr* John Meades /*Yorkshire TV* (UK) /2000+ x 30m col.

Count Duckula

Children's. ITV 1988–93

Animated misadventures of fowl Count Duckula, the world's first vegan vampire (courtesy of an accidental transfusion of tomato ketchup), which spoofed the horror genre to droll comic effect, most elaborately evidenced in the episode 'Return of the Curse of the Secret of the Mummy's Tomb meets Franken Duckula's Monster'. The Christopher Lee-like duck was accompanied on his disasters by sinister manservant Igor, and dim-bulb housekeeper Nanny. A spin-off from ➢*Danger Mouse*, it likewise featured the vocal talents of David Jason (with the addition of, among others, comic Ruby Wax) and made a calculated play for the mom'n'pop market, even punning Bob Dylan songs with the episode titles 'Transylvanian Homesick Blues' and 'I Don't Want to Work on Maggot's Farm No More'.

CAST (voices) *Count Duckula* David Jason *Igor* Jack May *Nanny* Brian Trueman *Von Goosewing* Jimmy Hibbert *Narrator* Brian Clayton /*cr* Mike Harding, Brian Trueman /*pr* Brian Cosgrove, Mark Hall, John Hambley /*dr* Chris Randall /*wr* Brian Trueman, Jimmy Hibbert, Peter Richard Reeves, Jan Needle, Jon Sayle, John Broadhead, Joyce McCleer /*Cosgrove Hall TV: Thames TV* (UK) /65 x 25m col /US tx Nickleodeon 1988.

The Count of Monte Cristo

Adventure. ITV 1956

The sword-rattling adventures of Alexander Dumas' 18th-century hero, Edmund Dantes, were a natural port of call for 50s ITV, given its post-➢*The Adventures of Robin Hood* proclivity for costume actioners. The role of the wrongly imprisoned Dantes, who breaks free of his shackles to seize lost treasure on the island of Monte Cristo and thence set himself up as a nobleman, was played by George Dolenz, father of ➢*The Monkees*'s Mickey Dolenz. Nick Cravat played Cristo's faithful mute companion, Jacopo, in the acrobatic style he had begun in the 1950 cinema swashbuckler *The Flame and the Arrow*. The show, which largely 'sequelized' Dumas' novel and transformed Cristo into a Gallic righter-of-wrongs, had the distinction of having its opening three-part episode directed by Hollywood veteran overseer Budd Boeticher. Like the subsequent episodes, it was shown on US TV before receiving its British screening. An animated *The Count of Monte Cristo* (17 x 30m col), with Dantes superheroed-up, was made by Halas and Batchelor (/RAI) for European television in 1973.

CAST *Edmund Dantes, the Count of Monte Cristo* George Dolenz *Jacopo* Nick Cravat *Rico* Robert Cawdron /*pr* Leon Fromkess, Hal Roach Jr, Sidney Marshall, Dennis Vance /*dr* inc Budd Boeticher, Charles Bennett, Dennis Vance, David McDonald, Sidney Salkow /*ITC* (UK) /39 x 30m bw /US tx Syndicated 1956.

Cracker

Crime. ITV 1993–6

Pessimistic, brooding *policier* featuring a psychologist who helps the Greater Manchester Police Force with their murder inquiries. Criminal profiles, interviewing techniques and mind reading were just a few of corpulent Dr Eddie 'Fitz' Fitzgerald's special skills. But that was his professional life. At home, like all the best TV crime beaters, his life was in tatters and his wife Judith walked out on him, leaving him free to embark on a tempestuous affair with Detective Sergeant Jane 'Panhandle' Penhaligon, the woman usually assigned to accompany him on missions. With deftly braided plots, a Dostoevskian central hero of Falstafian appetites (alcohol, cigarettes, gambling, women) who seeks not whodunit but whydunnit, *Cracker* was universally acclaimed. Even when the show dispensed with any real semblance of proper police work and creator Jimmy McGovern exhibited an inclination to masochistically kill off main characters, the performances of the cast, especially that of Robbie Coltrane (previously *A Kick Up the Eighties*, ➢*The Comic Strip Presents...*, ➢*Tutti Frutti*) as Fitz, held everything mesmerically together. Intense, graphic and unafraid to take on taboos – rape, serial killing, homosexuality the series had as its adviser psychologist Ian Stephen, the man who helped police track down the notorious serial killer Bible John in 1969.

CAST *Eddie 'Fitz' Fitzgerald* Robbie Coltrane *Judith Fitzgerald* Barbara Flynn *Det. Sgt Jane Penhaligon* Geraldine Somerville *Det. Chief Insp. David Bilborough* Christopher Eccleston *Det. Sgt Jimmy Beck* Lorcan Cranitch *Chief Insp. Wise* Ricky Tomlinson /*cr* Jimmy McGovern /*pr* Gub Neal, Paul Abbott, Hilary Bevan Jones /*dr* inc Roy Battersby, Julian Jerrold /*wr* Jimmy McGovern, Paul Abbott, Ted Whitehead /*Granada TV* (UK) /12 x 60m, 1 x 75m, 1 x 90m col.

Crackerjack

Children's. BBC 1955–84

Originally transmitted fortnightly at 5.15 p.m., it remains stuck in the memory as a weekly that opened: 'It's Friday, it's five to five, and it's *Crackerjack*!' Derived from the variety/music-hall tradition, *Crackerjack* mixed slapstick sketches (notably those of Leslie Crowther and former Crazy Gang extra, Peter Glaze, although Jack

'Carry On' Douglas, Ronnie Corbett, Don Maclean, and Little and Large also performed sterling comic service) and pop music. In between were segregated competitions for boys and girls, most famously the quiz *Double or Drop*, which rewarded the junior contestants' wrong answers with armfuls of booby-prize cabbages. Win or lose, competitors went home with a *Crackerjack* pencil, the envy of their scrub-kneed friends.

CAST (presenters) Eamon Andrews, Leslie Crowther, Michael Aspel, Ed 'Stewpot' Stewart & Stu Francis /*pr* Johnny Downes, Peter Whitmore, Brian S. Jones, Robin Nash, Paul Ciani /*dr* inc Johnny Downes /*wr* inc Bob Block /*BBC TV* (UK) /approx 400 x 30m bw:col.

Crane
Adventure. ITV 1963–65

Tired of suburban life, Richard Crane (lantern-jawed, boom-voiced Patrick Allen) emigrated to Morocco, where he donned a panama hat and opened a beachfront bar. He also did a lucrative trade in smuggling contraband (though nothing viewer-alarming like guns or drugs), despite the efforts of fastidious police chief, Colonel Mahmoud.

Popular, stylish nonsense which spun-off a children's show, *Orlando* (played by Sam Kydd), based around Crane's eccentric criminal accomplice of that moniker. After playing the adventurer abroad, Patrick Allen starred in numerous series (*Brett*, *Hard Times*, *Glencannon*, ➢*The Winds of War*) but is doomed to be forever remembered as the helicopter-borne salesman in the Barrett homes commercial.

CAST *Richard Crane* Patrick Allen *Orlando O'Connor* Sam Kydd *Colonel Mahmoud* Gerald Flood *Halima* Laya Raki /*cr* Patrick Allen, Jordan Lawrence /*pr* Jordan Lawrence /*dr* inc Raymond Menmuir, Richard Doubleday, Christopher Hodson /*wr* inc Terence Feely, Patrick Tilley, James Mitchell /*Associated Rediffusion* (UK) /120 x 30m bw.

Crapston Villas
Comedy. C4 1995–

Animated soap opera from the ➢*Spitting Image* team, set in a crumbling Victorian villa in south-east London, with piles of cat-sick humour. The characters were unnervingly well-observed, none more so than the 'resting' film-maker, Jonathan (complete with pretentious goatee), and down-trodden girlfriend, who lived in slug-ridden Flat B. They shared the pad with cutesie actress Flossie, who saw life in SE69 as 'just like being in a documentary', and the rest of the house with the dysfunctional, sex-crazed Stenson family, and gay couple Robbie and Larry. Modern urban life made video. Among the famous lending their voices (at Equity minimum) were Jane Horrocks and Alison Steadman.

CAST (voices) Jane Horrocks, Steve Steen, Alison Steadman, Liz Smith, Morwenna Banks /*cr* Sarah Anne Kennedy /*pr* Richard Bennett /*dr* Sarah Anne Kennedy /*wr* Sarah Anne Kennedy /*Spitting Image Productions* (UK) /9 x 30m col.

Crime Story
Crime. ITV 1989

Tough-looking period 60s cop show from Michael Mann which, like his uncharacteristically marsh-mallow ➢*Miami Vice*, mixed pulsating music (here such classics as Del Shannon's 'Runaway') with carefully posed visuals. Set in a Chicago beset by racketeering and almost constantly enveloped by night, *Crime Story* detailed the dogged efforts of Lieutenant Mike Torello (Dennis Farina) of the city's Major Crime Unit to bring slippery rising mobster Ray Luca (Anthony Denison) to book. Authenticity was provided by co-creator Chuck Adamson's having served 18 years on the Chicago PD, and casting half- and un-known actors from the right-stuff backgrounds: Farina had actually served in the unit which inspired the show and Denison was an ex-professional gambler. Post *Crime Story*, Mann has largely exercised his talents in the movies.

CAST *Lt Michael Torello* Dennis Farina *Pauli Taglia* John Santucci *Ray Luca* Anthony Denison *Attorney David Abrams* Stephen Lang /*cr* Chuck Adamson, Gustave Reininger /*exec pr* Michael Mann /*dr* inc Michael Mann /*mus* Del Shannon ('Runaway' theme) /*New World TV* (USA) /48 x 60m col.

Criss Cross Quiz
Light Entertainment. ITV 1957–67

Hugely popular (reaching No. 6 in the BARB ratings) general-knowledge game based on noughts and crosses, derived from the American format *Tic Tac Dough.* The host was Jeremy Hawk, father of Belinda ➢'*2 Point 4 Children*' Lang, who also presented a kiddie-time version, *Junior Criss Cross Quiz.* Other *Junior CCQ* presenters included Bob Holness, Bill Grundy (of Sex Pistols interview infamy) and soccer legend Danny Blanchflower.

CAST (presenters) Jeremy Hawk /*dr* inc Graeme Macdonald, Philip Casson /*Redifusion* (UK) / 342+ x 25m bw.

The Critic

Comedy. Bravo 1995

The success of ➢*The Simpsons* caused much pitching of 'toon' ideas at US networks; *The Critic* – made by the producers of *The Simpsons* – was one of the few to fruit, running to a single season. Its title character was unattractive Manhattan film critic Jay Sherman (any resemblance to reviewer Roger Ebert was, naturally, purely coincidental), host of the little-watched cable show 'Coming Attractions', where he bitterly pilloried the latest releases, none of which could meet his impossibly high standards. Workplace irritations came in the form of his megalomaniacal, brusque boss (any resemblance to CNN's Ted Turner was, of course, purely coincidental), and make-up lady Doris, who sprayed his shining pate with artificial hair.

CAST (voices) *Jay Sherman* Jon Lovitz *Duke Phillips* Charles Napier *Doris* Doris Grau *Margo* Nancy Cartwright *Jeremy Hawke* Maurice LaMarche *Marty Sherman* Christine Cavanaugh /*exec pr* James L. Brooks, Al Jean, Mike Reiss, Phil Roman /*pr* Richard Sakai, Richard Raynis /*Gracie Films: Columbia Pictures Television* (USA) /23 x 30m col /US tx TCC 1994.

Crossroads

Melodrama. ITV 1964–88

'Crossroads Motel, may I help you?'

These words opened ATV's sudster answer to ➢*Coronation Street*, but the production values and acting proved so legendarily poor that the IBA ordered its weekly output to be restricted to three (down from five) episodes per week. Set in King's Oak on the edge of a Midland's conurbation, the *Crossroad*'s motel was ruled over by matriarch Meg Richardson (ex-*Lunch Box* performer Noele Gordon) and her family. If Meg's life – injury in a bomb explosion, imprisonment for dangerous driving, desertion at the altar, poisoning by lover Malcolm Rider, husband Hugh's kidnapping by terrorists and his subsequent death – was tragic, much worse awaited her daughter Jill. Over *Crossroads*' near 24 years, Jill was married three times (once to a bigamist), had a baby by her stepbrother, became a drug addict, became an alcoholic, and had two miscarriages and a nervous breakdown. Somewhat surprisingly, perhaps, Jill was the only member of the orginal cast to make it to the final episode. Her brother Sandy, meanwhile, was disabled in a motor accident. After Tragedy, the most regular callers at Crossroads were Inconsistency and Improbability. Characters came and went without explanation. The motel idiot Benny (he of the woollen bobble hat and the 'Miss Dianes') once disappeared for six months after 'going to fetch a spanna', while Sandy went MIA for nearly a year before a minor character casually remarked that he had died. Bizarrely, the mole on the face of Barbara Hunter, wife of sometime motel manager David 'Hulloh' Hunter (Ronald Allen, ➢*Compact*, ➢*United!*) moved from episode to episode, and char Amy Turtle was accused of being a spy, Amy Turtleovski.

It has been estimated that 20,000 actors and actresses passed through the portals of *Crossroads*, among them Malcolm McDowell (➢*Our Friends in the North*), Diane Keen, Elaine Paige, Larry Grayson (Meg's wedding chauffeur), Gretchen Franklin (later in ➢*EastEnders*), black actor Carl Andrews (whose character Joe McDonald was the first Afro-Caribbean to be a regular in a British soap), and Stephanie de Sykes, whose motel rendition of 'Born with a Smile on My Face' reached No. 2 in the charts in 1974. Nor was Sykes the only motel singer; the Hon. Sue Nicholls, who later joined *Coronation Street*, released a single, 'Where Will You Be When I Need You?' Of the show's backroom staff, it is not without interest that *Crossroads*' initial producer, Reg Watson, went on to create Australian supersoap ➢*Neighbours* and prison melodrama ➢*Prisoner: Cell Block H.*

In 1981 a storyline was introduced which changed the face of *Crossroads* forever: the motel burnt down and Meg was presumed to be inside, but later disovered to be on the QE2 en route for the land of Oz. The end result, however, was the same. Richardson had left the motel forever – and *Crossroads* had lost its focus. The serial's producers tried several devices to boost the show's post-Meg appeal, most of which involved taking it upmarket, even retitling it *Crossroads, King's Oak.* Actress Gabrielle Drake (➢*UFO*, ➢*The Brothers*) was brought in as the new, sophisticated motel manager. All this was to *misunderstand* Crossroad's considerable allure (17.6 million viewers at its 1978 height); TV watchers liked the show because it *was* tacky and cheap and so thoroughly unbelievable as to be teetering on the edge of absurdist comedy. In its way it was a work of genius. The creators were Hazel Adair and Peter Ling, whose previous soap had been the altogether more ordinary *Compact.*

CAST *Meg Richardson* Noele Gordon *Jill Harvey (née Richardson)* Jane Rossington *Sandy Richardson* Roger Tonge *Penny Richardson* Diane Grayson *David Hunter* Ronald Allen *Barbara Hunter* Sue Lloyd *Diane Parker (née Lawton)* Susan Hanson *Vince Parker* Peter Brookes *Sandra Gould* Diane Keen *Clifford Leyton* Johnny Briggs *Doris Luke* Kathy Staff *Benny Hawkins* Paul Henry *Carlos Rafael* Anthony Morton *Amy Turtle* Anne George *Marilyn Gates* Sue Nichols *Paul Ross* Sandor Eles *Adam Chance* Tony Adams *Hugh Mortimer* John Bentley *Shughie McFee* Angus Lennie *Sid Hooper* Stan Stennett *Nichola Freeman* Gabrielle Drake /*cr* Hazel Adair & Peter Ling /*pr* Reg Watson, Pieter Rogers, Eric Fawcett, Jack Barton, Philip Bowman, William Smethurst, Michelle Buck /*dr* inc Jack Barton, Rollo Gamble, Jonathan Wright-Miller / *wr* Hazel Adair, Peter Ling, Jon Rollason, Malcolm Hulke, Michaela Crees, Paula Milne, Gerald Kelsey / *mus* Tony Hatch (theme), Max Early & Raf Ravenscroft /*ATV: Central TV* (UK) /4510 x 25m bw:col.

Crown Court
Melodrama. ITV 1972–84

Dramatized court trials, told over three half-hour episodes each week. The quintessence of 70s afternoon drama, *CC* languidly but effectively covered surprisingly substantial topics (rape, arson, murder). Those called to appear before fictitious Fulchester Crown Court in its various tribulations included such ranking actors as Juliet Stevenson, Michael Elphick, Arthur English, John LeMesurier and Fulton Mackay. The verdict to each trial was delivered by a jury of viewers. Loosely based on the 50s American show *The Verdict is Yours*, which also had a British run (1958–9) under Granada producer Denis Forman.

pr inc Dennis Woolf, Howard Baker /*dr* inc Bob Hird, Sarah Harding, Colin Bucksey /*wr* inc David Yallop / *Granada TV* (UK) /600 x 30m col.

The Crystal Maze
Light Entertainment. C4 1990–

Fairly diverting gameshow in which six competitors faced mental and physical challenges in different time zones – Futuristic, Aztec, Industrial (later replaced by Ocean World), Medieval – in pursuit of time points for a spell inside the Crystal Dome. There, gold tokens flurried about to be caught and exchanged for prizes. Presented initially by chrome-domed 'mazemaster' Richard O'Brien, creator of the *The Rocky Horror Picture Show*, the show was filmed in a studio which, despite its computerworld appearance, was actually situated in North Weald Airfield in Essex.

CAST (presenter) Richard O'Brien, Edward Tudor Pole /*pr* Malcolm Heyworth & David G. Croft /*dr* Dominic Brigstocke /*Chatworth Television* (UK) / 120+ x 30m col.

Crystal Tipps and Alistair
Children's. BBC1 1972–

Psychedelic cartoon (much influenced by George Dunning's 1968 feature, *Yellow Submarine*) concerning the adventures of a bushy-haired girl and her square-jawed dog in a Gandalf-garden setting, complete with exotic fluttering doves and butterflies. Created by Hilary Hayton, the series was a product of the short-lived BBC Animation Department. It was screened in the slot before the 6 p.m. news, previously occupied by another *rara avis* counter-culture children's series, ➢*The Magic Roundabout.* Narration was by Richard Briers.

CAST (narrator) Richard Briers /*cr* Hilary Hayton / *pr* Michael Grafton-Robinson /*wr* Hilary Hayton, Graham McCallum /*BBC TV* (UK) /25 x 25m col.

Cybill
Comedy. C4 1996–

After a period of conspicuous absence from the small screen, Cybill Shepherd (➢*Moonlighting*) did a Roseanne Barr and based a sitcom around herself, playing the eponymous bit-parting Hollywood actress (vampire's victims, etc.) with two daughters and fortysomething ageing worries. There was also a duo of intrusive ex-husbands, dunderheaded stuntman Jeff Robbins (a wondrously cast Tom Wopat from ➢*The Dukes of Hazzard*) and neurotic novelist Ira Woodbine. As well as savvy swipes at Tinseltown life, zingy one-liners, engaging characters (none more so than acid-tongued best friend Maryann, an Emmy-winning performance by Christine Baranski), it kept viewers awake spotting the weekly surprise guest star. Those obliging included Robert Wagner, Stephanie Powers and Shepherd's real-life ex-husband, director Peter Bogdanovitch.

CAST *Cybill Sheridan* Cybill Shepherd *Ira Woodbine* Alan Rosenberg *Jeff Robbins* Tom Wopat *Maryann Thorpe* Christine Baranski *Rachel Blanders* Dedee Pfeiffer *Zoey Woodbine* Alicia Witt *Rachel Blanders* Deedee Pfeiffer /*cr* Cybill Shepherd /*exec pr* Marcy Carsey, Caryn Mandabach, Cybill Shepherd, Tom Werner /*dr* inc Jonathan Weiss, Tom Moore, Robert Berlinger /*YBL: River Siren Productions: Carsey-Werner Productions* (USA) /87 x 30m col /US tx CBS 1995–8.

D

'Right then, pay attention men'. Some of the cast of sitcom classic *Dad's Army*, based on writer Jimmy Perry's own wartime experience with the Home Guard.

Dad's Army

Comedy. BBC1 1968–77

It was their finest half hour. Based on writer Jimmy Perry's youthful experiences with the WWII local defence corps, and developed with producer (and ex-army major) David Croft, this nostalgic comedy of the misadventures of a Home Guard platoon was initially rejected by the then BBC1 controller, Paul Fox, for fear that it denigrated the wartime heroes. This was gloriously to miss the point; the Walmington-on-Sea platoon, led by pompous Captain Mainwaring, may have been eccentric bumbling amateurs of the first rank, but there was never any doubt that should the Nazis have landed, they would have fought bravely to a man. Much of the humour of the show came from the mixing of the social classes that WWII occasioned (epitomized by the lower middle class Mainwaring outranking the public-school educated Sergeant Wilson), and from the inspired characters. Alongside Mainwaring ('Right then. Pay attention, men.') and the diffident Wilson ('Is that really wise, Sir?'), the other platoon members were: eternally volunteering Corporal Jones ('Don't panic!'); spivvy Private Walker; wild-eyed coffin-maker Private Frazer; mummy's boy Pike; and ageing, incontinent Private Godfrey ('Do you think I might be excused, Sir?'). The ARP warden, Hodges (who endlessly dismissed Mainwaring as 'Napoleon'), the vicar and the verger were constant irritations, continually competing for use of the church hall. Perhaps the quintessential moment, the perfect

Dad's Army synthesis of Ealing Films and Englishness, came in 'The Deadly Attachment' when the platoon captured a German submarine officer (Philip Madoc) who demanded the name of the Home Guardsman who had mocked him. 'Don't tell him, Pike,' Mainwaring shouted.

So identified did the cast become with their *Dad's Army* roles, that their other achievements are frequently overlooked. Arthur Lowe had previously starred in ➢*Coronation Street* and ➢*Pardon the Expression*, and would later lead ➢*Potter* and ➢*AJ Wentworth, BA*. John LeMesurier, of whom BBC comedy head Michael Mills once remarked 'he suffers so beautifully', had played the apparently bewildered foil before, in ➢*George and the Dragon*, as well as bringing an air of charm to reels of British films. Arnold Ridley OBE had 38 plays to his name, including the West End classic, *The Ghost Train*.

Filmed on location at Thetford, Norfolk, *Dad's Army* recruited a small army of guest actors, many of whom – Don Estelle, Jack Haig, Donald Hewitt, Michael Knowles, Carmen Silvera and Wendy Richard (Private Walker's girlfriend) – would be economically recycled in future Croft/Perry shows such as ➢*Are You Being Served?*, ➢*'Allo, 'Allo*, ➢*It Ain't Half Hot, Mum* and ➢*Hi-de-Hi!* A spin-off feature film was released in 1971, the same year in which *Dad's Army* was awarded the BAFTA for Best Comedy. Although the last original episode was filmed in 1977, the show remains timelessly popular, for it was Perry and Croft's great genius to create in *Dad's Army* a vision of the English as they like to see themselves.

CAST *Capt. Mainwaring* Arthur Lowe *Sgt Wilson* John LeMesurier *Cpl Jones* Clive Dunn *Pte Frazer* John Laurie *Pte Pike* Ian Lavender *Pte Godfrey* Arnold Ridley *Pte Walker* James Beck *ARP Warden Hodges* Bill Pertwee *Verger Yateman* Edward Sinclair *Vicar* Frank Williams *Mavis Pike* Janet Davies /*cr* Jimmy Perry, David Croft /*pr* David Croft /*dr* inc Bob Spiers, Harold Snoad /*wr* Jimmy Perry, David Croft /*mus* Ivor Novello (theme music), Jimmy Perry (theme lyrics), Bud Flanagan (theme vocal) /*BBC TV* (UK) /79 x 30m, 2 x 60m col.

Daktari

Children's. BBC1 1966–9

Taking its title from the Swahili for 'doctor', this Ivan Tors (➢*Flipper*, ➢*Sea Hunt*, ➢*Ripcord*) jungle show related the adventures of courageous vet Dr Marsh Tracy, head of Wameru game preserve in deepest darkest Africa. Assisting the cravat-wearing Marsh in his dedicated battle against predatory man (especially hunters and poachers) was teenage daughter Paula, handsome American conservationist Jack Dane, and faithful native helper Mike Makula (Hari Rhodes, ➢*Roots*). Hedley was the starched stiff British District Officer. Yet, as with other Tors shows, it was the animal characters who stole it, viz. lion Clarence (*Daktari* was derived from a Tors feature, *Clarence, the Cross-Eyed Lion*) and chimp, Judy (who also did a turn as Debbie in ➢*Lost in Space*, where her tendency to bite the cast resulted in the removal of all her teeth). Later human additions were safari guide Bart Jason, and orphan, Jenny Jones (played by Erin Moran, later Joanie in ➢*Happy Days*). Despite its apparently authentic African setting, *Daktari* was filmed at a wildlife park outside Los Angeles.

CAST *Dr Marsh Tracy* Marshall Thompson *Paula Tracy* Cheryl Miller *Jack Dane* Yale Summers *DO Hedley* Hedley Mattingly *Mike Makula* Hari Rhodes *Bart Jason* Ross Hagen *Jenny Jones* Erin Moran /*cr* Ivan Tors, Art Arthur /*exec pr* Ivan Tors /*pr* Leonard Kaufman /*dr* Otto Lang, Paul Landres, John Florea, Marshall Thompson, Dick Moder, Alan Crossland / *wr* inc Stephen Kandel, Robert Lewis, Alan Caillou, Richard Carlson /*MGM: Ivan Tors* (USA) /89 x 60m col /US tx CBS 1966–9.

Dallas

Melodrama. BBC1 1978–91

Everyday life of a Texan oil-rich clan, as viewed through the enlarging, irridescent perspective of the soap bubble. The first of the supersudsters, *Dallas* was initially produced by Lorimar as a mini-series, but quickly grew into a worldwide cult serial with 300 million viewers in 57 countries. The featured family were the Ewings of Southfork Ranch: patriarch Jock, matriarch Miss Ellie (Barbara Bel Geddes, from Hitchcock's *Vertigo*), and sons JR (Larry Hagman, the former straight man in ➢*I Dream of Jeannie*), Gary and Bobby (Patrick Duffy, ➢*The Man from Atlantis*). JR, a scheming business man and inveterate seducer of women, quickly became the show's main focus. An anti-hero of colossal proportions, JR symbolized 80s greed like no other TV creation. Also prominent was JR's alcoholic wife Sue Ellen, Bobby's wife Pamela and Gary's daughter Lucy. Most of the troubles and tragedies which befell the Ewings of Southfork in the early and mid years were (just) this side of believable: Jock's heart attack, Miss Ellie's cancer, the discovery that ranch cowhand Ray Krebbs (played by Steve Kanaly, the Vietnam veteran whose experiences inspired *Apocalypse Now* screenwriter John Milius) was Jock's illegitimate son, and the running feud with arch-enemy Cliff Barnes, son of Jock's embittered former pardner, Digger. The watershed came with the 1980 episode featuring the attempted murder of JR. After this cliffhanger – the assassin was revealed, in the highest-rated individual show in history to that date, to be Sue Ellen's sister, Kristin, pregnant with JR'S child – the scriptwriters had little place to go but into the fantastic. In 1985 Bobby was 'killed' in a car accident, but a full season later it transpired that wife Pamela (she was Cliff Barnes' sister) had dreamt the whole thing. Then JR bedded hayseed Cally, whose irate brothers imprisoned him on a work farm, only releasing him for a shotgun marriage. This proved small escape, for JR was then confined to a mental institution by un-beloved son James. In the final episode, 'Conundrum', JR's world seemed to have collapsed around him. The Ewings had dispersed or died, Southfork had been turned over to Bobby by Miss Ellie, and Ewing Oil had passed into the hands of Cliff Barnes. In an inversion of Frank Capra's movie *It's a Wonderful Life*, an 'angel' appeared unto JR as he contemplated suicide to show him what life would have been like if he had never been born. This done, the eyes of the angel – probably Lucifer – flashed red and a shot rang out. Bobby burst into the room and only he, not the viewer, saw what had happened.

The quintessential TV show of the Reagan era, *Dallas*'s success generated a rush of spin-offs for Lorimar – ➢*Knots Landing, Flamingo Road,* ➢*Falcon Crest* and *King's Crossing* – and enormous wealth for its stars (Hagman earned £15 million as JR). Celebs queued to jump aboard the gold train. Former Miss USA, Deborah Shelton, played Mandy Winger; rock widow Priscilla Presley appeared as Bobby's sometime girl, Jenna Wade; while English thespians Gayle Hunnicutt, Lesley-Anne Down and Ian McShane all appeared in the show's latter, dying days. But it was not all glamour on the *Dallas* lot. Charlene Tilton (Lucy Ewing) was given the cowboy boot in 1985 for being too fat.

CAST *John Ross (JR) Ewing* Larry Hagman *Eleanor Southworth Ewing (Miss Ellie)* Barbara Bel Geddes/ Donna Reed *John Ross (Jock) Ewing* Jim Davis *Bobby Ewing* Patrick Duffy *Pamela Barnes Ewing* Victoria Principal *Lucy Ewing Cooper* Charlene Tilton *Sue Ellen Ewing* Linda Gray *Ray Krebbs* Steve Kanaly *Cliff Barnes* Ken Kercheval *Gary Ewing* David Ackroyd/Ted Shackelford *Valene Ewing* Joan Van Ark *Kristin Shepard* Mary Crosby *Donna Culver Krebbs* Susan Howard *Mitch Cooper* Leigh McCloskey *John Ross Ewing III* Tyler Banks/Omri Katz *Afton Cooper* Audrey Landers *Clayton Farlow* Howard Keel *Katherine Wentworth* Morgan Brittany *Mickey Trotter* Timothy Patrick Murphy *Mark Graison* John Beck *Jenna Wade* Morgan Fairchild/Francine Tacker/Priscilla Presley *Vanessa Beaumont* Gayle Hunnicutt *Don Lockwood* Ian McShane *Stephanie Rogers* Lesley-Anne Down / *cr* David Jacobs /*exec pr* Philip Caprice /*pr* Leonard Katzman /*dr* inc Larry Hagman, Patrick Duffy, Leonard Katzman, Corey Alen, Linda Gray /*wr* inc David Jacobs, D.C. Fontana, Richard Fontana /*mus* Jerrold Imel (theme) /*Lorimar Studios* (USA) /356 x 60m col / US tx CBS 1978–91.

Dalziel and Pascoe

Crime. ITV 1994/BBC1 1996–

Adaptation of Reginald Hill's stories featuring a chalk-and-(Yorkshire) cheese cop duo. First, and risibly, breathed into TV life by comics ➢*Hale and Pace*, the show went over to the BBC for Warren Clarke to make the part of the gruff, arse-scratching Dalziel (pronounced Deeel, for those who care) his own, while Colin Buchanan passed muster as his caring, by-the-textbook, middle-class sidekick. A high-quality production, with treatments by the likes of Malcolm Bradbury and Alan Plater, but over-generous at 90 minutes.

CAST *Det. Supt Andy Dalziel* Warren Clarke *DS Peter Pascoe* Colin Buchanan /*pr* inc Chris Parr /*wr* inc Malcolm Bradbury, Alan Plater /*BBC TV* (UK) :A&E (US) /6 x 90m col /US tx A&E 1996–.

Dangerfield

Crime. BBC1 1994–

Police-cum-medical drama with dashing forensic surgeon/GP hero Dr Paul Dangerfield, whose tragic lot in life – wife killed in car crash leaving him the care of their truculent teenage children – was cynically designed to evoke viewer sympathies. The widowed Warwickshire workaholic, however, eventually found some solace in the arms of fellow colleague, Joanna Stevens (Amanda Redman, *Beck*, ➢*El C.I.D.*, and ex-wife of ➢*Soldier, Soldier*'s Robert Glenister). A buccolic crowd pleaser (like ➢*Peak Practice* and ➢*Heartbeat*), *Dangerfield* became disconcertingly directionless by the third series, with a wholesale introduction of new characters and the recasting of old ones.

CAST *Dr Paul Dangerfield* Nigel Le Vaillant *Joanna Stevens* Amanda Redman *Al Dangerfield* Tamzin Malleson *Marty Dangerfield* Sean Maguire *Dr Jonathan Paige* Nigel Havers/Tim Vincent / *exec pr* Tony Virgo / *pr* Peter Wolfes / *wr* inc Don Shaw / *BBC TV* (UK) / 38+ x 50m col.

Danger Man

Adventure. ITV 1960–9

'Every government has its Secret Service branch... NATO also has its own. A messy job? Well, that's when they usually call on me. Or someone like me. Oh yes, my name is Drake, John Drake.'

So were viewers introduced to *Danger Man*, a series of fast-paced espionage thrillers destined to make actor Patrick McGoohan an international name. As would become standard in 60s TV spy capers, episodes were played out against exotic locales, from Kashmir to the Austrian Alps, the scenery only improved by the presence of a beautiful woman. However, unlike his screen rivals, in particular ➢*The Saint*, laconic lone-wolf troubleshooter Drake was no philanderer, for McGoohan personally insisted that the show did not promote promiscuity. John Drake was thus the ultimate professional action man, a scrub-kneed boy's heroic ideal. In 1964 Drake (weapon of choice: old fashioned fisticuffs, by the quadfull) was transferred to Britain's M19 branch, where he received his orders from boss Hobbs. At the same time, episodes were expanded to 60 minutes, and there was also a new emphasis on gadgetry, including a tiepin which served as a camera (this three years before *From Russia With Love* hit the screen). Two 60 minute colour episodes (released as a TVM, *Koroshi*) were made as part of a projected fourth season, eventually scrapped because McGoohan was preoccupied with another project: ➢*The Prisoner*.

CAST *John Drake* Patrick McGoohan *Hobbs* Peter Madden / *cr* Ralph Smart / *exec pr* Ralph Smart / *pr* Ralph Smart, Aida Young, Sidney Cole / *dr* inc Ralph Smart, Patrick McGoohan, Charles Crichton, Don Chaffey, Peter Yates / *wr* inc Brian Clemens, Ralph Smart, Philip Broadley, Tony Williamson / *mus* Edwin Astley /ITC (UK) / 39 x 30m bw, 45 x 60m bw, 2 x 60m col /US tx CBS 1961 (as *Secret Agent*).

Danger Mouse

Children's. ITV 1981–92

The breathlessly exciting escapades of Danger Mouse, 'the greatest secret agent the world has ever known', and his trusty (if timorous) sidekick, Penfold. Sallying forth from his base in a Baker Street postbox, the eye-patch-wearing cartoon rodent superhero bested assorted colourful adversaries, prime among them the terrifying toad, Baron Greenback (said by some to be modelled on TV supremo, Sir Lew Grade), whose plans to take over the world incorporated everything from giant chickens to a bad luck ray. Superior animation, excellent character voice work (by David Jason and Terry Scott, among others) and enjoyable parodying of the 007 genre gave the show added adult appeal. A spin-off, ➢*Count Duckula,* was almost as successful. Shown on US network Nickelodeon, the sophisticated – by the standards of American toons – *Danger Mouse* prompted the cable service to develop its own oddball shows, among them ➢*Ren and Stimpy* and ➢*Rugrats.*

CAST (voices) *Danger Mouse/Narrator/Colonel K.* David Jason *Penfold* Terry Scott *Baron Greenback* Edward Kelsey *Stiletto Mafioso* Brian Trueman / *cr* Mike Harding, Brian Trueman / *exec pr* John Hambley / *pr* Brian Cosgrove, Mark Hall / *dr* Brian Cosgrove, Chris Randall / *wr* Brian Trueman, Mike Harding / *mus* Mike Harding / *Cosgrove Hall: Thames TV* (UK) / 145 x 5–10m col / US tx Nickelodeon 1984.

Danger UXB

Drama. ITV 1979

High-tension drama about the activities of a squad of sappers – bomb disposal experts – led by Lieutenant Ash RE (a pre-➢*Brideshead Revisited* Anthony Andrews) in WWII London. Based on the memoirs of Major A.P. Hartley, and produced by John Hawkesworth, whose previous forays into the past had been largely Edwardian (➢*Upstairs, Downstairs,* ➢*Duchess of Duke Street*).

CAST *Lt Brian Ash* Anthony Andrews *Sgt James* Maurice Roeves *Susan Ash (née Gillespie)* Judy Geeson *Capt. Mould* Norman Chappell *Wilkins* George Innes / *cr* John Hawkesworth / *exec pr* Johnny Goodman / *pr* John Hawkesworth / *wr* inc John Hawkesworth / *Euston Films* (UK) /13 x 60m col.

Daniel Boone

Western. ITV 1967

Biopic of the legendary Kentucky frontiersman for the kiddie end of the couch, calculated to trade on actor Fess Parker's earlier spectacular coonskin success, ➢*Davy Crockett.* With stirring outdoor action (typified by the opening sequence which showed Boone splitting a tree with a single throw of his axe), solid scripts, and production from rising powers Aaron Spelling and Barney Rosenzweig (➢*Cagney and Lacey*), it made the grade. A 1966 two-part episode was edited into the theatrical release *Daniel Boone – Frontier Trail Rider.* A 1977 revival, *Young Dan'l Boone*, however, bit the dust and was never screened in Britain.

CAST *Daniel Boone* Fess Parker *Yadkin* Albert Salmi *Mingo* Ed Ames *Rebecca Boone* Patricia Blair /*exec pr* Aaron Spelling, Aaron Rosenberg /*pr* Barney Rosenzweig /*dr* inc William Witney, George Sherman, George Marshall /*wr* inc Borden Chase, D.D. Beauchamp /*mus* The Imperials (theme vocal), Paul Sawtell /*Arcola: Fesspar: Fox TV* (USA) /165 x 52m bw:col /US tx NBC 1964–70.

Dark Skies

Sci-fi. C4 1997–8

The illegitimate child of ➢*The X-Files* and ➢*The Invaders.*

In 1961 Washington DC a Congressman's aide, John Loengard, discovers a secret government comspiracy called Majestic-12, which seeks to suppress the truth of alien landings. On the run from Majestic-12 and the alien Hive, Loengard and girlfriend Kimberley Shaw create a grassroots resistance movement – code-name Dark Skies – to fight the bodysnatching ETs.

Vaguely immoral for its shameless plagiarism, but a consistently fun tour of the high (and low) points of 60s history, from JFK's assassination to Woodstock, with hold-onto-your-seat fear and paranoia all the way.

CAST *John Loengard* Eric Close *Kimberley Sayers* Megan Ward *Capt. Frank Bach* J.T. Walsh /*cr* Bryce Zabel, Brent Friedman /*exec pr* James D. Parriott, Bryce Zabel /*dr* inc Tobe Hooper, Ric Kolbe, Lou Antonio, Tucker Gates /*wr* inc Bryce Zabel, Brent Friedman, James D. Parriott, J.T. Walsh, Melissa Rosenberg /*Bryce Zabel Productions Inc: Columbia Pictures Television* (USA) /1 x 120m, 18 x 60m col / US tx CBA 1996–7.

The Darling Buds of May

Comedy. ITV 1991–3

Perfick. Just what the audience needed in the early 90s: a return to the rural Kent of the 50s where the sun always shone and the Larkins always laughed and the whole was steeped in nostalgia. Based on H.E. Bates' five novels about the frolicsome farming family (and taking its name from the first novel), *Darling Buds* was brought to the screen by the late author's son, Richard, with the first series written by Bob Larbey. It was one of Yorkshire TV's greatest successes. David Jason was perfectly cast as cheery 'Pop' Larkin, who ran a 22-acre smallholding and did a bit of this and that on the side. He was united in perpetual cuddle with the buxom 'Ma' (Pam Ferris), his loveable common-law wife, a jovial, ever-baking woman. Together they had created a hearty brood of six, including smouldering beauty and eldest daughter Mariette (played by then-unknown Welsh actress Catherine Zeta Jones) who captured the heart of an innocent Inland Revenue official calling to investigate Pop's affairs. Ratings soared like the lark.

CAST *Sidney Charles 'Pop' Larkin* David Jason *Ma Larkin* Pam Ferris *Mariette Larkin* Catherine Zeta Jones *Cedric 'Charley' Charlton* Philip Franks *Primrose Larkin* Julie Davies/Abigail Romison *Montgomery Larkin* Ian Tucker *Petunia Larkin* Christina Giles *Zinnia Larkin* Katherine Giles *Victoria Larkin* Stephanie Ralph *Edith Pilchester* Rachel Bell *Ernest Bristow* Michael Jayston *The Brigadier* Moray Watson / *exec pr* Richard Bates /*pr* Robert Banks Stewart, Peter Norris, Simon Lewis /*dr* inc David Giles, Robert Tronson, Rodney Bennett /*wr* inc Bob Larbey, Richard Harris /*Yorkshire TV: Excelsior Group* (UK) /18 x 60m, 2 x 90m col.

Dastardly and Muttley in Their Flying Machines

Children's. BBC1 1970

Stop that pigeon... In WWI, spy Dick Dastardly and canine assistant Muttley take to the air in less than magnificent flying machines in an attempt to stop Yankee Doodle Pigeon flying his vital messages to Uncle Sam. Naturally, Dastardly never does succeed in his missions. 'Drat! and Double Drat!' Raucous, amusing animation, spun off from ➢*The Wacky Races.*

CAST (voices) *Dick Dastardly* Paul Winchell *Muttley:Klunk:Zilly* Don Messick /*exec pr* William Hanna, Joseph Barbera /*mus* Hoyt Curtain /*Hanna-Barbera* (USA) /17 x 22m col /US tx CBS 1969.

Dave Allen at Large

Comedy. BBC2 1971–6

Rambling monologues from Irish sit-on-stool comic (born David Tynan O'Mahony) with 9½ nicotine-stained fingers and a whisky glass; the rants being interspersed with filmed sketches. The favoured targets of sex and religion and bureaucracy were, at the time, risqué and Allen's comedic thrusts drew much appreciation from a viewership uneasy at the anachronism of conservative rules on screen and in society. Allen himself wrote much of the material which, the laid-back ease of its delivery aside, could be highly wrought and sophisticated. A virtuoso interlude in which Allen anagrammed the names of famous politicians (Revd Ian Paisley became 'Vile IRA Pansy') bears comparison with the product of any TV humorist.

Dave Allen ('Anal Delve') began his small-screen career with *Val Doonican*, graduating to his first solo series, *The Dave Allen Show*, in 1969. Others, for both ITV and BBC followed, but *At Large* was the creative high-water mark.

CAST (host) Dave Allen /*pr* Peter Whitmore /*wr* Dave Allen, Austin Steele, Peter Vincent /*BBC TV* (UK) / 50 x 35m col.

The David Nixon Show

Light Entertainment. ITV 1972–7

Chrome-headed, mellow-voiced conjuror David Nixon was a favourite small-screen personality from the 1950s, when he was a regular panellist on ➢*What's My Line?*, until his death in 1978. The first indigenous illusionist to become a TV star, he hosted a rope of magic-cum-variety shows for both ITV and BBC, of which *The David Nixon Show* was the longest-running, becoming a stalwart of ITV's early-evening output for the mid 70s, achieving an audience figure topping 11 million. He was also the man responsible for making a celebrity of the aristocratic fox puppet who went on to the solo ➢*The Basil Brush Show*.

CAST (host) David Nixon /*pr* Royston Mayoh, David Clark /*dr* inc Daphne Shadwell /*Thames TV* (UK) / 50 x 50m col.

Davy Crockett

Western. ITV 1956

Biopic about the life and times of the legendary American frontiersman, from his days as an Injun fighter to the stand at the Alamo. It led to 'Crockettmania' in the USA, with citizens spending upwards of $100 million on associated merchandise, while Walt Disney (from whose *Disneyland* anthology the show sprang) subsequently claimed it as the cause of the TV Western stampede of the 50s. Certainly the show, with its brutal hand-to-hand combat, marked a transition from the kiddie to the adult oater. Two theatrical features, made from re-edited episodes, *Davy Crockett, King of the Wild Frontier* and *Davy Crockett and the River Pirates*, were released in 1955. Actor Fess Parker made something of a speciality of coonskin roles, going on to star as ➢*Daniel Boone*. Buddy Ebsen (aka Christian Ebsen), who played Crockett's sidekick, went on to star in ➢*The Beverly Hillbillies* and ➢*Hec Ramsey*.

CAST *Davy Crockett* Fess Parker *Georgie Russell* Buddy Ebsen /*cr* Walt Disney /*exec pr* Walt Disney / *pr* Bill Walsh /*dr* Norman Foster /*mus* George Burns / *Walt Disney Productions* (USA) /5 x 52m bw /US tx ABC 1954–5.

Days of Hope

Drama. BBC1 1975

Leftist mini epic about Britain between 1916–26, as reflected in the lives of three related Yorkshire poor. Filmed by director Ken Loach in semi-documentary style (as per his famed ➢*Wednesday Play* offering, 'Cathy Come Home'), it came in four heartfelt, impressive parts, '1916: Joining Up'; '1921: Black Friday'; '1924: The First Labour Government', and '1926: The General Strike'. Despite a clutch of awards, it was never repeated by the BBC, mostly because its pacifist morality caused controversy in Conservative circles.

CAST *Ben Matthews* Paul Copley *Sarah Hargreaves* Pamela Brighton *Philip Hargreaves* Nikolas Simmonds / *cr* Jim Allen /*pr* Tony Garnett /*dr* Ken Loach /*wr* Jim Allen /*BBC TV* (UK) /1 x 95m, 1 x 100m, 1 x 80m, 1 x 135m col.

The Day Today

Comedy. BBC2 1994

TV news satire, similar to ➢*Drop the Dead Donkey* and ➢*KYTV* of the same era, but with a stronger political desire to expose media manipulation and the degrading of newscasting standards. In this, it was award-winningly successful. Sometimes, in moments of uninspiration, it relied on borrowed ➢*Monty Python*esque surrealism, e.g. the headline 'Dismantled Pope Found Sliding Along Road'. Steve Coogan, who took the part of ignorant Pringle-clad sportscaster Alan Partridge, found the show a boost to his already rising showbiz fortunes, later basking in the same year's ➢*Knowing Me, Knowing You... with Alan Partridge.* Among the other featured newzak folk were decapitated weatherman Sylvester Stuart, economics correspondent Peter O'Hanraha'hanrahan, business affairs reporter Collaterlie Sisters, with Christopher Morris (appearing under his own name) as the argumentative Paxman-like anchorman.

CAST Christopher Morris, Patrick Marber, Rebecca Front, Steve Coogan, Doon Mackichan, David Schneider /*cr* Christopher Morris, Armando Iannucci /*exec pr* Peter Fincham /*pr* Armando Iannucci /*dr* Andrew Gillman /*wr* Christopher Morris, Armando Iannucci /*Talkback* (UK) /14 x 30m col.

The Day of the Triffids

Sci-fi. BBC1 1981

Walking evil plants take over the Earth. Restrained adaptation of John Wyndham's classic tale, accurately following its central theme of the dehumanizing of man in a holocaust environment, but weakened by expensive *sfx* which failed to scare. John Duttine, previously in *To Serve Them All My Days*, played Bill Masen, the man who battled the Brobdingnagian flora. TV telefantasy again called at the Wyndham oeuvre in the 1980s, with ITV's *Chocky* (1984, 18 x 30m col), based on the author's tale of the same title about an intelligent alien life form who befriends an English boy.

CAST *Bill Masen* John Duttine *Jo* Emma Relph *Jack Coker* Maurice Colbourne /*pr* David Maloney /*dr* Ken Hannam /*wr* Douglas Livingstone /*mus* Christopher Gunning /*sfx* Steve Drewett /*BBC TV* (UK) /6 x 60m col.

Dear John

Comedy. BBC1 1986–7

Sitcom featuring a lonesome divorcee reduced to a West London bedsit and membership of a 1-2-1 group, run by the pryingly prurient Louise Williams. There, the wimpish schoolteacher John encountered a ring of equally sad people. Kate (Belinda Lang, ➢*The Bretts*, ➢*2 Point 4 Children*) was frigid and thrice married. Kirk St Moritz was a medallion man fantasist – his real name was Eric Morris – who had joined to pull 'frustrated chicks'. Ralph Dring (Peter Denyer, ➢*Please Sir!*) was simply bored. Also seen was Mrs Arnott, Sylvia and rock star of yesteryear, Ricky Fortune. Not the show's least virtue was that it demonstrated one compass point of the extraordinary acting range of star Ralph Bates (d. 1991), a former Hammer-horror turn and the brooding Warleggan in ➢*Poldark.* Written by John Sullivan (➢*Citizen Smith*, ➢*Only Fools and Horses*, ➢*Just Good Friends*), it sold to the US, where Judd Hirsch (➢*Taxi*) was cast as the lonely heart, John Lacey. This version, to which Sullivan contributed episodes, was then purveyed back to Britain, screening on BBC as *Dear John: USA.*

CAST *John Lacey* Ralph Bates *Kirk St Moritz* Peter Blake *Kate* Belinda Lang *Louise Williams* Rachel Bell *Ralph Dring* Peter Denyer *Mrs Arnott* Jean Challis *Mrs Lemenski* Irene Prador *Ricky Fortune* Kevin Lloyd *Sylvia Watkins* Lucinda Curtis /*cr* John Sullivan /*pr* Ray Butt /*wr* John Sullivan /*BBC TV* (UK) /13 x 30m, 1 x 60m col.

Dear Mother... Love Albert

Comedy. ITV 1969–71

Former ➢*Likely Lad* Rodney Bewes co-wrote and starred in this so-so sitcom about an unlikely lad, naive confectionary salesman Albert Courtney, who moved to racy London from grim-but-respectable Up North. Traditional trouble came in the form of girlfriends and their mothers, particularly when Albert's flatmates in season three were girls with 10 out of 10 for looks. Each week Albert wrote a letter home to his mother, in which he gave an exaggerated account of his life in the Big City. A 1972 sequel, *Albert!*, was more of the same except that the innocent's fiancée was no longer played by Liz Gebhardt (➢*Please Sir!*) but by Cheryl Hall (➢*Citizen Smith*).

CAST *Albert Courtney* Rodney Bewes *A.C. Stain (the manager)* Garfield Morgan *Vivian McKewan* Sheila White *Mrs McKewan* Geraldine Newman *Doreen Bissel* Liz Gebhardt *Mrs Bissel* Amelia Bayntun /*cr* Rodney Bewes, Derrick Goodwin /*exec pr* John Duncan /*pr* Rodney Bewes, Derrick Goodwin /*wr* Rodney Bewes, Derrick Goodwin /*mus* Mike Hugg /*Thames TV: Yorkshire TV* (UK) /19 x 30m col.

Death Valley Days

Western. BBC 1953–61

Oater anthology show of long-toothed longevity which depicted incidents in the lives of pioneer Westerners in California and Nevada in the 1880s. Originally begun on radio in 1930 by its sponsor, Twenty Mule Team Borax, it was hosted on TV by Stanley Andrews ('The Old Ranger', 1952–64), future US President Ronald Reagan (1964–7), Robert Taylor (1967–9), Dale Robertson (1969–72), and Merle Hagard (1975). Production standards were modest, although location filming in Death Valley gave the series a certain big-sky, wide-open space grandeur. Also known as *Call of the West* and *Western Star Theatre* (among others) during its numerous US reruns.

CAST *cr* Ruth Woodman /*exec pr* Armand Schaefer, Dorrel McGowan, Robert W. Stabler /*Flying A Productions: McGowan: Filmaster: Madison* (USA) /558 x 30m bw:col /US tx Syndicated 1952–75.

The Defenders

Crime. BBC2 1962–7

Legal drama about conscientious father and son attorneys, Lawrence and Kenneth Preston, rightly venerated for its adult scripting and social awareness. As producer Herbert Brodkin claimed with only slight exaggeration: 'We did subjects on television that no one had ever done before: subjects such as prostitution, rape, murder, whatever we saw in the daily papers... *The Defenders* almost changed the face of television.' Certainly the show mounted, in the 1964 episode 'Blacklist', TV's first dramatic examination of its own McCarthyite past (winning Emmy awards for actor Jack Klugman and writer Ernest Kinoy). Unusually for TV advocates, Preston & Preston did not always win.

The Defenders' pilot (starring William Shatner as Preston junior, and Steve McQueen as the defendant) appeared as part of *Studio One* in 1957, but was rejected as a series. It only got on air at the personal insistence of then CBS chairman, William Paley. Perhaps to appease low-brow tastes, *The Defenders* habitually employed guest stars from Hollywood and Broadway to grace episodes. Dustin Hoffman, Jon Voight and Robert Redford were among those who appeared over the years. The show was co-created by Reginald Rose, the author of *Twelve Angry Men.*

CAST *Lawrence Preston* E.G. Marshall *Kenneth Preston* Robert Reed /*cr* Reginald Rose, Herbert Brodkin /*pr* Herbert Brodkin /*dr* inc Paul Bogart, Buzz Kulik, Michael Powell, Elliott Silverstein /*wr* Ernest Kinoy /*Plautus* (USA) /132 x 50m bw /US tx CBS 1961–5.

Defenders of the Earth

Children's. BBC1 1988

Modernized cartoon makeover of the adventures of Flash Gordon who, with a band of ace warriors (Mandrake, Lothar, the Phantom), fights to protect Earth from old adversary, Ming the Merciless, ruler of planet Mongo. Like ➢ *The New Adventures of Flash Gordon,* this was a blatant attempt to ride the comet-tail success of the 1980 movie, *Flash Gordon.*

CAST (voices) inc Buster Jones, William Callaway, Adam Carl, Ron Feinberg, Loren Lester, Diane Pershing /*pr* Margaret Loesch, Lee Gunther, Bruce Paisner /*King Features Entertainment Ltd Production* (USA) /35 x 20m col /US tx Syndicated 1986.

The Demon Headmaster

Children's. BBC1 1996–8

'The headmaster is a marvellous man... The headmaster is a marvellous man... The headmaster is a marvellous man...'

The ➢*Dr Who* of the 90s, a super-scary sci-fi show for juveniles, the first series of which was watched by a phenomenal 60 per cent of those aged 4 to 14. Adapted by Helen Cresswell from the 1982 novel by Gillian Cross, it featured an evil headmaster with hypnotic eyes and a pet theory that 'childhood is such a useless waste of time.' Only stupendously bright pupil Dinah Hunter resisted his brainwashing powers. For the second series, the demon headmaster was transplanted into a secluded research centre in a small village where he plotted to alter the human race genetically to eradicate its brats. Strongly performed, written and directed, the show had grim underlying themes, certain to appeal to children: adults are untrustworthy; your peers will betray you.

CAST *The Demon Headmaster* Terrence Hardiman *Mrs Hunter* Tessa Peake-Jones *Mr Hunter* David Lloyd *Dinah Hunter* Frances Amey /*cr* Gillian Cross /*dr* Roger Singleton-Turner /*wr* Helen Cresswell, Gillian Cross /*BBC TV* (UK) /18 x 25m col.

Dempsey and Makepeace

Crime. ITV 1985–6

Mid-Atlantic mish-mash in which brash, trigger-happy New York police lieutenant James Dempsey (played by one-time Brooklyn gang member Michael Brandon) was sent over to Britain – for his own protection – after uncovering corruption amongst his Ninth Precinct colleagues. In Blighty he was partnered by Lady Harriet Makepeace (pneumatic Glynis Barber, ➢*Blake's 7*, BBC2's adaptation of the Daily Mirror's bimbo comic-strip ➢*Jane*), an upper-class English blonde with a Cambridge degree in science and distant claims to the throne. This uneasy pairing worked in and around London for Scotland Yard's covert division S1 10 and while 'Loot' Dempsey never left home without his .357 Magnum, 'Harry' Makepeace preferred to use her friends in high places. Overseeing the pair's antics was loudmouth Liverpudlian Gordon Spikings, while Detective Chas Jarvis (Tony Osoba, ➢*Porridge*) also lent his skills on occasion. Preposterous, all-action series with super-annuated plots, frequently forced to rely for watchability on the two cops' will-they-won't-they relationship. This, fortunately for the producers, gained considerable spice from the much publicised off-screen romance between its stars, who later married.

CAST *Lt James Dempsey* Michael Brandon *DS Harriet Makepeace (Harry)* Glynis Barber *Chief Supt Gordon Spikings* Ray Smith *DS Charles Jarvis (Chas)* Tony Osoba /*cr* Tony Wharmby *pr* Tony Wharmby, Nick Elliott, Ranald Graham /*dr* Tony Wharmby, William Brayne, Christian Marnham, Robert Tronson, Gerry Mill /*wr* Ranald Graham, Jesse Carr-Martindale, Murray Smith, Dave Humphries, Jonathan Hales / *mus* Alan Parker /*A Golden Eagle Films Production for London Weekend TV* (UK) /1 x 105m, 29 x 60m col.

Department S

Crime. ITV 1969–70

Cult TV caper about a fictional offshoot of Interpol, headed by flamboyant investigator Jason King, who also penned detective novels in his spare time. He formed a team (shades of ➢*The Champions*) with two co-agents, prosaic Stewart Sullivan and computer expert Anabelle Hurst. The trio's boss was Sir Curtis Seretse (played by black actor Dennis Alaba Peters), and it was he who gave them their assignments; these usually had a strong element of the fantastic about them, epitomized by the episode 'The Pied Piper of Hambledown' in which an entire village populace was abducted. The scripts were stylish, but much the most stylish aspect of the show was Peter Wyngarde's (aka Cyril Louis Goldbert) portrayal of the rakish King, with his trend-setting Zapata moustache and dandy shirts which played havoc with early colour TV cameras. To no one's surprise King was spun-off to solo show ➢*Jason King*.

CAST *Jason King* Peter Wyngarde *Stewart Sullivan* Joel Fabiani *Annabelle Hurst* Rosemary Nichols *Sir Curtis Seretse* Dennis Alaba Peters /*cr* Monty Berman, Dennis Spooner /*pr* Monty Berman /*dr* Cyril Frankel, Roy Ward Baker /*wr* Gerald Kelsey, Philip Broadley, Terry Nation, Tony Williamson, Harry H. Junkin, Donald James, Leslie Darbon /*mus* Edwin Astley /ITC (UK) / 28 x 60m col /US tx Syndicated 1971.

Deputy Dawg

BBC1 1963–4

A simpleton canine law officer tries to defend a hen coop from prankster varmints ('Just a cotton picking moment…') out in the old West. Timeless, amusing animation. Show director Ralph Bakshi later found fame as the overseer of strictly adult toon, *Fritz the Cat*.

CAST (voices) *Deputy Dawg* Dayton Allen /*cr* Larz Bourne /*exec pr* Bill Weiss /*dr* inc Ralph Bakshi, Bob Kuwahara /*wr* inc Larz Bourne /*Terrytoons* (USA) /104 x 25m col /US tx CBS 1960.

Designing Women

Comedy. Sky1 1993–6

American sitcom about a quartet of southern belles who work at Sugarbakers, an Atlanta interior-design firm. The brainchild of writer Linda Bloodworth-Thomason (an Arkansas friend of Bill and Hilary Clinton, no less) the show was dumped after several weeks by CBS but, like ➢*Cagney and Lacey*, was brought back from extinction by a viewer letter-campaign. The original drawling decorator foursome were employees Mary Jo Shively (Annie Potts, the record-store manager in *Pretty in Pink*) and Charlene Frazier, and the two Sugarbaker sisters who employed them, Julia and Suzanne. The sexpot latter, played by former Miss Florida, Delta Burke (who eventually went to fat and was fired), had fine lines in dumbery: 'I'm gonna turn the TV off – it's only the news and I saw that yesterday.' The only male in the women's room was black ex-convict Anthony, an assistant who eventually made the grade as partner (thus nicely puncturing any viewer notions that the Deep South was run entirely by redneck racists). Over the seasons the cast changed considerably but the character balance of sass, sex and stupidity was maintained throughout.

CAST *Suzanne Sugarbaker* Delta Burke *Julia Sugarbaker* Dixie Carter *Mary Jo Shively* Annie Potts *Charlene Frazier* Jean Smart *Anthony Bouvier* Meshach Taylor *Carlene Frazier Dobber* Jan Hooks *Allison Sugarbaker* Julia Duffy *B.J. Poteet* Judith Ivey *Bernice Clifton* Alice Ghostley /*cr* Linda Bloodworth–Thomason /*exec pr* inc Harry Thomason, Linda Bloodworth-Thomason, Pamela Norris, Tommy Thompson /*dr* inc Ellen Falcon, Jack Shea, Harry Thomason /*wr* inc Linda Bloodworth-Thomason, Pamela Norris /*Columbia TV* (USA) /163 x 30m col /US tx CBS 1986–93.

Desmond's

Comedy. Channel 4 1989–94

In a barbershop in Peckham, south London, the different generations of proprietor Desmond's family mingled and sparred with each other and selected locals over video games, food, tears, laughter and the occasional haircut. Testy yet tolerant Desmond (Norman Beaton, ➢*Empire Road*, ➢*The Fosters*) and fierce but loving wife Shirley (Carmen Munroe, ➢*General Hospital*, *The Fosters*) were a salt-of-the-earth partnership, parents to Michael, Sean and Gloria, and pillars of their community. With a rare sharp line struggling to be heard amongst predictable scripts and pantomime delivery, its almost exclusively black cast nonetheless won a fervent following for its depiction of ethnic mix and intergenerational difference. It ran to five series, won an appearance for Beaton on ➢*The Cosby Show* and spawned a spin-off, *Porkpie*, featuring Peckham's one-time lollipop man (played by Ram John Holder), now a lottery winner and millionaire (written and created, like *Desmond's*, by St Lucia-born Trix Worrell).

CAST *Desmond Ambrose* Norman Beaton *Shirley Ambrose* Carmen Munroe *Matthew* Gyearbuor Asante/ Christopher Asante *Porkpie* Ram John Holder *Lee* Robbie Gee *Tony* Dominic Keating *Sean Ambrose* Justin Pickett *Michael Ambrose* Geff Francis *Gloria Ambrose* Kim Walker *Louise* Lisa Geoghan *Beverley* Joan Ann Maynard *Mandy* Matilda Thorpe /*cr* Trix Worrell /*pr* Humphrey Barclay, Charlie Hanson /*dr* Trix Worrell, Charlie Hanson, Nic Phillips, Liddy Oldroyd, Mandie Fletcher /*wr* Trix Worrell, Joan Hooley /*Humphrey Barclay Productions* (UK) / 65 x 30m col.

Detective

Crime. BBC1 1964–9

Anthology of classic detective tales, introduced by Rupert Davies as Maigret. Sherlock Holmes, Albert Campion and Father Brown were among the more famous fictional sleuths exercising their ratiocinative talents. The series was an obvious launch pad for potential other series, and no less than three shows were spun off onto the airwaves: ➢*Sherlock Holmes*; R.A. Freeman's forensic scientist *Thorndyke* (BBC 1964, starring Paul Copley); and *Cluff* (BBC1 1964–5, with Leslie Sands), a contemporary Yorkshire policeman based on Gil North's character.

CAST inc *Maigret* Rupert Davies *Sherlock Holmes* Douglas Wilmer *Albert Campion* Brian Smith *Father Brown* Mervyn John /*pr* David Goddard, Verity Lambert, Jordan Lawrence /*dr* inc Jonathan Alwyn, John Frankau, Shaun Sutton, James Cellan Jones / *mus* John Addison /*BBC TV* (UK) /46 x 50m bw.

The Detectives
Comedy. BBC1 1994–7

Spoof version of macho ITV actioner ➢*The Professionals*, spun off from a *Canned Carrott* (➢*Carrott's Lib*) sketch, featuring Jasper Carrott and Robert Powell (➢*Doomwatch*, ➢*Jesus of Nazareth*, husband of ex-Pan's People dancer, Babs) as defective detectives Louis and Briggs. In a neat homage to his tough-guy ➢*Special Branch* persona, pockmarked actor George Sewell played the duo's exasperated boss, whilst numerous other actors famously associated with TV crime – Frank Windsor, John Nettles and James Ellis among them – made cameo appearances. Occasionaly sardonic ('You're coppers – why start telling the truth now?'), the show relied principally on clownery for its humour quotient.

CAST *Bob Louis* Jasper Carrott *Dave Briggs* Robert Powell *Supt Frank Cottam* George Sewell /*cr* Steve Knight, Mike Whitehill /*pr* Ed Bye /*dr* Ed Bye /*wr* Steve Knight, Mike Whitehill /*Celador* (UK) /29 x 30m col.

Dial 999
Crime. ITV 1958–9

Vintage but vigorous black and white police series about a Mountie, tough-sounding Mike Maguire (Canadian film star Robert Beatty), seconded to Scotland Yard. Naturally, he always got his man. Filmed almost entirely on location, it was a co-production with Stateside conveyor-belt programme maker, *Ziv-TV*, and contained a weekly chase plus a generous slug of fisticuffs with underworld hoodlums, these elements thought to be essential for the action-minded American viewer. Duncan Lamont, previously ➢*Quatermass*, played Detective Inspector Winter, Maguire's London counterpart.

CAST *Mike Maguire* Robert Beatty *Det. Insp. Winter* Duncan Lamont *Det. Sgt West* John Witty /*pr* Harry Alan Towers /*dr* inc Alvin Rakoff /*mus* Sidney Torch / *A Towers of London Production in Association with Ziv-TV* (UK:USA) /39 x 30m bw /US tx Syndicated 1959.

Diana: Her True Story
Drama. BSkyB 1993

Gloriously tacky mini-series, based on Andrew Morton's bestseller, reconstructing the soap-opera marriage of their RHs, Charles and Di. David Threlfall (*Paradise Postponed*, ➢*Nightingales*) excelled as the Prince of Wales, with every nervous tick, grimace and hand clasp down pat; Serena Scott Thomas (sister of Kirsten) passed muster as Diana. Filmed in soft focus around various des. piles and palaces, and with a sumptuous wardrobe, it looked two million dollars (which is what it cost). Executive producer Martin Poll argued inventively that *Diana* was 'the sequel' to his triple-Oscar-winning film *The Lion in Winter*, whereas those lucky or tasteless enough to view it on satellite recognized it as Britain's long-awaited answer to ➢*Dynasty*.

CAST *Prince Charles* David Threlfall *Princess Diana* Serena Scott Thomas *Camilla Parker Bowles* Elizabeth Garvie *Queen Elizabeth II* Anne Stallybrass /*exec pr* Martin Poll /*pr* Hugh Benson /*dr* Kevin Connor / *wr* Stephen Zito /*A Martin Poll Production* (USA) / 2 x 120m col.

Dick Barton – Special Agent
Crime. ITV 1979

TV version of the 40s radio detective show, which sensibly kept the derring-do theme music, but less sensibly gave the ex-commando hero unseemly seamy looks. The twice-weekly serial followed Barton's investigation – with help from old army chums Snowey and Jock – into the missing offspring of Sir Richard Marley. To no great surprise, arch-enemy Melganik, dunnit.

CAST *Dick Barton* Tony Vogel *Snowey White* Anthony Heaton *Jock Anderson* James Cosmo *Sir Richard Marley* John Gantrel *Melganik* John G. Heller /*exec pr* Terence Baker, Lewis Russ /*pr* Jon Schofield /*dr* Jon Schofield /*wr* Clive Exton, Julian Bond / *Southern* (UK) /31 x 15m col.

The Dick Emery Show

Comedy. BBC1 1963–81

'Ooh, you are awful – but I like you.'

Like Benny Hill, Sid James, Tony Hancock and a score of other old faces, Richard Gilbert Emery served his showbiz apprenticeship with a WWII entertainment unit (Ralph Leader's RAF Gang Show), before forging a post-war career in radio. His break on the wireless came with *Educating Archie*; initiation into the new medium of TV came shortly afterwards, via *Two's Company*, ➢*It's a Square World* and ➢*The Army Game*. The BBC was then persuaded to give Emery his own show, wherein (like Benny Hill) he purveyed a vulgar, anachronistic, sub-music-hall comedy of impressions. Most famous of his invented characters were the toothy vicar, the peroxide bombshell Mandy, Farmer Finch and, improbably enough, an ageing bovver boy who shook his leg after taking a piss. Audiences lapped it up for nearly two decades. There was also a 1972 feature film, *Oh ... You Are Awful*, several Christmas specials, a *Dick Emery Comedy Hour* for ITV, and a swansong comedy thriller, *Emery* (BBC1, 1982–3), in which Emery played PI, Bernie Weinstock.

CAST Dick Emery /*pr* Ernest Maxin, Colin Charman, Harold Snoad /*wr* inc Dick Emery, John Singer, John Warren /*BBC TV* (UK) /180 x 45–50m bw:col.

The Dickie Henderson Show

Comedy. ITV 1960–8

Former Hollywood child actor and variety trouper Dickie Henderson played himself (largely) in this sitcom about an entertainer with lightly comic troubles at work and home. Most of the former were caused by incompetent manager Jack Meadows, most of the latter by headstrong wife Jane and ten-year-old son Richard. A weekly guest star helped tease out the laughs. Styled closely on the American way of TV comedy, in particular ➢*I Love Lucy*, *Henderson* topped the UK ratings in 1961. The show was a knock-on from an earlier Henderson domcom vehicle, *The Dickie Henderson Half-Hour* (ITV, 1958–60).

CAST *Dickie Henderson* himself *Jane* June Laverick / Isla Blair *Richard* John Parsons/Danny Glover *Jack Meadows* Lionel Murton /*pr* Bill Hitchcock /*dr* Bill Hitchcock /*wr* inc Jimmy Grafton, Jeremy Lloyd, Stan Mars, Eric Newman /*Associated Rediffusion* (UK) / 220 x 30m bw.

The Dick Powell Show

Drama. BBC1 1962–4

One of Hollywood's leading men in the 40s, best remembered as Philip Marlowe in Edward Dymytryk's *Farewell, My Lovely*, Dick Powell moved into production in the 1950s, setting up the Four Star company with David Niven and Charles Noyer (there was no fourth star). Among its many TV programmes was this quality drama anthology, introduced by – and often starring – Powell himself. It acted as a launch pad for several series, notably ➢*Burke's Law*. The directors included Sam Peckinpah, Sam Fuller and, for the segment 'Open Hand', actor Ray Milland in a rare venture behind the camera. Also known as *Dick Powell Theatre*.

CAST (presenters) Dick Powell, June Allyson (stand in hosts) Robert Mitchum, Robert Taylor, James Stewart /*pr* inc Dick Powell, Aaron Spelling, Ralph Nelson /*dr* inc Sam Peckinpah, Marc Daniels, Ray Milland, Sam Fuller, Don Medford /*wr* inc Aaron Spelling, Richard Alan Simmons, Christopher Knopf /*Four Star Productions* (USA) /59 x 60m col /US tx NBC 1961–3.

Dick Spanner PI

Comedy. C4 1987

Puppet show from Gerry ➢'*Thunderbirds*' Anderson which spoofed the hardboiled private-eye films of the 30s, the name of the wise-cracking title 'tec intentionally echoing that of Dashiell Hammett's toolish Sam Spade and Mickey Spillane's Mike Hammer. Exuberantly loaded with puns which benefitted from at least a working familarity with the movies of yore (the story 'The Case of the Maltese Parrot' had a heavy by the name of George Lifeboat and a sexpot called Mae East), the show also traded in the sort of literalist comedy pioneered by ➢*Police Squad*. Originally shown as part of C4's *Network 7* Sunday morning series, *Dick Spanner* was later edited into five segments for late night stripping.

CAST (voices) *Dick Spanner* Shane Rimmer /*cr* Terry Adlam /*pr* Gerry Anderson, Christopher Burr /*mus* Christopher Burr /*Anderson Burr Partnership* (UK) / 2 x 55m col.

Dick Turpin

Adventure. 1979–82

Idealized version of the exploits of the famed 18th-century highwayman. Scripted by Richard Carpenter, it depicted Turpin as Robin Hood astride a horse, friend of the poor and enemy of the rich, especially the appositely-named Sir John Glutton and his henchman Spiker (David Daker, later in ➢*Boon*). Joining Turpin on his adventures was novice gentleman of the road, Swiftnick. What *DT* lacked in versimilitude it made up for in galloping, early evening excitement. Even the casting of sitcom star Richard O'Sullivan (➢*Man About the House*) as the swashbuckling hero worked. A spin-off mini-series, *Dick Turpin's Greatest Adventures* (1981), saw Mary Crosby of ➢*Dallas* play an American girl petitioning the Attorney-General for justice on behalf of her fellow colonists.

CAST *Dick Turpin* Richard O'Sullivan *Nick Smith (Swiftnick)* Michael Deeks *Sir John Glutton* Christopher Benjamin *Captain Spiker* David Daker / *cr* Richard Carpenter / *pr* Paul Knight, Sidney Cole / *dr* inc Charles Crichton, Gerry Poulson, James Allen / *wr* Richard Carpenter / *Gatetarn: Seacastle Prods: LWT* (UK) /25 x 30m col.

The Dick Van Dyke Show

Comedy. BBC1 1963–6

Top-rated US sitcom from the 60s golden age, starring Dick Van Dyke as Rob Petrie, a comedy writer for the fictional *The Alan Brady Show*. The settings, unusually, were two: Petrie's office, where he shenaniganed with assistants Buddy Sorrell and man-eater Sally Rogers (also seen was pompous producer, Melvin Cooley); and his home in the New York suburb of New Rochelle, which he shared with perky, capri-pants wearing wife Laura and son Ritchie.

Originally, creator Carl Reiner intended to play Petrie himself, but was persuaded to step down by executive producer Sheldon Leonard, who cast in his place a former game-show host, Dick Van Dyke. After much searching, unknown actress Mary Tyler Moore was chosen for the part of Laura. Tyler Moore's hitherto most substantial roles had been as the secretary, Sam – filmed only from the hips down – in *Richard Diamond, Private Eye* and the 'Happy Hotpoint' elf in the TV commercial.

Though it would eventually rise to No. 3 in the Nielsens, *DVDS* started inauspiciously, partly because CBS chief Jim Aubrey ('the Smiling Cobra') disliked it and even had to be persuaded to air it by sponsors Proctor and Gamble. When their enthusiasm, in turn, flagged, the show was saved by the Television Academy, which bestowed a cabinet's worth of Emmys. There were, in total, 15 awarded to the show, including Outstanding Writing in Comedy (1962, 1963, 1964, 1965), Outstanding Comedy Program (1963, 1964, 1966) and Outstanding Program Achievement in Entertainment (1965). Van Dyke and Tyler Moore both received Emmy's for their performances. Famously liberal and optimistic of human nature, it was financed initially by money from the Kennedy clan, via JFK's brother-in-law, Peter Lawford. As if to underline the show's embodiment of the spirit of the Kennedy age, Tyler Moore even looked like Jackie Kennedy.

The show came to an end in 1966 due to a pact between the producers and cast made in 1961 that they would do five year's worth of episodes and no more. Van Dyke, 'the male Julie Andrews' as he called himself, moved over into the movies, but returned to TV in 1971 with *The New Dick Van Dyke Show* playing Dick Preston, host of a TV chat show. Meanwhile, Tyler Moore progressed to her own, and even more fabulous ➢*The Mary Tyler Moore Show*. *DVDS* continues to be repeated to this day, its timeless appeal helped by being originally shot without any slang expressions and few topical references.

CAST *Rob Petrie* Dick Van Dyke *Laura Petrie* Mary Tyler Moore *Ritchie Petrie* Larry Matthews *Alan Brady* Carl Reiner *Jerry Helper* Jerry Paris *Millie Helper* Ann Morgan Guilbert *Buddy Sorrell* Morey Amsterdam *Sally Rogers* Rose Marie *Mel Cooney* Richard Deacon / *cr* Carl Reiner / *exec pr* Sheldon Leonard, Danny Thomas, Carl Reiner / *pr* Carl Reiner / *dr* inc Sheldon Leonard, Carl Reiner, John Jerry Paris / *wr* inc Carl Reiner, Bill Persky, Sam Denoff / *Calvada Productions: T&L Productions* (USA)156 x 25m bw /US tx CBS 1961–5.

Diff'rent Strokes

Comedy. ITV 1980–6

Interracial American sitcom which premised the adoption of two black Harlem orphans, Arnold (Gary Coleman) and Willis Jackson, by a white, Park Avenue millionaire. Developed by NBC executive Fred Silverman as a vehicle for the precocious eight-year-old Coleman (he of the extraordinary comic timing and savvy self-confidence), the show sought to bridge the colour divide in the American audience. This it did, but not without criticism from black organizations that Coleman was just the grinning, wire-haired piccaninny from yesteryear's TV and film, filling the life of the soulless white folks with joy. Unfortunately, a kidney transplant stunted Coleman's growth and led to health problems, making his face look prematurely aged, which gave his performance a diverting oddness. Janet Jackson, in the days before she became a pop megastar, appeared as Willis' girlfriend.

CAST *Arnold Jackson* Gary Coleman *Willis Jackson* Todd Bridges *Philip Drummond* Conrad Bain *Kimberley Bail* Dana Plato *Mrs Garrett* Charlotte Rae *Charlene DuPrey* Janet Jackson /*cr* Jeff Harris, Bernie Kukoff /*pr* Budd Grossman, Howard Leeds, John Maxwell Anderson /*TAT Productions* (USA) / 84 x 30m col /US tx NBC:ABC 1978–86.

District Nurse

Drama. BBC1 1984–7

Dreary drama starring former ➢*Liver Bird* Nerys Hughes as bicycling Welsh Florence Nightingale, Megan Roberts. It was set in the impoverished mining village of Pencwm in the 1920s, where the prissy, middle-class Roberts struggled to win respect from the clannish prole locals. A second series moved the story up to the 1930s and the setting to a Cymric seaside town, where she lived in the house of Dr Emlyn Isaacs. It was the work of future ➢*EastEnders* creators, Julia Smith and Tony Holland.

CAST *Megan Roberts* Nerys Hughes *Dr Emlyn Isaacs* Freddie Jones /*cr* Julia Smith, Tony Holland /*pr* Julia Smith /*wr* inc Julia Smith, Tony Holland /*BBC TV* (UK) /15 x 30m col.

Dixon of Dock Green

Crime. BBC1 1955–76

Evening all. Jack Warner (born John Waters) played wise old copper George Dixon who kept an eye out for errant kids, and villains straight out of the catalogue of stereotypes, in this televisual institution, the longest-running police show in the history of British TV. The character of Dixon first appeared in the 1950 Rank movie *The Blue Lamp*, in which he was shot by a young villain (Dirk Bogarde). Kindly, tea-drinking Dixon, however, so caught the public's imagination (or need for a reassuring representation of ordered, honest bobbery), that he was resurrected from the dead by the BBC as a replacement for ➢*Fabian of the Yard*, with his co-creator Ted Willis penning most of his early small-screen appearances. For his ideas, Willis spent some weeks researching at Paddington Green station, eventually recruiting 250 officers onto his 'payroll' to provide him with anecdotes. Although Willis genuflected at the, then, vogue for documentary-style visuals, he intentionally constructed the series as a cosy, non-violent entertainment suitable for all the family. Episodes famously ended with the uniformed Dixon intoning a homily – invariably to the effect that crime doesn't pay – beneath the station's blue lamp before disappearing into the night whistling 'Maybe It's Because I'm a Londoner'. By the mid 1960s, however, Dixon was beginning to look jaded in comparison to the coppers of ➢*Z Cars*, while his pro-establishment views (including support for capital punishment) were embarrassingly anachronistic. With Dixon's promotion to desk sergeant, the station's younger officers – especially Andy Crawford (Peter Byrne, later in ➢*Bread*) and 'Laudy' Lauderdale – came to the fore. Even so, the advent of hyper-realistic police actioner ➢*The Sweeney* in the 1970s, which was set on the same London streets, showed the series to be irredeemably outmoded. But not forgotten. When Warner died in 1981 at the age of 85 (he had fought in WWI, winning an MSM [Meritorious Service Medal]) his coffin was borne by police officers from Paddington Green station, with the show's theme 'An Ordinary Copper' playing over the PA. It was not only Jack Warner who was buried that day. Into the grave with him went George Dixon, the emblematic old-fashioned British bobby. Never again would the police be so well served on the small screen.

CAST *PC/Sgt George Dixon* Jack Warner *PC/DS Andy Crawford* Peter Byrne *Mary Crawford (née Dixon)* Billie Whitelaw/Jeannette Hutchinson *PC 'Laudy' Lauderdale* Geoffrey Adams *Desk Sgt Flint* Arthur Rigby *PC 'Tubb' Barrell* Neil Wilson *Sgt Grace Millard* Moira Mannion /*cr* Ted Willis, Jan Read /*pr* inc Douglas Moodie, Ronald Marsh, Philip Barker, G.B. Lupino, Eric Fawcett, Robin Nash, Joe Waters /*dr* inc Vere Lorrimer, Michael Goodwin, Douglas Argent /*wr* inc Ted Willis, Eric Price, Gerald Kelsey, N.J. Crisp, Jack Trevor Story, Robert Holmes, P.J. Hammond, Tony Williamson /*mus* Jeff Darnell ('Ordinary Copper' theme) /*BBC TV* (UK) /429 x 30–45m bw:col.

Doctor in the House

Comedy. ITV 1969–70

Medical sitcom which pleased in small doses. Loosely derived from the book by Richard Gordon, at the instigation of LWT's comedy supremo, Frank Muir, it updated the story to feature a fresh intake of students at famed St Swithins' teaching hospital. Most prominent amongst the beery, leery, cheery freshmen quacks were Michael Upton, Duncan Waring, Paul Collier (George Layton) and upper-class Dick Stuart-Clark. Professor Loftus and the Dean were the haughty figures of aghast authority. The show proved useful writing work for Cambridge contemporaries John Cleese, Graham Chapman, Bill Oddie, Graeme Garden and Jonathan Lynn (who also appeared as mad Irish medic Danny Hooley), with the follow-up show, *Doctor at Large* (ITV, 1971), even allowing Cleese a try-out episode about a rude hotel keeper that would aid the gestation of ➢*Fawlty Towers. Doctor at Large* saw Upton *et al* newly qualified, and puritan kill-joy Bingham (Richard O'Sullivan, ➢*Man About the House*, ➢*Dick Turpin*) joining the department of incompetence and comic crises. Thereafter, *Doctor* series emanated with laxative regularity: *Doctor in Charge* (ITV, 1972–3), *Doctor at Sea* (ITV, 1974), *Doctor on the Go* (ITV, 1975–7) and the antipodean *Doctor Down Under* (ITV, 1980), by which time Waring and Stuart-Clark were the only surviving original characters. Alas, the sequel shows tended merely to illustrate the law of diminishing returns. As did the BBC's ill-advised revival *Doctor at the Top* (BBC, 1991), which saw Waring, Collier and Stuart-Clark 20 years on and the holders of (improbably and unfunnily) high office at St Swithins. A 1983 film, *Doctor in the House* (ITV), segued clips from the *Doctor* series thus far.

CAST *Michael Upton* Barry Evans *Duncan Waring* Robin Nedwell *Dick Stuart-Clark* Geoffrey Davies *Paul Collier* George Layton *Huw Evans* Martin Shaw *Prof. Geoffrey Loftus* Ernest Clark *The Dean* Ralph Michael *Dave Briddock* Simon Cuff *Danny Hooley* Jonathan Lynn /*cr* Richard Gordon, Frank Muir /*pr* Humphrey Barclay /*dr* inc Bill Turner, David Askey /*wr* inc John Cleese, Graham Chapman, Bill Oddie, Graeme Garden, Jonathan Lynn /*BBC TV* (UK) /26 x 30m col.

Dr Katz

Comedy. Paramount 1995–

The (head) cases of 'Dr Katz, Professional Therapist', whose workload was not helped by a contemptuous, nail-filing secretary and wimpily inadequate son.

American animated sitcom of acerbic humour, drawn with distinction – only the characters were in colour, the backgrounds were monochrome – and written with casual brilliance. A loony toon for intelligent adults.

CAST (voices) *Dr Katz* Jonathan Katz *Ben* H. Jon Benjamin *Laura* Laura Silverman *Stanley* Will LeBow /*cr* Tom Snyder, Jonathan Katz /*exec pr* Tom Snyder, Tim Braine, Nancy Geller /*pr* inc Jonathan Katz, Julianne Shapiro, H. Jon Benjamin /*wr* inc Jonathan Katz, H. Jon Benjamin, Loren Bouchard, Karen LeBlanc, Anette LeBlanc Cates, Will LeBow /*mus* Tom Snyder and Shapiro Music /*HBO Downtown Productions: Tom Snyder Productions: Popular Arts* (USA) /46+ x 30m col.

The Doctors

Melodrama. BBC1 1969–71

Early and typically cautious BBC attempt to slum it in the genre of soap opera (see ➢*Compact*, ➢*United!*). Set in a north London NHS practice run by Dr John Somers, it lacked the tacky heart of the successful sudster, overweighting the personal lives of the practice staff with gloomy, gritty medical storylines (this despite having Fay Weldon in the writing department). Notable, though, for being the first bi-weekly soap to be shot in colour. A spin-off, *Owen, MD*, featured the surgery's Welsh GP of that surname.

CAST *Dr John Somers* John Barrie *Dr Roger Hayman* Richard Leech *Dr Elizabeth McNeal* Justine Lord *Tom Durham* Paul Massie *Dr Thomas Owen* Nigel Stock /*pr* Colin Morris, Bill Sellars /*wr* inc Fay Weldon, Elaine Morgan /*BBC TV* (UK) /120 x 30m col.

Doctor Who

Sci-fi. BBC1 1963

Not just a space-opera for children, but a national institution. The eponymous Time Lord, with a blood temperature 20 degrees below that of humans, first landed on the Earth's TV screens on 22 November 1963, his appearance being delayed

Five the Daleks missed. Patrick Troughton (second from left) heads a gathering of Time Lords in a celebration of sci-fi classic *Doctor Who.* The show was originally intended as a children's educational programme.

17 minutes by nothing less than the assassination of JFK. Originally, *Dr Who*'s adventures were intended by the then head of BBC drama, Sydney Newman, to be of educational benefit, a means of explaining past times and physical concepts. 'No cheap-jack bug-eyed monsters,' he instructed the show's first producer, Verity Lambert (later ➢*Minder*, ➢*Edward and Mrs Simpson*). To the joy of all future TV generations, Lambert ignored the caution and introduced Terry Nation's (➢*Blake's 7*, ➢*The Survivors*) Daleks in episode two, 'The Dead Planet'. Fearsome creations of cardboard and Morris Minor indicator lights, the Daleks – with their cry of 'Ex-ter-min-ate! Ex-ter-min-ate!' – would become the Doctor's most constant adversary. They also shot the show up the charts. Its peak viewing would reach 16 million.

A mere 720 years old (900 according to some), the Doctor was a native of planet Gallifrey, who stole a faulty time travel machine or TARDIS (standing for Time and Relative Dimension in Space), and set out to wander the cosmos. Eventually, he moved from being an objective observer of events to a fighter against evil. As the TARDIS had defective navigation, it could land anywhere, anytime.

To date there have been seven TV series incarnations of the Doctor, all different in character, explained by the need for Time Lords to 'regenerate'. The first, played by ➢*The Army Game* regular William Hartnell, was grandfatherly and Edwardian, but was replaced by a Chaplinesque hobo version (Patrick Troughton) who, in turn, was replaced by the dandyish, gadget-crazy interpretation of Jon Pertwee (➢*Worzel Gummidge*). Tom Baker – who married *Who* girl Lalla Ward – then played the Doctor for seven years as a scarf-trailing wit ('Hello, I'm the Doctor – have a jelly baby'), before the character was reinvented as a sensitive preppy by Peter Davison (➢*All Creatures Great and Small*). Colin Baker's tenure gave the character an abrasive, anti-authoritarian persona, while Sylvester McCoy was a clownish extrovert.

Aiding the Doctor have been numerous female 'companions', most of them helpless women. More advanced female characters appeared on occasion – the Liberationist Sarah Jane and the warrior Leela – but the tendency has always been to slip back towards the norm. As for the Doctor's enemies, these, like the Daleks, have tended to be made out of sheer inventiveness. Of the 140+

species of alien to appear on *Dr Who*, most have been humanoid, purely because an actor could be dressed to play them. Memory says that all the action took place in either a wobbly set or the BBC sandpit, while the TARDIS – a police phone box – was simply claimed to be bigger inside than out.

But the attraction of *Dr Who* was always the quality of its ideas and scriptwriting (Douglas Adams and Chris ➢'*Star Cops*' Boucher were regular writers), not the quantity of its budget. When the ideas began to go awry in the late 80s, the show lost its appeal, becoming a parody of itself, with narratives viewed like sitcoms. Ken Dodd appeared on set, as did Nicholas Parsons and even Bonnie Langford. Ratings slumped to 4.5 million, and the BBC put the serial on 'hiatus'. However, the Doctor regenerated yet again in 1996 for a TVM, produced by the BBC and America's Universal TV, starring Paul McGann, with the promise of a follow-up series. As the Doctor put it in 1967's 'The Tomb of the Cybermen', 'We [Time Lords] can live for ever, barring accidents.'

As the longest running sci-fi serial in the world, *Doctor Who* has proved a useful training ground for young actors. Serial regulars Peter Purves and Frazer Hines went on to ➢*Blue Peter* and ➢*Emmerdale Farm*, while Martin Clunes (➢*Men Behaving Badly*) was among the many who received their first substantial screen role playing a *Who* baddie.

CAST *Dr Who I (1963–6)* William Hartnell *Susan Foreman* Carole Ann Ford *Ian Chesterton* William Russell *Barbara Wright* Jacqueline Hill *Vicki* Maureen O'Brien *Steven Taylor* Peter Purves; *Dr Who II (1966–9)* Patrick Troughton *Polly* Anneke Wills *Ben* Michael Craze *Jamie* Frazer Hines *Zoe* Wendy Padbury; *Dr Who III (1969–74)* Jon Pertwee *Liz Shaw* Caroline John *Jo Grant* Katy Manning *Brigadier Lethbridge-Stewart* Nicholas Courtney; *Dr Who IV (1974–81)* Tom Baker *Sarah Jane Smith* Elizabeth Sladen *Harry Sullivan* Ian Marter *Leela* Louise Jameson *Romana* Mary Tamm/Lalla Ward *K9* John Leeson (voice); *Dr Who V (1982–4)* Peter Davison *Tegan* Janet Fielding *Nyssa* Sarah Sutton *Adric* Matthew Waterhouse *Turlough* Mark Strickson; *Dr Who VI (1984–6)* Colin Baker *Perpugillian 'Peri' Brown* Nicola Bryant *Melanie Brush* Bonnie Langford; *Dr Who VII (1987–92)* Sylvester McCoy *Ace* Sophie Aldred; *The Master* Roger Delgado (also Anthony Ainley) /*cr* Sydney Newman /*pr* inc Verity Lambert, Barry Letts, John Nathan-Turner /*dr* inc Waris Hussein, Douglas Camfield, Mervyn Pinfield, Derek Martinus, Christopher Barry, Julia Smith, George Spenton Foster, Michael E. Briant, Paddy Russell, Pennant Roberts, Graeme Harper /*wr* inc Terry Nation, Dennis Spooner, John Lucarotti, Kid Pedler, Gerry Davis, Robert Holmes, Malcolm Hulke, Robert Banks Stewart, Chris Boucher, Douglas Adams, Peter Grimwade /*mus* Ron Grainer (theme) /*BBC TV* (UK) / 679 x 30m, 15 x 50m, 1 x 90m bw:col.

Dr Finlay's Casebook

Melodrama. BBC 1962–7

Venerable, much-loved medical series of bucolic cosiness, set in the small Scottish town of Tannochbrae in the late 1920s. Episodes revolved around elderly, irascible Dr Angus Cameron and his young, newly-arrived junior at Arden House practice, Dr Finlay (newsreader Bill Simpson). As with US 60s rivals ➢*Dr Kildare* and ➢*Ben Casey*, the doctorly generations disputed dramatically, only to learn the value of the other's point of view. Down-to-earth housekeeper, Janet, looked on disdainfully.

Like all the best whimsical Scottish screen products, the series found its strength in its evocation of place (it was filmed in and around the Perthshire village of Callader) and slightly larger than life characters. It thus provided gainful employment for Scottish character actors galore, among them John Laurie, Gordon Jackson and James Robertson-Justice. For those who care to know, Finlay's car was a 1913 Sunbeam. The series was adapted from A.J. Cronin's stories, *The Adventures of a Black Bag*.

With the 90s revival of pastoral nostalgia, seen most obviously in ➢*The Darling Buds of May* and ➢*Heartbeat*, it was perhaps only a matter of time before *Dr Finlay's Casebook* was taken out of the morgue and revived. Despite a strong cast in David Rentoul, Annette Crosbie and Ian Bannen, *Dr Finlay* (Scottish TV, 1993–) the remake, however, was only moderately successful.

CAST *Dr Angus Cameron* Andrew Cruickshank *Janet* Barbara Mullen *Dr Alan Finlay* Bill Simpson *Dr Snoddie* Eric Woodburn *Mistress Niven* Effie Morrison *Barbara Davidson* Tracy Reed *Bruce Cameron* Anthony Valentine /*cr* A.J. Cronin /*pr* Campbell Logan, Andrew Osborn, Gerard Glaister, Royston Morley, John Henderson, Douglas Allen /*dr* inc Julia Smith, Laurence Bourne, William Slater, Prudence Fitzgerald / *wr* inc N.J. Crisp, Elaine Morgan, Donald Bull, Robert Holmes, Pat Dunlop /*BBC TV* (UK) /178 x 50m bw:col.

Dr Kildare

Melodrama. BBC1 1961–6

Based on novelist Max Brand's (aka Fredrick Schiller Faust) stories, *Dr Kildare* was translated to TV in 1961 (via a reel of successful movies starring Lew Ayres) and promptly set the formula for an epidemic of medical melodramas: impetuous young doctor has to be taught the value of experience by aged mentor, while the mentor is forced to acknowledge that new-fangled ideas work. After a misfiring pilot episode, veteran actor Raymond Massey was hired as craggy, wise Gillespie and William Shatner was cast as Kildare. Shatner, however, decided to accept another offer of work (*For the People*), leaving unknown Richard Chamberlain to the role of the new intern at metropolitan Blair General Hospital. Blond and boyish, Chamberlain was every mother's dream son, every girl's dream boyfriend. Within a year the show had a 15 million (largely distaff) audience in the USA. As well as enjoying Chamberlain's female appeal, the show shamelessly exploited patient dramas, standardly incorporating two or three tear-jerking storylines per episode. After five years, Chamberlain was vocally tired of playing Kildare ('I had worn out every facet') and complained of the show's shift towards an anthology format in which the focus was the ailing weekly guest star. With the ratings dipping anyway, NBC cancelled the show in the autumn of 1966. Chamberlain himself was more than a flash in the bedpan, becoming the 'king of the mini-series' in the 1970s (➢*Shogun*, ➢*The Thorn Birds inter alia*). In 1972 MGM tried artificial respiration on Brand's character, producing *Young Dr Kildare*, which managed a short run in syndication.

CAST *Dr James Kildare* Richard Chamberlain *Dr Leonard Gillespie* Raymond Massey *Nurse Zoe Lawton* Lee Kurty *Dr Simon Agurski* Eddie Ryder *Dr Thomas Gerson* Jud Taylor *Dr John Ross* Robert Paget *Dr Kapish* Ken Berry *Nurse Conant* Jo Helton *Mrs Salt* Cynthia Stone /*exec pr* David Victor /*pr* Norman Felton, Hebert Hirschman, David Victor /*dr* inc Leonard Horn, Alf Kjellin, Don Medford, Ralph Senensky, Lawrence Dobkin /*mus* Jerry Goldsmith / *Arena Productions: MGM–TV* (USA) /142 x 60m bw, 58 x 30m col /US tx NBC 1961–6.

Dr Quinn: Medicine Woman

Western. ITV 1992–

Mild, rather than Wild, Western show. Out in the frontier town of Colorado Springs folks didn't take kindly to the notion of a female sawbones. Still, Dr Quinn just jutted her jaw, got on with her job and asserted her proto-feminist viewpoint.

Like fellow Brit actress gone to Hollywood Joan Collins, former Bond girl Jane Seymour (born Joyce Frankenburg) found her niche in middle life as the mainstay of a US TV show. And there was gold in dispensing them thar pills. Playing the gingham-clad embodiment of the female frontier spirit made Seymour Britain's highest-earning woman with, in 1995, a £2 million contract for 25 episodes. Part of the revival of the screen Western inaugurated by ➢*Lonesome Dove*, *Dr Quinn*'s patented mixture of soft-focus teletography, hokey feminism, spectacular scenery (the Santa Monica Mountains National Recreation Area, California), old-fashioned oater action, and refined sugary sentiment slipped down with painless ease. Seymour's third husband, James Keach (brother of Stacy, ➢*Mickey Spillane's Mike Hammer*) was one of the show's principal directors.

CAST *Dr Michaela 'Mike' Quinn* Jane Seymour *Byron Sully* Joe Lando *Matthew Cooper* Chad Allen *Brian Cooper* Shawn Toovey *Colleen Cooper* Erika Flores/ Jessica Bowman /*exec pr* inc Beth Sullivan, Sara Davidson, Tim Johnson /*pr* Tim Johnson, Carl Binder /*dr* inc James Keach, Alan J. Levi, Chuck Bowman, Jerry Jameson /*wr* inc Melissa Rosenberg, Sara Davidson, Andrew Lipitz, Philip Gerson /*The Sullivan Company: CBS Entertainment Productions* (USA) / 147 x 60m col /US tx CBS 1993–8.

Dogtanian and the Three Muskehounds

Children's. BBC1 1985

Cartoon canine version of Alexandre Dumas' *The Three Musketeers*. Dogtanian, an endearingly gauche puppy from Gascony, travels to Paris to join the King's Own Guard, falling in love en route with the beautiful Juliette, but eventually teaming up with swordsters Athos, Porthos and Aramis to fight for the underchien throughout France. A minor classic, with engaging characterization, despite some crudity of drawing.

cr Claudio Biern Boyd /*exec pr* Claudio Biern Boyd /*dr* Tom Wiener, Robert Barron, Byrd Ehlmann /*wr* Claudio Biern Boyd /*mus* Guido & Maurisio de Angelis /*sfx* Luis Castro /*BRB International SA* (Sp) / 12 x 25m col.

Do Not Adjust Your Set

Children's. ITV 1967–9

Subtitled *The Fairly Pointless Show*, a zany children's review of fast-footed sketches and visual gags, written and performed by Oxbridge graduates Michael Palin, Terry Jones and Eric Idle. Co-stars were a young (and decidely more proletarian) David Jason and Denise Coffey, whose cod super-hero *Captain Fantastic* slot eventually acquired an existence beyond *DNAYS* as an insert into other shows. Music was courtesy of the surreal Bonzo Dog Doodah Band (of 'Monster Mash' celebrity). During the run of the show John Cleese introduced animator Terry Gilliam and thus were the seeds of ➢*Monty Python* born.

CAST Eric Idle, Michael Palin, Terry Jones, David Jason, Denise Coffey /*pr* Humphrey Barclay, Ian Davidson /*dr* inc Daphne Shadwell, Adrian Cooper / *wr* inc Eric Idle, Michael Palin, Terry Jones / Rediffusion (UK) /30 x 30m bw.

Don't Wait Up

Comedy. BBC1 1983–90

Father and son medical mirth. Recently divorced GP Tom Latimer (Nigel Havers, *The Charmer*, scion of former Attorney-General Sir Michael Havers) is scandalized to find that his own parents are separating. Worse, his father Toby, a Harley Street dermatologist, moves into his tiny flat. Episodes played on the universal truth that children expect impossibly high standards of behaviour from their parents, plus Tom's frosty relations with his ex-wife Helen, and his political disagreement with his private-medicine-practising pater.

CAST *Dr Tom Latimer* Nigel Havers *Dr Toby Latimer* Tony Britton *Angela Latimer* Dinah Sheridan *Helen Latimer* Jane How *Madeleine Forbes (later Latimer)* Susan Skipper *Dr Charles Cartwright* Richard Heffer /Simon Williams /*cr* George Layton /*pr* Harold Snoad /*wr* George Layton /*BBC TV* (UK) /38 x 30m col.

Doogie Howser, MD

Comedy. BBC1 1990–3

Improbable but diverting sitcom featuring a boy genius who becomes a fully qualified doctor at 16. The fresh-faced one practised – to the jaw-dropping panic of patients – at the Eastman Medical Center in LA. Dotingly supported by his parents, Howser was astutely kept the right side of precious by typical teen friend Vinnie. Developed by Steven Bochco as part of his ten-pilot contract with America's ABC network, the show was co-created with David Kelley, with whom Bochco again teamed for ➢*LA Law*.

CAST *Dr Douglas 'Doogie' Howser* Neil Patrick Harris *Dr David Howser* James B. Sikking *Katherine Howser* Belinda Montgomery *Vinnie Delpino* Max Casella *Dr Benjamin Canfield* Lawrence Pressman /*cr* Steven Bochco, David Kelley /*dr* inc Paul Newman, Bill D'elia, Kris Tabori, Steven Cragg, Joan Darling, Matia Karrell, Eric Laneuville /*Steven Bochco Productions* (USA) /60 x 30m col /US tx ABC 1989–93.

Doomwatch

Sci-fi. BBC1 1970–2

Prescient eco-drama, which donated a new word to the English lexicon. *Doomwatch* – which stood for Department of Measurement of Science Work – related the activities of a crack British agency dedicated to protecting Earth from the effects of uncontrolled scientific experiments. Head of the agency was abrasive Dr Spencer Quist, while smooth John Ridge and conscientious Tobias 'Toby' Wren (Robert ➢'*Jesus of Nazareth*' Powell in his debut) were the main operatives. A dour Yorkshireman from a stereotype mill, Colin Bradley, did the lab work. Theatrical but intelligent, it covered a gamut of incipient environmental problems, from sonic noise pollution ('The Red Sky') to drug-aided sub-liminal advertising of cigarettes ('The Devil's Sweets'). It also raised viewer goosepimples as well as consciousness; the veritible ➢*Hammer House of Horror* segment 'Tomorrow the Rat', about genetically-engineered, flesh-eating rodents, caused questions to be asked in the House of Commons. The show reached its artistic peak with the season one finale, 'Survival Code' (in which Tobias Wren died defusing a bomb), the series thereafter declining into dramatic OTTness, exemplified by Ridge going mad and threatening to kill off humanity with a flask of anthrax. Its run was marked by controversy, and it was only appropriate that *Doomwatch* should end with the banning of its ultimate episode, 'Sex and Violence', which provoked the Corporation's ire because it contained real footage of a military execution. A 1972 feature-film version only accorded the usual cast cameo roles, giving the starring part to actor Ian Bannen.

CAST *Dr Spencer Quist* John Paul *Dr John Ridge* Simon Oates *Tobias Wren* Robert Powell *Colin Bradley* Joby Blanshard *Pat Hunisett* Wendy Hall *Dr Fay Chantry* Jean Trend /*cr* Kit Pedler, Gerry Davis /*pr* Terence Dudley /*dr* inc Paul Ciappessoni, Jonathan Alwyn, Terence Dudley /*wr* Kit Pedler, Gerry Davis, Dennis Spooner, Terence Dudley, Ian Curteis /*mus* Max Harris /*BBC TV* (UK) /38 x 50m col.

Dorothy L. Sayers Mystery

Crime. BBC2 1987

More than a decade after Ian Carmichael hung up his gumshoes as ➢*Lord Peter Wimsey*, Edward Petherbridge starred in these further cases of Sayers' aristo amateur sleuth. Solidly made, faithful to Sayers' conception, with laudable period atmosphere and supporting acting from Harriet Walter as Wimsey's saved-from-the-gallows *femme* companion, Harriet Vane, the show nonetheless never quite grabbed the fancy as much as Carmichael's idiosyncratic 'cheer-frightfully-ho!' version of 1972–5. The three stories dramatized were: *Strong Poison*; *Have His Carcase*; *Gaudy Night*.

CAST *Lord Peter Wimsey* Edward Petherbridge *Bunter* Richard Morant *Harriet Vane* Harriet Walter /*pr* Michael Chapman /*dr* Christopher Hodson, Michael Simpson /*wr* Philip Broadley, Rosemary Ann Sisson /*mus* Joseph Horowitz /*BBC TV* (UK) /10 x 55m col / US tx WGBH Boston 1987.

Dotto

Light Entertainment. ITV 1959–60

Extraordinarily popular quiz show, reaching No. 1 in the ratings in its launch year. Correct answers from contestants enabled them to join dots to reveal a celebrity's face to win money. Presenters included Shaw Taylor, who later lent his voice of doom to the pioneer aid-the-constabulary series, *Police Five*.

The American blueprint of *Dotto* achieved notoriety when it was removed from the screen in the 'Quiz Show Scandal', after an allegation that questions were rigged for the advantage of favoured, telegenic punters.

CAST (presenters) Robert Gladwell, Jimmy Hanley, Shaw Taylor /*pr* John Irwin /*ATV* (UK) /60 x 30m bw /US tx NBC 1958.

Double Your Money

Light Entertainment. ITV 1955–64

Early ITV quiz show, hosted by Canadian actor-showman Hughie Green (previously in Hollywood's ➢*Lassie* cycle), in which contestants doubled their money for giving correct answers to general-knowledge questions. When they hit the £1000 'Treasure Trail' the mood switched to serious and they were shunted off into a soundproof booth for the ultimate questions. A 1966 episode was presented from the USSR, with the top prize of a television set.

Based on America's famous *The $64,000 Question*, which had an economy British replicate, *The 64,000 Question* (ITV 1956–8), in which the contestants won prize units of sixpence. It was resurrected in 1990 under its original title with Bob Monkhouse as the questioner.

CAST (presenter) Hughie Green (hostesses) Nancy Roberts, Monica Rose, Julie de Marco /*cr* John Beard /*dr* inc Eric Croall, Don Gale, Jim Pople, Peter Croft /*Arlington Television and Radio Ltd* (UK) /260 x 30m bw:col.

Douglas Fairbanks Jr Presents

Drama. ITV 1955–9

The son of the Hollywood matinée idol hosted and produced this drama anthology of enormously wide-ranging subject matter (psycho-thrillers, swashbucklers, farce and all). Mass produced at Britain's National Studios at Elstree, with British casts and crews, the series was of erratic – though generally solid – quality and sold to fill screens worldwide. In the UK, the series topped the ratings in 1956. Some quarter of the episodes starred Fairbanks Jr himself, a leading man in his own, not just his father's reflected, light.

CAST (presenter) Douglas Fairbanks Jr /*pr* Lance Comfort, Douglas Fairbanks Jr /*dr* inc Lance Comfort, Bernard Knowles, Leslie Arliss, Terence Fisher /

Douglas Fairbanks Productions (UK) /117 x 30m bw / US tx Syndicated 1953–7.

Dragnet

Crime. ITV 1952–8

'Ladies and gentlemen, the story you are about to see is true. Only the names have been changed to protect the innocent.'

Thus opened every episode of the hyper-realistic *Dragnet*, featuring Jack Webb (also creator, executive producer, director) as downbeat LAPD Detective Sergeant Joe Friday, master of the minimalist sentence ('Just the facts, Ma'am.'/'I carry a badge.'/'That's my job.'). Though Friday plodded stiffly through his cases in almost real time, tension was maintained by dynamic, documentary-style photography, Webb's terse narration and Walter Schumann's moody music (Schumann's famous 'dum-de dum-dum' theme even became a hit record). Authenticity was guaranteed by basing stories on cases pulled from the files of the real-life LAPD. Among the most popular and influential TV shows ever, *Dragnet*'s main fault was a sententious moralizing on behalf of the upstanding nature of Los Angeles' finest. It originated from a 1949 movie, *He Walked By Night*, in which Webb played a lab technician, then went to radio, before being transmitted as part of TV's *Chesterfield Sound Off Time* in 1951. It debuted in Britain in 1955, the first cop show to be screened there. On the conclusion of *Dragnet*'s US prime-time run in 1959, by which time Friday had gone through three partners (Romero, Jacobs, Smith), the series went into syndication as *Badge 714* (Friday's warrant number); it was revived in colour for NBC network in 1967 as *Dragnet 67*, then *Dragnet 68* and so on annually until *Dragnet 70*. Nagging hypochondriac Bill Gannon (Harry Morgan, later in ➢*M*A*S*H*) was brought in as Friday's new sidekick.

Since the death of Jack Webb (a sometime head of Warner TV, and producer of such hits as *O'Hara, US Treasury* and ➢*Hec Ramsey*) in 1982, *Dragnet* has been resurrected for TV once again, as a syndicated US series starring Jeff Osterhage as the Fridayesque detective Vic Daniels. A 1987 *Dragnet* movie-parody, with Dan Aykroyd and Tom Hanks, featured Harry Morgan in affectionate homage to his years on the show.

CAST *Sgt (later Lt) Joe Friday* Jack Webb *Sgt Ben Romero* Barton Yarborough *Sgt Ed Jacobs* Barney Phillips *Off. Frank Smith* Herb Ellis /Ben Alexander *Off. Bill Gannon* Harry Morgan /*cr* Jack Webb, Richard L. Breen /*exec pr* Jack Webb /*dr* Jack Webb /*wr* Jack Webb, Richard L. Breen, Jerry Cohen, James Doherty, James Moser /*mus* Walter Schumann /*MCA TV: Mark VII: Universal TV* (USA) /263 x 30m bw, 98 x 30m col / US tx NBC 1952–8, 1967–70.

Dream On

Comedy. C4 1991–

Made for cable American 'adult comedy' (i.e. spiced with naked embonpoint) in which sex-mad NY book editor Martin Tupper, a TV child of the 50s, becomes a newly divorced guy of the 90s. With scant sympathy from gloriously pugnacious secretary Toby, and dubious advice from womanizing friend Eddie, Tupper (facially expressive Brian Benben, *Dark Angel*) sank into comic neuroses and bed with almost every passing good-looking woman. Expertly written and produced – by the team who would later create ➢*Friends* – its main gimmick was to illustrate Tupper's every thought with a clip from archive black and white shows – *GE Theatre* and *Alcoa Premiere* being favourites. The device was borrowed by the show's creator, movie director John Landis (*An American Werewolf in London*, *The Blues Brothers*) as a lucrative means of utilizing MCA's back catalogue.

CAST *Martin Tupper* Brian Benben *Judith Tupper* Wendie Malick *Toby Pedalbee* Denny Dillon *Jeremy Tupper* Chris Demetral *Eddie Charles* Charles Jeffrey /Dorien Wilson /*cr* David Crane, Marta Kauffman /*exec pr* Kevin S. Bright, John Landis /*pr* Robb Idels, David Crane, Marta Kauffman /*dr* inc John Landis, Eric Laneuville, Anson Williams, Betty Thomas, Rob Thompson /*wr* inc Marta Kauffman, David Crane /*Kevin S. Bright Productions: MCA Television Entertainment* (USA) /100 x 30m col /US tx Home Box Office 1990–6.

Drop the Dead Donkey

Comedy. C4 1990–8

In the beginning this acclaimed, behind-the-scenes sitcom set in the fictional newsroom of Sir Royston Merchant's Globelink was heavily topical in its humour. Yet, as the seasons passed, the current-affairs gags were reduced in number (from around 25 per episode down to 12) and the comedy came to rely on the caricatured characters who were Globelink's staff: Gus Hedges, the virginal, jargon-spouting chief executive; Alex, his acerbic right-hand woman, later replaced by lesbian Helen; Damien (Stephen Tompkinson, ➢*Ballykissangel*), the deranged, disaster-chasing reporter; Henry, the dissolute news anchor who was permanently at war with snobbish but stupid newsreader, Sally; George, the hopeless, hypochondriac, be-cardiganed news editor; Dave Charnley (Neil Pearson, ➢*Between the Lines*) the permanently philandering gambler; and Joy, the PA with attitude. Transmogrified into a character-com and an unnervingly realistic depiction of office backbiting, the show became a massive international hit, selling to such diverse countries as Turkey and Iceland. In 1992 the show was awarded the Emmy for International Popular Arts with an episode about the office Christmas party, which contained the timeless gag of a John-Major-a-gram entering the room but nobody noticing. Other awards showered on *DTDD* included another International Emmy and two BAFTAS for Best Comedy. The show was the creation of Guy Jenkin and Andy Hamilton (formerly producer of ➢*Who Dares Wins*).

CAST *Gus Hedges* Robert Duncan *George Dent* Jeff Rawle *Alex Pates* Haydn Gwynne *Damien Day* Stephen Tompkinson *Dave Charnley* Neil Pearson *Henry Davenport* David Swift *Sally Smedley* Victoria Wicks *Joy Merryweather* Susannah Doyle *Helen Cooper* Ingrid Lacey /*cr* Andy Hamilton, Guy Jenkin /*exec pr* Denise O'Donoghue /*pr* Andy Hamilton, Guy Jenkin /*dr* Liddy Oldroyd /*wr* Andy Hamilton, Guy Jenkin, Ian Brown, Nick Revell, Malcolm Williamson /*Hat Trick* (UK) /65 x 25m col.

Duchess of Duke Street

Melodrama. BBC1 1976–80

John Hawkesworth's Edwardian TV drama to follow ➢*Upstairs, Downstairs* watchably fictionalized the story of real-life Rosa Lewis, a cockney cook who worked her way up – despite snobbery and sexism – to become owner of the select Cavendish Hotel. For the dramatic purposes of the period-perfect series, Lewis was renamed Louisa Trotter (a sparky performance by Gemma Jones), the Cavendish retitled the Bentinck and a generous dollop of shocking cross-class romance (between Trotter and Lord Haslemere, played by Christopher Casanove) added in. On the lower echelons of the *dramatis personae*, Lalla Ward was cast as Trotter's illegitimate daughter, Lottie. A stint in the Tardis with ➢*Dr Who* (and marriage to Tom Baker) shortly followed.

CAST *Louisa Trotter* Gemma Jones *Lord Haslemere* Christopher Casanove *Major Toby Smith-Barton* John Vernon *Merriman (Head Waiter)* John Welsh *Starr (Head Porter)* John Cater *Mary* Victoria Plunkett *Lottie* Lalla Ward /*cr* John Hawkesworth /*pr* John Hawkesworth /*dr* Bill Bain, Cyril Coke, Simon Langton, Raymond Menmoui, Gerry Mill /*wr* inc Julian Bond, John Hawkesworth, Jack Rosenthal, Rosemary Ann Sisson /*mus* Alexander Faris /*BBC TV: Time-Life Television* (UK) /31 x 50m col.

Duckman

Comedy. BBC2 1995–

'What the hell you starin' at?'

Anarchic animation featuring an irascible fowl-man detective which parodied the TV formats of its subtitle – 'Private Dick/Family Man' –with an acidly caustic humour and avant-garde cartoon style that took it to the edge of art. Scripted by duo Jeff Reno and Ron Osborn, whose credits include ➢*Mork and Mindy* and ➢*Moonlighting*, its voice cast featured Jason Alexander (➢*Seinfeld*), Nancy Travis, Dweezil (son of Frank) Zappa and Tim 'Rocky Horror Show' Curry. Although it failed to get the major league of celebrity guests, it did secure the B team (Heather ➢*'Melrose Place'* Locklear, Jim Belushi, Ice T, Leonard Nimoy, Burt Reynolds).

CAST (voices) *Duckman* Jason Alexander *Cornfed Pig* Gregg Berger *Ajax* Dweezil Zappa *Bernice* Nancy Travis *King Chicken* Tim Curry /*cr* Everett Peck /*exec pr* Jeff Reno, Ron Osborn /*wr* inc Jeff Reno, Ron Osborn /*Fox TV* (USA) /70 x 30m col /US tx USA Network 1994–7.

Due South

Crime. Sky1/BBC1 1995–6

Odd Canadian caper about a straight-arrow Mountie, Fraser (Paul Gross, *Tales of the City*), assigned to duty in Chicago, where he buddied-up with cynical detective Ray Vecchio (*Lethal Weapon II*). Naturally, Fraser always got his man, though quirky powers (heightened sense of smell and sight, the ability to see the ghost of his dead father) and a lip-reading wolf-husky called Diefenbaker helped some. Pitched somewhere between ➢*Northern Exposure* and ➢*McCloud*, with exemplary wisecracking scripts (some by Gross himself), the show was filmed in squeaky-clean Toronto, where streets had to be 'dirtied' to pass for the Windy City. Topping the guest cast was Leslie 'Police Squad' Nielsen, who taught Gross how to lace his boots in correct RCMP manner; Nielsen's father had been a Mountie. A hit in Canada and the UK, the show was unable to defeat bad US ratings, causing its cancellation after two series. It rose again, but *sans* Marciano, in a joint Canadian–BBC1 (the Corporation being the terrestrial transmitter of the show in the UK) production.

CAST *Cons. Benton Fraser* Paul Gross *Det. Ray Vecchio* David Marciano *Lt Harding Welsh* Beau Starr *Det. Louis Gardino* Daniel Kash *Det. Jack Huey* Tony Craig /*cr* Paul Haggis /*exec pr* Paul Haggis, Jeff King, Kathy Slevin /*dr* inc George Bloomfield, Paul Lynch, Paul Haggis, Steve DiMarco /*wr* inc Paul Haggis, Jeff King & Kathy Slevin, Paul Gross /*Alliance Communications* (Can): *BBC* (UK) /1 x 120m, 61 x 50m col.

The Dukes of Hazzard

Adventure. BBC1 1979–85

In which hayseeds Bo and Luke Duke sped around mythical Hazzard County in souped-up car, 'The General Lee' (complete with Confederate flag painted on the roof), getting themselves into kidult-type comedy adventures. They may have been moonshinin' outlaws but 'them Duke boys' were good guys, latter-day knights in a '69 Dodge Charger, constantly foiling the dastardly schemes of corrupt corpulent politician Boss Hogg (Sorrell Booke, ➢*Soap*) and his dimwitted henchmen, Sheriff Rosco P. Coltrane (screenwriter James Best) and Deputy Enos Strate. Occasionally, the Dukes stopped the tyre-screechin' action (300 Dodge Chargers lost their lives during the show's course) to fill up on blueberry pie from cutoff-clad cousin Daisy and moral homilies from bearded Uncle Jesse at stereotype Southern homestead. Derived from Guy Waldron's 1974 action–comedy feature *The Moonlighters*, the show went to No. 2 in the Nielsens in 1981. A pay dispute the following year saw stars Schneider and Wopat walk out, to have their places in the General Lee taken by Christopher Mayer and Byron Cherry; in practice the replacements were lacklustre, and Schneider and Wopat returned – after a pay rise – to the General Lee's seats. There were two spin-offs: a cartoon version, *The Dukes* (1983, Hanna-Barbera) and a short-lived series, *Enos* (1980–1), in which the grinning deputy was seconded to the LAPD.

CAST *Luke Duke* Tom Wopat *Bo Duke* John Schneider *Daisy Duke* Catherine Bach *Uncle Jesse Duke* Denver Pyle *Sheriff Rosco P. Coltrane* James Best *Jefferson Davis 'Boss' Hogg* Sorrell Booke *Deputy Enos Strate* Sonny Shroyer *Deputy Cletus* Rick Hurst *Coy Duke* Byron Cherry *Vance Duke* Christopher Mayer *The Balladeer /Narrator* Waylon Jennings /*cr* Guy Waldron /*exec pr* Paul R. Picard, Philip Mandelker /*pr* Guy Waldron, Rod Amateau, Myles Wilder, Ralph Riskin, Hy Averback, Joseph Gantman /*dr* inc Rod Amateau, Denver Pyle, Guy Waldron /*wr* inc Guy Waldron, Myles Wilder, Martin Roth, Leonard Kaufman /*mus* Waylon Jenning (theme song) /*Lou-Step Productions: Warner Bros TV* (USA) /147 x 60m col /US tx CBS 1979–85.

The Dustbinmen

Comedy. ITV 1969

Already controversial for his cutting-edge scripts for ➢*Coronation Street* and ➢*That Was The Week That Was*, Jack Rosenthal reached down into the bottom of the garbage for his 1968 Playhouse piece, 'There's a Hole in Your Dustbin, Delilah', and came up with handfuls of narrative comedic gold. A follow-on series following his smutty Northern binmen – Smellie, Cheese and Egg, Winston, dim-bulb Eric and ladies man Heavy Breathing – as they wended their rounds on their 'Thunderbird 3' dustcart, ogling housewives and dodging depot manager Bloody Delilah, topped the ratings. There was much criticism of its vulgarity and vernacular language; arguably it began the 70s drift towards crudity in ITV sitcoms, exemplified by ➢*Love Thy Neighbour*.

CAST *Bloody Delilah* John Woodvine/Brian Wilde *Cheese and Egg* Bryan Pringle *Smellie Ibbotson* John Barrett *Heavy Breathing* Trevor Bannister *Eric* Tim Wylton *Winston Platt* Graham Haberfield /*cr* Jack Rosenthal /*pr* Jack Rosenthal, Richard Everitt /*dr* Les Chatfield /*wr* Jack Rosenthal /*Granada TV* (UK) /20 x 30m bw.

Duty Free
Comedy. ITV 1984–6

Good clean British holiday romp (lightweight division), in which adultery was much hinted at but never accomplished. When David Pearce (Keith Barron, *Leaving*, Dennis Potter's 'Vote, vote for Nigel Barton', king of the TV advertising voice-overs, the Andrex puppy amongst them) was made redundant, he and his wife Amy used part of the payout for a package holiday in the Costa del Sol. Likewise at leisure were Robert Cochran and his wife, Linda (Joanna Van Gyseghem, ➢*Fraud Squad*), a blonde and would-be refined woman who brought out the upwardly mobile man in David. While David postured and wooed and made countless failed assignations with Linda, Amy remained deadpan and stole the show. Confused waiter, Carlos, meanwhile looked on with bemusement at the antics of these foreign visitors. A ratings topping farce, the show ran to three series and a Christmas special.

CAST *David Pearce* Keith Barron *Amy Pearce* Gwen Taylor *Robert Cochran* Neil Stacy *Linda Cochran* Joanna Van Gyseghem *Carlos* Carlos Douglas /*pr* Vernon Lawrence /*wr* Eric Chappell, Jean Warr /*mus* Peter Knight /*Yorkshire TV* (UK) /20 x 30m, 1 x 60m col.

Blake Carrington gets to grips with ex-wife Alexis in *Dynasty*, an everyday tale of Denver oil folk. The show topped the US Nielsen ratings in 1984.

Dynasty
Melodrama. BBC1 1982–9

Like ➢*Dallas*, the supersoap it emulated, Aaron Spelling's *Dynasty* featured a western oil family (indeed, the show's working title was *Oil*), but here the setting was Denver, Colorado. Head of the Carrington dynasty was the slick, smooth Blake (John Forsythe, aka John Lincoln Freund, the voice of Charlie in ➢*Charlie's Angels*), who had several wacko kids, a beautiful young(ish) new wife, Krystle, an embittered ex-wife, Alexis, and a host of business enemies, most of whom slept with each other in complicated permutations. Initially, ratings were modest, but at the end of the first season Blake was put on trial for the murder of gay offspring Steven's boyfriend. Into the courtroom swept a mysterious female figure with padded shoulders, oozing malice. Alexis Carrington – for it was she – was prime witness for the prosecution. Now *Dynasty* had its villain (witchily, wonderfully overplayed by Joan 'The Bitch' Collins OBE), and its direction, for the show came to centre on Alex's baroque plots to either woo back or demolish Blake. And if Alexis loathed Blake she positively detested Krystle ('that blonde tramp'), causing her to lose her baby. Krystle, in turn, memorably slugged it out with Alexis in the lily pond at the Carrington mansion, then in the mud outside a burning log cabin. Intentionally more camp than its *Dallas* model, *Dynasty* soon topped even the ridiculousness of these catfights with the wedding of Alexis' daughter Amanda to Prince Michael (Michael Praed, ➢*Robin of Sherwood*, ➢*Riders*) of Moldavia. The reception was interrupted by revolutionaries who machine-gunned the guests. But the best was saved till last: in the final episode Blake's daughters Fallon and Krystina were buried in a tunnel with a Nazi art hoard and a psychopath, while Blake shot it out with a crooked blackmailing murderous cop, and Adam Carrington, Blake's long-lost son, pushed Alexis and husband Dexter off a balcony. The outcome of this cliffhanger was revealed in a 1991 TVM, *Dynasty: The Reunion.* Alexis managed to turn in the air, land on Dexter – and walk away unscathed.

Stupendously unbelievable, badly written, poorly characterized – *Dynasty* was all these things. It was also, in the inimitable Aaron Spelling (➢*Charlie's Angels*, ➢*Beverly Hill 90210*, ➢*Savannah*) style, glossy to a lustrous degree. Each episode cost $1.2 million to make (much of it spent on the wardrobe) and it hired American guest actors from the A list: Rock Hudson (as Krystle's dalliance Daniel Reece, Hudson's last screen role), Diahann Carroll (as Blake's half-sister), Blaxploitation star Richard Lawson, Ali MacGraw and George Hamilton. From Britain it imported, as well as La Collins and Praed, Kate O'Mara (as Alexis' sister), Emma Samms (Fallon, Mk II), Christopher Casenove, and Stephanie Beacham (bitch Sable Colby, later a stalwart of *Dynasty* spin-off ➢*The Colbys*. Beacham was well versed in bitchery, having played the title rag-trade tycoon in Central TV's 1985 torrid *Connie*). But the ultimate touch of glamour was to feature appearances from ex-US President, Gerald Ford, and former Secretary of State, Henry Kissinger, guests at a 1983 ball. Such soap opera class saw *Dynasty* rise in the US ratings, even overtaking *Dallas,* to reach pole position in 1984.

Strange but true facts. *Dynasty* was something of a second soap chance for actress Linda Evans (➢*The Big Valley*), who played limpid-eyed Krystle. Originally *Dallas* had been invented as a vehicle for her, but she had turned it down as beneath her talents ... Evans and Forsythe had starred together in a show before, the family sitcom *Bachelor Father.*

CAST *Blake Carrington* John Forsythe *Krystle Jennings Carrington* Linda Evans *Alexis Carrington Colby* Joan Collins *Fallon Carrington Colby* Pamela Sue Martin /Emma Samms *Steven Carrington* Al Corley/Jack Coleman *Michael Torrance (Adam Carrington)* Gordon Thomson *Jeff Colby* John James *Claudia Blaisdel* Pamela Bellwood *Sammy Jo Dean* Heather Locklear *Farnsworth 'Dex' Dexter* Michael Nader *Amanda Carrington* Catherine Oxenburg/Karen Cellini *Dominique Devereaux* Diahann Carroll *Prince Michael* Michael Praed *Ben Carrington* Christopher Casenove *Caress Morell* Kate O'Mara *Krystina Carrington* Jessica Player *Sable Colby* Stephanie Beacham *Monica Colby* Tracy Scoggins *Daniel Reece* Rock Hudson *Joel Abrigore* George Hamilton *Nick Kimball* Richard Lawson *Lady Ashley Mitchell* Ali MacGraw /*cr* Richard & Esther Shapiro /*exec pr* Aaron Spelling, Douglas Kramer, Richard & Esther Shapiro /*pr* inc Elaine Rich /*dr* inc Don Medford, Ed Ledding, Gwen Arner, Irving Moore, Alf Kjellin, Philip Leacock /*wr* inc Richard & Esther Shapiro, Edward De Blasio, Denis Turner, Samuel J. Pelovitz, Leah Markus, Eileen Mason Pollock, Robert Mason Pollock /*mus* Bill Conti (theme), Peter Myers /*Aaron Spelling Productions: Fox TV* (USA) /169 x 50m col /US tx ABC 1981–9.

Earth 2

Sci-fi. Sky1 1995

Or ➢*Wagon Train* goes to another planet. When a colonizing mission of future humanoids crash-lands on the wrong side of new world G889, they must trek 3,400 miles through alien badlands to the only fertile region. Show plus-points were stunning locations (the New Mexico desert), special effects (especially the creatures of Oscar-winning designer Greg Cannon), and a captivating baddie (Tim Curry, *The Rocky Horror Show*). Alas, the expeditioners were unable to beat off long-winded plotting and attacks of melodrama, with the result that US network NBC suspended *E2* with the characters still many miles from Eden. Made by Steven Spielberg's Amblin company.

CAST *Devon Adair* Debrah Farentino *Alonzo Solace* Antonio Sabato Jr *John Danziger* Clancy Brown *Yale* Sullivan Walker *Gaal* Tim Curry /*cr* Michael Duggan, Carol Flint, Mark Levin /*exec pr* Michael Duggan, Carol Flint, Mark Levin /*pr* P.K. Simmonds, Tony To, Cleve Landsberg, John Melfi /*dr* inc Scott Winnant / *mus* David Bergeaud /*sfx* Greg Cannon (creature design) /*Amblin Television: Universal TV* (USA) / 1 x 120m, 18 x 60m col /US tx NBC 1994–5.

Earthworm Jim

Children's. TCC 1995–

Not so long ago, and not so far away, on the planet Insectika, lived a slimy cartoon despot called Queen Slug-for-a-Butt, whose bad sense of humour and lust for power posed a threat to peace-loving lifeforms across the galaxy. Who could save them? Enter Earthworm Jim, an innocent multi-celled organism transformed into the unlikeliest of heroes by a supersuit which one day happened out of the sky. Accompanied by Peter Puppy, Earthworm Jim tirelessly set forth to defeat Slug-for-a-Butt (and save her nice sister, Insectika's rightful ruler, Princess What's-Her-Name), all the while avoiding the clutches of his many enemies: Professor Monkey-For-Head; bounty hunter with bad breath Psy-Crow; Evil, the Cat from Heck; and Bob, the Killer Goldfish. Engaging $5 million lunacy, which began life as a video game. Dan Castellaneta, Homer in ➢*The Simpsons*, graced the voice cast as Earthworm Jim himself.

CAST (voices) Charlie Adler, Jeff Bennett, Dan Castellaneta, Jim Cummings, Edward Hibbert, John Kassir, Andrea Martin, Kathi Souci /*cr* Doug Tennapel /*pr* Kathi Castilo, Roy Allen Smith /*wr* inc Doug Langdale /*mus* William Anderson /*Flextech: Shiny Entertainment: Universal* (USA) /13+ x 29m col / US tx WB Network 1995–.

EastEnders

Melodrama. BBC1 1985–

'Why do they live there?' Queen Mary, after a flying visit to London's East End.

If HM had enjoyed the benefit of this 80s soap, she might have found the answer: fings ain't boring in postal code area E. Devised by producer Julia Smith and script editor Tony Holland, who had previously collaborated on ➢*Z Cars*, ➢*Angels* and ➢*District Nurse*, *EastEnders* was the Corporation's long-awaited sudster success (after the disappointments of ➢*Compact*, ➢*The Newcomers*, and ➢*United!*) to equal ITV's ➢*Coronation Street*, even pushing the Granada product off the top of the BARB ratings. Set in the fictitious London borough of Walford E20, the series centred on dilapidated Albert Square, with the Queen Vic pub at its centre, run by rough diamonds Den and Angie Watts. The Square, with attached market, was home to many, but especially the archetypal close-knit London families of Beale and Fowler (loosely based on Holland's own relatives).

The serial might have been set in a square, but its chief geometric shape was always the love triangle. The key storyline of early years was the

Dirty Den/Angie/Michelle Fowler (Susan Tully, ➢*Grange Hill*) triangle, with the lecherous and shifty Den getting the schoolgirl pregnant. (The episode in which Den gave Angie divorce papers for Christmas was watched by a then BARB record of 30.15 million viewers.) Over the subsequent seasons, the triangle was made flesh by, among others, Phil Mitchell/Grant Mitchell/Sharon Watts, Arthur Fowler/Pauline Fowler (Wendy Richard, ➢*Are You Being Served?*)/Christine Hewitt, Samantha Butcher/Ricky Butcher/Bianca Jackson and Ian Beale/Cindy Beale/David Wicks.

Obeying the dictum of London's finest chronicler, Charles Dickens, that good stories play to collective nostalgia, *EastEnders* tapped into any and every myth of cockneydom – in particular, the good old, bad old days of the Kray gangsters. Den Watts (played by Leslie Grantham who, as the press gleefuly uncovered, had served a long prison sentence for the murder of a German taxi driver), the bullet-headed Mitchell brothers, chirpy car dealer Frank Butcher and rattish car dealer David Wicks were all part-representations of the Krays. When the BBC broke its *EastEnders* 'no stars' policy to admit actress Barbara 'Carry On' Windsor to the Square, it merely confirmed the soap's debt to the allure of London villainy. As a young actress, Windsor (born Barbara-Ann Deeks) had 'gone out' with Charlie Kray; her husband, Ronnie Knight, was imprisoned for seven years for his part in the 1983 Security Express Robbery.

And yet, *EastEnders* also displayed more social conscience than its soapish older rivals, routinely and grittily dramatizing such issues as rape (Kathy Beale by James Wilmott-Brown of the Dagmar pub), prostitution (punk Mary Smith), unemployment (Arthur Fowler, Arthur Fowler and Arthur Fowler again), HIV infection (Mark Fowler, played by *Grange Hill*'s Todd Carty after actor David Scarboro committed suicide), abortion (the baby of Michelle and Lofty Holloway), and homosexuality (Colin and Barry). Less successful was the show's earnest (thus patronizing) articulation of the problems of the immigrant community through the lives of the Osmans, the Carpenters, the Karims, the Kapoors and the Taverniers. (Playing Hattie Tavernier was Michelle Gayle, who subsequently embarked on a pop career of some note; others from the *EastEnders* cast to enter the music charts, although without quite such street cred, were Anita Dobson with 'Anyone Can Fall in Love', Nick Berry – later ➢*Heartbeat* – with 'Every Loser Wins', Letitia Dean and Paul Medford with 'Something Outa Nothing', and Patsy Palmer and Sid Owen with 'Better Believe It'.)

Initially broadcast twice a week, with a Sunday omnibus edition added in mid 1985, *EastEnders* went thrice weekly in April 1994. Alas for Smith and Holland, the midas touch spectacularly departed them on their follow-up soap for the BBC – ➢*Eldorado*.

CAST *Arthur Fowler* Bill Treacher *Pauline Fowler* Wendy Richard *Michelle Fowler* Susan Tully *Mark Fowler* David Scarboro/Todd Carty *Lou Beale* Anna Wing *Kathy Beale (later Mitchell)* Gillian Taylforth *Peter Beale* Peter Dean *Ian Beale* Adam Woodyatt *Dennis Watts* Leslie Grantham *Angie Watts* Anita Dobson *Sharon Watts (later Mitchell)* Letitia Dean *Ethel Skinner* Gretchen Franklin *Dot Cotton* June Brown *Nick Cotton* John Altman *Debbie Wilkins* Shirley Cheriton *Andy O'Brien* Ross Davidson *Simon Wicks* Nick Berry *Pat Wicks (later Butcher)* Pam St Clement *Dr Harold Legg* Leonard Fenton *Mary Smith* Linda Davidson *George 'Lofty' Holloway* Tom Watt *Ali Osman* Nejdet Salih *Sue Osman* Sandy Ratcliff *Tony Carpenter* Oscar James *Cassie Carpenter* Delanie Forbes *Kelvin Carpenter* Paul J. Medford *Hannah Carpenter* Sally Sagie *James Wilmott-Brown* William Boyde *Cindy Williams (later Beale)* Michelle Collins *Colin Russell* Michael Cashman *Barry Clark* Gary Hailes *Magda 'Mags' Czaijkowski* Kathryn Apanowicz *Frank Butcher* Mike Reid *Diane Butcher* Sophie Lawrence *Janine Butcher* Rebecca Michael/Alexia Demetriou *Ricky Butcher* Sid Owen *Samantha Butcher* Danielle Westbrook *Eddie Royle* Michael Melia *Grant Mitchell* Ross Kemp *Phil Mitchell* Steve McFadden *Peggy Mitchell* Jo Warne/Barbara Windsor *Jules Tavernier* Tommy Eytle *Celstine Tavernier* Leroy Goldin *Etta Tavernier* Jacqui Gordon-Lawrence *Clyde Tavernier* Steven Woodcock *Hattie Tavernier* Michelle Gayle *Lloyd Tavernier* Garey Bridges *Kofi Tavernier* Marcel Smith *Christine Hewitt* Elizabeth Power *Nigel Bates* Paul Bradley *Sanjay Kapoor* Deepak Verma *Gita Kapoor* Shobu Kapoor *Bianca Jackson* Patsy Palmer *David Wicks* Michael French /*cr* Julia Smith, Tony Holland /*pr* inc Julia Smith, Tony Holland, Corine Hollingworth, Helen Greaves, Leonard Lewis, Josephine Ward /*dr* inc Tony Virgo, Nicholas Prosser, Barry Letts, Matthew Robinson, Chris Clough, Steve Goldie /*wr* inc Julia Smith, Tony Holland, Tony McHale, Bill Lyons, Gerry Huxham, Michael Robartes, Jane Hollowood, Tony Jordan, Christopher Reason, Jeff Povey /*BBC TV* (UK) /1 x 45m, 1000 x 30m col.

Edge of Darkness

Crime. BBC2 1985

If TV is ever faced with judgement day, it might usefully cite Troy Kennedy Martin's paranoid nuclear thriller in its defence. Fortuitously for the left-leaning Martin (also ➢*Z Cars*, the movie *The Italian Job*) he took his script to BBC2 at a time when it wished to move away from costume drama into something contemporary, even dangerous. This it got, and then some. *Edge of Darkness* concerned a Yorkshire police detective, Ronald Craven (Bob Peck), whose beloved scientist daughter Emma (Joanne Whalley, ➢*The Singing Detective*) is killed by an Irish gunman. At first, Craven believes the murder a botched attempt to assassinate himself, but as Emma returns to him (as a ghost) and he discovers her connection with a radical environmentalist group, Gaia, he stumbles upon a nuclear conspiracy which threatens the very future of the planet. With its pessimistic scenario of a nuclear state composed of warring ruling-class groups (Craven's only real ally turned out to be a maverick Texan CIA agent, Jedburgh) and megalomaniac big business, none of whom cared for man or planet, it made deeply unsettling viewing. This was exacerbated by Eric Clapton's bluesy incidental guitar music, discordant sound techniques, and the visually oppressive, gloomy *noir* film style adopted by director Martin Campbell. More, perhaps, than any other TV product, it captured the mood of mid-80s Thatcherite Britain, post-miners' strike but still pre-boom. And the final frame, of Craven falling to a sniper's bullet on a lonely hillside and shouting out his daughter's name (Peck's own suggestion), will long haunt the blank depths of the small screen.

Such was the clamour on the series' original release that it was repeated on BBC1 only weeks later. There were BAFTAs in 1986 for Best Drama Series and for Peck as Best Actor. As well as its intrinsic value, *Edge of Darkness* also sent careers upwards. Peck went Hollywoodwards (and later starred in *Jurassic Park*), as did Joanne Whalley and composer Michael Kamen (to become responsible for *Lethal Weapon*), while Martin Campbell ended up at the helm of Bond blockbuster *Golden Eye*.

CAST *DI Ronald Craven* Bob Peck *Darius Jedburgh* Joe Don Baker *Emma Craven* Joanne Whalley *Pendleton* Charles Kay *Harcourt* Ian McNeice *Clementine* Zoë Wanamaker *Terry* Tim McInnerny *Ross* John Woodvine *Grogan* Kenneth Nelson /*cr* Troy Kennedy Martin /*pr* Michael Wearing /*dr* Martin Campbell /*wr* Troy Kennedy Martin /*mus* Michael Kamen (played by Eric Clapton) /*BBC TV* (UK) / 6 x 50m col.

Edward and Mrs Simpson

Drama. ITV 1978

Adaptation by Simon Raven of Frances Donaldson's account of the infatuation between King Edward VIII and American divorcee Wallis Simpson, and the subsequent abdication crisis of 1936. Raven's scripts (accentuated by fine performances from Edward Fox and Cynthia Harris) portrayed HM as weak and malleable and her as a scheming ermine-digger. From Paris, the real life Mrs Simpson (aka the Duchess of Windsor) objected and even succeeded in getting the drama banned in France.

CAST *King Edward VIII* Edward Fox *Wallis Simpson* Cynthia Harris /*pr* Andrew Brown /*dr* Waris Hussein /*wr* Simon Raven /*BBC TV* (UK) /7 x 60m col.

Edward the Seventh

Drama. ITV 1975

Seventies British TV continued its fascination with kings and queens (see ➢*The Six Wives of Henry VIII*, ➢*Elizabeth R*) in Cecil Clarke's all-star reconstruction of the life of sybaritic petticoat-chaser Edward VII. Lavish in its period settings and location filming (including, by permission, several royal residences), the show was co-penned by David Butler, better known as Dr Nick Williams in ➢Emergency – Ward 10. Annette Crosbie's portrayal of Queen Victoria won her a BAFTA. Based on the biography by Philip Magnus, the show spawned a short-lived spin-off featuring Edward's mistress ➢*Lillie* Langtry. When aired in the USA, *EtS* was retitled *The Royal Victorians* and shown on a conglomeration of stations specially put together by Mobil Corporation. To the surprise of nearly all, several episodes beat network competition.

CAST *Edward VII* (child) Charles Sturridge/Timothy West *Queen Victoria* Annette Crosbie *Prince Albert* Robert Hardy *Princess Alexandra* Deborah Grant /Helen Ryan *Princess Vicky* Felicity Kendall *Lord Palmerston* Andre Morell *Benjamin Disraeli* John Gielgud *William Gladstone* Michael Hordern *Lillie*

Langtry Francesca Annis *Prince Eddy* Charles Dance / *pr* Cecil Clarke / *dr* John Gorrie / *wr* David Butler, John Gorrie / *ATV* (UK) /13 x 60m col /US tx PBS 1979.

Eerie Indiana

Horror. C4 1993

'Nobody believes me but Eerie Indiana is the centre of weirdness for the entire planet...'

So says teenager Marshall Teller (Omri Katz, JR's son in ➢*Dallas*) on moving to the weird small American town of the title, in this kidult version of ➢*Twin Peaks*. In the opening episode Teller was required to save his family from a body-snatcher-like cult of tupperware fanatics; similar bizarrities occurred with weekly regularity. Movie helmsman Joe Dante (*Gremlins*, *The Burbs*) managed gothic visual panache on his segments but generally direction was mediocre. But not as mediocre as the heavy-handed, moralizing scripts. A 1998 revival aired as *Eerie Indiana: The Other Dimension*.

CAST *Marshall Teller* Omri Katz *Simon Holmes* Justin Shenkarow *Syndi Teller* Julie Condra *Edgar Teller* Francis Guinan *Marilyn Teller* Mary-Margaret Humes / *cr* Karl Schaefer & Jose Rivera / *exec pr* Karl Schaefer, John Cosgrove, Terry Dunn-Meurer / *pr* Jose Rivera, Gary Markowitz, Walter Barnett / *dr* inc Joe Dante, Tim Hunter, Bob Balaban / *wr* inc Gary Markowitz / *Unreality Inc: Cosgrove Meurer Productions* (USA) /18 x 30m col /US tx NBC 1991–2.

El C.I.D

Comedy. ITV 1990–2

Criminous comedy in which two Scotland Yard officers took early retirement and sailed off to España to open a bar. The bar, however, is maliciously destroyed, leaving Bromley and Blake to join a local father and daughter PI agency in a battle against expat gangster, Gus Mercer. Humour tended not to be above the modest level of the show's punning title, and stemmed from the inept attempts of Bromley to sleuth it. When actor Alfred Molina left in the third series, he was replaced by Amanda Redman (later ➢*Dangerfield*, *Beck*) who played Bromley's daughter, Rosie. Co-created by Chris Kelly, most famous as the host of BBC2's *Food and Drink*. Inoffensive.

CAST *Douglas Bromley* John Bird *Bernard Blake* Alfred Molina *Gus Mercer* Kenneth Cranham *Frank* Tony Haygarth *Metcalf* Donald Churchill *Delgado* Simon Andreu *Mercedes* Viviane Vives *Stevie Blake* Robert Reynolds *Rosie Bromley* Amanda Redman *Graham* Niven Boyd / *cr* Chris Kelly, Ian Roy / *exec pr* Sally Head / *pr* Matthew Bird / *dr* inc Robert Tronson / *wr* inc Paul Anderson / *Granada TV* (UK) /21 x 30m col.

Eldorado

Melodrama. BBC1

Thrice-weekly sun and sangria soap which, despite an investment of £10 million from the BBC (including the building of a village production lot), was prematurely cancelled due to poor ratings. Created by ➢*EastEnders* masterminds Julia Smith and Tony Holland, it was set among a British expatriate community in southern Spain. The warm weather certainly encouraged the sexual activity the Corporation hoped would have viewers's eyeballs glued to the screen: episode two opened with child bride Fizz (16-year-old model Kathy Pitkin) stripping off for her nuptials. Alas, awarding roles on the basis of who looked good in underwear and swimsuits left a cast (particularly the Spanish and other Europeans) who had no discernible ability to act. Most of the Los Barcos characters anyway were sorry contrivances – teenage tearaway Lockhead, worried mum Lockhead, disabled daughter Lockhead, alcholic dad Lockhead, poor man's baddie Marcus Tandy (Jesse Birdsall, later ➢*Bugs*) – all oddly at variance with the exotic locale. Even this was poorly exploited, with some characters barely seeming to step outside into the *al fresco*. After just a year *Eldorado*, the biggest series yet awarded by the BBC to an independent company (Cinema Verite) was terminated by incoming BBC1 head Alan Yentob.

CAST *Gwen Lockhead* Patricia Blake *Drew Lockhead* Campbell Morrison *Nessa Lockhead* Julie Fernandez *Blair Lockhead* Josh Nathan *Trish Valentine* Polly Perkins *Joy Slater* Leslee Udwin *Marcus Tandy* Jesse Birdsall *Snowy White* Patch Connolly *Bunny Charlson* Buki Armstrong *Dieter Schultz* Kai Maurer *Roberto Fernandez* Franco Rey *Abuela Fernandez* Maria Vega *Isabelle Leduc* Framboise Gommendy *Philippe Leduc* Daniel Lombart *Pilar Moreno* Sandra Sandri *Stanley Webb* William Lucas *Rosemary Webb* Hilary Crane / *cr* Julia Smith, Tony Holland / *exec pr* Verity Lambert, John Dark / *pr* Julia Smith, Corinne Hollingworth / *Cinema Verite: J Dy T* (UK) /300 x 30m col.

Elizabeth R

Drama. BBC2 1971

Majestic costume drama charting the life of the Tudor monarch from effervescent princesshood to grotesque balding death prior to handing over the throne to the Stuarts. Seven months in the making, historically accurate to an almost pedantic degree, it singularly succeeded – thanks largely to Glenda Jackson's understated acting and the insightful scripts by, among others, John Prebble and John Hale – in capturing the psychological and political complexities of the Virgin Queen. There was also fine thespian support work from Robert Hardy, Robin Ellis and Michael Williams. Winner of no less than five Emmy Awards, the series was virtually a sequel to ➢*The Six Wives of Henry VIII.*

CAST *Elizabeth R* Glenda Jackson *Mary Tudor* Daphne Slater *Earl of Leicester* Robert Hardy *Earl of Essex* Robin Ellis *Duke of Alènçon* Michael Williams *Sir Francis Drake* John Woodvine *Earl of Southampton* Peter Egan /*pr* Roderick Graham /*wr* John Hale, John Prebble, Rosemary Ann Sissons /*BBC TV* (UK) / 6 x 90m col /US tx PBS 1973.

Ellen

Comedy. C4 1994–

Kooky ➢*Seinfeld*-type sitcom from the USA about mixed up single people. It starred stand-up comic Ellen DeGeneres as an LA book/coffee-shop manager around whom orbited a coterie of goofy friends: ambitious Paige, irriating 'Coffee' Joe, lecherous Adam, and whiney airhead Audrey. Filmed in feel-good warm lighting reminiscent of lavatory roll adverts, it excelled in probing the corners of friendship paranoia. And, as with *Seinfeld,* there were the occasional moments of surrealism. But unlike that show, the humour was as much miss as hit. There was a brief brouhaha in 1997 when star DeGeneres came out of the closet to announce on the cover of *Time*, 'Yep, I'm gay!'

CAST *Ellen* Ellen DeGeneres *'Coffee' Joe Farrell* David Anthony Higgins *Paige Clark* Joely Fisher *Audrey Penney* Clea Lewis *Adam Green* Ayre Gross /*cr* Carol Black, Neal Marlens, David Rosenthal /*exec pr* inc Eileen Heisler, DeAnne Heline, Vic Kaplan /*pr* Tracy Newman, Jonathan Stark, Lisa Debenedicitis, Daryl Rowland /*dr* inc Robby Benson, Tom Cherones, Gil Junger /*The Black-Marlens Company: Touchstone TV* (USA) /109 x 30m col /US tx ABC 1994–8.

Ellery Queen

Crime. BBC1 1976

Cases of a NY mystery-writer turned supersleuth. Invented in a 1929 novel, *The Roman Hat Mystery*, by Frederic Dannay and Manfred Bennington Lee, Ellery Queen was first brought to the small screen by Richard Hart in the 1950s series *The Adventures of Ellery Queen.* When Hart died of a heart attack the title role passed to Lee Bowman, then to George Nader and then to Lee Phillips. After 15 years the character was revived by American network NBC in this 40s period piece, overseen by Richard Levinson and William Link. They added a pleasant leavening of self-conscious humour, epitomized by Queen's turning to the audience just before the denoument to ask 'Have *you* figured it out?' Here, the part of Queen was taken by Jim Hutton, later cast in the abortive US version of ➢*Butterflies.* David Wayne, who played Queen's policeman father, was previously on the other side of the law as ➢*Batman* villain, 'Mad Hatter'. Two years after handing in his badge as Queen Snr Wayne resurfaced as Willard 'Digger' Barnes in ➢*Dallas.*

CAST *Ellery Queen* Jim Hutton *Insp. Richard Queen* David Wayne *Sgt Velie* Tom Reese *Frank Flanigan* Ken Swofford *Simon Brimmer* /*cr* Richard Levinson, William Link /*exec pr* Richard Levinson, William Link / *pr* Peter S. Fischer, Michael Rhodes /*dr* inc David Greene, Charles Dubin, Peter Hunt, Jack Arnold, James Sheldon, Seymour Robbie /*mus* Elmer Bernstein, Hal Mooney /*A Fairmont-Foxcroft Production: Universal TV* (USA) /1 x 120m, 22 x 60m col /US tx NBC 1975–6.

Emergency – Ward 10

Melodrama. ITV 1957–67

Britain's first indigenous medical soap opera, also with a claim to the record books as the nation's first twice-weekly serial. Those actors playing doctors and nurses in the fictitious Oxbridge General Hospital included John Alderton (who married show phwoar Jill Browne), Charles Tingwall and Ray Barrett, all of whom found the show a useful fast ambulance drive towards stardom, while Jane Rossington (➢*Crossroads*), Paul Darrow (➢*Blake's 7*) and patients Joanna Lumley and Albert Finney found it at least an acceptable stretcher ride in the right direction. Originally to be titled *Calling Nurse Roberts* after the initial central character, bumpkin Nurse Pat Roberts, the show later spun off Dr John

Rennie (Richard Thorp, later ➢*Emmerdale Farm*) to a series of his own, *Call Oxbridge 2000.* There was also a forgettable movie version, *Life in Emergency Ward Ten.* Created by Tessa Diamond, *EW10* reached No. 2 in the ratings in 1960, but slippage in the mid 60s saw ATV supremo Lew Grade unplug the life support in 1967. This decision, Grade later admitted, was 'one of the two biggest mistakes of my life' and he tried to rectify the error by launching another medical sudster, ➢*General Hospital.*

CAST *Nurse Pat Roberts* Rosemary Miller *Nurse Carole Young* Jill Browne *Dr Patrick O'Meara* Glyn Owen *Dr Alan Dawson* Charles Tingwell *Simon Forrester* Fredrick Bartman *Sister Cowley* Elizabeth Kentish *Dr Richard Moone* John Alderton *Dr Chris Anderson* Desmond Carrington *Dr Don Nolan* Ray Barrett *Mr Lester Large* John Carlisle *Dr John Rennie* Richard Thorp *Nurse Kate Ford* Jane Rossington *Dr Nick Williams* David Butler *Mr Verity* Paul Darrow */cr* Tessa Diamond */pr* Anthony Kearey, John Cooper, Cecil Petty, Josephine Douglas */dr* inc Anthony Kearey, Rex Firkin, Eric Price */wr* inc Tessa Diamond, Hazel Adair, Rachel Grieves, Rosemary Ann Sisson */An ATV Network Production* (UK) /966 x 30m, 50 x 60m bw.

Emmerdale Farm

Melodrama. ITV 1972–

Rural soap – *The Archers* of the screen – initiated by ITV to fill the void in afternoon programming that existed before the advent of all-day TV in the early 70s. Transmitted twice weekly, it focused on the Yorkshire farming community of Beckindale, in particular the agricultural enterprise of the title, left in the will of Jacob Sugden to wife Annie, sons Jack and Joe, and daughter Peggy. Although only other people seemed to watch it, *Emmerdale Farm* achieved respectable ratings (and a move to an early evening slot), selling its audience beautiful scenery, an insider's glimpse into farming life, and a steady trickle of illicit affairs and family discords. The plots, however, moved more slowly than sheep, and in the mid 80s the producers administered a revamp, adding more sex and sensationalism. In 1989 the programme title was changed to the snappier *Emmerdale.* Still perturbed by the show's low profile, especially amongst young adults, the producers hired soap-maestro Phil Redmond (➢*Brookside*) to cast his magic. A lesbian character, Zoe, was introduced (before *Brookside*'s famous sapphic shenanigan) and, in an infamous 1993 'Christmas Special', Beckindale suffered a Lockerbie-type disaster, with an airliner crashing on the centre of the village and culling half the cast. A *ménage à trois* between Dave Glover, and Kim and Frank Tate at Home Farm was also the stuff of which extended editions were made. Few shows have pursued reinvention more determinedly. The cow did change its spots, and *Emmerdale* achieved cult and chattering-class status.

CAST *Annie Sugden* Sheila Mercier *Jack Sugden* Andrew Burt/Clive Hornby *Joe Sugden* Frazier Hines *Peggy Skilbeck* Jo Kendall *Matt Skilbeck* Frederick Pyne *Amos Brierly* Ronald Magill *Henry Wilks* Arthur Pentelow *Marian Wilks* Gail Harrison *Rev. Donald Hinton* Hugh Manning *Seth Armstrong* Stan Richards *Alan Turner* Richard Thorp *Kate Hughes (née Sugden)* Sally Knyvette *Sarah Sugden* Alyson Spiro *Karen Moore* Annie Hulley *Vic Windsor* Alun Lewis *David Glover* Ian Kelsey *Linda Glover* Tonicha Jeronimo *Ned Glover* Johnny Leeze *Jan Glover* Roberta Kerr *Roy Glover* Nicky Evans *Kim Tate* Claire King *Zoe Tate* Leah Bracknell *Frank Tate* Norman Bowler */cr* Keith Laffan */exec pr* Peter Holmans, David Cunliffe, Michael Glynn, Keith Richardson */pr* David Goddard, Robert D. Cardona, Michael Glynn, Anne W. Gibbons, Richard Handford, Michael Russell, Stuart Doughty, Morag Bain, Nicholas Prosser, Mervyn Watson */dr* inc Michael Snow, Tristan de Vere Cole, Paddy Russell, David Reynolds, Darroll Blake */wr* inc Keith Laffan, Andy Baker, William Humble, Anthony Couch, David Crane, Neville Siggs */Yorkshire Television* (UK) / approx. 1000 x 30m col (not networked until 1978).

Empire Road

Drama. BBC2 1978–9

The first British TV drama to be written by a black writer (Michael Abbensetts) for an all-black cast. Set in a suburban Birmingham street populated by West Indians and Asians, it centered on Guyanan landlord Everton Bennett (Norman Beaton, later ➢*Desmond's*), whose son Marcus was dating an Asian girl, Ranjanaa – a Romeo and Juliet device which allowed inter-racial hostility and generational differences to be explored. Bennett's stammering brother-in-law, Walter, supplied the light relief. During the second series, ➢*Love Thy Neighbour*'s Rudolph Walker did a pleasantly heavy turn as a black Rachman.

CAST *Everton Bennett* Norman Beaton *Marcus Bennett* Wayne Laryea *Walter Isaacs* Joseph Marcell *Hortense Bennett* Corinne Skinner-Carter *Ranjanaa*

Kapoor Nalini Moonasar *Sebastian Moses* Rudolph Walker /*pr* Peter Ansorge /*wr* Michael Abbensetts /*BBC TV* (UK) /15 x 30m col.

Empty Nest

Comedy. C4 1989–92

A knock-on from the ➢*The Golden Girls*, set in Miami. Likewise created by Susan Harris, it starred Richard Mulligan, from her earlier hit ➢*Soap*, as widowed paediatrician Harry Weston whose daughters – neurotic Carol and undercover cop Barbara – had flown the nest. But only to return. Paternal anxiety and misunderstanding ensued, while Weston sought to deal with the mature female suitors who washed up at his door (the *GG* among them) and his lascivious neighbour Charley. A friendly, sympathetic ear was lent by dog Dreyfuss. *EN*, in turn, spun off another sitcom, *Nurses* (1991).

CAST *Dr Harry Weston* Richard Mulligan *Carol Weston* Dinah Manoff *Barbara Weston* Kirsty McNichol *Nurse LaVerne Todd* Park Overall *Charley Dietz* David Leisure /*cr* Susan Harris /*Witt Thomas Harris: Touchstone Productions* (USA)170 x 30m col /US tx NBC 1988–95.

Enemy at the Door

Drama. ITV 1978–80

WWII yarn about the German occupation of the Channel Islands, as seen (primarily) through the eyes of 20-year-old Guernsey girl, Clare Martel, and her family. Alfred Burke (➢*Public Eye*, ➢ *The Borgias*) heel-clicked nicely as Nazi Major Richter.

CAST *Clare Martel* Emily Richard *Olive Martel* Antonia Pemberton *Dr Philip Martel* Bernard Horsfall *Major Richter* Alfred Burke *Oberleutnant Kluge* John Malcolm *Hauptmann Reinicke* Simon Cadell *Peter Porteous* Richard Heffer /*exec pr* Tony Wharmby /*pr* Michael Chapman, Jonathan Alwyn /*LWT* (UK) /26 x 60m col.

ENG

Drama. C4 1991–2

Canadian series which sought to do for the TV newsroom – the title abbreviation stood for Electronic News Gathering – what ➢*Hill Street Blues* had done for the police precinct and ➢*St Elsewhere* had done for the hospital ward. And, to an extent, it succeeded. Shot with admirable panache and pace, it featured the ratings-driven staff of a major independent station, Channel 10, in downtown Toronto. Inevitably, their coverage of the city's doings always posed them a BMI (Big Moral Issue): child molestation, AIDS, the telephone sex business – and so on and so forth. It received a number of awards from, incestuously enough, the real TV industry, including, in 1991, Geminis for Best Series, Best Performance by an Actor (Art Hindle) and Best Writing.

CAST *Mike Fennell* Art Hindle *Ann Hildebrant* Sara Botsford *Jake Antonelli* Mark Humphrey *John Elman* Eugene A. Clark /*exec pr* Robert Lantos /*pr* Jeff King, Robert B. Carney /*Alliance Entertainment: CTV TV Network: Baton Broadcasting Inc* (Can) /1 x 120m, 24 x 60m col.

The Equalizer

Crime. ITV 1986–

➢*Callan* with an American dressing (plus a pinch of Bronson's *Death Wish*); no more, and much less. Edward Woodward played a muttering Manhattan former secret service agent turned PI/bodyguard who drove a Jaguar, dressed immaculately and righted wrongs, usually by dint of his gun. Careful to avoid anything too strenuous 'The Equalizer' passed over the legwork to assistant Mickey Kostmayer. A violent vigilante fantasy – most of those to die were NY muggers and rapists – the show was lapped up in the USA and did tolerably well over here. The theme music was composed by Stewart Copeland from sub-punk band The Police. Woodward was later to be seen laconically presenting the true crime show, *In Suspicious Circumstances* and evidencing unsuspected talent in the garbagemen comedy ➢*Common as Muck*.

CAST *Robert McCall, 'The Equalizer'* Edward Woodward *Control* Robert Lansing *Lt Isadore Smalls* Ron O'Neal *Lt Burnett* Steven Williams *Mickey Kostmayer* Keith Szarabajka *Scott McCall* William Zabka /*cr* Michael Sloan, Richard Lindheim /*exec pr* James McAdams /*pr* inc Alan Barnette, Colman Luck, Scott Shepherd, Daniel Lieberstein, Peter A. Runfolo /*dr* inc Russ Mayberry, Richard Compton, Alan Metzger /*mus* Stewart Copeland (theme) /*A Universal TV Production* (USA) /88 x 60m col /US tx CBS 1985–9.

ER

Drama. C4 1995–

'IV drip, 5,000 units of heparin and TPA 10 milligrams – stat…'

Developed from Michael 'Jurassic Park' Crichton's unmade 1974 movie script at the behest of Steven Spielberg's Amblin TV company, *ER* – standing for Emergency Room – made its debut in the USA in September 1994 as the highest-rated drama in just under a decade. Its key gimmick was its frenetic, emotionally wringing pace, termed by Crichton – who had served time himself as a medical student at Massachussetts General Hospital – 'rock 'em – sock 'em'. The result was channel surfing without pressing the button, as scenarios and stories progressed through the ER room of Cook County Hospital in Chicago at dizzying speed. The opening 90-minute pilot had no less than 45 medical stories. To heighten the tension and realism still further, sequences were filmed in claustrophobic sets (constructed, unusually, with four walls and a ceiling) by hand-held standicam. There was also blood by the bucket load.

Unlike rival slick hospital show *Chicago Hope* (starring Mandy Pantinkin, *pr* David E. Kelley), *ER* dwelt little on the patients, instead focussing almost entirely on its ensemble of doctor and nurse characters, whose professional lives and (shambolic) personal loves were explored in winning anatomical detail. Dr Mark Greene (Goose in *Top Gun*, ➢*Northern Exposure*) was the balding saintly surgeon whose ex-wife fought him bitterly for the custody of their daughter and whose boss, chief resident Kerry Weaver, was a constant thorn. Douglas Ross (George Clooney, later in the movie *Batman and Robin*) was the handsome paediatrician given to destructive drinking, who rescued his esteem by saving a drowning boy in 'Hell and High Water' (an archetypal *ER* episode, pitting the individual against seemingly impossible odds). Peter Benton was the tough-guy surgeon, seemingly foreign to emotion until he punched an obnoxious salesman after Jeannie Boulet ended their affair. Nurse Hathaway was the attempted suicide who was miraculously revived (after audience appreciation figures were studied by the producers – they decided well, for actress Julianna Margulies went on to win an Emmy). John Carter was the medical student whose ineptitude provided light relief before he got ambitious and callous, and then became committed and caring. Susan Lewis (Sherry Stringfield, headhunted from ➢*NYPD Blue*) was the ambitious high achiever, burdened by her family's expectations and then the care of her baby niece. Once asked by a patient if she was married, Lewis could only reply, 'No. I'm a doctor.' It could have been said by any *ER* doc.

Winning eight Emmys in its first year, a record only matched by ➢*Hill Street Blues*, *ER* was made as a co-production between Amblin and Crichton's own company, Constant-C, and co-executive produced by John Wells, previously the writer/producer of *China Beach* (1988–91), set in a female MASH in Vietnam. *ER*'s directors included Quentin Tarantino, making a rare excursion into TV – presumably since the show was a chance to splatter blood on an even grander scale than *Reservoir Dogs*.

CAST *Dr Mark Greene* Anthony Edwards *Dr Susan Lewis* Sherry Stringfield *Dr Douglas Ross* George Clooney *Charge Nurse Carol Hathaway* Julianna Margulies *Dr Peter Benton* Eriq LaSalle *John Carter* Noah Wyle *Kerry Weaver* Laura Innes *Jeannie Boulet* Gloria Reuben *Dr Anna Del Amico* Maria Bello *Dr Elizabeth Corday* Alex Kingston /*cr* Michael Crichton /*exec pr* Michael Crichton, John Wells /*pr* Mimi Leder, Lydia Woodward, Chris Culack, Paul Manning /*dr* inc Rod Holcomb, Mimi Leder, Anthony Edwards, Donna Deitsch, Richard Thorpe, Quentin Tarantino /*wr* inc Michael Crichton, Lance A. Gentile, Neal Baer, John Wells /*Contant-C: Amblin TV* (USA) /1 x 90m, 90+ x 60m col /US tx NBC 1994–.

Eurovision Song Contest

Light Entertainment. BBC1 1957–

Declared a 'monument to drivel and mediocrity' by the French when they withdrew (temporarily), the Eurovision Song Contest began in 1956 as a starry-eyed televisual attempt to promote international friendship in the era of the Cold War. It grew out of the San Remo Song Festival, with the nations of the European Broadcasting Union presenting an original song and performer(s) to be judged by 'juries' of viewers – via the Eurovision interconnect link – from the other participant countries. By the early 90s, so popular was the *ESC* that over 40 nations were warbling their wares in the annual competion, including much of the former Eastern Bloc and swathes of North Africa and the Middle East.

Far, however, from promoting peace and understanding, the *ESC* is a festival of chauvinism; the Jordanians, famously, pulled the plug in 1978 because Israel was winning, replacing the contest with the screening of a detective film. When lyrics in English began to predominate, a rule was made in 1975 that every entry had to be sung in one of the major languages of the country concerned. To overcome the unfortunate fact that, in some tongues, romantic sentiments sound like a docker eating fish stew, many entries are composed of meaningless sounds, like A Ba Ni Bi (Israel, 1978, winner), Diggi Loo Diggi Ley (Sweden, 1984, winner) and Bana Bana (Turkey, 1989). This notwithstanding, upwards of 500 million viewers tune in each year to watch Norway, the laughing stock of the competition, fail ignominiously ('La Norvege, nil points...'), although the British audience has declined from its peak in the 70s to only 10 million in the 90s. For much of this period, the BBC commentary has been provided by a sardonic Terry Wogan, whose support for the proceedings is similar to that lent by a rope to a hanged man.

Britain itself first competed in the contest in 1957, since when she has notched up four wins: barefoot Sandie Shaw in 1967, Lulu in 1969, Brotherhood of Man in 1976 and Bucks Fizz in 1981 with 'Making Your Mind Up'.

CAST (British presenters) inc David Jacobs, Tom Sloan, David Gell, Dave Lee Travis, Tom Fleming, David Vine, Pete Murray, Michael Aspel, John Dunn, Terry Wogan /*BBC TV: European Broadcasting Union* (UK /Eur) 20+ x 120m bw:col.

Evening Shade

Comedy. C4 1992–4

After 40 movies, most of them forgettable, Burt Reynolds returned to TV (he came up in *Gunsmoke*) to make his sitcom debut – and promptly walked off with the 1991 Emmy Award for Best Comedy Actor for his role as *Evening Shade*'s Wood Newton, an over-the-hill football hero who goes back to his home town in Arkansas to become High School coach. Naturally, the team was hopeless and the local folk eccentric. As well as providing an opportunity to show Reynolds' talent for self-deprecating humour (winning him a Golden Globe to place alongside the Emmy), the show tapped neatly and nostalgically into traditional American small-town mythology. Even more so than ➢*Northern Exposure*, gently funny *ES* was the sunshine antidote to ➢*Twin Peaks*. Marilu Henner of ➢*Taxi* fame played Newton's politically ambitious wife, Ava. Reynolds, as if to demonstrate his versatility, also directed several episodes.

CAST *Wood Newton* Burt Reynolds *Ava Newton* Marilu Henner *Evan Evans* Hal Holbrook *Dr Harlan Elldridge* Charles Durning *Taylor Newton* Jay R. Ferguson *Molly Newton* Melissa Martin/Candace Hutson *Will Newton* Jacob Parker *Herman Stiles* Michael Jeter *Ponder Blue* Ossie Davis *Fontana Beausoleil* Linda Gehringer /*pr* Tommy Thompson, Don Rhymer /*dr* inc Burt Reynolds /50 x 30m col / US tx CBS 1990–92.

Ever Decreasing Circles

Comedy. BBC1 1984–9

From the prolific pens of writing duo Esmonde and Larbey (➢*Please Sir!*, ➢*Get Some In*, ➢*The Good Life*, ➢*Brush Strokes*) and featuring Richard Briers as Martin Brice, pernickety pillar of the local community, chair of every neighbourhood club that could raise a committee, and loyal employee of Mole Valley Valves. While Martin fussed, meddled and failed to delegate the whole day through, his implausibly desirable and patient wife Ann (Penelope Wilton), soothed and smoothed his brow. The arrival of new neighbour Paul Ryman (Peter Egan, also *A Perfect Spy*, *Big Breadwinner Hog*, *Paradise Postponed*), the suave, understanding and effortlessly effective proprietor of a beauty salon, was presumably intended to inject a little piquancy to the proceedings. It served only, however, to add a degree of tetchiness to Martin's character that made him still more unpalatable. Simple and sartorially challenged neighbours, Howard and Hilda Hughes, meanwhile, were friends to all alike.

CAST *Martin Brice* Richard Briers *Ann Brice* Penelope Wilton *Paul Ryman* Peter Egan *Howard Hughes* Stanley Labor *Hilda Hughes* Geraldine Newman /*cr* John Esmonde, Bob Larbey /*pr* Sydney Lotterby, Harold Snoad /*wr* John Esmonde & Bob Larbey / *BBC TV* (UK) /27 x 30m col.

F

Fabian of the Yard

Crime. BBC 1954-6

Legendary British police series from the 50s fictionalizing the cases of the Yard's real-life DI Fabian. Shot on film, with Bruce Seton, stiff upper lip clamped on pipe, as the consummately dedicated Fabian, it cast a giant TV shadow. For the post-war generation Fabian was not just the first British police hero of the small screen, but the best. The show sold to America where it was screened as *Inspector Fabian of Scotland Yard* or – in reference to the hero's Black Humber Hawk – *Patrol Car*. The real Fabian, incidentally, retired from the force to become 'Guardian of the Questions' on quiz show *The 64,000 Question.*

CAST *DI Robert Fabian* Bruce Seton /*pr* John Larkin, Anthony Beauchamp /*dr* inc Anthony Beauchamp, John Lemont, Bernard Knowles, Alex Bryce /*wr* inc Arthur La Bern, Rex Rienits, Arnold Goldsworthy, Donald Bull /*Anthony Beauchamp Prods: Trinity Prods* (UK) /39 x 30m bw /US tx Syndicated 1955.

Fairly Secret Army

Comedy. C4 1984–6

Sitcom veteran Geoffrey Palmer (➢*Butterflies, Last Song, As Time Goes By,* etc.) played retired Major Harry Kitchener Wellington Truscott, a right-wing fanatic who believed the country was overrun by 'right on feminists, do gooders, and left-wing anarchist sympathisers'. Accordingly, he founded a private army (inevitably, and comically, a rag-tag affair of half-brained fascists and no-brained military toffs) to whip the nation into shape. Truscott was loosely based on the military-minded Jimmy (also played by Palmer) in David Nobbs' earlier ➢*The Fall and Rise of Reginald Perrin.*

CAST *Major Harry Kitchener Wellington Truscott* Geoffrey Palmer *Nancy* Diana Fletcher *Sgt Major Throttle* Michael Robbins *Doris Entwistle* Liz Fraser *Stubby Collins* Ray Winstone *Beamish* Jeremy Child /*cr* David Nobbs /*pr* Peter Robinson /*dr* Robert Young, Roy Ward Baker /*Video Arts* (UK) /12 x 30m col.

Falcon Crest

Melodrama. ITV 1982

From – improbably enough – the pen of Earl Hamner Jr, the man who brought the world the lachrymose ➢*The Waltons, Falcon Crest* was a companion soap to Lorimar's ➢*Dallas*, merely swapping oil for sour grapes. The setting was 'Tuscany Valley' (the real life Napa Valley) in California, with dowager vintner Angela Channing as a JR figure who presided malevolently over a power struggle for the family vineyard. So appalling was the show pilot ('The Vintage Years') that it was never televised; the transmitted episodes themselves were banal agglomerations of OTT soap-opera clichés, viz. murder, kidnapping, comas, sexual shenanigans, long-lost offspring, white slavery, international epsionage and gangster-type larceny. The series caught light (reaching No. 7 in the Nielsens) largely because of its prestige cast, headed by Ronald Reagan's ex-wife, Jane Wyman (as Angela Channing), a semi-legendary actress in the USA and winner of an Oscar for *Johnny Belinda* (1948). *Falcon Crest* marked her first TV appearance since her own anthology show (*The Jane Wyman Show*) of the late 50s. She was joined at the head of the dramatis personae by Robert Foxworth (the actor who had previously turned down JR in *Dallas* and Trapper John in ➢*M*A*S*H*) as Channing's nephew-nemesis, Chase Gioberti. Below these actors, the producers recruited a parade of movie stars seldom seen on the small screen: Lana Turner, Gina Lollobrigida, Kim Novak, Mel Ferrer, John Saxon (from *Enter the Dragon*), Rod Taylor and Cesar Romero. It was spotting and watching movie icons slumming it in a soap that gave *FC* its real appeal. Others in the cast included Roy Thinnes (➢*The Invaders*), Jane Badler (➢*V*), Simon MacCorkindale and Ken Olin (later ➢*Thirtysomething*). Unusually for a soap opera, *FC* allowed its characters a happy ending, with Angela Channing re-united with her family, the dynastic squabble over.

CAST *Angela Channing* Jane Wyman *Chase Gioberti* Robert Foxworth *Maggie Channing (née Gioberti)* Susan Sullivan *Lance Cumson* Lorenzo Lamas *Tony Cumson* John Saxon *Phillip Erikson* Mel Ferrer *Jacqueline Perrault* Lana Turner *Nick Hogan* Roy Thinnes *Francesca Gioberti* Gina Lollobrigida *Greg Reardon* Simon MacCorkindale *Jordan Roberts* Morgan Fairchild *Father Christopher* Ken Olin *Peter Stavros* Cesar Romero *Kit Marlowe* Kim Novak *Meredith Braxton* Jane Badler *Frank Agretti* Rod Taylor /*cr* Earl Hamner Jr /*exec pr* Earl Hamner Jr, Michael Filerman, Joanne Brough, Jeff Freilich, Camille Marchetta, Jerry Thorpe /*dr* inc Jerry Thorpe, Robert Foxworth, Fernando Lamas, Jack Bender /*wr* inc Earl Hamner Jr, Sandra Siegel, Michael Filerman /*mus* Bill Conti (theme) / *Lorimar* (USA) /220 x 60m col /US tx CBS 1981–90.

The Fall and Rise of Reginald Perrin

Comedy. BBC1 1976–9

David Nobbs' inspired serial satire on middle everything (age, class, England), based on his novel, *The Death of Reginald Perrin.*

After 20 years as an executive for Sunshine Desserts, Reginald Iolanthe Perrin (Leonard Rossiter, ➢*Rising Damp*) walked out on his surreally monotonous life and faked a seaside suicide. After a spell as a labourer on a pig farm, he assumed the persona of Martin Welbourne, remarried wife Elizabeth and started a company, Grot, selling useless items (son-in-law Tom's abysmal homemade wine, square footballs) at hugely inflated prices. Alas, this sly critique of consumerism became a capitalist success, and Reggie entered the ranks of the tycoonery. When Sunshine Desserts collapsed, Reggie employed all his old colleagues – gimlet-eyed boss CJ, ever cross-legged secretary Joan (Sue Nicholls, ➢*Crossroads*, ➢*Coronation Street*), sycophantic juniors Tony 'Super' Webster and David 'Great' Harris-Jones. This seemed a form of pleasant revenge, until Reggie realized that he had simply recreated his former existence. At the end of season two, Reggie and the whole cast staged a counterfeit suicide. They were brought back for a third season, in which Reggie founded a community for stressed executives, Perrins. There was also room for an impenetrable Scottish cook, McBlane, and Reggie's militaristic brother-in-law Jimmy (played by Geoffrey Palmer, who largely reprised the character in ➢*Fairly Secret Army*), constantly on the scrounge for the odd scrag end with an apologetic, 'Bit of a cock up on the catering front.' (The show also donated at least one other enduring catchphrase to the English language: CJ's 'I didn't get where I am today…')

Markedly cerebral for a late 70s sitcom, *The Rise and Fall of Reginald Perrin* avoided dessication thanks to the virtuoso performance of Rossiter as Reggie, who took a cipher and made it into an outstanding tragi-comic creation, the patron saint of those on the 7.50 from Purley Oaks. An American version, simply entitled *Reggie*, (starring Richard Mulligan from ➢*Soap*, together with a pre-➢*Thirtysomething* Timothy Busfield) was broadcast by ABC in 1983.

Against all reason, the BBC belatedly sequelized the show in 1996 with Reggie killed by an insurance hoarding (Rossiter himself had died in 1984), leaving his cronies to perform absurd tasks in the hope of receiving several million pounds from his will. Although nearly all the original cast returned for *The Legacy of Reginald Perrin*, their characters, stripped of their social context, were mere walking sitcom clichés.

CAST *Reginald Iolanthe Perrin* Leonard Rossiter *Elizabeth Perrin* Pauline Yates *CJ* John Barron *Joan Greengross* Sue Nicholls *Doc Morrisey* John Horsley *Tony Webster* Trevor Adams *David Harris-Jones* Bruce Bould *Prue Harris-Jones* Theresa Watson *Jimmy* Geoffrey Palmer *Linda* Sally-Jane Spencer *Tom* Tim Preece /Leslie Schofield *McBlane* Joseph Brady /*cr* David Nobbs /*pr* John Howard Davies, Gareth Gwenlan /*dr* Gareth Gwenlan /*wr* David Nobbs /*mus* Ronnie Hazlehurst /*BBC TV* (UK) /21 x 30m col.

The Fall Guy

Crime. ITV 1982–6

Actor Lee Majors' (➢*The Big Valley*, ➢*The Men from Shiloh*, ➢*The Six Million Dollar Man*) fourth prime-time hit saw him play Colt Seavers, a Hollywood stuntman who earned extra bucks tracking down bail jumpers. Naturally, this latterday bounty hunting required stuntwork of even greater spectacularness than that which Seavers performed for the movie biz. He was assisted by eager-beaver cousin Howie, and beautiful stuntwoman Jody Banks. To distract from the oft routine plotlines, the producers plied such old tricks of the TV trade as parades of beautiful women (one episode alone included former Bond girls Britt Ekland and Lana Wood), slapstick, and glamorous locales. Majors also sang the theme song.

CAST *Colt Seavers* Lee Majors *Howie Munson* Douglas Barr *Jody Banks* Heather Thomas *Samantha 'Big Jack' Jack* Jo Ann Pflug *Terrie Shannon (Michaels)* Markie Post *Pearl Sperling* Nedra Volz /*cr* Glen A. Larson /*exec pr* Glen A. Larson /*pr* inc Robert Jones, Harry Thompson /*dr* inc Tom Connors, Daniel Haller, Ray Austin, Vincent Edwards /*wr* inc Larry Brand, Rebecca Reynolds /*mus* David Somerville, Gail Jensen, Glen Larson ('The Unknown Stuntman' theme) /*20th Century-Fox TV* (USA) /120 x 60m col /US tx ABC 1983–6.

Fame

Melodrama. BBC1 1982–4

Fascinating schmaltz, based on Alan Parker's movie of the same name, relating the dreams, struggles and heartaches of youthful showbiz wannabees at New York's High School for the Performing Arts. Among the featured students were: Leroy, a dancer from the ghetto (played by Gene Anthony Ray, an expellee from the real NYHSPA); Bruno, a nerdishly brilliant musician; Doris, a comedienne-writer (Valerie Landsberg, daughter of Hollywood producer Alan); Coco, a singer-dancer in hurry for the big time; and Julie, the quiet out-of-towner cellist (Lori Singer, later ➢*VR5*). Even more dedicated than the students were the staff, headed by glamorous, tough-minded dance teacher Lydia Grant (Debbie Allen, sister of ➢*The Cosby Show*'s Phylicia), bearded oldster music professor Shorofsky and English teacher Elizabeth Sherwood.

The show was an enormous critical success in the USA, where it was singled out for the quality of its acting and the acuteness of its portrayal of the angsts of the urban young in competitive contemporary society. An Emmy went to Debbie Allen for her choreography of the leotarded song and dance numbers that *Fame* students were wont to break into at the drop of a hint. Inexplicably, it flopped with the viewers and was cancelled by NBC network after just 18 months, although the producers continued to make episodes for syndication, picking up a pre-famous Janet Jackson and Eric Pierpoint (➢*Alien Nation*) for the cast along the way. In Britain, meanwhile, *Fame* became a kind of craze, racking up 11 million viewers and even zooming songs from the show ('Hi-Fidelity', 'Starmaker') into the record charts.

Four of the original movie cast reprised their roles in the TV series. They were Allen, Hague, Ray and Curreri.

CAST *Lydia Grant* Debbie Allen *Leroy Johnson* Gene Anthony Ray *Coco Hernandez* Erica Gimpel *Danny Amatullo* Carlo Imperato *Professor Shorofsky* Albert Hague *Elizabeth Sherwood* Carol Mayo Jenkins *Doris Schwartz* Valerie Landsburg *Bruno Martelli* Lee Curreri *Julie Miller* Lori Singer *Montgomery MacNeil* P.R. Paul *Cleo Hewitt* Janet Jackson *Paul Singer* Eric Pierpoint /*pr* William Blinn, Gerald I. Isenberg, Mel Swope, Stanley C. Rogow /*dr* inc Robert Scheerer /*wr* inc Hindi Brooks, Ralph Farquhar and Kevin Sullivan /*mus* 'Fame' theme, Michael Gore & Dean Pitchford (theme lyrics), Erica Gimpel (theme vocal) /60 x 60m col / US tx NBC 1982–3, Syndication 1983–7.

Family Ties

Comedy. C4 1985–9

Reportedly President Ronald Reagan's favourite TV show. *Family Ties*' other distinction was that it provided the vehicle for the diminuitive Michael J. Fox to achieve screen stardom. Fox played Alex P. Keaton, the bemused, arch-conservative teen-age son of former flower children Elyse and Steve Keaton, who continued to espouse liberal values in the cold climate of the 80s. The Ohio couple's other progeny were fashion-plate Mallory and cutesie Jennifer, later joined by baby Andrew. Although the show's main theme was the generation gap, it also parodied Reaganite values; Fox's besuited, monetarist-espousing Alex was intended as a ridiculous figure but, as with Gordon Gecko in *Wall Street*, curiously ended up a hero. Tom Hanks appeared in some early episodes as Elyse's embezzling brother, Ned. The theme song, 'Without Us', was crooned by Johnny Mathis and Deniece Williams.

CAST *Elyse Keaton* Meredith Baxter-Birney *Steve Keaton* Michael Gross *Alex P. Keaton* Michael J. Fox *Mallory Keaton* Justine Bateman *Jennifer Keaton* Tina Yothers *Andrew Keaton* Brian Bonsall /*cr* Gary David Goldberg /*exec pr* Gary David Goldberg /*dr* inc Debbie Allen, Alan Bergman /*wr* inc Gary David Goldberg, Ruth Bennett /*mus* Jeff Barry & Tom Scott (theme) /*Paramount TV* (USA) /180 x 30m, 1 x 60m col /US NBC tx 1982–9.

Family Affair

Comedy. ITV 1969

Archetypal American 'heart' comedy. Brian Keith (*The Westerner*, *The Brian Keith Show*, ➢*The Zoo Gang*) starred as Bill Davis, a playboy NY millionaire who becomes the foster parent of his orphaned nephew and nieces. This was to the dismay of Davis' disdainful butler, French, the dry catalyst for most of the laughs. Despite the sitcom's hit status in the USA, only a smattering of episodes were screened in the UK.

CAST *Bill Davis* Brian Keith *Mr Giles French* Sebastian Cabot *Jody* Johnnie Whittaker *Buffy* Anissa Jones *Cissy* Kathy Garver /*cr* Don Fedderson /*dr* inc James Sheldon /*pr* Don Fedderson /*Don Fedderson Productions* (USA) /138 x 30m col /US tx CBS 1966–71.

A Family at War

Drama. ITV 1970–2

Relentlessly gloomy Granada serial about the tribulations of a middle-class Liverpool family, the Ashtons, beginning with the Depression(!) year of 1938 and continuing through the dark days of WWII. Always expensively produced, sometimes evocative (the scripts of war novelist Alexander Baron), never subtle (the opening 'symbolic' shot was of a sandcastle being eroded by waves). Fortuitously, perhaps, it was released in the dog days of the Ted Heath government (power blackouts, striking miners, the three-day week) and struck a therapeutic glum chord with its audience, who watched it into the uppermost reaches of the ratings.

CAST *Edwin Ashton* Colin Douglas *Jean Ashton* Shelagh Fraser *Margaret Porter (née Ashton)* Lesley Nunnerley *Sheila Ashton* Coral Atkins *Philip Ashton* Keith Drinkel *Freda Ashton* Barbara Flynn *Sefton Briggs* John McKelvey /*cr* John Finch /*exec pr* Richard Doubleday /*pr* Richard Doubleday, Michael Cox, James Brabazon /*dr* inc June Howson, Bob Hird, Gerry Mill, Baz Taylor /*wr* inc John Finch, Alexander Baron, Jonathan Powell /*Granada TV* (UK) /52 x 50m col.

Fantasy Football League

Comedy. BBC2 1994–

The lads' night in. Pleasantly inebriating mix of batchelor-pad humour and socceralia, hosted by alternative(ish) comedians David Baddiel (➢*The Mary Whitehouse Experience*) and Frank Skinner (*Blue Heaven*, *Packet of Three*). Each week 'guest managers' – among them Patsy Kensit, Jimmy Tarbuck, ➢*Basil Brush* – joined the couch duo to report on the progress of dream football teams, while the dressing-gown-clad Statto sat on the sidelines with the facts and figures. The banal technical talk of scoring points for 'saves and assists' was a turn off, but the 'Phoenix from the Flames' recreations of great footie moments became hugely, cultishly popular. Flatmates in real life as well as in the studio confines, Baddiel and Skinner also presented several *FFL* 'Specials' for the key events of the home and international soccer calendar.

CAST (presenters) David Baddiel, Frank Skinner /*pr* Andy Jacobs /*dr* Peter Orton /*Avalon* (UK) / 30+ x 30m col.

Fantasy Island

Drama. ITV 1978–84

Stories of guests on a remote tropical island who pay its mysterious ruler to have their dreams come true. Aiding Mr Roarke in his benevolent sorcery – the visitors went away with not only the experience of a lifetime, but also Self Knowledge – was a dwarf, Tattoo (later replaced by new assistant Lawrence). The show was developed by America's ABC as a follow-up to another romantic drama anthology, ➢*Love Boat*, in the hopes that large dollops of glamour, beachfuls of bikini babes, and the occasional dash of danger would persuade humdrum millions to tune into the network again. To nobody's surprise, they did.

CAST *Mr Roarke* Ricardo Montalban *Tattoo* Herve Villechaize *Julie* Wendy Schaal *Lawrence* Christopher Hewett /*exec pr* Aaron Spelling, Leonard Goldberg /*A Spelling Goldberg Production* (UK) /120 x 60m col / US tx ABC 1979–84.

The Far Pavilions

Drama. C4 1984

In the tumultuous hey days of the Raj a young British army officer, Ash Pelham-Martyn, is torn between his loyalty to his country and his class, and his forbidden love for Indian Princess Anjuli.

Opulent adventure epic costing £8 million (a not-inconsiderable portion of it spent on seducing big name stars Gielgud, Sharif and Lee), based on M.M. Kaye's novel. Beautiful to look at (director of photography was the great Jack Cardiff), but ultimately to no mind-moving message. Like fellow Raj drama ➢*Jewel in the Crown*, which debuted in the same year, it was prompted into screen life by the success at the box office of Attenborough's *Gandhi* (1982).

CAST *Ashton Pelham-Martyn* Ben Cross *Kaka-Ji Rao* Christopher Lee *Koda Dad* Omar Sharif *Cavagnari* John Gielgud *Princess Anjuli* Amy Irving *Biju Ram* Saeed Jaffrey *The Commandant* Robert Hardy *Princess Shushila* Sneh Gupta *The Rana of Bhithor* Rossano Brazzi /*pr* Geoffrey Reeve /*dr* Peter Duffell /*wr* Julian Bond /*mus* Carl Davis /*Geoff Reeve and Associates: Goldcrest* (UK) /1 x 120m, 2 x 115m col.

The Fast Show
Comedy. BBC2 1995–

Furiously inventive and pacy comedy skit show (averaging a machine-gun-like 25 sketches per 30 minutes), judiciously apolitical, fuelled by playground-friendly catchphrases (the Latin weather girl's 'Scorchio') and *Viz*-like creations. The Fat Sweaty Cops, Arthur 'Where's Me Washboard' Atkins, tongue-tied toff Ralph, coughing gardener Bob Fleming, the Alcoholics, and jinxed geriatric Unlucky Alf (provider of unusually hilarious small-screen slapstick) were among the most famous characters. Paul Whitehouse, former plasterer and ex-➢*Harry Enfield's Television Programme* 'chum', Charles Higson and Caroline Aherne (➢*The Mrs Merton Show*) led the team of players and writers in a series which re-established the art of comic-sketch timing, against the self-indulgence shown by such comtemporaries gone to flab as ➢*French and Saunders* ... which was nice.

CAST inc Paul Whitehouse, Charles Higson, Caroline Aherne (aka Hook), Simon Day, John Thomson, Arabella Weir, Mark Williams /*pr* Paul Whitehouse, Charles Higson /*dr* Mark Mylod, Sid Robertson /*wr* inc Paul Whitehouse, Charles Higson, Simon Day, Caroline Aherne /*BBC TV* (UK) /32+ x 30m col.

Father Brown
Crime. ITV 1974

Affable period detective series featuring Kenneth More as G.K. Chesterton's clumsy-but-cerebral clerical sleuth (motto: 'Have Bible – will travel'). Solidly made, excellently cast (thanks to Sir Lew Grade badgering More until he acquiesced to the role), a last sigh of the gentle school of deduction before the screen was overrun by the action men of ➢*The Sweeney* and ➢*Starsky and Hutch.*

CAST *Father Brown* Kenneth More *Det. Flambeau* Dennis Burgess /*pr* Ian Fordyce /*dr* Robert Tronson, Peter Jeffries /*wr* Hugh Leonard, Peter Wildeblood, Michael Voysey, John Portman /*mus* Jack Parnell / *An ATV Network Production* (UK) /13 x 60m col / US tx PBS 1982.

Father Dear Father
Comedy. ITV 1968–73

Mild, middle-class sitcom with Patrick Cargill as a divorced novelist whose romantic assignations and attempts to scribe in peace were farcically interrupted by his mother, his agent, his ex-wife (Barbara), his wife's lover (Bill, *his* best friend), his housekeeper, and his two luscious teenage daughters, whose legs apparently stretched to heaven. A St Bernard named H.G. Wells spent its life asleep on the sofa. The series' producer was future ➢*Fifteen To One* presenter William G. Stewart. An Australian version was made in 1977, with Cargill leaving Hampstead to care for a couple of inherited colonial nieces. Only Noel Dyson from the original cast joined him Down Under.

CAST *Patrick Glover* Patrick Cargill *Anna Glover* Natasha Pyne *Karen Glover* Ann Holloway *Matilda 'Nanny' Harris* Noel Dyson *Barbara Glover/Mossman* Ursula Howells *Mrs Glover* Joyce Carey *Georgie* Sally Bazely/Dawn Addams *Bill Mossman* Patrick Holt *Howard* Richard O'Sullivan/Tony Briton /*cr* Johnny Mortimer, Brian Cooke /*pr* William G. Stewart /*dr* inc William G. Stewart /*wr* Johnny Mortimer, Brian Cooke /*Thames TV* (UK) /36 x 30m bw:col /US tx Syndicated 1977.

Father Dowling Investigates
Crime. ITV 1990–4

Tom Bosley, in his first starring role since ➢*Happy Days*, played a Chicago Catholic priest whose hobby was amateur 'tec work. He was aided in his investigations by a credulity-breaking streetwise nun, Sister Steve, and in his screen charm by a clapped-out station wagon. Not good enough for TV Heaven but not quite offensive enough for TV Hell. Purgatory, perhaps. Based on Ralph McInerny's novels which, suspicion says, were an updated American steal of Chesteron's ➢*Father Brown* cycle.

CAST *Father Frank Dowling* Tom Bosley *Sister Stephanie ('Sister Steve')* Tracy Nelson *Father Prestwick* James Stephens *Marie* Mary Wickes *Sgt Clancy* Regina Krueger /*cr* Ralph McInerny, Dean Hargrove, Joel Steiger /*exec pr* Fred Silverman, Dean Hargrove /*pr*

Barry Steinberg /*dr* inc Harry Harris, Sharron Miller /*mus* Dick DeBenedictis /*Viacom: Dean Hargrove Productions: Fred Silverman Productions* (USA) / 45 x 60m col /US tx NBC 1987, ABC 1990–1 (as *Father Dowling Mysteries*).

Father Knows Best

Comedy. ITV 1956

Epitome of the 'Hi honey, I'm home' family sitcoms of the affluent Eisenhower 50s, depicting the idyllic life of the American family Anderson. Transferring to TV after a successful radio run, the show novelly played on all three main US networks. Star Robert Young, a Hollywood front man in the 30s and 40s, later went on to to play the equally iconic ➢*Marcus Welby MD.*

CAST *Jim Anderson* Robert Young *Margaret Anderson* Jane Wyatt *Betty Anderson* Elinor Donahue *Bud Anderson* Billy Gray *Kathy Anderson* Lauren Chaplin / *pr* Eugene B. Rodney, Robert Young/*Rodney–Young Productions* (USA) /191 x 25m bw /US tx CBS/NBC 1954–1962 (re-runs on ABC).

Father Ted

Comedy. C4 1995–8

Superlative clerical sitcom following the exploits of an unholy trinity of priests – relatively sensible Ted, permanently inebriated Jack ('Drink! Gurrls! Feck!'), transcendentally dim Dougal – living on godforsaken Craggy Island, somewhere off the west coast of Ireland. Dithering old Mrs Doyle was the housekeeper. Blessed with a tendency towards surrealism (a minor character, Father Larry Duff, repeatedly appeared and died), innocent daftness and outstanding performances, it was deluged with BAFTAs, although it took a repeat run of the first season for many people to see the joke. Creators Graham Linehan and Arthur Mathews later donated their talents to numerous other TV comedy products, among them ➢*The Fast Show* and *Coogan's Run. Father Ted* was brought to a premature end by the death of star Dermot Morgan (aged 45) in 1998.

CAST *Father Ted Crilly* Dermot Morgan *Father Dougal McGuire* Ardal O'Hanlon *Father Jack Hackett* Frank Kelly *Mrs Doyle* Pauline McLynn /*cr* Graham Linehan & Arthur Mathews /*pr* Geoffrey Perkins, Lissa Evans /*dr* Declan Lowney /*wr* Graham Linehan & Arthur Mathews /*Hat Trick* (UK) /19 x 30m, 1 x 40m col.

Fawlty Towers

Comedy. BBC2 1975–9

Much loved BBC sitcom, born during a ➢*Monty Python* location shoot in Torquay, when an over-zealous hotel owner threw Eric Idle's briefcase into the street as a precaution against it containing a bomb. John Cleese and his then wife, Connie Booth, wrote the manic hotelier into a ➢*Doctor in the House* sequel, before giving him his own series in 1975 as Basil Fawlty, proprietor of Fawlty Towers. Each episode took six weeks to write (the TV norm is ten days), and combined situation comedy that exposed British smugness and hypocrisy (Basil's fawning over the U-class, his cruel dismissal of foreigners – immortalized in the 'Don't mention the war!' sequence with Basil goosestepping before a group of German tourists – and those he considered socially inferior), with outstanding performances. Cleese himself played Basil, while Prunella Scales was cast as 'sour old bag' wife Sybil, Connie Booth as sensible chambermaid Polly, and Andrew Sachs as Manuel the waiter. In the name of comedy, Manuel was used as a battering ram to open the fire exit, hit over the head with a frying pan and dragged round by his ear. He also tried to expand his command of English beyond 'I know nothing, I ham from Barcelona', but was usually reduced to an immortal, uncomprehending 'Que?'. US show, *Amanda's* (starring ➢*The Golden Girls*' Bea Arthur), tried to duplicate the formula, but without success.

CAST *Basil Fawlty* John Cleese *Sybil Fawlty* Prunella Scales *Polly* Connie Booth *Manuel* Andrew Sachs *Major Gowen* Ballard Berkely *Miss Tibbs* Gilly Flower *Miss Gatsby* Renee Roberts /*cr* John Cleese, Connie Booth /*pr* John Howard Davies, Douglas Argent /*dr* Bob Spiers /*wr* John Cleese, Connie Booth /*mus* Dennis Wilson /*BBC TV* (UK) /12 x 30m col /US tx PBS 1976–9.

The FBI

Crime. ITV 1965–70

Tough-guy show featuring the Federal Bureau of Investigation, which received an encomium from no less than J. Edgar Hoover, the real-life chief of the FBI himself. Efrem Zimbalist Jr (➢*77 Sunset Strip*) played incorruptible G-Man Inspector Lewis Erskine, a robot-like pursuer of commies and crooks whose daughter was killed off by the producers so that he would suffer no distraction from his mission. Of Erskine's succession of Bureau partners, Tom Colby lasted longest. Episodes frequently ended with an appeal to viewers to help catch the FBI's 'Most Wanted'. So enamoured with the propagandistic *FBI* was Hoover – despite the show's rudimentary and pedestrian artistic levels – that he allowed scenes to be filmed at the Bureau's Washington HQ. The official sponsors of the programme, meanwhile, were the Ford Motor Company, whose gleaming sedans were the agents' standard means of transportation. It came from Quinn Martin (➢*The Fugitive*, ➢*Cannon*).

CAST *Insp. Lewis Erskine* Efrem Zimbalist Jr *Assistant Director Arthur Ward* Philip Abbott *Barbara Erskine* Lynn Loring *Special Agent Tom Colby* William Reynolds *Special Agent Jim Rhodes* Stephen Brooks *Chris Daniels* Shelly Novack *Narrator* Marvin Miller / *exec pr* Quinn Martin / *pr* Charles Larson, Anthony Spinner, Philip Saltzman / *dr* inc Earl Bellamy, Richard Donner, Walter Grauman, Jesse Hibbs, Allen Reisner, William Wiard / *wr* inc John D.F. Black, Richard Landau, Norman Lessing, Andy Lewis / *Quinn Martin Productions* (USA) /236 x 60m col /US tx ABC 1965–74.

Fifteen To One
Light Entertainment. C4 1988–

Deliciously malicious general-knowledge quiz show in which 15 contestants sought to eliminate each other, leaving one survivor. The 15 winners from each season then gathered in a semicircle around presenter William G. Stewart for a final showdown, from which the champion walked away rich in kudos if not in money: the prize was a trophy. Before *FTO*, Stewart had earned the family bacon as the producer of some of British TV's greatest hits: ➢*Bless This House*, ➢*Father Dear Father*, and ➢*The Price is Right*.

CAST (presenter) William G. Stewart / *cr* John M. Lewis / *pr* William G. Stewart / *dr* inc Richard Bardley, Nick Bigsby / *Regent Productions* (UK) 400+ x 30m col.

Filthy Rich and Catflap
Comedy. BBC1 1987

Ben Elton-scripted sitcom about a ruthless TV star (played by Rik Mayall) whose attempts to hobnob with the celebrity likes of 'Tarby' are undone by his incompetent agent (Nigel Planer) and brainless bodyguard (Adrian Edmondson). Dismissed as 'The Young Ones: The Next Generation', *FRC* certainly continued that show's attack on the traditional sitcom (repetitive use of extreme violence, scatological jokes, absurdist interludes). Yet, viewed through a generous frame of mind, it was also a decent tilt at the arrogance of showbiz and the corrupting nature of fame.

CAST *Filthy Ralph* Nigel Planer *Richard Rich* Rik Mayall *Eddie Catflap* Adrian Edmondson / *cr* Ben Elton / *pr* Paul Jackson / *wr* Ben Elton, Rik Mayall / *BBC TV* (UK) /6 x 30m col.

A Fine Romance
Comedy. ITV 1981–4

Bob Larbey sitcom which cast real-life husband and wife, Dame Judi Dench (Shakespeare galore, *As Time Goes By*, Sheba cat-food ads) and Michael Williams, as a couple of mid-lifers eventually fumbling their way into marriage. She was proactive Laura, he was cautious Mike, a landscape gardener. Impeccably, seemingly effortlessly, performed, it was a rare portrayal of believable middle-aged characters. By the end of its run it had pushed itself to No. 3 in the ratings.

CAST *Laura* Judi Dench *Mike* Michael Williams *Helen* Susan Penhaligon *Phil* Richard Warwick / *cr* Bob Larbey / *exec pr* Humphrey Barclay / *pr* James Cellan Jones, Don Leaver / *dr* James Cellan Jones, Don Leaver / *wr* Bob Larbey / *LWT* (UK) 24 x 30m col.

Fireball XL5
Children's. ITV 1963

Puppet master Gerry Anderson's second 'supermarionation' (after ➢*Supercar*) featured the fearless exploits of the crew of rocketship Fireball XL5 (complete with detachable nose cone, Fireball Jnr) as they guarded Sector 25 of the solar system in AD 2067 on behalf of the World Space Patrol. Commanding the vessel was quintessential square-jawed Andersonesque hero Colonel Steve Zodiac; also aboard were delectable blonde space physician Venus, eccentric bespectacled scientist Prof. Matt(hew) Matic, transparent co-pilot Robert the Robot (voiced by Gerry Anderson) and mascot Zoonie, a monkey-like being known as a Lazoon (favourite food: Martian delight). The XL5's missions were assigned by Commander Zero, based at WSP HQ in Earth's Space City.

Notable for its advanced scripts (writers included Dennis Spooner) and sfx (courtesy of new recruit Derek Meddings), the series achieved sales around the world, and marked Anderson's entrée into the TV big time.

CAST (voices) *Col Steve Zodiac* Paul Maxwell *Prof. Matic/Lt 90/Zoonie* David Graham *Venus* Sylvia Anderson *Robert the Robot* Gerry Anderson *Commander Zero* John Bluthal /*cr* Gerry Anderson /*pr* Gerry Anderson /*dr* Gerry Anderson, Alan Pattillo, David Elliott, Bill Harris, John Kelly /*wr* Gerry & Sylvia Anderson, Alan Fennell, Anthony Marriott, Dennis Spooner /*mus* Barry Gray /*sfx* Derek Meddings (visuals) /*An AP Films Production: ATV: ITC* (UK) / 39 x 30m bw.

First Born

Sci-fi. BBC1 1988

Adaptation by Ted Whitehead of Maureen Duffy's darkly disturbing novel, *Gorsaga.* Charles Dance (➢*Jewel in the Crown*, ➢*Rebecca*) starred as Edward Forester, a geneticist who mixed his own sperm with cells from a female gorilla to create an infant man-ape, Gor(don). This grew into a fine and human-looking son who, when told the facts of his cross-species birth, demanded to see his gorilla mother – who beat him to death. To pile on the horrors (and the dire warnings about the dangers of playing God) Forester's incestuous daughter gave birth to Gor's child, who was plainly a hybrid.

CAST *Edward Forester* Charles Dance *Ann Forester* Julie Peasgood *Lancing* Philip Madoc *Gor* Peter Wiggins (child), Jamie Foster *Nell Forester* Beth Pearce (child), Gabrielle Anwar *Nancy Knott* Rosemary McHale *Chris Knott* Peter Tilbury /*pr* Sally Head /*dr* Philip Saville /*wr* Ted Whitehead /*BBC TV: Australian Broadcasting Corporation: Television New Zealand* (UK:Aus:NZ) /3 x 50m col.

The First Churchills

Drama. BBC2 1969

Costume drama charting the rise to glory – and the Dukedom of Marlborough – of Sir Winston Churchill's soldierly 17th-century ancestor, John. The demure Susan Hampshire, who rather put it about in 60s/70s period pieces (➢*The Forsyte Saga*, ➢*The Pallisers*), played Churchill's demure wife. Passable.

CAST *John Churchill* John Neville *Sarah Churchill* Susan Hampshire *Sidney Godolphin* John Standing *Charles II* James Villiers /*pr* Donald Wilson /*dr* Donald Wilson /*wr* Donald Wilson /*BBC TV* (UK) /12 x 60m col.

Five O'Clock Club

Children's. ITV 1963–6

Met on Tuesdays and Fridays with Muriel Young and Howard Williams hosting a pre-teen agenda of interviews with studio guests (usually pop singers) and badinage with puppet characters Ollie Beak and Fred Barker. Bert 'Play in a Day' Weedon gave tips on guitar-playing, while Jimmy Hanley and Grahame Dangerfield advised on hobbies and pets. Williams was later replaced by Wally Whyton (of the Vipers skiffle group) and in 1965 the programme title was changed to *Ollie and Fred's Five O'Clock Club.* In the same year Ollie and Fred were to be found moonlighting on *Five O'Clock Funfair* with Majorie Sigley. *Club* evolved out of Associated-Rediffusion's ➢*Lucky Dip* via *Tuesday Rendezvous* (1961–3).

CAST (presenters) Muriel Young, Howard Williams, Wally Whyton /*Associated-Rediffusion* (UK) / 120 x 30m bw.

Flambards

Drama. ITV 1979

Adaptation of K.M. Peyton's romantic trilogy, set against WWI, concerning the weepie tribulations of a young orphan girl growing up in the country house of her tyrannical uncle. An over-testosteroned cousin, Mark, made life at Flambards 'beastly', while nice cousin William was more interested in the invention of the new-fangled aeroplane.

CAST *Christina Parsons* Christine McKenna *Uncle Russell* Edward Judd *Mark Russell* Steven Grives *William Russell* Alan Parnaby *Dick* Sebastian Abineri *Sandy* Peter Sethelen /*cr* K.M. Peyton /*exec pr* David Cunliffe /*pr* Leonard Lewis /*dr* inc Michael Ferguson / *wr* inc Alan Plater, K.M. Peyton, Alex Glasgow / *Yorkshire TV* (UK) /12 x 60m col.

The Flame Trees of Thika

Drama. ITV 1981

Immensely popular, visually stunning adaptation of the autobiography of Elspeth Huxley OBE (born Grant) relating her childhood in Africa on the eve of WWI. Filmed entirely on location in Kenya, it was scripted by John Hawkesworth (➢*Upstairs, Downstairs*, ➢*The Duchess of Duke Street*). Hayley Mills played the authoress's mother, Tilly.

CAST *Elspeth* Holly Aird *Tilly* Hayley Mills *Major Grant* John Nettleton /*exec pr* Verity Lambert /*pr* John Hawkesworth, Christopher Neame /*dr* Roy Ward Baker /*wr* John Hawkesworth /*Euston Films* (UK) / 7 x 60m col.

The Flintstones

Comedy. ITV 1961–6

'Yabba Dabba Doo!'

Originally to be called 'The Flagstones', William Hanna and Joseph Barbera's prehistoric comedy was the first prime-time animation in TV history. Set in the city of Bedrock, Cobblestone County, it featured blowhard optimist Fred (a crane driver), patient wife Wilma, and their Bedrock neighbours Barney and Betty Rubble. These were, as Hanna-Barbera acknowledged, shameless cartoon versions of Jackie Gleeson's ➢*The Honeymooners.* The show's real novelty in content was its neat Stone Age satirizing of American suburban consumerism, seen most obviously in the famous anachronistic Flintstone gadgets: the gramophone operated by a long-billed bird, the baby mastodon vacuum cleaner, the famished buzzard tied under the sink serving as a garbage disposer. Reviews of the opening episodes were largely critical (the *New York Times* dubbed it an 'inked disaster'), but the show was awarded a Golden Globe and, by season two, had become an essential fixture in the American TV watcher's schedule. In 1963 the Flintstone family was expanded to include baby daughter Pebbles, born at the Rockapedic Hospital (after panicking Fred had initially admitted pet Dino instead of Wilma). Not to be outdone, the Rubbles adopted a boy, Bamm Bamm, they found on their doorstep, and the two *Kinder* eventually spun off to their own series, *Pebbles and Bamm Bamm.* Along with numerous other classic 60s TV shows, *The Flintstones* was revived as a (live action) feature in the 90s. Almost inevitably, corpulent domestic sitcom star John Goodman of ➢*Roseanne* was cast as Fred.

CAST (voices) *Fred Flintstone* Alan Reed *Wilma Flintstone/Pebbles* Jean Vander Pyl *Barney Rubble / Dino* Mel Blanc *Betty Rubble* Bea Benaderet /Gerry Johnson *Bamm Bamm* Don Messick /*cr* Joseph Barbera, William Hanna /*pr* William Hanna, Joseph Barbera /*dr* inc William Hanna, Joseph Barbera, Charles A. Nichols /*wr* inc Joseph Barbera, Warren Foster, Mike Maltese, Tony Benedict /*mus* Hoyt Curtin (theme) /*Hanna-Barbera* (USA) /166 x 30m col /US tx ABC 1960–6.

Flipper

Children's. ITV 1966–9

Whenever trouble threatened the Coral Key Marine Preserve, a clever dolphin was on fin to help out ranger Porter Ricks and his freckle-faced sons, Sandy and Bud.

Enduring, morally fibrous adventure serial for the short-trousered, with excellent underwater sequences; it was derived from Hungarian–American Ivan Tors' (➢*Daktari*) 1963 feature of the same title. Western star Andy 'Stagecoach' Devine appeared in early episodes as exaggerating sea dog Hap Gorman. The show's dolphin trainer was Ricou Browning, who had previously played the title role in the 1954 horror-flick *The Creature from the Black Lagoon.*

The series was remade in the 90s with an entirely new cast and setting, the Bal Harbor Institute. A ➢*Baywatch*-style makeover, with endless air and sea rescues, it was a charmless exercise in money-making.

CAST *Porter 'Po' Ricks* Brian Kelly *Sandy Ricks* Luke Halpin *Bud Ricks* Tommy Nordon *Hap Gorman* Andy Devine *Flipper* Susie /*cr* Ivan Tors /*exec pr* Ivan Tors / *pr* Leon Benson, James Buxbaum /*dr* inc Ivan Tors, Leon Benson, Ricou Browning, Paul Landres /*wr* inc Lee Erwin, Leonard Kaufman, Peter C. Dixon, James Buxbaum /*mus* Ruby Raskin, Frankie Randall (theme vocal) /*MGM-TV: Ivan Tors Films* (USA) /88 x 60m col /US tx NBC 1964–8.

The Flowerpot Men

Children's. BBC1 1952–4

'Flobadob.'

Wednesday's ➢*Watch with Mother* featured the twin flowerpot dwellers, Bill and Ben, who lived in a shed at the bottom of the garden. Their legs were made out of inverted clay pots, and they wore outsize garden boots and gloves. Between them lived Little Weed ('We-e-e-e-d'), who informed them when it was safe to come out and play, and when the gardener was returning. Peter Hawkins (later ➢*Captain Pugwash*, the Daleks in ➢*Doctor Who*) invented the famous 'flobadob' language – criticized by some for promoting immaturity – as well as supplying the puppet duo's voices. Manipulation, music and scripts were by Maria Bird, Audrey Atterbury and Molly Gibson, the team responsible for ➢*Andy Pandy*. The invention of Hilda Brabban, based on the childhood antics of her brothers and sister, *The Flowerpot Men* made their media debut on radio's *Listen With Mother* in 1951.

CAST (voices) *Bill and Ben* Peter Hawkins *Others* Gladys Whitred, Julia Williams /*cr* Hilda Brabban, Freda Lingstrom /*wr* Freda Lingstrom /*BBC TV* (UK) /approx. 120 x 15m bw.

The Flying Doctors

Melodrama. BBC1 1988–

Soapy afternoon adventure serial about the Royal Flying Doctor Service in the Oz outback town of Cooper's Crossing. Unluckily for the staff of the cottage hospital, but to the advantage of the viewer, the bush was chock-a-block with social and medical problems, these ferried in by the RFDS's alarmingly tiny twin-prop plane. Intelligence flickered through the stories and this, together with decent acting (and attractive scenery), set the show above other Australian TV imports of the 80s.

CAST *Dr Tom Callaghan* Andrew McFarlane *Dr Chris Randall* Liz Burch *Dr Geoff Standish* Robert Grubb *Dimitrius Ionniadis* George Kapiniaris /*Crawford* (Aus) /200+ x 30m col.

Follyfoot

Children's. ITV 1971–3

Popular kid–teen stories of a Yorkshire horse sanctuary, run by an engagingly daffy retired army colonel and his two youthful helpers, Dora and Steve. The theme song, 'The Lightning Tree' (in reference to the burnt-out trunk in the yard of Follyfoot Farm), was sung by the New Seekers and made a brief trot into the charts. Derived from Monica Dickens' 1963 novel *Cobblers Dream*.

CAST *The Colonel* Desmond Llewellyn *Dora* Gillian Blake *Steve* Steve Hodson *Slugger* Arthur English *Ron Stryker* Christian Rodska *Lewis Hammond* Paul Guess /*exec pr* Tony Essex /*pr* Audley Southcott /*dr* Claude Watham /*wr* Francis Stevens /*mus* New Seekers (theme vocal) /*Yorkshire TV* (UK) /39 x approx. 30m col.

Forest Rangers

Children's. ITV 1966–8

Stories of the Junior Rangers Club of Indian River as they assist Ranger Keeley trackin' bad guys and savin' injured good guys in the wilderness woods of Canada. Popular outdoor actioner for the junior crew, well cast (especially Ralph Endersby as city kid, Chub, sent north for his moral health) and with the benefit of stunning scenery. Woody direction, alas.

CAST *Ranger Keeley* Graydon Gould *Joe Two Rivers* Michael Zenon *Sgt Scott* Gordon Pinsent *Uncle Raoul* Rolland Bedad *Chub* Ralph Endersby *Kathy* Susan Conway *Denise* Barbara Pierce *Steve* Don Mason *Ted* George Allen *Mike* Peter Hagon/Peter Tully /*pr* William Davidson /*mus* Joseph J. Lilley /ASP (Can) /104 x 30m col /US tx Syndicated 1965–7.

Forever Knight

Adventure. Sky1 1996–7

Tales of a blood-sucker who seeks to atone for his sins by becoming a homicide cop. Derivative and pretentious mix of ➢*Highlander* and *Interview with a Vampire*, which began life as a 1989 two-hour pilot, *Nick Knight*, with acid rock star Rick Wakeman in the title role. For the series, the fanged part fell to Welsh-born actor Geraint Wyn Davies, who had previously starred in the revival of ➢*Airwolf*. Courtesy of some occasional humour and a stylishly Gothic atmosphere, *Forever Knight* lifted itself up the US ratings above the other vampiric TV offerings (e.g. *Kindred: The Embraced*) which sought to trade on the 90s return of the undead to the big screen.

CAST *Det. Nick Knight* Geraint Wyn Davies *Det. Don Schanke* John Kapelos *Dr Natalie Lambert* Catherine Disher *LaCroix* Nigel Bennett *Janette* Deborah Duchene *Tracey Vetter* Lisa Ryder /*exec pr* Jon Slan, James D. Parriott /*dr* inc Geraint Wyn Davies, John Kapelos /*Paragon: Tristar Television* (USA) /69 x 30m col /US tx CBS 1992–6.

The Forsyte Saga

Drama. BBC2 1967

Dramatization of John Galsworthy's chronicle of a London merchant family between 1879–1926.

Although sold as worthy period drama, Donald Wilson's production was but soap opera in high disguise. It began with Jo Forsyte (Kenneth More, ➢*Father Brown*) leaving his wife for his pregnant mistress, then proceeded to the wedding of calculating lawyer Soames (Eric Porter) and the beautiful Irene (Nyree Dawn Porter, later ➢*The Protectors*). This marriage, however, quickly fell apart, leaving Irene to dally with architect Philip Bosinney. To reclaim his property, Soames brutally raped Irene – one of the most infamous scenes in TV history. The couple divorced and Irene fell in love with Jo Forsyte, married him and produced a son, Jon. Meanwhile, Soames married Annette and forced her to have a child – who, to his disappointment, turned out to be a girl, Fleur (Susan Hamphire, ➢*The First Churchills*, ➢*The Pallisers*). The impetuous but brittle Fleur was the main focus of the *Saga* as it moved into the flapper age, where she partook of a tempestuous and extra-marital affair with Jon Forsyte.

The last major British serial to be filmed in black and white, *The Forsyte Saga* found in actors Eric Porter and Nyree Dawn Porter alchemists of an unusually potent TV sexual chemistry. This, more than any other factor, was the key to the *Saga*'s success. Which was phenomenal. In Britain the serial reached No. 3 in the ratings, despite being screened on minority channel BBC2, while sales around the world more than offset the £250,000 the Corporation had lavished on the project (their most expensive drama to that date). Ironically, among the countries who bought in the show was the Soviet Union, where the authorities, much like viewers in Surbiton, were able to relish the scandalous screen goings-on by pretending that they constituted Art. In America the show was transmitted on public television, where its popularity prompted the commercial networks to develop the mini-series form of literary adapations (e.g. ➢*QB VII*, ➢*Rich Man, Poor Man*).

CAST *Jolyon 'Jo' Forsyte* Kenneth More *Soames Forsyte* Eric Porter *Irene Forsyte (née Heron)* Nyree Dawn Porter *Jolyon Forsyte* Joseph O'Connor *James Forsyte* John Welsh *Winifred Forsyte* Marageret Tyzack *Montie Dartie* Terence Alexander *Fleur Forsyte* Susan Hampshire *Annette Forsyte* Dallia Penn *Jolyon 'Jon' Forsyte* Martin Jarvis *June Forsyte* Susan Pennick /June Barry *Joylon 'Jolly' Forsyte* Michael York /*pr* Donald Wilson /*dr* David Giles, James Cellan Jones /*wr* inc Lennox Philips, Constance Cox, Anthony Steven, Donald Wilson, Vincent Tilsley, Lawrie Craig /*mus* Marcus Dods /*BBC: MGM-TV* (UK) /26 x 50m bw / US tx National Educational TV 1969–70.

For the Love of Ada

Comedy. ITV 1970–1

Two seventysomethings, widow Cresswell (who had buried her late husband) and gravedigger Bingley fall gently in love, set up a nest in Cemetery Lodge and eventually marry. Popular Vince Powell and Harry Driver sitcom, sometimes mawkish, but distinguished by the unusualness of its OAP subject matter and the cheerfully exuberant performances of Wilfred Pickles and pudding-shaped character actress Irene Handl. A feature film version was produced under the same title by Tigon British in 1972.

CAST *Ada Cresswell* Irene Handl *Walter Bingley* Wilfred Pickles *Leslie Pollitt* Jack Smethurst *Ruth Pollitt* Barbara Mitchell /*cr* Vince Powell & Harry Driver / *pr* Ronnie Baxter /*wr* Vince Powell & Harry Driver / *mus* Ron Grainer /*Thames TV* (UK) /19 x 30m, 1 x 45m col.

The Fortunes of War

Drama. BBC1 1987

WWII mini-epic. Adapted by Alan Plater from Olivia Manning's *The Balkan Trilogy* and *The Levant Trilogy*, the serial followed the story of two young Brits, Guy and Harriet Pringle, caught in the German advance through S-E Europe. Especially under the lens was the fate of their young marriage. Costing £6 million to make, Betty Willingale's self-consciously 'quality' production cast relative unknowns, Kenneth Branagh and Emma Thompson, in the Pringle parts (in a prime case of life imitating art, the actors later married), setting them on the stairway to celebrity. There were complaints that *TFOW* was long-winded and action-short, but in this it was faithful to the novels.

CAST *Guy Pringle* Kenneth Branagh *Harriet Pringle* Emma Thompson *Prince Yakimov* Ronald Pickup /*pr* Betty Willingale /*dr* James Cellan Jones /*wr* Alan Plater / *BBC TV* (UK) /7 x 60m col.

The Fossett Saga
Comedy. ITV 1969

Victorian-set sitcom, its title punning on ➢*The Forsyte Saga*, starring Jimmy Edwards as James Wellington Fossett, an author of penny dreadfuls with delusions of grandeur and a taste for the fast life. This included frequent visits to the Music Hall, where he encountered singer Millie Goswick (played by June Whitfield, proving the truth of Roy Hudd's immortal adage that she was 'the comedians' tart', since she had served them all). Fossett's unpaid manservant at 14 Old Cobblers Street was the obsequious but cunning Quince. Undemanding.

CAST *James Fossett* Jimmy Edwards *Herbert Quince* Sam Kydd *Millie Goswick* June Whitfield /*cr* Dave Freeman /*pr* David Askey /*wr* Dave Freeman /LWT (UK) /7 x 30m col.

The Fosters
Comedy. ITV 1976–7

Sitcom about a black South London family, hailed as ground-breakingly original, but in fact based on the format of US show *Good Times* (itself a descendant of ➢*All in the Family* via ➢*Maude*). The tower-block-living Fosters were: hassled pater Samuel, phlegmatic mother Pearl, artistic elder son Sonny (a painfully overacting Lenny Henry), teenage sexpot daughter Shirley and younger son Benjamin. Shirley's gossipy friend and neighbour Vilma also figured prominently. Criticized for perpetuating racial stereotypes, it did well enough in the ratings (no doubt helped by such episode titles as 'Sex and the Black Community') to earn a second season. Norman Beaton and Carmen Munro were later reunited for another, and superior, black-cast Sarf London comedy, ➢*Desmond's*.

CAST *Samuel Foster* Norman Beaton *Pearl Foster* Isabelle Lucas *Sonny Foster* Lenny Henry *Shirley Foster* Sharon Rosita *Benjamin Foster* Lawrie Mark /*pr* Stuart Allen /*dr* Stuart Allen /*wr* inc Jack Elinson, Norman Paul, Jon Watkins, Lou Derman, Bill Davenport /*LWT* (UK) /26 x 30m col.

Four Feather Falls
Children's. ITV 1960

Early puppet show from Gerry Anderson. Out in the Old West Kansas town of the title, Tex Tucker – the 'nicest cowpoke you could ever meet' – kept the peace, helped by four magic feathers. Given to Tex by Chief Kalamakooya as a reward for saving his injured son, the feathers enabled Tex's dog, Dusty, and horse, Rusty, to speak, and the pistols on Tex's gunbelt to swivel and fire automatically. Most of Tex's problems arose from the no-good activities of bandits Pedro, Fernando and Big Bad Ben. Nicholas Parsons (previously the straight man in *The Eric Barker Half-Hour*, *The Arthur Haynes Show* and ➢*Benny Hill*, later the genial host of ➢*Sale of the Century*) voiced Tex, except when the lawman crooned à la Roy Rogers – at which point Michael Holliday lent his vocal cords.

CAST (voices) *Tex Tucker* Nicholas Parsons *Tex Tucker (singing)* Michael Holliday *Rocky/Dusty/Pedro* Kenneth Connor *Grandpa Twink/Fernando* David Graham *Ma Jones/Little Jake* Denise Bryer /*cr* Gerry Anderson /*pr* Gerry Anderson /*dr* Gerry Anderson /*wr* inc Gerry Anderson /*sfx* Reg Hill /*An AP Films Production for Granada TV* (UK) /39 x 15m bw.

Frank Stubbs Promotes/Frank Stubbs
Comedy. ITV 1993–4

Starred hamster-faced Timothy Spall (➢*Auf Wiedersehen, Pet*, ➢*Outside Edge*) as a chronically optimistic – but ever-destined to fail – latterday spiv who threw over his ticket tout business to promote an array of comically dodgy products, from kit cars to the memoirs of an ex-con. The show was adapted by Simon ➢'*Men Behaving Badly*' Nye from his novel, *Wideboy*, though in the process of being made into television it conspicuously stole from the ➢*Only Fools and Horses* and ➢*Minder* schools of light criminous comedy. Any cavils, however, were assuaged by a wondrous performance from Spall and dialogue drier than a communion wafer.

CAST *Frank Stubbs* Timothy Spall *Archie Nash* Trevor Cooper *Dave Giddings* Nick Reding *Diane Stubbs* Hazel Ellerby *Petra Dillon* Lesley Sharp *Dawn Dillon* Daniella Westbrook *Blick* Roy Marsden /*cr* Simon Nye /*pr* Hilary Bevan /*wr* inc Simon Nye /*mus* Brian May /*Carlton: Noel Gay* (UK) /13 x 30m col.

Frasier

Comedy. C4 1994–

'Hi, you're on the air with Dr Frasier Crane. If you can feel, I can heal.'

A spin-off from ➢*Cheers* which relocated the elegantly pompous Dr Frasier Crane (Kelsey Grammer) to his home town of Seattle, where he moved into a luxury apartment and began a psychiatrist phone-in show on radio station KACL-780. However, any hopes for a tranquil life were ended when analy-retentive brother (and fellow shrink) Niles off-loaded their crotchety ex-cop father Martin on him, complete with dog Eddie. Soon afterwards, daffy Brit, Daphne (Jane Leeves, a former ➢*The Benny Hill Show* dancer), moved into the apartment as home help and physiotherapist for Martin, becoming in the process the earthy object of lust for the fragile Niles, who was married to (and later separated from) the unseen, but rich, Maris. A steady stream of guest appearances by former ➢*Cheers* stars (Bebe Neuwirth, Shelley Long, Ted Danson) underlined the show's connection with the Boston barcom, but *Frasier* was much more than therapy for *Cheers* fans suffering withdrawal. It enjoyed fine ensemble acting and a dazzling range of comedy techniques that could acrobat from verbal wit ('The man is a fascist. He's like Himmler without the whimsy.') to near physical slapstick in the flash of a cathode ray tube. What it lacked, perhaps, was the dark, soulful bite that made *Cheers* matchless. Sublime, even so. It virtually monopolized the comedy Emmys in the early to mid-90s, with Grammer – who learned the art of comic timing by watching Jack Benny – picking up the Best Comedy Actor Emmy in 93, 94, and 95.

As no shortage of clever pundits pointed out, there was irony in Grammer playing a psychiatrist, since he was unable to straighten out his own conspicuously troubled life. His father and sister were murdered (in separate incidents), he was a cocaine addict, a battered husband, a two-time divorcee and served a prison sentence for alcohol-related offences. Yet his public willingness to discuss the intimate parts of his psyche (and that in him which he lent to the character of Frasier) only increased his celebrity in America, making him one of the brightest stars in the TV firmament. In acknowledgment, Paramount paid him £250,000 per 30-minute episode.

A spin-off from *Cheers, Frasier* garnered Emmys galore. And $250,000 per episode for star Kelsey Grammar (centre).

CAST *Dr Frasier Crane* Kelsey Grammer *Dr Niles Crane* David Hyde Pierce *Martin Crane* John Mahoney *Eddie* Moose *Daphne Moon* Jane Leeves *Roz* Peri Gilpin *Kate Costas* Mercedes Ruehl /*cr* David Angell, Peter Casey, David Lee /*exec pr* inc Christopher Lloyd / *pr* Maggie Randall /*dr* inc Kelsey Grammer, Andy Ackerman, James Burrows /*wr* inc Steve Levitan /*Grub Street: Paramount* (USA) /100+ x 30m col /US tx NBC 1993–.

Fraud Squad

Crime. ITV 1969–70

Fictionalized files of Scotland Yard's Fraudulent Crime Squad. Created by former ➢*Dixon of Dock Green* writer Ivor Jay, the series made a strength of procedural realism, but counterbalanced any tendency towards dowdiness – this was the age of ➢*Jason King* – by making DI Gamble's sidekick the glamorous DS Vicky Hicks. Something of a ceiling-breaking character in the male-dominated world of the British TV *policiers*, Hicks was played by Joanna Van Gyseghem, later to descend to the holiday farce, ➢*Duty Free*.

CAST *DI Gamble* Patrick O'Connell *DS Hicks* Joanna Van Gyseghem *Supt Proud* Ralph Nossek /*cr* Ivor Jay / *pr* Nicholas Palmer, Robert D. Cardona /*dr* inc Paul Annith, John Sichel /*wr* inc Ivor Jay, Robert Holmes, Jack Trevor Story, Richard Harris /*An ATV Network Production* (UK) /26 x 60m col.

French and Saunders

Comedy. BBC2 1987–

Award-winning comedy sketch show from the distaff duo of ➢*The Comic Strip Presents...*, which created a gallery of characters (the two country women who thought any hardship or injury 'stuff and nonsense', the fat male slobs who constantly anthemed 'I'd give her one') of unnerving comic exactitude. Equally meritorious were the economically-worked, female-centred sketches concerning the idiosyncracies of contemporary life, such as the shamingly perfect piece in which two middle-class mothers gave their children 'quality time' (but screamed at them when they did something spontaneous). Alas, the later seasons depended heavily on generously-budgeted pastiches of Hollywood movies; when reduced to their elements, these parodies only contained two jokes (the painstaking perfection of the spoof and the fact that French and Saunders always broke out of character to bicker bitterly) and their appeal dimmed markedly. They continued to dominate BBC comedy, in quantity if not in quality, however, with a slew of character-led shows: Saunders (wife of Adrian ➢'*The Young Ones*' Edmondson) in ➢*Absolutely Fabulous*, and French (wife of Lenny Henry) in ➢*Murder Most Horrid* and ➢*The Vicar of Dibley*.

CAST Jennifer Saunders, Dawn French: plus Simont Brint, Rowland Rivron and others /*pr* Geoff Posner, Jon Plowman /*dr* John Birkin, Bob Spiers /*wr* Dawn French, Jennifer Saunders /*BBC TV* (UK) /2 x 40m, 40+ x 30m col.

The Fresh Prince of Bel Air

Comedy. BBC2 1991–

Sitcom featuring a black homeboy from a Philadelphia ghetto sent to live with uppercrust relatives in their Californian mansion. There he was under the care of pompous Uncle Philip and mediating Aunt Vivian. The Banks had three children of their own, preppy Carlton, narcissistic Hilary and puppyish Ashley. There was also – shades of ➢*Soap* – a snooty butler, Geoffrey (played by British RSC actor Joseph Marcell), to whom fell the silver salver delivery of many of the show's best one-liners. A rare example of a US sitcom doing 'class' (even rarer, of course, for doing race simultaneously), it starred likeable rap singer Will Smith, who displayed a captivating easy enthusiasm with both physical and verbal comedy. The show was based on an idea by record executive Benny Medina who, as a (poor) boy, had been fostered by Beverly Hills musician Jack Elliot, composer of music for such TV titles as ➢*Barney Miller*.

CAST *Will Smith* himself *Philip Banks* James Avery *Vivian Banks* Janet Hubert-Whitten/Daphne Reid *Carlton Banks* Alfonso Ribeiro *Hilary Banks* Karyn Parsons *Ashley Banks* Tatyana M. Ali *Geoffrey the Butler* Joseph Marcell *Jazz* Jeff Townes ('DJ Jazzy Jeff') /*cr* Benny Medina /*exec pr* Susan Borowitz, Andy Borowitz, Quincy Jones, Kevin Wendle /*pr* Werner Wallan, Samm-Art Williams, Cheryl Gard, Benny Medina, Jeff Pollack /*dr* inc Debbie Allen, Jeff Melman, Rita Rogers Blye /*wr* inc Susan Borowitz, Andy Borowitz, Samm-Art Williams, Shannon Gaughan, Cheryl Gard, Rob Edwards, Lisa Rosenthal /*A Stuffed Dog Company and Quincy Jones Entertainment Production in Association with NBC Productions* (USA) /125 x 30m col /US tx NBC 1990–6.

Friends

Comedy. C4 1995–

Comedic version of ➢*Thirtysomething* for twentysomethings. The 'friends' of the title were six shiny, happy New Yorkers – Rachel (Jennifer Aniston, daughter of soap actor John and god-daughter of Telly ➢'*Kojak*' Savalas), Ross, Phoebe, Monica, Chandler, Joey – who all drank inordinate amounts of café latte at Central Perk and pontificated on relationships and life. Although incurably schmaltzy, the sitcom boasted sharp writing and one-liners, most of which issued from the lips of Chandler (viz. Chandler on the virtues of breast feeding: 'The packaging is attractive to adults.'). As star David Schwimmer astutely observed: '*Friends* works because it's a fantasy family at a time when the family is so dysfunctional for this generation.' And it worked to an unprecedented degree; one episode of the show was watched by half the households in America, the nation's highest ever audience rating. Elliott Gould, Julia Roberts,

Jean-Claude Van Damme, Tom ➢'*Magnum PI*' Selleck (as Monica's fortysomething regular boyfriend, Richard Burke) and Charlie Sheen headed the queue of guest appearances. From the creators of ➢*Dream On*.

CAST *Chandler* Matthew Perry *Ross* David Schwimmer *Rachel* Jennifer Aniston *Monica* Courteney Cox *Phoebe* Lisa Kudrow *Joey* Matt LeBlanc /*cr* David Crane & Marta Kauffman /*exec pr* Kevin S. Bright, David Crane, Marta Kauffman /*dr* inc James Burrows, Michael Lembeck, Kevin Bright, Peter Bonerz /*wr* inc David Crane, Marta Kauffman, Alexa Junge, Jeffrey Astrof & Mike Sikowitz /*Warner Bros* (USA) /1 x 60m, 78+ x 30m col /US tx NBC 1994–.

The Frost Report

Comedy. BBC1 1966–7

Before he assumed gravitas David Frost fronted ➢*That Was The Week That Was* and this similarly satrical offering, which came complete with the immortal opening words, 'Hello, good evening, and welcome.' Each week a topical institution or subject was debunked in a series of sketches (which included the famous 'class' skit in which upper-class John Cleese looked down on middle-class Ronnie Barker, who in turn looked down on working-class Ronnie Corbett) and songs. Not the least of *The Frost Report*'s claims to historical importance is that it brought together the anarchic writing team of John Cleese, Graham Chapman, Terry Jones, Michael Palin and Eric Idle – the ➢*Monty Python* team, bar one – for the first time. A selection of the show's best moments, *Frost Over England*, was awarded the Golden Rose at the 1967 Montreux Festival.

CAST David Frost, John Cleese, Ronnie Barker, Ronnie Corbett, Nicky Henson, Tom Lehrer, Julie Felix, Nicholas Smith, Sheila Steafel /*pr* Duncan Wood, James Gilbert /*BBC TV* (UK) /30 x 30m bw.

The Fugitive

Crime. ITV 1963–6

Phenomenally popular 60s show in which David Janssen (aka David Harold Meyer, previously the star of PI show *Richard Diamond*) played Dr Richard Kimble, on the run for a crime he did not commit, the slaying of his wife Helen. Over four seasons Kimble traversed the USA, eluding the ruthless manhunt of Lieutenant Gerard whilst simultaneously searching for the real murderer, a mysterious one-armed man. To subsist, Kimble took a long line of odd jobs. Only his sister, Donna, believed in his innocence. The series, which maintained almost constant tension, concluded with a two-parter in which Kimble cornered the one-armed man atop a water tower. The killer confessed and Lt Gerard arrived in time to shoot him and save Kimble's life. In order to keep the outcome secret, the final episode was broadcast on the same day (29 August 1967) throughout the world. Its viewing share in the USA was 72 per cent of the audience, the largest recorded for a single episode of a regular dramatic series until the 'Who Shot JR?' cliff-hanger of ➢*Dallas* in 1980. Similar ratings were achieved in other countries. Such success inspired a cycle of similar 'manhunt' shows, among them *Run for Your Life*, *Run, Buddy, Run* and ➢*The Invaders* (also a Quinn Martin production), while *The Fugitive* itself ran again as a movie in 1993.

David Janssen, who was raised to international stardom by the series, continued his career in screen crime with Jack Webb's propagandist *O'Hara, US Treasury* and the distinctly downbeat shamus show ➢*Harry O*. Though Quinn Martin tended not to broadcast it, *The Fugitive* borrowed heavily from Victor Hugo's classic novel *Les Miserables*. For good dramatic measure, the producers also added a dash of the 1954 real-life case of Ohio physician Dr Sam Shepard, wrongly imprisoned for the homicide of his spouse.

CAST *Dr Richard Kimble* David Janssen *Lt Philip Gerard* Barry Morse *The One-Armed Man (aka Fred Johnson)* Bill Raisch *Donna Taft* Jacqueline Scott /*cr* Roy Huggins /*exec pr* Quinn Martin /*dr* inc Sutton Roley, Jerry Hopper, Don Medford, Robert Butler /*wr* inc Larry Cohen, William Link, Richard Levinson, Harry Cronman /*mus* Peter Rugolo /*A Quinn Martin Production* (USA) /120 x 60m bw:col /US tx ABC 1963–7.

Game for a Laugh

Light Entertainment. ITV 1981–5

'Watching us, watching you.'

Taste-challenged derivative of ➢*Candid Camera* and 50s US series *People Are Funny.* At the bidding of four permanently smiling hosts sat on high stools, contestants performed asinine stunts in the studio, these interspersed with pre-filmed hidden-camera pranks. Usually embarrassing, always graceless. Throughout, the audience collectively brayed like a donkey. The original four presenters were Henry Kelly, Matthew Kelly, Sarah Kennedy and Jeremy Beadle. The bearded Beadle made something of a speciality of *Candid Camera*-type shows, following *Game for a Laugh* with *Beadle's About* (ITV, 1986–90), *People Do the Funniest Things* (ITV, 1986–7) and *Beadle's Box of Tricks* (ITV, 1989). He also hosted *You've Been Framed* (ITV, 1990–), a showcase of allegedly amusing home video howlers.

CAST (presenters) Matthew Kelly, Jeremy Beadle, Sarah Kennedy, Henry Kelly, Rustie Lee, Martin Daniels, Lee Peck, Debbie Rix /*exec pr* Alan Boyd /*pr* Phil Bishop, Keith Stewart, Brian Wesley, Bob Merilees /*dr* inc Phil Bishop, John Longley, John Gorman /*LWT* (UK) /100 x 30m col.

Game On

Comedy. BBC2 1995–6

Three friends, products of the 'nervous nineties', share a flat and their problems – mostly about sex. The sitcom debut of Andrew Davies (➢*A Very Peculiar Practice*, the adapter of ➢*Pride and Prejudice*, ➢*Middlemarch*, ➢*House of Cards*) it achieved late night cultdom. Actress Samantha Janus was the dish that also adorned ➢*Pie in the Sky*, while Neil Stuke had previously served as DS Nash in YTV's ➢*A Touch of Frost.*

CAST *Matthew Malone* Ben Chaplin/Neil Stuke *Martin Henson* Matthew Cottle *Mandy Wilkins* Samantha Janus /*cr* Andrew Davies & Bernadette Davis /*pr* Geoffrey Perkins & Sioned William /*dr* John Stroud /*wr* Andrew Davies & Bernadette Davis / *Hat Trick* (UK) /12 x 30m col.

Gangsters

Crime. BBC1 1976–8

Graphically violent underworld thriller. Episodes – or 'Incidents' – related the attempt of former SAS man John Kline (Maurice Colbourne, later ➢*Howard's Way*) to penetrate the Birmingham underworld circa 1975 as an undercover agent for D16. Shot on video, it made for a high-tension tour through the low life (gang wars, prostitution, drug smuggling) of British urbana. Stylish. Developed from a 1975 ➢*Play for Today* directed by Philip Saville.

CAST *John Kline* Maurice Colbourne *Khan* Ahmed Khalil *Anne Darracott* Elizabeth Cassidy *Dermot Macavoy* Paul Antrim *Rafiq* Saeed Jaffrey /*cr* Philip Martin /*dr* Alistair Reid /*wr* Philip Martin /*mus* Dave Greenslade, Chris Farlowe (theme vocals) /*BBC Birmingham* (UK) /12 x 50m col.

GBH

Drama. C4 1991

Epic tragi-comedy from Alan Bleasdale (➢*The Boys from the Blackstuff*), which narratively followed the personal clash of wills between megalomaniac socialist Liverpool council leader Michael Murray (Robert Lindsay, ➢*Citizen Smith*), and moderate headmaster Jim Nelson, who dared defy his strike call. At a deeper level *GBH* was about the dark imprint Murray's tormented childhood had left on the adult man. This was particularly eased to the surface in Murray's affair with the mysterious Barbara and scenes with his senile mother (played by Julie

Walters). Perceived fictional parallels with the early 80s political turmoil in Liverpool attracted the ire of sartorial militant Derek Hatton, and disorientated those (just about everyone) who viewed Bleasdale as a pen of the Left. While *GBH* failed to win the expected 'best series' BAFTA, its provocative satirizing, inspired casting (with nice Michael Palin from ➢*Monty Python's Flying Circus* as Nelson) and finely written set pieces made it a non-mainstream hit.

CAST *Michael Murray* Robert Lindsay *Jim Nelson* Michael Palin *Barbara Douglas* Lindsay Duncan *Mrs Murray* Julie Walters /*cr* Alan Bleasdale /*pr* Verity Lambert, David Jones, Alan Bleasdale /*dr* Robert Young /*wr* Alan Bleasdale /*GBH (Films) Ltd* (UK) / 10 x 30m col.

Gemini Man

Sci-fi. BBC1 1976

Transparently obvious American remake of ➢*H.G. Wells' The Invisible Man*, starring a bemused Ben Murphy (from ➢*Alias Smith and Jones*) as a special investigator for INTERSECT, who had the power to make himself ... invisible. The show itself disappeared after a single season. It came courtesy of Harve Bennett, previously the producer of ➢*The Six Million Dollar Man*.

CAST *Sam Casey* Ben Murphy *Dr Abigail Lawrence* Katherine Crawford *Leonard Driscoll* William Sylvester /*exec pr* Harve Bennett /*pr* Leslie Stevens /*dr* inc Alan Levi /*wr* Leslie Stevens /*A Harve Bennett Production in Association with Universal TV and NBC TV* (USA) /1 x 95m, 11 x 50m col /US tx NBC 1976.

General Hospital

Melodrama. ITV 1972–9

One of several ITV romantic melodramas (see ➢*Emmerdale Farm*) created to take advantage of the 1972 lifting on afternoon broadcasting restrictions. Aimed uncompromisingly at bored housewives, *General Hospital* contained large prescriptions of lurve and upset amongst the dreamboat doctors, pretty nurses and crotchety patients of a Midlands hospital. Over the seasons distaff viewers swooned to the bedside manner of Dr Bywaters (gay actor Tony Adams, later ➢*Crossroads*), thrilled to the power struggle between Dr Armstrong and difficult Dr Parker-Brown, and admired the Nightingalesque work of black Sister Washington (Carmen Monroe, later ➢*The Fosters*, ➢*Desmond's*) and Nurse Hilda Price (Lynda Bellingham, ➢*All Creatures Great and Small*, Oxo adverts uncountable). Initially twice weekly at lunchtime, the series was elevated in 1975 to a Friday hour-long slot. It took its title from the venerable US stethoscope saga, which ran on the ABC network from 1963 onwards and was responsible for giving Demi Moore her screen break.

CAST *Dr Matthew Armstrong* David Garth *Dr William Parker-Brown* Lewis Jones *Dr Martin Baxter* James Kerry *Dr Peter Ridge* Ian White *Dr Robert Thorne* Ronald Leigh-Hunt *Dr Bywaters* Tony Adams *Sister Washington* Carmen Monroe *Sister Ellen Chapman* Peggy Sinclair *Nurse Hilda Price* Lynda Bellingham *Student Nurse Katy Shaw* Judy Buxton /*pr* Ian Fordyce, Royston Morley /*dr* inc Shaun O'Riordan, David Foster, Pembroke Dutson, Alan Tarrant /*wr* inc Brian Finch /*ATV* (UK) /110 x 30m /54 x 60m col.

The Generation Game

Light Entertainment. BBC1 1971–82/1990–

Game-show vehicle created for lisp-voiced Bruce Forsyth (aka Bruce Forsyth Johnson), a TV trouper whose stardom stretched back to the 50s and *Sunday Night at the London Palladium*. Two pairs of contestants – who had to be related to each other and of a different generation – were required to perform arts and crafts (icing cakes, throwing clay pots) after watching an expert, this topped off by participation in a farcical sketch. The winning duo were then placed in front of the 'conveyor belt' and obliged to memorize 'goodies' (which always included a cuddly toy) as these passed by. Those items recalled could be taken home.

Broadcast for some of its run under the title *Bruce Forsyth and the Generation Game*, the series enabled the perma-smiling Forsyth to add several catchphrases to his already existing stock of 'Nice to see you, to see you nice.' These were 'Didn't he do well?' and 'Give us a twirl', the latter directed at hostess Anthea Redfern, whom Brucie later married.

From 1978 to 1981 *The Generation Game* was hosted by camp comedian Larry 'Shut that door!' Grayson (as *Larry Grayson's Generation Game*), with the assistance of Scottish balladeer Isla St Clair. Vying with Bob Monkhouse for the title King of the Game Shows, Forsyth (also *Play*

Your Cards Right, Bruce's Price Is Right, You Bet!) relaunched the *Generation Game* in 1990, with Rosemary Ford as his accomplice.

CAST (presenters) Bruce Forsyth, Larry Grayson /*pr* inc James Moir, Alan Boyd, Marcus Plantin, David Taylor, Robin Nash /*dr* inc Alan Tarrant, Alan Boyd, John Gorman /*BBC TV* (UK) /approx. 300 x 45m col.

Gentle Ben

Children's. BBC 1968–9

More animal magic from Ivan ➢'*Flipper*' Tors. A young boy befriends a bear cub and enjoys adventures in the great outdoors under the kindly eye of his game-warden pa Tom (Dennis Weaver, from ➢*Gunsmoke*). Flawless family entertainment, the homo–ursine theme of which was later picked up in another series-for-all-the-sofa, ➢*Life and Times of Grizzly Adams.*

CAST *Tom Wedloe* Dennis Weaver *Mark Wedloe* Clint Howard *Elen Wedloe* Vera Miles /Beth Brickell /*pr* Ivan Tors, Andy White, George Sherman /*Ivan Tors Films* (USA) /56 x 25m col /US tx CBS 1967–9.

The Gentle Touch

Crime. ITV 1980–4

Introduced Britain's first starring female cop, DI Maggie Forbes (beating ➢*Juliet Bravo* by a mere five months) of Soho's Seven Dials station. The widowed mother of a teenage son, much of Forbes' initial attention – and thus the viewers' – was given over to her downbeat homelife. As the seasons passed, however, the series moved into actioner mode (although non-driving actress Gascoine had always to be filmed behind the wheel of a tiresomely stationary car) and eventually transmogrified into ➢*C.A.T.S. Eyes*, in which Forbes led an intelligence squad.

CAST *DI Maggie Forbes* Jill Gascoine *DCI Russell* William Marlowe *DI Bob Croft* Brian Gaspari /*cr* Brian Finch /*exec pr* Tony Wharmby, Nick Elliott /*pr* Kim Mills, Jack Williams, Michael Verney-Elliott /*dr* inc Tony Wharmby, John Reardon, Christopher Hodson / *wr* inc Brian Finch, Roger Marshall, Terence Feely / *mus* Roger Webb /*An LWT Network Production* (UK) / 56 x 60m col.

George and Mildred

Comedy. ITV 1976–9

Domestic sitcom which moved proletarian landlords George and Mildred Roper from their basement abode in ➢*Man About the House* to a twee, modern home in suburbia, 46 Peacock Crescent, Hampton Wick. He was working class and lazy, she was sex-starved (witness her Freudian banana print trousers) and socially aspirant. Their next-door neighbours were middle-class Jeffrey Fourmile and family, which allowed class conflict to raise its comic head, with Fourmile constantly complaining that George's motorbike and sidecar lowered the tone of the neighbourhood. George (Brian Murphy) also led the Fourmile's bespectacled son into distinctly ungenteel ways like gambling. More acerbic and satisfying than its parent show (also by Johnnie Mortimer and Brian Cooke), *George and Mildred* sold to America, where it was remade by ABC as *The Ropers* (1979–80).

CAST *George Roper* Brian Murphy *Mildred Roper* Yootha Joyce *Jeffrey Fourmile* Norman Eshley *Anna Fourmile* Sheila Fearn *Tristram Fourmile* Nicholas Bond-Owen *Jerry* Roy Kinnear /*cr* Johnnie Mortimer & Brian Cooke /*pr* Peter Frazer-Jones /*dr* Peter Frazer-Jones /*wr* Johnnie Mortimer & Brian Cooke /*Thames TV* (UK) /38 x 30m col.

George and the Dragon

Comedy. ITV 1966–8

A forgotten classic of black and white British TV, from the typewriter of Vince Powell and Harry Driver (➢*Bless This House*, ➢ *Love Thy Neighbour*). To the chagrin of retired Colonel Maynard, his country house had a 'bigger female' staff turnover than Selfridges, thanks to the lascivious attentions of his chaffeur-cum-dogsbody, George. That is, until the formidable, bellow-lunged Gabrielle Dragon is employed as housekeeper, a woman even George cannot fancy. Scheming, comic warfare between George and the Dragon ensued, as epitomized in the episode 'The Not So Tender Trap' when Dragon, with the connivance of the Colonel and meek gardener Ralph, conned a grotesquely horrified George into believing he had drunkenly proposed marriage. On paper it would have been passable fare; in the hands of Peggy Mount, ravaged *Carry On* star Sid James, and the languid John LeMesurier (➢*Dad's Army*), it was superlative.

CAST *George Russell* Sid James *Gabrielle Dragon* Peggy Mount *Colonel Maynard* John LeMesurier *Ralph* Keith Marsh /*cr* Vince Powell & Harry Driver /*pr* Alan Tarrant, Jack Williams /*dr* Shaun O'Riordan /*wr* Vince Powell & Harry Driver /*mus* Tom Springfield (theme) /*Thames TV* (UK) /26 x 30m bw.

Get Smart

Comedy. BBC1 1966–70

Spoof espionage show. Inspired by the mid-60s screen spy craze (especially the 007 movies) *Get Smart* featured the farcical cases of Maxwell Smart, enthusiastic but incompetent Agent 86 for the Washington-based CONTROL organization. They provided him with such useful spook equipment as a telephone in a shoe, a cover occupation (salesman for the Pontiac Greeting Card Co.) and Hymie, a robot with a 200+ IQ had a marked tendency to interpret orders literally. When told to 'kill the lights', Hymie blasted them with bullets. Thaddeus was Max's exasperated boss, and Agent 99 (Barbara Feldon, previously a Revlon model and winner of *The $64,0000 Question*) his beautiful female partner. In a November 1970 episode Max and Agent 99 – her name was never given – were married and soon after had twins. One of the most successful TV parodies ever (winning a Best Comedy Emmy, and donating the world such enduring catchphrases as 'Sorry about that, Chief' and 'The old ... trick'), *Get Smart* nonetheless had a troubled broadcast career; it was originally commissioned by US network ABC, who then jettisoned it because of a 'dirty and un-American' pilot scene in which the Statue of Liberty was blown up; the show then sold on to NBC, who cancelled it after the 1969 season, leaving the last two seasons to be broadcast on CBS. It was co-created by Mel Brooks, later the director of such Hollywood features as *Blazing Saddles*.

CAST *Maxwell Smart, Agent 86* Don Adams *Agent 99* Barbara Feldon *Thaddeus, the Chief* Edward Platt *Agent 13* Dave Ketchum *Carlson* Stacey Keach *Hymie, the CONTROL robot* Dick Gautier *Conrad Siegfried* Bernie Kopell /*cr* Mel Brooks, Buck Henry /*exec pr* Arne Sultan, Mel Brooks /*pr* inc Leonard B. Stern, Jess Oppenheimer, Arnie Rosen, Jay Sandrich /*dr* inc Paul Bogart, Richard Donner /*wr* inc Mel Brooks, Buck Henry, Leonard B. Stern /*Talent Artists: Heyday Productions* (USA) /138 x 30m col /US tx NBC / CBS 1965–70.

Get Some In

Comedy. ITV 1975–8

Successful but sometimes raggedly turned out military sitcom from prolific author duo Esmonde and Larbey (➢*Please Sir!*, ➢*The Good Life*, etc.), set during the austere National Service years of the 50s. On arriving at RAF Skelton training camp, four draftees – Teddy-boy Jakey, grammar-school boy Ken Richardson, uncoordinated Scot Bruce Leckie, and effete vicar's son Matthew Lilley – find their worst nightmare realized in the form of sadistic NCO, Corporal Marsh (as in 'My name is Marsh. B.A.S.T.A.R.D. Marsh.'). Predictably, however, the dense Marsh was easily outwitted by the recruits, particularly 'Poof House' Richardson. After basic training the squad were transferred to RAF Midham for instruction in nursing (much to the amusement of accompanying nemesis, Marsh), before postings to Malta and RAF Hospital Druidswater. Tony Selby made Marsh one of ITV's great comic sitcom creations of the 70s, and the series started the TV bigtime for Robert Lindsay. Those who also served included Lori Wells as Marsh's platinum blonde wife Alice, Madge Hindle as Min the Naafi woman, and Jenny Cryst as Bruce's manly girlfriend (later wife), Corporal Wendy Williams.

CAST *Ken Richardson* David Janson *Jakey Smith* Robert Lindsay *Matthew Lilley* Gerard Ryder *Bruce Leckie* Brian Pettifer *Corp. Marsh* Tony Selby /*cr* John Esmonde & Bob Larbey /*pr* Michael Mills, Robert Reed /*dr* Michael Mills, Robert Reed /*wr* John Esmonde & Bob Larbey /*mus* Alan Braden /*Thames TV* (UK) /1 x 60m, 34 x 30m col.

The Ghost and Mrs Muir

Comedy. ITV 1970

Fantasy-comedy about a young widow in love with the old sea-dog ghost (played by Edward Mulhare, to find greater fame in ➢*Knight Rider*) who inhabits her New England seaside cottage. Based on the R.A. Dick novel and the 1947 movie (starring Gene Tierney and Rex Harrison) of the same title. Nicely made, but to little ratings avail. Richard Dreyfuss made an early screen appearance in the 1969 segment, 'Buried on Page One'.

CAST *Carolyn Muir* Hope Lange *Captain Gregg (the ghost)* Edward Mulhare *Jonathan Muir* Harlen Carraher *Candy Muir* Kellie Flanagan *Marta (the housekeeper)* Reta Shaw *Claymore Gregg* Charles Nelson Reilly /*pr* Howard Leeds /*dr* inc Gene Reynolds, Ida Lupino, Lee Phillips, Hollingsworth Morse, John Erman /*wr* inc Peggy Elliott & Ed Scharlach, Joseph Bonaduce /20th Century Fox (USA) / 50 x 30m col /US tx NBC 1968–9, ABC 1969–70.

The Ghosts of Motley Hall
Comedy. ITV 1976–8

The ghosts of stately 400-year-old Motley Hall resent and repel prospective purchasers. Exuberant supernatural sitcom with convincing sfx and a decidedly solid cast, headed by Freddie Jones, Peter Sallis (➢*Last of the Summer Wine*) and Sheila Steafel.

CAST *Sir George Uproar* Freddie Jones *Fanny, the footman* Nicholas Le Prevost *Matt, the stable boy* Sean Flanagan *Bodkin* Arthur English *The White Lady* Sheila Steafel *Mr Gudgin* Peter Sallis /*pr* Quentin Lawrence /*wr* Richard Carpenter /*mus* Wilfred Josephs / *Granada TV* (UK) /20 x 30m col.

Ghost Squad
Crime. ITV 1961–4

An elite Scotland Yard unit infiltrates the British underworld. Efficient thriller, graced by the presence of Shakespearean actor Sir Donald Wolfit as the Squad's first head man, while busy Australian Ray Barrett (➢*Emergency – Ward 10*, ➢*Stingray*, ➢*Thunderbirds*) played the quietly lethal agent, Peter Clarke. The other main operatives were: American master of disguise Nick Craig, strong-armed Tony Miller, and typist turned 'tec Jean Carter. For the latter part of its run the series was transmitted as *GS5*. Inspired by the memoirs of Scotland Yard's real-life undercover detective, John Gosling.

CAST *Nick Craig* Michael Quinn *Sir Andrew Wilson* Sir Donald Wolfit *Tony Miller* Neil Hallett *Helen Winters* Angela Browne *Geoffrey Stock* Anthony Marlowe *Jean Carter* Claire Nielson *Peter Clarke* Ray Barrett /*pr* Connery Chappell, Anthony Kearey, Dennis Vance /*dr* inc Don Sharp, Norman Harrison / *wr* Lindsay Galloway, Robert Stewart, Patrick Campbell /*mus* Philip Green /*Rank Organization: ATV* (UK) /52 x 60m bw.

Gideon's Way
Crime. ITV 1965–6

Cases of a CID copper in gritty London. Efficient police procedural made visually arresting by use of documentary-style photography, courtesy of the influence of US cop show ➢*Dragnet*. Even in the mid 60s, however, the 'chalk and cheese cop' routine (here the intuitive Gideon conflicting with his scientifically minded young sidekick) was old policeman's hat. Based on the novels of the prolific John Creasey, under the pen name of J.J. Maric, the series came to TV via a successful 1958 cinema film, *Gideon's Day*, starring Jack Hawkins.

CAST *Cmdr George Gideon* John Gregson *DCI David Keen* Alexander Davion *DCS Bell* Ian Rossiter *Kate Gideon* Daphne Anderson /*pr* Monty Berman, Robert S. Baker /*mus* Edwin Astley /*ATV* (UK) /26 x 60m bw / US tx Syndicated 1966 (aka *Gideon CID*).

Gilligan's Island
Comedy. ITV 1965–6

Slapstick-inclined US sitcom in which a buffoonish group of rich vacationers were marooned on an uninhabited South Pacific island after the foundering of their sightseeing boat, SS Minnow. Alan Hale Jr (➢*Casey Jones*) played the good-natured skipper, Grumby, while Bob Denver (from the grocery-store sitcom *Dobie Gillis*) took the role of Gilligan himself, the hapless first mate whose attempts to return to civilization started and ended in ineptitude. There were two spin-off animations: *The New Adventures of Gilligan* (1974) and *Gilligan's Planet* (1982–9 in which Professor Hinkley's try at escaping the island by rocket accidentally landed the latter-day Robinson Crusoes on an unknown celestial body).

Nearly ten years after the original series was pulled from the airwaves, NBC made a slew of nostalgic TV movie sequels: *Rescue from Gilligan's Island* (1978), *Castaways on Gilligan's Island* (1979), and the thoroughly unlikely *The Harlem Globetrotters on Gilligan's Island* (1981). For the record, Gilligan's first name, never used in the series but later revealed by Bob Denver, was Willie.

CAST *Jonas Grumby* Alan Hale Jr *Gilligan* Bob Denver *Thurston Howell III* Jim Backus *Lovey Howell* Natalie Schafer *Ginger Grant* Tina Louise *Prof Roy Hinkley*

Russell Johnson *Mary Ann Summers* Dawn Wells /*cr* Sherwood Schwartz /*pr* Sherwood Schwartz /*Gladasya Productions: United Artists TV* (USA) /98 x 25m bw.

The Girl from UNCLE
Spy adventure. BBC1 1966–7

Deeply dippy follow-on from ➢*The Man From UNCLE*, featuring Stefanie Powers (*The Feather and Father Gang*, later ➢*Hart to Hart*) as girl agent April Dancer. Noel Harrison, son of Rex, played spyman Mark Slate, transferred to UNCLE'S NY HQ from its London bureau to aid Dancer in her far fetched capers. The character of Dancer first appeared in *TMFU* episode 'The Moonglow Affair', where she was interpreted by former Miss America, Mary Ann Mobley.

CAST *April Dancer* Stefanie Powers *Mark Slate* Noel Harrison *Alexander Waverly* Leo G. Carroll /*cr* Norman Felton /*pr* Douglas Benton /*Arena Productions: MGM* (USA) /29 x 50m col /US tx NBC 1966.

Girls on Top
Comedy. ITV 1985–6

Distaff version of ➢*The Young Ones* in which four assortedly out-to-lunch girls shared a Chelsea pad. This was owned by Lady Carlton, a daffy romantic authoress (and as close a parody of Dame Barbara Cartland as lawyers would allow) who lived downstairs. Her tenants were: the habitual feminist Amanda, who worked for *Spare Cheeks* magazine; the habitually dull Jennifer; the habitually mendacious Candice; and the habitually loud-mouthed Shelley, an American would-be actress entirely devoid of talent. At the start of the second season Candice departed for America (as had actress Tracey Ullman). Created by ➢*The Comic Strip Presents...* veterans Dawn French and Jennifer Saunders, along with US comedienne Ruby Wax.

CAST *Amanda* Dawn French *Jennifer* Jennifer Saunders *Shelley* Ruby Wax *Candice* Tracey Ullman *Lady Carlton* Joan Greenwood /*cr* Dawn French, Jennifer Saunders, Ruby Wax /*dr* Ed Bye /*wr* Dawn French, Jennifer Saunders /*Central TV* (UK) /13 x 30m col.

Gladiators
Light Entertainment. ITV 1991–

Stylized sport-combat spectacle, derived from *American Gladiators* (syndicated in the US from 1989 onwards). Each week four earnest members of the public pitted their pecs against the 'Gladiators', muscle-bound professionals (of both sexes) with such names as 'Saracen' and 'Wolf', in a sequence of physical challenges. These were nasty, brutish and short. Among them were Sumo, Hang Tough (in which contestants had to progress along rings suspended in the air, whilst the Gladiators sought to bring them to earth) and Danger Zone. Contenders earned points towards a cash prize and a place in the grand finals. Most of the Gladiators came from the usual ranks of failed wrestlers, boxers and bodybuilders, although former Olympic medallist Sharron Davies was recruited in 1995. A mirror to an age obsessed with the lycra-clad, gym-honed body beautiful, cartoon-like superheroes and violent video games. Sometime TV weather girl Ulrika Jonsson (➢*Shooting Stars*) and former footballer John Fashanu presented from the National Indoor Arena, Birmingham.

CAST (hosts) John Fashanu, Ulrika Jonsson (Gladiators) inc Hawk, Phoenix, Warrior, Saracen, Flame, Shadow, Jet, Scorpio, Wolf, Panther, Vogue, Amazon, Rebel, Rio, Ace, Trojan /*exec pr* John Kaye Cooper, Nigel Lythgoe /*pr* inc Nigel Lythgoe, Ken Warwick /*dr* inc Jonathan Glazier /*An LWT Production* (UK) /100+ x 60m col

The Glittering Prizes
Drama. BBC2 1976

Critically acclaimed sextet of teleplays by novelist Frederick Raphael charting the ever-changing lives of a group of Cambridge students, from heady undergraduate days in 1953 to the traumas of middle age in the mid 70s. Much more than a rewarmed ➢*Brideshead Revisited* (the fault of most screen works on the 'Oxbridgers grow-up' theme), it was sharply incisive on the era's varied social determinants, and brought Scottish actor Tom Conti to screen prominence as lead character Adam Morris. It also gave a useful leg up to Anna Carteret (➢*Juliet Bravo*) and Mark Wing-Davey (➢*The Hitchhiker's Guide to the Galaxy*).

CAST *Adam Morris* Tom Conti *Barbara Morris* Barbara Kellerman *Lionel Morris* Leonard Sachs *Dan Bradley* Malcolm Stoddart *Barbara Ransome* Anna

Carteret *Mike Clode* Mark Wing-Davey /*pr* Mark Shivas /*dr* Waris Hussein, Robert Knights /*wr* Frederick Raphael /*BBC TV* (UK) /6 x 80m col.

Godzilla

Children's. BBC1 1979

Animated adventures of a 600-ton radioactive dinosaur who aids scientist Carl Majors, of the good ship *Calico*, in his battle against evil. Comic relief came in the cowardly shape of Godzilla's baby nephew, Godzooky. ➢*The Addams Family*'s Ted 'Lurch' Cassidy headed the voice cast of a raucous kiddie crowd-pleaser from Hanna-Barbera. In the USA it was screened with *Jana of the Jungle* (a female Tarzan) in *The Godzilla Power Hour.*

CAST (voices) *Godzilla* Ted Cassidy *Carl Majors* Jeff David *Godzooky* Don Messick /*A Hanna-Barbera Production* (USA) /26 x 25m col /US tx NBC 1978–81.

Going Straight

Comedy. BBC1 1978

So-so sequel to ➢*Porridge* following the fortunes of Norman Stanley Fletcher (Ronnie Barker) on his release from HM Slade Prison. Outside the confines of authority, however, the subversive Fletcher had little comic purpose or interest and only six episodes were made. Nicholas Lyndhurst, in his first starring role, played Fletch's son, Raymond.

CAST *Norman Fletcher* Ronnie Barker *Lennie Godber* Richard Beckinsale *Ingrid Fletcher* Patricia Blake *Raymond Fletcher* Nicholas Lyndhurst /*cr* Dick Clement & Ian La Frenais /*pr* Sydney Loterby / *BBC TV* (UK) /6 x 30m col.

The Golden Girls

Comedy. C4 1986–3

Situation comedy from Susan Harris (➢*Soap*, ➢*Empty Nest*) which centred on four oldster women living together in Miami, Florida, mecca of retirees. Dorothy (Bea Arthur from ➢*Maude*) was the acid-tongued teacher whose husband, Stan, had left her for an air stewardess. Rose (Betty White, ➢*The Mary Tyler Moore Show*, *The Betty White Show*) was a dippy widow who worked as a grief counsellor and frequently harked on her Norwegian roots (her mother's maiden name was Gerkelnerbigenhoffstettlerfrau). Blanche, who owned the house, was also recently widowed; however, she was no gentle flower, but a Southern belle of prodigious sexual appetites. Sophia was Dorothy's octogenarian, tactless mother who moved in when her retirement home, Shady Pines, was burned to the ground. Brazenly sentimental, the show was also sharply written and conspicuously unafraid to discuss taboo subjects, from dating midgets to drooping breasts and, of course, ageing itself. The first comedy show to depict women senior citizens positively, *GG* was directly commissioned by NBC chief, Brandon Tartikoff, because he had noted the shifting demographics of the US population and wanted a show to suit. A smash popular hit and highly regarded by the TV industry, *GG* won ten Emmys, including best comedy (twice). The show ended its run with a two-parter, 'One Flew Out of the Cuckoo's Nest', in which Dorothy married Blanche's Uncle Lucas (Leslie Nielsen, ➢*Police Squad*, *The Naked Gun* movies) and relocated to Atlanta. A spin-off series, *The Golden Palace*, saw the remaining Miami matrons enter the hotel trade, where their staff included a Mexican chef, Chuy, played by Cheech Marin from film comedy duo Cheech and Chong. An attempted anglicization of the *GG* format, *The Brighton Belles* (Carlton TV, 1993) with Jean 'Bread' Boyt, Wendy Craig, Sheila Hancock and Sheila Gish, became a TV industry byword for disaster, being withdrawn by the ITV Network Centre before the conclusion of its opening season.

CAST *Dorothy Zbornak* Bea Arthur *Rose Nylund* Betty White *Blanche Devereaux* Rue McClanahan *Sophia Petrillo* Estelle Getty *Stan Zbornak* Herb Edleman /*cr* Susan Harris /*exec pr* Paul Junger Witt, Tony Thomas, Susan Harris /*dr* inc Jay Sandrich, Paul Bogart, Terry Hughes, Lex Passaris, Peter Beyt /*wr* inc Susan Harris, Kathy Speer, Terry Grossman /*mus* Andrew Gold ('Thank You for Being a Friend' theme) /*Witt-Thomas-Harris in Association with Touchstone Television* (USA) /180 x 30m col /US tx NBC 1985–93.

The Golden Shot

Light Entertainment. ITV 1967–75

Compulsive game show in which contestants were required to guide a blindfolded cameraman on a 'tele-bow' and instruct him ('left a bit, down a bit') to fire at targets in return for prizes. The ultimate booty was secured by piercing a thread hung before an apple, on which a cache of coins spilled over the studio floor. Initially a moderate Saturday nighter hosted by Jackie Rae, *The Golden Shot* became a Sunday teatime classic under the command of the oleaginous Bob Monkhouse, who later cribbed the show's catchphrase 'Bernie the Bolt' for *Bob's Your Uncle*, where it came out as the unlikely 'Donna the Dart'. Originally devised in Germany as *Der Goldener Schuss*, the show departed from the generally Spartan air of the British game genre by decorating the set with glamorous 'Golden Girl' hostesses (blonde Anne Aston being the most prevalent of them) and celebrities by the score.

CAST (presenters) Jackie Rae, Bob Monkhouse, Norman Vaughan, Charlie Williams (hostesses) inc Anne Aston, Andrea Lloyd, Carol Dilworth, Anita Richardson /*pr* Colin Clews, John Pullen, Edward Joffe, Mike Lloyd, Les Cocks, Dicky Leeman /*dr* inc John Pullen, Mike Lloyd, Dicky Leeman /*ATV* (UK) /240 x 30m bw:col.

The Goodies

Comedy. BBC2 1970–80/ITV 1981–2

Madcap goonery from the same Cambridge and ➢*The Frost Report* background as ➢*Monty Python's Flying Circus*, with Tim Brooke-Taylor (the patriot with the Union-Jack waistcoat), Bill Oddie (the hirsute skeptic) and Graeme Garden (the mad prof) as a trio of do-gooders who would do 'anything, anyplace, anytime' to help humanity. Venturing forth from their quintessential 70s flat (complete with portraits of the Queen and Chairman Mao) on a tandem, they saved the world from a giant white kitten, protected the Crown Jewels and took over the British film industry, amongst other assignments. Wildly parodying film, politics and pop culture fads (such as kung fu, given a North County spin in 'Ecky Thump') and politics, episodes were a potage of slapstick, sight gags, and inventive visual sfx which received their due recognition in two Silver Roses at Montreux. A number of Goodies' records also reached the higher reaches of the pop charts, led by 'Funky Gibbon' and 'The In-Betweenies'. Despite all this and high audience ratings too, the BBC persistently considered *The Goodies* (originally to be called *Super Chaps Three*) to be little more than children's entertainment. Demoralized, Oddie, Brooke-Taylor and Garden decamped to ITV in 1981 for a six-part series. But by then the moment of The Goodies, who were as much of the 70s as Sport biscuits and Glam rock, had passed.

Ecky Thump. *The Goodies* were (l to r), Bill Oddie, Tim Brooke-Taylor, Graeme Garden.

CAST Graeme Garden, Tim Brooke-Taylor, Bill Oddie /*cr* Garden, Brooke-Taylor & Oddie /*pr* John Howard Davies, Jim Franklin, Bob Spiers (for LWT) /*dr* inc John Howard Davies, Bob Spiers /*wr* Graeme Garden & Bill Oddie /*BBC TV: LWT* (UK) /73 x 30m, 2 x 50m col.

The Good Life

Comedy. BBC1 1975–8

Along with ➢*Happy Ever After* and ➢*Terry and June*, the epitome of the British 'middle everything' situation comedies of the 70s. It centred on the attempt of 40-year-old Tom Good, a draughtsman of cereal gifts for the JJM Company, to drop out of the rat race and go self-sufficient. Thus Tom and his improbably perky wife Barbara, dug up the back garden and turned it over to a pig, a goat and numerous hens. Tom's hit and miss DIY and agricultural methods were a major source of the show's twee yet uplifting (even feel-good) humour, as were the shocked reactions of class-conscious next-door neighbour Margo Leadbetter, leading light of the local music society, who feared that the Goods would bring the social tone of 'The Avenue' irrevocably down. Yet, as sitcoms cannot contain genuinely unpleasant characters, Margo's snootiness was more than tempered by her generous friendship to the odd-couple Goods in their times of need. Meanwhile, Margo's husband Jerry (who still worked for JJM), looked on the Goods with a bemused affection, occasionally suggestive of envy. Accorded the accolade of a special Royal Command performance, the enduringly popular show established the cast foursome as some of the most loved faces on TV. All went on to continued small-screen success: Briers in ➢*Ever Decreasing Circles* (another Esmonde and Larbey series), Keith in to ➢*To The Manor Born* and *Next of Kin*, Felicity Kendal (whose coquettish sex-appeal was the unacknowledged key to *The Good Life*'s popularity) in ➢*The Mistress* and Eddington in the ➢*Yes, Minister* cycle. Kendal and Eddington also appeared together in Mary Wesley's infamously steamy upper-crust saga, *The Camomile Lawn* (C4, 1992, 5 x 65m col, *dr* Peter Hall in his first venture from theatre into TV).

CAST *Tom Good* Richard Briers *Barbara Good* Felicity Kendal *Margo Leadbetter* Penelope Keith *Jerry Leadbetter* Paul Eddington /*cr* John Esmonde & Bob Larbey /*pr* John Howard Davies /*wr* John Esmonde & Bob Larbey /*mus* Burt Rhodes /*BBC TV* (UK) / 28 x 30m, 2 x approx. 45m col.

Goodnight Sweetheart

Comedy. BBC1 1993–

Time-travel comedy in which a 90s TV repairman, Gary Sparrow (Nicholas Lyndhurst), walked down Duckett's Passage in London's East End to find himself in the warring 1940s. There he began a dalliance with publican's daughter Phoebe (Dervla Kirwan, ➢*Ballykissangel*), despite his marriage to demanding 90s wife Yvonne. The dilemmas of Sparrow's ensuing double life provided most of the humour and storylines in a cleverly likeable mainstream mixture of romantic sitcom and telefantasy from Marks and Gran (➢*Birds of a Feather*). At the end of season two building work seemingly threatened Sparrow's portal to the past, but no series with 13 million viewers was going to be blitzed for such flimsy reasons, and Duckett's Passage became Duckett's Plaza, with Sparrow opening a shop on the site selling 40s memorabilia. *Goodnight Sweetheart* was produced by the independent company Alomo, whose name derived from its three main creative talents: Allan McKeown, Laurence Marks and Maurice Gran – Al, Lo and Mo. Marks and Gran dreamed up the idea for the show when sitting in Bloom's restaurant, London, and noticing an alley opposite untouched by half a century of time.

CAST *Gary Sparrow* Nicholas Lyndhurst *Phoebe Bamford* Dervla Kirwan/Elizabeth Carling *Yvonne Sparrow* Michelle Holmes/Emma Amos *Ron Wheatcroft* Victor McGuire *Reg Deadman* Christopher Ettridge /*cr* Laurence Marks & Maurice Gran /*pr* John Bartlett /*dr* inc Robin Nash /*wr* Laurence Marks & Maurice Gran, Paul Maki /*Alomo: SelecTV* (UK) / 44+ x 30m col.

The Good Old Days

Light Entertainment. BBC 1953–83

Long-running music-hall revival show, most famously compèred by the preposterously prolix Leonard Sachs (father of Andrew 'Manuel' Sachs from ➢*Fawlty Towers*), showcasing such artistes as Danny La Rue, Ken Dodd, John Inman and ventriloquist Ray Alan (with 'Lord Charles'). It was broadcast from a genuine music hall (one of the last), the City Varieties in Leeds, the audience adding to the nostalgic atmosphere by dressing in Victorian/Edwardian costume. A rousing chorus of 'Down at the Old Bull and Bush' brought each episode to its conclusion.

CAST (chairmen) Don Gemmell, Leonard Sachs /*pr* Barney Colehan /*mus* (director) Bernard Herrmann / *BBC TV* (UK) /700 x approx. 45m bw:col.

Grange Hill

Children's. BBC1 1978–

Pioneeringly realistic school-soap for kids, devised by Phil Redmond (➢*Brookside*, ➢*Hollyoaks*, *All You Need is Love*), and set in the London comprehensive of the title. Plotlines such as Zammo's heroin addiction and 15-year-old Chrissy's pregnancy, alongside routine hair-pulling and shop-lifting scenes outraged many but, as the show's producers constantly pointed out, its twice-weekly tales were cautionary ones. Ingenious use of low camera angles gave ownership of the show to young people; it was watched by 25 per cent of the 15 to 18 age group teatime audience. Recipient of the 1979 BAFTA for Best Children's Programme, it attracted writers of the calibre of playwright John Godber. Several *Grange Hill* alumni passed on to other TV series, notably Todd Carty who went on to *Tucker's Luck*, then ➢*EastEnders*. Susan Tully, Letitia Dean and Michelle Gayle all also made the short walk from Grange Hill (actually Kingsbury High School in northwest London) to Albert Square.

CAST *Peter 'Tucker' Jenkins* Todd Carty *Justin Bennett* Robert Morgan *Benny Green* Terry Sue Patt *Trisha Yates* Michelle Herbert *Mr Llewellyn* Sean Arnold *Pogo Patterson* Peter Moran *Pamela Cartwright* Rene Alperstein *Suzanne Ross* Susan Tully *Mr Bronson* Michael Sheard *Samuel 'Zammo' McGuire* Lee MacDonald *Lucinda*

Letitia Dean *Chrissy Mainwaring* Sonya Kearns *Fiona Wilson* Michelle Gayle *Kevin* George Stark /*cr* Phil Redmond /*exec pr* Anna Home, Richard Callanan /*pr* Colin Cant, Susi Hush, Kenny McBain, Ben Rea, Ronald Smedley, Albert Barber, Christine Seacombe / *dr* inc Colin Cant, Brian Lennane, Carol Wilks, Roger Singleton-Turner, Margie Barbour /*wr* inc Phil Redmond, Barry Purchese, Alan Janes, Margaret Simpson, Chris Ellis, John Godber /*BBC TV* (UK) /500+ x 30m col.

Great Expectations

Drama. ITV 1989

Sunday teatime adaptation of the Dickens classic, faithfully done. It enjoyed a perfect cast, notably Anthony Hopkins as the criminal Magwitch and Jean Simmons as bitter Miss Havisham. The presence of Simmons gave the production gravitas, for she had played Havisham's beautiful young companion, Estella, in David Lean's 1946 classic film version.

CAST inc Anthony Hopkins, Jean Simmons, Ray McAnally /*HTV: Walt Disney (UK/USA))* /6 x 50m col.

Green Acres

Comedy. BBC1 1966–8

➢*The Beverly Hillbillies* in reverse. Successful Manhattan lawyer Oliver Wendell Douglas, transposes himself and socialite wife Lisa – to her considerable dismay – to ramshackle 160-acre Haney Farm, Hooterville, in a bid to get back to nature ('fresh air!').

Originating in the radio series *Granby's Green Acres*, the broad-brush humour of *GA* came from the culture clash of city meets country, plus the language difficulties of the Hungarian-accented Lisa (played by Eva Gabor, younger sister of Zsa Zsa) who misunderstood most everything said to her. There was also a pig, Arnold, owned by neighbour Fred Ziffel, who performed party tricks to order. The show was closely related to another US sitcom, *Petticoat Junction*, also set in Hooterville and produced by Paul Henning.

CAST *Oliver Wendell Douglas* Eddie Albert *Lisa Douglas* Eva Gabor *Fred Ziffel* Hank Patterson *Ed Dawson* Tom Lester *Eustace Haney* Pat Buttram /*cr* Jay Sommers, Paul Henning /*exec pr* Paul Henning /*pr* Jay Sommers /*dr* inc Richard Bare /*wr* inc Jay Sommers, Dick Chevillat /*mus* Eddie Albert, Eva Gabor (theme vocal) / *Filmways* (USA) /170 x 25m col /US tx CBS 1965–71.

The Green Hornet

Crime. Bravo 1996

TV version of a 30s American radio favourite. Britt Reid, editor of Washington DC's *Daily Sentinel*, secretly 'protects the rights and lives of decent citizens' as masked crime-buster The Green Hornet. His dual identity is known only to his Oriental chauffeur (played by the legendary Bruce Lee, aka Lee Jun Fan, in his small-screen debut), secretary Leonore Case and DA Scanlon.

Despite the eye-catching martial arts of Lee and a slew of techno-gimmicks, among them the Hornet's non-lethal sonic Sting gun and 'rolling arsenal', the Black Beauty (a customized Chrysler Imperial), the show barely lasted its introductory season, undone as it was by melodramatic earnestness. This, despite being executive produced by William Dozier, previously the mover and shaker of the camp classic ➢*Batman*, and introduced on the heels of its success.

The creator of *The Green Hornet* was George W. Trendle, also the inventor of ➢*The Lone Ranger*. Britt Reid, in Trendle's invented genealogy for the Reid clan, was no less than the son of Dan Reid, the Lone Ranger's nephew.

CAST *The Green Hornet/Britt Reid* Van Williams *Kato* Bruce Lee *Leonore 'Case' Case* Wende Wagner *Mike Axford* Lloyd Gough *District Attorney F.P. Scanlon* Walter Brooke /*cr* George W. Trendle /*exec pr* William Dozier /*pr* Richard Bluel /*dr* inc Leslie Martinson, Allen Reisner, Darrel Hallenbeck, Norman Foster, William Beaudine /*wr* inc Art Weingarten, William L. Stuart, Lorenzo Semple, Ken Pettus /*mus* Rimsky-Korsakov's 'Flight of the Bumble Bee', updated by Al Hirt (theme), Billy May /*Greenway Productions: Fox TV* (USA) /26 x 30m col /US tx ABC 1966.

The Grove Family

Melodrama. BBC 1954–7

The first authentic British soap, *The Grove Family* featured the domestic and social concerns of a lower middle-class family from Hendon. Named after the BBC's Lime Grove studios, the Grove clan consisted of Mr and Mrs, plus librarian daughter Pat, teenage schoolgirl daughter Daphne, National Service-doing son Jack, young son Lenny (played by Christopher Beeny) and irascible Gran. Conscious of its public-service role, the Corporation insisted on installing obtrusively informative storylines (e.g. on protecting the home from burglary) in the show, but even these failed to dent its enormous popularity. A spin-off, *It's A Great Day*, was released in 1955 and starred the TV cast.

CAST *Bob Grove* Edward Evans *Gladys Grove* Ruth Dunning *Pat Grove* Sheila Sweet/Carole Mowlam *Daphne Grove* Margaret Downs *Jack Grove* Peter Bryant *Lenny Grove* Christopher Beeny *Gran* Nancy Roberts */cr* Michael & Roland Pertwee */pr* John Warrington */wr* Michael & Roland Pertwee */BBC TV* (UK) /approx. 220 x 15–20m bw.

Gunsmoke

Western. ITV 1956–70

Together with ➢*Cheyenne*, the series most responsible for the stampede of TV Westerns in the 50s. *Gunsmoke* began life on radio with William Conrad (➢*Cannon*) in the lead role of righteous frontier marshal Matt Dillon, but when it transferred to TV the part was offered to the more photogenic John Wayne. He, however, refused, recommending instead his drawling friend James Arness, previously the star of Howard Hawk's creeper feature *The Thing*. Arness (born Aurness, and brother of ➢*Mission: Impossible*'s Peter Graves) proved felicitously cast, the square-jawed personification of the Western hero. Wayne lent his support by introducing the first episode, thus conferring on *Gunsmoke* a mythic oater legitimacy.

Set in Dodge City in 1873, the show's other principal characters were Kitty Russell, the owner of the Long Branch Saloon, Dillon's limping deputy, Chester B. Goode (an Emmy-winning performance by Dennis Weaver, later ➢*McCloud*), and bullet-removing 'Doc' Adams. In 1964 Deputy Chester, the constant brewer of a 'mean cup of coffee' (a phrase borrowed by ➢*Twin Peaks*) was replaced by hillbilly deputy, Festus Hagen. Half-breed blacksmith Quint Asper (Burt Reynolds) featured for a while, as did young gunsmith Newly O'Brien.

Debuting in the same week as ➢*The Life and Legend of Wyatt Earp*, *Gunsmoke*'s adult approach and prime-time production values garnered viewers by the drove. In January 1958 it topped the Nielsens. Such success soon spawned imitators; within 18 months there were over 30 Westerns a week showing on US TV. *Gunsmoke*, however, outstayed them all, not riding off into the televisual sunset until 1975, by which time it was the last Western left – and also the longest-running dramatic series of any sort. Of the original cast, only Arness and Stone were left, and the show had subtly changed from an action-adventurer to a frontier soap, with Dillon heading what was effectively a 'family' of characters (with Russell as his 'wife').

Transmitted in the UK as *Gun Law*, *Gunsmoke* boasted a number of top-calibre directors, including Joseph H. Lewis and double Oscar-winner Harry Horner (the segment 'The Guitar' was written by no less than Sam Peckinpah). The revival of the Western in the late 80s saw two TV movies based on the show: *Gunsmoke: Return to Dodge* and *Gunsmoke: The Last Apache*, with Arness and Blake in their famed roles as the screen West's greatest lawman and saloon gal.

CAST *Marshal Matt Dillon* James Arness *Kitty Russell* Amanda Blake *Doc Galen Adams* Milburn Stone *Deputy Chester B. Goode* Dennis Weaver *Deputy Festus Hagen* Ken Curtis *Quint Asper* Burt Reynolds *Sam* Glenn Strange */cr* Charles Marquis Warren */exec pr* Robert Stabler, Charles Marquis Warren, John Mantley, Philip Leacock */pr* inc James Arness */dr* inc Andrew V. McLaglen, Harry Horner, William Conrad, Joseph H. Lewis, John Rich, Tay Garnett, Richard Sarafian */wr* inc Charles Marquis Warren, Clyde Ware, Sam Peckinpah */mus* Glenn Spencer & Rex Koury ('Old Trails' theme) */Filmaster Productions: Arness & Company* (USA) /233 x 26m, 402 x 52m bw:col /US tx CBS 1955–75.

The Guyver

Sci-fi. Paramount 1996

A hyper-violent and visually intoxicating 'Japanimation' or *animé*, based on the Manga comic strip of the same name. The Guyver was the ultimate weapon, a 'bioarmour' mechanism which interfaced with a group of teenagers to make them futuristic, robot-like warriors. Thus endowed, they fought the evil Kronos syndicate and its hulking zoanoid henchmonsters. Also known as *Bio-Booster* Armor Guyver.

CAST (voices) *Sho Fukamachi* Tom Charles *Agito Makeshima* Steve Blum *Tesuro Sagawa* Victor Garcia *Mizuki Segawa* Melissa Charles *Murakami* Steve Areno *Fumia Fukmachi* Sonny Byrkett *Tetsuro Segawa* Kozo Shioya */cr* Yoshiki Takaya */pr* Osamu Shimizu, Katsutoshi Sasaki, Yutaka Maseba */dr* Masachiro Otami, Naoto Hashimoto */wr* Brother Noppo */mus* Mad Dog Winston ('Guyver Rock' theme) */Takaya Productions* (Japan, 1989) /6 x 30m col.

H

Hadleigh

Melodrama. ITV 1969–74

Once described by director Carl Foreman as 'the world's idea of a gentleman', Gerald Harper (also ➢*Adam Adamant Lives!*) was at his languidly aristocratic best as divorced country squire and champion of the underdog James Hadleigh, owner of stately Melford Park. The mansion and the problems posed by the cost of its upkeep provided the main storylines (with Hadleigh occasionally obliged to freelance for his old employer, the Treasury), though interludes for romantic dalliance were frequent. (Hadleigh's innate pulling power was only increased by his white Monteverdi 375L sportscar and thoroughbred horse, The Drummer.) Towards the end of the soapish series, watched by 17 million at its peak, Hadleigh married the lower-class but fortuitously rich Jennifer Caldwell. The character of Hadleigh first appeared in YTV's *Gazette*, a series about a local newspaper owned by his father.

CAST *James Hadleigh* Gerald Harper *Jennifer Caldwell* Hilary Dwyer /*pr* Terence Williams, Jacky Stoller / *dr* inc Brian Parker, Tony Wharmby, Peter Cregeen, Mike Newell /*wr* inc Ian Kennedy Martin, Ian Curteis / *A Yorkshire Television Production* (UK) /52 x 60m col.

Hale & Pace

Comedy. ITV 1988–98

Skits and spoofs featuring comedians Gareth Hale and Norman Pace and their invented characters, most celebratedly the cockney gangsters The Two Rons (a parody of the Krays, developed into a short LWT series *The Management*), and patronizing children's TV presenters Billy and Johnny. Occasionally lacking sophistication and ideas, Hale & Pace were deliciously unafraid to push at the boundaries of TV taste: a sketch involving the microwaving of a cat caused a typhoon of controversy. Former teachers, Hale & Pace arose on the alternative comedy circuit, making their debut on TV in C4's mid-80s shows *Pushing Up Daisies* and *Coming Next...*, before exposure in ➢*The Young Ones* and ➢*Saturday Live* persuaded LWT to give them a show of their own. In the 90s the comic twosome tried their hand at straight acting in an adaptation of the ➢*Dalziel and Pascoe* stories of Reginald Hill, but to no success.

CAST Gareth Hale, Norman Pace, with Ainsley Harriott, Annette Badland, Paula Hannis, Maggie Henderson /*pr* Charlie Hanson /*LWT* (UK) /approx 70 x 25m, 1 x 60m col.

Hamish Macbeth

Crime. BBC1 1995–7

Rural police drama featuring Robert Carlyle (the movies *Trainspotting* and *The Full Monty*) as the eponymous easy-going PC of the remote (and fictional) Scottish village of Lochdubh. Accompanied by West Highland terrier Wee Jock, Hamish Macbeth pursued bucolic villains and a troublesome lovelife, torn between the blonde (Alex) and the brunette (Isobel). Evidently influenced by such offbeat US shows as ➢*Northern Exposure*, *HM* mixed light whimsy with dark tragedy, and backgrounded a stock of quaint characters (among them the grocer Rory Campbell, played by Brian Pettifer from ➢*Get Some In*).

CAST *Hamish Macbeth* Robert Carlyle *Alex* Valerie Grogan *Isobel* Shirley Henderson *Rory Campbell* Brian Pettifer *Esme Murray* Anne Lacey *TV John* Ralph Riach /*pr* Deidre Keir, Charles Salmon /*dr* inc Nicholas Renton, Mandie Fletcher, Patrick Lan /*wr* inc Daniel Boyle, Dominic Minghella /*Zenith-Skyline for BBC Scotland* (UK) /20 x 50m col.

Hammer House of Horror
Drama. ITV 1980

Anthology of spine-shiverers produced for TV by cult horror-flic firm, Hammer Films. Those taking the helm included such HF veterans as the talented Don Sharp (maker of the classic *The Brides of Fu Manchu*, 1962) and Peter Sasdy, with Peter Cushing, Diana Dors and Denholm Elliott topping the cast. Subject matter covered the usual suspect stuff – voodooism, cannibalism, witchcraft – the overall result being decently shocking. A follow-on collection of Hitchcockian type thrillers appeared in 1984 under the rubric *Hammer House of Mystery and Suspense.*

CAST inc Peter Cushing, Diana Dors, Denholm Elliott /*pr* Roy Skeggs /*dr* inc Peter Sasdy, Don Sharp, Alan Gibson /*wr* inc Murray Smith, Don Shaw /*ATV: Hammer Film Productions: Chips Productions: Cinema Arts* (UK) /13 x 60m col.

Hancock's Half Hour
Comedy. BBC 1956–61

At 23 Railway Cuttings, East Cheam, the bumptious Anthony Aloysius Hancock dreamed of rising above his humble origins whilst gloomily observing life's petty frustrations. Room-mate Sid provided the common-sense foil. Transferring from radio, the series' bitter-sweet scripts (by Alan Simpson and Ray Galton) perfectly suited the deadpan delivery and comic timing of Hancock, 'the lad himself'. The final season was transmitted under the title *Hancock* and, despite the absence of Sid James (and Hancock's trademark black homburg hat), produced *Hancock's* classic episodes: 'The Blood Donor' ('A pint? That's nearly an armful!') and 'The Radio Ham'. Thereafter, Hancock defected to ITV and unwisely dispensed with the scripts of Simpson and Galton (who went on to create ➢*Steptoe and Son*). This, plus Hancock's decision to read his lines off autocue rather than memorize them, saw quality drop through the floor. Alternative comic Paul Merton (➢*Have I Got News For You, The Paul Merton Show*) remade a number of *Hancock's* scripts for BBC2 in the mid 90s.

CAST *Anthony Aloysius Hancock* Tony Hancock *Sid* Sid James (plus Bill Kerr, Irene Handl, June Whitfield, Warren Mitchell, Patricia Hayes) /*cr* Ray Galton & Alan Simpson /*pr* Duncan Wood /*dr* Duncan Wood / *wr* Ray Galton & Alan Simpson /*mus* Wally Stott / *BBC TV* (UK) /63 x 25m bw.

The archetypal sad clown, Tony Hancock committed suicide in a hotel room in 1968. His *Hancock's Half Hour* remains immortal.

The Hanged Man
Crime. ITV 1975

The boss of an international construction company, Lew Burnett, becomes the target of an unknown assassin. To find out who and why, Burnett plays dead and goes undercover into his past to discover which of his rivals or loved ones hated him enough to have him murdered. Tense, well-made thriller which succeeded despite its unglamorous brickie-business background. A spin-off series, *Turtle's Progress* (ITV, 1979–80), followed the fortunes of two villains and their haul of safe deposit boxes.

CAST *Lew Burnett* Colin Blakely *John Quentin* Gary Watson *Alan Crowe* Michael Williams /*cr* Edmund Ward /*pr* Marc Miller, Edmund Ward /*dr* Marc Miller / *wr* Edmund Ward /*Yorkshire TV* (UK) /8 x 60m col.

Hannay

Spy. ITV 1988–9

Prequel of John Buchan's novel *The Thirty Nine Steps*, in which his officer-adventurer Hannay (Robert Powell), pits *Boys Own* spunk and wits against the agents of Imperial Germany. Painstaking Edwardian period detail undermined by childish writing and inanely constructed plots.

CAST *Richard Hannay* Robert Powell *Count Von Schwabing* Gavin Richards /*pr* Richard Bates /*dr* inc David Giles /*wr* inc Michael Robson /*Thames* (ITV) / 6 x 60m col.

Happy Days

Comedy. ITV 1975–84

Nostalgia fest set in smalltown Milwaukee in the rock'n'roll 50s, begun as a sketch on *Love, American Style* in 1972 but finding its impetus in the movie *American Graffiti*. Initially, the show centred on 'humdrum' teenager Richie Cunningham (Ron Howard, one of the stars of *American Graffiti*) and his family, but by the second season it became apparent that the real focus was biker Arthur 'the Fonz' Fonzarelli (Henry Winkler), a minor character invented to lessen *Happy Days*' tendency towards middle-American schmaltz. With his thumbs up 'aayyhh' and inestimably cool, finger-clicking ability to pull girls at Arnold's Drive-In malt bar, the Fonz became a pop culture phenomenon (the Smithsonian Institute even exhibited his leather jacket). To incorporate the Fonz more into the narrative action, scriptwriters devised a scenario whereby he rented the loft apartment over the Cunningham's garage. Cast changes were surprisingly few until the 1980s, when Ron Howard, along with Danny Most and Anson Williams – who played Richie's friends Ralph and Potsie – left the show, their teenage characters having long since become adults, gone to college and, in the case of Richie, married Lori Beth. The main addition to the cast was Chachi, Fonz's cousin, who fell in and out of love with Richie's sister, Joanie (played by Erin Moran from ➢*Daktari*; she and Scott Baio were equally on–off lovers in real life). At one stage the youthful twosome were given their own spin-off show, *Joannie Loves Chachi*. It flopped. However, two other spin-offs, ➢*Mork and Mindy* and ➢*Laverne & Shirley* became major ratings successes. *Happy Days* ended its 255-episode run in 1984, still popular but no longer an object of fanatical devotion. Ron Howard subsequently forged himself a career as a top Hollywood director (*Backdraft*, *Cocoon*) and Henry Winkler became an award-winning producer. Tom Bosley, who played Cunningham pater, reappeared in 1990 wearing gumshoes in the TV crime caper ➢*Father Dowling Investigates*.

CAST *Richie Cunningham* Ron Howard *Arthur 'the Fonz' Fonzarelli* Henry Winkler *Howard Cunningham* Tom Bosley *Marion Cunningham* Marion Ross *Joanie Cunningham* Erin Moran *Potsie Weber* Anson Williams *Ralph Malph* Danny Most *Chachi* Scott Baio /*cr* Garry Marshall /*pr* Garry Marshall, Edward K. Milkis, Thomas L. Miller, Jerry Paris /*dr* inc Jerry Paris /*mus* Bill Haley ('Rock Around the Clock' theme), Gimel & Fox ('Happy Days' theme) /*Miller-Milkis: Paramount TV* (USA) /255 x 30m col /US tx ABC 1974–84.

Happy Ever After

Comedy. BBC1 1974–8

Standard model suburban sitcom about a couple, the Fletchers, whose children flew the nest allowing them to get into silly middle-aged scrapes. Ancient Aunt Lucy, who moved in with her Mynah bird, helped. Originating in a *Scott On...* sketch performed by Terry Scott and June Whitfield, and developed into a series via ➢*Comedy Playhouse*, *Happy Ever After* finally ended its days as ➢*Terry and June*.

CAST *Terry Fletcher* Terry Scott *June Fletcher* June Whitfield *Aunt Lucy* Beryl Cooke *Susan Fletcher* Lena Clemo /Pippa Page *Debbie Fletcher* Caroline Whitaker /*cr* John Chapman & Eric Merriman /*pr* Peter Whitmore /*dr* inc Ray Butt /*wr* John Chapman & Eric Merriman, Christopher Bond, Jon Watkins, John Kane /*BBC TV* (UK) /32 x 30m col.

Happy Families

Comedy. BBC1 1985

Ben Elton-scripted comedy in which an about-to-expire mad dowager sends her doltish grandson, Guy Fuddle, to find his four sisters, who are scattered to the corners of the world. Specifically, Madelaine was living in an arty French commune, Joyce was a novice nun, Roxanne in jail and Cassie a Hollywood soap actress. All the sisters and the grandmother were played by a virtuoso Jennifer Saunders (shades of Alec Guinness in *Kind Hearts and Coronets*), and Guy's quests were smartly filmed in an appropriate style, e.g. grainy documentary for the jail shots, soft focus for the Tinseltown episode. Even so, it never quite sparked enough enthusiasm to counter its far-fetchedness.

CAST *Guy Fuddle* Adrian Edmondson *Edith /Madelaine/Joyce/Roxanne/Cassie* Jennifer Saunders *Cook* Dawn French *Dr De Quick* Stephen Fry *Flossie* Helen Lederer /*cr* Ben Elton /*pr* Paul Jackson /*wr* Ben Elton /*BBC TV* (UK) /6 x 30m col.

Hark at Barker

Comedy. ITV 1969–70

Starred Ronnie Barker as Lord Rustless of Chrome House, a lascivious ageing aristo. Spun off from Alun Owen's play 'Ah, There You Are' for 1968's *The Ronnie Barker Playhouse*, the sitcom also found David Jason on the cast list as the gardener Dithers (this five years before Barker and Jason would man the corner shop together in ➢*Open All Hours*). Bill ➢'*The Goodies*' Oddie was among those who contributed scripts. In 1972 the opinionated Rustless and his comically inadequate staff defected to the airwaves of the BBC, appearing as *His Lordship Entertains*. As with *Hark at Barker*, the star played most of the occasional characters himself.

CAST *Lord Rustless* Ronnie Barker *Badger, the butler* Frank Gatliff *Dithers, the gardener* David Jason *Mildred Bates, the secretary* Josephine Tewson *Cook* Mary Baxter *Effie, the maid* Moira Foot /*pr* Humphrey Barclay /*dr* Maurice Murphy /*wr* Bill Oddie, Peter Caulfield, Chris Miller, Gerald Wiley, Bernard McKenna /*LWT* (UK) /16 x 30m col.

Harpers West One

Melodrama. ITV 1961–3

Soap-like series about the office and sales staff of a bustling West End department store. It lathered well for a season (topping the ratings in mid 1961) before the bubble burst, largely pricked by its own intentions of serious dramatic purpose. Co-created by future IBA Director-General, John Whitney.

CAST *Edward Cruickshank* Graham Crowden *Mike Gilmore* Tristram Jellinek *Harriet Carr* Jan Holden *Philip Nash* Bernard Horsfall *Charlie Pugh* Tenniel Evans *Frances Peters* Jayne Muir /*cr* Geoffrey Bellman & John Whitney /*pr* inc Hugh Rennie, Rex Firkin, Royston Morley /*dr* inc Philip Dale, Royston Morley, Phil Brown /*wr* inc Geoffrey Bellman & John Whitney /*ATV* (UK) /approx. 30 x 60m bw.

Harry and the Hendersons

Comedy. BBC1 1991–2

When vacationing in the Pacific Northwest, the Henderson family run over a large hairy creature. This turns out to be a Bigfoot (also known as a Sasquatch), which the Hendersons take home for its convalescence. To protect Harry – for it was he – from the authorities, the Hendersons were duly obliged to perform farcical acts of secrecy. Lively family fare, based on the 1987 movie *Bigfoot and the Hendersons*, with Kevin Peter Hall reprising his role as the hirsute one.

CAST *Harry* Kevin Peter Hall/Dawan Scott/Brian Steele *George Henderson* Bruce Davison *Nancy Henderson* Molly Cheek *Ernie Henderson* Zachary Bostrom *Sarah Henderson* Carol-Ann Plante /*pr* Lin Oliver /*mus* Leon Redbone ('Your Feets Too Big' theme) /*Amblin* (USA) /72 x 30m col /US tx Syndicated 1991–3.

Harry Enfield's Television Programme

Comedy. BBC2 1991–2

After a celebrated stint on ➢*Saturday Live*, comedian Harry Enfield gained his own BBC2 show, which introduced a gallery of new comic caricatures (usually performed in cooperation with Paul Whitehouse or Kathy Burke): upper-class Tim-Nice-But-Dim, the Old Gits, wideboys Lee and Lance, Wayne and Waynetta Slob (who gave birth to a daughter, Spudulika), Mr 'You Don't Want To Do That', The Scousers (a lampoon of ➢*Brookside*), and Mr Cholmondley-Warner and Mr Greyson, whose 40s-style documentary presentations were later translated into a series of advertisements for a telephone company. Though Enfield's performances were highly controlled, the satire was barely restrained: his spoof DJs Mike Smash and Dave Nice (fave rave: 'You Ain't Seen Nothing Yet' by Bachman-Turner Overdrive) demolished any lingering credibility of an entire generation of ageing Radio 1 presenters. Unwilling to preserve characters beyond a short screen life (the said 'poptabulous' DJs went to TV heaven in a 'tip-top tippety-top'

1992 special, *Smashey & Nicey – The End of an Era*), Enfield was obliged to invent new ones at prodigious rate. *Harry Enfield & Chums* (BBC1 1994–), effectively *HETP* under a new title and channel, accordingly saw the birth of the Self-Righteous Brothers, Kevin the Teenager, Tory Boy, Lovely Wobbly Randy Old Ladies, and Considerably Richer Than You, amongst others. More uneven in quality than *HETP*, it also suffered in comparison with the rapid-fire pace of ➢*The Fast Show* from, ironically enough, Enfield's own 'chum' Paul Whitehouse. While sketch shows remained Enfield's major contribution to British TV comedy, he also tried his face in sitcoms *Gone to the Dogs* (as Little Jim Morley) and ➢*Men Behaving Badly*. A 1989 spoof documentary on the life of a thespian, *Norbert Smith... A Life* (C4) was awarded an International Emmy.

CAST Harry Enfield, Paul Whitehouse, Kathy Burke / *exec pr* Denise O'Donoghue /*pr* Geoff Posner, Geoffrey Perkins /*dr* Geoffrey Perkins /*wr* Harry Enfield, Charlie Higson, Paul Whitehouse, Geoffrey Perkins /*Hat Trick* (UK) /16 x 30m col.

Harry O

Crime. BBC1 1974–7

Was Harry Orwell, an invalided (bullet in the back) LA police officer turned PI. He lived in a bohemian beachfront home, only took those cases which interested him, leaving him acres of time to restore a sailboat he called 'The Answer' and to eye up women. The latter included air-stewardess neighbour Sue Ingrim, played by a pre-➢*Charlie's Angels* Farrah Fawcett. Laconic and almost actionless (since Orwell's injury forbade rough stuff), the show needed no less than two pilots – *Harry O* and *Smile Jenny You're Dead* (with a 12-year-old Jodie Foster) – to get it off the ground, and then it lost out to rival cynical 'loser' private-eye show ➢*The Rockford Files*. Aside from his disability, Orwell's gimmick was an MG sports car which never worked, leaving him to bus it. The series was the last starring role for David Janssen (*Richard Diamond, Private Eye,* ➢*The Fugitive, O'Hara, US Treasury*), save for the epic historical drama *Centennial*, before his death from a heart attack in 1980.

CAST *Harry Orwell* David Janssen *Det. Lt Manny Quinlan* Henry Darrow *Lt K.C. Trench* Anthony Zerbe *Lester Hodges* Les Lannon /*cr* Howard Rodman /*exec pr* Jerry Thorpe /*dr* inc Barry Crane, Richard Lang, Jerry Thorpe, Don Weis, Paul Wendkos /*wr* inc John Meredyth Lucas, Robert Dozier, Steven Kandel /*mus* Jerry Goldsmith /*Warner Bros TV* (USA) /2 x 120m, 43 x 60m col /US tx ABC 1974–6.

Harry's Game

Drama. ITV 1982

Tensely realistic thriller concerning an intelligence operative, Captain Harry Brown, sent undercover in Northern Ireland with the mission impossible of tracking down an IRA assassin. Adapted by former ITN journalist Gerald Seymour from his own novel, with the evocative theme music by Clannad entering the charts. Also shown as a 145-minute film.

CAST *Capt. Harry Brown* Ray Lonnen /*exec pr* David Cunliffe /*pr* Keith Richardson /*dr* Lawrence Gordon Clark /*wr* Gerald Seymour /*mus* Clannad (theme) / Yorkshire TV (UK) /3 x 60m col.

Hart To Hart

Crime. ITV 1980–5

'This is my boss, Jonathan Hart, a self-made millionaire. Quite a guy. This is Mrs H. She's gorgeous. She's one lady who knows how to take care of herself... By the way, my name is Max. I take care of them both, which ain't easy – 'cause when they met it was moider.'

Thus spoke the Hart's gravel-voiced retainer over the opening credits of Aaron Spelling's *Hart to Hart*, a glossy romantic crime caper ostensibly created by Sidney Sheldon, but in fact an update of ➢*The Thin Man* husband-and-wife amateur-sleuth movies of the 30s, down to the accompanying pooch (here called Freeway). A particular peril for the Harts (played to schmaltzy perfection by Robert ➢*'Colditz'* Wagner and Stephanie ➢*'The Girl from UNCLE'* Powers) as they jet-setted around the world encountering corpses galore was Jennifer's proneness to serial kidnap. This danger not-withstanding, episodes standardly ended with the frolicking Harts under the duvet indulging in such repartee as: 'What could be better than milk and fortune cookies in bed?' 'You'll find out in a few minutes.' Annoyingly watchable goo.

Their hobby was moider. Stephanie Powers, Lionel Stander (er, standing) and Robert Wagner in *Hart to Hart*, Aaron Spelling's 70s make-over of the *Thin Man* films.

CAST *Jonathan Hart* Robert Wagner *Jennifer Hart* Stephanie Powers *Max* Lionel Stander /*cr* Sidney Sheldon /*exec pr* Aaron Spelling, Leonard Goldberg /*dr* inc Tom Mankiewicz, Stuart Margolin, Sam Wanamaker, Peter Medak /*wr* inc Stephen Kandel, Allan Folsom, David Levinson, Anthony Yerkovich /*mus* Mark Snow /*Spelling: Goldberg* (USA) /1 x 90m, 110 x 60m col /US tx ABC 1979–81.

Have Gun, Will Travel

Western. ITV 1959–62

Oater actioner which rose above the TV Western herd of the late 50s, due to an unusual protagonist, an erudite, black-dressed loner called Paladin (menacingly performed by Richard Boone, later ➢*Hec Ramsey*), who hired out his gun for righteous causes. The telegrammed assignments were delivered to Paladin's base at San Francisco's Hotel Carlton by Oriental servant Hey Boy. (During the 1960–1 season, when actor Kam Tong worked on the series *Mr Garlund*, the messages were ported by Lisa Lu as Hey Girl.) Principal writers were Gene Roddenberry (➢*Star Trek*) and Sam Peckinpah. Although officially created by Sam Rolfe (later ➢*The Man From UNCLE*) and Herb Meadow, the show was later the subject of a successful $3 million plagiarism suit by a variety performer called Paladin, whose business cards – like those of the show's hero – read: 'Have Gun, Will Travel.'

CAST *Paladin* Richard Boone *Hey Boy* Kam Tong *Hey Girl* Lisa Lu /*pr* inc Frank Pierson, Don Ingalls /*dr* inc Andrew V. McLaglen, Buzz Kulik, Ida Lupino, Richard Boone /*wr* inc Gene Roddenberry, Sam Peckinpah, Sam Rolfe, Bruce Geller, Ken Kolb /*mus* Johnny Western, Sam Rolfe, Richard Boone ('The Ballad of Paladin' theme vocals) /*Filmaster Productions* (USA) /156 x 26m bw /US tx CBS 1957–63.

Have I Got News For You

Light Entertainment. BBC2 1990–

Current-affairs game-show-cum-satire, derived from Radio 4's *The News Quiz*. Angus Deayton (➢*One Foot in the Grave*) asked questions about the preceeding week's events of Ian Hislop (editor of *Private Eye*) and comic Paul Merton (*The Paul Merton Show*), each accompanied by a celebrity guest (usually a politician or entertainer). Many were called to appear as team-mates on *HIGNFY*, and many – fearing either a mauling or an overshadowing by the irreverent and able-tongued Hislop and Merton – declined. Perhaps the classic edition was that in which an angered Paula Yates, ex-presenter of *The Tube* and daughter of Jess Yates (*Stars on Sunday*), called Hislop 'the sperm of the devil'. Yet the guest celebs were virtually dispensable, the wit and sometimes the necessary political truths delivered by *HIGNFY* came almost entirely from the trinity of Deayton, Hislop and Merton, who maintained a sardonically rivalrous relationship. Although there were frequent Conservative complaints of left-wing bias, *HIGNFY* producer Harry Thompson (*Harry Enfield and Chums*, ➢*The Mary Whitehouse Experience*, sports quiz *They Think It's All Over*) described the politics of the show as 'neutrally cynical'.

CAST (presenters) Angus Deayton, Paul Merton, Ian Hislop /*pr* Harry Thompson, Colin Swash, Richard Wilson /*dr* inc John F.D. Northover, Steve Smith, Paul Wheeler /*wr* inc Harry Thompson, Colin Swash, Angus Deayton /*Hat Trick* (UK) /90+ x 30m col.

Hawaiian Eye

Crime. ITV 1960–3

A private-eye series from the same slick but ultimately vacuous Warner Bros drawer as ➢*77 Sunset Strip*, this set in Honolulu, where 'tecs Tracy Steele and Thomas Jefferson Lopaka worked out of the swish Hawaiian Village Hotel. (The resident chanteuse was Cricket Blake, played by Connie Stevens, who used her time on the show to build a successful singing career.) Jack Nicholson made an early appearance before the camera in the 1962 episode 'Total Eclipse'.

CAST *Thomas Jefferson Lopaka* Robert Conrad *Tracy Steele* Anthony Eisley *Cricket Blake* Connie Stevens *Phil Barton* Troy Donahue *Poncie Ponce* Kazuo Kim *Gregg Mackenzie* Grant Williams /*exec pr* William T. Orr /*pr* Charles Hoffman, Stanley Niss, Ed Jurist /*dr* inc Robert Altman, Leslie H. Martinson /*mus* Mack David, Jerry Livingston /*A Warner Bros Television Production* (USA) /133 x 60m bw /US tx ABC 1959–62.

Hawaii Five-0

Crime. ITV 1970–82

'Book'em, Dan-O.'

The longest-running cop show in US TV history. Jack Lord (aka John Joseph Ryan, previously bronco-rider *Stoney Burke*) starred as Steve McGarrett, head of a special detective squad of the Hawaii State Police. Too important for everyday crime-busting, the squad – principally McGarrett himself, boyish Danny 'Dan-O' Williams, Chin Ho Kelly and Kono Kalakaua – concentrated on fighting psychopathic killers and Triad-like gangs, especially that led by arch-enemy Wo Fat. As with Lewis Erskine in ➢*The FBI*, McGarrett was denied any life outside the job and was often a mere cipher for the hard-action, and sometimes routine, plots. However, the exotic scenery (exquisitely photographed, as with the opening credit sequence of Polynesians powering an out-rigger canoe to Morton Steven's exhilarating theme) covered over the blemishes. In gratitude to the boost given the Hawaiian tourist industry by the show, Hawaii added a 'Jack Lord' day to its calendar.

CAST *Steve McGarrett* Jack Lord *Det. Danny Williams* James MacArthur *Det. Chin Ho Kelly* Kam Fong *Det. Kono Kalakaua* Zulu *Gov. Philip Grey* Richard Denning *Lt Lori Wilson* Sharon Farrell *Wo Fat* Khigh Dhiegh / *cr* Leonard Freeman, Jack Lord /*exec pr* Leonard Freeman, Philip Leacock, Douglas Greene /*pr* inc B.W. Sandefeur, Leonard Katzman, Leonard B. Kaufman, Jack Lord /*dr* inc Jerry Thorpe, Jack Lord, John Moxey, Michael O'Herlihy, Sutton Roley, Nicholas Colasanto, Marvin Chomsky /*wr* inc Robert Lewin, Leonard Freeman, Stephen Kandel, John D.F. Black, Glen Olson, Robert Hamner /*mus* Morton Stevens (theme) / *Leonard Freeman Productions* (USA) /270 x 50m col / US tx CBS 1968–80.

'Book 'em, Dan-O!' Steve McGarrett (played by the late Jack Lord, second left) plots the apprehension of another villain in *Hawaii Five-0*, US TV's longest-running crime show.

Hawkeye and the Last of the Mohicans

Western. ITV 1957

Kiddietime tales of James Fenimore Cooper's trapper hero and his Indian sidekick as they battled the Hurons on the wild frontier of upstate New York in the 1750s. It hit the mark with rousing buckskin action, solid performances by John Hart (once upon a brief time ➢*The Lone Ranger*) and Lon Chaney Jr (son of the famed 'man of a thousand faces' thespian), and glorious big country scenery.

CAST *Nat 'Hawkeye' Cutler* John Hart *Chingachgook* Lon Chaney Jr /*pr* Sigmund Neufeld /*Normandie Productions* (Can) /39 x 26m bw.

Hazell

Crime. ITV 1978–9

Private-eye capers featuring London gumshoe James Hazell (played by Nicholas Ball, *The Crezz, Colin's Sandwich,* and the first husband of Pamela Stephenson). Made in *film noir*ish style, with the ex-alcholic Hazell (favourite phrase: 'Kin'ell') working the capital's seedy streets like a cockney Philip Marlowe, complete with cynical voice-over commentary, the series deserved a better fate than its premature cancellation. The theme music was by Andy McKay of Roxy Music. Derived from the novels of P.B. Yuill (the *nom de plume* of Gordon Williams and ex-England football manager Terry Venables).

CAST *James Hazell* Nicholas Ball *'Choc' Minty* Roddy McMillan *Cousin Tell* Desmond McNamara /*cr* Gordon Williams & Terry Venables /*pr* June Roberts, Tim Aspinall /*dr* inc Don Leaver, Alistair Reid, Jim Goddard, Peter Duguid /*wr* Richard Harris, Gordon Williams, Tony Hoare, Peter Ransley, Trevor Preston, Terry Venables /*mus* Andy McKay (theme) /*A Thames Television Network Production* (UK) /22 x 60m col.

Heartbeat

Drama. ITV 1992–

In 1964 a cockney bobby, PC Nick Rowan, is transferred to the Yorkshire village of Aidensfield (real life Goathland), where his GP wife sets up in practice.

Nostalgic and gentle pan-generational confection for Sunday evenings, replete with picturesque countryside, upbeat storylines (save for a 1995 weepie in which Kate Rowan died of leukaemia) and period pop hits. It boasted an audience of 17 million, toppled ➢*Coronation Street* from the top of the ratings, and made Nick Berry (late of ➢*EastEnders*) the highest paid TV actor in Britain – a remuneration seemingly in direct inverse proportion to his acting talent. Also featured were Niamh Cusack (daughter of Irish thepsian Cyril), Derek Fowlds (➢*The Basil Brush Show*, ➢*Yes, Minister*), and Juliette Gruber (niece of Walter Matthau).

CAST *PC Nick Rowan* Nick Berry *Dr Kate Rowan* Niamh Cusack *Sgt Oscar Blaketon* Derek Fowlds *Claude Jeremiah Greengrass* Bill Maynard *Gina Ward* Tricia Penrose *George Ward* Stuart Golland *PC Ventress* William Simmons *PC Bellamy* Mark Jordon *Eileen* Anne Stallybrass *Jo Weston* Juliette Gruber *Maggie Bolton* Kazia Pelka /*exec pr* Keith Richardson /*pr* inc Stuart Doughty, Steve Lanning, Carol Wilks /*dr* inc Alister Hallum, Tim Dowd, Gerry Mill, Ken Horn /*wr* inc Brian Finch, David Lane, Peter Gibbs /*Yorkshire TV* (UK) /42+ x 50m col.

Heartbreak High

Children's. TCC 1994–

Teenage drama set in a multi-racial Sydney high school, which skillfully combined the hip and the grit (thus something like a racy Oz version of ➢*Byker Grove*). Based on the 1993 film *The Heartbreak Kid,* shot on film and pacily edited with Alex Dimitriades reprising his lead film role. Attracted 70 per cent of the youth audience in Australia.

CAST *Nick* Alex Dimitriades *Jodie* Abi Tucker *Peter* Scott Major *Con* Salvatore Coco *Matt* Vince Poletto *Kurt* Jeremy Lindsay Taylor /*exec pr* Ben Gannon, Michael Jenkins /*dr* inc Ian Gilmour /*Gannon Television* (Aus) /70+ x 60m col.

Hec Ramsey

Western. ITV 1973–4

1901. With the end of the West in sight, grizzled gunfighter-turned-deputy Hec Ramsey (Richard Boone, ➢*Have Gun, Will Travel,* and descendant of the frontiersman Daniel) sought to keep pace with the changing times by employing the latest developments in forensic science to catch the bad guys. However, since the town of New Prospect, Oklahoma, was still on the wild side, he continued to tote a gun as well as a microscope. Sheriff Oliver B. Stamp was Ramsey's greenhorn boss, and Doc Coogan (Harry Morgan, ➢*Dragnet*, ➢*M*A*S*H*) the narrator and town barber. Directors included Nicholas Colasanto, better known for his before-the-camera role as Coach in ➢*Cheers*. An innovative and classy combination of Western and detection which rotated as part of US network NBC's *Sunday Mystery Movies*, alongside ➢*McMillan and Wife*, ➢*Columbo* and ➢*McCloud*.

CAST *Hec Ramsey* Richard Boone *Sheriff Oliver B. Stamp* Richard Lenz *Doc Amos B. Coogan* Harry Morgan /*exec pr* Jack Webb /*dr* inc Douglas Benton, Nicholas Colasanto, Andrew McLaglen, Harry Morgan / *wr* inc S. Bar-David, Simon Wincelberg, William R. Cox, John Meston /*Mark VII Limited: Universal TV* (USA) /10 x 90–120 m col /US tx NBC 1972–4.

Hector's House

Children's. BBC1 1968

Known in its native France as *La Maison de Tu Tu*, *Hector's House* featured a sad-eyed dog of that name, breathy Zaza the cat (voiced by breathy Joanna Lumley) and giggling gingham overall-clad Mrs Kiki the frog. The two-note adventures took place in Zaza and Hector's garden, with the helpless *femmes* forever asking gentlemanly Hector for help in their latest miniature distress, or having japes at his expense. Episodes finished with the puppet dog addressing camera with a variation on his catchline: 'I'm a great big silly old Hector.' A pre-news filler to take the place of ➢*The Magic Roundabout*, it appealed across the generations.

CAST (voices) inc Joanna Lumley /*cr* Georges Croses / (Fr) /50 x 6m col.

Heimat

Drama. BBC2 1993

Epic 11-part film for TV from Edgar Reitz charting life in the fictional German village of Sabbach between 1919 and 1982. An arty soap opera, mesmerically filmed in monochrome (with resonant, sudden sequences of colour), full of symbolism and sometimes meaning. It was followed by *The Second Heimat: A New Generation*, which trod much the same homeland for no great purpose.

CAST inc Marita Breuer, Dieter Schaad, Jarin Kienzler, Michael Lesch, Eva Maria Bayerswalter, Ruediger Weigang, Peter Harting, Gertrud Bredel, Gabriele Brum, Johannes Lobewein, Willi Burger, Jorg Hube /*cr* Edgar Reitz /*dr* Edgar Reitz /*wr* Edgar Reitz, Peter Steinbach /*mus* Nikos Mamangakis /*WDR: SFB* (Ger) /1 x 120m, 10 x approx. 80m bw:col.

Help! It's the Hair Bear Bunch

Children's. BBC1 1973

Three cartoon ursines (Hair, Square and Bubi) seek to improve conditions at Wonderland Zoo. Moderately funny cartoon antics from Hanna-Barbera.

CAST (voices) *Hair Bear* Daws Butler *Bubi Bear* Paul Winchell *Square Bear* Bill Callaway *Botch* Joe E. Ross *Mr Peevley* John Stephenson /Hanna-Barbera (USA) / 16 x 22m col /US tx CBS 1971–2.

He-Man and the Masters of the Universe

Children's. BBC1 1983

Upon holding aloft his magic sword and speaking the words 'By the power of Greyskull', Prince Adam of Eternia was transformed into He-Man, the mightiest mortal in the universe. This was fortuitous since his castle and his life were constantly attacked by Skeletor, an evil being from another dimension. Sword'n'sorcery animation, with a welcome sardonic humour flickering through the garish predictability. Based on the mega-selling range of Mattel toys of the same name.

CAST (voices) *He-Man* John Erwin; also Linda Gary, Alan Oppenheimer (as Skeletor), Eric Grunden / *pr* Lou Scheimer, Arthur H. Nadel /*Filmation: Mattel* (USA) /65 x 25m col /US tx Syndicated 1983.

Henry's Cat

Children's. BBC1 1983–93

Off-the-wall animation from Bob Godfrey Films (➢*Roobarb and Custard*) about a cockney feline given to fanciful adventures, usually of film inspiration: 'Captain Goodcat' was a take on *Star Wars*, 'The Case of the Pilfered Pilchard' was a spoof on Sherlock Holmes. Rambaba the sheep and Chris the Rabbit (the latter given to wearing a cardboard-cutout TV set on his head) also featured. Drolly narrated by Godfrey himself, the low-budget series won a BAFTA for Best Animation.

CAST (narrator) Bob Godfrey /*cr* Stan Hayward /*wr* Stan Hayward /*Bob Godfrey Films Ltd* (UK) /60 x 10m col /US tx Showtime 1990.

The Herbs
Children's. BBC1 1970–2

Created by Michael 'Paddington' Bond, a quaintly quirky puppet show for the ➢*Watch with Mother* slot. It was set in the walled English country garden of Sir Basil and Lady Rosemary, and also featured tail-chasing Dill the dog, Sage the owl, Bayleaf the gardener, Constable Knapweed, Mr Onion, Aunt Mint, The Chives, Tarragon, Pashana Bedhi, Belladonna and the undoubted luminary of the show, large-headed lion Parsley (later given his own spin-off, *The Adventures of Parsley*). The magic word which opened the garden was 'Herbidacious'. The series' director was Ivor Wood, who had worked with Serge Danot in Paris on ➢*The Magic Roundabout*.

CAST (narrator) Gordon Rollins /*cr* Michael Bond /*exec pr* Graham Clutterbuck /*dr* Ivor Wood /*wr* Michael Bond /*mus* Tony Russell, Brenda Johnson /*Filmfair* (UK) /40 x 15m col.

Hercules: The Legendary Journeys
Adventure. Sky1 1996–

Think *Conan: The TV Series*, then you have it. Originating in MCA's *Action Pack* TV slot, *Hercules* spun off into a hugely successful ongoing fantasy-adventure series filmed (for reasons of stunning scenery, as well as economy) in Auckland, New Zealand, despite being all-American in production. The half-mortal son of Zeus, Hercules, together with sidekick Iolaus, wandered across the ancient world on a mission to protect humanity and avenge the brutal murder of his wife and children by evil stepmother, Hera. Handsomely produced (by Sam Raimi), with superb CGI effects (especially the mythical monsters that habitually blocked Hercules' progress) and with nicely choreographed swordster heroics, the show, in a none-too-subtle pitch at its male viewing base, habitually paraded babe-tastic beauties in diaphanous, barely restraining gossamer. A spin-off, ➢*Xena: The Warrior Princess* also did good business.

CAST *Hercules* Kevin Sorbo *Iolaus* Michael Hurst *Ares* Kevin Smith *Salmoneus* Robert Trebor /*exec pr* Sam Raimi, Rob Tapert /*pr* Eric Gruendemann /*dr* inc John Cameron, Harley Cokliss, Doug Lefler, Garth Maxwell, Gus Trikonis, Timothy Bond, Bruce Seth Green /*mus* Joseph LoDuca /*MCA Television Entertainment Inc: Renaissance Pictures* (USA) /30+ x 60m /US tx Syndicated 1995–.

Here Come the Double Deckers
Children's. BBC1 1971

Zany 70s children's sitcom about seven young heroes who used a London Transport double-decker bus for escapades galore, usually of musical bent. Clearly inspired by the 1962 Cliff Richard film *Summer Holiday*, the series was initially rejected by ITV, only to be snapped up by US network ABC. It was then screened in Britain by the BBC. For the record, the titular do-gooders were: leader of the gang Scooper (Peter Firth, who grew up to be a film actor), Brains, Spring (Brinsley Forde, later of the reggae group Aswad), the American Sticks, sensible Billie, podgy Doughnut and little Tiger. The sole regular adult in the show was Albert (played by Melvyn Hayes, who had, coincidentally, starred in *Summer Holiday*; he later resurfaced in ➢*It Ain't Half Hot, Mum*). The guest cast included Clive Dunn, Jane Seymour and Sam Kydd.

CAST *Scooper* Peter Firth *Billie* Gillian Bailey *Brains* Michael Audreson *Doughnut* Douglas Simmonds *Spring* Brinsley Forde *Sticks* Bruce Clark *Tiger* Debbie Russ *Albert* Melvyn Hayes /*cr* Roy Simpson, Harry Booth /*pr* Roy Simpson /*dr* inc Harry Booth, Charles Crichton, Jeremy Summers /*wr* inc Harry Booth, Melvyn Hayes /*mus* Ivor Slaney /*Fox TV* (UK) / 17 x 20m col /US tx ABC 1970–1.

Here's Harry
Comedy. BBC 1960–5

Starred Harry Worth as a bumbling busybody with a penchant for tackling local officialdom. He lived at 52 Acacia Avenue, in the northern town of Woodbridge, with his cat, Tiddles, and housekeeper Mrs Williams (later Mrs Benson). An aunt, Mrs Amelia, was oft referred to but never seen. A memorable opening credit sequence saw the trilby-hatted Worth perform an illusion in a shop window which made him look as though he was standing in mid-air. The sitcom developed from the earlier, and similar, *The Trouble With Harry*, was specifically created as a vehicle to take Worth, a former stage comedian and ventriloquist, into TV land.

CAST *Harry Worth* himself *Mrs Williams* Vi Stevens *Mrs Benson* Doris Gambell *Tommy* Reginald Marsh *Alf* Joe Gladwin /*pr* John Ammonds, John Street /*wr* inc Vince Powell & Harry Driver /*BBC TV* (UK) / approx. 40 x 30m bw.

Hergé's Adventures of Tin Tin
Children's. BBC1 1962–4

Breathless five-minute animated escapades of the famous Belgian boy reporter and his dog Snowy. The other featured characters were: grog-swilling Captain Haddock of the *Karaboudjan*; the bowler-hatted Thompson Twins (who inspired the 80s pop band); General Alcazar; and absent-minded Professor Calculus. Based on the comic-strip created by Hergé (alias George Remi) for newspaper *Le Petit Vingtieme* in 1929. The series was dubbed – extremely well – into English by Peter Hawkins (➢*Captain Pugwash*, ➢*The Flowerpot Men*) from the 1961 French production.

CAST (narrator) Peter Hawkins /*pr* Peggy Miller (UK) / *Tele-Hachette* (Fr) /50 x 5m col.

Hetty Wainthrop Investigates
Comedy. BBC1 1996–

Whimsical drama in which a sprightly Lancashire pensioner (Patricia Routledge, naturally) staved off mindless old age by setting up a detective agency. For her 'devoted sidekick' she press-ganged a teenage shoplifter, Geoff, who usefully transported her around TV's version of the North (dreary streets, corny brass-band theme music, sub-Alan Bennett dialogue) on the back of his scooter. Although the series largely failed to deliver its intended gentle giggles, it was preserved through the seasons by the sheer vigour of Routledge's performance.

CAST *Hetty Wainthrop* Patricia Routledge *Robert Wainthrop* Derek Benfield *Geoffrey Shawcross* Dominic Monaghan /*cr* David Cook /*pr* Carol Parks /*dr* John Glenister, Roger Bamford, David Giles, Robert Tronson /*wr* John Bowen, David Cook /*BBC TV* (UK) / 12 x 50m col.

H.G. Wells' The Invisible Man
Sci-fi. ITV 1958–9

While testing his theory of optical density in the 1950s, brilliant young scientist Dr Peter Grady accidentally rendered himself transparent. Grady was the Invisible Man. Initially, HM Government saw him as a security risk, but them employed him for espionage work, usually against communist adversaries. He also constantly searched for an antidote to his clear predicament, with moral support forthcoming from sister Diane and niece Sally.

Early adaptation of Wells' classic novel, lacking its dark madness and burdened with somewhat monotone plots, but particularly notable for its excellent-for-the-time special effects (usually achieved by an elaborate system of wires), including: the sight of a wineglass raised to unseen lips, springs on chairs going down as though sat upon and a cigarette puffing in mid air. To maintain the mystique of the Invisible Man, producer Ralph Smart (➢*The Adventures of William Tell*, ➢*Danger Man*) refused to reveal the identity of the actor who played the part. It is now known, however, that his voice was dubbed by Tim Turner and stuntman Johnny Scripps provided the body of Grady, standardly indicated on screen by suit, bandaged head and sunglasses.

The other *The Invisible Man* series were an American version by Harve Bennett in 1975 (with ➢*The Man from UNCLE*'s David McCallum in the title role), the 1976 US ➢*Gemini Man*, and a literalist BBC six-parter in 1984 from Barry Letts (starring Philip Donaghy).

CAST *Dr Peter Grady/The Invisible Man* Tim Turner (voice), Johnny Scripps (body) *Diane* Lisa Daniely *Sally* Deborah Watling /*cr* Ralph Smart /*pr* Ralph Smart /*dr* Pennington Richards, Peter Maxwell, Ralph Smart, Quentin Lawrence /*wr* inc Michael Connor, Ralph Smart, Leslie Arliss, Ian Stuart Black, Tony O'Grady (aka Brian Clemens) /*mus* Sidney John /*sfx* Jack Whitehead /*Official Films: ITP: Ralph Smart* (UK) 26 x 30m bw /US tx CBS 1958–60.

Hi-De-Hi!
Comedy. BBC1 1980–9

Good morning campers! After lampooning the British armed forces in ➢*Dad's Army* and ➢*It Ain't Half Hot, Mum,* and the British department store in ➢*Are You Being Served?*, Jimmy Perry and David Croft turned their comedic attentions to another Great British Institution – the holiday camp. Set in Maplins (a very thinly veiled Butlins, where Perry had worked as a Red Coat) at Crimpton-on-Sea circa 1959, *Hi-De-Hi!* captured in nostalgic broad farce the misadventures of the camp's entertainment staff as they sought to forcibly jolly along the holidaying proles. The Chief Entertainments Officer was the donnishly misplaced Jeffrey Fairbrother (played by Simon Cadell, later Croft's real-life son-in-law), under whom served the spivvy Camp Host Ted Bovis, Welsh senior Yellowcoat Gladys Pugh

The Cannon clan in *High Chaparral*, a ranch-building Western from the same creative stable as *Bonanza*.

(who sought to speak 'posh' but only malapropped), and young comic Spike. Dimwitted and accident-prone maid Peggy, meanwhile, sought to rise above her chalet and don a yellow blazer. Also prominent were the snobby ballroom dancers Barry and Yvonne, ex-jockey Fred Quilley, now in charge of the camp horses, and child-hating Punch and Judy Man, Mr Partridge. In the later seasons Fairbrother was replaced as CEO by Squadron Leader Clive Dempster DFC. Many of the main cast came back for Croft and Perry's spoof of ➢*Upstairs, Downstairs*, ➢*You Rang M'Lord*, and the Croft and Spendlove railway sitcom, ➢*Oh, Doctor Beeching!*.

CAST *Jeffrey Fairbrother* Simon Cadell *Ted Bovis* Paul Shane *Gladys Pugh* Ruth Madoc *Spike Dixon* Jeffrey Holland *Mr Partridge* Leslie Dwyer *Fred Quilly* Felix Bowness *Yvonne Stuart-Hargreaves* Diane Holland *Barry Stuart-Hargreaves* Barry Howard *Peggy Ollerenshaw* Su Pollard *Sylvia* Nikki Kelly *Betty* Rikki Howard *Mary* Penny Irving *Squadron Leader Clive Dempster* David Griffin *The Yellowcoat Boys* Terence Creasey, the Webb twins /*cr* David Croft & Jimmy Perry /*pr* David Croft, John Kilby /*dr* David Croft, Jimmy Perry, John Kilby /*wr* David Croft & Jimmy Perry /*mus* Jimmy Perry ('Holiday Rock' theme) /*BBC TV* (UK) /approx. 70 x 30m col.

The High Chaparral

Western. BBC1 1967–70

Cowboy soap relating the efforts of Big John Cannon to build a ranch empire, The High Chaparral, in an Arizona desert beset by drought, Cochise Indians and avaricious Mexican cattle-barons. Aside from the granite-hewn Big John, the other members of the Cannon clan were: intellectually-challenged son Billy Blue, fun-loving brother Buck, second wife Victoria de Montoya, and sharp-suited brother-in-law Manilito (Henry Darrow, *Zorro and Son*). Occasionally the trouble at the ranch got too much even for the Cannons and their hired hands, in which case they sent for help pronto from Victoria's nobleman father, Don Sebastian.

From the same creative stable as ➢*Bonanza*, *THC* was among the TV oaters most influenced by the spaghetti Westerns of the cinema (see *THC*'s opening credits and stylish use of colour photography), and also the political liberalism of the 60s: no other major TV Western has maintained such a balanced attitude towards White–Indian relations. It was only fitting, then, that when Blue was written out of *THC* towards its close, his place at the High Chaparral table was taken by a half-breed, Wind.

CAST *Big John Cannon* Leif Erickson (aka William Anderson) *Victoria Cannon* Linda Cristal *Buck Cannon* Cameron Mitchell *Billy Blue Cannon* Mark Slade *Manilito de Montoya* Henry Darrow *Sam Butler* Don Collier *Joe* Bob Hoy *Pedro* Roberto Contreras *Ted Reno* Ted Markland *Wind* Rudy Ramos *Don Sebastian de Montoya* Frank Silvera /*cr* David Dotort /*exec pr* David Dotort /*pr* William F. Claxton, James Schmerer / *dr* inc Seymour Robbie, Harry Harris, William F. Claxton, Virgil W. Vogel, William Witney /*wr* inc Laird Konig, Peter L. Dix, Walter Black /*mus* David Rose (theme) /*Xanadu* (USA) /98 x 52m col /US tx NBC 1961–71.

Highway to Heaven

Drama. ITV 1987–9

A probationary angel, Jonathan Smith, seeks to bring love and understanding to mortals on Earth. Fantasy drama from Michael Landon (➢*Bonanza*), oozily sentimental but sensibly restrained from tipping into complete gush by tongue-in-cheekedness: a Halloween special, 'I Was a Middle-Aged Werewolf', was even a skit on Landon's movie debut, the 1957 *I Was A Teenage Werewolf.* Victor French, who played the angel's acerbic cop convert, Mark Gordon, had previously starred with Landon in ➢*Little House on the Prairie.*

CAST *Jonathan Smith* Michael Landon *Mark Gordon* Victor French /*cr* Michael Landon /*exec pr* Michael Landon /*dr* inc Michael Landon /*NBC Productions* (USA) 11 x 60m col /US tx NBC 1984–9.

Highway Patrol

Crime. ITV 1956–60

Immensely popular police actioner starring Broderick Crawford as Chief Dan Matthews, a gravel-voiced traffic cop who worked the sprawling freeways of Western USA. Bitter gun-play and thundering car chases were the prime (even sole) ingredients of this Ziv TV Production, its elemental effectiveness influencing the genre for a generation. Matthews' radio-acknowledgement 'Ten Four' passed into common parlance around the world.

CAST *Chief Dan Matthews* Broderick Crawford *Narrator* Art Gilmore /*exec pr* Vernon E. Clark /*mus* Richard Llewellyn /*A Ziv-TV Production* (USA) / 156 x 30m bw /US tx Syndicated 1955–9.

Highlander

Adventure. Sky1 1994–

'I was born 400 years ago in the Highlands of Scotland. I am IMMORTAL ... In the end there can be only one...'

Sword and sorcery show, derived from the Christopher Lambert/Sean Connery movies of the same title, depicting the adventures of Duncan MacLeod as he battles evil immortals through history with the help of NY street kid and neophyte immortal, Richie Ryan. Cast in the role of the brooding hero was Adrian Paul, a British former ballet dancer who made his TV debut in the frothy ➢*The Colbys.* With swirling action and tight-knit plots, the series was at least the equal of its cinematic forebear.

There can be more than one ... an animated spin-off appeared in 1995 featuring Quentin MacLeod.

CAST *Duncan MacLeod* Adrian Paul *Richie Ryan* Stan Kirsch *Joe Dawson* Jim Byrnes /*cr* Gregory Widen /*exec pr* Bill Panzer, Peter Davis, Marla Ginsburg, Christian Charret /*mus* Queen ('Princes of the Universe' theme) /*Davus-Panzer: Gaumont Television: France Productions: Rysher Entertainment* (USA) /44+ x 60m col /US tx Syndicated 1992–.

Hill Street Blues

Crime. ITV 1981–4/C4 1984–9

Semi-serial police drama following everyday life at Hill Street Station in a rundown eastern US city (Chicago provided the exteriors). In command was divorcee Captain Frank Furillo, whose affair with contentious public defender Joyce Davenport turned into marriage. Under Furillo served Hispanic second-in-command Ray Calletano, station conscience Henry Goldblume, trigger-happy SWAT lieutenant Howard Hunter, tooth-pick-chewing Neal Washington, the vaguely off-beam undercover detective Mick Belker, and the black/white patrol team of Bobby Hill and Andy Renko. Paternal head sergeant Phil Esterhaus ended the morning roll-call with the standard warning, 'And hey, let's be careful out there.' Prominent recruits of later seasons included Sergeant Stan Jablonski – who replaced Esterhaus when the latter died of a heart attack during intercourse with widow Grace Gardener – the abrasive Norman Buntz (spun off into a series of his own, *Beverly Hills Buntz*) and Detective Harry

'And, hey, let's be careful out there...' Daniel Travanti (centre) and the cast of *Hill Street Blues*. The show was cancelled when Travanti refused to do an eighth season.

Garibaldi (Ken Olin, later ➢*Thirtysomething*). With its innovative admix of hyper-realistic texture (hand-held camera work and eight-track sound), its elements of soap opera, cop action, comic relief and unwieldy, multi-strand narratives (frequently left unresolved), it was arguably the most influential TV *policier* of the 80s (winning eight Emmys in its first season), with co-creator Steven Bochco taking its basic ingredients into a spree of other acclaimed crime shows – ➢*Hooperman*, ➢*LA Law*, ➢*NYPD Blue* ➢*Murder One*, to name but four.

CAST *Capt. Frank Furillo* Daniel J. Travanti *Sgt Phil Esterhaus* Michael Conrad *Off. Bobby Hill* Michael Warren *Det. Mick Belker* Bruce Weitz *Lt Howard Hunter* James B. Sikking *Det. Neal Washington* Taurean Blacque *Lt Ray Calletano* Rene Enriquez *Off. Andy Renko* Charles Haid *Joyce Davenport* Veronica Hamel *Sgt/Lt Henry Goldblume* Joe Spano *Off./Sgt Lucy Bates* Betty Thomas *Fay Furillo* Barbara Bosson *Det. Harry Garibaldi* Ken Olin *Sgt Stanislaus Jablonski* Robert Prosky *Lt Norman Buntz* Dennis Franz *Sidney Thursto ('Sid the Snitch')* Peter Jurasik /*cr* Steven Bochco, Michael Kozoll /*exec pr* Steven Bochco /*pr* Gregory Hoblit, David Anspaugh, Anthony Yerkovich /*dr* inc Robert Butler, Gregory Hoblit, Georg Stanford Brown, Arnold Laven, Jack Starrett, Corey Allen /*wr* inc Steven Bochco, Michael Kozoll, Geoffrey Fischer, Robert Crais, Robert Earll, Mark Frost, David Milch / *mus* Mike Post ('Hill Street Blues' theme) /*MTM Enterprises* (USA) /145 x 60m col /US tx NBC 1981–7.

The History Man

Drama. BBC2 1981

Professor Malcolm Bradbury's cynical, satirical novel about a trendy 70s Marxist lecturer (in sociology, naturally) at Watermouth University made TV. Anthony Sher as the sexually adventuring, Zapata-moustachioed Howard Kirk, shone brilliantly in Christopher Hampton's superlative adaptation.

CAST *Howard Kirk* Anthony Sher *Barbara Kirk* Geraldine James /*pr* Michael Wearing /*dr* Robert Knights /*wr* Christopher Hampton /*BBC TV* (UK) / 2 x 50m, 2 x 60m col.

The Hitchhiker's Guide to the Galaxy

Sci-fi. BBC2 1981

Seconds before Earth was destroyed by a Vogon Constructor Fleet (to make way for a hyperspace bypass), Ford Prefect, an alien from planet Betelgeuse and researcher for the best-selling intergalactic reference book *The Hitchhiker's Guide*, rescued typical Englishman Arthur Dent from the impending doom. Arthur, surprised to hear that Ford Prefect is not, in fact, from Guildford, found himself on a journey through space, where he met such exotic beings as part-time Galactic President Zaphod Beeblebrox and his girlfriend Tillian (Sandra Dickinson), Marvin the Paranoid Android, the unpoetic Vogons, the useless Golgafrinchians, and a pair of pan-dimensional beings who are searching for the Ultimate Question to Life, the Universe and Everything (they have the answer: it's 42).

Douglas Adams' brilliant satire on modern times and SF conventions began as a radio play then became a novel, before this serializaton under the hand of Alan J.W. Bell. Notorious for its low sci-fi budgets, the BBC graced the serial with superior sfx and sophisticated computer animation converting the viewers' screen into the *Guide* when necessary. The guest stars (who formed something of an in-joke) were headed by

Peter Davison (Dickinson's husband, and ➢*Doctor Who*) and David Prowse, Darth Vader in *Star Wars*. Adams himself appeared in the second episode, where he disrobed and, in an echo of the credits of ➢*The Fall and Rise of Reginald Perrin*, walked into the sea.

CAST *Arthur Dent* Simon Jones *Ford Prefect* David Dixon *Voice of the Book* Peter Jones *Zaphod Beeblebrox* Mark Wing-Davey *Trillian* Sandra Dickinson *Marvin* David Learner *Voice of Marvin* Stephen Moore /*cr* Douglas Adams /*pr* Alan J.W. Bell /*wr* Douglas Adams /*mus* Paddy Kingsland /*BBC TV* (UK) 6 x 35m col / US tx NBC 1982.

Hogan's Heroes

Comedy. ITV 1967–70

POW farce set in WWII's Stalag 13, ostensibly ruled by pompous Nazi Colonel Clink and dim sidekick Sergeant Schultz but, in fact, throughly under the command of rugged US inmate Colonel Hogan (Bob Crane). With his Allied pals – chiefly French cook Le Beau (Robert Clary, who had been imprisoned in a German camp as a child), Sergeant James Kinchloe (Ivan Dixon, later director of the movie *The Spook Who Sat By the Door*) and cockney Corporal Newkirk – Crane ran rackets galore and circles around Klink. The POWs also lived in a state of some luxury, including a sauna. To justify their continued presence in the camp – since they could leave at any time through a special door in the fence – Hogan's merry men were charged with regular anti-Jerry sabotage and espionage missions. Despite a similarity to the stage play, *Stalag 17*, which invited a successful law suit, the show ran for six raucous seasons. It once again made the news in 1978 when actor Bob Crane was found beaten to death at his home in Arizona.

CAST *Col. Robert Hogan* Bob Crane *Col. Wilhelm Klink* Werner Klemperer *Sgt Hans Schultz* John Banner *Cpl Peter Newkirk* Richard Dawson *Louis LeBeau* Robert Clary *Sgt James Kinchloe* Ivan Dixon *Sgt Andrew Carter* Larry Hovis /*cr* Bernard Fein, Albert S. Ruddy /*pr* Edward H. Feldman /*dr* inc Gene Reynolds, Edward H. Feldman /*wr* inc Lawrence Marks /*Bing Crosby Productions* (USA) /168 x 25m col /US tx CBS 1965–71.

Hollyoaks

Children's. C4 1995–

Teen soap from Phil Redmond, suprisingly free of social conscience and angst (see his track record of *Going Out*, ➢*Grange Hill*, ➢*Brookside*), set in leafy Chester. Indeed, with its 'Britpack' cast of hunks and hunkesses and Ray Bans perspective on the life of British 17/18 year olds (all puppy lurve and consumer-goods worship), the show was quickly dubbed 'Chester 90210'. Yet Redmond was unable to let old habits go completely: a prominent early storyline saw Natasha die of a drug OD. Scheduled against US imports, *Hollyoaks* was shot on video but with the tapes manipulated in post production to give it the quality look of film. Originally a weekly series with a Sunday omnibus, it went twice weekly in September 1996. In an inexplicable piece of casting, aged rock star Alvin Stardust (and some-time husband of Lisa Goddard) played Natasha's ill-fated father, landlord of the Dog and Duck public house.

CAST *Kurt* Jeremy Edwards *Jambo* William Mellor *Dawn* Lisa Williamson *Louise* Brett O'Brien *Maddie* Yasmin Bannerman *Tony* Nick Pickard *Bazz* Toby Sawyer *Jude* Davinia Taylor *Natasha* Sheba Ronay /*cr* Phil Redmond /*exec pr* Phil Redmond /*dr* inc Gill Wilkinson, Jeremy Woolf, Ric Mellis /*wr* inc Roy Boulter, Andy Lynch /*Mersey TV* (UK) /250+ x 30m col.

Home and Away

Melodrama. ITV 1989–

Australian sudster, created by Seven Network as a rival to ➢*Neighbours* (ITV in the UK also using it for the same 'knocking' purpose against the BBC's transmission of the Ramsey Street saga), and set in the fictitious resort of Summer Bay. Here, foster parent Pippa Fletcher, initially accompanied by husband Tom (later killed off in a car crash), watched over the scandals and relationships of her youthful, troubled charges. In a calculatedly shrewd piece of headhunting *Home and Away* recruited ➢*Neighbours* star Craig MacLachlan to play unorthodox teacher Grant Mitchell. Also on the list of dramatis personae were Dannii Minogue (sister of Kylie) and Terence Donovan (father of Jason, and himself to end up in *Neighbours*).

CAST *Pippa Fletcher* Vanessa Downing/Debra Lawrence *Tom Fletcher* Roger Oakley *Marilyn Chambers* Emily Symons *Donald Fisher* Norman Coburn *Bobby Simpson* Nicolle Dickson *Al Simpson* Terence Donovan *Alf Stewart* Ray Meagher *Ailsa Stewart (née Hogan)* Judy Nunn *Shannon Reed* Isla Fisher *Grant Mitchell* Craig MacLachlan *Sally Keating* Kate Ritchie *Ben Lucini* Julian McMahon *Emma Jackson* Dannii Minogue *Carly Lucini (née Morris)* Sharyn Hodgson *Steven Matheson* Adam Willit /*cr* Alan Bateman /*exec pr* Alan Bateman /*dr* inc Sean Nash, Cathie Roden, David Gould /*A Seven Network Presentation* (Aus) /2000+ x 30m col.

Home Improvement

Comedy. C4 1994–

A smash-hit US sitcom from Matt Williams (creator of ➢*Roseanne*) starring Tim Allen as the gadget-crazy, know-it-all presenter of a DIY cable programme called 'The Tool Show'. Largely misread as a piece of macho-posturing by UK critics (who accordingly advised viewers to tune out), *HI* effectively and amusingly satirized the unreconstructed male (down to the wife at home, Jill, who truly held all the power). There were other notable comedic elements to the show: as with any domestic sitcom, there was a next-door neighbour, but in the case of Wilson he was permanently hidden from view by the fence and uttered mystic, Confucius-like sayings; and, as with *Roseanne*, the closing credits showed 'bloopers' committed by the cast. Most funny of all, Pamela Denise Anderson got her break into TV playing Lisa, the 'Tool Time Girl'.

CAST *Tim Taylor* Tim Allen *Jill Taylor* Patricia Richardson *Brad Taylor* Zachery Ty Bryan *Randy Taylor* Jonathan Taylor Thomas *Mark Taylor* Taran Noah Smith *Wilson* Earl Hindman *Al Borland* Richard Karn *Lisa* Pamela Denise Anderson /*cr* Matt Williams /*exec pr* Matt Williams, David McFadzean, Carmen Finestra /*Disney: Touchstone: Wind Dancer: Buena Vista* (USA) /70 x 30m col /US tx ABC 1991–8.

Homicide: Life on the Street

Crime. C4 1994–

Police drama from Barry Levinson (director of *Diner*, *Rainman*) featuring the detectives of a Baltimore Homicide Squad. Shot on 16mm film, entirely on location, with what Levinson termed a 'down and dirty sensibility', episodes followed an individual murder case from report to solution (sometimes). However, crim-catching was a priority below the inter-relationships of the detectives in the squad room, these headed by black Italian Lieutenant Giardello (Yaphet Kotto, the Bond movie *Live and Let Die*). Based (loosely) on David Simon's journalistic account of a year spent with Baltimore's murder squad, *Homicide.*

CAST *Lt Al Giardello* Yaphet Kotto *Det. Stanley Bollander* Ned Beatty *Det. Frank Pembleton* Andre Braugher *Det. John Munch* Richard Belzer *Det. Beau Felton* Daniel Baldwin *Det. Kay Howard* Melissa Leo *Det. Tim Bayliss* Kyle Secor *Det. Meldrick Lewis* Clark Johnson *Det. Steve Crosetti* Jon Polito *Sgt Kay Howard* Melissa Leo /*cr* Barry Levinson, Tom Fontana /*dr* inc Barry Levinson, Kathy Bates, Kathryn Bigelow /*NBC: Fatima* (USA) /170+ x 60m col /US tx NBC 1994– .

The Honeymooners

Comedy. ITV 1958 /BBC2 1987

The character of blowhard but ineffectual NY bus driver Ralph Kramden (Jackie Gleason) first appeared in skits on *DuMont's Cavalcade of Stars* and *The Jackie Gleason Show*, before being spun off into a series, set (entirely) in a rundown apartment at 328 Chauncey Street, Brooklyn, NY. This was shared by Kramden's level-headed wife Alice, constantly puncturing his fantastic schemes to make or save money, these ranging from attempting to offload a warehouseful of useless can-openers on late night TV to withholding a rent increase. Although Ralph and Alice argued like cat and dog ('One of these days, Alice, right in the kisser ... pow!') they loved each other deeply, episodes ending in a 'clinch' the producers called 'kissville'. Upstairs from the Kramdens lived Ralph's best friend, the cheery but incompetent sewer cleaner Ed Norton (Art Carney), and his wife Trixie. The Gleason–Carney partnership had an inspired whiff of Laurel and Hardy about it and this, plus skilled scripts which tapped into the frustrations of the US working classes (the show has a claim to being the first blue-collar sitcom), gave *The Honeymooners* instant classic status in the USA. The Buick Motor Company backed it to the tune of $6 million, the largest sponsorship commitment in history to that date; the ultimate compliment, however, was Hanna-Barbera's shameless cartoon imitation of the show as ➢*The Flintstones*. A revival of *The Honeymooners* in 1966 took the form of one-hour episodes of Gleason's then current series (with Broadway-style musicals padding out episodes by some 30 minutes). A collection of reruns aired as a 'new' series in 1971. In the 1980s 'lost episodes' of *The Honeymooners* were broadcast, but these in fact were skits from *DuMont Calvalcade* and *The Jackie Gleason Show* edited together to make 68 new *Honeymooner* half-hours.

CAST *Ralph Kramden* Jackie Gleason *Ed Norton* Art Carney *Alice Kramden* Audrey Meadows/Sheila MacRae (1971) *Trixie Norton* Joyce Randolph/Jane Kean (1971) /*cr* Jackie Gleason, Joe Bigelow, Harry Crane /*exec pr* Jack Philbin /*pr* Jack Hurdle /*dr* inc Frank Satenstein, Jackie Gleason /*wr* Jackie Gleason, Marvin Marx, Walter Stone, Andy Russell, Herbert Finn, Leonard Stern, Sydney Zelinka /*mus* Jackie Gleason (theme) /*CBS* (USA) /39 x 30m bw: 13 x 60m col (1971): 68 x 30m col (1984–5).

Honey West

Crime. ITV 1966

One of the first PI shows to feature a woman hero. Publicized as 'television's pretty private eye-ful', Honey West was a blonde, judo-kicking investigator with an ex-Marine, Sam, and an ocelot (called Bruce) for company. The gimmicks, alas, failed to make up for poor production values, unimaginative scripts and obvious use of a stuntman in a blonde wig for the fight scenes. Based on the novels of the husband-and-wife writing team of G.G. Fickling; developed for a TV series via an episode of ➢*Burke's Law*.

CAST *Honey West* Anne Francis *Sam Bolt* John Ericson /*pr* Jules Levy, Arthur Gardiner, Arnold Laven /*mus* Joseph Mullendore /*A Four Star Production* (USA) /30 x 30m col /US tx ABC 1965–6.

Hong Kong Phooey

Children's. TV BBC1 1975–6

Hanna-Barbera spoof on the martial arts craze which swept the Western world in the 70s (thanks to Bruce Lee's *Enter the Dragon* and David Carradine's ➢*Kung Fu*), featuring a seemingly mild-mannered police station janitor, Penrod Pooch. But when trouble of the type of the Gumdrop Kid ('He's gonna eat every candy bar in town.') came around, Penrod leapt into a filing cabinet to emerge in a dressing gown as Hong Kong Phooey, Mutt of Steel. Peculiarly inept, however, Phooey was accompanied in the

With a drop of his janitor's bucket and mop, Penry Pooch turned into Hong Kong Phooey, in Hanna-Barbera's loony 'toon spoof of the kung-fu craze of the 70s.

animated underworld by pet cat Spot, a snickering, horizontally-striped feline who usually solved the case. Also seen were grouchy Sergeant Flint (voiced by Joe E. Ross from ➢*The Phil Silvers Show*), and sexbomb receptionist Rosemary, 'the cutie beauty who's always on duty'.

CAST (voices) *Penrod 'Penry' Pooch* Scatman Crowther *Sgt Flint* Joe E. Ross *Rosemary* Kathi Gori *Spot* Don Messick /*pr* William Hanna, Joseph Barbera, Iwao Takamoto /*Hanna-Barbera* (USA) /16 x 22 col /US tx ABC 1974–6.

Hooperman

Comedy. ITV 1988

'Dramedy' starring John Ritter (son of Western legend Tex) as sensitive San Francisco cop Harry Hooperman, who inherits an apartment block – and a dog, Bijoux – when his landlady dies. The irate tenants proved to be as troublesome as his lady boss at work, the abrasively demanding Captain 'CZ' Stern. Hooperman's on/off relationship with tenant handywoman Susan, offered scant solace. A skilled amusement from Steven Bochco and Terry Louise Fisher (the duo responsible for ➢*LA Law*) which never quite achieved hit status.

CAST *Det. Harry Hooperman* John Ritter *Susan Smith* Debrah Farentino *Capt. Celeste 'CZ' Stern* Barbara Bosson *Off. Boris Pritzger* Clarence Felder /*cr* Steven Bochco, Terry Louise Fisher /*exec pr* Robert Myman, Leon Tokatyan, Rick Kellard /*mus* Mike Post /*An Adam Production: Fox TV* (USA) /42 x 30m col /US tx ABC 1987–89.

Hopalong Cassidy

Western. ITV 1955–6

After 13 years in the B-movie saddle as Hopalong Cassidy, actor William Boyd turned to TV in 1945, editing down the Hopalong features for American network NBC. By 1948 these proved so successful that Boyd decided to produce 52 low-budget episodes made especially for the small screen, with Edgar Buchanan (*The Adventures of Judge Roy Bean*, ➢*Cade's County*) as his sidekick, Red Connors. A saintly pursuer (astride horse Topper) of the West's badguys, 'Hoppy' – like contemporary ➢*The Lone Ranger* – was strong on moral codes. Thus he bore little relation to author Clarence E. Mulford's original foul-mouthed character, but was infinitely more palatable to TV tastes. The show was hugely popular with children; in 1950 American clothing manufacturers ran out of black dye because of small fry demand for black clothes in the style of their favourite Western hero. The same year saw 108 licensed manufacturers sell $70 million-worth of Hoppy products. A herd of juvenile oaters followed hard on its trail, dominating small-screen viewing until the mid 50s. In a notable case of life imitating art Boyd, previously known for his pastimes of women and whisky, became a clean-living paragon of virtue in the mould of Hoppy himself. Said Boyd: 'When you've got parents saying what a wonderful guy Hoppy is, what the hell do you do? You've got to be a wonderful guy.' Boyd died in 1972, a multi-millionaire, still faithful to his fourth wife, whom he had married in 1937.

CAST *Hopalong Cassidy* William Boyd *Red Connors* Edgar Buchanan /*pr* William Boyd /*dr* inc George Archainbaud, Derwin Abbe /*wr* inc Doris Schroeder, Harrison Jacobs /*William Boyd Productions* (USA) / 52 x 26m bw /US tx NBC 1951–2.

House of Cards

Drama. BBC1 1990

'You may think that: I couldn't possibly comment...'

Drama serial charting the rise to No. 10 of ambitious Tory minister Francis Urquhart (appropriately known as 'FU' to all and political sundry), this topped – or rather bottomed – when he pushed his young mistress, Mattie, from the parapet of the House of Commons into perdition. Despite FU's amoralism, he cunningly drew the viewer into complicity through intimate, Shakespearian soliloquies to camera. By the good fortune of the programming gods, its broadcast coincided with Mrs Thatcher's downfall and it went on to become a best-selling drama around the world. A sequel, *To Play the King* (1993), followed the problems of Urquhart's tenure as it came under pressure from a new, trendy monarch. Rounding off the trilogy was *The Final Cut* (1995), which saw FU besieged, amidst declining electoral fortunes, by his own bestial cabinet. Liberally – even leftishly – adapted by Andrew Davies from the novels of Michael Dobbs, a former deputy chairman of the Conservative Party, the dramas had the strange ring of prophecy, with their scenarios of sexual scandals, leadership scheming and a ruling party oblivious to any interest save the maintenance of power.

CAST *Francis Urquhart* Ian Richardson *Elizabeth Urquhart* Diane Fletcher *Mattie Storin* Susannah Harker *Stamper* Colin Jeavons /*pr* Ken Riddington / *wr* Andrew Davies /*BBC TV* (UK) /4 x 60m col.

House of Eliott

Drama. BBC1 1991–4

Two beautiful sisters fall on hard times after the death of their GP father, before rising to the cat-walk of success with their own fashion house in 1920s London.

Slowly addictive period drama, colourfully dressed up in the highest production values, stitched together with 90s sensibilities (notably, the Eliott gals' feministic professional and personal lives). Devised by ➢*Upstairs, Downstairs* creators Eileen Atkins and Jean Marsh.

CAST *Beatrice Eliott* Stella Gonet *Evangeline 'Evie' Eliott* Louise Lombard *Lady Lydia Eliott* Barbara Jefford *Arthur Eliott* Peter Birch *Jack Maddox* Aden

Gillett *Daniel Page* Richard Lintern /*cr* Eileen Atkins & Jean Marsh /*exec pr* Ken Riddington /*pr* Jeremy Gwilt /*BBC TV* (UK) /24 x 60m col.

How

Children's. ITV 1966–81

Much-loved kid's programme that explained – as its title suggested – how things worked. Even in the politically uncomplicated 60s and 70s, however, the Native American-style greeting (palms raised) used by the presenters – pontificating old Jack Hargreaves, twinkle-eyed Fred Dinage, Jon Miller and Bunty James – was embarrassing; it was dropped for a 1990 revival *How 2*, hosted by Dinage, ➢*Countdown*'s Carol Vorderman and Gareth 'Gaz Top' Jones.

CAST (presenters) Bunty James (later replaced by Marian Davies), Jack Hargreaves, Jon Miller, Fred Dinage, Jill Graham /*Southern TV* (UK) /approx 500 x 30m bw:col.

Howard's Way

Melodrama. BBC1 1985–90

Launched by the BBC as the Corporation's £3 million answer to ➢*Dynasty*, *HW* was a lush drama set along Hampshire's River Hamble, the mooring place of the rich and their vessels. The serial initially told the story of Tom Howard (Maurice Colbourne, ➢*Gangsters*), a redundant aircraft designer who bought into a local boatyard, The Mermaid, run by Jack Rolfe. As the season's passed, however, the serial began to concentrate more and more on extra-boatyard activities: Tom had an affair with Jack's daughter Avril, his wife Jan embarked on liaisons with her fashion-house boss, Ken Masters (a wonderful medallion-man performance by Stephen Yardley), and businessman Sir Edward Frere. Meanwhile, the Howard's student drop-out son was obsessed with the moody Abby, while their bratty daughter Lynne married Frenchman Claude Dupont (decapitated whilst water-skiing) before ending up with the ruthless tycoon Charles Frere. (The romantic complications spilled curiously over into real life, with Stephen Yardley and Jan Harvey pairing up, and Tracey Childs and Tony Anholt getting spliced.) Co-created by Gerard Glaister, the show's seamy fascination with naked capitalism and sexual adventuring harkened back to his ➢*The Brothers*, but with the elements of glossy lifestyle added. Alongside ➢*Capital City*, *Howard's Way* was the quintessential British soap of the Thatcherite eighties.

CAST *Tom Howard* Maurice Colbourne *Jan Howard* Jan Harvey *Leo Howard* Edward Highmore *Lynne Howard* Tracey Childs *Jack Rolfe* Glyn Owen *Avril Rolfe* Susan Gilmore *Ken Masters* Stephen Yardley *Kate Harvey* Dulcie Gray *Abby Urquhart* Cindy Shelley *Charles Frere* Tony Anholt *Sir Edward Frere* Nigel Davenport *Claude Dupont* Malcolm Jamieson *Vanessa Andenburg* Lana Morris *Laura Wilde* Kate O'Mara *Phil Norton* Anthony Head /*cr* Gerard Glaister, Allan Prior /*pr* Gerard Glaister /*dr* Sarah Hellings, Keith Washington, Frank W. Smith, Alister Hallum, Peter Rose, Jeremy Summers /*wr* Raymond Thompson, Jeremy Burnham, Mervyn Haisman, Douglas Watkinson /*BBC TV* (UK) /80 x 50m col.

How Do You Do!

Children's. BBC1 1977

Educational and entertaining blend of counting games, tales and music for tiny tots. Shown in the generic *See-Saw* series, the successor to ➢*Watch with Mother*, it was introduced by Carmen Munro (➢*General Hospital*, ➢*The Fosters*, ➢*Desmond's*). Only 13 episodes were made, but repeats kept it almost constantly on screen until 1981.

CAST (presenter) Carmen Munro /*BBC TV* (UK) / 13 x 30m col.

How the West Was Won

Western. BBC1 1977

The sprawling saga of the pioneer Macahan family as they journey westwards to Wyoming (where they eventually founded a ranch empire), based on John Ford's 1963 motion picture of the same title. ➢*Gunsmoke*'s James Arness played clan head, mountain man Zeb, while Bruce Boxleitner (later ➢*Babylon 5*) took the part of the troublesome Luke, and a wagon-load of veteran Western actors lent genre credibility, among them Woody Strode, Cameron Mitchell (➢*High Chaparral*) and Jack Elam. Narratively long-winded, but spectacularly mounted and filmed on location in Utah, Arizona, Southern California and Colorado.

CAST *Zeb Macahan* James Arness *Kate Macahan* Eve Marie Saint *Luke Macahan* Bruce Boxleitner *Laura Macahan* Kathryn Holcomb *Molly Culhane* Fionnula Flanagan /*exec pr* John Mantley /*pr* John G. Stephens, Jeffrey Hayden /*dr* inc Daniel Mann, Burt Kennedy, Vincent & Bernard McEveety, Barry Crane, Joseph Pevney /*wr* inc John Mantley, Calvin Clements, Earl W. Wallace, Howard Fast, Ray Goldrup /*Albert S. Ruddy Prod: MGM: John Mantley Prods* (USA) / 1 x 124m pilot (*The Macahans*), 2 x 150m, 4 x 52m col /US tx ABC 1976–9.

H.R. Pufnstuf

Children's. ITV 1970

Enjoyable derivation of *The Wizard of Oz* in which a boy, Jimmy, and his talking flute are beckoned to a fantasy land by evil Witchiepoo. Luckily, the nice dragon mayor of Living Island, H.R. Pufnstuf, is on claw to help them fight the dastardly sorcerer. Among the voice cast was Felix Silla, better known as Cousin Itt in ➢*The Addams Family*. Made to the highest production values (both monetary and artistic), with the non-humans represented by elaborately gaudy life-size puppets, it spawned a feature-film version in 1970. It was from Sid and Marty Krofft, also repsonsible for the kiddie sci-fi classic ➢*Land of the Lost.*

CAST (voices) *Jimmy* Jack Wild *Witchiepoo* Billie Hayes, also Joan Gerber, Walker Edmiston, Felix Silla, Jerry Landon /*cr* Sid & Marty Krofft /*pr* Sid & Marty Krofft /*Krofft Communications* (USA) /17 x 30m col /US tx NBC 1969–70.

The Huckleberry Hound Show

Children's. ITV 1960–4

Animated adventures of a genial, none-too-smart Southern pooch, who stumbed obliviously from one comic disaster (falling trees) to the next (exploding rockets), whilst whistling an off-key rendition of 'Clementine'. Each week the corn-pone 'Huck' turned up in a different guise – lion tamer, medieval chivalrous knight, professor, swashbuckling Purple Pumpernickel – but calamity always awaited. A loose imitation of Tex Avery's sad-eyed hound Droopy, *Huckleberry Hound* was the first TV cartoon superstar, winning an Emmy for Outstanding Achievement in Children's Programming. Also seen on the show, in self-contained segments, were: *Pixie and Dixie*, two Southern mice who tormented Jinks the cat (who 'hated those meeces to pieces'); picnic-snatching ➢*Yogi Bear*; and lupine con-artist *Hokey Wolf.*

Creators Bill Hanna and Joseph Barbera had risen to fame as the animators behind Warner Brothers' *Tom & Jerry* film shorts and had moved into TV when the studio had wound down its cartoon department. For the new medium they pioneered an inexpensive method of animation, which reduced lip movements to a simple vowel-to-vowel cycle, and body movements to a minimum. Their first TV show was *Ruff and Ready*, but it was *Huckleberry Hound* who took them into the small-screen big time.

CAST (voices) *Huckleberry Hound* Daws Butler /*cr* William Hanna, Joseph Barbera /*pr* William Hanna, Joseph Barbera /*wr* Joseph Barbera, Warren Foster / *mus* Joseph Barbera, Hoyt Cutin (theme lyrics) / *Hanna–Barbera: Screen Gems* (USA) /195 x 30m bw / US tx Syndicated 1958–62.

The Human Jungle

Melodrama. ITV 1963–5

Case files of an eminent psychiatrist. Intense and somewhat brooding melodrama starring Herbert Lom (later Clouseau's manic boss in the *Pink Panther* films) as widower analyst Dr Roger Corder MD DPM, whose off-duty hours were filled by concern for his teenage daughter Jennifer. Eminently watchable.

CAST *Dr Roger Corder* Herbert Lom *Jennifer Corder* Sally Smith /*cr* Julian Wintle /*pr* Julian Wintle, Leslie Parkyn /*dr* inc Vernon Sewell, Sidney A. Hayes /*wr* inc John Kruse /*mus* Bernard Ebbinghouse /*Independent Artists Production* (UK) /26 x 50m bw.

I

I, Claudius

Drama. BBC2 1976

Robert Graves' 1934 novel charting the decline of Ancient Rome was initially intended to see the light of a screen as a movie starring Charles Laughton. This, however, was abandoned and the book was deemed 'unfilmable' for 40 years, until adapted in 12 finely written pieces by Jack Pulman for the BBC. Using Graves' own literary device, Pulman had Emperor Claudius narrate (as flashbacks) the intrigues, violence and depravity of his reign and those of his immediate predecessors. Somewhat uneasy over the 'high brow' nature of Graves' material, the BBC had Pulman embroider the historical tapestry with Mafia-esque family drama and a pail of gore, notably an invented scene in which the crazed Caligula eats the foetus of his incestuously conceived unborn child. For his virtuoso performance as the stammering but wily Claudius, actor Derek Jacobi (➢*Cadfael*) earned the critical laurel of a BAFTA; the golden supporting cast included John Hurt, Brian Blessed, George Baker, Sian Phillips, Patrick Stewart (later to beam up in time to ➢*Star Trek: TNG*) and, improbably enough, Christopher Biggins as Nero. When shown in the USA on PBS, *I, Claudius* single-handedly redefined the parameters of acceptable taste on American TV. Despite particular unease over its episodes of sexual immorality (incest, orgies, nymphomania – including a famous sequence in which the Empress Messalina engaged in a sex tournament – adultery, rape *ad infinitum*) all PBS stations broadcast the series, under the *Masterpiece Theater* label, to sitting ovations.

CAST *Claudius* Derek Jacobi *Augustus* Brian Blessed *Livia* Sian Phillips *Tiberius* George Baker *Caligula* John Hurt *Sejanus* Patrick Stewart *Drusus* Ian Ogilvy *Nero* Christopher Biggins *Gratus* Bernard Hill *Pallus* Bernard Hepton *Messalina* Sheila White /*pr* Martin Lisemore /*dr* Herbert Wise /*wr* Jack Pulman /*BBC TV* (UK) /1 x 100m, 11 x 50m col /US tx PBS 1978.

I Dream of Jeannie

Comedy. ITV 1966

When NASA astronaut Tony Nelson (Larry Hagman, later ➢*Dallas*) crashes on a deserted Pacific Island, he finds a beautiful genie in a bottle. She accompanies him back to Cape Canaveral, where she seeks magically to improve his lot in life. Unfortunately, Jeannie – who is only visible to Nelson and buddy Roger Healey – is both overzealous and petulantly jealous (ousting Nelson's fiancée Melissa by episode four, eventually to install herself in the post). Still, with a blink of her eyes she soon undoes each episode's mayhem.

Likeable, light supernatural sitcom, engagingly played, intended by US network NBC to ride the success of rival ABC's ➢*Bewitched.* With starette Barbara Eden in skimpy hareem attire, it also pandered to an obvious male fantasy (would she really do *anything* for him?) and many turned on.

CAST *Jeannie* Barbara Eden *Capt. Anthony 'Tony' Nelson* Larry Hagman *Capt. Roger Healey* Bill Daily *Dr Alfred Bellows* Hayden Rorke /*cr* Sidney Sheldon /*exec pr* Sidney Sheldon /*dr* inc Gene Nelson, Alan Rafkin, E.W. Swackhamer, Hal Cooper, William Asher, Claudio Guzman /*wr* inc Sidney Sheldon, Arthur Alsberg, Bob Fisher /*mus* Hugh Montenegro /*Screen Gems* (USA) /139 x 25m col /US tx NBC 1965–9.

I Love Lucy

Comedy. ITV 1955–65

The scatterbrained antics of NY housewife and showbiz-wannabe Lucy Ricardo, snap the patience of fiery bandleader husband Ricky, while nosy apartment neighbours the Mertzes look on.

Prototype, much-imitated sitcom, from its live audience and four-camera (later three) technique, to its basic structure of neighbouring, interrelating couples. It grew from Ball's CBS radio show *My Favourite Husband*, with Richard Denning slated to be her TV co-star; instead she decided to film a pilot with her real-life spouse, Cuban musician-actor Desi Arnaz (the two had met on the set of Arnaz's Hollywood feature, *Too Many Girls*), which sold them and the concept to CBS. A smash-hit in its first season, *I Love Lucy* became a kind of mania in the USA; the 1953 episode in which the Ricardos' baby boy was born (its transmission, extraordinarily enough, coinciding with Ball giving birth to Desi Arnaz Jr) actually headlined in newspapers above Eisenhower's inauguration. The high classiness of the show's production (it was made on film by Ball and Arnaz's own company, Desilu), scripts and acting secured it five Emmys. These factors, plus such timeless slapstick gags as Lucy pinned to the kitchen wall by an over-yeasted bread mix, have made *I Love Lucy* virtually indestructible – it is estimated that the show has always been on the air somewhere in the world for the last 40 years – although Lucy's dizzy femininity can grate on modern sensibilities.

After her 1961 divorce from Arnaz, the former speakeasy hostess Ball went on the next year to star in the sitcom *The Lucy Show* (CBS, co-produced with new husband Gary Morton), in which she played Connecticut widow and mother of two, Lucy Carmichael. Despite a shift down in quality, hampered by a volatile cast list and a change in title to *Here's Lucy*, its longevity alone (until 1972) established Ball, if proof was needed, as American TV's comedienne without peer.

CAST *Lucy Ricardo* Lucille Ball *Ricky Ricardo* Desi Arnaz *Ethel Mertz* Vivian Vance *Fred Mertz* William Frawley *Little Ricky Ricardo* Richard Keith *Mrs MacGillicuddy (Lucy's mother)* Kathryn Card *Jerry, the agent* Jerry Hausner /*cr* Jess Oppenheimer, Madelyn Pugh, Bob Carroll /*exec pr* Desi Arnaz /*pr* Jess Oppenheimer, Desi Arnaz /*dr* Marc Daniels, William Asher, Ralph Levy, James V. Kern /*wr* Jess Oppenheimer, Madelyn Pugh, Bob Carroll /*mus* Eliot Daniel (theme), Wilbur Hatch & the Desi Arnaz Orchestra /*Desilu Productions* (USA) /179 x 30m bw /US tx CBS 1951–61.

I'm Dickens, He's Fenster

Comedy. ITV 1964

The slapstick capers of two carpenter-cum-builders who had a penchant for Trouble.

Intermittently amusing series, something like Abbott and Costello rewarmed for the 60s, which provided a step up the career ladder for John Astin (➢*The Addams Family*).

CAST *Harry Dickens* John Astin *Arch Fenster* Marty Ingels *Kate Dickens* Emmaline Henry *Mel Warshaw* Dave Ketchum *Banister* Frank DeVol *Mulligan* Henry Beckman /*cr* Leonard Stern /*pr* Leonard Stern /*Heyfay* (USA) /32 x 25m bw /US tx ABC 1962.

The Impossibles

Children's. BBC1 1967

Cartoon adventures of a pop trio who, on command from boss Big D, turned into government superheroes – Coil Man, Multi Man (able to make unlimited copies of himself) and Fluid Man. 'Rally-Ho!'

Adequate afternoon filler, transmitted in a package with *Frankenstein Jr* (sometimes under the title *Frankenstein Jr and The Impossibles*), this latter Frankenstein being a 50-feet tall robot (voiced by ➢*The Addams Family*'s Ted Cassidy), the invention of boy scientist Buzz Conroy, who activated the metallic scourge of supervillains everywhere with the magic word 'Allakazoom!'

CAST (voices) *Multi Man* Don Messick *Coil Man* Hal Smith *Fluid Man* Paul Frees *Frankenstein Jr* Ted Cassidy *Buzz Conroy* Dick Beals /*exec pr* William Hanna, Joseph Barbera /*Hanna-Barbera* (USA) /18 x 25m bw /US tx CBS 1966–8.

Inch High, Private Eye

Children's. BBC1 1974

Almost amusing cartoon twist on ➢*Get Smart*, replacing the inept Smart with the inept – and miniscule – detective Inch High. Emanating a completely unfounded confidence, the 'World's Biggest Little Detective' usually stumbled into success, with the aid of his misnamed dog Braveheart, his normal-sized teenage niece Lori, and her boyfriend Gator.

CAST (voices) *Inch High* Lennie Weinrib *Lori* Kathi Gori *Gator* Bob Luttell /*Hanna-Barbera* (USA) / 13 x 25m col /US tx NBC 1973.

The Incredible Hulk

Sci-fi. ITV 1978–82

When compassionate scientist Dr David Banner is accidentally injected with an overdose of gamma rays, he acquires the uncontrollable tendency, in moments of anger, to transform into a raging man-beast of Herculean strength – The Incredible Hulk. As such, he is remorselessly pursued o'er America by hard-nosed reporter Jack McGee, who believes him a killer. A latterday take on R.L. Stevenson's *Dr Jekyll and Mr Hyde* (plus elements of Mary Shelley's *Frankenstein* and Quinn Martin's ➢*The Fugitive*), the Hulk started life as a Stan Lee *Marvel* kiddie comic character, transferring to TV at the instigation of prodigious sci-fi writer–producer Kenneth Johnson (➢*The Bionic Woman*, ➢ *V*, ➢*Alien Nation*), who played up the Hulk's existential angst for crossover appeal. Any pretensions, however, were pricked by the show's crass production; sharp-eyed viewers noted that footage from movies (among them *Duel* and *Airport*) was often edited in. Bill Bixby (previously ➢*My Favourite Martian*, ➢*The Magician*) played Banner, Lou Ferrigno his green *alter ego*. A former Mr Universe, Ferrigno had made his screen debut in Arnold Schwarzenegger's 1976 film *Pumping Iron*.

CAST *Dr David Bruce Banner* Bill Bixby *The Incredible Hulk* Lou Ferrigno *Jack McGee* Jack Colvin /*cr* Stan Lee /*exec pr* Kenneth Johnson /*pr* inc Chuck Bowman, Jim Parriott, Nicholas Corea, Bob Steinhauer /*dr* inc Reza S. Badiyi, Bill Bixby, Sig Neufeld, Ray Danton, Chuck Bowman, Alan J. Levi, Frank Orsatti /*wr* inc Kenneth Johnson, Richard Matheson, Karen Harris, Jim Hirsch /*mus* Joseph Harnell /*An MCA Television Production* (USA) / 2 x 120m, 80 x 60m col.

The Informer
Crime. ITV 1966–7

Starred Ian Hendry as a disbarred barrister who used his underworld contacts to forge a risky career as a police informant for DS Piper. Tense, pungent thriller with broad-couch appeal (it also covered the lawyer Lambert's strained marriage and todding relationship with an ex-client's sympathetic girlfriend), touched by the directorial hand of, among others, a young Ridley Scott.

CAST *Alex Lambert* Ian Hendry *Janet Lambert* Heather Sears *DS Piper* Neil Hallett *Sylvia Parrish* Jean Marsh *Cass* Tony Selby /*cr* John Whitney, Geoffrey Bellman /*exec pr* Stella Richman /*pr* Stella Richman, Peter Collinson /*dr* inc Ridley Scott, Michael Lindsay-Hogg, Richard Doubleday /*wr* inc Jack Trevor Story, Richard Harris /*Rediffusion* (UK) /21 x 55m bw.

Insektors
Children's. C4 1996

Animated eco-allegory about two insect species, the hippy-like Verigreens (the nice guys) and the grey, hegemonic Kruds (the nasty guys), who inhabited different sides of the black planet. The Queen of the Kruds, Katheter, had ice in her soul and to keep her warm her minions constantly raided the daffodil woods of the Verigreens using such pleasantly bizarre means as a giant mechanical frog.

The series, which used a computer graphic technique similar to Disney's celebrated film *Toy Story*, won the 1994 International Emmy for Children's Programmes. This notwithstanding, the British versions of the original French scripts made an obvious pitch for a crossover audience; one line, for instance, described a bridge as being 'very Richard Rogers', a reference obviously beyond childish grasp.

pr Georges Lacroix (Fr): Teddy Kempner, Andy Secombe (UK) /*dr* Gilbert Louet /*wr* Teddy Kempner, Andy Secombe /*mus* Jacques Davidovici /*Santome* (Fr): *Lunchtime Productions* (UK) /26 x 15m col.

Inspector Morse
Crime. ITV 1987–

Languid, exquisitely filmed police procedurals featuring Colin Dexter's Chief Inspector Morse of Thames Valley Police (Oxford beat). Accompanied by prosaic Geordie sidekick Lewis, the cerebral, irascible Morse (hobbies: Wagner, crosswords, real ale) pursued plots of true middle-browness, in that they bridged lowly whodunnit teleplays and cryptic, high-minded allegories. A case in point was Julian Mitchell's 'Masonic Mysteries', which was not only a murder mystery but a parody of *The Magic Flute and* freemasonry within HM's Constabulary; another was Mitchell's 'Promised Land', which took a tilt at real life policing by making Morse the subject of a wrongful conviction. With each episode developed over two hours – a leisurely cinematic length insisted on by early producer Kenny McBain – there was a plenitude of time for plot, character and nostalgic atmosphere to develop. Heavily redolent of Oxford's dreaming spires, bicycling lanes and the ghost of Sebastian Flyte, *Morse* proved complusive viewing for 75 million around the world. It was also a singular case of the box being better than the book.

Some *Morse* trivia: novelist Colin Dexter

appeared as an extra in every episode; Morse drove a red 1960 Mk II Jaguar; his first name, long hidden was revealed as the thoroughly contrived Endeavour; although the programme officially ended in 1993, 'one offs' appeared thereafter at an almost annual rate; in the original books, Lewis was an elderly Welshman; *Morse* scriptwriter Anthony Minghella went on to write the film *Truly, Madly, Deeply* and direct *The English Patient.* Barrington Pheloung's theme music spelt out M-O-R-S-E in Morse code; Morse's new sidekick was Adrian Kershaw.

CAST *Chief Insp. Morse* John Thaw *DS Robbie Lewis* Kevin Whately/Peter Woodthorpe *Dr Grayling Russell* Amanda Hillwood *Chief Supt Strange* James Grout /*exec pr* Ted Childs, John Thaw /*pr* Kenny McBain, Chris Burt, David Lascelles, Deidre Keir /*dr* inc Danny Boyle, Alastair Reid, Brian Parker, Adrian Shergold, Roy Battersby /*wr* inc Julian Mitchell, Anthony Minghella, Thomas Ellice, Charles Wood, Ray Bradbury /*mus* Barrington Pheloung (theme) /*Zenith: Central TV: Carlton* (UK) /32+ x 120m col.

Interpol Calling

Crime. ITV 1959–60

Police drama series about a brace of investigators, Duval and Mornay, working for Interpol's Paris HQ. The detecting-in-the-European-underworld dangers were tensioned-up, providing plenty of action (heralded by a credit sequence of a car smashing through a barrier) under the executive eye of F. Sherwin Green.

CAST *Insp. Paul Duval* Charles Korvin *Insp. Mornay* Edwin Richfield /*exec pr* F. Sherwin Green /*pr* Anthony Perry, Connery Chappell /*A Rank /Wrather Production* (UK) /39 x 25m bw.

In the Heat of the Night

Crime. ITV 1988–90

Any screen retread of John Ball's novel was bound to suffer in comparison with the 1967 multi-Oscared Steiger/Poitier movie, but this James Lee Barrett TV version held up tolerably well. Cast in the role of (white) Police Chief Gillespie of Sparta, Mississippi, was Carroll O'Connor from ➢*All in the Family,* with Howard Rollins, from the film *Ragtime,* as returned-home (black) detective Virgil Tibbs. Obliged by the local mayor to work together on the murder case of a teenage white girl, the two policemen related abrasively but (unlike novel and film) this was less racial in nature than generational. In particular, Gillespie resented the new-fangled methods Tibbs advocated.

The Hugh O'Connor on the cast list was Carroll O'Connor's son. Larry 'JR' Hagman was among those on the director's roster.

CAST *Chief Bill Gillespie* Carroll O'Connor *Det. Virgil Tibbs* Howard Rollins *Sgt Bubba Skinner* Alan Autry *Althea Tibbs* Anne-Marie Johnson *Deputy Lonnie Jamison* Hugh O'Connor *Tom Duggan* Jon Don Baker /*cr* James Lee Barrett /*exec pr* Fred Silverman, Juanita Bartlett, David Moessinger, Jeri Taylor, Carroll O'Connor /*dr* inc Larry Hagman, Harry Harris, Carroll O'Connor /*mus* Quincy Jones, Alan & Marilyn Bergman (theme) /*An MGM Television Production* (USA) /US tx NBC /40+ x 60m col /1988–94.

The Invaders

Sci-fi. ITV 1967–9

The TV show most closely related to the paranoid 'They're here!' sci-fi films of the 50s (exemplified by *The Invasion of the Body Snatchers*), though shorn of their McCarthyite political content. It also drew heavily on the Cassandra myth and executive producer Quinn Martin's classic 'running man' adventure, ➢*The Fugitive.*

One night, on a remote country road, architect David Vincent (Roy Thinnes) witnesses the landing of a flying saucer. He tries to tell the authorities but nobody believes him, leaving Vincent to wage a lone, monomaniacal crusade against the Invaders, whose infiltration of earth is caused by the death of their own planet. Able to take human form, The Invaders need to regenerate every 10–12 days, and are given away by a lack of heartbeat, emotions and the inability to bend their little fingers. Their most frightening accessory is a small disc which, when applied to the back of the human neck, produces death by apparent cardiac arrest.

Occasionally succeeding in its aim of scaring the audience to refuge behind the couch, *The Invaders* was predominantly predictable (the person Vincent trusted always turned out to be One of Them) and depressing, for no matter how many aliens the hero vaporized, more came along. The producers' introduction of allies to Vincent's side, 'The Believers' led by millionaire electronics businessman Edgar Scoville, gave no fillip to the ratings. The show itself was vaporized after 43 episodes.

CAST *David Vincent* Roy Thinnes *Edgar Scoville* Kent Smith /*cr* Larry Cohen /*exec pr* Quinn Martin /*dr* inc Paul Wendkos, Joseph Sargent, Don Medford, Sutton Roley /*wr* inc Jerry Sohl, Earl Hamner Jr, Don Brinkley, Clyde Ware, Larry Cohen /*mus* Dominic Frontiere /*A Quinn Martin Production* (USA) / 43 x 60m col /US tx ABC 1967–8.

The Irish RM

Comedy. C4 1983–5

At the turn of the century Major Sinclair Yates resigns his commission to become a Resident Magistrate in western colonial Ireland. Duly installed, he is the uncomprehending gull for blarneying natives and his sly landlord, Flurry Knox.

Colourful adaptation of the comic Anglo-Irish novel *Some Experiences of an Irish RM* by cousins Edith Sommerville and Martin Ross (aka Violet Martin) which gave Peter Bowles one of his better roles.

CAST *Major Sinclair Yates* Peter Bowles *Flurry Knox* Bryan Murray *Philippa Yeates* Doran Godwin *Mrs Knox* Beryl Reid *Sally* Lise-Ann McLaughlin /*pr* James Mitchell /*Little Bird Films: Rediffusion Films: Ulster TV: RTE: James Mitchell Productions* (UK /Eire) /26 x 30m col.

Iron Horse

Western. BBC1 1967–8

Under the fighting leadership of Ben Calhoun (Dale Roberston from ➢*Tales of Wells Fargo*), the Buffalo Pass, Scalplock & Defiance railroad is driven through the untamed West of the 1870s. Passable oater series, which numbered future Oscar-winning actress Ellen Burstyn (née McRae) among its cast. Developed from a TVM, *Scalplock*, in which gambler Calhoun won the BPS&D in a poker game.

CAST *Ben Calhoun* Dale Robertson *Dave Tarrant* Gary Collins *Nils Torvald* Roger Torrey *Barnabas Rogers* Bob Random *Julie Parsons* Ellen McRae /*cr* Stephen Kandel, James Goldstone /*exec pr* Charles Marquis Warren /*dr* inc Sam Fuller /*Screen Gems* (USA) /47 x 52m col /US tx ABC 1966–8.

Raymond Burr as wheelchair-bound San Francisco detective Ironside. So convincing was Burr's performance that viewers thought him paraplegic.

Ironside

Crime. BBC1 1967–75

After being paralyzed by a sniper's bullet, former police chief Robert T. Ironside is given a permanent post as special consultant to the San Francisco PD and an operations base in a converted attic of its HQ. Recruited to help the wheelchair-bound master 'tec are Sergeant Ed Brown, Officer Eve Whitfield (Barbara Anderson, ➢*Mission: Impossible*, later replaced, after a salary dispute, by Elizabeth Baur), and black, former petty crook Mark Sanger (Don Mitchell, also the blaxploitation pic *Scream, Blacula, Scream*), bodyguard and chauffeur of Ironside's customized van.

Spun off from a surprise hit TVM, *Ironside* avoided the potential tastelessness of its 'defective detective' gimmick through star Burr's (➢*Perry Mason*) commanding, sympathetic performance. This, plus solid helmsmanship from a strong duty list of directors, transported the show into a long (185 episode) run and an enduring place in the TV viewer's affections.

Transmitted in the UK as *A Man Called Ironside.*

CAST *Chief Robert T. Ironside* Raymond Burr *Sgt Ed Brown* Don Galloway *Off. Eve Whitfield* Barbara Anderson *Mark Sanger* Don Mitchell *Fran Belding* Elizabeth Baur /*cr* Collier Young /*exec pr* Cy Chermak, Joel Rogosin, Frank Price, Collier Young /*dr* inc Michael Caffey, Charles S. Dubin, Jeannot Swarc, Jimmy Sangster, Christian I. Nyby II, Leon Penn, Boris Sagal /*wr* inc Don Mankiewicz, Christopher Trumbo, Cy Chermak, Ken Kolb /*mus* Monty Paich, Oliver Nelson /*Harbour Productions: Universal TV: NBC* (USA) /197 x 60m, 3 x 120m col /US tx NBC 1967–75.

I Spy

Adventure. ITV 1967–9

Espionage entertainment of some slickness, but primarily interesting as the first major American TV series to co-star a black actor with a white one. The black actor was Bill Cosby, who played agent Alexander Scott to Robert Culp's Kelly Robinson, the spook duo travelling the exotic corners of the globe disguised as a tennis ace and his trainer. Not wishing to strain the intolerance of Southern viewers, NBC ensured that Culp took the more masterful roles (he was the player not the coach), and that Cosby never appeared opposite white women. That said, Cosby won three Emmys for his role, forged a precedent for inter-racial bonding on the small screen (seen more latterly in ➢*Miami Vice* and ➢*NYPD Blue*), and made himself into a national institution, the eventual pinnacle of which was ➢*The Cosby Show.* In 1972 Cosby and Culp paired up again, this time for the feature *Hickey & Boggs* (*dr* Culp), in which they played a pair of down-at-heel private investigators.

CAST *Kelly Robinson* Robert Culp *Alexander Scott* Bill Cosby /*exec pr* Danny Thomas, Sheldon Leonard /*pr* Mort Fine, David Friedkin /*dr* inc Tom Gries, Paul Wendkos, Richard Sarafian /*wr* inc Mort Fine, Arthur Dales /*mus* Earle Hagen (theme) /*NBC: Sheldon Leonard* (USA) /82 x 60m col /US tx NBC 1965–8.

It Ain't Half Hot, Mum

Comedy. BBC1 1974–81

From the authorial partnership of Croft and Perry a sitcom set, like their meisterwerk ➢*Dad's Army*, during WWII, but of coarser comedy cut. It featured the Royal Artillery Concert Party of India and, especially, the efforts of blustering Welsh Sergeant Major Williams to instil in the 'boys to entertain you' (as the theme song had it; to Williams they were a 'bunch of poofs') some semblance of military order. On parade alongside Williams were diminutive 'Lofty' Sugden, Bombadier Solomons, Scotsman Gunner Mackintosh, Gunner Parkin (possessor of a 'fine pair of shoulders'; Williams thought he was the boys' father), egg-headed pianist 'Lah-de-Da' Gunner Graham, and Bombadier Beaumont, who cross-dressed into 'Gloria' for the cabarets. Their idiotic commissioned officers were Colonel Reynolds and effete Captain Ashwood. Also seen were the local wallahs (including a blacked up Michael Bates), whose stereotyped pidgin English caused suggestions that the programme be retitled 'It Ain't Half Racist, Mum'.

A spin-off single, *Whispering Grass*, performed by Windsor Davies and Don Estelle, became a No. 1 hit in 1975.

CAST *RSM B.L. Williams* Windsor Davies *Bombadier Solomons* George Layton *Bombadier 'Gloria' Beaumont* Melvyn Hayes *Gunner 'Lofty' Sugden* Don Estelle *Gunner 'Paderuski' Graham* John Clegg *Gunner Mackintosh* Stuart McGugan *Gunner Parkin* Christopher Mitchell *Colonel Reynolds* Donald Hewlett *Capt. Ashwood* Michel Knowles *Rangi Ram* Michael Bates *Gunner 'Nosher' Evans* Mike Kinsey *Gunner 'Nobby' Clarke* Kenneth MacDonald *Char Wallah Muhammed* Dino Shafeek *Punkar Wallah* Babar Bhatti /*cr* Jimmy Perry & David Croft /*pr* David Croft /*dr* John Kilby, Phil Bishop, Bob Spiers /*wr* Jimmy Perry & David Croft /*mus* Jimmy Perry & Derek Taverner (theme) /*BBC TV* (UK) /56 x 30m col.

It's a Knockout

Light Entertainment. BBC1 1966–82

Daft team games, with torrents of water splashed about, as towns competed (in silly, usually medieval-type costumes) for the right to represent Blighty in the European finals of *Jeux Sans Frontières.* The weekly competition was interspersed with the Mini-Marathon, a multi-element game overseen by Rugby League's whining sportscaster Eddie 'up and under' Waring. Former football referee Arthur Ellis supervised the games. Stuart Hall provided the corpsing commentary. The show was derived from a 50s series, *Top Town*, in which the local amateur artistes represented their town in competition.

There were a host of *It's a Knockout* specials – *It's a Celebrity Knockout, It's a Christmas Knockout, It's a Championship Knockout* and the nadir, *The Grand Knockout Tournament*, which involved most of the younger members of the Royal Family. The sight of Princess Anne, Prince Edward and the Duke and Duchess of York playing with giant beach balls ended the mystique of the monarchy in one swift hour, and began the institution's terminal decline in the affection of the British public.

CAST (presenters) David Vine (1967–71), Stuart Hall (1972–82), Eddie Waring (1967–79) /*pr* inc Barney Colehan, Cecil Korer, Geoff Wilson, John Street /*dr* inc Geoff Wilson, Philip S. Gilbert, John Rooney /*BBC TV* (UK) /approx. 300 x 45 /60m bw:col.

It's a Square World

Comedy. BBC 1960–4

Madly surreal sketch and gag comedy series, built around ex-Goon Michael Bentine, who was often in the pose of a lecturer/commentator. Not infrequently, Bentine's illustrative models came to life in animations and visual techniques which prefigured ➢*Monty Python's Flying Circus*. The most celebrated of the gags saw a Chinese junk sailing up the Thames to attack the House of Commons (that one was temporarily banned by the Corporation for fear it was too political at election time) and another depicted a 40-feet-long white whale trying to enter the Natural History Museum. (The filming of the sequence, which required 25 men standing inside the model whale to propel it along, caused traffic chaos on the streets of London.) Those assisting Bentine included Clive Dunn, Frank Thornton, Dick Emery and, in his first TV starring role, Ronnie Barker. Arguably the founding father of the satirical skit genre which would flower in the 60s, Bentine followed *Square World* with *All Square* (ITV, 1966–7), ➢*Michael Bentine's Potty Time* and 1977 BBC1 special, *Michael Bentine's Square World*.

CAST Michael Bentine, Frank Thornton, Clive Dunn, Ronnie Barker, Benny Lee, Dick Emery, Leon Thau, Joe Gibbons, Freddie Earlie, John Bluthal, Louis Mansi, Janette Rowsell, Len Lowe, Anthea Wyndham /*cr* Michael Bentine /*pr* G.B. Lupino, John Street, Joe McGrath /*wr* Michael Bentine, John Law /*BBC TV* (UK) /32 x 30m bw.

It's Gary Shandling's Show

Comedy. BBC2 1987–90

Unconventional comedy series in which toothsome American Gary Shandling played a fictitious version of himself and talked directly to the studio audience. Although set exclusively in Shandling's sitting room, the plots could go far, far off-beam: they included hosting the 1988 elections and creating the 'Shandlingland' theme park in the comfort of home. Elaborately designed to satirize the artificiality of TV (the credits began with the self-referential gag, 'This is the theme to Gary's Show'), the show was kept within the bounds of mainstream watchability by Shandling's own goofy persona and the subject matter which – the wilder plots notwithstanding – usually involved the staple of US sitcoms: family and friends. Almost symbolically, then, *Shandling's Show*, for all its post-modernist referencing of ➢*I Love Lucy* (the single set), *The Jack Benny Show* (the opening monologue) and *The Burns and Allen Show* (the addresses to the audience), ended its run with Gary marrying girlfriend Phoebe. Perhaps its sophisticated 'wackiness' was more apparent in Britain, where it ran against such home-grown products as the utterly predictable *No Place Like Home*.

CAST *Gary Shandling* Gary Shandling *Mrs Ruth Shandling* Barbara Cason *Nancy Bancroft* Molly Cheek *Leonard Smith* Paul Wilson *Pete Schumaker* Michael Tucci *Jackie Schumaker* Bernadette Birkett *Grant Schumaker* Scott Nemes *Phoebe Bass* Jessica Harper /*cr* Gary Shandling, Alan Zweibel /*exec pr* Bernie Brillstein, Brad Gery, Gary Shandling /*dr* inc Alan Rafkin, Paul Miller, Stan Lathan, Thomas Schlamme /*wr* Gary Shandling, Alan Zweibel, Jeff Franklin /*mus* Joey Carbone /*Showtime* (USA) /approx. 60 x 30m col /US tx Fox TV 1986–90.

It Takes a Thief

Adventure. ITV 1969

Tongue-in-cheek espionage series starring Robert Wagner (later ➢*Colditz*, ➢*Hart to Hart*) as a Raffles-like cat burglar, Alexander Mundy, paroled from San Jobel prison to ply his trade on behalf of the US government's SIA intelligence agency. Foreign travel, fast cars and faster women ensued. Fred Astaire appeared in several episodes as the hero's father, Al Mundy, the master of master thieves.

CAST *Alexander Mundy* Robert Wagner *Noah Bain* Malachi Throne *Wallie Powers* Edward Binns *Al Mundy* Fred Astaire /*cr* Collier Young /*pr* Frank Price, Jack Arnold, Gordon Oliver /*dr* inc Don Weis /*wr* inc Roland Kibbe, Glen A. Larson, Stephen J. Cannell / *mus* Dave Grusin /*Jack Arnold: Universal TV* (USA) / 65 x 50m col /US tx ABC 1968–7.

Ivanhoe

Adventure. ITV 1958–9

'Ivanhoe, Ivanhoe to adventure, bold adventure watch him go/There's no power on earth can stop what he's begun…' (theme song).

Sir Walter Scott's novel about the knightly scourge of evil Prince John was a natural port of call for ITV in the 50s, given its penchant for costume swashbucklers. Filmed at Beaconfield studios, the series had all the elements for actioner success – rousing swordplay, excellent stuntwork, clean-limbed direction – but was primarily raised above the throng by the casting of smooth Roger Moore (it was his TV series debut). The former cardigan model caught the notice of many and followed up the transatlantic success of *Ivanhoe* with ➢*Maverick*, ➢*The Saint*, ➢*The Persuaders!* and a sequence of James Bond movies. Two of the more noteworthy *Ivanhoe* guest appearances were by Christopher Lee, in 'The German Knight' segment, and actor–director John Schlesinger, in 'The Masked Bandits'.

A television industry clearly short of ideas or any sense of adventure itself has returned to *Ivanhoe* several times since Moore hung up his chain-mail. A BBC TV series (10 x 25m) was broadcast in 1970 with Eric Flynn in the title role; in 1982 an American TVM starring Anthony Andrews was presented; and in 1997 the BBC serialized the novel (in 6 x 55m parts) with a decidedly hirsute Steven Waddington as Wilfred of Ivanhoe – high on 12th-century atmosphere, romantic passion and action, but low on heroic charisma, it was produced by Jeremy Gwilt.

CAST *Ivanhoe* Roger Moore *Gurth* Robert Brown *Bart* John Pike *Prince John* Andrew Keir /*exec pr* Peter Rogers /*pr* Bernard Coote /*dr* inc Lance Comfort, Pennington Richards, Arthur Crabtree /*wr* inc Shirl Hendryx, Anthony Verney, Saul Levitt /*mus* Albert Elms /*A Sydney Box Television Presentation* (UK) / 39 x 30m bw /US tx Syndicated 1959.

Ivor the Engine

Children's. ITV 1959–63/BBC1 1976–7

Railway stories for when we were young, starring a tiny green puffer-train which worked for Merioneth and Llantisilly Rail Traction Company Limited. Jones the Steam was Ivor's driver, Dai Station was the man in charge of Llaniog station and Owen the Signal did the obvious.

Quaintly irresistible animation from Smallfilms. With the fantasy typical of their oeuvre (➢*The Clangers*, ➢*Noggin the Nog et al*), Ivor's boiler was fired by Idris, a small, homeless Welsh dragon.

CAST (narrators) Oliver Postgate, David Edwards, Anthony Jackson, Olwen Griffiths /*pr* Oliver Postgate /*wr* Oliver Postgate /*Smallfilms* (UK) /approx 50 x 5m bw:col.

J

Jackanory

Children's. BBC1 1965–

Long-running series of kid's stories read (from autocue) in 15-minute instalments by the thespian great and good. Standardly illustrated with drawn pictures (Quentin Blake and Barry Wilkinson were among those donating their talents), the tales have been presented in everything from a bare studio to one filled with packs of dogs (Judi Dench's reading of Philippa Pearce's *A Dog So Small*).

Begun as a short-term experiment, *Jackanory* grew into a quality TV institution (with parents entirely comfortable leaving their progeny at the feet of a Marks and Spencers of the airwaves). Thus it was that Rik Mayall's (➢*The Young Ones*) 1988 anarchic reading of Roald Dahl's anti-adult *George's Marvellous Medicine* caused apoplexy in Purley and a storm of mail to the BBC Duty Office.

In 1972 a sister series of playlets, *The Jackanory Playhouse*, was introduced and in 1983 an original *Jackanory* creation, *Jonny Briggs*, was spun off to a series of his own.

Some facts: Bernard Cribbins holds the record for the most story-telling appearances (111 plus), followed by Kenneth Williams; *The Hobbit* by J.R.R. Tolkien was presented for the 3000th edition; and in 1984 HRH Prince of Wales – one of the few non-showbiz narrators – read his own *The Old Man of Lochnagar*.

CAST (narrators) inc Bernard Cribbins, Kenneth Williams, Rik Mayall /*exec pr* Anna Home, Angela Beeching /*pr* Joy Whitby, David Coulter, Anna Home, Angela Beeching, David Turnball, Christine Secomble, Roger Singleton-Turner, Margie Barbour, Nel Romano /*dr* inc Michael Kerrigan /*BBC TV* (UK) /3500 x 15m bw:col.

The Jack Benny Show

Comedy. BBC 1956–60

Among the first comedians to see the possibilities of TV, Jack Benny (born Benjamin Kubelsky) transferred his long-running radio show over to the new medium virtually complete. This centred on his fictionalized persona as a pompous, ageing actor and outstanding miser, regularly and comically brought low by the foils who were his workmates. As such, the programme's intrinsic elements of extended sketches, invented characters and a 'family' of regulars marked a departure from the variety model of early television humour; *The Jack Benny Show* was the prototype situation comedy.

The show's regulars – all veterans from the radio run – were: Don Wilson, Benny's announcer and friend; secretary Mary Livingstone (Benny's real-life wife); Eddie Anderson who played black manservant Rochester; and Mel Blanc (later a Hanna–Barbera star), who voiced the engine of Benny's antique Maxwell car and appeared as his hapless violin teacher, Professor Le Blanc.

CAST Jack Benny, Mary Livingston, Eddie Anderson, Mel Blanc, Don Wilson, Russ Conway, Dennis Day, Phil Harris, Artie Auerbach, Ronald Coleman /*pr* inc Irving Fein, Fred DeCordova, Ralph Levy /*mus* Leo Robin, Ralph Rainger ('Love in Bloom' theme) /*Dumont* (USA) /approx. 170 x 30m bw /US tx CBS 1950–65 /NBC 1977.

The Jack Dee Show

Comedy. C4 1992–4

Stand-up routines from the deadpan comic, interpersed with music from guest artistes of a quality-kitsch type (Tom Jones, Leon Redbone, Alison Moyet), filmed at the fictitious Bohemia Club, a modern homage to the Talk of the Town. Dee's much noted sarcasm was largely superficial, hid no real malice and, therefore, after a series of beer advertisements which considerably raised his sharp-suited profile, the comedian easily crossed from alternative C4 to prime-time ITV with *Jack Dee's Saturday Night.*

CAST (host) Jack Dee /*pr* Dave Morley /*dr* Juliet May /*wr* Jack Dee /*mus* Seamus Beaghan / *Wonderdog Productions: Open Mike Productions* (UK) /18 x 35m, 2 x 60m col.

Jake and the Fatman
Crime. ITV 1989–91

After playing corpulent detectives ➢*Cannon* and ➢*Nero Wolfe,* William Conrad stayed within typecasting to play the Fatman, a former Hawaiian cop turned Honolulu DA, in this serviceable vehicle from Viacom. The Fatman's constant companion was his pet bulldog, Max, while the Jake of the title was the Fatman's pet PI, suave Jake Styles. A fair ratings runner in the USA, it received only sporadic screenings across the ITV network, and then invariably in the midnight hour.

CAST *J.L. 'Fatman' McCabe* William Conrad *Jake Styles* Joe Penny *Derek Mitchell* Alan Campbell /*cr* Dean Hargrove, Joel Steiger /*exec pr* Fred Silverman, Dean Hargrove, David Moessinger, Ed Waters /*dr* inc Bernard Kowalksi, Christian I. Nyby II, Russ Mayberry, Ron Satlof, Dale White, David Moessinger, Alexander Singer /*mus* Dick DeBenedictis /*A Viacom Production* (USA) /100+ x 60m col /US tx CBS 1987–.

Jane
Comedy. BBC2 1982

Starred curvacious, be-stockinged Glynis Barber (from ➢*Blake's 7,* later ➢*Dempsey and Makepeace*) as the famous WWII cartoon heroine whose escapades always ended in inadvertent disrobement. Innovatively placing live actors against drawn backgrounds, the consecutive nightly instalments were complimented by a weekend omnibus edition. Jane, originally drawn by Norman Pett for the *Daily Mirror,* returned in another sequence of clothes-losing adventures, *Jane in the Desert* (BBC2, 5 x 10m) in 1984, again with Barber as the heroine.

CAST *Jane* Glynis Barber /*pr* Ian Keill /*wr* Mervyn Haisman /*BBC TV* (UK) /5 x 10m col.

Jason King
Crime. ITV 1972–3

Spin-off from ➢*Department S,* in which the dandy detective-cum-author went solo on intrigues, these invariably necessitating foreign travel and girls, girls, girls. Nicola Harvester was King's publisher, Sir Brian and Ryland the men from the ministry who blackmailed him (over tax evasion) into working for them. In place of the beguiling baroque plots of *S,* the series substituted a not-altogether-successful parodying of fellow ITC actioners.

CAST *Jason King* Peter Wyngarde *Sir Brian* Dennis Price *Ryland* Ronald Lacey *Nicola Harvester* Ann Sharp /*cr* Dennis Spooner, Monty Berman /*pr* Monty Berman /*wr* inc Robert Banks Stewart /*mus* Laurie Johnson /*A Scroton Production for ITC* (UK) /26 x 60m col.

Jaycee and the Wheeled Warriors
Children's. ITV 1986

Animated adventures of 19-year-old Jaycee, as he searches the cosmos for his scientist father so that the roots of a magic plant can be reunited with each other and the evil Monster Minds destroyed. The Wheeled Warriors were Jaycee's space age crew, namely: Oon, a mechanical slave; Flora, a half-woman, half-plant; and Merc, a pilot for hire. Based on the line of Mattel toys.

CAST (voices) *Audric (Jaycee's father)* Dan Hennessey *Jaycee* Darin Baker *Oon* Luba Goy *Merc* Len Carlson *Flora* Valerie Politis *Saw Boos (leader of the Monster Minds)* Giulio Kukurugya /*A DIC Enterprise Production in association with WWP Productions* (USA) /66 x 30m col /US tx Syndicated 1985.

Jeeves and Wooster
Comedy. ITV 1990–3

Irresistible TV version of P.G. Wodehouse's stories of dimwit socialite Bertie Wooster and his capable valet Jeeves, starring Hugh Laurie and Stephen Fry (the pair seemingly born to play the title roles) in lively plots that contained the perfect formulaic blend of mad disastrous pashes, hair-brained moneymaking schemes and frightening dowager aunts. The sumptuous period 30s look was the responsibility of designer Eileen Diss. Later episodes were set in New York, after Bertie's escape from his imminent marriage to Honoria Glossop.

A previous BBC adaptation, *P.G. Wodehouse's World of Wooster* (BBC1, 1965–7), starred Ian Carmichael with Dennis Price as the gentleman's gentleman. What ho!

CAST *Bertie Wooster* Hugh Laurie *Jeeves* Stephen Fry *Aunt Agatha* Mary Wimbush /Elizabeth Spriggs *Aunt Dahlia* Brenda Bruce/Vivian Pickles /*pr* Brian Eastman /*dr* Robert Young, Simon Langton, Ferdinand Fairfax /*wr* Clive Exton /*mus* Anne Dudley /*Picture Partnership Productions: Carnival Films* (UK) /23 x 52m col.

Jennie, Lady Randolph Churchill

Drama. ITV 1974

Mini-series tracing the life of Jennie Jerome, the wealthy American who married Lord Randolph Churchill to become *mater* of Winston. A contrived transatlantic money-spinner of an idea (and timed to coincide with the centenary of the statesman's birth), it was redeemed by a flair for contextualizing history and the slick ease of Cellan Jones' direction.

CAST *Jennie Jerome/Lady Randolph Churchill* Lee Remick *Lord Randolph Churchill* Ronald Pickup *Duke of Marlborough* Cyril Luckham *Duchess of Marlborough* Rachel Kempson *Count Kinsky* Jeremy Brett *Winston Churchill* Warren Clarke *George Cornwallis-West* Christopher Cazenove *Mrs Patrick Campbell* Sian Philipps /*exec pr* Stella Richman /*pr* Andrew Brown /*dr* James Cellan Jones /*wr* Julian Mitchell /*Thames TV* (UK) /7 x 60m col /US tx PBS 1975.

Jesus of Nazareth

Drama. ITV 1977

Monumental biopic of Jesus Christ, as authorized by Franco Zefferelli and Lord Lew Grade. Humanistic rather than religious, co-written by Anthony Burgess, it appealed across religious boundaries (even unto the non-religious) to become a transworld hit. Much of the £9 million cost went on the star-studded cast, headed by Robert Powell as Christ, and three years of location filming in Tunisia and Italy.

CAST *Jesus Christ* Immad Cohen (boy)/Robert Powell (adult) *Virgin Mary* Olivia Hussey *Joseph* Yorgo Voyagis *Mary Magdalene* Anne Bancroft *Judas Iscariot* Ian McShane *Simon Peter* James Farentino *John the Baptist* Michael York *Simeon* Ralph Richardson *Nicodemus* Laurence Olivier *Balthazar* James Earl Jones *Melchior* Donald Pleasence *Gaspar* Fernando Rey *Joseph of Arimathea* James Mason *Herod the Great* Peter Ustinov *Salome* Isabel Mestres *Herod Antipas* Christopher Plummer *Caiaphas* Anthony Quinn *Pontius Pilate* Rod Steiger *Barabbas* Stacy Keach *The Adulteress* Claudia Cardinale *Joel* Oliver Tobias *Amos* Ian Bannen *Yehuda* Cyril Cusack /*exec pr* Bernard J. Kingham /*pr* Vincenzo Labella /*dr* Franco Zefferelli / *wr* Anthony Burgess, Suso Cecchi d'Amico, Franco Zeffirelli /*mus* Maurice Jarre /*ATV: RAI-TV* (UK /It) / 2 x 120m col.

The Jetsons

Children's. ITV 1963

➢*The Flintstones* gone space-age. A straight reversal of Hanna–Barbera's stone-age animation, *The Jetsons* sent a suburban American family not into the past but way into the future: the late 21st century AD.

Paterfamilias of the Jetson clan was harried George, who worked as a 'digital index operator' for Orbit City's Spacely Space Age Sprockets; his wife Jane (voiced by Penny Singleton of the *Blondie* movie series) was a shopaholic; daughter Judy was a teenybopper pupil at Orbit High; while nine-year-old son Elroy (voiced by Daws ➢'*Yogi Bear*' Butler) was an electronics whizzkid. Keeping clean the Jetsons' abode in Skypad Apartments – which could be raised and lowered according to the weather – was sarcastic robotmaid Rosie.

Against the pessimism endemic in sci-fi TV, *The Jetsons* presented a reassuringly optimistic vision of the future, complete with an abundance of technological labour-saving goods. Indeed, in popular memory the Jetsons' neat push-button, meal-dispensing 'Food-a-rac-acycle' and a seeing-eye vacuum cleaner are more usually recalled than the (fairly vapidly characterized) Jetsons themselves.

Although the series performed poorly on US prime time TV, it proved durable enough in syndication to merit the making of 41 more episodes in 1985. These introduced the suction-footed Orbity, an alien pet to join the Jetsons' dog, Astro. Ten more episodes were added in 1987, plus two full length features, *The Flintstones Meet the Jetsons* and *Rockin' With Judy Jetson*.

CAST (voices) *George Jetson* George O'Hanlon *Jane Jetson* Penny Singleton *Judy Jetson* Janet Waldo *Elroy Jetson/Cogswell/Henry* Daws Butler *Rosie/Stella Spacely* Jean Vander Pyl *Astro* Don Messick *Orbity* Frank Welker /*exec pr* William Hanna, Joseph Barbera /*dr* William Hanna, Joseph Barbera /*wr* Warren Foster, Mike Maltese, Harvey Bullock, Larry Markes, Tony Benedict /*mus* Hoyt Curtin, William Hanna, Joseph Barbera (theme) /*Hanna-Barbera* (USA) /24 x 39m, 51 x 30m col.

Jewel in the Crown

Drama. ITV 1985

Truly epic (four years in the making) Granada production of Paul Scott's literary *The Raj Quartet*, set during the dying years of British colonial rule in India, 1942 to 1947. The plot concerned the cross-race affair between new English arrival to Mysore nurse Daphne Manners, and Indian reporter Hari Kumar, which turned to tragedy when Manners was raped in the Bibighar Gardens. Despite his protestations of innocence, Kumar was arrested by vindictive security officer Ronald Merrick (Tim Pigott-Smith), a repressed homosexual jealous of Kumar's privileged upbringing. Sensitive, stunning performances (by, among others, Peggy Ashcroft, Geraldine James and Charles Dance) brought out all the pathetic immoralities and snobberies of colonialism in a rare televisual engagement of heart, head and, thanks to visually stunning teletography, the eye. (Although most filming took place on location in India, parts of Britain were also mocked up to look like the sub-Continent, with Salford Dock even passing for Bombay.) After being awarded five BAFTAs (including Best Actor for Piggott-Smith), the £5 million jewel in Granada's dramatic crown went on to win the 1984 International Emmy for Best Drama.

CAST *Daphne Manners* Susan Wooldridge *Hari Kumar* Art Malik *Supt Ronald Merrick* Tim Piggott-Smith *Sarah Layton* Geraldine James *Susan Layton /Bingham* Wendy Morgan *Sgt Guy Perron* Charles Dance *Lady Manners* Rachel Kempson *Count Dimitri Bronowski* Eric Porter *Barbie Batchelor* Peggy Ashcroft *'Sophie' Dixon* Warren Clarke *Mildred Layton* Judy Parfitt /*pr* Christopher Morahan /*dr* Christopher Morahan, Jim O'Brien /*wr* Ken Taylor /*Granada TV* (UK) /1 x 120m, 13 x 60m col.

Jim'll Fix It

Children's. BBC1 1975–8

'Now then, now then...'

Saturday teatime show in which ageing, peroxided medallion-man DJ Sir Jimmy Savile made the pipe dreams of kiddie (and occasionally adult) viewers come true. The requests, sent in by the postbag-full, ranged from interviewing the PM to piloting Concorde, with the lucky selectees not only having their wishes made real but getting a 'Jim Fixed It For Me Badge' to boot.

CAST (presenters) Sir James Savile OBE /*pr* Roger Ordish /*dr* inc Stanley Appel, Phil Bishop, Paul Ciani, Rick Gardner, Peter Campbell, Marcus Mortimer, Tony Newman /*BBC TV* (UK) /approx. 500 x 30m col.

Joe 90

Children's. ITV 1968

In which bespectacled, nine-year-old Joe McClaine has the ability to acquire temporarily the intelligence and abilities of anyone on the globe, thanks to a gadget – the Brain Impulse Galvanoscope Record and Transfer, or BIG RAT – invented by his equally bespectacled scientist father, Prof. 'Mac' McClaine. Luckily for humanity, both boy and machine are put to the use of good, in the form of the World Intelligence Network, which sends Joe on its most secret missions (stealing Russian jet fighters, obtaining the antidote to a building-eating Oriental virus, recovering gold stolen by a dictator) and accords him the status 'Most Special Agent'. Although Joe's fresh-faced visage is his best disguise, he hides his WIN code book in his school case.

Largely unloved Gerry Anderson 'Supermarionation', whose juvenile hero prevented the crossover essential to the success of other 21st-century shows. Rupert Davies (➢*Maigret)* and Keith Alexander (*Topo Gigio*) were among those giving voice to the puppets on strings.

CAST (voices) *Joe 90* Len Jones *Mac* Rupert Davies *Shane Weston* David Healy *Sam Loover* Keith Alexander *Mrs Harris* Sylvia Anderson /*cr* Gerry & Sylvia Anderson /*exec pr* Reg Hill /*pr* David Lane /*dr* Desmond Saunders, Alan Perry, Leo Eaton, Ken Turner, Gerry Anderson /*wr* Gerry & Sylvia Anderson, Tony Barwick, Shane Rimmer, David Lane, Desmond Saunders & Keith Wilson, Donald James, John Lucarotti, Pat Dunlop /*mus* Barry Gray /*A*

Century 21 Production in Association with ATV for ITV World-Wide (UK) /30 x 30m col /US tx 1968.

John Craven's Newsround
Children's. BBC1 1972–

The day's news digested for thc 7–12 sct in a manner child-friendly but not (usually) patronizing.

Like the BBC's earlier *Children's Newsreel*, introduced in 1950, *John Craven's Newsround* bent towards youthful matters but unlike that programme it did not eschew 'hard' news, even breaking such stories as the Challenger shuttle disaster in 1986. When anchorman Craven departed the series in 1989 (eventually to tip up on the airwaves as presenter of *Country Files*), it carried on as, simply, *Newsround*. A brace of programmes developed from the series: a 1977–8 round-up entitled *Newsround Weekly* and the more enduring mini-documentary slot, *Newsround Extra* (BBC1, 1981–).

Initially transmitted twice weekly at 5.00 p.m., *Newsround* went daily (weekends excepting) in 1979.

CAST (presenters) John Craven, Paul McDowell, Roger Finn, Helen Rollason, Juliet Morris, Julie Etchingham, Krishnan Guru-Murthy, Chris Rogers /*cr* Edward Barnes /*pr* inc Jill Roach, Eric Rowan /*BBC TV* (UK) /2000 x 10m col.

Johnny Ringo
Western. Lifestyle 1992

Once upon a time in the West a gunfighter called Johnny Ringo swapped his black hat for a tin star to become sheriff of Velardi, Arizona. There he kept order with a smoking LeMat Special (one barrel fired .45 bullets, the other shotgun shells), with young Deputy Cully providing back-up.

Saddled with the occasional clunking horse-opera cliché (in one episode Ringo sang, *à la* Roy Rogers), this early production from Aaron Spelling (later to become the master of the American sudster) was top-hand stuff, particularly in its psychologically inclined scripts.

Although Ringo was a real-life historical figure, a minor participant in the Earp–McLaury feud which led to the gunfight at the OK Corral, Don Durant's clean-cut character bore no relation.

CAST *Johnny Ringo* Don Durant *Deputy Cully 'Kid' Adonas* Mark Goddard *Cason Thomas* Terence DeMarney *Laura Thomas* Karen Sharpe /*cr* Aaron Spelling /*pr* Aaron Spelling /*wr* inc Richard Levinson, William Link /*mus* Don Durant (theme vocal) / *Four Star: Pamaron: Zane Grey Productions* (USA) / 38 x 25m bw /US tx CBS 1959–60.

Johnny Staccato
Crime. ITV 1969

Noir-ish cases of a 1950s jazz musician turned private detective.

Much criticized on its US debut for being a carbon copy of ➢*Peter Gunn*, this John Cassavetes series more than made up for its lack of originality with sharp performances (especially from Cassavetes himself) and stylish teletography, both underscored by use of pulsating jazz rhythms. The theme was composed by Elmer Bernstein, while jazz men Barney Kessel, Red Mitchell and John Williams (who would later compose the music for *Star Wars*) were frequently to be glimpsed playing in the background shadows of Waldo's club in downtown NY, Staccato's HQ.

Cassavetes used the money made from the show to finance his directorial debut film, *Shadows* (1959); as with his subsequent work as director, the movie was experimental and Cassavetes remains one of the biggest influences on American avant-garde film. He is probably more familiar, however, for his before-the-camera roles in *The Dirty Dozen* (1967) and as Mia Farrow's betraying husband in *Rosemary's Baby* (1968).

CAST *Johnny Staccato* John Cassavetes *Waldo* Eduardo Cianelli /*cr* John Cassavetes /*pr* William Freye /*dr* inc John Cassavetes, Bernard Gaird, Joseph Pevney, Paul Henreid /*wr* inc John Cassavetes /*mus* Elmer Bernstein (theme) /*MCA: Universal* (USA) /27 x 25m bw /US tx NBC 1959–60 (as *Staccato*): ABC 1960.

Joking Apart
Comedy. BBC2 1993–5

'My wife left me. She said I was incapable of taking anything seriously. I just laughed.'

Developed from a 1991 one-off *Comedy Aside*, Stephen Moffat's (➢*Press Gang*) acidic sitcom related, via flashbacks, the brief and failed marriage of flippant scriptwriter Mark Taylor. A second series was dominated by the complicated carnal consequences of his mistaken bedding of Tracy, a friend's wife.

CAST *Mark Taylor* Robert Bathurst *Becky Johnson* Fiona Gillies *Tracy* Tracie Bennett *Robert* Paul Raffield *Trevor* Paul-Mark Elliott /*cr* Stephen Moffat /*pr* Andre Ptaszynski /*dr* Bob Spiers, John Kirby /*wr* Stephen Moffat /*Pola Jones Film Production* (UK) /12 x 30m col.

Jonny Quest

Children's. BBC1 1965

Superlative *Boy's Own* cartoon from Hanna–Barbera featuring the 11-year-old of the title, who jetted around the world with his bearded scientist father investigating strange phenomena. Jonny's travelling companions were a mystical Indian boy called Hadji, a bulldog called Bandit and his tutor-bodyguard, Roger 'Race' Bannon, whose pecs tended to get them out of the trouble that Dr Quest's wits could not. Character voice work was supplied by, among others, Tim Matthieson (aka Matheson), later to take his thespian career to the movies.

In 1986, after doing the rounds of Saturday morning US TV for nearly two decades, a tranche of 13 new *JQ* episodes was added. Expensively animated, their style was less red blooded than the originals, in line with the general jitters about violence which gripped the industry in the mid-80s. Then, in a clear trade on the revival of the action-adventure format led by the *Batman* movies, the show was updated in 1996 as *The Real Adventures of Jonny Quest.* This tampered with the unique essence of Jonny Quest – that he was an ordinary boy, not a superhero – by drawing him as a gym-freak. The adventures themselves took place in a virtual reality environment called Quest World. Hollywood star George Segal voiced the part of Dr Benton Quest.

CAST (voices) *Jonny Quest* Tim Matthieson *Race Bannon* Mike Road *Dr Benton Quest* John Stephenson/Don Messick *Hadji* Danny Bravo *Dr Zin* Vic Perrin /*pr* William Hanna, Joseph Barbera /*dr* William Hanna, Joseph Barbera /*wr* inc Arthur Pierson, Doug Wildey /*mus* Hoyt Curtin /*Hanna–Barbera* (USA) /26 x 25m col /US tx ABC 1964–5.

Josie and the Pussycats

Children's. BBC1 1971–2

Animated adventures of a globe-gigging all-girl band.

Adequate Hanna–Barbera cartoon filler, modelled on *The Archies*, succeeded by the incredulity-breaking *Josie and the Pussycats in Outer Space* (1972–4). Among the singers was one 'Cherie Moore' (aka Cheryl Jean Stopelmoor), later to ascend to *Charlie's Angels* in her married name of Cheryl Ladd.

CAST *Josie* Janet Waldo (speaking)/Cathy Douglas (singing) *Melody* Jackie Joseph (speaking)/Cherie Moore (singing) *Valerie* Barbara Pariot (speaking) / Patricia Holloway (singing) *Alexandra* Sherry Alberoni *Alexander* Casey Kaseem *Sebastian* Don Messick /*pr* William Hanna, Joseph Barbera /*Hanna–Barbera* (USA) /104 x 22m col /US tx CBS 1970–2.

Jossy's Giants

Children's. BBC1 1986

One of a dribble (along with *Striker* and *Murphy's Mob*) of 80s soccer sagas for the junior viewer. The comically inclined *Jossy's Giants* followed the fortunes of a team of 13-year-old school children – the Clipton Grasshoppers – as managed by retired pro-footballer Jossy Blair. Created by Sid Waddell, the Tyneside darts commentator.

CAST *Jossy Blair* Jim Barclay /*cr* Sid Waddell /*pr* Paul Stone /*dr* Edward Pugh /*wr* Sid Waddell /*BBC TV* (UK) /12 x 25m col.

Journey to the Centre of the Earth

Children's. BBC1 1968–9

On their voyage to the Earth's core, Professor Lindenbrook and his expedition are trapped underground by evil Count Sacknussem. To reach the surface they must battle past the usual nasties (swampmen, icemen, cavemen) who inhabit the land of kiddie television.

A crude animated adaptation of Jules Verne's sci-fi novel, whose implausibility was only attested to by the fact that the expeditioners could apparently see underground without the aid of lights.

CAST (voices) *Prof. Oliver Lindenbrook/Count Sacknussem* Ted Knight *Cindy Lindenbrook* Jane Webb *Alec Hewitt/Lars/Torg* Pat Harrington Jr /*exec pr* Louis Scheimer, Norman Prescott /*dr* Hal Sutherland /*wr* inc Ken Sobel /*mus* Gordon Zahler /*Filmation: Fox TV* (USA) /17 x 30m col /US tx ABC 1967–9.

Journey to the Unknown

Drama. ITV 1968

Hammer Films' second TV venture (after *Tales of Frankenstein*) was an American-financed anthology, mostly of supernatural suspensers but also incorporating sci-fi and murder most foul. Executive producer Joan Harrison was an associate of Alfred Hitchcock and a suitably Hitchcockian tone of chill menace lay over the eclectic proceedings. With starry Americans in the lead roles (the episode 'Do Me A Favour – Kill Me!' even drew Joseph Cotton on to the payroll) and dependable, actorly Brits in support, *Journey to the Unknown* premiered in the USA to decent ratings. In Britain, however, screenings were scattered across the ITV regions (beginning with LWT) for several years.

CAST inc Joseph Cotton, Barbara Bel Geddes, Edward Fox, Jane Asher, Roddy McDowall, Julie Harris, Dennis Waterman, David Hedison, Stefanie Powers, Nanette Newman, Edward Hardwicke, George Mahraris /*exec pr* Joan Harrison, Norman Lloyd /*pr* Anthony Hinds /*dr* Peter Sasdy, Alan Gibson, Michael Lindsay-Hogg, Gerry O'Hara, Rex Firkin, Don Chaffey, Robert Stevens, Roy Ward Baker, John Gibson, Peter Duffell, Noel Howard, James Hill / *wr* inc Oscar Millard, Anthony Skene, Robert Bloch / *mus* Harry Robinson (theme) /*Hammer Films Productions: 20th Century Fox TV* (UK /USA) / 17 x 60m col /US tx ABC 1968.

Judge Dee

Crime. ITV 1969

Praiseworthy attempt to try something televisually new in the TV-crime genre, being the cases of a 7th-century Chinese judge-detective. These were adapted from Robert Van Gulik's novels, themselves based on a real-life investigative magistrate of the T'ang dynasty. Although the production was excellently executed, the casting suffered a laughable yellowing-up of Caucasian actors, among them Michael Robbins from sitcom ➢*On the Buses*. Only six of the seven produced episodes were screened.

CAST *Judge Dee* Michael Goodliffe *Tao* Garfield Morgan /*pr* Howard Baker /*wr* John Wiles /*mus* Derek Hilton /*A Granada Television Network Production* (UK) /6 x 60m col.

Julia

Comedy. ITV 1970

The first TV series since *Beulah* (1950) to star a black woman and, unlike that show's maid-heroine, one in a 'prestige' occupation. Diahann Carroll (later ➢*Dynasty*) took the title role as a beautiful nurse trying to raise a son after her pilot husband was KIA in Vietnam. There were criticisms that the lack of discrimination shown to Julia at work (an aerospace factory) and home (a housing 'project') made the show unrealistic, but it nevertheless broke the studio colour ceiling to emerge as a fully fledged hit. It was ironic, then, that US network NBC had only aired the series (in a coffin-spot, opposite CBS's *The Red Skelton Show*) for the moral kudos of making a show with a black principal and had no expectation of it succeeding.

CAST *Julia Baker* Diahann Carroll *Corey Baker* Marc Coppage *Dr Morton Chegley* Lloyd Nolan *Marie Waggerdorn* Betty Beaird *Earl J. Waggerdorn* Michael Link *Hannah Yarby* Lurene Tuttle /*pr* Hal Kanter / *Twentieth Century Fox TV* (USA) /86 x 30m col / US tx NBC 1968–71.

Juliet Bravo

Crime. BBC1 1980–5

A policewoman's lot is not a happy one. Inspector Jean Darblay (Stephanie Turner) endures sexism from male officers at fictional Hartley station in Lancashire; however, she manages to solve the pettily realistic, thoroughly human cases that come her way.

Debuting in the same year as another British policewoman series, ➢*The Gentle Touch*, this effective, low-key show came somewhat surprisingly from Ian Kennedy Martin, creator of actioner ➢*The Sweeney* (in which Turner had served briefly as George Carter's wife). When, in the fourth season, Darblay was promoted upstairs, her shoes were filled by Kate Longton (Anna Carteret), who kept the police call sign that gave the show its title.

CAST *Insp. Jean Darblay* Stephanie Turner *Insp. Kate Longton* Anna Carteret *Tom Darblay* David Hargreaves *Sgt Joe Beck* David Ellison *Sgt Joe Parrish* Noel Collins *PC Danny Sparks* Mark Botham *PC Brian Kelleher* C.J. Allen /*cr* Ian Kennedy Martin /*pr* Terence Williams, Peter Cregeen, Geraint Morris /*dr* inc Adrian Shergold, Paul Ciappessoni, Jan Sargent, Carol Wilks, Jonathan Alwyn, Pennant Roberts, Tristan de Vere Cole /*wr* inc Ian Kennedy Martin, Paula Milne, Tony Parker, Wally K. Daly /*BBC TV* (UK) /82 x 50m col.

Jupiter Moon
Sci-fi. BSB 1990

The world's first sci-fi soap opera. Invented by William Smethurst of ➢*Crossroads* infamy, and only viewable on its original transmission by those possessing a fantastic satellite device called a 'squarial'; few did, and of those even fewer cared for amateurish *Jupiter Moon*. For the record, it followed the lives of the students and crew of a college on the Christopher Columbus space station in the year 2050.

CAST *Eliot Creasy* Andy Rashleigh *Finbow Lewis* Phil Willmott *Chantal de Grecy* Caroline Evans *Cats Kitebrook* Toby Rolt/Nick Hutchison *Piers Gilpin* Dominic Arnold *Jorge Amado* Peter Polycarpou /*cr* William Smethurst /*pr* William Smethurst /*Primetime, Andromeda* (UK) /150 x 30m col.

Just Good Friends
Comedy. BBC1 1983–6

Class-based sitcom from John Sullivan with sometime songster Paul Nicholas (he of the unforgettable 'Dancing with the Captain') as cockney turf accountant Vince and Jan Francis as his jilted-at-the-altar middle-class girlfriend Penny. Five years on, the twosome meet by chance and, almost against their wills, enter into a relationship (off, on, love, hate) again. After a somewhat protracted will-they-won't-they agony, the pair eventually tie the knot.

Of gentle, even semi-tragic stripe, *Just Good Friends* retained Sullivan's eye for pleasing caricature, here in the shape of Vince's grotesquely coarse scrap-metal-merchant father, Les, and brassy mother, Rita.

CAST *Vince Pinner* Paul Nicholas *Penny Warrender* Jan Francis *Rita Pinner* Ann Lynn *Les Pinner* Shaun Curry *Clifford 'Cliffy' Pinner* Adam French *Daphne Warrender* Sylvia Kay *Norman Warrender* John Ringham /*cr* John Sullivan /*pr* Ray Butts /*wr* John Sullivan /*BBC TV* (UK) /22 x 30m col.

Just Jimmy
Comedy. ITV 1964–6

Translation to TV of the radio favourite about the naughty schoolboy, *The Clitheroe Kid*. Diminutive Lancashire comedian James Robertson 'Jimmy' Clitheroe played the lead role in both mediums. The sitcom gained little in the change of medium, save for Molly Sugden as the exasperated Ma Clitheroe.

CAST *Jimmy Clitheroe* himself *Mrs Clitheroe* Mollie Sugden *Danny* Danny Ross /*cr* Jimmy Clitheroe /*pr* Ronnie Baxter /*wr* Ronnie Taylor, Frank Roscoe, Alick Hayes, Fred Robinson /*ABC* (UK) /90 x 25m bw.

Just William
Children's. BBC TV (UK) 1962–3

Richmal Crompton's famous tales of mischievous schoolboy William Brown were first prepared for broadcast by the authoress herself, in a BBC radio adaptation which ran from 1945–52. Obvious stuff for television, the material translated easily to the small screen, not least because adaptor C.E. Webber strayed little from Crompton's characterizations, therefore astutely avoiding upsetting viewer preconceptions. A 14-year-old Dennis Waterman played the leader of the Outlaws in the first series, to be replaced by Denis Gilmore in the second. Adequate stuff.

Far superior was LWT's 1977 *Just William*, which played to colourful caricature (and against fautless period settings), and was only made more pleasing by the superb casting of Diana Dors as Mrs Bott and Bonnie Langford as her lisping daughter Violet Elizabeth, the boy anti-hero's arch-enemy. William was played by Adrian Dannatt. The adaptor was Keith Dewhurst.

As if to prove that you cannot keep a bad boy down, *Just William* returned again to the screen in 1994, with Oliver Rokison in the short trousers.

CAST *William Brown* Dennis Waterman/Denis Gilmore *Ginger* Christopher Witty *Henry* Kaplan Kaye *Douglas* Carlo Cura *Violet Elizabeth Bott* Gillian Gostling /*pr* Leonard Chase /*wr* C.E. Webber /*BBC TV* (UK) /12 x 25m bw.

Karaoke/Cold Lazarus
Drama. BBC1/C4 1996

The valedictory dramas of Dennis Potter, dutifully produced and transmitted by the BBC and C4 in joint collaboration as per his dying wish. Half drama, half knowing Potter-pastiche (complete with references to the playwright's previous work, non-linear narratives, cockney tarts and grouchy middle-aged men), *Karaoke* followed screenwriter Daniel Feeld as he prowled the streets of London under the heavy burdens of cancer, alcoholism and the feeling that his latest gangster-film script seems to be coming to life around him. Although few critics dared say it, the work was alienatingly arch and self-indulgent. Most lingered on the positive: Renny Rye's stylish direction (which fully justified Potter's faith in him), the intoxicatingly garish sets, Albert Finney's most genuine performance for years, and a masterful cameo by Roy Hudd as the spooneristic agent, Baglin. BBC1 struggled to find four million viewers.

CAST *Daniel Feeld* Albert Finney *Nick Balmer* Richard E. Grant *Ben Baglin* Roy Hudd *Sandra Sollars* Saffron Burrows *Arthur 'Pig' Mailion* Hywel Bennett / *cr* Dennis Potter / *pr* Kenith Trodd, Rosemarie Whitman / *dr* Renny Rye / *wr* Dennis Potter / *Whistling Gypsy* (UK) /4 x 60m col.

And then there was *Cold Lazarus*, linked to *Karaoke* by the character of Feeld, but entirely different in type. A sci-fi show set 374 years after Feeld's death, it featured the attempts of a tight-budget group of cryogenic scientists to break into the screenwriter's synapses. Outside the hi-tech Masdon Science Centre laboratory, a corporate mogul (shades of Potter's *bête noire*, Rupert Murdoch) schemed to exploit Feeld's freed memories on the worldwide screen and a London terrorist organization called Reality or Nothing (RON) sought to explode society's quietude. Allusive, politically engaged, its elements of overblown sci-fidom a pleasing parody of a bad sci-fi serial. *Cold Lazarus* made for a stunning exit. It was also a hard gripping futuristic thriller.

CAST *Daniel Feeld* Albert Finney *Emma Porlock* Frances de la Tour *Martina Matilda Masdon* Diane Ladd *David Siltz* Henry Goodman *Fyodor Glazunov* Ciaran Hinds / *cr* Dennis Potter / *pr* Kenith Trodd, Rosemarie Whitman / *dr* Renny Rye / *wr* Dennis Potter / *Whistling Gypsy* (UK) /4 x 60m col.

Kate
Drama. ITV 1970–2

The personal problems of a London magazine agony aunt, widowed Kate Graham, scribe of the 'Dear Monica' page for *Heart and Home*.

Reasonably successful Yorkshire TV drama-soap, which had Penelope Keith (playing Penelope Keith to perfection) on the payroll. Fay Weldon contributed several scripts.

CAST *Kate Graham* Phyllis Calvert *Wenda Padbury* Penelope Keith *Donald Killearn* Jack Hedley *Miss Wren* Isabel Dean / *pr* Stanley Miller, Peter Mortimer, Pieter Rogers / *dr* inc Michael Currer-Briggs, June Wyndham-Davies, Paul Annett / *wr* inc Alan Falconer, Susan Pleat, Fay Weldon / *Yorkshire TV* (UK) /38 x 60m col.

Kate and Allie
Comedy. C4 1982–9

Were two NY divorcees obliged by impecunious finances to share an apartment. Their kids came too. Although Kate, a hi-energy swinging 60s liberal, and Allie, a quiet conservative, had little in common, they female-bonded like glue, even setting up in business (catering) together. Towards the end of the show's run Allie remarried but continued to live with Kate since her sportscaster husband worked the week in Washington DC. A distaff version of ➢*The Odd Couple*, but intelligently done. Jane Curtin collected two Emmys for her portrayal of Allie.

CAST *Kate McCardle* Susan Saint James *Allie Lowell* Jane Curtin *Emma McCardle* Ari Meyers *Chip Lowell* Frederick Koehler *Jennie Lowell* Alison Smith /*cr* Sherry Kobin /*exec pr* Mort Lachman, Merrill Grant, Bill Persky, Saul Turtletaub, Bernie Orenstein /*pr* Bob Randall, Anne Flett, Chuck Ranberg /*dr* inc Bill Persky, Linda Day /*wr* inc Bob Randall /*Reeves Entertainment* (USA) /111+ x 30m col /US tx CBS 1984–8.

Kavanagh QC

Crime. ITV 1995–

Marked icon John Thaw's return to TV after the drubbing he recieved for *A Year in Provence*. Tailor-made for Thaw at the behest of ➢*Inspector Morse* commissioner and Central Films MD, Ted Childs, the actor played a bewigged QC in a legal series of glossy professionalism and gripping courtroom detail. And made to an absolutely safe dramatic formula: Kavanagh was a working-class northerner (anti-hero outsider, champion of the underdog) married to a daughter of the aristocracy (colour-supplement lifestyle), whose relationship was affected by extra-marital liaisons (soap opera). Not infrequently the problems occupying *chez* Kavanagh – which also included two teenage progeny – were morally similar to those filling Kavanagh's in-court hours. The programme garnered 13 million viewers in its debut season alone. It was produced by Chris Kelly, also presenter of BBC2's *Food and Drink* show.

CAST *James Kavanagh QC* John Thaw *Lizzie Kavanagh* Lisa Harrow *Kate Kavanagh* Daisy Bates *Matt Kavanagh* Tom Brodie *Peter Foxcott* Oliver Ford Davies *Jeremy Aldermarten* Nicholas Jones *Julia Piper* Anna Chancellor /*exec pr* Ted Childs /*pr* Chris Kelly /*dr* Renny Rye, Andrew Grieve, Paul Greengrass, Colin Gregg /*wr* Adrian Hodges, Matthew Hall, Russell Lewis, Paul Hines /*Carlton UK* (UK) /212+ x 90m col.

Keeping Up Appearances

Comedy. BBC1 1990–5

Roy Clarke situation comedy featuring Mrs Hyacinth Bucket ('It's pronounced Bouquet!'), a matronly class-climber – she dressed for elevenses, and polished the leaves of her trees – permanently undone by her own social gaffes and her embarrassing council-house relatives. Patricia Routledge bloomed as the matron from suburban hell, with fine support work from Clive Swift as her long-suffering husband, Judy Cornwall and Shirley Stelfox as her slutty sisters Daisy and Rose, and Geoffrey Hughes (➢*Coronation Street*) as her be-vested, S-reg-Cortina-driving brother-in-law Onslow. Josephine Tewson and David Griffin were the next-door brother and sister who cowered at the sight of the advancing Hyacinth. The aural joke of bucket/bouquet was not new, dating back to British black and white cinema, but Clarke turned the screw of social observation to full effect and hit-status.

CAST *Hyacinth Bucket* Patricia Routledge *Richard Bucket* Clive Swift *Daisy* Judy Cornwall *Rose* Shirley Stelfox/Mary Millar *Onslow* Geoffrey Hughes *Elizabeth* Josephine Tewson *Emmett Hawksworth* David Griffin *Vicar* Gerald Sim /Jeremy Gittins *Daddy* George Webb /*cr* Roy Clarke /*pr* Harold Snoad /*dr* Harold Snoad /*wr* Roy Clarke /*BBC TV* (UK) /40 x 30m; 4 x approx. 60m col.

Keep It in the Family

Comedy. ITV 1980–3

Ho-hum domestic sitcom about the ups and downs of the Rush family: cartoonist *pater* Dudley, *mater* Muriel, and lightly troublesome daughters Susan and Jacqui. It pleased in its day, with a peak viewing of 18.1 million. Robbie Coltrane guested in the episode 'A Matter of Principle'.

The same programme title had been used by David Nobbs and Peter Vincent for their familial sitcom for YTV, transmitted in 1971.

CAST *Dudley Rush* Robert Gillespie *Muriel Rush* Pauline Yates *Susan Rush* Stacy Dorning *Jacqui Rush* Jenny Quayle /Sabrina Franklyn *Duncan Thomas* Glyn Houston /*cr* Johnnie Mortimer, Brian Cooke /*pr* Mark Stuart, Robert Reed /*wr* Johnnie Mortimer, Brian Cooke, Alex Shearer, Dave & Greg Freeman /*Thames TV* (UK) /31 x 30m col.

Kelly Monteith

Comedy. BBC2 1979–84

Homelife with wry American comedian Kelly Monteith and his wife.

A BBC-produced hybrid of sitcom and sketch-show, this likeable, bright series cast Gabrielle Drake (➢*UFO*, ➢*Crossroads*) as Monteith's British spouse. Unusually, much of the wit was delivered by Monteith directly to camera in asides as he wandered his flat.

CAST Kelly Monteith, Gabrielle Drake, Louis Mansi, Nicholas McCardle, Michael Stainton / *pr* James Moir / *wr* Kelly Monteith, Neil Shand / *mus* Ronnie Hazelhurst / *BBC TV* (UK) /24 x 30m col /US tx TEC 1982–3.

The Ken Dodd Show

Light Entertainment. BBC 1959–63/BBC1 1966

Those living in the 60s and early 70s knew when they would reach senility, for that would be the moment when they found Liverpudlian comedian Ken Dodd OBE funny. A spiritual heir of crude music hall, Dodd – with his trademark mop hair and buck teeth (the result of a boyhood cycling accident) – purveyed idiot routines and unsubtle caricatures. He was abetted in this stagey TV production by a troupe of miniature 'Diddymen' characters and a prop called a 'tickling stick' (to you and me a feather duster), and ended in a ditty that became a record that became a No. 1 hit in 1965, 'Tears'. The catchphrase was 'How're you diddling, Missus?' Among Dodd's other TV shows were *Ken Dodd in 'Funny You Should Say That'* (ATV, 1972), *The Ken Dodd Laughter Show* (Thames, 1979), and *Ken Dodd's World of Laughter* (BBC1, 1974–6).

CAST inc Ken Dodd, David Hamilton, Arthur Mullard, the Irving Davies Dancers, Ruth Kettlewell / *pr* Barney Colehan, Duncan Wood, Michael Hurll / *wr* Eddie Braben, Ken Dodd / *BBC TV* (UK) / 70 x 60m bw: col.

The Kenny Everett Video Show

Comedy. ITV 1978–80

A 'shock-jock' before the term was invented, the radio DJ first took his patented madcap humour to TV in 1968 with a Granada series forgotten by everyone, even those who made it. This was *Nice Time*, in which Everett's unlikely co-hosts were ➢*Candid Camera*'s Jonathan Routh and feminist academic Germaine Greer. The director was John Birt, who would rise without trace to become Director General of the BBC. Everett was awarded his own series in 1970, *The Kenny Everett Explosion* (LWT, 1970), but it was *The Kenny Everett Video Show* for Thames that produced his best TV. He was then still enthusiastic about the medium, especially the possibilities of the new video gadgetry. Presented in a studio empty except for a wall of TV monitors, the show was an adolescent half-hour of gleeful erotics (courtesy of Arlene Philips' dance troupe, Hot Gossip) and comic sketches, with Everett playing the caricatures Sid Snot, Marcel Wave, an animated sci-fi version of himself known as Captain Kremmen, punk Gizzard Puke, and a Dolly Parton character (known off-air as Cupid Stunt) of mountainous *décolletage.* Similarly breaking the boundaries of 'the best possible taste' was Everett's buxom assistant Miss Whiplash (Cleo Rocas).

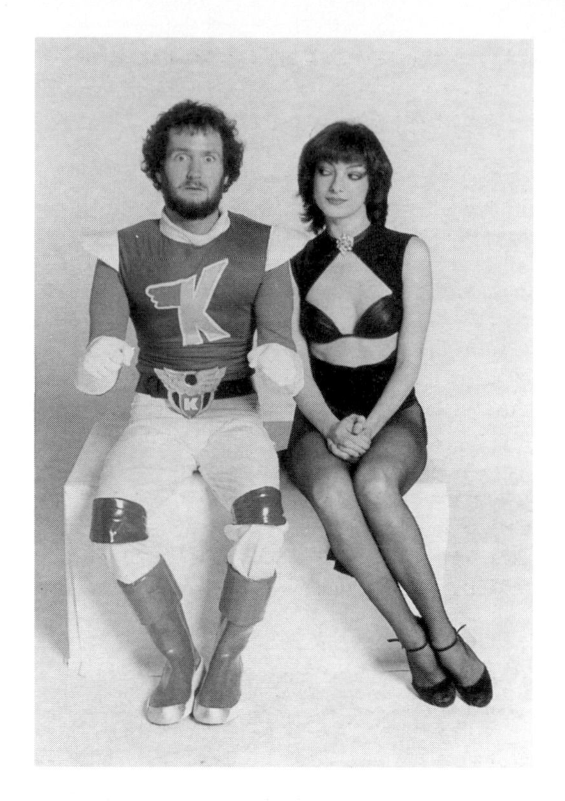

It was all done in the worst possible taste ... *The Kenny Everett Video Show.* The star – who was born Maurice Cole – died of an AIDS-related illness.

After numerous appearances on ➢*Blankety Blank* and fronting the short-lived *The Kenny Everett Video Cassette* (Thames TV, 1981), Everett presented the *The Kenny Everett Television Show* (1982–88) for BBC1. Lacking the originality of the *Video Show* (and Hot Gossip), it nonetheless produced one of Everett's greatest video gags, a Bee Gees sketch in which Everett played all three toothsome, Tandoori-tanned brothers at the same time. Interviewed (by Everett), the 'Bee Gees' answered all questions with lines from their songs: 'How do you sell so many records?'/ 'Because we're living in a world of fools…'

Kenny Everett (aka Maurice Cole) died of an AIDS-related illness in 1995.

CAST Kenny Everett, Cleo Rocas /*pr* David Mallet /*wr* Ray Cameron, Barry Cryer, Kenny Everett /*Thames TV* (UK) /24 x 30m col.

Kessler

Drama. BBC1 1981

The sadistic Gestapo chief of ➢*Secret Army* resurfaces 35 years later as a businessman (called Manfred Dorff), and with the Nazi-hunters closing in. Clifford Rose menaced pleasingly, and the tension was kept just taut enough to prevent a trip to the set for a change of channel.

CAST *Ludwig Kessler* Clifford Rose /*cr* Gerard Glaister, John Brason /*pr* Gerard Glaister /*dr* Tristan de Vere Cole /*wr* John Braon /*BBC TV* (UK) /1 x 55m, 5 x 50m col.

A Kick Up the 80s

Comedy. BBC2 1981–4

Sketch show from BBC Scotland, which mined the same iconoclastic post-punk humour as ➢*Not the Nine O'Clock News* and ➢*Who Dares Wins*. It featured a host of rising talent (including Robbie Coltrane and Tracey Ullman), although only Rik Mayall's monologues as opinionated, brain-dead Brummie Kevin Turvey (perfectly finished off by a pose as 'The Thinker'), achieved immortality. The anchorman was the rather Old Turk-ish Richard Stilgoe.

CAST Richard Stilgoe, Rik Mayall, Tracey Ullman, Robbie Coltrane, Miriam Margoyles, Ron Bain, Roger Sloman /*pr* Tom Gutteridge, Colin Gilbert /*BBC Scotland* (UK) /18 x 30m col.

Kidnapped

Children's. ITV 1979

Kilt-swinging serialization of Robert Louis Stevenson's classic novel about the rebellious Highlanders of mid-18th-century Scotland. Former ➢*The Man from UNCLE* David McCallum starred as hero Alan Breck. Peter Graham Scott supervised a production enterprisingly financed by marks as well as pounds, which accounted for the Teutonic as well as the tartan names on the cast list.

CAST *Alan Breck* David McCallum *David Balfour* Ekkehardt Belle *Catriona* Aude Landry /*pr* Peter Graham Scott /*HTV West: Tele-Munchen* (UK/Ger) / 13 x 30m col.

The Kids From 47A

Children's. ITV 1974

On the death of their widowed mother, the flat-living Gathercole kids decide to look after themselves without adult help.

A comedy of youthful trials and errors which also tackled pertinent subjects in a serious way. One Phil Redmond, then an unknown tyro, was among the scriptwriters.

CAST *Jess Gathercole* Christine McKenna *George Gathercole* Russell Lewis *Willy Gathercole* Nigel Greaves *Binny Gathercole* Gaynor Hodgson /*pr* Richard Bramall /*dr* Jonathan Wright Miller /*wr* inc Phil Redmond, John Kane /*ATV* (UK) /approx. 30 x 25m col.

King and Castle

Comedy. ITV 1986–8

Ian Kennedy Martin sitcom about a duo of London debt collectors, the heavy Ronald King and the gimpy David Castle (➢*The Young Ones*' Nigel Planer in an orthodox role). The characters never appealed, although some ➢*Minder*-ish moments flickered briefly through the apathy. Spun off from a 1985 pilot in Thames' *Storyboard* showcase series.

CAST *Ronald King* Derek Martin *David Castle* Nigel Planer /*cr* Ian Kennedy Martin /*pr* Peter Duguid /*dr* inc Jan Sargent /*wr* inc Ian Kennedy Martin /*Thames TV* (UK) /16 x 30m col.

King of the Hill

Comedy. C4 1997–

Mike Judge's follow-up to ➢*Beavis and Butt-Head* was a benign cartoon satirization of a non-too-bright family out of Arlen, Texas. Head of the clan was Hank Hill, assistant manager of the Strickland Propane Co., father to dumpy 12-year-old son Bobby, and husband to the preternaturally plain Peggy. Sharing their suburban home was niece Luanne, a sexy teenager whose trailer-trash parents had busted up in an 'argument over beer'. An archetype of Southern Bubba culture, Hank (hobbies: beer, power tools, mowing the grass) tried to keep life simple in a world gone awry, but was constantly undone by his own idiosyncracies, and continually embarrassed and perplexed by the vulgar realities of modern life (explaining the facts of life to Bobby, hugging, foreplay). After the tendency to baroque of the later ➢*The Simpsons* episodes (on which co-creator Greg Daniels had once scribed) the outlandishness of ➢*Ren & Stimpy* and ➢*South Park*, *KOTH* consciously sought a more accessible, family-based humour. To this end, it eschewed quirky graphics in favour of a lo-fi primitive cartoon style (*pace Beavis and Butt-Head* itself). A major prime-time hit, *KOTH* was the almost perfect family sitcom. That it was an animation was almost incidental.

CAST *Hank Hill/Boomhauer/Dooley* Mike Judge *Peggy Hill* Kathy Najimy *Bobby Hill* Pamela Segall *Luanne Platter/Joseph Gribble* Britanny Murphy *Dale Gribble* Johnny Hardwick *Bill Dauterive* Stephen Root /*cr* Mike Judge, Greg Daniels /*exec pr* Howard Klein, Phil Roman, Michael Rotenberg, Greg Daniels, Mike Judge /*dr* inc Jeff Myers, Tricia Gracia, John Rice, Chuck Sheetz /*wr* inc Mike Judge, Greg Daniels /*mus* Brian David Blush & Roger Meade Clyne (theme) /*20th Century-Fox Television: Film Roman Productions: 3 Arts Entertainments* (USA) /30+ x 30m col /US tx FOX 1997–.

Kinvig

Sci-fi. ITV 1981

Earth boys are easy. Whimsical, ultimately unsuccessful sci-fi comedy from Nigel Kneale (creator of ➢ *Quatermass*), that satirized believers in alien abduction. The hero of the piece was electrical repairman Des Kinvig, who found refuge from his mundane life – and the dotings of wife Netta and dog Cuddley – in the fantasies of UFOlogist friend Jim. And then one night Des was apparently transported to the planet Mercury by the beautiful alien Miss Griffin, only to find a plot afoot by the ant-like inhabitants, Xux, to replace Earth's *Homo sapiens* with androids. The adventures were, in fact, all a figment of Des' imagination, though there was sufficient ambiguity to confuse some viewers.

CAST *Des Kinvig* Tony Haygarth *Netta Kinvig* Patsy Rowlands *Jim Piper* Colin Jeavons *Miss Griffin* Prunella Gee *Buddo* Simon Williams /*cr* Nigel Kneale /*pr* Les Chatfield /*dr* Les Chatfield, Brian Simmons /*wr* Nigel Kneale /*London Weekend Television* (UK) / 7 x 30m col.

Knight Errant '59

Drama. ITV 1959–61

Middling British adventure series chronicling the crime-solving and damsel-saving capers of Adam Knight, a debonair crusader for hire. He was joined in his Knight Errant Agency by ex-*Daily Clarion* reporter Liz Parrish and writer Peter Parker (played by Richard Carpenter, later to forge a glittering career as a TV playwright with such series as ➢*Catweazle*, ➢*The Ghosts of Motley Hall* and ➢*Robin of Sherwood*). With the advent of a new year, the programme title changed to *Knight Errant '60*, and then again to *Knight Errant Ltd.* By that time the agency personnel had altered somewhat, with Knight himself departing to the wilds of Canada, a new boss, Stephen Drummond, taking over the reins (with help from secretary Frances Graham), and new investigators added in the faces of Colonel Cope-Addams and Greg Wilson.

CAST *Adam Knight* John Turner *Liz Parrish* Kay Callard *Peter Parker* Richard Carpenter *Stephen Drummond* Hugh David *Frances Graham* Wendy Williams *Tony Hollister* William Fox *Greg Wilson* Stephen Cartwright *Colonel Cope-Addams* Alan Webb /*cr* Philip Mackie /*pr* Warren Jenkins, Kitty Black /*Granada TV* (UK) /76 x 50m bw.

Knightmare

Children's. ITV 1987–94

Conscious of the 80s popularity of home-video games, TV stations sought to keep kiddie viewers watching their output by making shows that were virtually indentical to home video games. The lead was given by BBC TV's *The Adventure Game* (1980–6), followed by Anglia's *Knightmare.* Invented by Tim Child, this targetted 8–16 year-old viewers with a computerized dungeon fantasy whereby teams of four youngsters were pitched into a tournament of wits against medieval jousting knights, wizards, ghouls and the like. ➢*The Crystal Maze*, played much the same format to a slightly older audience.

CAST *Treguard/Host* Hugo Myatt /*cr* Tim Child / *pr* Sally Freeman /*dr* Sally Freeman /*sfx* (computer graphics) Robert Harris /*Anglia* (UK) /90 x 25 / 30m col.

Knight Rider

Sci-fi. ITV 1983–7

The hokum crime-fighting adventures of rebuilt ex-policeman Michael Knight and his talking automobile KITT (standing for Knight Industries Two Thousand). Almost amusingly, this 300 m.p.h. black Pontiac Trans Am – which boasted more firepower than most Third World Nations – had its own, somewhat truculent personality.

Alledgedly tailor-created for handsome, but hardly loquacious, actor David Hasselhoff (➢*The Young and the Restless*), *Knight Rider* proved a big success with kids who liked techno-gimmicks, women who liked a man in tight jeans, and men who realized the show was not intended to be wholly serious. Richard Basehart from ➢*Voyage to the Bottom of the Sea* played dying industrialist Wilton Knight, the do-gooder responsible for financing the Foundation for Law and Government vigilante mission, of which the cop and his car were the business end.

After *Knight Rider* Hasselhoff flexed his pecs as Lt Mitch Buchannon in ➢*Baywatch.*

CAST *Michael Knight* David Hasselhoff *Devon Miles* Edward Mulhare *Bonnie Barstow* Patricia McPherson *Voice of KITT* William Daniels *April Curtis* Rebecca Holden *Reginald Cornelius III ('RC3')* Peter Parros *Wilton Knight* Richard Basehart /*cr* Glen A. Larson / *exec pr* Glen A. Larson, Robert Cinader, Robert Forster / *dr* inc Virgil Vogel, Rick Kolbe, Peter Crane, Bruce Kessler /*wr* inc Glen A. Larson, Karen Harris, Stephen B. Katz, Richard Matheson /*Universal TV: Glen A. Larson* (USA) /1 x 105m, 90 x 60m col.

Knights of God

Sci-fi. ITV 1987

Epic telefantasy positing a 2020 AD Britain devastated by civil war. From the carnage there arises a new order, the brutal, militaristic zealots of the Knights of God, led by dictator Prior Mordrin. Those joining the anti-Mordrin resistance include teenagers Gervase and Julia, who begin an Arthurian-type quest to find the deposed King of England and restore him to the throne. Stylishly combining Dark Age-like settings with future technology, the £1 million series assured its credentials by the employment of such sci-fi actors as Gareth Thomas (➢*Blake's 7*) and Patrick Troughton (➢*Doctor Who*) among its 50-strong cast.

CAST *Gervase Edwards* George Winter *Julia* Claire Parker *Mordrin* John Woodvine *Arthur* Patrick Troughton *Owen* Gareth Thomas *Hugo* Julian Fellowes *Colley* Don Henderson *Simon* Nigel Stock *Nell* Ann Stallybrass /*cr* Richard Cooper /*exec pr* Anna Home / *pr* John Dale /*dr* Andrew Morgan, Michael Kerrigan / *wr* Richard Cooper /*TVS* (UK) /13 x 30m col.

The Knock

Crime. ITV 1996–

An elite unit of undercover Customs and Excise officers hunt down modern-age smugglers.

One of ITV's slicker, tighter dramas of the mid-90s, which posed new possibilities for a tired cops'n'robbers format. There was money too, for exotic location filming and big name guest stars (including Anthony Valentine and Dennis Waterman) to play the various Mr Bigs. Alex Kingston (➢*Moll Flanders*) played agent Katherine Roberts in the opening seasons. Produced by Paul Knight, previously the guiding hand behind ➢*Dick Turpin,* ➢*Robin of Sherwood* and ➢*London's Burning.*

CAST *George Webster* Anthony Valentine *Bill Adams* Malcolm Storry *Diane Ralston* Caroline Lee Johnson *Katherine Roberts* Alex Kingston *George Andreotti* Enzo Squillino Jr *Barry Christie* Steve Toussaint *Arnie Reinhardt* Marston Bloom *Kevin Whitwell* Andrew Dunn *Alex Murray* Daniel Brown *Lynn Hickson* Sarah Malin /*cr* Paul Knight, Anita Bronson /*exec pr* Sally Head /*pr* Paul Knight /*dr* inc Gerry Poulson, Frank Smith, James Hazeldine /*wr* inc Geoffrey Case, Ian Kennedy Martin /*Bronson Knight Productions* (UK) / 16 x 60m col.

Knots Landing

Melodrama. BBC1 1980–9

Spin-off from ➢*Dallas* in which the weak-willed, alcoholic Gary Ewing (brother of Bobby and JR, pa of Lucy) remarried estranged wife Val and fled to the small town of Knots Landing, California. There they settled in a *chichi* suburban close, and Gary (played by Ted Shackleford, later to be beamed aboard ➢*Space Precinct)* took a job as a classic-car salesman with Knots Landing Motors. Although the domestic traumas of Gary and Val were the show's initial focus, it soon expanded to include those of the other prominenti in the cul-de-sac: Sid Fairgate (who owned K.L. Motors) and his wife Karen; Sid's no-good, divorced sister Abby Cunningham; womanizing attorney Richard Avery and his real-estate agent wife Laura; record-company executive Kenny Ward and wife Ginger. And, of course, Immorality and Tragedy. Thus it was that Gary was divorced from Val (for adultery), married to Abby, indicted for murder, dumped by Abby, and had his two sons (by Val) sold to the black market. Meanwhile, his neighbours dizzily swapped partners, before disappearing or dying (usually in suspicious circumstances); by 1988 only Gary, Val and Karen Fairgate survived from the original residents. This culling of characters allowed the introduction of a noticeably younger cast (prefiguring the youth-oriented soaps like ➢*Melrose Place*) and allowed the series overall to evolve to an unusual degree for a sudster. American viewers approved, but for British viewers *Knots Landing*'s middle-class setting provided little pull after the glamorous fantasy of life at Southfork. Screened for two years by the BBC at Saturday prime time, it was dropped from the schedule entirely before finding a place as an afternoon filler.

There was some overlap between *Knots Landing* and *Dallas*, with members of the Ewing clan making occasional appearances in California, and Gary visting the old ranch home. In a moment of happiness rare for either series, Gary and Val married yet again in 1991. Alec Baldwin, Ava Gardner, Howard Duff, Red Button and Michael York were guest stars.

CAST *Gary Ewing* Ted Shackelford *Valene Ewing /Gibson/Waleska* Joan Van Ark *Sid Fairgate* Don Murray *Karen Fairgate/MacKenzie* Michele Lee *Michael Fairgate* Pat Petersen *Kenny Ward* James Houghton *Ginger Ward* Kim Lankford *Richard Avery* John Pleshete *Laura Avery/Sumner* Constance McCashin *Abby Cunningham/Ewing/Sumner* Donna Mills *Olivia Cunningham/Dyer* Tonya Crowe *Gregory Sumner* William Devane *M. Patrick 'Mack' MacKenzie* Kevin Dobson *Joshua Rush* Alec Baldwin *Paul Galveston* Howard Duff *Ruth Galveston* Ava Gardner *Al Baker* Red Buttons *Charles Cott* Michael York */cr* David Jacobs */exec pr* Lee Rich, Michael Filerman, David Jacobs */dr* inc Peter Levin, Alexander Singer, David Moessinger, Kate Swofford, Kevin Dobson, Reza S. Badiyi, Robert Lewis, William Devane, Joseph Manduke, Joan Van Ark, Harvey Laidman */mus* inc Jerrold Immel ('Knots Landing' theme) */Roundlay: MF Productions: Lorimar Television* (USA) /approx. 320 x 60m col /US tx CBS 1979–93.

Knowing Me, Knowing You ... with Alan Partridge

Comedy. BBC2 1994–

Spoof chat show hosted by the smarmy, logorrhoeic and incompetent 'Alan Partidge'. A-ha.

A transfer to TV (via ➢*The Day Today*) from radio of comedian Steve Coogan's presenter persona which, in the new medium, proved an even more squirmingly acute send-up of the self-importance and deceitful mechanics of broadcasting.

The most telegenic of the wave of 90s absurdist humorists which grew up around R4's 'On the Hour', Coogan (previously ➢*Spitting Image*, the portentous advertising voice of Allied Carpets) also invented a long line of other characters who found TV infamy, although only lager-drinking Mancunian Paul 'bag o'shite' Calf and his shag-happy sister Pauline and their 'video diaries' (of which the pinnacle was the BAFTA-winning *Three Fights, Two Weddings and A Funeral*) rivalled Partridge for accuracy. The satirical progress of Partridge continued in 1997's *I'm Alan Partridge*.

CAST *Alan Partridge* Steve Coogan */pr* Armando Iannucci */dr* Dominic Brigstocke */wr* Steve Coogan, Henry Normal, Patrick Marber */BBC TV* (UK) / 12 x 30m.

Kojak

Crime. BBC1 1974–8

Although a long-established movie actor, Greek–American Telly Savalas did not achieve screen celebrity until he took on the role of TV homicide cop Kojak in 1973. Premiering in an Emmy-winning feature-length episode, 'The Marcus–Nelson Murders' (based on the real-life Wylie–Hoffert case), the series was an instant hit, ranking seventh in the Nielsens in its debut season. If most plaudits went to Savalas for his performance (which charismatically combined brute power with soft-hearted tenderness) as the balding, lollipop-sucking, 'Who loves ya, baby?'-saying Lieutenant Theo Kojak, the show's graphic, street-level realism made for a powerful screen intoxicant. A fine support cast in Kevin Dobson

'Who loves ya baby?' Telly Savalas as the eponymous NY homicide cop Kojak. A former war hero (winning a Purple Heart in Korea), Savalas turned to acting after a career behind the screen as a director.

(who played Kojak's youngster partner at Manhattan South Precinct), Dan Frazier (long-suffering Chief McNeil) and George – brother of Telly – Savalas (as corpulent, cuddlesome Stavros) also did their bit. Sylvester Stallone, then a virtual unknown, was among the guest cast.

Kojak was successfully dubbed throughout the world – in Germany it was known as *The Lion Without a Mane* and in Egypt as *The Man of Honour* – and even enjoyed a brief revival in the mid-1980s, beginning with the CBS telemovies *Belarus* (1985) and *Kojak: The Price of Justice* (1989). High ratings prompted the ABC network to feature the tough NYPD detective – now an Inspector – in a quintet of TVMs (*Ariana, Fatal Flaw, Flowers for Matty, It's Always Something* and *None So Blind*) in 1989.

Savalas died in January 1994, a year after suing the makers of *Kojak*, Universal TV, for $6 million, his claimed 25-per-cent share of the programme's profits.

CAST *Lt Theo Kojak* Telly Savalas *Chief Frank McNeil* Dan Frazer *Lt Bobby Crocker* Kevin Dobson *Det. Stavros* George Savalas *Det. Rizzo* Vince Conti *Det. Saperstein* Mark Russell /*cr* Abby Mann /*exec pr* Matthew Rapf /*pr* Chester Krumholz, James McAdams, Jack Laird /*dr* inc Jack Sargent, Telly Savalas, Richard Donner, Jerry London, Jerrold Friedman, David Freidkin /*wr* inc Mort Fine, Robert Swanson, Richard Nelson, Donald P. Bellisario / *mus* Billy Goldenburg (theme) /*Universal TV* (USA) / 2 x 120m, 1 x 180m, 112 x 60m col /US tx CBS 1973–8.

Kolchak: The Night Stalker

Sci-fi. ITV 1983–5

Cult fright-night series, of interest in its own right, but also as the inspiration for 90s TV sensation ➢*The X-Files*. Based on Jeff Rice's 1970 novel *The Kolchak Papers*, and preceded by two TVMs (*The Night Stalker* and *The Night Strangler*), *Kolchak* starred Darren McGavin as the eponymous down-at-heel newshound who pursued strange phenomena down the dark alleyways of America. To maximize viewer frisson, the show adopted documentary-style photography, suggesting that its content of bug-eyed monsters, vampires, serial killers and werewolves was fact rather than fiction. Perhaps the epitome of *Kolchak*'s ability to tingle the spine was the Jimmy Sangster-directed segment 'Horror in the Heights' (guest star: Phil Silvers) which featured a monster who insidiously cosied up to its victims by assuming the shape of their dearest. Mainstream US of A was unsettled and switched over to easier fare. To ram a final nail in *Kolchak*'s coffin, novelist Rice sued ABC network for producing the series without his permission.

CAST *Carl Kolchak* Darren McGavin *Tony Vincenzo* Simon Oakland /*exec pr* Darren McGavin /*pr* Paul Playdon, Cy Chermak /*dr* Don Weiss, Gene Levitt, Bruce Kessler, Vincent McEveety /*wr* inc Paul Playdon, Jimmy Sangster, Michael Kozoll, Stephen Lord, Steve Fisher /*mus* Gil Melle /*Francy Productions for Universal TV* (USA) /20 x 60m col /US tx ABC 1974–5.

Krypton Factor

Light Entertainment. ITV 1976–95

Composite TV quiz and physical-endurance test, designed to find the 'Super Being of Great Britain'. Their eyes on the fabulous Krypton

'Ah, Grasshopper...' David Carradine as Caine in the chop-suey Western, *Kung Fu.* The show was based on an idea by martial arts master Bruce Lee.

Factor Prize (a trophy), competitors were tested for their brawn over a military assault course and for their brains in a series of IQ, observational and general-knowledge exams. Somewhat earnest and self-important, the show achieved popularity (and a sale of the format to ABC in the USA) without becoming a must-view. In 1988 Granada introduced a short-lived kiddie version, *Young Krypton*, hosted by Ross King.

The title was taken from the name of Superman's home planet.

CAST (presenters) Gordon Burns, Penny Smith /*cr* Jeremy Fox /*exec pr* Stephen Leahy, David Liddiment / *pr* Jeremy Fox, Stephen Leahy, David Jenkins, Geoff Moore, Patricia Pearson, Nick Turnbull, Kieran Roberts, Rod Natkiel, Caroline Gosling /*dr* inc Peter Walker, Patricia Pearson, Rod Natkiel, Graham C. Williams, Nick Abson, Stephen Leahy, Brian Lennane / *Granada TV* (UK) /approx. 100 x 60m col.

Kung Fu

Western. ITV 1973–4

A chop suey Western, originally developed by martial arts star Bruce Lee (➢*The Green Hornet*) as a vehicle for himself, but given by Warner Bros. to the Caucasian actor David Carradine because the studio believed an American audience would not accept the Asiatic Lee as a lead player(!). Thus Carradine – son of the cadaverous Hollywood thespian John and formerly TV's *Shane* – played Kwai Chang Caine, a shaven-headed Sino-American Shaolin priest who wandered the Old West in search of his long-lost brother and wisdom. Though tutored in inner harmony and prone to Confucius-him-say sort of utterances, Caine was a master of Kung Fu – which proved altogether more useful than meditation at dealing with the bad guys who populated the TV frontier.

Aside from its novelty value, which inspired a worldwide craze for Oriental combat arts, the series pioneered eye-catching visual techniques. The fight scenes were filmed by cameraman Fred Koencamp in a highly stylized slo mo, while flashbacks were used to relate Caine's boyhood training as a priest in China, where he had been affectionately known as 'Grasshopper'. The episode 'Eye for an Eye' won Jerry Thorpe an Emmy for direction. Only a stale manhunter narrative element, whereby Caine was pursued by assassins from the Chinese legation for his youthful self-defence killing of a Ming prince, jarred the show's joys.

A 90s follow-on, *Kung Fu: The Legend Continues*, starred Carradine as Caine's grandson in an absolutely standard urban cop drama, not redeemed by the occasional martial manoeuvre.

CAST *Kwai Chang Caine* David Carradine *Caine (as boy)* Radamas Pera/Stephen Manley *Master Po* Keye Luke *Master Kan* Philip Ahn /*cr* Bruce Lee, Ed Spielman /*pr* Jerry Thorpe, Alex Beaton, Herman Miller, Bill Perry /*dr* inc Jerry Thorpe, Gordon Hessler, Marvin Chomsky, Richard Lang, Robert Butler, Charles S. Dubin /*wr* inc Ed Spielman, Howard Friedlander /*mus* Jim Helms (theme) /*Warner Bros TV* (USA) /62 x 52m col /US tx ABC 1972–5.

KYTV

Comedy. BBC2 1990–3

Topical – in its day – parody of satellite TV, named after the sitcom's fictitious station-owner, Sir Kenneth Yellowhammer. (The programme title was also clearly intended to suggest a brand lubricating jelly commonly used as a sex aid.) Every aspect of extraterrestrial TV was sent up, particularly its financial deficiencies and cultural crudity. Some of the neatest skewerings were the self-explanatory 'Herne Bay Watch', a behind-the-scenes look at the making of classic drama entitled 'Martin Chizzlenut', and a fly-on-the-wall special examining the life of a suburban family. From the same team – prime among them Angus Deayton – who brought the wireless listener the local radio spoof *Radio Active* (R4).

CAST *Mike Channel* Angus Deayton *Mike Flex* Geoffrey Perkins *Anna Daptor* Helen Atkinson Wood *Martin Brown* Michael Fenton Stevens *Mr Hartford* Philip Pope /*cr* Angus Deayton, Geoffrey Perkins /*pr* Jamie Rix, /*dr* John Kilby, John Stroud /*wr* Angus Deayton, Geoffrey Perkins /*BBC TV* (UK) /18 x 30m col.

L

Lace

Melodrama. ITV 1984

A Hollywood porn star, Lili, goes in search of her mother.

Subtle, polysemic and enigmatic *Lace* was not, but prurient and shrewdly pitched schlock (16.2 million tuned in) it most assuredly was. Adapted from the novel by Shirley Conran. A sequel, *Lace II*, charted Lili's quest for her father.

CAST *Lili* Phoebe Cates *Maxine* Arielle Dombasle *Judy* Bess Armstrong *Pagan* Brooke Adams *Dr Geneste* Anthony Quale /*dr* Billy Hale /*wr* Elliott Baker /*CBS Entertainment* (USA) /2 x 90m col.

Lady Killers

Drama. ITV 1980–1

Dramatized cases of prominent distaff murderers of the evil ilk of Ruth Ellis. Introduced by Robert Morley, the seven hour-long plays hovered suspiciously between fact and fiction, but pleased enough of the gallows crowd (up to 10.9 million) to warrant a follow-on series entitled, with subtle difference, *Ladykillers*, about famous murderers of women. Rita Tushingham (as Charlotte Bryant) and Joan Sims (as Amelia Dryer) were among the criminal cast.

CAST (presenter) Robert Morley (actors) inc Georgina Hale, Rita Tushingham, Joan Sims, Elaine Paige /*pr* Pieter Rogers /*dr* Valerie Hanson, Nicholas Ferguson /*wr* inc Jeremy Sandford, Edwin Pearce /*Granada TV* (UK) /14 x 60m col.

LA Law

Crime. ITV 1987–92 /BSkyB 1994–5

Emmy Award-winning legal drama, the brainchild of Steven Bochco (➢*Hill Street Blues*) and former Deputy DA, Terry Louise Fisher (➢*Cagney and Lacey*). Sexier and soapier than its creators' previous televisual offerings, *LA Law* concerned the ambitious and attractive attorneys of the prestigious LA law firm of McKenzie, Brackman, Chaney & Kuzak, who devoted as much time to their labyrinthine sexual affairs as they did to case work. Kuzak (played by Harry Hamlin, voted the sexiest man alive by *People Magazine* in 1987) lusted after idealist DA Grace Van Owen, but she became pregnant by the Hispanic Sifuentes, while sleazy divorce lawyer Becker chased anything remotely female and Markowitz had the hots for Kelsey... In one of the most famous episodes, 'Venus Butterfly'(which won a best teleplay Emmy for Fisher), Markowitz was taught a sexual technique by a client which meant that Kelsey succumbed to his charms overnight. (Actors Tucker and Eikenberry were, incidentally, married; life, TV, art – what's the difference?) Other prominent members of the firm – which met every morning in a meeting of minds reminiscent of ➢*Hill Street Blues*' dawn roll call – were fatherly senior lawyer McKenzie, the egotistical Brackman, black lawyer Rollins, and secretary Melman. In 1989 Roz Shays joined McKenzie Brackman and almost destroyed it – after an affair with McKenzie – in a boardroom power struggle. The firm, though, had the last laugh when Shays stepped into an empty elevator in 'Good to the Last Drop' and fell to her death. Another later addition was Cara Jean ('CJ') Lamb, played by Golden Globe-winning English actress Amanada Donohoe (the film *Castaway*).

The series' liberal airing of 'problem' issues generated (almost) as much coverage as its characters' sex lives. Cases taken by the resident legal eagles frequently covered topical concerns, among them AIDS, racial discrimination, drug use and Tourette's Syndrome. The American media went into a frenzy when CJ and intern Abby Perkins enjoyed an on-screen lesbian kiss, and the firm's Benny Stulwicz (played to double Emmy-winning effect by Larry Drake) was one of the few mentally retarded characters – along with Chris Burke's teenager Corky in *Life Goes On* – ever to be portrayed on the small screen.

Devised by small-screen wunderkind Steven Bochco, *LA Law* featured the affairs – personal and professional – of the firm of McKenzie Brackman, Chaney & Kuzak.

With the departure of several key players (Hamlin, Smits, Donohoe) the series began to lose it way and audience share. To put some chutzpah back into *LA Law*, William Finkelstein, the original producer, was rehired, bringing with him two characters, Eli Levinson and Densie Iannello, from his cancelled *Civil Wars* (the first occasion in prime-time history that characters were transferred from one programme to another which was not a spin-off). Finkelstein, however, was unable to stop the drift and on 19 May 1994 the firm of McKenzie Brackman, Kelsey, Markowitz & Morales closed its doors forever.

CAST *Leland McKenzie* Richard Dysart *Douglas Brackman Jr* Alan Rachins *Michael Kuzak* Harry Hamlin *Grace Van Owen* Susan Dey *Arnie Becker* Corbin Bernsen *Ann Kelsey* Jill Eikenberry *Victor Sifuentes* Jimmy Smits *Abby Perkins* Michele Green *Roxannne Melman* Susan Ruttan *Stuart Markowitz* Michael Tucker *Jonathan Rollins* Blair Underwood *Benny Stulwicz* Larry Drake *Rosalind Shays* Diana Muldaur *Tommy Mullaney* John Spencer *Carl Jean Lamb* Amanda Donohoe *Daniel Morales* A. Martinez *Eli Levinson* Alan Rosenberg *Denise Iannello* Debi Mazar /*cr* Steven Bochco, Terry Louise Fisher / *exec pr* Steven Bochco, Gregory Hoblitt, Rick Wallace, David E. Keley, William Finkelstein, Mark Tinker, Elodie Keene /*dr* inc Gregory Hoblitt, Elodie Keene, Mimi Leder, Janet Greek, Mervin Bennett Dayan, E.W. Swackhamer, Eric Laneuville /*wr* inc Terry Louise Fisher, David E. Kelley, John Masius, D. Keith Mano / *mus* Mark Post /*Twentieth Century Television* (USA) / 150 x 60m col /US tx NBC 1986–94.

Lancer

Western. BBC1 1969

The San Joaquin Valley in California in the 1870s was the setting for this saga of an old rancher, Murdoch Lancer, forced to call on the help of his estranged sons – gunfighter Johnny and college boy Scott – to keep the family spread out of the hands of local land pirates.

Adequate oater series, though very much a calculated amalgam of ➢*Bonanza* (a male family of three) and ➢*The Big Valley* (the SJ Valley backdrop). It was co-produced by Sam Wanamaker.

CAST *Old Murdoch Lancer* Andrew Duggan *Johnny Madrid Lancer* James Stacy *Scott Lancer* Wayne Maunder *Teresea O'Brien* Elizabeth Baur *Jelly Hoskins* Paul Brinegar /*cr* Sam Peeples /*pr* Sam Wanamaker, Alan A. Armer /*dr* inc Walter Grauman, Leo Penn, Alexander Singer, Sam Wanamaker, Gene Nelson / *mus* Jerome Moross ('Lancer' theme) /*Fox-TV* (USA) 51 x 52m col /US tx CBS 1968–71.

Land of the Giants

Sci-fi. ITV 1968–72

En route to London, the US rocketship 'Spindrift' enters a 'spacewarp' and descends on a world where everything is Earth-like – but 12 times normal size. The crew and passengers trapped in this land of the giants are: Captain Steve Burton, co-pilot Dan Erickson, engineer-tycoon Mark Wilson, stewardess Betty Hamilton, heiress Valerie Scott, mystery passenger Fitzhugh and orphaned boy Barry Lockridge (plus dog Chipper). Menaced by close encounters with giant cats and pursued by Inspector Kobick of the SIB Security Service, the castaways seek to repair their ship and escape the Brobdingnagian planet.

Classic Irwin Allen 60s telefantasy (see also ➢*Voyage to the Bottom of the Sea*, ➢*Time Tunnel*, ➢*Lost in Space*), inspired by *Gulliver's Travels*. Elaborate trick photography and clever props constructed on an enormous scale, such as bread made from from four-foot slabs of rubber, were the show's main switch-on factor, funded by a budget of $250,000 per episode (making LOTG one of the most expensive TV dramas to that date). A curiosity on the guest-cast roster was Sugar Ray Robinson, ex-world-champion boxer, in the episode 'All That Jazz'.

CAST *Capt. Steve Burton* Gary Conway *Dan Erikson* Don Marshall *Betty Hamilton* Heather Young *Alexander Fitzhugh* Kurt Kaznar *Mark Wilson* Don Matheson *Valerie Scott* Deanna Lund *Barry Lockridge* Stefan Arngrim *Insp. Kobick* Kevin Hagen /*cr* Irwin Allen /*exec pr* Irwin Allen /*pr* Irwin Allen, Bruce Fowler /*dr* inc Irwin Allen, Harry Harris, Sobey Martin /*wr* inc Dan Ullman, Anthony Wilson, Bob & Esther Mitchell, Richard Shapiro, Sheldon Stark /*mus* John Williams /*sfx* L.B. Abbott, Art Cruickshank, Emil Kosa Jr /*An Irwin Allen Production for Fox TV* (USA) / 51 x 60m col /US tx ABC 1968–70.

Land of the Lost

Children's. Sci-fi Channel 1994

Sci-fi serial by Sid and Marty Krofft, masters of American Saturday morning TV.

When the Marshall family plunge over a waterfall on the Colorado River they enter a time vortex and wash up in a parallel jungle universe: the Land of the Lost. Episodes related the struggle of the Marshall family to adjust to the hostile land and find a way back to their own time and world. Along the way they encountered prehistoric monsters, ape-men (the Pakuni), other human accidental explorers, the ruins of a once-great civilization, and a barbaric species of intelligent lizard (the Sleestak).

While it trod the well-worn footsteps of ➢*Journey to the Centre of the Earth* and Irwin Allen's time-warp classics, ➢*Land of the Giants* and ➢*Lost in Space*, it did so with considerable intelligence and fright-making from the script and direction departments. (➢*Star Trek* actor Walter Koenig was, incidentally, among those contributing teleplays.) The only cavil was special-effects work, a mix of animation and models, whose crudity sometimes caused even babies to laugh behind their dummies.

A 1991 remake, in which it was the turn of the unfortunate Porter family to fall into the Land of the Lost, starred Timothy Bottoms, Jennifer Druggan and Robert Gavin.

CAST *Rick Marshall* Spencer Milligan *Will Marshall* Wesley Eure *Holly Marshall* Kathy Coleman *Cha-Ka* Philip Paley *Uncle Jack Marshall* Ron Harper *Enik* Walker Edminston /*cr* Sid & Marty Krofft, Allan Foshko /*exec pr* Albert J. Tenzer, Sid & Marty Krofft /*pr* Dennis Steinmetz, Sid & Marty Krofft /*dr* inc Dennis Steinmetz, Bob Lally /*wr* inc D.C. Fontana, Larry Niven, David Gerrold, Walter Koenig /*mus* Linda Laurie (theme), Jimmie Haskell, Michael Lloyd, John D'Andrea /*Krofft Communications* (USA) /43 x 30m col /US tx NBC 1974–7.

Laramie

Western. BBC 1959–64

After their father is killed by an outlaw, young Slim Sherman and his 14-year-old brother Andy (Bobby Crawford, sibling of ➢*The Rifleman*'s Johnny Crawford) carry on the family's Wyoming ranch. Saddle tramp Jess Harper drifts in as a partner, while old amigo Jonesy (played by no less than music master Hoagy Carmichael) takes the position of top hand.

Solid oater for all on the sofa. The Sherman ranch's other purpose, as a depot for the Great Overland Mail Stage Line, allowed a steady supply of characters to mosey through, all with a tale on their tail.

CAST *Slim Sherman* John Smith *Jess Harper* Robert Fuller *Jonesy* Hoagy Carmichael *Andy Sherman* Bobby Crawford Jr *Mort Corey* Stuart Randall *Mike Williams* Dennis Holmes *Daisy Cooper* Spring Byington *Gandy* Don Durant /*pr* John Champion, Richard Lewis, Robert Pirosh /*dr* inc Lesley Selander, Tay Garnett, Virgil W. Vogel, Douglas Heyes, Earl Bellamy, William Whitney, Hollingsworth Morse /*mus* Cyril Mockridge (theme song) /*Revue Productions* (USA) /124 x 52m bw:col /US tx NBC 1959–63.

The Larkins

Comedy. ITV 1958–64

Early ATV sitcom about a cockney family who lived a cor-blimey comedy of domestic mishaps at 66 Sycamore Street, somewhere in London's outer limits. Dad Alf was henpecked, Ma Ada was a battleaxe (show-stealingly played by a fearsome Peggy Mount, ➢*George and the Dragon*), son Eddie was a layabout, and daughter Joyce was married to an American writer of Western comics. The Prouts were the next-door neighbours. Such was the show's popularity that a spin-off, *Inn For Trouble* (1959), was made for cinema, which had the Larkins running a country pub. Shaun O'Riordan shortly afterwards changed occupations to go from a middling actor to a distinguished producer.

CAST *Alf Larkin* David Kossoff *Ada Larkin* Peggy Mount *Eddie Larkin* Shaun O'Riordan *Jeff Roger* Ronan O'Casey *Joyce Roger* Ruth Trouncer *Myrtle Prout* Hilary Bamberger *Hetty Prout* Barbara Mitchell *Sam Prout* George Roderick /*cr* Fred Robinson /*pr* Bill Ward, Alan Tarrant /*wr* Fred Robinson /*ATV* (UK) / 40 x 30m bw.

The Larry Sanders Show

Comedy. BBC2 1995–

Fictitious TV chat show. Modelled on David Letterman and Jerry Langford (the character played by Jerry Lewis in *King of Comedy*), 'host' Sanders oozed schmooze on screen and vitriol off, and paranoid ego all the time. A cruelly brilliant spoof of the talk-show genre, with masterful performances by Garry Shandling (grown inestimably in comic maturity since ➢*It's Garry Shandling's Show*) in the title role, veteran Rip Torn as the producer Artie, and Jeffrey Tambor as Sanders' second banana, the obsequious Hank 'Hey Now!' Kingsley (modelled on Johnny Carson's number two, Ed McMahon). Viciousness, expletives and art-house overlapping conversations ensured the programme low ratings on HBO cable channel. However, those who loved it, loved it well, and numbered among them were the intelligentsia of US TV and the glitterati of US film. Robin Williams, Sharon Stone and David Duchovny all appeared as guests; as did Jay Leno and Letterman himself. In a proof positive that life and art are the same, actress Linda Doucett (who played Hank's comely assistant Darlene) was removed from the show when she ceased to be star Shandling's girlfriend. She was replaced by Scott Thompson from the Canadian sitcom *Kids in the Hall.*

CAST *Larry Sanders* Garry Shandling *Artie* Rip Torn *Hank* Jeffrey Tambor *Paula* Janeane Garafalo /*pr* inc John Ziffren /*wr* inc Peter Tolan, Garry Shandling, Jon Vitti /*HBO: Brillslein-Grey* (USA) /88 x 30m col /US tx HBO 1992–8.

Lassie

Children's. ITV 1956–73

More kiddie-time dog tales (see also ➢*The Adventures of Rin Tin Tin*, ➢*The Littlest Hobo*), originating in Eric Knight's best-selling 1940 novel *Lassie Come Home*, filmed for cinema with Elizabeth Taylor and Roddy McDowall.

The original TV owner of Lassie was Jeff Miller (played by Tommy Rettig; arrested in the 80s for cocaine smuggling), who lived on a small farm outside Calverton, USA. In 1957 young orphan Timmy arrived on the doorstep and stayed. Soon after, the Millers sold up the old homestead leaving Lassie and Timmy in the care of new owners, the Martins. Some seven years later, the Martins and Timmy left for Australia, abandoning poor Lassie behind them because of quarantine restrictions. She then became the canine pal of old man Cully – but he suffered a heart attack and gave Lassie up to the care of forest ranger Corey Stuart. By 1968 Lassie, understandably tired of such fickle human company, went solo walkabout, fell in love with a male collie and bore him a litter of pups (sharp-eyed viewers may have been bemused by this, since all the dogs to play Lassie were in fact males). Then, in 1972, Lassie trotted onto the Californian ranch of Garth Holden (whose assistant, Dale Mitchell, was played by Larry Wilcox, later to ride to fame in ➢*CHiPS)*, where she enjoyed a semi-detached relationship until the end of the show's run. Filmed in Canada, *Lassie* was co-executive produced by Jack Wrather from ➢*The Lone Ranger*.

As if to prove that you can't keep a good dog down, Lassie bounded back in the animated *Lassie's Rescue Rangers* and a 1988 dramatic series *The New Lassie*.

CAST *Jeff Miller* Tommy Rettig *Ellen Miller* Jan Clayton *Gramps Miller* George Cleveland *Timmy* Jon Provost *Ruth Martin* Cloris Leachman/June Lockhart *Corey Stuart* Robert Bray *Garth Holden* Ron Hayes *Keith Holden* Larry Pennell *Dale Mitchell* Larry Wilcox *Ron Holden* Skip Burton *Mike Holden* Joshua Albee /*exec pr* Jack Wrather, Robert Maxwell /*pr* Jack Wrather, Robert Maxwell, Bonita Granville Wrather, William Beaudine Jr, Rudy E. Abel, Sherman A. Harris, Robert Golden /*dr* inc Joseph Sargeant, Sheldon Leonard, Dick Moder, William Witney / *The Wrather Corp* (USA) /186 x 25m col /US tx CBS 1954–71: Syndicated 1971–4.

Last of the Mohicans

Western. BBC1 1971

British-made production of James Fenimore Cooper's tales of pathfinder Hawkeye and his Indian soulmate, Chingachgook, with the west of Scotland doing a surprisingly good stand-in for the New York frontier of the 1750s. Stirring, faithful to source, it was a credit to its makers, who followed it up with *Hawkeye, The Pathfinder* (1973, 5 x 55m col; co-funded by Fox TV).

CAST *Hawkeye* Kenneth Ives *Chingachgook* John Abineri /*pr* John McRae /*dr* David Maloney /*wr* Harry Green /*BBC TV* (UK) /8 x 45m col.

Last of the Summer Wine

Comedy. BBC1 1972–

Long-running, gently whimsical sitcom about three reprobate Yorkshire pensioners, developed from a 1973 *Comedy Playhouse*, 'Of Funerals and Fish', by Roy Clarke (later ➢*Open All Hours*, ➢*Rosie*, ➢*Keeping Up Appearances*). Filmed on location in Holmfirth, the series was novel in that it asked viewers to laugh with OAPS, not at them, making it a British male anticipation of ➢*The Golden Girls*. The original terrible three were the unkempt Compo (Bill Owen, ex-lyricist for Ken Dodd), widower Norman 'Cleggy' Clegg and ex-Signals sergeant Blamire, their adventures turning into misadventures either through Compo's delinquent behaviour or Blamire's ill-founded self-confidence. Over the passing seasons Blamire (Michael Bates, also ➢*It Ain't Half Hot, Mum*, d. 1976) was replaced by another ex-army man, Foggy Dewhurst, then by a former teacher, Seymour Utterthwaite, before Dewhurst returned again. It was notable that, whatever the configuration of the three, their essentially overgrown schoolboy antics were always met with stony-faced disapproval by the village's womenfolk, especially Nora Batty (Compo's improbable, wrinkle-stockinged object of desire) and café prorietor Ivy – underneath the geriatric novelty of *Last of the Summer Wine* lurked the old stalwart of British TV humour: the battle of the sexes. In 1988–9 a prequel, *First of the Summer Wine*, was aired on BBC1 (12 x 30m) featuring Compo, Cleggy, Utterthwaite and Dewhurst in their pre-War Dales youth.

CAST *Compo Simmonite* Bill Owen *Norman 'Cleggy' Clegg* Peter Sallis *Blamire* Michael Bates *Foggy Dewhurst* Brian Wilde *Seymour Utterthwaite* Michael Aldridge *Sid* John Comer *Ivy* Jane Freeman *Nora Batty* Kathy Staff *Wally Batty* Joe Gladwin *Wesley Pegden* Gordon Wharmby *Edie Pegden* Thora Hird *Eli* Danny O'Dea *Smiler* Stephen Lewis *Auntie Wainright* Jean Alexander /*cr* Roy Clarke /*pr* James Gilbert, Bernard Thompson, Sydney Lotterby, Alan J.W. Bell /*wr* Roy Clarke /*BBC TV* (UK) /171 x 30m, 4 x 60m col.

Late Night Horror

Drama. BBC2 1968

Misnomer for an anthology only scary in its gruesome dullness; several of the playlets, anyway, fell outside the horror genre, and those which did not were the usual vampire stuff. Perhaps the best of the pieces was Robert Aickman's vaguely erotic tale 'The Bells of Hell'; Roald Dahl and Sir Arthur Conan Doyle were among the other sources adapted. One of the first BBC2 series to be made in colour.

pr Harry Moore /*dr* Paddy Russell, Richard Martin, Rudolph Cartier, Naomi Capon /*wr* Hugh Leonard, Roald Dahl, David Campton, Hugh Whitemore, John Hawkesworth /*BBC TV* (UK) /7 x 25m col.

Laverne & Shirley

Comedy. ITV 1977–83

Started out as double dates for Fonzie and Richie in ➢*Happy Days*, before being spun off to their own series, in which they worked as bottle-cappers at Milwaukee's Shotz Brewery and roomed together at 730 Hampton Street. For the last seasons the setting changed to California, where the girls hoped to break into the movies but ended up behind the counter in the Bardwell Department Store. When, in 1982, actress Cindy Williams left the hit show in a contract dispute, her character was married off to a medic (so ending a long-running comedic worry about Shirley retaining her virginity in the increasingly permissive 50s) and Laverne struggled on for a year as a single gal wage-slaving for the Ajax Aerospace Company.

One of America's few blue-collar comedies, *Laverne & Shirley* was the creation of Garry K. Marshall, who cast his sister in the raucous role of Laverne. Penny Marshall went on to become a bigwig Hollywood director, helming such movies as *Big* and *League of their Own.*

Two cartoon versions of the series were made by Hanna–Barbera, *Laverne and Shirley in the Army* (1981–2) and *Laverne and Shirley with the Fonz* (1982–3). They were equally dire.

CAST *Laverne DeFazio* Penny Marshall *Shirley Feeney* Cindy Williams *Andrew 'Squiggy' Squigman* David Lander *Lenny Kosnoski* Michael McKean *Carmine Ragusa* Eddie Mekka /*cr* Garry K. Marshall /*exec pr* Thomas L. Miller, Edward K. Milkis, Garry K. Marshall /*dr* inc James Burrows, Jay Sandrich, Howard Storm, Joel Zwick /*wr* inc David L. Lander, Michael McKean /*mus* Norman Grimble & Charles Fox ('Making Our Dreams Come True' theme music and lyrics), Cyndi Grecco (theme vocal) /*Miller-Miklis: Henderson: Paramount TV* (USA) /178 x 25m col /US tx ABC 1976–83.

Law and Order

Crime. BBC2 1978

Four linked plays in drama-doc style by G.F. Newman on the theme of crime and punishment, as seen through the respective eyes of a Detective, a Villain, a Lawyer and a Prisoner. To the loud ire of many, Newman suggested that cops, robbers and 'screws' were cut from much the same corrupt human material. A piece of outrageous, pinko propaganda. And pretty good, really.

The producer was Tony Garnett.

cr G.F. Newman /*pr* Tony Garnett /*dr* Leslie Blair / *wr* G.F. Newman /*BBC TV* (UK) /4 x 75m col.

Law and Order (USA)

Crime. BBC1 1991 /BSkyB 1992–

Update of ➢*Arrest and Trial*, likewise devoting the first half of the show to the crime and apprehension of the (alleged) felon, and the second to the ensuing court case.

Tight scripts, atmospheric NY locales, gritty camerawork and an able cast (including some, like Sam Waterston, seduced from the movies), brought just Awards.

CAST *DS Max Geevey* George Dzunda *Det. Phil Cerreta* Paul Sorvino *Det. Mike Logan* Christopher Noth *Det. Lennie Briscoe* Jerry Orbach *Lt Anita Van Buren* S. Epatha Merkerson *Asst DA Ben Stone* Michael Moriarty *Asst DA Paul Robinette* Richard Brooks *Asst DA Claire Kincaid* Jill Hennessy *Asst DA Jack McCoy* Sam Waterston *DA Adam Schiff* Steven Hill /*exec pr* Dick Wolf /*pr* Robert Palm, Dan Sackheim /*dr* inc Ed Sherin, Vigil W. Vogel, Bill D'Elia, Bruce Seth Green, Kris Tabori, Steve Robman, James Rawley /*A Wolf Films Production: Universal TV* (USA) /180 x 60m; 1 x 90m col /US tx NBC 1990–.

The Lenny Henry Show

Comedy. BBC1 1984–

Comedy showcase for the former ➢*New Faces* winner. Over the seasons it changed humorous hue, as Henry flirted with formats (stand-up and sketches) and alternative-type comedy, although a constant was his talent for developing broad comic caricatures, such as PC Ganga, drag queen Deeva, Jamaican pensioner Deakus, and testosteroned crooner Theophilus P. Wildebeeste (who once asked a female member of the audience: 'Do you have any African in you? Do you want some?'). For the years 1987–8, the *Show* was given over entirely to a sitcom built around Henry's 'crucial' Brixton DJ, Delbert Wilkins.

CAST Lenny Henry /*pr* Geoff Posner, Geoff Atkinson / *dr* inc Juliet May /*wr* inc Lenny Henry, Stan Hey, Andrew Nickolds /*BBC TV* (UK) /36 x 30m col.

Lenny the Lion
Children's. BBC 1957–8/1960

Featured ventriloquist Terry Hall and his leonine puppet (who was famously unable to pronounce his 'r's) in gag woutines interspersed with pop music. Initially screened on *Children's Television*, the hugely popular show was followed by *Lenny's Den* (BBC, 1959–61), then *Pops and Lenny* (BBC, 1962–3) which once included The Beatles as guest artistes.

CAST (presenter) Terry Hall /*pr* Johnny Downes, Ronald Eyre /*BBC TV* (UK) /approx. 60 x 25m bw.

L for Lester
Comedy. BBC1 1982

Underrated farce about the disaster-prone driving instructor of a small West Country town. The casting of Brian Murphy (➢*Man About the House*) was perfect, if obvious.

CAST *Lester Small* Brian Murphy *Mrs Davies* Hilda Braid *Mr Davies (the bank manager)* Richard Vernon *Chief Insp. Rodgers* James Cossons *Sally Small* Amanda Barrie /*pr* Dennis Main Wilson /*dr* John B. Hobbs /*wr* Dudley Long /*BBC TV* (UK) /6 x 30m col.

The Life and Legend of Wyatt Earp
Western. ITV 1956–7

The story of how, armed with his trusty long-barrelled Buntline Special .45 pistols, Marshal Wyatt Earp tamed the towns of the West.

Quality adult Western, with an unusual semi-serial format, based heavily on Stuart N. Lake's 1931 biography of the lawman. In addition to Hugh O'Brian (aka Hugh Krampke), other actors to play Earp on the small screen include Med Flory in ➢*Maverick* and Bruce Boxleitner in *I Married Wyatt Earp*, a TV movie from the Osmond Corporation.

CAST *Wyatt Earp* Hugh O'Brian *Ben Thompson* Denver Pyle *Bat Masterson* Mason Alan Dinehart III *Ned Buntline* Lloyd Corrigan *Doc Holliday* Douglas Fowley *Morgan Earp* Dirk London *Virgil Earp* John Anderson *Old Man Clanton* Trevor Bardette *Sheriff Johnny Behan* Lash LaRue /*cr* Frederick Hazlitt Brennan /*pr* Louis F. Edelman, Robert Sisk, Roy Roland /*dr* inc Paul Landres /*wr* inc Frederick Hazlitt Brennan, Frank Gruber /*mus* The Ken Darby Singers (theme vocal) /*Wyatt Earp Enterprises: Desilu* (USA) / 226 x 26m bw /US tx ABC 1955–61.

Life and Loves of a She Devil
Drama. BBC2 1986

Ultra-black comedy in which one ugly and maligned wife became a glorious avenging angel for womankind. When husband Bobbo informed wife Ruth he had fallen in love with glamorous novelist Mary Fisher, she did not go meekly. Instead, the huge woman with the shoulders of a stevedore, four hairy moles and a moustache on her face, and eyes that turned the red of hell in anger, burned down the lighthouse where the superwomanish authoress lived, surrounded herself with a gang of outcasts from male society (including Tom Baker's decadent vicar), destroyed her runaway husband's assets, home and career and, to complete the transformation, had plastic surgery. Triumphant and macabre, this adaptation of Fay Weldon's novel was big girl Julie T. Wallace's finest hour. Women cheered, men cowered in their seats and the BAFTA Award-winning drama was picked over Dennis Potter's ➢*The Singing Detective* as best drama of 1986. ITV attempted to emulate its success with their own Weldon productions, *The Cloning of Joanna May* and *Growing Rich,* but failed to achieve its inspired combination of outrageous fantasy and devastating truth. Directed for the small screen by Philip Saville (*Fellow Traveller, The Fruit Machine*), it was produced as a feature film, *She-Devil,* in 1989, starring Roseanne Barr and Meryl Streep and directed by Susan Seidelman.

CAST *Ruth Patchett* Julie T. Wallace *Bobbo Patchett* Dennis Waterman *Mary Fisher* Patricia Hodge /*cr* Fay Weldon /*pr* Sally Head /*dr* Philip Saville /*wr* Ted Whitehead /*BBC TV* (UK) /4 x 60m col.

Life and Times of Grizzly Adams

Western. ITV 1978

Foolproof Western drama (from a Mormon company) for the family audience, containing weepy sentiment, stunning scenery, nature stories, a catchy hit theme and a personable animal star.

When James Adams is falsely accused of murder in the late 1880s, he flees to the mountains, where he is befriended by an old prospector, Mad Jack (Denver Pyle), and an Indian, Nakuma. But his real boon companion is a grizzly bear cub rescued from a ledge: Ben.

Loosely based on the real story of trapper John Adams, who ended his days as an exhibit in P.T. Barnum's circus.

CAST *James 'Grizzly' Adams* Dan Haggerty *Mad Jack* Denver Pyle *Nakuma* Don Shanks *Robbie Cartman* John Bishop /*cr* Charles E. Sellier Jr /*exec pr* Charles E. Sellier Jr /*pr* Leonard B. Kaufman, Jim Simmons, Art Stolnitz /*dr* James Conway, Sharron Miller /*mus* Tom Pace ('Maybe' theme vocals), Bob Sumners /*Schick Sunn Classics* (USA) /2 x 74m, 34 x 50m col /US tx NBC 1977–8.

A Life of Bliss

Comedy. BBC TV 1960 1

Transfer to TV of a popular radio comedy, taking with it George Cole as the shy hapless bachelor, David Alexander Bliss. A congenital maker of misunderstandings and mishaps, Bliss found solace in the company of fox terrier dog Psyche (voiced by Percy Edwards). Though but a single joke oft repeated, the show ran for two series. It was most notable for being Cole's first small-screen role, beginning a TV career which would stretch into four decades.

CAST *David Alexander Bliss* George Cole *Psyche* Percy Edwards (voice) *Anne Fellows* Isabel Dean *Tony Fellows* Colin Gordon *Pam* Frances Bennett *Bob* Hugh Sinclair /*cr* Godfrey Harrison /*pr* Graeme Muir, Godfrey Harrison /*wr* Godfrey Harrison /*BBC TV* (UK) /14 x 30m bw.

Life of Riley

Comedy. ITV 1959

Misadventures of Chester A. Riley, a none-too-bright riveter who lived at 1313 Blue View Terrace, Los Angeles, where he opined from his armchair on the world's problems – when not being henpecked by his wife, that is.

Prototypical sitcom of the Bumbling Pop type, it starred Jackie Gleason – it was his first TV series – in its 1949 (Emmy-winning) season, but the version shown in Britain had William Bendix in the lead role – the actor who had originally created the part for radio.

The same title was also used by Granada TV for a 1975 comedy series starring Bill Maynard as an insurance agent with a lecherous eye.

CAST *Chester A. Riley* Herb Vigran /Jackie Gleason /William Bendix *Peg Riley* Alice Drake /Rosemary DeCamp /Marjorie Reynolds *Jim Gillis* Lou Krugman /Sid Tomack /Tom D'Andrea *Olive 'Honeybee' Gillis* Jo Gilbert /Maxine Semon *Veda* /Ann Borg *Barbara 'Babs' Riley* Gloria Winters /Lugene Sanders *Chester Riley Jr* Lanny Rees /Wesley Morgan *Honeybee's mother* Bea Benaderet /*pr* Andy Potter, Irving Brecher, Tom McKnight /*NBC Entertainment* (USA) /60 x 30m bw /US tx NBC 1948, DuMont 1949–50, NBC 1953–8.

Life with Father

Comedy. ITV 1963

Situation comedy based on the popular book, play and film by Clarence Day. Set in 1880s New York, it chronicled the domestic misadventures of the upper middle class Day family, as ruled over by their stubbornly Victorian *pater*. It had an easy likeability and convincing period air. Of note, also, for being the first live colour show made in Hollywood for US network TV. Actress Marion Ross, later to find immortality in ➢*Happy Days*, was hidden in the lower depths of the show's thespian pool as the maid.

CAST *Clarence Day Snr* Leon Ames *Vinnie Day (wife)* Lurene Tuttle *Clarence Day Jr* Ralph Reed/Steven Terrell *Whitney Day* Ronald Keith /B.G. Norman /Freddy Ridgeway *Harlan Day* Harvey Grant *John Day* Freddie Leiston /Malcolm Cassell *Margaret* Dorothy Bernard *Nora* Marion Ross /*pr* Ben Feiner, Fletcher Markle /*McCadden* (USA) /26 x 25m bw /US tx CBS 1953–5.

Life Without George

Comedy. BBC1 1987–9

When her live-in lover walks out the door, dance instructor Jenny Russell finds love on the rebound with a drippy divorced estate agent, Larry. Whimsical romantic sitcom, in the vein of many others.

CAST *Jenny Russell* Carol Royle *Larry Wade* Simon Cadell *Amanda* Rosalind March/Elizabeth Estensen *Ben Morris* Michael Thomas *Harold Chambers* Ronald Fraser /*cr* Penny Croft /*exec pr* Robin Nash /*pr* Susan Belbin /*wr* Penny Croft, Val Hudson /*mus* Penny Croft (theme vocals) /*BBC TV* (UK) /14 x 30m col.

Lift Off

Children's. ITV 1969–74

Pop-music show aimed at the same pre-pubescents audience who learned the words to the latest chart hits from *Record Mirror and Disc.* Originally presented by Graham Bonney and Wally 'Pussy Willum' Whyton, it was at its zenith under the sultry pouting Ayshea Brough (➢*UFO*), and the show's title was changed to *Lift Off With Ayshea* accordingly. In addition to bands in the studio miming their latest disc, there was chat with the stars and a resident dance troupe. The producer was former ➢*Five O'Clock Club* presenter Muriel Young, who was also responsible for the Granada pop-music series *Get It Together* (with Roy North, Meg Nicoll, puppet Ollie Beak), *Discotheque* (with Billy J. Kramer), *Shang-A-Lang* (with the Bay City Rollers) and *Arrows.*

CAST (presenters) Ayshea Brough, Wally Whyton, Graham Bonney /*pr* Muriel Young /*Granada TV* (UK) / approx. 50 x 25m col.

The Likely Lads

Comedy. BBC2/BBC1 1965–9

As with all the best British sitcoms of the 60s (➢*Dad's Army*, ➢*Till Death Us Do Part*, ➢*Steptoe and Son*), *The Likely Lads* found its humour in the vagaries of the nation's class system. Originating out of a sketch Dick Clement wrote with friend Ian La Frenais for his BBC director's course, it concerned two young electrical workers in Northumberland, Terry Collier and Bob Ferris, who were markedly different in ambitions and attitudes. Terry was brash, aggressive, only interested in girls and resigned to his proletarian station in life; Bob was Terry's alter ego, diffident, scared of authority (particularly if it had a posh accent) and almost pitiful in his belief that if he worked hard enough he could escape the class trap. (It was not difficult to see the show as a critique of the supposed social mobility of the Swinging Sixties.) Despite their pub-and-birds friendship, they always viewed each other with leaden horror; unsurprising, perhaps, since their escapades, initiated by Terry, always ended tears.

In 1973 Terry and Bob were brought back for a revival, *Whatever Happened to the Likely Lads?* (BBC1, 27 x 30m col), which, unusually enough, was a sequel as well written as the original. Here the ill-fated pair were four years older, with Terry having spent the intervening period in the Army (and marrying, badly). Bob, meanwhile, had become engaged to the fearsome Thelma (Brigit Forsyth), bought a house of his own, and taken to foreign holidays and meals in restaurants. Terry's disdain towards such bourgeois delusions was remorseless. There was also a touching vein of social commentary on the bewildering changes to the industrial North East of the 70s.

A disappointing *Likely Lads* cinema film was released in 1976.

CAST *Terry Collier* James Bolam *Bob Ferris* Rodney Bewes *Audrey* Sheila Fearn /*cr* Dick Clement & Ian La Frenais /*pr* Dick Clement /*wr* Dick Clement & Ian La Frenais /*mus* Ronnie Hazlehurst /*BBC TV* (UK) / 20 x 25m bw.

Lillie

Drama. ITV 1978

Biopic of Lillie Langtry, the Jersey actress who became the mistress of the Prince of Wales and the darling of America. Francesca Annis reprised her ➢*Edward the Seventh* role as Langtry in a colourful adaptation of James Brough's book, *The Prince and the Lily.* A bodice-fumbler dressed up in the finery of historical drama.

CAST *Lillie Langtry* Francesca Annis *Edward, Prince of Wales (Edward VII)* Dennis Lill *Edward Langtry* Anton Rodgers *Oscar Wilde* Peter Egan /*pr* Jack Williams /*dr* John Gorrie /*wr* David Butler, John Gorrie /*LWT* (UK) /13 x 60m col /US tx PBS 1979.

Lipstick on Your Collar

Drama. C4 1993

A return by playwright Dennis Potter to the romantic comedy style of ➢*Pennies From Heaven.* Set against the Suez Crisis of 1956, *Lipstick on Your Collar* centred on two National Service conscripts in the War Office, Private Mick Hopper and Private Francis Francis, who sought to break free of the stifling, pin-striped conventions which bound them. They did so by embracing the new sexual promiscuity and rock'n'roll music sweeping the land from the USA, with Francis falling moonily for the streetwise blonde wife (played by Potter's personally selected ingénue, Louise Germaine) of the hated Corporal Berry, and Hopper smitten by the dark-haired American, Lisa. Light and accessible, it joined *Pennies From Heaven* and ➢*The Singing Detective* as a singalong Potter piece liked by all.

CAST *Pte Mick Hopper* Ewan McGregor *Pte Francis Francis* Giles Thomas *Sylvia Berry* Louise Germaine *Cpl Peter Berry* Douglas Henshall *Lisa* Kymberley Huffman *Harold Atterbow* Roy Hudd *Col. Harry Bernwood* Peter Jeffrey /*cr* Dennis Potter /*pr* Rosemarie Whitman /*dr* Renny Rye /*wr* Dennis Potter /*Whistling Gypsy* (UK) /6 x 60m col.

A Little Bit of Wisdom

Comedy. ITV 1974–6

A hot star after the success of the 1953 movie *Trouble in Store*, the gump-suited, peak-capped Norman Wisdom – Britain's belated answer to Charlie Chaplin – became a regular fixture on the small screen in such variety-oriented shows as *It's Norman* (ATV, 1953), and *The Norman Wisdom Show* (BBC, 1956). He also tried his hand at sitcom with *Norman* (ITV, 1970), *Nobody is Norman Wisdom* (ITV, 1973) and the last season of *A Little Bit of Wisdom* (the first two seasons presented non-linked playlets). For this seven-week stint, Wisdom was given a permanent job as a clerk in a builder's office, where he caused slapstick mayhem in between blushes at the boss's daughter. It persuaded 7.8 million to watch it.

CAST *Norman Wisdom* himself *Albert Clark* Robert Keegan *Linda Clark* Frances White *Alec Potter* Neil McCarthy /*pr* Les Chatfield /*wr* Lew Schwarz, John Kane, Jon Watkins, Ronnie Taylor /*ATV* (UK) / 7 x 25m col (1976 sitcom season).

Little House on the Prairie

Western. BBC1 1974–82

The struggles of the Ingalls family (seen through the uplifting eyes of second-born daughter Laura) as they eked out a living on a small frontier farm at Walnut Grove, Plumb Creek, Minnesota, in the late 19th century. Also featured were the settlement's shopkeepers Nels and Harriet Oleson (plus bratty kids), mill owner Mr Hanson, and neighbouring farmer Mr Edwards. When Edwards left the story, his place was temporarily taken by Jonathan Garvey (played by ex-Los Angeles Rams star Merlin Olsen).

It was developed for TV from the autobiographical books of Laura Ingalls Wilder by ex-➢*Bonanza* star Michael Landon, who also served as co-executive producer, occasional director and writer, in addition to taking the role of Pa Ingalls. Seamlessly made and played, *Little House* became US network NBC's highest-rated weekly programme for 1978–9. When Landon (born Michael Orowitz) left the series in 1982 to develop ➢*Highway to Heaven*, the show was retitled *Little House: A New Beginning* and the focus shifted to Laura and her husband Almanzo. Meanwhile, two supporting players, Oleson and Victor French, were spun off to their own series, *Father Murphy* and *Carter Country*, respectively.

The show's sentimentality made it easy to ridicule, but not so to forget; the opening credit sequence of skipping children through a sunny buttercup meadow and that tinklingly optimistic theme music (by David Rose, ➢*The High Chaparral*) is doomed to play in a loop of the viewer's memory forever.

CAST *Charles Ingalls* Michael Landon *Caroline Ingalls* Karen Grassle *Laura Ingalls Wilder* Melissa Gilbert *Mary Ingalls Kendall* Melissa Sue Anderson *Carrie Ingalls* Lindsay Greenbush /Sidney Greenbush *Nels Oleson* Richard Bull *Harriet Oleson* Katherine MacGregor *Nellie Oleson Dalton* Alison Arngrim *Willie Oleson* Jonathan Gilbert *Isaiah Edwards* Victor French *Lars Hanson* Karl Swenson *Jonathan Garvey* Merlin Olsen *Almanzo Wilder* Dean Butler /*cr* Michael Landon /*exec pr* Michael Landon, Ed Friendly /*pr* Michael Landon, John Hawkins, Winston Miller, B.W. Sandefur, William F. Claxton /*dr* inc Michael Landon, Victor French, William F. Claxton, Leo Penn, Alf Kjellin /*wr* inc Michael Landon, Blanche Hanalis, Harold Swanton, Arthur Heinemann /*mus* David Rose (theme) /*NBC Productions: Ed Friendly Productions* (USA) /1 x 96m, 216 x 52m col /US tx NBC 1974–82.

The Littlest Hobo

Children's. BBC 1966

Adventures of London, a masterless German Shepherd dog, who helps the sick, the lost, the lonely and the injured. A cross between ➢*Lassie* and ➢*The Adventures of Rin Tin Tin*, with even more slush, making it a perennial loved by almost everybody under five.

CAST inc David Connely, Brian Reid /*pr* Darrell McGowan, Stuart McGowan /*Canamac* (Can) /57 x 25m bw.

The Little World of Don Camillo

Comedy. BBC2 1980

Giovanni Guareschi's classic short stories about the feud between the priest and the communist mayor of a small Italian village, translated for TV by Hugh Leonard, who produced a character comedy which lasted over rather too many episodes. A raucous performance by Brian Blessed helped some.

CAST *Don Camillo* Mario Adorf *The Mayor* Brian Blessed /*pr* Bill Sellars /*dr* Peter Hammond /*wr* Hugh Leonard /*BBC TV* (UK) /13 x 30m col.

Live and Kicking

Children's. BBC1 1993–

Fourth in the BBC's illustrious quartet (with ➢*Multi-coloured Swap Shop*, *Saturday Superstore*, and the Sarah Greene/Philip Schofield presented *Going Live*) of Saturday morning children's TV shows. So laid back as to be almost reclining, it was presented by Andi Peters and Emma Forbes in post-modern style (references to the tele-making process, calling the cameraman by name) and avoided the usual patronizing air of the genre. This, plus a menu of music, chat with the youthful stars of the record biz and small screen (including a hot-seat interrogation of a special guest by junior questioners), cartoons and humour (not least the excruciating puns of comedic duo Trevor and Simon), gave *Live and Kicking* an audience way beyond its 10–16 target group. Edited by Chris Bellingham, who had worked on the show's three predecessors.

CAST (presenters) Andi Peters, Emma Forbes, Zoe Ball, Jamie Theakston /*pr* Angela Sharp, Cathy Gilbey / *BBC TV* (UK) /100+ x 180m col.

The Liver Birds

Comedy. BBC1 1969–78

Developed from a 1969 ➢*Comedy Playhouse*, a classic flat-share sitcom, usually attributed to Carla Lane alone but in fact created with fellow housewife Myra Taylor and veteran scribe Lew Schwarz. The first two Birds to share the poky bedsit in Huskisson Street were Pauline Collins as the prim Dawn and Polly James as the raucous, tomboyish Beryl, but James and Collins never gelled and in January 1971 Nerys Hughes arrived to play the diffident, socially aspirant Sandra; the perfect foil. Beryl and Sandra then set forth on fella-chasing misadventures around Liverpool, with the perfect Merseybeat theme music for their chirpy antics provided by The Scaffold. By the third season, however, Lane had gone solo as writer (although the BBC engaged Eric Idle to script edit) and began to introduce the undertone of lonesome tragedy that would become her hallmark. Thus the Birds, though they continued to room together, began to have separate lives: Sandra began a steady relationship with Paul (a before-➢*Bergerac* John Nettles) and in 1974, on the same day as Princess Anne's wedding, Beryl got married to Robert (played by Jonathan Lynn, later to write ➢*Yes, Minister*) and left the series. Her successor was Carol Boswell, who wore multi-coloured jumpsuits and had red hair and a morose brother called Lucien whose hobby of leporidy led to the catchphrase: 'It's me rabbits…' Carol's Catholic, gin-swilling Ma, meanwhile, became the prototype for ➢*Bread*'s Nellie Boswell, down to the shared surname. The series ended with Sandra finding a suitable match in vet Derek, and becoming pregnant. It was 1978 and the days of the freewheeling Liver Birds was finally over.

A 1996 revival (*pr* Philip Kampff), with Nerys Hughes and Polly James playing their original characters grown older and not necessarily wiser, only proved the point. Shorn of their relative youth and context they were but embarrassing sad cases.

'T'ra.'

CAST *Beryl Hennessey* Polly James *Dawn* Pauline Collins *Sandra Hutchinson* Nerys Hughes *Mrs Hutchinson* Mollie Sugden *Carol Boswell* Elizabeth Estensen *Mrs Boswell* Eileen Kennally/Carmel McSharry *Lucien Boswell* Michael Angelis *Paul* John Nettles *Robert* Jonathan Lynn *Derek Paynton* Tom Chadbon /*cr* Carla Lane, Myra Taylor, Lew Schwarz /*pr* Sydney Lotterby, Douglas Argent, Roger Race /*dr* inc Ray Butt, Bernard Thompson, Douglas Argent /*wr* Carla Lane, Myra Taylor, Lew Schwarz /*mus* The Scaffold (theme), Ronnie Hazlehurst /*BBC TV* (UK) / 79 x 30m bw:col.

Logan's Run

Sci-fi. ITV 1978

Futuristic man-on-the-lam series, set on a post-nuclear Earth (AD 2319, to be exact).

Faced with ritual euthanasia at the age of 30, Logan, a Sandman (policeman) in the City of Domes, decides to give it a miss and flee for a mythical (or maybe not) place called Sanctuary. Accompanying him on his run is a member of the underground, Jessica; en route, at Mountain City, they pick up an android called Rem. Naturally, their flight does not go unpursued and hot on their hovercraft trail is a posse of Sandmen, led by Logan's former partner Francis.

Based on the William F. Nolan/George Clayton Johnson novel and 1976 feature film of the same name (starring Michael York and Jenny Agutter), and therefore suffering the same deficiency: a trite and corny plot.

CAST *Logan* Gregory Harrison *Jessica* Heather Menzies *Rem* Donald Moffat *Francis* Randy Powell /*exec pr* Ivan Goff, Ben Roberts /*dr* inc Alexander Singer, Irving J. Moore, Paul Krasny, Nicholas Colasanto, Michael Caffey /*wr* inc William F. Nolan, James Schmerer, D.C. Fontana, Simon Wincelberg, Harlan Ellison, Richard L. Breen, Katharyn Michaelian Powers, John Meredyth Lucas /*An MGM Television Production* (USA) /1 x 80m, 13 x 60m col /US tx CBS 1977–8.

London's Burning

Drama. ITV 1988–

Action soap about the firefighters of Blue Watch B25, Blackwall, which began life as a one-off 1986 TVM by Jack Rosenthal. Combining colourful characters ('Sicknote', 'Bayleaf', 'Vaseline'), fear-some pyrotechnics, cold-sweat stunts and melo-drama-ish dwelling on the crew's off-duty domestic problems, it was a programme for all viewers of low- to middle-browish mood and became the mainstay of ITV's Sunday evening line up for a decade. Although never sent onto the schedules with anything less than basic professionalism, each passing series was ever more reliant on sfx and spectacular conflagrations until it looked like a serial version of the Great Fire of London.

CAST *Mike 'Bayleaf' Wilson* James Hazeldine *Station Off. Sidney Tate* James Marcus *Bert 'Sicknote' Quigley* Richard Walsh *Roland 'Vaseline' Cartwright* Mark Arden *Sub-Officer John Hallam* Sean Blowers *Malcolm Cross* Rupert Baker *Leslie 'Charisma' Appleby* Gerard Horan *Josie Ingham* Kartharine Rogers *Kate Stevens* Samantha Beckinsale *Stuart 'Recall' Mackenzie* Ben Onwukwe *Geff 'Poison' Pearce* Michael Garner *Nick Georgiadis* Andrew Kazamia *Billy Ray* John Alford *Kevin* Ross Boatman /*cr* Jack Rosenthal /*exec pr* Linda Agran, Nick Elliott, Sarah Wilson /*pr* Paul Knight, Gerry Poulson /*dr* inc Gerry Poulson, Gerry Mill, Rank W. Smith /*wr* Simon J. Sharkey, David Humphries /*LWT* (UK) /120+ x 60m col.

The Lone Ranger

Western. BBC1 1956–60

'Who was that masked man?'

Legendary Western show for children, which began life as a radio programme for Detroit's WXYZ in 1933, where it was created by station owner George W. Trendle, writer Fran Striker and producer James Jewell. Almost overnight the show was taken up nationally and, by 1939, had been turned into two film serials by Republic. In 1949, *The Lone Ranger* debuted as a TV show on America's ABC network, to become one of the new medium's biggest hits.

Helpfully, the first episode provided a résumé of how the Lone Ranger received his *nom de justice*: as Texan Ranger John Reid he had been the only survivor of a bushwhack and was saved from death by a kindly Indian called Tonto, who had declared, 'You only Ranger left. You lone ranger now.' And, stopping only to don a mask, 'The Lone Ranger' set off to avenge his comrades and right the wrongs of 19th-century Texas, accompanied by his Indian companion and his horse Silver.

The plots of the show, mostly cannibalized from the radio scripts, were elementary bestings of baddies, but there was enough stirring action and gunplay to keep younger viewers ogling the set. Parents loved it for its patriotism and high-minded moralism, while FBI chief J. Edgar Hoover termed it 'one of the forces for juvenile good in the country.' The production company's list of 'Lone Ranger's Don'ts' for potential scriptwriters included: 'At all times, The Lone Ranger uses perfect grammar and speech'; 'The Lone Ranger never shoots to kill'; 'the ultimate objective of his story ... is the development of the west of our country...'

Selected to play the The Lone Ranger was former trapeze artist and male model Clayton Moore, the so-called 'King of the Serials' at Republic film studios. During a contract dispute between Moore and *The Lone Ranger*'s producers, the part was briefly taken by John Hart (later ➢*Hawkeye and the*

Last of the Mohicans) before Moore was lassoed back. Tonto was played by Jay Silverheels who, despite being the genuine son of a Mohawk Indian chief, was really named Harold Smith. Aside from the Lone Ranger and Tonto, the only other recurring characters were: their respective horses, Silver and Scout; the Lone Ranger's nephew Dan Reid (whose son, in turn, would become ➢*The Green Hornet*); and oldtimer Jim Blaine, who ran the Lone Ranger's private silver-mine, the source of the silver for his bullets.

Aside from numerous reruns, the series has spun off a 1966 cartoon version and some 13 Lone Ranger TV movies, all edited from existing episodes. Hi-ho, Silver, and away!

CAST *The Lone Ranger* Clayton Moore/John Hart *Tonto* Jay Silverheels *Dan Reid* Chuck Courtney *Jim Blaine* Ralph Littlefield /*pr* George W. Trendle, Jack Chertok, Sherman Harris, Paul Landres, Harry H. Poppe /*dr* inc George B. Seitz, Charles Livingtone, Paul Landres /*wr* inc Fran Striker, George G. Seitz, Ed Earl Repp, Walker A. Tompkins /*mus* Rossini ('William Tell Overture' theme) /*Alberto Columbo / Apex Film Corp: Wrather Corp* (USA) /182 x 25m bw:col.

Lonesome Dove

Western. BBC1 1991

Epic adaptation of Larry McMurtry's epic Pulitzer-winning novel.

Robert Duvall and Tommy Lee Jones played a pair of ageing Texas Rangers, the reprobate Gus McCrae and the control-freak Call, who, in a final flicker of frontier spirit, resolve to lead a cattle drive north from Texas through Indian Country to the wide-open range of Montana. With painterly visuals and a deliberately stately pace that allowed the emotional exploration of character (particularly the tangled relationship between McCrae, Call and his old flame Clara), *Lonesome Dove* was both high drama and high art. In retrospect it is possible to carp that the mini-series was *too* studied, but there is no doubting its success or its place in screen history: it lassoed no less than seven Emmys and single-handedly revived the Western, causing the networks to rush a number of oater shows into production (*The Young Riders*, ➢*Paradise* and *Bordertown*) and the studios to dust off the old horse-opera lots.

A sequel to *Lonesome Dove* itself was inevitable. *Return to Lonesome Dove* picked up where the first series ended, with Call returned to Texas pulling the tin coffin of his old friend. However, despite an obviously lavish budget and a comparably star-spangled cast, it remained content simply to repeat the story of *Lonesome Dove* by substituting wild horses for cows.

CAST *Gus McCrae* Robert Duvall *Capt. Call* Tommy Lee Jones *Jake Spoon* Robert Urich *Clara* Anjelica Huston *Newt* Ricky Schroder /*exec pr* Suzanne De Passe, Bill Wittliff, Robert Halmi Jr /*pr* Dyson Lovell / *dr* Simon Wincer /*wr* Bill Wittliff /*mus* Basil Poledouris /*Motown Productions: Pangaea Productions: Qintex Entertainment* /4 x 120m col /US tx CBS 1989.

Longstreet

Crime. ITV 1973

Crime cases of a blind New Orleans private investigator and his Alsatian guide dog, Pax.

Meretricious 70s detective show, only worth sick-humour viewing for its unintentional comedy and some scintillating chop-chop appearances from Bruce Lee as Longstreet's self-defence teacher; in particular the opening episode 'The Way of the Intercepting Fist'.

CAST *Mike Longstreet* James Franciscus *Nikki Bell* Marilyn Mason *Duke Paige* Peter Mark Richman *Mrs Kingston* Ann Doran /*exec pr* Stirling Silliphant /*pr* Joel Rogosin /*dr* inc Joseph Sargent /*wr* inc Stirling Silliphant /*mus* Billy Goldenburg, Robert Drasnin / *Paramount TV* (USA) /24 x 60m col /US tx ABC 1971–2.

Lord Peter Wimsey

Crime. BBC1 1972–5

In which Ian Carmichael impersonated novelist Dorothy L. Sayers' titled detective in a set of mini-serials of particularly flavoursome 20s atmosphere. Glyn Houston (➢*Minder*) and Peter Newark alternately roughed it as his manservant Bunter in the adapted puzzles, which began with 'Clouds of Witness', progressed through 'The Unpleasantness at the Bellona Club', 'Murder Must Advertise', and 'The Nine Tailors', to conclude with 'Five Red Herrings'. As if to prove that Snobbery with Violence is the TV opiate of the English, three further Wimsey serials were produced in 1987 under the title ➢*A Dorothy L. Sayers Mystery*, starring Edward Petherbridge.

CAST *Lord Peter Wimsey* Ian Carmichael *Bunter* Glyn Houston/Peter Newark /*pr* Richard Beynon, Bill Sellars / *dr* Hugh David, Ronald Wilson, Raymond Menmuir,

Rodney Bennett, Robert Tronson /*wr* Anthony Steven, Bill Craig /*BBC TV: BBC Scotland* (UK) /21 x 45–50m col.

Lost in Space
Sci-fi. ITV 1965–70

After his success with ➢*Voyage to the Bottom of the Sea,* Irwin Allen looked spacewards for his next project, the story of the American Family Robinson who, in the year 1997, left overcrowded Earth for uninhabited Alpha Centauri. Alas, their *Jupiter 2* spaceship was sabotaged by evil (thus foreign) agent Dr Zachary Smith, who blew them – and himself – off course. For three dreary years Smith, the Robinsons and their Robot wandered a low-budget cosmos in a repeat plot where Smith connived with the episode's extraterrestrials to disastrous effect. An attempt to emulate the camp of ➢*Batman* only succeeded in making the show ridiculous.

Robot design was by Bob Kinoshita, who had previously created Robby the Robot for the classic sci fi film, *Forbidden Planet.*

CAST *Prof. John Robinson* Guy Williams *Maureen Robinson* June Lockhart *Judy* Marta Kristen *Penny* Angela Cartwright *Will* Bill Mumy *Don West* Mark Goddard *Dr Zachary Smith* Jonathan Harris *Robot* Bob May /Dick Tufeld (voice) /*cr* Irwin Allen /*exec pr* Irwin Allen /*dr* inc Tony Leader, Alex Singer, Leo Penn, Sobey Martin, Alvin Ganzer, Leonard Horn, Robert Douglas /*wr* inc Shimon Wincelberg, Carey Wilbur, Robert Hamner, Jack Turley /*mus* Johnny Williams /*sfx* L.B. Abbott, Hal Lydecker /*Irwin Allen: Jodi Production Inc: Van Bernard Productions for Fox TV* (USA) /83 x 60m bw /US tx CBS 1965–8.

The Lotus Eaters
Drama. BBC2 1972–3

Serial set around a small taverna in the Cretan resort of Aghios Nicholaos, used by expat Brits as home from home. Their intriguing, often dark personal histories were interlaced with the troubled story of the bar's owners, Erik (Ian Hendry from *Police Surgeon*) and Ann Shepherd.

Insidiously addictive trouble-in-paradise melodrama.

CAST *Erik Shepherd* Ian Hendry *Anne Shepherd* Wanda Ventham *Major Edward Woolley* Thorley Walters *Mrs Miriam Wolley* Sylvia Coleridge *Ruth Stewart* Cyd Hayman *Nester Turton* Maurice Denham / *cr* Michael J. Bird /*pr* Anthony Read /*wr* Michael J. Bird /*BBC TV* (UK) /9 x 50m col.

Lou Grant
Drama. ITV 1979–82

The character of Lou Grant first appeared as the newsroom boss in the comedy ➢*The Mary Tyler Moore Show.* At the end of *MTM*, Grant was fired from Minneapolis radio station WJM–TV only to reappear in this newpaper drama, where he worked as the crusading city editor of the *Los Angeles Tribune*, owned by the redoutable Margaret Pynchon. Unlike *MTM*'s previous spin-offs (➢*Rhoda, Phyllis*), *Lou Grant* dropped outright comedy for a format of hour-length drama that innovatively mixed workplace sitcom with soap and intense social conscience. Usually, several plotlines ran in each episode, making the show something of a precursor to production company MTM's ➢*Hill Street Blues.* After a slow start in the ratings, *LG* picked up, thanks to the popularity of the charismatic Asner as the gruff but lovable Grant, a public interest in the journalistic trade in the wake of Watergate, and a gallery of strong supporting characters: Pynchon, hotshot reporter Joe Rossi, 60s leftover photographer Animal, assistant city editor Art Donovan, and career-minded reporter Billie Newman.

After winning 11 Emmys in five years (including two for Asner as best Actor, and two for Outstanding Drama), the show ended in 1982 in a controversy worthy of an *LG* episode. Asner, the head of the Screen Actors Guild, clashed noisily with President Reagan over the US intervention in Central America, and CBS, concerned over a consequent drop in the ratings and right-wing critcism, pulled the plug.

CAST *Lou Grant* Edward Asner *Billie Newman McCovey* Linda Kelsey *Joe Rossi* Robert Walden *Charlie Hume* Mason Adams *Margaret Pynchon* Nancy Marchand *Dennis 'Animal' Price* Daryl Anderson *Carla Mardigian* Rebecca Balding *Art Donovan* Jack Bannon /*cr* Allan Burns, James L. Brooks, Gene Reynolds /*exec pr* Allan Burns, Gene Reynolds, James L. Brooks /*dr* inc Gene Reynolds, Mel Damski, Roger Young, Burt Brinckerhoff, Jay Sandrich, Charles Dubin, Richard Crenna, Corey Allen /*wr* inc Leon Tokatyan, Michele Gallery, Gary David Goldberg, Gene Reynolds, Allan Burns /*mus* Patrick Williams, Michael Melvoin, Hod David /*MTM* (USA) /113 x 60m col /US tx CBS 1977–82.

Love, American Style

Comedy. ITV 1970

Skits, vignettes and playlets on the theme of lurve, played to humorous effect. There was no regular cast, outside of a rep company of extras (which included Stuart Margolin, later the ➢*The Rockford Files*), with weekly guest artists performing the lead roles. Burt Reynolds and Tiny Tim were among the many celestial ones to do so. It enjoyed a hit run in the USA, and one of its better pieces provided the start for ➢*Happy Days*.

CAST inc Stuart Margolin /*cr* Douglas S. Cramer, Tom Miller /*exec pr* Jim Parker, Arnold Margolin /*pr* Ray Allen, Harvey Bullock, Jim Parker, Arnold Margolin /*mus* The Charles Fox Singers ('Love American Style' theme vocals) /*Paramount* (USA) / 112 x 30–60m col /US tx ABC 1969–74.

Love Boat

Melodrama. ITV 1978–86

Anthology of light romantic playlets set aboard luxurious liner, the *Pacific Princess*.

It leaked a slick of insincere sentiment but stayed afloat in the ratings for years, buoyed up by B-list Hollywood guest talent. The show sunk finally in 1986, with an episode in which Captain Stubing married a passenger, Emily Heywood, played by Marion Ross from ➢*Happy Days*. Aaron Spelling produced.

CAST *Capt. Merrill Stubing* Gavin MacLeod *Julie McCoy* Lauren Tewes *Judy McCoy* Pat Klous *Dr Adam Bricker* Bernie Kopell *Burl 'Gopher' Smith* Fred Grandy *Isaac Washington* Ted Lange *Vicki Stubing* Jill Whelan /*exec pr* Aaron Spelling, Douglas S. Cramer /*dr* inc Kim Friedman, Neil Cox, Hy Averback, Jerome Courtland, Bob Claver, Richard Lang, Gordon Farr, Ted Lange, James Sheldon /*Aaron Spelling Productions* (USA) /120 x 60m col /US tx ABC 1977–86.

Love Hurts

Comedy. BBC1 1992–4

A drop-out businesswoman and self-made millionaire plumber in mismatch romance.

Low-key, low-appeal comedy from Marks and Gran, full of cringe-making discussions between the characters on the relative merits of social conscience and Mammon. The poor casting of Zoë Wanamaker as the non-credible Tessa (director of an aid agency, Seed) and Adam Faith as the unlikeable Frank did not help, since the former was too good for her role and the latter barely adequate. In the second series Tessa and Frank married, and in the third became parents to baby Alice, but by then there were few viewers left to care.

CAST *Frank Carver* Adam Faith *Tessa Piggott* Zoë Wanamaker *Diane Warburg* Jane Lapotaire *Max Taplow* Tony Selby *Hugh Marriner* Stephen Moore /*cr* Laurence Marks & Maurice Gran /*pr* Guy Slater, Tara Brem, Irving Teitlebaum /*wr* Laurence Marks & Maurice Gran /*BBC TV* (UK) /18 x 30m col.

Lovejoy

Comedy. BBC1 1986–94

From the novels of Jonathan Gash. A comedy thriller in which (a nicely cast) Ian McShane played an East Anglian antiques dealer of some knowledge and equal dodginess. Lovejoy was assisted on his capers by bewildered chums Tinker and Eric, a vintage Morris Minor called Miriam, and local aristo Lady Jane Felsham, who also supplied the flirtatious romantic interest (until replaced by auctioneer Charlotte Cavendish.) Developed for TV by the sublimely assured hand of Ian La Frenais (➢*The Likely Lads*), the show cleverly stimulated viewer affection for its central character by the use of plots in which he protected innocent punters from dealers more shady than he, and his asides to camera, which gave those at home the feeling of privileged conspirator.

CAST *Lovejoy* Ian McShane *Lady Jane Felsham* Phyllis Logan *Tinker Deal* Dudley Sutton *Eric Catchpole* Chris Jury *Lord Felsham* Pavel Douglas *Beth* Diane Parish *Charlotte Cavendish* Caroline Langrishe *Charlie Gimbert* Malcolm Tierney *Amanda* Cassie Stuart /*cr* Ian La Frenais /*pr* Richard Everitt, Robert Banks Stewart, Jo Wright, Colin Shindler, Emma Hayter /*dr* inc Francis Megahy, Bill Brayne, Geoff Love, Baz Taylor, Ian McShane, John Crome, Sarah Hellings, Peter Barber-Fleming /*wr* inc Ian La Frenais, Terry Hodgkinson, Robert Banks Stewart, Douglas Watkinson /*Tamariska: Witzend: McShane* (UK) / 71 x 30m col.

The Lovers

Comedy. ITV 1970–1

Jack Rosenthal sitcom in which Paula Wilcox sought to preserve her virginity on the sitting room sofa against the desperate advances of Richard Beckinsale (later ➢*Rising Damp*, ➢*Porridge*). A big screen version, with Wilcox still resisting 'Percy Filth', came out in 1972. The actress virtually reprised her frigid role in ➢*Man About the House.*

CAST *Geoffrey ('Bubbles Bon Bon')* Richard Beckinsale *Beryl* Paula Wilcox *Mum* Joan Scott *Roland* Robin Nedwell /*cr* Jack Rosenthal /*pr* Jack Rosenthal, Les Chatfield /*dr* Michael Apted /*wr* Jack Rosenthal, Geoffrey Lancashire /*mus* Derek Hilton (theme) / *Granada TV* (UK) /14 x 30m col.

Love Story

Drama. ITV 1963–7/1969/1972–4

An anthology of romantic plays, screened intermittently by ATV over the 60s and 70s. It was at its peak vitality in its youth, when contributors included the likes of Stan Barstow, Doris Lessing and Edna O'Brien, who in turn attracted a quality cast: Marguerite Duras' 1965 mini-masterpiece 'La Musica' starred Vanessa Redgrave, while in the same year Roman Polanski penned 'The Girl Opposite', putting Dudley Moore in a rare straight role. The same title was also used by the BBC in the early 80s for runs of mini-serials of much the same romantic sort.

CAST inc Vanessa Redgrave, Dudley Moore, Anton Rodgers, Angharad Rees, Gabrielle Drake, Penelope Keith, Frances Cuka, Johnny Briggs, Judi Dench, Julia Foster, Patrick Macnee, Robert Hardy /*pr* inc Hugh Rennie, Stella Richman, Josephine Douglas, Pieter Rogers, Rex Firkin, Henri Safran, Nicholas Palmer /*dr* inc Josephine Douglas, Valerie Hanson, Ian Fordyce, Mike Newell /*wr* inc Edna O'Brien, Marguerite Duras, Roman Polanski, Doris Lessing, Mordecai Richler, Robert Muller, Robert Holles /*ATV* (UK) /40 x 50m bw:col.

Love Thy Neighbour

Comedy. ITV 1972–6

The first British sitcom to deal exclusively with the subject of race relations, placing bigoted white trade unionist Eddie Booth and his wife next door to a West Indian couple, Bill and Barbie Reynolds. Eddie, whose aim was to 'preserve our white heritage' called his neighbour 'nig-nog'; Bill traded the insult back by calling him 'snowflake' and 'honky'. Creators Harry Driver and Vince Powell (➢*Never Mind the Quality, Feel the Width*, ➢*George and the Dragon*, ➢*Bless This House*) claimed to expose these racial 'insults is to the public to take the sting out of them and make them less hurtful.' Meanwhile, as is so often the case in British domestic comedies, the wives got on like a house on fire.

It was unedifying, unfunny stuff, but its novel subject matter kept it high in the ratings for five years (usually in No. 1 position). Almost certainly it paved the way for Britain's first all-black comedy series, ➢*The Fosters.*

A feature-length *Love Thy Neighbour*, with the TV cast, was made by Hammer (*dr* John Robbins) for cinema release in 1973, while an American attempt to format the show for ABC network managed just one season.

CAST *Eddie Booth* Jack Smethurst *Joan Booth* Kate Williams *Barbie Reynolds* Nina Baden-Semper *Bill Reynolds* Rudolph Walker *Jacko Jackson* Keith Marsh /*cr* Vince Powell & Harry Driver /*pr* Stuart Allen, Ronnie Baxter, Anthony Parker /*dr* Stuart Allen, Ronnie Baxter /*wr* inc Vince Powell Harry Driver, Johnnie Mortimer, Sid Colin /*Thames TV* (UK) /40 x 25m col.

Lucky Dip

Children's. ITV 1958–61

A Tuesday bag of assorted surprises, subtitled *The Junior Newspaper*, and first presented by Nevil Whiting and then Howard Williams. 'Correspondents' included Grahame Dangerfield (nature), Bert Weedon (music), Muriel Young (roving reporter), and Fanny and Johnnie Craddock ('Happy Cooking'). Light relief was provided in the lively puppet shapes of Ollie Beak and Pussy Cat Willum. The series evolved into *Tuesday Rendezvous* (1961–3) and then ➢*Five O'Clock Club.*

CAST (presenters) inc Nevil Whiting, Howard Williams, Fanny Craddock /*cr* Eric Spear /*pr* Nevil Whiting, Howard Williams /*Associated Rediffusion* (UK) /approx 60 x 25m bw.

Luna

Children's. ITV 1983–4

Imaginative space-age comedy for children, which sought to show – not least through its use of absurdly funny techno-babble – the need for human ethics in a future world. Created by Mickey Dolenz, the ex-drummer for ➢*The Monkees*, the series starred Patsy Kensit as the title teenager.

CAST *Luna* Patsy Kensit/Joanna Wyatt *Brat* Aaron Brown *Gramps* Frank Duncan *40D* Natalie Forbes *Andy* Colin Bennett *80H* Roy Macready /*cr* Mickey Dolenz /*pr* Mickey Dolenz /*dr* Mickey Dolenz, Chris Tookey /*wr* Colin Bennett, Colin Prockter /*Central Production* (UK) /12 x 30m col.

Richard Dean Anderson, the star of adventure series *Macgyver*, exec. produced by former actor Henry 'the Fonz' Winkler.

Macgyver

Spy adventure. ITV 1987–94

Espionage actioner with a likeable hero who always managed to escape deadly perils – flaming oil pits, primed rockets – in the nick of time, armed only with a paper clip or disposable pen. For the first season 'Mac' (played in suitably comic-strip style by Richard Dean Anderson), a former Special Forces soldier, troubleshot for the US Government, but from season two he was employed by the privately owned Phoenix Corporation. In the last season it was revealed that the hero's less-than-heroic-sounding first name was Angus.

The show was co-executive produced by Henry Winkler, formerly 'The Fonz' in ➢*Happy Days*. Randy Edelman provided the theme music.

CAST *(Angus) Macgyver* Richard Dean Anderson *Peter Thornton* Dana Elcar *Murdoc* Michael Des Barres / *cr* Lee David Zlotoff / *exec pr* Henry Winkler, John Rich, Stephen Downing / *pr* inc Stephen Kandel / *dr* inc Michael Caffey, William Gereghty, Michael Vejar, James L. Conway, Bruce Kessler, Dana Elcar / *wr* inc Lincoln Kibbee, Rick Mittleman, John Considine, David Rich, Stephen Kandel / *mus* Randy Edelman (theme) / *John Rich Productions: Paramount TV* (USA) / 139 x 60m; 2 x 90m col / US tx ABC 1985–94.

Madigan

Crime. ITV 1973

Stemmed from the 1968 film of the same title (*dr* Don Spiegel), with Richard Widmark reprising his role as the abrasive loner NY homicide cop, here sent on a clutch of cases requiring foreign travel. To forgettable avail.

CAST *Sgt Dan Madigan* Richard Widmark / *exec pr* Dean Hargrove, Frank Rosenberg / *pr* Roland Kibbee / *dr* Alex March, Boris Sagal, Jack Smight / *wr* inc William McGovern, Roland Kibbee, Dean Hargrove / *Oden Productions: Universal Television* (USA) / 6 x 90m col / US tx NBC 1972–3.

The Magician

Crime. ITV 1974

Starred a pre- ➢*The Incredible Hulk* Bill Bixby as a magician who used his illusionist skills to help those in trouble. Moderately unusual sleuth show, but as substantial as spun sugar. To Bixby's credit, however, he performed the wizard tricks himself. Hollywood's Magic Castle was a frequent location.

CAST *Anthony Blake (Anthony Dorian in pilot)* Bill Bixby *Max Pomeroy* Keene Curtis *Dennis Pomeroy* Todd Crespi /*cr* Bruce Lansbury /*pr* Laurence Heath /*dr* Marvin Chomsky, Alexander Singer, Barry Crane /*mus* Patrick Williams (theme) /*Paramount TV* (USA) /1 x 73m, 24 x 50m col /US tx NBC 1973–4.

The Magic Roundabout
Children's. BBC1 1965–77

'Time for bed,' said Zebedee.

Cult 60s and 70s puppet show from French *animateur* Serge Danot, written and dryly narrated for British TV by Eric Thompson (ex-➢*Play School*, and father of Oscar-winning actress Emma). Set in Mr Rusty's blue, red and white garden, the featured creatures were sensible Florence, boorish ginger dog Dougal (whose nose was seven inches in diameter), Brian the snail, silly old moo Ermintrude, bicycling Mr McHenry, spring-man Zebedee and dopey Dylan the rabbit, who appeared to smoke grass rather than eat it. Surreal, funny and frequently sardonic about real events (such as Dr Beeching's swingeing rail cuts) in its scripting, it built up an eight-million-strong audience (many of them adults) in its slot before the weekday six o'clock news. Notable also for its pioneering use of mixed animation and marionettes, it prompted a feature film *Pollux et le Chat Bleu*, released as *Dougal and the Blue Cat* (1972) in the UK.

A new series of 52 stories appeared in 1992 on C4, written and narrated by Nigel Planer (ex-➢*The Comic Strip Presents...*, ➢*The Young Ones*).

CAST (narrator) Eric Thompson /*cr* Serge Danot /(Fr) /302 x 5m col.

Magnum, PI
Crime. ITV 1981–7

Private-eye vehicle for muscles-and-moustache actor Tom Selleck, who had caught the eye of Universal TV when playing smug gumshoe Lance White in ➢*The Rockford Files*. Economically recycling *Rockford*'s penchant for parody, plus the paradise setting and scantily-clad-girls formula of ➢*Hawaii Five-0* (even using that show's production facilities), *Magnum*'s conceit was that its title 'tec was a rakish ex-Vietnam vet who had the job – as well as doing some genereal gumshoeing – of protecting the Oahu estate of permanently absent writer Robin Masters (voiced by Orson Welles); this

Down boy! Tom Selleck as laid-back Honolulu 'tec Magnum, PI. Not the least of the show's appeal to network CBS was that they were able to re-use the production facilities of *Hawaii Five-0.*

gave Magnum *gratis* use of a red Ferrari, as well as a palatial ceiling over his head. The downside was Masters' crusty British manservant, Higgins, who disliked Magnum's casual air and freeloading ways to the extent of encouraging Dobermann pinschers Zeus and Apollo to take bites out of his hide. Developed from a pilot entitled 'Don't Eat the Snow in Hawaii', the show relied too frequently on Selleck's sex-appeal and shining talent for comedy to cover up creaking plots to be entirely successful. It lasted, however, for eight much-loved seasons before anybody noticed and pulled the trigger on it.

CAST *Thomas Magnum* Tom Selleck *Jonathan Quale Higgins III* John Hillerman *Theodore 'TC' Calvin* Roger E. Mosley *Orville 'Rick' Wright* Larry Manetti *Robin Masters* (voice) Orson Welles /*cr* Donald P. Bellisario, Glen A. Larson /*exec pr* Donald P. Bellisario, Glen A. Larson /*dr* inc David Hemmings, Peter Medak, Joan Darling, Donald P. Bellisario, Bernard Kowalski, Rich Kolbe, Burt Kennedy, Alan Levi, Leo Penn, Russ Mayberry, John Llewellyn Moxey, Harry Harris, Michael O'Herlihy /*Universal TV* (USA) / 6 x 120m, 150 x 60m col /US tx CBS 1980–8.

Magpie
Children's. ITV 1968–80

'One for sorrow, two for joy, three for a girl, four for a boy...'

Magpie was ITV's groovy, twice-weekly magazine-answer to the BBC's primly middle-class ➢*Blue Peter.* Intially presented by the triumvirate of Susan Stranks, former R1 DJ Pete Brady and Tony Bastable, *Magpie* specialized in pop music, fashion and fun (including for a period David Jason's Captain Fantastic character from ➢*Do Not Adjust Your Set*), though the educational element was present in slots such as 'A Date With Tony', an in-depth examination of past ages. In 1971 a teenager saved a boy by giving him the kiss of life he'd seen demonstrated on the show. As on *Blue Peter,* there were charity appeals, although *Magpie*, unlike that show which regarded money as too base to mention, had no inhibitions about asking kiddies for the pennies in their pocket, the total amount of lucre raised indicated by a red line which ran around the Teddington Studio. The name of the magpie mascot, for those who wish to know it, was Murgatroyd. Jenny Hanley, Tommy Boyd and the Marc Bolanesque Mick Robertson (later *Free Time*, and producer of C4's *Wise Up*) were the most prominent of the later presenters.

CAST (presenters) Pete Brady, Susan Stranks, Tony Bastable, Mick Robertson, Douglas Rae, Tommy Boyd, Jenny Hanley /*cr* Susan Turner /*exec pr* Lewis Rudd / *pr* Sue Turner, David Hodgson, Randal Beattie, Tim Jones, Tony Bastable, Leslie Burgess /*Thames TV* (UK) / approx. 1000 x 30m col.

Maid Marian and Her Merry Men
Children's. BBC1 1989–94

Award-winning, politically correct, spoof of the Robin Hood legend by Tony Robinson (the luckless Baldrick in ➢*Blackadder*), which posited Maid Marian as the real outlaw leader of Sherwood Forest – and Robin as a wimpy yuppie known as Robin of Kensington who took all the credit. The merry men included a Rastafarian (played by Danny John-Jules from ➢*Red Dwarf*) and a midget. Anarchic and original, with quivers of kiddie-friendly visual jokes. Robinson himself played the Sheriff of Nottingham in the style of Adolf Hitler, only without the charm.

CAST *Maid Marian* Kate Lonergan *Robin of Kensington* Wayne Morris *Rabies* Howard Lew Lewis *Little Ron* Mike Edmonds *Barrington* Danny John-Jules *Sheriff of Nottingham* Tony Robinson *Prince John* Forbes Collins /*cr* Tony Robinson /*pr* Richard Callanan /*cr* David Bell /*wr* Tony Robinson /*BBC TV* (UK) /26 x 30m col.

Maigret
Crime. BBC 1960–3

Starred Rupert Davies as Georges Simenon's famous pipe-smoking detective from the Paris Sûreté, who solved cases by analysing character rather than wielding a magnifying glass in a hunt for clues. The casting of Davies delighted Simenon (who had given the BBC the rights to his work ahead of global competition), though Davies would later claim: 'I didn't have a life as an actor after I put on his [Maigret's] trilby and struck that match against a wall at the opening of every episode.' Typecast and damned, Davies returned as Maigret to host the 1964 series ➢*Detective* and to feature in a 1969 ➢*Play for Today*, 'Maigret at Bay'. In 1988 HTV released a 120 minute TVM *Maigret* (with a miscast Richard Harris), before the character was resurrected in series form by Granada TV in 1992. Michael Gambon (from ➢*The Singing Detective*) assumed the title role of Maigret in a production that interpreted the sleuth as a stolid plodder; Geoffrey Hutchings was Sergeant Lucas, while Ciaran Madden/Barbara Flynn shared the playing of Madame Maigret. Sponsored by Kronenbourg, the series was filmed in Hungary because it was cheaper and looked more like the Paris of *temps perdu*.

CAST *Chief Insp. Maigret* Rupert Davies *Lucas* Ewen Solon *Mme Maigret* Helen Shingler /*exec pr* Andrew Osborn /*dr* inc Andrew Osborn /*wr* inc Giles Cooper / *mus* Ron Grainer /*BBC TV: Winwell* (UK) /52 x 50m bw.

The Main Chance
Crime. ITV 1969–75

Quality legal drama starring charismatic John Stride as an ambitious solicitor on the career-up – this, despite a tendency to take on progressive underdog cases for free. Whatever the work, David Main approached it in an instinctive, no-nonsense manner beloved of his clients – and the TV audience; the series topped the ratings in October 1970. Kate O'Mara played Main's wife in the debut season.

CAST *David Main* John Stride *Julia Main* Kate O'Mara *Sarah Courtenay/Lady Radchester* Anna Palk /*cr* Edmund Ward /*exec pr* Peter Willes, David Cunliffe /*pr* Peter Willes, David Cunliffe, John Frankau, Derek Bennett /*dr* John Frankau /*wr* inc Edmund Ward, John Malcolm /*YTV* (UK) /45 x 50m col.

Making Out

Comedy. BBC1 1989–91

Debbie Horsfield comedy drama – from a Franc ➢'*Auf Wiedersehen, Pet*' Roddam idea – set in the fictitious Manchester factory of New Line Electronics, where the poor but far from down-trodden women workers toiled uppitily and complained about men lengthily. Margi Clarke ('the Merseyside Monroe', wife of punk artist Jamie Reid) headed the cast as gobby Queenie; also included were Brian Hibbard (ex-The Flying Pickets a capella group and ➢*Coronation Street*) as Queenie's lay-about hubbie and Keith Allen (➢*The Comic Strip Presents...*) as boss Rex. Unlike the workplace comedies of yore, such as ➢*The Rag Trade*, it reeked of authenticity and real characters, and there were often as many tears as there were giggles by the conveyor belt.

CAST *Queenie* Margi Clarke *Rex* Keith Allen *Chunky* Brian Hibbard *Carol May* Shirley Stelfox *Pauline* Rachel Davies *Norma* Tracie Bennett *Klepto* Moya Brady *Donna* Heather Tobias /*cr* Franc Roddam /*pr* John Chapman, Carol Wilks /*dr* Chris Bernard, Richard Spence, Noella Smith, John Woods /*wr* Debbie Horsfield /*BBC TV* (UK) /24 x 50m col.

The Mallens

Melodrama. ITV 1979

Catherine Cookson's saga of a ruthless 19th-century Northumberland squire and his bastard offspring (each of whom had inherited his flash of white hair known as 'The Mallen Streak'), adapted by Jack Russell. Full of the sound of ripping bodices and familial discord, but signifying nothing at all. Except perhaps to boost the career of actress Juliet Stevenson, who played the squire's illegitimate daughter.

CAST *Thomas Mallen (father)* John Hallam *Donald Radlett* John Duttine *Dick* David Rentoul *Constance Farrington (later Radlett)* Julia Chambers/June Ritchie *Barbara Farrington* Pippa Guard *Barbara Mallen* Juliet Stevenson *Anna Brigmore* Caroline Blakiston /*pr* Roy Roberts /*dr* Ronald Wilson, Mary McMurray /*wr* Jack Russell /*Granada TV* (UK) /13 x 60m.

Man About the House

Comedy. ITV 1973–6

Popular Johnnie Mortimer and Brian Cooke sitcom about two chicks (prissy Chrissy, dumb-blonde Jo) who inadvertently end up sharing their Earls Court flat with a guy (student chef Robin). In the 70s mixed-sex households were considered risqué, resulting in lots of 'whoops, I-didn't-know-you-were-in-the-bath' gags and hiding from visiting Victorian-leftover mums. The trio's basement mean-minded landlord and his sex-minded wife were eventually spun off to their own show, ➢*George and Mildred*, while Robin (played by Richard O'Sullivan) went on to culinary disasters in ➢*Robin's Nest.* A feature film version of *Man About the House* was released by Hammer/EMI in 1974 and the format sold to America as *Three's Company.*

CAST *Chrissy Plummer* Paula Wilcox *Jo* Sally Thomsett *Robin Tripp* Richard O'Sullivan *George Roper* Brian Murphy *Mildred Roper* Yootha Joyce /*cr* Johnnie Mortimer, Brian Cooke /*pr* Peter Frazer-Jones /*wr* Johnnie Mortimer, Brian Cooke /*Thames TV* (UK) /39 x 25m col.

The Manageress

Drama. C4 1989

Soccer drama, the twist being that the new manager of the struggling club was of the distaff persuasion. On-field activities were strictly amateur league, the drama was unmemorable, though the mere presence of Cherie 'luscious' Lunghi drove some reviewers to fever pitch.

CAST *Gabriella Benson* Cherie Lunghi *Gary Halliwell* Mark McGann *Eddie Johnson* Tom Georgeson *Jina Wilson* Stephen Tompkinson /*pr* Glenn Wilhide, Sophie Balhetchet /*dr* inc Christopher King /*wr* Neville Smith, Stan Hey /*Zed Ltd* (UK) /12 x 52m col.

Man at the Top

Drama. ITV 1970–2

The continuing adventures of Joe Lampton, northern anti-hero on the make, begun in John Braine's classic 50s novel (subsequently a cinema film, *Room at the Top*). Since marriage and settlement in suburban Surrey as a management consultant had done little to diminish Lampton's financial and sexual amorality, it was eventually moved to a post-watershed slot. Among the producers was the co-deviser of ➢*The Prisoner*, George Markstein. A feature film version was released by Hammer/Dufton in 1973 (also with Kenneth Haig).

CAST *Joe Lampton* Kenneth Haig *Susan Haig* Zena Walker /*cr* John Braine /*pr* George Markstein, Lloyd Shirley, Jacqueline Davis /*dr* inc Mike Vardy, Dennis Vance, Don Leaver /*wr* John Braine, Tom Brennand & Roy Bottomley /*Thames TV* (UK) /39 x 50m col.

A Man Called Shenandoah

Western. ITV 1966

Post-Civil War oater about an amnesiac who wanders the West in a search for his identity. Virtually tailor-made for star Robert ➢'*Wagon Train*' Horton on his return to TV from the movies, it was too similar to ➢*Branded* to take. Received only sporadic screenings across the ITV networks in Britain.

CAST *Shenandoah* Robert Horton /*cr* E. Jack Neuman /*pr* Vincent Fennelly /*MGM TV* (USA) /34 x 26m bw.

Mancuso FBI

Crime. UK BBC1 1990–1

A veteran G-man pursues public enemies in a rufty-tufty loner style not to the liking of his buttoned-down young boss. Predictable crime-buster series, seamlessly made.

CAST *Nick Mancuso* Robert Loggia *Eddie McMasters* Frederic Lehne *Jean St John* Randi Brazen /*cr* Steve Sohner /*exec pr* Steve Sohner, Jeff Bleckner /*pr* Jacob Epstein, Ken Solarz /*mus* Dennis McCarthy /*A Steve Sohner Production: NBC* (USA) /19 x 60m col.

Man Dog

Children's. BBC1 1972

Teen-time sci-fi serial, commissioned from award-winning children's writer Peter Dickinson, in which a band of freedom fighters from the 26th century escapes back to the present. There, the renegades – who have the 26th-century's secret police hot on their time-travelling trail – are helped by schoolkids Kate, Sammy and Duncan. The title canine was Sammy's pet, Radnor, into whose head renegade leader, Levin, transferred his mind for safe-keeping. *Man Dog* was produced and part-directed by Anna Home, future head of BBC Children's TV.

CAST *Levin* Christopher Owen *Gala 1* Derek Martin *Gala 2* Ray Taylor *Halmar* Jonathan Hardy *Kate* Caroll Hazell *Sammy* Jane Anthony *Duncan* Adrian Shergold *Mrs Morris* Mollie Sugden /*cr* Peter Dickinson /*pr* Anna Home /*dr* Anna Home, Paul Stone /*wr* Peter Dickinson /*BBC TV* (UK) /6 x 25m col.

Man From Atlantis

Sci-fi. ITV 1977–8

After a heavy storm a humanoid with gills and webbed appendages is washed up on a Californian beach. He is the last survivor from a lost civilization; he is The Man from Atlantis (a pre-➢*Dallas* Patrick Duffy, *avec* yellow swimming trunks and green contact lenses). Nursed back to health and named Mark Harris, he is then recruited to the beautiful Dr Elizabeth Merrill's Foundation for Oceanic Research, on behalf of which he descends into the deep (often in the super-sub Cetacean) to battle a familiar array of extraterrestrial monsters and evil villains. None of these, even mad scientist Mr Schubert, proves a match for the Atlantean's faster-than-a-speeding-dolphin swimming abilities, super-strength and supersenses.

Familiar undersea bunkum which literally plumbed the depths, reaching its absolute nadir in an episode where a mudworm developed human characteristics. The first Amercian entertainment TV show to be shown in mainland China.

CAST *Mark Harris* Patrick Duffy *Dr Elizabeth Merrill* Belinda Montgomery *C.W. Crawford* Alan Fudge *Mr Schubert* Victor Buono /*exec pr* Herbert F. Solow /*pr* Herbert F. Solow, Herman Miller, Robert Justman /*dr* inc Paul Krasny, Reza Badiyi, Charles Dubin, Marc Daniels, Harry Harris, Virgil Vogel, Michael O'Herlihy / *wr* inc Mayo Simon, Robert Lewin, John D.F. Black, Alan Caillou, Stephen Kandel, Shimon Wincelberg, Larry Alexander /*mus* Fred Karlin /*sfx* Tom Fisher / *A Solow Production for NBC* (USA) /3 x 100m, 1 x 75m, 13 x 60m col.

The Man From Interpol

Crime. ITV 1960

Was Commander Anthony Smith who, whilst on secondment from Interpol to Scotland Yard, pursued big-time international villains around the globe. But ploddingly and on a low budget.

Barely adequate black and white *policier.*

CAST *Cmdr Anthony Smith* Richard Wyler *DI Mercer* John Longden /*pr* Edward J. Danziger /*mus* Tony Crombie /*A Danziger Brothers Production* (UK) / 39 x 30m bw /US tx NBC 1960.

The Man From UNCLE

Spy adventure. BBC1 1965–8

Prompted by the cinematic success of James Bond, the US TV channel NBC invited 007's creator, Ian Fleming, to outline a spy serial for the small screen. The result, conceived over lunch in London, was *The Man from UNCLE* (originally *Solo*, until the Bond films' producers objected), in which super-agent Napoleon Solo (Robert Vaughn, who had ridden to fame in the *The Magnificent Seven*) pitted his wits on behalf of UNCLE, initially a meaningless collection of letters, but eventually to stand for United Nations Command for Law Enforcement. The agency's HQ was behind the secret wall of a New York dry-cleaners. If Fleming was the father of *TMFU*, the man who brought up the baby was Sam Rolfe, previously the writer-producer of ➢*Have Gun, Will Travel.* It was Rolfe who invented Solo's sidekick, Ilya Kuryakin (British actor David McCallum), and who gave him his blonde-haired, polo-necked cool. Moreover, Kuryakin's Russian nationality enabled *TMFU* to be the first spy show to transcend the Cold War. Of course, Solo and Kuryakin still needed bad guys to trounce: usually these were provided by THRUSH, an international crime syndicate.

The show's episodes – or 'Affairs' as they were called – were as rigidly constructed as Noh plays: the agents would be briefed by boss Alexander Waverly, the case would always involve some innocent in trouble, and the fate of the world would rest on its outcome. Another stock ingredient was a large measure of spoof, while the show's gadgetry (which included radio-receiver pens, a blue two-seat Piranha coupé, and the 'UNCLE Special' pistol, which could be converted into a rifle or machine-gun) cemented its following among young be-shorted boys. One of the more intriguing pairings of the guest stars who graced every segment was William Shatner and Leonard Nimoy, who appeared in 'The Project Strigas Affair' two years before they stood on the bridge of the USS Enterprise together. The series survived until 1968 (spinning off ➢*The Girl from UNCLE* en route), by which time its lapse into the ridiculous – epitomised by the popsicle grenades of 'The Suburbia Affair' – made it unwatchable even for the spy-crazy Sixties.

'Open Channel D'. Robert Vaughn (right) and David McCallum, the stars of *The Man from UNCLE*, a spy spoof co-conceived by 007's creator, Ian Fleming.

CAST *Napoleon Solo* Robert Vaughn *Ilya Kuryakin* David McCallum *Mr Alexander Waverly* Leo G. Carroll / *cr* Ian Fleming, Sam Rolfe /*pr* Sam Rolfe, David Victor, Anthony Spinner /*dr* inc Don Medford, Richard Donner, Alf Kjellin /*wr* inc Harlan Ellison, Robert Towne /*mus* Jerry Goldsmith /*MGM: Arena* (USA) /105 x 50m bw:col /US tx NBC 1964–7.

Manhunt

Drama. ITV 1970

Atmospheric WWII drama about a British intelligence agent, a female Resistance fighter and a shot-down RAF pilot seeking to escape Occupied France. They were the quarry; the hunters in this edge-of-the-seat chase were Abwehr Sergeant Gratz (a limelight-pulling performance by Robert Hardy), and SS Officer Lutzig. Only the characters' tendency to pontification caused cavils. Hollywood-bound actor Brian Cox appeared low down the cast list as Resistance fighter Anton.

CAST *Nina* Cyd Hayman *Sqn Ldr Jimmy Porter* Alfred Lynch *Vincent* Peter Barkworth *Sgt Gratz* Robert Hardy *Lutzig* Philip Madoc /*cr* Red Firkin /*exec pr* Red Firkin /*pr* Andrew Brown /*wr* Vincent Tilsley /*mus* Beethoven ('Fifth Symphony' theme) /*LWT* (UK) / 26 x 50m col.

Manimal

Sci-fi. BBC1 1984

In which criminology professor Jonathan Chase has the ability, inherited from his father, to transform himself into any animal at will (hence the title, 'man-into-animal'). With the help of ole Vietnam War buddy Ty Earl (a camp black in the excruciating style of Huggy Bear in ➢*Starsky and Hutch*) and NYPD detective Brooke McKenzie, Chase uses his supernatural powers to bring the guilty to justice, vigilante style.

Intriguing, if flawed, fantasy crime series from Glen A. Larson. The 'manimal' tranformations of Jonathan Chase (played by amiable British leading man Simon MacCorkindale, ➢*Jesus of Nazareth*) were a nice idea, but took so long to effect that even the most decrepit villain could hardly have failed to escape. Curio value only.

CAST *Jonathan Chase* Simon MacCorkindale *Brooke McKenzie* Melody Anderson *Tyrone 'Ty' Earl* Michael D. Roberts /*cr* Glen A. Larson /*exec pr* Glen A. Larson, Paul Mason /*pr* inc Donald R. Boyle, Paul Radin, Michael Berk /*dr* Russ Mayberry, Sidney Hayers, Dan Haller, Chuck Bail, Les Martinson, George J. Fenady /*wr* Glen A. Larson, Donald R. Boule, Michael Berk, Douglas Schwartz, Sam Egan, Paul Mason, Joseph Gunn /*sfx* Stan Winston, Al Wright /*A Glen A. Larson Production: Twentieth Century-Fox Television* (USA) / 1 x 120m, 7 x 50m col /US tx NBC 1983–4.

Man in a Suitcase

Crime. ITV 1967–8

Superlative mid-Atlantic crime caper from ITC, starring rugged Richard Bradford as McGill, a CIA man forced into PI work after being falsely accused of treason. With only a suitcase of clothes for company, McGill scoured Europe for clues to clear his name and any job that paid $500 a day (plus expenses). There was tough-guy action galore, but only rarely did it require the laconic McGill to remove the cigarette from the corner of his mouth. Due to Sir Lew Grade's lust for American sales, the series engaged quality scribes and directors, among the latter John Glen (who would later helm such Bond movies as *For Your Eyes Only*), Charles Crichton (*The Lavender Hill Mob, A Fish Called Wanda*) and Hammer veteran Freddie Francis.

CAST *John McGill* Richard Bradford /*cr* Richard Harris, Dennis Spooner /*pr* Sidney Cole /*dr* inc Charles Crichton, Robert Tronson, Freddie Francis, Don Chaffey, John Glen, Charles Frend /*wr* inc Edmund Ward, Philip Broadley, Wilfred Greatorex, Roger Parkes, Vincent Tilsley, Reed de Rouen /*mus* Albert Elms, Ron Grainer /*ITC* (UK) /30 x 60m col / US tx ABC 1968.

The Man in Room 17

Crime. ITV 1965–6

Actually there were two men from the ministry, Oldenshaw and Dimmock (later replaced by Denholm Elliott's Defraits), who solved crimes and espionage cases without leaving the confines of isolated Room 17.

A peculiar, sometimes fascinating 60s crime/spy series which borrowed heavily (from ➢*The Avengers*, Len Deighton's Cold War novels and the English whodunnit school, to name but three) to good purpose. A spin off, *The Fellows* (ITV, 1967), followed the exploits of Oldenshaw and Dimmock as academic criminologists on behalf of the Peel Research Fellowship, Cambridge.

CAST *Oldenshaw* Richard Vernon *Dimmock* Michael Aldridge *Defraits* Denholm Elliott *Sir Geoffrey* Willoughby Goddard /*cr* Robin Chapman /*pr* Richard Everitt /*A Granada Television Network Production* (UK) /26 x 60m bw.

Mannix

Crime. ITV 1971/1980–3

Private-eye series starring the muscular Mike Connors (born Kreker Ohanian) as Joe Mannix, initially an op with the hi-tec Los Angeles agency Intertect before he went solo, renting an office (under his apartment) at 17 Paseo Verde. There he received secretarial favours from the black Peggy Fair (part of the show's draw was the novel thrill of possible miscegenation).

Almost laughable in its attempt to out-tough-guy the adventures of Mike Hammer and Phil Marlowe, *Mannix* was the most violent small-screen product until the Manga-influenced animations of the 90s. The wonder is not that it was popular (the No. 1 rated crime show in the USA in 1971), but how it lasted eight years before being cancelled. Actor Larry Linville, later Frank Burns in ➢*M*A*S*H*, played LAPD Lieutenant George Kramer.

CAST *Joe Mannix* Mike Connors *Peggy Fair* Gail Fisher *Lou Wickersham* Joseph Campanella *Lt Adam Tobias* Robert Reed *Lt George Kramer* Larry Linville /*cr* Richard Levinson, William Link /*exec pr* Bruce Geller / *pr* Ivan Goff, Ben Roberts /*dr* inc Corey Allen, Reza S. Badiyi, Richard Benedict, Marvin Chomsky, Seymour Robbie, Fernando Lamas, John Llewellyn Moxey, Fernado Lamas /*wr* inc Ric Vollaerts, Shirl Hendryx, Stephen Kandel, Don M. Mankiewicz, John Meredyth Lucas, Robert Lewin, Chester Krumholz /*mus* Lalo Schifrin /*Paramount Television* (USA) /191 x 60m col / US tx CBS 1967–75.

The Many Wives of Patrick

Comedy. ITV 1976–7

Sitcom vehicle for Patrick Cargill which featured him as a serially divorced antiques dealer. It taxed him little and reassured his fans much, since the part was a virtual reprise of his rakish, but flappish, role as ➢*Father Dear Father* and was likewise produced by future ➢*Fifteen to One* host William G. Stewart.

CAST *Patrick Woodford* Patrick Cargill *Elizabeth Woodford* Ursula Howells *Mother* Agnes Lauchlan /*cr* Richard Waring /*pr* William G. Stewart /*wr* Richard Waring /*LWT* (UK) /21 x 30m col.

Marcus Welby MD

Melodrama. ITV 1969–76

At the age of 62, actor Robert Young – previously best known as Jim Anderson in sitcom ➢*Father Knows Best* – ambled out of retirement to play the title role in this medical melodrama about a kindly Santa Monica GP. James Brolin played young assistant Dr Steven Kiley, who made his house calls on a motorbike. Inevitably, the two clashed over methods, Welby being of the by-the-gut-feeling-school and Kiley being of the by-the-academic-textbook-type. The warm and wise Welby usually diagnosed the patient's problems as stemming from something beyond the illness, so giving himself the opportunity to concern himself with the patient's psychological well-being. Such uplifting drama soon achieved healthy ratings, and *Marcus Welby MD* became American network ABC's biggest hit up to that date. It also earned the approval of the TV industry, winning the 1970 Emmy for Outstanding Dramatic Programme. Developed from a 1968 pilot, the series was retitled *Robert Young, Family Doctor* in syndication. Sharon Gless (➢*Cagney and Lacey*) appeared as Nurse Faverty.

CAST *Dr Marcus Welby* Robert Young *Dr Steven Kiley* James Brolin *Nurse Consuelo Lopez* Elena Verdugo *Nurse Kathleen Faverty* Sharon Gless *Janet Blake* Pamela Hensley /*cr* David Victor /*exec pr* David Victor / *pr* David O'Connell /*dr* inc Jeannot Swarc, Joseph Pevney, Marc Daniels, Richard Benedict, Arnold Laven / *wr* inc Robert Collins, Don Mankiewicz /*mus* Leonard Rosenman (theme song) /*Universal TV* (USA) / 172 x 50m col /US tx ABC 1969–76.

Marine Boy

Children's. BBC1 1969–70

'It's Marine Boy, brave and free, fighting evil beneath the sea…'

Cartoon show imported from Japan about a fearless aquaboy, who works as a top agent for his father's international peace-keeping organization, Ocean Patrol. Drawing oxygen from Oxygum (O-producing bubblegum), Marine Boy took to the watery depths in his P-1 submarine at every threat of danger from Captain Kidd, Dr Slime and Count Shark, using his sonic boomerang, jet-propelled boots and his bullet-proof wet suit to emerge triumphant. Aiding Marine Boy in his campy trouncing of the baddies were crew-mates

Bulton and Piper and talking pet dolphin Splasher. The Japanese title was: 'Kaitai Shonen Marine'. Although produced in colour, it was first transmitted in Britain in black and white.

CAST (voices) *Marine Boy/Neptina/Cli Cli* Corinne Orr *Dr Mariner (Marine Boy's father)* Jack Curtis *Bulton* Peter Fernandez *Piper/Splasher/Dr Fumble / Commander* Jack Grimes */pr* Hinoru Adachi */A Japan Tele-cartoons Production* (Jap) /78 x 30m col.

Market in Honey Lane

Melodrama. ITV 1967–9

Soap opera set in a fictitious London street market overburdened with chirpy barrow-people, all with a line in sales spiel. Created by former ➢*Doctor Who* script editor Louis Marks, it topped the ratings in its debut year, but was always overlong at an hour; it was shortened to a twice-weekly half-hour afternoon serial in September 1968 and retitled *Honey Lane*, but still the TV punters drifted away. It was dismantled for good a year later. Among the cast was Anna Wing, who would return to cod cockneydom as the Fowler-Beale matriarch in ➢*EastEnders.*

CAST *Billy Bush* John Bennett *Sam English* Michael Golden *Dave Sampson* Ray Lonnen *Jacko Bennett* Peter Birrel *Jimmy Benthall* Jack Bligh *Polly Jessell* Pat Nye *Danny Jessell* Brian Rawlinson */cr* Louis Marks */pr* John Cooper */dr* inc David Reid */wr* inc Louis Marks / *ATV* (UK) /approx 220 x 30–60m col.

Mark Saber

Crime. ITV 1957–9

The character of Mark Saber initially appeared on the small screen in the American shows *Mystery Theatre* and *Inspector Mark Saber – Homicide Squad* (played by Tom Conway as a British police officer seconded to the NYPD), before his most famous incarnation as a one-armed private detective portrayed by Donald Gray. Although based in London, Gray's dapper Mark Saber frequently left dowdy British shores for glamorous European locations in pursuit of assorted villainy. He was helped in his endeavours by side-kick Barney O'Keefe and secretary Stephanie Ames.

A second series, entitled ➢*Saber of London*, by the same team, was produced for syndication in the States, again starring the former BBC announcer Gray as Saber, but with an entirely different team of characters in support.

CAST *Mark Saber* Donald Gray *Stephanie Ames* Diane Decker *Barney O'Keefe* Michael Balfour *Insp. Brady* Patrick Holt *Insp. Chester* Colin Tapley */pr* Edward & Harry Lee Danziger */wr* Brian Clemens */Danzigers* (USA) /52 x 30m bw /US tx ABC 1955–7 (as *The Vise*).

Marlowe – Private Eye

Crime. ITV 1984

A British-made collection of cases featuring America's most famous fictive PI, Philip Marlowe. Powers Boothe's portrayal spiritedly sought to recapture Chandler's original concept of Marlowe as a compassionate knight-errant (hence the medieval-sounding moniker); unfortunately, Humphrey Bogart's world weary interpretation of Marlowe in the film *The Big Sleep* set an audience expectation difficult to shake, and this was only confirmed by the subsequent movie casts of cynical Robert Mitchum, James Garner and Elliot Gould. The cases/episodes filmed, on location in London and California, were: 'The Pencil', 'Nevada Gas', 'Finger Man', 'The King in Yellow' and 'Smart-Aleck Kill'.

CAST *Philip Marlowe* Powers Boothe *Lt Magee* William Kearns */pr* David Wickes */mus* John Cameron / *A David Wickes Production: London Weekend TV* (UK) /5 x 60m col.

Marriage Lines

Comedy. BBC 1963–6

Ex-actor turned playwright Richard Waring specially tailored this comedy series for Richard Briers (the two had appeared together in the 1962 legal comedy *Brothers in Law*). Briers played George Starling, a young newly-wed City clerk trying to adjust to life with spouse Kate (Prunella Scales), their unease with each other exacerbated by his low wages and their confining Earls Court flat. The prototypical show of the 'Darling, I'm home' sort, it was lively enough to last five seasons (the third of which saw a baby Starling, Helen, added to the chaotic nest), and minted Briers as one of the domcom genre's leading men (see ➢*The Good Life*, ➢*Ever Decreasing Circles*).

CAST *George Starling* Richard Briers *Kate Starling* Prunella Scales *Peter* Ronald Hines *Norah* Christine Finn / *cr* Richard Waring / *pr* Graeme Muir, Robin Nash / *wr* Richard Waring / *BBC TV* (UK) / 43 x 30m bw.

Married... With Children

Comedy. ITV 1990 /Sky1 1994–

Like ➢*Roseanne* and ➢*The Simpsons*, a domestic comedy which kicked against the usual idealized portrayal of US suburban family life on TV – only more so. Centring on the bickering white trash Bundy household, the show featured Al, a former high-school football star turned salesman of women's footwear (for Gary's Shoe Accessory), and his couch-potato wife Peg. Their quarrels were invariably about sexual dissatisfaction, leaving Ed to peruse his favourite reading matter, *Playboy* and *Big'Uns*. Their children were equally unwholesome: daughter Kelly spent her evenings leaving heel prints on the ceilings of assorted boy-friends' cars, while girlfriendless son Bud enjoyed the company of a blow-up doll.

Comic accomplishment small, popularity big; it was one of America's longest-running sitcoms ever.

CAST *Al Bundy* Ed O'Neill *Peggy Bundy* Katey Sagal *Kelly Bundy* Christina Applegate *Bud Bundy* David Faustino *Steve Rhoades* David Garrison *Marcy Rhoades* Amanda Bearse / *cr* Ron Leavitt, Michael G. Moye / *pr* Ron Leavitt, Michael G. Moye, Katherine Green, Richard Gurman / *dr* inc Zane Busby, Amanda Bearse, Gerry Cohen, Sam W. Orender, Arlando Smith, Gerry Cohen / *Columbia: ELP: Leavitt* (USA) / 259 x 30m col / US tx Fox TV 1987–97.

The Martian Chronicles

Sci-fi. BBC1 1980

Star-spangled American treatment of Ray Bradbury's allusive, haunting novel, *The Silver Locusts*, about Earth's rapacious colonization of Mars between 1999 and 2006. Rock Hudson, Gayle Hunnicutt and Roddy McDowall headed the cast.

CAST *Col John Wilder* Rock Hudson *Ruth Wilder* Gayle Hunnicutt *Father Stone* Roddy McDowall *Sam Parkhill* Darren McGavin *Elma Parkhill* Joyce Van Patten / *pr* Andrew Donally, Milton Subotsky / *dr* Michael Anderson / *wr* Richard Matheson / *A Charles Fried Production* (USA) / 3 x 92m col.

Martin Kane, Private Investigator

Crime. ITV 1958–9

The progenitor of TV private eyedom, Martin Kane began his career on US TV in 1949, reaching No. 12 in the Nielsens the following season. Actor William Gargan reprised the hardboiled, wisecracking role (also taken by Lloyd Nolan, Lee Tracy and Mark Stevens in the US) for this British-made show, which set Kane gumshoeing on the streets of London. His contact was Superintendent Page of the Yard.

CAST *Martin Kane* William Gargan *Supt Page* Brian Reece / *pr* Harry Alan Towers / *Towers of London: Ziv-TV* (UK) / 39 x 30m bw / US tx Syndicated 1957 (as *The New Adventures of Martin Kane*).

Marty

Comedy. BBC2 1968–9

So long the backroom scribbler and third banana, bug-eyed Marty Feldman finally got a show of his own with this BBC2 late-evening slot. There was plenty of off-the-wall visual gagging – most of the future ➢*Monty Python* team contributed 'additional material' to the scripts – and studio tomfoolery, but with typical Corporation caution this was tempered by such middle-England guests as ➢*The Black and White Minstrels*. To, of course, some success; with something for almost everyone the show earned a quick repeat on BBC1, where it reached No. 4 in the ratings. *The Marty Feldman Comedy Machine* (ATV, 1971–2) and *Marty Back Together Again* (BBC1, 1974) followed, before Feldman decamped to Hollywood to make the Mel Brooks movies *The Young Frankenstein* and *Silent Movie*, which would bring him international renown. Feldman, the brother of actress Fenella Fielding, died in Mexico City in 1982.

CAST Marty Feldman, Tim Brooke-Taylor, John Junkin / *pr* Dennis Main Wilson / *wr* Marty Feldman, Barry Took, John Cleese, Graham Chapman, Terry Jones, Michael Palin, Philip Jenkinson, Donald Webster / *BBC TV* (UK) / 12 x 30m bw.

The Mary Tyler Moore Show

Comedy. BBC1 1972–5

With the demise of ➢*The Dick Van Dyke Show*, Mary Tyler Moore spent several years ill-advisedly seeking to emulate Ginger Rogers, before starring in this situation comedy about Mary Richards, a liberal career girl-about-Minneapolis-town. The character represented a landmark in TV comedy, since she was the first major small-screen woman who was single by choice (Marlo Thomas in the 1966 *That Girl*, little known in the UK, was the actual first solo-by-wish femme). At WJM-TV her boss was the irascible Lou Grant, with sarcastic newscaster Murray Slaughter, vain anchorman Ted Baxter, and *Happy Homemaker* hostess Sue Ann Nivens (Betty White, ➢*The Golden Girls*) comprising the rest of the eccentric main workforce. While many of the laughs in this highly polished show – to many fans and critics alike it represented the apotheosis of the sitcom form – came from workplace antics, it also (like ➢*The Dick Van Dyke Show*) focused on the principle character's homelife. Those featured on the domestic set were Richards' best friend, window dresser Rhoda Morgenstern and busybody neighbour Phyllis Lindstrom (Cloris Leachman).

Over a seven-year run, the show won a record 27 Emmys, including Outstanding Comedy awards in 1975, 1976 and 1977. All 120 episodes were filmed live before a studio audience. Co-created by James L. Brooks (later ➢*Taxi*, ➢*The Simpsons*) *Mary Tyler Moore* provided a windfall of spin-offs and knock-ons for MTM Enterprises (the company owned by Moore and her then husband Grant Tinker). They were: ➢*Rhoda*, ➢*The Love Boat*, ➢*Lou Grant*, *The Betty White Show* and *Phyllis*.

CAST *Mary Richards* Mary Tyler Moore *Lou Grant* Ed Asner *Ted Baxter* Ted Knight *Murray Slaughter* Gavin McLeod *Rhoda Morgenstern* Valerie Harper *Phyllis Lindstrom* Cloris Leachman *Sue Ann Nivens* Betty White /*cr* James L. Brooks, Allan Burns /*pr* James L. Brooks, Allan Burns, David Davis, Stan Daniels, Ed Weinberger /*dr* inc Jay Sandrich, James Burrows, Mel Ferber, Joan Darling /*wr* inc James L. Brooks, Allan Burns, Treva Silverman, Ed Weinberger, Stan Daniels, David Lloyd, Bob Ellison /*mus* Sonny Curtis (theme), Pat Williams /*MTM Productions* (USA) /120 x 25m col / US tx CBS 1970–7.

The Mary Whitehouse Experience

Comedy. BBC2 1990–2

Transfer to TV of the R1 alternative comedy show, unusual in alternating (at frenetic rate) between stand-up and sketches. Irreverent and controversial (the programme's contents were anything but the sort of thing moral watchdog Mary Whitehouse liked to experience on her TV), *TMWE* comprised the writer/performer teams of Steve Punt and bishop's son Hugh Dennis (also ➢*Carrott's Lib*), and David Baddiel (later ➢*Fantasy Football League*) and Rob Newman. At a time when nearly all the other rock'n'roll 90s comedians were appearing on C4, *TMWE* proved a positive blush-saver for BBC, so long the home of cutting-edge small-screen humour.

CAST Steve Punt, Hugh Dennis, David Baddiel, Rob Newman /*pr* Marcus Mortimer /*dr* Marcus Mortimer / *wr* Steve Punt, Hugh Dennis, David Baddiel, Rob Newman /*Spitting Image Productions: BBC TV* (UK) / 13 x 30m col.

M*A*S*H

Comedy. BBC2 1973–84

Developed from Robert Altman's 1970 movie about the weary surgeons and staff of the 4077th Mobile Army Surgical Hospital during the Korean War, *M*A*S*H* was the most improbable hit comedy of the 70s. Unlike the long line of military comedies which preceded it (➢*Hogan's Heroes*, *You'll Never Get Rich*, *F Troop*, ➢*McHale's Navy*), the show was a dark anti-war satire – and this at a time when the USA was losing the Vietnam conflict. It also foregrounded such taboo TV subjects as adultery and homosexuality. On its side, it had frequently flawless scripts, high production values (including the set left over from the movie version), and constant inventiveness (one episode, 'The Interview', was improvised by the cast, another shot in black and white). Best of all, it had a collection of likeable oddballs. Captain Hawkeye Pierce (Alan Alda, aka Alphonso D'Abruzzo) was the inveterate joker – although also the most inclined to muse on the dehumanizing nature of war – ably assisted by Trapper John McIntyre. Head nurse Major Margaret 'Hotlips' Hoolihan, though censorious about other people's morals, was having an affair with the arrogant Frank Burns, the most incompetent surgeon in unit. Henry Blake, the commanding officer, ignored all antics as long as his doctors performed in the operating theatre. Radar O'Reilly was the extremely shy clerk. Unsurprisingly, given the show's longevity, there were significant cast changes over the years. Transvestite Corporal Max Klinger (played by Jamie Farr, the only member of the cast to have served in Korea) was added to the 4077th as a theatre aide. When Colonel Blake was killed in a plane crash, he was replaced by the homely mid-Westerner Sherman Potter (played by veteran

The staff of the 4077th mobile hospital in the anti-war *M*A*S*H*. It was based on the novel by Richard Hooker, who disowned the TV version because of its liberalism.

Harry Morgan ➢*Dragnet*, ➢*Naked City*, *The American*, ➢*That Was The Week That Was*). In the summer of 1975 Trapper John spun off to a show of that name (*Trapper John MD*) and B.J. Hunnicutt took over as Hawkeye's main conspirator. At the beginning of the 1977–8 season Frank Burns went AWOL when Hotlips rejected him for Lt Col Penobscott, Burns being succeeded as arch pain in the butt by aristocratic Bostonian Charles Emerson Winchester. Behind the scenes, writer Larry Gelbart quit *M*A*S*H* in 1976 (declaring 'War is hell. So is TV'), leaving Alda as 'creative consultant'; his character gradually became more prominent and episodes simultaneously more sentimental and less inclined to banana-skin madcappery, relying on the irreverent wisecracking between the characters for the laughs.

*M*A*S*H* itself finally bowed out in 1983 with a two-and-a-half-hour special, 'Goodbye, Farewell and Amen', to that date the most watched programme in history (it has since been pipped by Bostonian bar-com ➢*Cheers* and *Friends*). As Alda claimed, with pardonable exaggeration, 'We came to tell jokes and stayed to touch the edges of art.'

And, to production company joy, make mountains of dollars along the way. Reportedly, Twentieth Century-Fox Television reaped $25 million from the first round of syndication in America, and five times that figure on the second round. It can safely be said that *M*A*S*H* has earned more money than any other programme in the history of TV.

A number of *M*A*S*H* characters were brought back from the TV dead in a sequel *AfterMASH*, which followed their adjustment to civilian life.

CAST *Capt. Benjamin Franklin 'Hawkeye' Pierce* Alan Alda *Capt. 'Trapper John' McIntyre* Wayne Rogers *Major Margaret 'Hotlips' Houlihan* Loretta Swit *Cpl Maxwell Klinger* Jamie Farr *Lt Col. Henry Blake* McLean Stevenson *Major Frank Burns* Larry Linville *Capt. B.J. Hunnicutt* Mike Farrell *Cpl Walter 'Radar' O'Reilly* Gary Burghoff *Major Charles Emerson Winchester III* David Ogden Stiers *Col. Sherman Potter* Harry Morgan *Father Francis Mulcahy* George Morgan /William Christopher /*cr* Richard Hooker, Larry Gelbart /*pr* Burt Metcalfe, Gene Reynolds /*dr* inc Alan Alda, Harry Morgan, Jackie Cooper, Don Weis, Gene Reynolds, Burt Metcalfe /*wr* inc Alan Alda, Larry Gelbart, Glen Charles, Les Charles, Jim Fritzell, Everett Greenbaum, Den Wilcox, Thad Mumford /*mus* Johnny Mandel ('Suicide is Painless' theme music) /*Twentieth Century-Fox* (USA) / 1 x 150m, 250 x 30m col /US tx CBS 1972–83.

The Master
Children's. ITV 1966

Begins as a Blytonesque-jaunt (two children, plus dog, become marooned on Rockall), continues through sci-fi chiller (the island is inhabited by the title telepathic despot) and ends with an action-bang (Rockall is blown up).

Adapted by Rosemary Hill from T.H. White's novel, the six-part serial was Southern TV's most prestigious children's drama of the 60s (perhaps ever). In particular, it assumed a certain IQ on behalf of its audience, not least whether they could understand the philosophical conundrum which eventually faces the junior adventurers Nicky and Judy: should The Master be murdered for the greater good? Quite, quite exceptional, with a cast which included John Laurie, George Baker and Adrienne Posta to boot.

CAST *Nicky* Paul Guess *Judy* Adrienne Posta *The Master* Olaf Pooley *Chinaman* Terence Soall *McTurk* John Laurie *Father* Richard Vernon *Frinton* George Baker /*pr* John Braybon /*dr* John Braybon, John Frankau /*wr* Rosemary Hill /*Southern Independent TV* (UK) /6 x 30m bw.

Mastermind
Light Entertainment. BBC1 1972–97

'I've started so I'll finish...'

Resolutely high-brow quiz show presented by Magnus Magnusson KBE (born Magnus Sigursteinnson) which attracted a mass viewership, largely because of the Gestapo-like (thus sadistically enjoyable) method of questioning used. Each contender – there were four per episode – was obliged to sit alone in a black leather chair in a darkened auditorium and answer rapid-fire questions from Magnusson for two minutes while spotlighted. Twice. Once in a specialist subject round, once in a general-knowledge round. Some of the winners of the cut-price, cut-glass *Mastermind* trophy went on to celebrity, among them taxi driver Fred Housego and train driver Christopher Hughes.

CAST (presenter) Magnus Magnusson /*cr* Bill Wright /*pr* Bill Wright, Roger Mackay, David Mitchell, Peter Massey /*dr* Peter Massey, Antonia Charlton, Laurence Vulliamy, Andrea Conway, Martin L. Bell /*BBC TV* (UK) /160 x 50m col.

Matlock
Crime. ITV 1987–

Mystery series about a canny Atlanta lawyer with a penchant for last-minute, trial-winning revelations, concocted from a jigger of ➢*Perry Mason* and a splash of the sort of Southern country US charm star Andy Griffith had previously displayed in his sitcom *The Andy Griffith Show.* Aiding Matlock in his legal labours were daughter Charlene, black stock-market whizz Tyler Hudson who moonlighted for Matlock & Matlock as a PI, clerk Cassie and junior brief Michelle.

CAST *Benjamin L. Matlock* Andy Griffith *Tyler Hudson* Kene Holliday *Charlene Matlock* Linda Purl *Michelle Thomas* Nancy Stafford *Cassie Phillips* Kari Lizer *Conrad McMaster* Clarence Gilyard Jr *Leanne McIntyre* Brynn Thayer /*cr* Dean Hargrove /*exec pr* Dean Hargrove, Fred Silverman /*pr* Rich Collins /*dr* inc Chris Hibler, Russ Mayberry, Nicholas Sgarro, Leo Penn, Burt Brinckerhoff, Bill Duke, Charles Dubin, Michael O'Herlihy, Seymour Robbie /*mus* Dick De Benedictis /*A Strathmore Production: Viacom* (USA) /195 x 60m col /US tx NBC 1986–95.

Matt Houston
Crime. BBC1 1983–7

Aaron Spelling crime caper featuring Matlock 'Matt' Houston, the playboy scion of a Texan oil clan turned amateur (later pro) peeper. Houston was helped on the new job by beautiful lawyer friend C.J. and obliging LA policeman friend Lieutenant Novelli; he was hindered by the lightly comic elements of cowhand employees Bo and Lamar. It was merely routine, for all its parades of Mercedes and swimming pools full of hot babes, not even lifted by the use of Buddy Ebsen as Houston's retired detective uncle, Roy.

CAST *Matt Houston* Lee Horsley *C.J. Parsons* Pamela Hensley *Lamar* Paul Brinegar *Bo* Dennis Fimple *Lt Vince Novelli* John Aprea *Roy Houston* Buddy Ebsen /*cr* Lawrence Gordon /*exec pr* Aaron Spelling /*pr* Michael Fisher /*dr* inc Cliff Bole, Hy Averback, Jerome Courtland, Michael Vejar, Peter Crane, Corey Allen, Richard Land, William Crain, Barbara Peters, Charles Picerni /*Aaron Spelling: Warner Bros TV* (USA) / 50 x 60m col /US tx ABC 1982–5.

Maude

Comedy. ITV 1976

Controversial domcom spin-off from ➢*All In the Family* centring on Archie Bunker's middle-aged and middle-class cousin-in-law, Maude Findlay, from the 'burb of Tuckahoe, NY. Uncompromisingly pro-Women's Lib (in the spirit of the times), Maude involved herself in topical issues guaranteed to cause heat; in the process she became a classic character of US TV. In one episode she had an abortion, in another she was treated for manic depression, in another she called her fourth husband Walter 'a son of a bitch'. The series, which flew as high as No. 4 in the US Nielsens, projected Bea Arthur to stardom and to a 1977 Emmy for Oustanding Lead Actress in a Comedy Series. Curiously, another of the future ➢*Golden Girls* also starred in the show, Rue McClanahan, who played Maude's best friend, Vivian. Only a smattering of episodes were screened in the UK.

CAST *Maude Findlay* Beatrice Arthur *Walter Findlay* Bill Macy *Carol* Adrienne Barbeaud *Philip* Brian Morrison/Kraig Metzinger *Dr Arthur Harmon* Conrad Bain *Vivian Cavender Harmon* Rue McClanahan *Florida Evans* Esther Rolle /*pr* Norman Lear /*dr* inc Hal Cooper, Tony Csiki /*Tandem Production* (USA) / 140 x 30m col /US tx CBS 1972–8.

Maverick

Western. ITV 1959–62

Classic small-screen series which spoofed the Western genre mercilessly. Moseying from one daft-sounding town (Oblivion) to another (Bent Fork), James Garner's eponymous gambler lived by lying, cheating and stealing; when trouble threatened he followed Pappy's sage advice: 'Run!'

The casting of Garner was perfect and launched him to stardom. He was later joined by Jack Kelly as straight-laced brother Bart. When Garner quit the series in a contract dispute, he was replaced by Roger Moore as cultured cousin Beau. For the last season, Robert Colbert (later the ➢*The Time Tunnel*) played another Maverick, Brent. The show's mocking of the oater form was deliriously well pitched, being both affectionate and savage. Perhaps the best segment was a lampoon on ➢*Bonanza*, in which Bart encountered a cattle baron called Joe Wheelwright, owner of the vast Sub Rosa ranch, who was trying to marry off his three idiot sons, Moose, Henry and Small Paul. Series directors included Robert Altman, Richard Sarafian and Budd Boetticher.

The show was revived as a 1979 TVM *The New Mavericks* (starring Garner) and as a series *Bret Maverick* (1981–2, again with Garner). In 1994 a big screen version was released with Australian Mel Gibson as the West's ultimate anti-hero. None captured the brilliant subversiveness of thc Emmy-winning original.

CAST *Bret Maverick* James Garner *Bart Maverick* Jack Kelly *Samantha Crawford* Diane Brewster *Beauregard Maverick* Roger Moore *Brent Maverick* Robert Colbert / *cr* Roy Huggins /*pr* Roy Huggins /*dr* inc Robert Altman, Budd Boetticher, Paul Henreid, Richard Sarafian, Douglas Heyes, Richard L. Bare, Abner Biberman /*wr* inc Roy Huggins /*mus* David Buttolph / *Warner Bros TV* (USA) /124 x 52m bw /US tx ABC 1957–62.

Max Headroom: The Series

Sci-fi. C4 1989

Began its screen life as 1985 TVM for C4. Set 'twenty minutes in the future' it depicted, in bleak parody, a world dominated by TV neworks, one of whom, Network 23, was winning the ratings battle by secret use of 'blipverts' – 30-second commercials condensed into a three-second burst. A side-effect of the blipverts was that they caused some viewers to explode. On discovering this scandal, investigative reporter Edison Carter is promptly terminated; however, in order to preserve his knowledge, his memory and appearance are scanned into a computer. The result was a stuttering, wise-cracking computer-generated TV presenter, named Max Headroom after the last words Carter ever saw.

The idea for *Max Headroom* came from British record producer Peter Wagg and C4 commissioning editor Andy Park as a means of linking pop videos. And this is exactly what C4 provided with *Max Headroom* in which the character only existed within a TV set. In America, however, Lorimar Television saw more mileage in the idea, producing a series of 14 episodes (reworking the British film for the opener) in which Edison's computer-generated alter ego roved the city armed with a minicam exposing corruption, his movements monitored by assistant, Theora Jones, and network whizz-kid, Bryce Lynch. This version was shown on C4 in 1989.

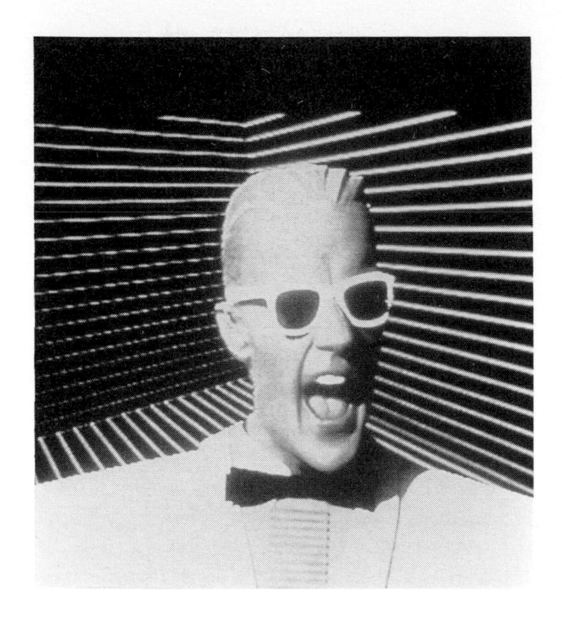

A trans-Atlantic sci-fi thriller hit, *Max Headroom* was originally developed by a record executive as a means of linking pop videos.

CAST *Edison Carter/Max Headroom* Matt Frewer *Theora Jones* Amanda Pays *Bryce Lynch* Chris Young *Ben Cheviot* George Coe /*cr* Peter Wagg, Andy Park, Steve Roberts, Rocky Morton, Annabel Jankel /*exec pr* Philip De Guere, Peter Wagg /*pr* Peter Wagg, Brian Frankish, Steve Roberts /*dr* Farhad Mann, Thomas J. Wright, Francis De Lia, Tommy Lee Wallace, Victor Lobl, Janet Greek, Todd Holland, Maurice Phillips /*wr* inc Steve Roberts, Joe Gannon, James Crocker, Michael Cassutt, Chris Ruppenthal /*mus* Cory Lerios, Michael Hoenig, Chuck Wild /*Chrysalis: Lakeside: Lorimar Telepictures* (USA) /14 x 60m col.

May to December

Comedy. BBC1 1989–94

Age-gap sitcom with Anton Rodgers (from *Fresh Fields*) as an ageing solicitor, Alec Callender, who marries a younger woman. Eventually she begat a child, whom they named Fleur. As well as scenes *chez* Callender, the family firm's offices in Pinner also figured prominently, where the secretarial desks were occupied by the prim Miss Vera Flood and the daffy 'h'-dropping 'ilary. When the latter left the employ of Semple, Callender and Henty for the Isle of Wight, she was replaced by the daffy, but Scottish Rosie MacConnachy. Also working at the law firm was Jamie, Callender's son from his first marriage, who eventually became a partner (on which the company name changed to Semple, Callender and Callender). It didn't exactly tickle the ribs, but it wasn't exactly hateworthy either.

CAST *Alec Callender* Anton Rodgers *Zoë Callender née Angell (wife)* Eve Matheson/Lesley Dunlop *Jamie Callender (son from first marriage)* Paul Venables *Simone (daughter from first marriage)* Carolyn Pickles *Miss Vera Flood/Tipple* Frances White *Hilary* Rebecca Lacey *Rosie MacConnachy* Ashley Jensen *Dot (Zoë's mother)* Kate Williams /*cr* Paul A. Mendelson /*exec pr* Verity Lambert /*pr* Sydney Lotterby, Sharon Bloom /*dr* Verity Lotterby, Paul Harrison, John Kilby /*wr* inc Paul A. Mendelson, Geoffrey Deane /*Cinema Verity* (UK) /39 x 30m col.

McCloud

Crime. ITV 1972–6

'There you go.'

The exploits of a cowboy-lawman in the big city, loosely based on the 1968 Clint Eastwood feature *Coogan's Bluff.* Dennis Weaver (already familar with stetson wearing from ➢*Gunsmoke*) played Sam McCloud, a New Mexican in New York ostensibly studying the policing methods of the 27th Precinct. In fact, Deputy Marshal McCloud studiously ignored local *modus operandi* and treated Manhattan like the Wild West, wore a cowpoke hat and boots, talked in down-on-the-range homilies and even rode his horse. A crime show with its tongue in both cheeks, *McCloud* worked the idea of an urban oater effortlessly well, helped by assuredly smooth acting. Also in the cast were Terry Carter as black sergeant Joe Broadhurst (dragged into constant trouble by McCloud), Diana Muldaur as McCloud's love interest Chris Coughlin, while Sharon Gless got in some early genre practice for ➢*Cagney and Lacey* as Sergeant Maggie Clinger.

The series originated as part of American NBC's *Four-in-One* series, moving to the *Mystery Movie* slot in 1971, where it rotated with ➢*Columbo* and ➢*McMillan and Wife.*

CAST *Deputy Marshal Sam McCloud* Dennis Weaver *Police Chief Peter B. Clifford* J.D. Cannon *Sgt Joe Broadhurst* Terry Carter *Chris Coughlin* Diana Muldaur *Sgt Maggie Clinger* Sharon Gless /*cr* Herman Miller, Glen A. Larson /*exec pr* Glen A. Larson, Leslie Stevens, Richard Irving /*pr* inc Michael Gleason, Dean Hargrove, Winrich Kolbe /*dr* inc Glen A. Larson, Richard A. Colla, Douglas Heyes, Nicholas Colasanto, Jerry Paris, Russ Mayberry, Jimmy Sangster, Boris Sagal /*wr* inc Leslie

Stevens, Dean Hargrove, Nicholas Baehr, Robert Hamner /*mus* Richard Clements /*Universal TV* (USA) /6 x 60m, 19 x 90m, 21 x 120m col /US tx NBC 1970–7.

McHale's Navy
Comedy. BBC 1963

US navy lark featuring the hustlers who crewed PT 73 (a motor torpedo boat) in the Pacific during WWII. Ernest Borgnine – taking a break from playing psychopathic heavies in Hollywood – revealed a suprising comic touch as the sly McHale. For the last season, McHale and men were transferred to the Mediterranean where their smileable antics continued undimmed. Based on the TV play *Seven Against the Sea*, in which Borgnine had also starred.

CAST *Lt Cmdr Quinton McHale* Ernest Borgnine *Capt. Wallace B. Binghampton* Joe Flynn *Ensign Chuck Parker* Tim Conway *Harrison 'Tinker' Bell* Billy Sands *Happy Haines* Gavin MacLeod /*pr* Edward J. Montagne, Si Rose /*dr* inc Sidney Lanfield /*MCA: Sto–Rev: Universal* (USA) /138 x 25m bw /US tx ABC 1962–6.

McMillan and Wife
Crime. ITV 1972–9

Hollywood star Rock Hudson, in his first TV series, played debonair San Francisco Police Commissioner Stewart McMillan, whose sexy but scatty wife Sally had the unfortunate knack of finding corpses in the glitzy mansions they were invited to for cocktails every weekend.

Like ➢*Hart to Hart*, another small-screen steal of Dashiell Hammett's *Thin Man* books of the 30s, the whodunnit cases were a plod, and much the most enjoyable aspect of the show – as with the affair featuring the Harts – was the frolicsome relationship between the lead characters. In the USA the show rotated as part of NBC's *Mystery Movies*. When Susan Saint James quit in 1976, it changed format leaving Mac to sleuth alone as plain *McMillan* for a final season.

CAST *Commissioner Stewart McMillan* Rock Hudson *Sally McMillan* Susan Saint James *Sgt Charles Enright* John Schuck *Mildred (the housekeeper)* Nancy Walker /*cr* Leonard B. Stern /*exec pr* Leonard B. Stern /*pr* Jon Epstein, Paul Mason, Ted Rich /*dr* inc John Astin, Hy Averback, Lou Antonio, E.W. Swackhamer /*wr* inc Steven Bochco, Robert Lewin, Don M. Mankiewicz /*Talent Associates: Norton Simon Inc: Universal TV* (USA) /39 x 90m col /US tx NBC 1971–7.

Melrose Place
Melodrama. Sky1 1993–

Sudster spin-off from ➢*Beverly Hills 90210*, also by that show's creator, Darren Star, and inspired by his own youthful experiences of living in a West Hollywood condo complex. Though defended by Star as having 'a tiny strain of reality', the night-time soap was a gloriously OTT depiction of yuppie life; almost without exception the residents who tanned themselves around Melrose Place's pool were libidinous, neurotic and infinitely ambitious. Initially, however, the show lingered – in true 90210 manner – on 'issues', which generated disappointing ratings. This was solved by the invention of double-crossing Amanda Woodward (played to bitchy, sirenesque perfection by ex-➢*Dynasty*, ex-➢*T.J. Hooker*, ex-*Return of the Swamp Thing* actress Heather Locklear, sometime wife of rock drummer Tommy Lee – later Mr Pamela Anderson – and then Bon Jovi guitarist Richie Sambora). No sooner installed as artistic director of the D&D advertising agency, than Woodward began seducing most of the pec-perfect Melrose Place men, even token nice guy Billy Campbell and the boyfriend of her mother (played by ➢*Dallas*'s Linda Gray). Such dastardliness only prompted the other women of Melrose Place to out-bed and out-scheme Woodward: the most improbable plot saw photographer Jo Reynolds in a custody battle for her son – after she had killed his father, the drug smuggler, Carter – then lose her child to her sister, get the boy back, then hire the babysitter from hell, then give him away. Almost as ridiculous was the story in which Dr Kimberly Shaw ran over her lover Michael Mancini while disguised as his ex-wife. The motive was revenge, for Kimberly had been disfigured (but only on the top of her pretty head) in a car accident she blamed on Mancini. Later, the psychopathic Shaw blew 4616 Melrose Place – but, conveniently, not all its occupants – into the Californian heavens.

Such melodramatic characters and addictive storylines made *Melrose Place* the second top drama series amongst the 18 to 25 age group in the US. Fox TV used the series to spin off *Model's Inc*, based around Linda Gray's Hillary Michaels character, while wunderkind Star went on to invent the soap *Central Park West*, set amidst New York's publishing scene. Somewhat immodestly, the launch episode was transmitted on a giant screen in Times Square.

CAST *Billy Campbell* Andrew Shue *Amanda Woodward* Heather Locklear *Jane Mancini* Josie Bissett *Michael Mancini* Thomas Calabro *Matt Fielding* Doug Savant *Jake Hanson* Grant Show *Alison Parker* Courtney Thorne-Smith *Jo Reynolds* Daphne Zuniga *Kimberly Shaw* Marcia Cross *Hillary Michaels* Linda Gray *Kyle McBride* Rob Ester /*cr* Darren Star /*exec pr* Aaron Spelling, E. Duke Vincent, Darren Star /*dr* inc Charles Braverman, Janet Greek, Daniel Attias, Steve Robman /*wr* inc Darren Star /*Darren Star Productions: Spelling Television Inc.* (USA) /60 x 60m col /US tx Fox TV 1992–.

Men Behaving Badly

Comedy. ITV 1991–4/BBC1 1994–

Politically incorrect – but funny – sitcom about two flat-sharing adolescently-minded males, which was the standard bearer of New Laddism on TV (also exemplified by ➢*Fantasy Football League* and ➢*Beavis and Butt-Head*). In the first season, the two men behaving were Gary (jug-eared Martin Clunes, whose first TV role was in ➢*Doctor Who*) and Dermot (the busy Harry Enfield), but then Dermot went off around the world and new lodger Tony (Neil Morrisey, formerly Sammy the Shammy in ➢*Noel's House Party*, and in ➢*Boon*) moved in. For Tony, a principle attraction of his new abode was the upstairs neighbour, the Twiggy-like Deborah (Leslie Ash, *Quadrophenia*, ➢*C.A.T.S Eyes*), whom he relentlessly lusted after. Meanwhile, Gary – in-between lagers down the pub with Tony – maintained a romantic entanglement of sorts with long-suffering State Registered Nurse Dorothy (Caroline Quentin, sometime wife of Paul Merton). Written in its entirety by Simon Nye (➢*Frank Stubbs Promotes*, *Is it Legal?*, *True Love*), and based on his novel of the same title, *MBB* cleverly balanced the cathartic and the cynical. It allowed male viewers to indulge in vicarious pubescent antics, while allowing female viewers (and the sensible side of the male brain) to ridicule the bad but loveable Tony and Gary. Produced by the venerable Beryl Vertue (a former artists' agent who moved into production with Eric Sykes' *The Plank* and whose daughter was Enfield's main squeeze when *MBB* began), the show received the first National Television Award for comedy. When ITV, inexplicably, decided not to film a third series, Vertue sold the show to the BBC. A past master at purveying British sitcom formats to the Americans (among them ➢*Steptoe and Son* and ➢*Till Death Us Do Part*), it was small suprise that Vertue also secured a US 're-version'. This starred stand-up comic Rob Schneider and Ron Eldard (Shep in ➢*ER*) and was from Carsey Werner.

CAST *Gary* Martin Clunes *Dermot* Harry Enfield *Tony* Neil Morrissey *Deborah* Leslie Ash *Dorothy* Caroline Quentin *George* Ian Lindsay *Anthea* Valerie Minifie *Les* Dave Atkins /*cr* Simon Nye /*pr* Beryl Vertue /*dr* Martin Dennis /*wr* Simon Nye /*mus* Alan Lisk /*Thames TV: Hartswood Films* (UK) /25+ x 30m col.

Men From Shiloh

Western. BBC1 1972

➢*The Virginian* refurbished. The Wyoming setting was moved up in time by a decade to the 1890s, with Stewart Granger brought in as the new Shiloh ranch owner, retired British Army officer Colonel Alan MacKenzie. Also introduced to the cast was Lee Majors (ex-➢*The Big Valley*) as Roy Tate. The update was heavily influenced by the spaghetti Westerns of the movies, down to a rousing theme by the great Ennio Morricone himself.

CAST *The Virginian* James Drury *Trampas* Doug McClure *Col. Alan MacKenzie* Stewart Granger *Roy Tate* Lee Majors *Parker* John McLiam /*pr* Glen A. Larson /*mus* Ennio Morricone (theme) /*Universal TV* (USA) /24 x 90m col /US tx NBC 1970–1.

Men into Space

Sci-fi. BBC 1960

Little known American space adventure serial featuring US Air Force moon explorer Colonel Edward McCauley. Made with the co-operation of the Defence Department it eschewed Bug Eyed Monsters in favour of realism (even adopting a documentary look) and the scientifically possible. As a a result, it was so boring that even Buzz Aldrin must have switched over. Series actor Corey Allen later went to work calling the shots and became a bigtime TV director. Angie Dickinson starred as McCauley's wife in the pilot episode.

CAST *Col Edward McCauley* William Lundigan *Mary McCauley* Angie Dickinson (pilot)/Joyce Taylor *Lt Johnny Baker* Corey Allen /*pr* Lewis Rachmill /*mus* David Rose /*United Artists* (USA) /38 x 25m bw /US tx CBS 1959–60.

Crockett (right) and Tubbs get their guns out in *Miami Vice*, a show conceived in response to a two-word memo from NBC's chief: 'MTV cops'.

Metal Mickey

Children's. ITV 1980–3

Sci-fi sitcom for children featuring a robot (catchphrase: 'Boogie, Boogie') invented by wunderkind Ken as a help in the family home. Naturally, where there was previously domestic order it brought zany chaos (plus travel in time, close encounters with aliens, etc. etc.). The show was produced by Mickey Dolenz, the former star of ➢*The Monkees.*

CAST *Ken* Ashley Knight *Father* Michael Stainton *Mother* Georgina Melville *Granny* Irene Handl *Haley* Lucinda Bateson *Janey* Lola Young *Steve* Gary Shail /*pr* Mickey Dolenz /*dr* Mickey Dolenz, David Crossman, Nic Phillips /*wr* Colin Bostock-Smith /*mus* Phil Coulter /*LWT* (UK) 39 x 30m col.

Miami Vice

Crime. BBC1 1985–90

Took its direction from a two-word memo from NBC boss Brandon Tartijoff: 'MTV cops'. A triumph of sound and vision over narrative content, the show cast two relative unknowns in the starring roles: Don Johnson as Causcasian designer-stubbled detective Sonny Crockett; and Philip Michael Thomas as his black partner, Ricardo Tubbs. Undercover vice cops in sleazy, neon-toned Miami, Crockett and Tubbs pursued bad guys whilst looking good in Versace clothing and Crockett's Ferrari Spider (later Ferrari Testarossa), all done to the adrenalin-pumping accompaniment of rock music trax (either specially commissioned, or brought in from established stars such as the Rolling Stones and Tina Turner).

Created and executive produced by Michael Mann, the series entered the top ten of the US Nielsens in its first season and celebrities queued for cameos. Among them was Briton Sheena Easton, whose chanteuse character briefly became Mrs Crockett before the producers, fearful that she would disturb the cop buddies' relationship, gunned her down, leaving Crockett to singledom (save for pet crocodile Elvis) aboard his boat *St Vitus* once again. Watergate burgler G. Gordon Liddy appeared as a real estate agent.

After lighting up the TV sky like a rocket, *Vice*

Ex-Goon Michael Bentine continued the madcap laughs with children's show *Potty Time*. Although born in darkest Watford, Bentine was the grandson of the vice president of Peru.

died a quick death. NBC placed it against ➢*Dallas*, and the hipster cop show proved no match for the glossy sudster. By its fifth season the show – now costing an estimated $1.2 million per installment – had fallen to 53rd place. Keen to recoup their dollars, makers Universal TV administered the axe and sold the show into syndication.

Michael Mann, meanwhile, took his distinctive talents to ➢*Crime Story* and the helming of such cinema features as *Manhunter* (1986) and *Last of the Mohicans* (1992).

CAST *Det. James 'Sonny' Crockett* Don Johnson *Det. Ricardo Tubbs* Philip Michael Thomas *Lt Martin Castillo* Edward James Olmos *Det. Gina Navarro Calabrese* Saundra Santiago *Det. Trudy Joplin* Olivia Brown *Caitlin Davies* Sheena Easton *Valerie Gordon* Pam Grier /*cr* Anthony Yerkovich, Michael Mann /*exec pr* Michael Mann /*dr* inc Michael Mann, David Soul, Don Johnson, Paul Michael Glaser, Edward James Olmos, Paul Krasny, Lee Katzin, Abel Ferrara /*wr* inc Miguel Pinero /*mus* Jan Hammer (theme) /*Universal TV* (USA) /3 x 120m, 108 x 60m col /US tx NBC 1984–9.

Michael Bentine's Potty Time

Children's. ITV 1973–80

Ex-Goon Michael Bentine (born Bentin, the grandson of the vice-president of Peru) made his first venture into children's programming with the 1954 puppet show *The Bumblies*. A sequence of adult shows followed, most famously ➢*It's A Square World*, before Bentine returned to tiny TV with *Potty Time* in which a cast of marionettes with ever changing wigs and moustaches acted out narratives of surreal nonsense on a studio table with bystanding blazered Bentine egging them on. Pure goonery. A masterpiece, though probably wasted on children.

CAST (voices) Michael Bentine /*Thames TV* (UK) / 60 x 25m col.

Mickey Spillane's Mike Hammer

Crime. ITV 1984–6

Cases of a NY private dick, so tough he never even had to remove the cigarette from his mouth while beating the villain to a pulp.

Likeable trash, based on Mickey Spillane's lurid novels, updated for the 1980s. Not for the weak stomached though; if Vietnam vet Hammer wasn't mashing the faces of baddies he was giving them lead injections from pistol Betsy. Voluptuous secretary Velda headed the parade of smoke-voiced babes who passed through every episode. On the detecting job, Hammer received assistance from grass Ozzie the Answer, and NYPD contact Captain Pat Chambers.

Production of the series was halted, somewhat ironically given its loud pro-law views, when actor Stacy Keach (brother of director James, Jane Seymour's spouse) was imprisoned in Britain's Reading Gaol for drug offences.

Keach, incidentally, wasn't the first actor to portray Hammer on the small screen: that honour went to Darren McGavin (also ➢*Kolchak: The Night Stalker*) in Revue's 78 x 30m bw series for syndication in the USA, 1957–60.

CAST *Mike Hammer* Stacy Keach *Velda* Lindsay Bloom *Capt. Pat Chambers* Don Stroud *Ozzie the Answer* Danny Goldman *Asst DA Lawrence Barrington* Kent Williams /*exec pr* Jay Bernstein /*pr* Lew Gallo /*dr* inc John Nicolla, Bernard Kowalski, Paul Krasny, Michael Preece, James Frawley, Leo Penn, Stacy Keach / *mus* Earle Hagen /*Columbia Pictures TV* (USA) / 1 x 120m, 46 x 60m col.

Middlemarch

Drama. BBC2 1994

BBC's lavish mini-series based on George Eliot's classic 19th-century novel, set in an English Everytown. Although on the surface it was a period story of how Dorothea Brooke erroneously follows her head and marries the dessicated Casaubon, it was also – courtesy of Andrew Davies' adaptation – full of resonant modern dilemmas, most pointedly the clash between money and ideals. A cast veritably stuffed full of veteran thespians and talented tyros turned in engrossing performances. If it required viewer alertness (there were 13 principle characters and multiple storylines), many thought the effort worthwhile. A torrent of Corporation costumiers (a TV form always close to the Beeb's Reithian bosom) followed, with ITV jumping on the cart with ➢*Moll Flanders* and Jane Austen's *Emma* among others.

CAST *Dorothea Brooke* Juliet Aubrey *Rev. Edward Casaubon* Patrick Malahide *Dr Tertius Lydgate* Douglas Hodge *Arthur Brooke* Robert Hardy *Nicholas Bulstrode* Peter Jeffrey *Mr Standish* Ronald Hines *Fred Vincy* Jonathan Firth *Rosamond Vincy* Trevyn McDowell *Will Ladislaw* Rufus Sewell *Peter Featherstone* Michael Hordern /*wr* Andrew Davies /*BBC TV* (UK) /1 x 90m, 5 x 60m col.

Mighty Morphin Power Rangers

Children's. Sky1 1993–6

The major kiddie-TV fad of the early 90s. Created by Israeli-born schlock-meister Haim Saban (➢*Sweet Valley High*) and musician-composer Shuki Levy, it featured five (later six) squeaky-clean Californian teenagers who could 'morph' into superheroes. Equipped with dinosaur-like vehicles, Dinozords (subsequently upgraded to Thunderzords), the Rangers, episode in and episode out, battled the evil Rita Repulsa. The wicked witch was aided and abetted by her husband Lord Zedd (over whom she had cast a spell), her brother Rio Revolto, and such henchfiends as the Tenga warriors Baboo, Finster and the Putty Patrol. *MMPR* was never, as Saban declared it, an 'excellent role model for today's youth', although complaints concerning its glorification of the martial arts somewhat missed its barn door sized tendency towards humour; moreover, the fight scenes were invariably between the Rangers and machines (i.e. not person-to-person). The real cavil was its cheap-skate production. In a shoddy, if astute, piece of cost cutting, the Rangers were masked for the action sequences, simply because this enabled the producers to incorporate uncredited footage from a Japanese live-action *sentai* show, *Zyu Ranger*. *MMPR* may have been a no-expense-spent programme, but it caused a merchandizing bonanza ($350 million in 1993 alone), which was eked out by periodic updates (such as title change, to *Power Rangers Zeo, Power Ranger Turbo*) which required new uniforms and equipment – and thus new merchandise lines. There was also a 1995 *Morphin* movie and a companion series, *VR Troopers*.

The original five Rangers were karate black belt Jason, gymnast Kimberly, reflective Trini, brainy Billy and exuberant Jack. The sixth Ranger, Tommy, was a turned agent of Rita.

CAST *Kimberly, the Pink Ranger* Amy Jo Johnson /Catherine Sutherland *Billy, the Blue Ranger* David Yost *Tommy, the White Ranger* Jason David Frank *Jason, the Red Ranger* Austin St John *Rocky, the Red Ranger* Steve Cardenas *Trini, the Yellow Ranger* Thuy Trang *Aisha, the Yellow Ranger* Karan Ashley *Zack, the Black Ranger* Walter Jones *Adam, the Black Ranger* Johnny Yong Bosch *Rita Repulsa* Barbara Goodson *Zordon* Bob Manahan /*cr* Haim Saban, Shuki Levy / *exec pr* Haim Saban, Shuki Levy /*pr* Ronnie Halder, Jonathan Tzachor /*Saban Entertainment Inc* (USA) / 145+ x 30m col /US tx Fox TV Children's Network 1993–6.

Millennium

Crime. Sky1 1996–

Detective drama from ➢*The X-Files* creator Chris Carter. Virtually tailor-written for mesmerizing, craggy-faced actor Lance Henriksen (*Aliens*, *Omen II*, *Terminator*), it featured him as an ex-FBI agent who joined an undercover law enforcement project in Seattle, The Millennium Group, designed to track down America's most wanted serial killers. The twist was that Henriksen's Frank Black had the psychic ability to enter his quarry's mind ('I put myself in his head. I become the horror.'). Black's wife, meanwhile, was the subject of a sicko's looming intentions. Although it trod the same dark and foreboding ground as ➢*Twin Peaks* and the movie *Seven*, it did so with semi-decent shock value. The turn-off was the pseudo mind-reading babble *à la* the Society of Psychics' weekly meet.

CAST *Frank Black* Lance Henriksen *Catherine Black* Megan Gallagher *Jordan Black* Britanny Tiplady *Lara Means* Kirstern Cloke *Det. Bob Gibelhouse* Stephen J. Lang *Terry O'Quinn* Peter Watts /*cr* Chris Carter /*exec pr* Chris Carter /*pr* Thomas J. Wright /*dr* inc Cliff Bole, Thomas J. Wright, David Nutter, Winrich Kolbe, Allen Coulter, Jim Chaleston /*mus* Mark Snow /*Ten Thirteen Productions: 20th Century-Fox TV* (USA) / 24 x 50m col /US tx FTV 1995–.

Minder

Comedy. ITV 1979–94

Originally created as a post-➢*The Sweeney* vehicle for Dennis Waterman, this sarf London-based serial about a gold-hearted bodyguard-gofer, Terry McCann (Waterman), and his shady entrepreneurial boss, Arthur Daley (George Cole), began with thrillerish intentions. However, low ratings and critical dislike caused a reduction in the violence quotient, and 'when AIDS came along, the sex had to go: all we were left with was the comedy' (Cole). The change was perfectedly suited to the sharp comic timing of Cole, who had honed his skills in the long-running ➢*A Life of Bliss* and, especially, as Flash Harry in the *St Trinians* films. Though the *Minder* title remained, the series became in reality the Arthur Daley Show (with Waterman's McGann assuming the role of stooge), based entirely around the trilby-hatted wheeler-dealer's scams. These were usually the flogging of something dodgy from his lock-up or used car lot, or the hiring out of the hapless McGann as a piece of minder meat. Such antics attracted the attention of 'plod' in the humourless form of Detective Sergeant Chisholm, whose *raison d'être* was to put Daley behind bars. Naturally he never did, but then Daley always emerged from his escapades with the pockets of his camel-hair coat as empty as when he began. Along with Del Boy – a fellow Thatcherite spiv – in ➢*Only Fools and Horses*, Arthur Daley was the great comic creation of the 80s, his name and expressions ('Er Indoors', 'nice little earner') passing into the everyday lexicon – the true test of a show's cultural impact.

By 1991, however, Waterman had tired of the series and refused to do more episodes. Unwilling to let a 'nice little earner' that had sold around the world die, Thames TV gave Daley a new sidekick, nephew Ray (played by virtual unknown Gary Webster). Not at all in the streetwise mould of McCann, the mineral water drinking Ray Daley proved both a filip and excuse to move the series further into outright sitcom. Brilliantly so.

The show's pub anthem theme song, 'I Could Be So Good For You' (sung by Waterman), was a top five hit in 1980.

CAST *Arthur Daley* George Cole *Terry McCann* Dennis Waterman *Dave* Glynn Edwards *DS Chisholm* Patrick Malahide *Sgt Rycott* Peter Childs *Des* George Layton *Ray Daley* Gary Webster *DS Morley* Nicholas Day *DC Park* Stephen Tompkinson /*cr* Leon Griffiths / *exec pr* Verity Lambert, Johnny Goodman /*pr* Lloyd Shirley, George Taylor, Ian Toynton /*dr* inc Roy Ward Baker, Peter Sasdy, Tom Clegg, Francis Megahy /*wr* inc Leon Griffiths, David Yallop, Tony Hoare, Willis Hall / *mus* Dennis Waterman & Gerard Kenny 'I Could Be So Good For You' theme song) /*Thames TV: Euston Films* (UK) /2 x 90m, 106 x 60m col.

The Mind of Mr J.G. Reeder

Crime. ITV 1969–71

A private investigator attached to the Public Prosecutor's office conceals a brilliant, villain-catching brain underneath his timid, pince nez-wearing appearance.

Passable televisualizations of Edgar Wallace's 1925 detective story collection of the same title.

CAST *J.G. Reeder* Hugh Burden *Sir Jason Toovey* Willoughby Goddard *Mrs Houchin* Mona Bruce *Miss Belman* Gillian Lewis /*exec pr* Lloyd Shirley /*pr* Kim Mills, Robert Love /*Thames TV* (UK) /16 x 50m col.

Mind Your Language

Comedy. ITV 1977–86

After quitting the cycle of medical comedies which began with ➢*Doctor In the House*, fresh-faced actor Barry Evans spent several years in theatre, where the rewards were more spiritual than monetary. In debt, he approached LWT for more TV work. The result was *Mind Your Language*, a low-brow comedy in which he starred as the lively but put-upon Jeremy Brown, a teacher of English to a class of assorted stereotyped foreigners. Evans died in 1997, after spending the last years of his life as a Leicestershire taxi driver.

CAST *Jeremy Brown* Barry Evans *Miss Courtney* Zara Nutley *Ali Nadim* Dino Shafeek *Danielle Faure* Françoise Pascal *Juan Cervantes* Ricardo Montez *Jamila Ranjha* Jamila Massey *Anna Schmidt* Jacki Harding /*cr* Vince Powell /*pr* Stuart Allen /*wr* Vince Powell /*LWT* (UK) 42 x 30m col.

Mission: Impossible

Adventure. ITV 1967–74

'Your mission, Jim, should you decide to accept it ...'

Spoken on a tape recorder that self-destructed five seconds later, these words introduced each week's instalment of *Mission: Impossible*, a glossy actioner about the activities of elite Amerian espionage agency IMF (Impossible Missions Force). Head of the IMF was Jim Phelps (Peter Graves, brother of ➢*Gunsmoke*'s James Arness, although Steven Hill as Briggs held the post for season one), under whom worked a team of skilled agents: Rollin Hand (Martin Landau), master of disguise; muscle-man Willie Armitage; female seductress Cinnamon Carter (Barbara Bain, wife of Landau); and electronics whizz-kid Barney Collier (a breakthrough black TV character, a professional on equal terms with his white colleagues). Although towards the end of the show's run the IMF tackled organized crime, its initial assignments always involved saving some poor country from communism. To say that the US flag flew high and wide over *Mission* would be an understatement, but saving graces were provided by tight scripts, honed direction, neat gadgetry and a charismatic cast, later to include Leonard 'Spock' Nimoy as Paris and Lesley Ann Warren as Dana Lambert. Emmys for Outstanding Dramatic Series were accordingly bestowed in 1967 and 1968. Barbara Bain also picked up best actress Emmys in 1967, 1968 and 1969. There were sales to 71 countries, and Lalo Schifrin's uptempo theme became a hit on both sides of the Atlantic.

'Your mission, Jim, should you decide to accept it...' Peter Graves (right) and the cast of *Mission: Impossible.* Lalo Schifrin's famous theme entered the charts on both sides of the Atlantic.

A *Mission: Impossible* revival was attempted by American ABC network in 1988, with episodes produced in Australia to avoid the American Writers' Guild strike. (In a technological update, the details of the mission were given to Jim on a self destructing laser disk.) And of course, with the Hollywood mania of the 90s for remaking TV classics for the big screen, a starry movie version was forthcoming. This appeared in 1996.

CAST *Daniel Briggs* Steven Hill *Jim Phelps* Peter Graves *Cinnamon Carter* Barbara Bain *Rollin Hand* Martin Landau *Willy Armitage* Peter Lupus *Barney Collier* Greg Morris *Paris* Leonard Nimoy *Dana Lambert* Lesley Ann Warren *Mimi Davis* Barbara Anderson *Lisa Casey* Lynda Day George /*cr* Bruce Geller /*exec pr* Bruce Geller /*pr* inc Stanley Kallis, Lee H. Katzin, Joseph E. Gantman, Alan Balter /*dr* inc Bruce Geller, Allen H. Miner, Alvin Ganzer, Bernard Kowalski /*wr* inc Bruce Geller /*mus* Lalo Schifrin (theme) /*Paramount TV* (USA) 171 x 50m col /US tx CBS 1966–73.

Miss Jones and Son

Comedy. ITV 1977–8

Mildly risqué for its time, a comedy from Richard Waring which cast Paula Wilcox (from ➢*The Lovers*, ➢*Man About the House*) as the unmarried mother of baby Roly. During a second season, Wilcox's artist character fell romantically for her next door neighbour, a writer, played by David Savile. It topped the ratings in both years of broadcast, any moral concern about its subject matter ultimately counterbalanced by British sympathy for the underdog.

CAST *Elizabeth Jones* Paula Wilcox *Roland 'Roly' Desmond Geoffrey Jones* Luke Steensil *Mrs Jones (mother)* Charlotte Mitchell/Joan Scott *Mr Jones (father)* Norman Bird *Rose Tucker* Cass Allen *Geoffrey* Christopher Beeny *David* David Savile /*cr* Richard Waring /*pr* Peter Frazer-Jones /*wr* Richard Waring /*mus* Roger Webb /*Thames TV* (UK) /12 x 30m col.

Miss Marple

Crime. BBC1 1984–92

Agatha Christie's busybody spinster sleuth Miss Marple was interpreted on the screen by numerous fine thespians (notably Margaret Rutherford) before Joan Hickson assumed the role in this occasional BBC series; but Hickson's tea-sipping, slightly hunched gentility was Marple as written by Christie. Simply definitive. It helped that the pieces were consumately crafted (Ray Boulting and Chris Petit were among the directors).

For the production, Nether Wallop in Hampshire doubled as 1930s St Mary Mead. There were 12 TV cases (ranging from feature length one-parters to three-parters of 50m) before Hickson OBE retired, aged 82.

CAST *Miss Jane Marple* Joan Hickson *Chief Insp. Slack* David Horowitz /*pr* Guy Slater, George Gallacio /*dr* inc Silvio Narizzano, Roy Boulting, Chris Petit, Norman Stone /*wr* inc Alan Plater, T.R. Bowen, Michael Frayn /*mus* Ken Howard, Alan Blaikey /*BBC TV: Arts and Entertainment Network: Network 7* (UK: USA: Aus) /16 x 50m, 1 x 115m, 3 x 110m, 1 x 100m col.

Mister Magoo

Children's. BBC 1962–4

The myopic and irritable Mr Magoo began his slapstick misadventuring as a character in a reel of 1949 cinema cartoon shorts, eventually transferring to TV in this UPA series of half hour episodes. Spectacularly unable to tell a moose from a woman, a phone kiosk from a policeman, Quincy Magoo was oft aided in his comic doings by nephews Prezley and Waldo (the latter a smart beatnik parody). His popularity reborn, Mr Magoo featured in numerous encores, from prime-time specials to a follow-up series, *The Famous Adventures of Mr Magoo* in which he impersonated famous Americans. The character was revived again, by DePatie-Freleng, in 1977, with *What's New, Mr Magoo?*

CAST (voices) *Mr Quincy Magoo/Mother Magoo* Jim Backus *Waldo* Jerry Hausner/Daws Butler *Prezley* Daws Butler/Paul Frees /*pr* John Hubley, Henry Saperstein, Glen Heisch /*UPA Productions* (USA) /127 x 30m col /US tx Syndicated 1960–1.

The Mistress

Comedy. BBC1 1985–7

Another Carla Lane sitcom about a single gal, Felicity Kendal, though a tad more upbeat than ➢*Solo*. Here Kendal played florist Maxine, the bit on the side for businessman Luke Mansel, married to Helen (played by Jane Asher), who was suspicious. The casting of Kendal, of course, was spot on, and played to the fantasy of the serried ranks of middle-Englishmen who considered her a sex object.

CAST *Maxine* Felicity Kendal *Luke Mansel* Jack Galloway/Peter McEnery *Helen Mansel* Jane Asher *Jenny* Jenny McCracken /*cr* Carla Lane /*pr* Gareth Gwenlan /*dr* Gareth Gwenlan /*wr* Carla Lane /*BBC TV* (UK) /12 x 30m col.

Moll Flanders

Drama. ITV 1996

Corset-ripping adaptation of Daniel Defoe's 1722 novel about a heroine, born in Newgate Prison and sold to gypsies, who used her feminine wiles to advance her fortune through serial marriage. Actress Alex Kingston (estranged wife of Ralph – or Rafe – Fiennes, and former star of ➢*The*

The 'pre-fab four' (left to right, Mike Nesmith, Peter Tork, Davy Jones, Mickey Dolenz) in *The Monkees*, an American TV aping of The Beatles' movies *A Hard Day's Night* and *Help!*

Knock) made a suitably voluptuous Flanders and the script by Andrew Davies (who also did the adapting jobs on ➢*Middlemarch* and ➢*Pride and Prejudice*), though occasionally tedious and anachronistic, had 17 sex scenes, enough to cause massed ranks of class CD men – not usually the first to switch on costume dramas – to ogle the screen. To critical ridicule, Davies even invented a lesbian lover, Lucy Diver, for Flanders. (In fact, scriptwriting licence was not stretched too far; Defoe himself had intimated that his other heroine, Roxana, went to bed with her maid, Amy.) When screened on the American Public Broadcasting Service (PBS) it attracted a 4.6 rating, the highest in the Service's history.

CAST *Moll Flanders* Alex Kingston *Jemmy Seagrave* Daniel Craig *Lucy Diver* Nicola Walker *Mrs Golightly* Diana Rigg *Sir Richard Gregory* Ronald Fraser *Roland* Colin Buchanan /*pr* David Lascelles /*dr* David Attwood /*wr* Andrew Davies /*Granada TV* (UK) / 4 x 60–65m col /US tx PBS 1996.

The Monkees

Comedy. BBC1 1966–7

'Hey, hey, we're the Monkees/And people say we monkey around.'

So opened the theme tune of the weekly life-on-the-road misadventures of an artificially-created American mop-top pop group based on The Beatles (of *A Hard Day's Night* and *Help!* vintage). More than 400 applicants were screened by producers Bert Schneider and Bob Rafelson before they chose, as the 'pre-fab four', English actor Davy Jones (previously Ena Sharples' grandson in ➢*Coronation Street*), folk-singer Peter Tork, former ➢*Circus Boy* actor Mickey Braddock (here called Dolenz, the name by which he would also go on to produce such TV shows as ➢*Metal Mickey*) and Michael Nesmith, whose mother invented the correcting fluid used for typing errors. Each episode featured picaresque madcap antics (emphasized by ingenious and innovative shooting techniques, such as fast-mo and distorted focus) and zany humour, plus a couple of musical numbers, to which The Monkees only contributed the vocals since, despite TV appearances, most could not play instruments.

Better than a manipulated product had a right to be, *The Monkees* won the 1966 Emmy for

Outstanding Comedy. Several of the band's songs even reached No. 1 in the charts ('Last Train to Clarksville', 'Daydream Believer', 'I'm a Believer'), though lyricists such as Neil Diamond helped. A Monkees' film, *Head* (directed by Rafelson, co-written with Jack Nicholson, in a partnership which would find further fruition with the movie *Five Easy Pieces*), proved too off the wall for the teenyboppers who were the main Monkees maniacs and died a death by box office. By then, anyway, the band had split up.

Until 1997, that is. Then, without a trace of doubt in their minds, the Monkees (now in their 50s) took the last train to nostalgiaville and announced a new album and a TV special. '...ooh I'm a believer believer, I'm a believer, I'm a believer ... yes I am.'

CAST Davy Jones, Peter Tork, Mickey Dolenz, Mike Nesmith /*cr* Bert Schneider, Bob Rafelson /*pr* Bert Schneider, Bob Rafelson /*dr* inc Bob Rafelson, James Frawley, Bruce Kessler /*mus* inc Neil Diamond / *Columbia TV* (USA) /28 x 25m col /US tx NBC 1966–7.

Monkey

Adventure. BBC2 1979–82

M O N K E Y! Japanese fantasy series about a 7th-century Buddhist priest, Tripitaka, who journeys from China to India escorted by three supernatural companions, Monkey (an outrageous clown, played by Masaaki Sakai from Nipponese popsters, The Spiders), Sandy (a moody philosopher) and Pigsy (a sex-mad hedonist). A sort of Eastern *Pilgrim's Progress*, adapted from the 16th-century book by Wu Ch'eng-en, it was dubbed for English audiences by David Weir, who had previously exercised his translating talents on ➢*The Water Margin.* As with the British pantomime tradition of Dick Whittington, the part of Tripitaka was taken by a woman, Masako Natsume, who died of leukaemia shortly after completion of the show.

CAST *Tripitaka* Masako Natsume *Monkey* Masaaki Sakai *Pigsy* Toshiyuki Nishida/Tonpei Hidari *Yu-Lung* Shunji Fujimura *Sandy* Shiron Kishibe /*dr* inc Yusuke Watanabe, Daisuke Yamazaki, Jun Funda /*wr* (English script) David Weir /*NTV: Kokusai Hoei* (Jap) / 39 x 45m col.

The Monocled Mutineer

Drama. BBC1 1986

Mesmerizing 'faction' about the WWI British Army mutiny at Etaples training camp, 1917, led by the dashing Private Percy Toplis (Paul McGann), a Nottinghamshire miner. Alan ➢'*Boys from the Blackstuff*' Bleasdale's scenic script, adapted from the history by William Allison, also followed Toplis's post-mutiny flight, dressed as a British officer, to Blighty, his love affair with the young widow Dorothy (Cherie Lunghi, ➢*The Manageress*), and assassination by MI5 on a bleak Lakeland hillside. It attracted establishment condemnation for its suggestion that British soldiers had been executed for desertion (they had) and viewer acclaim in equal measure.

CAST *Percy Toplis* Paul McGann *Dorothy* Cherie Lunghi *Charles Strange* Matthew Marsh *Woodhall (MI5 assassin)* Philip McGough /*pr* Richard Broke / *dr* Jim O'Brien /*wr* Alan Bleasdale /*BBC TV* (UK) / 2 x 75m, 1 x 80m, 1 x 95m col.

Monty Python's Flying Circus

Comedy. BBC1 1969–74

'And now for something completely different...'

Landmark BBC comedy series, originally to be called *Owl Stretching Time*, of free-form sketches and blackouts. The *Python* team shared an Oxbridge comedy background (with the exception of illustrator Gilliam, an American) and honed their separate TV talents on ➢*Do Not Adjust Your Set*, ➢*At Last the 1948 Show* and ➢*The Frost Report*, before coming together in *Python* at the instigation of Barry Took. Their targets were often quintessentially British: small-minded bureaucrats (John Cleese's Minister of Silly Walks), upper-class twits, lower-class wearers of knotted handkerchiefs ('Gumbies'), and accountants. (Unlike contemporary shows such as *The Frost Report* there was no political point to *Python* humour.) They also delighted in undermining the conventions of TV. Jokes failed to have punch lines, episodes were concluded with false endings, and characters – notably the blimpish Colonel and the Spanish Inquistion Cardinals, Ximanez, Fang and Biggles – flitted from skit to skit. Often the only link was a surreal Gilliam cartoon (the descending giant foot) or Cleese's 'And now for something completely different...' Yet for all its inspired brilliance and

And now for something completely different ... the cast of *Monty Python*, provisionally titled *Cynthia Fellatio's Flying Circus.*

cultural impact, the anarchic series was as often miss as hit; for every quotable Dead Parrot, Cheese Shop, Spam and Argument Clinic sketch, there were two of instant forgettableness. After a five year run and with Cleese in particular tiring of the 'anything goes' structurelessness, the group pulled down the *Python* TV big top to pursue brilliant individual careers (with ➢*Fawlty Towers*, ➢*Rutland Weekend Television*, and ➢*Ripping Yarns* among the results). To the relief of their admirers, however, *Python* continued to exist as a cinema being, continuing its collective craziness in a cycle of movies: *Monty Python and the Holy Grail* (1974), *Monty Python's Life of Brian* (1979), and *Monty Python's Meaning of Life* (1983).

CAST John Cleese, Eric Idle, Terry Jones, Michael Palin, Graham Chapman, Terry Gilliam (with Carol Cleveland) /*cr* Barry Took, John Cleese, Eric Idle, Terry Jones, Michael Palin, Graham Chapman, Terry Gilliam /*pr* John Howard Davies, Ian MacNaughton / *wr* John Cleese, Eric Idle, Terry Jones, Michael Palin, Graham Chapman, Terry Gilliam /*BBC TV* (UK) / 45 x 30m col.

Moonbase 3

Sci-fi. BBC1 1973

Semi-educational space show which launched itself on a proud tank of realism (the consultant was BBC scientific correspondent James Burke) and crash-landed ignominiously because the producers forgot to fit a decent dramatic engine. Set in 2003 it concerned colonization of the Moon by competing communities from the earthly powers. Strictly quotidian stuff. This, despite being the creation of illustrious ➢*Doctor Who* personnel Terrance Dicks and Barry Letts.

CAST *David Caulder* Donald Houston *Dr Helen Smith* Fiona Gaunt *Michel Lebrun* Ralph Bates *Tom Hill* Barry Lowe *Stephen Partness* Tom Kempinski /*cr* Barry Letts, Terrance Dicks /*pr* Barry Letts /*dr* Ken Hannam, Christopher Barry /*wr* Terrance Dicks & Barry Letts, John Lucarrotti, John Brason, Arden Winch /*mus* Dudley Simpson /*BBC TV* (UK) / 6 x 50m col.

Moonlighting

Comedy. BBC2 1986–9

Stylish romantic comedy, inspired by the 1940 film *His Girl Friday*, that rescued the stalled career of Cybill Shepherd (last seen in Bogdanovich's awesomely evocative movie, *The Last Picture Show*, and Texan ranch Western *The Yellow Rose*) and made that of Bruce Willis, whose previous screen performances had been limited to a bit part in ➢*Miami Vice*. Shepherd played former model Maddie Hayes (not too difficult a part for Shepherd to relate to; she was the 1968 Model of the Year) who, after being swindled by embezzlers, decides to turn the Los Angeles PI agency among her assets from a tax dodge to a profit-making concern. As partner in the Blue Moon Detective Agency she takes in Willis' lascivious and wisecracking David Addison. Their lust-hate relationship was the essence of the show, 'tec case work merely secondary, and by season two the producers succumbed to the obvious: a heavily hyped bed scene between Maddie and David, which moved the ratings to heavenly heights. The other leading cast members were Allyce Beasley as daffy receptionist Miss Dipesto and Curtis Armstrong as clerk Herbert Violam, the object of her unrequited sighs.

Created by Glenn Gordon Caron, the show was the epitome of post-modern TV, with its quirky effective rummages through the cutting floors of history: one episode, 'Atomic Shakespeare', was written in iambic pentameters; another, dealing with an unsolved 40s murder, was filmed in *noir* style; and nearly every instalment incorporated some tricksy self-referential statement or aside to camera.

Loved to almost fanatical degree by its devotees, the show was nevertheless beset by production problems. The off-screen three-way conflicts between Shepherd, Willis and Caron were legendary, and episodes ran over length and budget. A hasty cancellation in 1989 resulted.

CAST *Maddie Hayes* Cybill Shepherd *David Addison* Bruce Willis *Agnes Dipesto* Allyce Beasley *Herbert Violam* Curtis Armstrong /*cr* Glenn Gordon Caron /*exec pr* Glenn Gordon Caron /*pr* Jay Daniel /*dr* inc Alan Arkush, Peter Werner, Will Mackenzie, Christian I. Nyby, Paul Krasny, Robert Butler, Sam Weismam / *wr* inc Glenn Gordon Caron /*mus* Lee Holdridge & Al Jarreau (theme) /*Picturemaker Productions* (USA) / 1 x 120m, 66 x 60m col /US tx BC 1985–9.

The Morecombe and Wise Show

Comedy. ITV 1961–8/BBC2: BBC1 1968–76/ITV 1980–83

Not so much a comic double act as a beloved national institution, Eric Morecombe (born John Eric Bartholomew; Morecombe was his home town) and Ernie Wise (Ernest Wiseman) began their partnership in 1941. This was interrupted by Morecombe's wartime service as a miner, but resumed in 1947 as part of *Lord George Sanger's Variety Service*, the duo eventually finding their way into the new medium of TV in 1951 as part of BBC's *The Youth Parade*. They received their first TV series in the dismal shape of *Running Wild* (BBC, 1954). Extensive touring, however, perfected their timing and rapport and when offered another chance at their own series, by ATV in 1961, they did not waste it. Playing their stage personae of Eric, the mischievious pipe-smoking sceptic, and Ernie, the pompous, short-fat-hairy-legged foil (with '23 A Levels, all of them in Maths'), they mugged and sight-gagged happily (Eric holding Ern by the throat with the challenge 'Get outta that!'), in between introducing musical artistes, The Beatles included. In 1968 the duo were poached by the BBC where they produced their greatest work. The catchphrase 'you can't see the join' (about Ern's wig), Eric's pretence of being strangled behind the stage curtain, Ern's play 'wot I wrote', all date from this era. Most of the scriptwriting was done by Eddie Braben, who oft gave the sketches a touch of genuine quirkiness: a mock TV cold-remedy advertisement ended with an unseen questioner asking Morecombe if he was 'Fed up?' and then suggested, 'Why not try –' at which point a gun sounded. Morecombe and Wise's Christmas Specials, meanwhile, entrapped stellar celebrities (Glenda Jackson, Shirley Bassey, André Previn, and the never paid Peter Cushing) in affectionate antics and were, for almost two decades, as much a part of Yuletide as the Queen's Speech and plum pudding. A spell at Thames TV followed before Morecombe, who had long suffered with heart problems, died in 1984. The work of Morecombe and Wise, however, continues to be preserved in frequent repeats, video collections and the post-modernist plagiarism of the Morecombe lookalike Vic Reeves (see ➢*Vic Reeves' Big Night Out*).

CAST Eric Morecombe, Ernie Wise /*pr* inc Colin Clews (ATV), John Ammonds (BBC) /*wr* inc Sid Green & Dick Hills (ATV), Eddie Braben (BBC) / *ATV: BBC: Thames TV* (UK) /approx 60 x 30m, 100 x 60m bw:col /US tx Syndicated 1980–3.

Shazbat! Robin Williams starred as the extra-terrestrial visitor to Boulder, Colorado, in *Mork & Mindy*, a spin-off from *Happy Days.*

Mork & Mindy

Comedy. ITV 1979–83

Shazbat! A spin-off from a 1978 episode of ➢*Happy Days* in which Mork (Robin Williams) from planet Ork landed on Earth and tried to kidnap Richie Cunningham. Audience reaction to the story was so favourable that the childlike alien, an innocent abroad in the universe, was given a show of his own.

For his second coming to Earth, Mork landed at Boulder, Colorado, in a giant egg and with a mission to study the planet's human life. The findings were reported back to His Immenseness, Orkan leader, Orson. In Boulder, Mork was befriended by Mindy McConnell, daughter of music store owner Fred; initially Mork and Mindy's relationship was platonic (if apartment sharing), though they eventually married, honeymooning on Ork – where Mork discovered he was pregnant and laid an egg. From this emerged their son, Mearth, played by veteran US comedian Jonathan Winters; on Ork beings grew younger, not older.

The role of Mork, initially offered to Dom DeLuise, was perfectly suited to the wacky stream of consciousness style of Robin Williams, then a stand-up comic at LA's Comedy Store. Understanding this, *M&M* producers allowed Williams to improvise much, marking scripts 'Mork can go off here'. The zappy, zany show made Williams a star.

Like previous ET-in-an-American-home comedies, a genre which began with ➢*My Favourite Martian*, *M&M* juxtaposed the Alien against the Human to comment on the latter's foibles. Unfortunately, in the case of *M&M* these tended to be platitudinous rather than meaningful. Funny, though.

Na nu, na nu.

CAST *Mork* Robin Williams *Mindy McConnell* Pam Dawber *Frederick McConnell* Conrad Janis *Cora Hudson (Mindy's grandmother)* Elizabeth Kerr *Orson* Ralph James *Exidor (the UFO prophet)* Robert Donner *Mearth* Jonathan Winters /*cr* Garry K. Marshall, Tony Marshall, Dale McRaven, Joe Gauberg /*exec pr* Garry K. Marshall, Tony Marshall /*pr* Bruce Johnson, Dale McRaven /*dr* inc Bob Claver, Jeff Chambers, Howard Storm /*wr* inc Robin Williams, April Kelly, Deborah Raznicka, Ed Scharlach /*Miller-Milkis Prods: Henderson Production Co: Paramount TV* (USA) / 92 x 30m, 1 x 60m col /US tx ABC 1978–82.

Mouse and Mole

Children's. BBC1 1988

Animated rural tales of a cottage-sharing mouse and mole, based on the best-selling books by Joyce Dunbar and James Mayhew. Cartoon quality fine, voice-acting (by Richard Briers and Alan Bennett) divine.

CAST (voices) Alan Bennett, Richard Briers / *Grasshopper Productions* (UK) /26 x 5m col.

Mr and Mrs

Light Entertainment. ITV 1972–88

Quiz show from the slow and saccharine depths of Afternoon TV Hell, in which married couples were tested on their knowledge of each other's habits (e.g. 'Which leg does he put in his trousers first?'). Hosted by Alan Taylor and former radio ventriloquist Derek Batey it ran for several years in the Television Wales and West/HTV region before being networked, with HTV and Border sharing the production chores and charges. A Welsh language version, *Sion a Sian*, followed, as did a stage show for the Blackpool holiday season, and the format was revived for a satellite channel, UK Living (a natural home, if ever there was one) as *The New Mr and Mrs Show* in 1992.

CAST (presenters) Alan Taylor (HTV), Derek Batey (Border) /*cr* Roy Ward Dickson /*pr* Derek Batey, William Cartner, Derek Clark /*HTV: Border* (UK) / 400+ x 30m col.

Mr Bean

Comedy. ITV 1990–6

Near-silent comedies starring rubber-faced Rowan Atkinson (➢*Blackadder*, ➢*Not the Nine O'Clock News*) as the clueless and clumsy Mr Bean. The mini-misadventures had their side-splitting moments, if only because of Atkinson's impeccable timing, and at times viewed like important TV portraits of the human condition. At others, they were dumb antics, telegraphed a century in advance and wholly derivative of Charlie Chaplin and Monsieur Hulot. There were many specials, with *Merry Christmas Mr Bean* pulling in a crowd of 18.48m in December 1995, making it the most watched programme, save for soaps, in the Yuletide week.

CAST *Mr Bean* Rowan Atkinson *Irma Gobb* Matilda Ziegler /*pr* John Howard Davies, Sue Verne /*wr* Rowan Atkinson, Richard Curtis, Robin Driscoll, Ben Elton / *Thames TV: Central TV: Tiger TV* (USA) /114 x 30m col.

Mr Benn

Children's. BBC1 1971

Classic series of ➢*Watch with Mother* animated films about bowler-hatted Mr Benn, of 52 Festive Road, London, who visited a special costume shop. There, 'as if by magic', the shopkeeper allowed Mr Benn to try on any costume in the changing room, from which Mr Benn would proceed through 'the door that always led to adventure' and emerge in the world of whichever dress (cowboy, spaceman, pirate, etc.) he had donned. Mr Benn, who was a very nice man, would then aid some poor unfortunate animal or person, the end of the adventure being signalled by the arrival of the shopkeeper, who escorted Mr Benn back to his emporium. Afterwards, Mr Benn returned home (doing his famous stif-legged walk) to No. 52, clutching some memento of his magic travel

Created by David McKee (*King Rollo*, *Not Now, Bernard*), the series has been repeated every year since its original 1971 transmission, making it the UK's longest-running children's show after ➢*Blue Peter*. The narrator was Ray Brooks (➢*Armchair Theatre's* 'Cathy Come Home', ➢*Big Deal*, *Growing Pains*).

NARRATOR Ray Brooks /*cr* David McKee /*dr* Pat Kirby /*wr* David McKee /*mus* Don Warren /*Zephyr Film Productions: BBC TV* (UK) /13 x 15m col.

Mr Ed

Comedy. ITV 1962–5

On moving to the country, architect Wilbur Post finds that he has also bought a palomino horse who can talk.

American fantasy sitcom (one of the first, prefiguring ➢*My Favourite Martian*, ➢*Bewitched*, etc.), derived from the movie series *Francis* by its director, Arthur Lubin. Studio-bound and too feebly nonsensical to swallow. Equine scatology, in fact. Mr Ed was voiced by the great B-Western hardman, Allan 'Rocky' Lane (1901–73), while English actor Alan Young (born Angus Young) played his human foil.

CAST *Wilbur Post* Alan Young *Carol Post* Connie Hines *Roger Addison* Larry Keating *Kay Addison* Edna Skinner *Col. Gordon Kirkwood* Leon Ames *Winnie Kirkwood* Florence MacMichael *Mr Ed* (voice) Allan 'Rocky' Lane /*cr* Arthur Lubin /*pr* inc Al Simon, Arthur Lubin /*dr* inc Arthur Lubin /*wr* inc Bob O'Brian, William Burns, Lou Derman, Ben Starr /*Filmways* (USA) /143 x 25m bw /US tx Syndicated 1960–1, CBS 1961–6.

Mr Pastry

Children's. BBC 1960–2

Was a bewhiskered bungler (invented and lovingly portrayed by Richard Hearne) in coat tails who first appeared in the cinema and then on *Sunday Night at the London Palladium* and other adult-oriented TV variety shows, before starring in a roll of BBC live action series for children: *Leave It To Mr Pastry*, (1960), *Ask Mr Pastry* (1961), *Mr Pastry's Pet Shop* (1962), and *Mr Pastry's Progress* (1962), in which he reminisced about past misadventures. Also seen was his elderly postmistress friend, Miss Print.

CAST *Mr Pastry* Richard Hearne *Miss Print* Barbara Hicks /*cr* Richard Hearne /*BBC TV* (UK) /24 x 10m bw.

The Mrs Merton Show

Comedy. BBC2 1995–7

With the death of the British chat show in the 90s, there were only spoofs left, such as ➢*Knowing Me, Knowing You ... with Alan Partridge* and this effort featuring studio pensioner Mrs Merton (played by thirtysomething comedienne Caroline Aherne, previously a fixture on Granada's *The Dead Good Show*). It was full of winking innuendo and vicious snipes.

Brilliant, in fact. Merton's archly styled questions (to Debbie McGee: 'So tell me. What attracted you to millionaire Paul Daniels?') were simply devastating. A BAFTA Award followed, though ultimately the idea burst its bubble since cautious A and B list celebs refused the invitation to have the Mancunian granny's verbal knitting needles stuck in them. And *Mrs Merton*'s heavily manufacured irony suited the iconclastic mid 90s but not all times. The show's band featured Peter Hook from rock music combo New Order, who was also Aherne's sometime husband. Mrs Merton's famed piercing look was actually because Aherne suffers partial blindness in one eye.

CAST *Mrs Merton* Caroline Aherne /*pr* Peter Kessler, Mark Gorton /*dr* Pati Marr /*BBC TV* (UK) /18 x 30m col.

M Squad

Crime. ITV 1958–60

There have been hundreds of crime shows set in the naked city of Chicago and this thick-ear actioner was one of them. Tyro Lee Marvin starred as Lieutenant Frank Ballinger, the leader of the ruthless M Squad of crack plain-clothes homicide detectives (the role creating at one punch Marvin's screen persona as a heavy). Hard-hitting and fast-moving, it built up a popular folowing, but is always destined to be viewed as the warm up act for Quinn Martin's landmark ➢*The Untouchables*. The jazz theme used from season two onwards was composed by Count Basie. Robert Altman was among the directors sharing the chores.

CAST *Lt Frank Ballinger* Lee Marvin *Capt. Grey* Paul Newlan /*exec pr* Richard Lewis /*pr* John Larkin /*dr* inc Robert Altman, John Brahm, Bernard Girard, Allen H. Miner, Don Weis, Don Taylor /*mus* Count Basie ('Theme from M Squad' theme), Stanley Wilson / *Latimer Productions: Revue Studios: Universal TV* (USA) /115 x 30m bw /US tx NBC 1957–60.

Muck and Brass

Drama. ITV 1982

Starred Mel Smith (from ➢*Not the Nine O'Clock News*), in a rare straight role, as a ruthless property developer on the up in a fictitious Midlands city beset by corruption. A potent TV anticipation of the worst excesses of boomtime Thatcherism. Nasty stuff, nicely done.

CAST *Tom Craig* Mel Smith /*pr* Margaret Matheson / *dr* Martin Campbell, Marek Kanievska /*wr* Tom Clarke /*Central TV* (UK) /6 x 50m col.

Muffin the Mule

Children's. BBC 1946–55/ITV 1956/BBC 1957

Piebald Muffin the Mule was the first star of tiny TV, appearing in a 1946 edition of *For the Children* (the predecessor of ➢*Watch With Mother*) in which he capered around a piano top while the awfully English Annette Mills sang songs. Afterwards, the wooden puppet and Mills (sister of actor John and one-time rival for Mistinguett's title of 'woman with the most beautiful legs') were given a show of their own, in which they were joined by other puppet animals, among them: Peregrine the penguin, Oswald the ostrich, Monty the monkey, Louise the lamb and kittens Prudence and Primrose. The puppets were worked by Ann Hogarth (who had originally bought Muffin for 15 shillings) from behind a striped screen across the piano top. When Mills died in 1955, Muffin transferred to ITV, before returning to the Corporation stable for a final season with Jan Bussell as his singing stooge.

The theme song was: 'Here comes Muffin, Muffin the Mule/Dear old Muffin, playing the fool/Here comes Muffin, everybody sing/Here comes Muffin the Mule.'

CAST (presenters) Annette Mills, Jan Bussell /*cr* Annette Mills /*pr* David Boisseau, Peter Thompson, John Warrington, Gordon Murray, Peggy Bacon, Dorothea Brooking, Nan McDonald /*dr* inc Jan Bussell /*wr* inc Ann Hogarth, Annette Mills /*mus* Annette Mills /approx 300 x 16m bw.

The Multi-coloured Swap Shop
Children's. BBC1 1976–81

Saturday morning show for the junior to teen bracket, combining star chats, cartoons and an interactive slot where kids could swap items on the air (pets excepted). Keith Chegwin went out on the road to arrange live swaps amongst the unsuspecting public, Maggie Philbin hostessed around the studio, John Craven supervised 'The News Swap', and Noel Edmonds fronted with the assistance of a dinosaur toy called Posh Paws. Always emanating a slight air of Corporation goodygoodyness, *Swap Shop* would never snicker in the popular memory like its anarchic ITV rival, ➢*Tiswas*, and much the most important of its legacies was that it minted the shiny happy persona Edmonds would take to such chart-topping adult projects as *The Late, Late Breakfast Show* and ➢*Noel's House Party*. It was replaced by the identikit *Saturday Superstore*, hosted by Mike Reid.

CAST (presenters) Noel Edmonds, Keith Chegwin, Maggie Philbin, John Craven /*pr* Rosemary Gill / *BBC TV* (UK) /220 x 120m col.

The Munsters
Comedy. BBC 1965–71

Spoof horror show created by Bob Mosher and Joe Connelly (➢*Amos'n'Andy, Leave it to Beaver*), contemporary with ➢*The Addams Family* with which it has spooky similarities; they aired within weeks of each other) though generally cruder in execution.

The Munsters lived at number 43 Mockingbird Lane, a decrepit Victorian gothic mansion with a dungeon in the basement. Head of the Transylvanian clan was Herman (Fred Gwynne from ➢*Car 54, Where Are You?*), a 7-foot double of Frankenstein's monster who toiled at Gateman, Goodbury & Grave Funeral Home to provide for his family; wife Lily (née Dracula); 378-year-old Grandpa (played by Al Lewis, also *Car 54*); werewolf son Eddie; and niece Marilyn.

Stories were standard domestic fare (such as Herman dieting for his army reunion in 'Lo cal Munster') or, more usually, clash of culture comedies derived from the ghoulish family's contact with suburban America. As with *The Addams Family*, this meant that the 'inversion of the norm' gag (for instance, 'poor Marilyn', treated by the family as if she was ugly, was actually a ravishing Monroe lookalike) was overworked until it wore out its welcome. There was, however, an explicit message of liberal racial tolerance behind the humour (the Munsters were but a caricatured, cartoonized immigrant family) which had, and will always have, a place.

A movie, *Munster Go Home*, featuring the TV cast was released in 1966. Gwynne, DeCarlo and Lewis again reprised their roles for a 1981 TVM, *The Munsters Revenge*, before new players (John Shuck, Lee Meriwether, Jason Marsden, Hilary Van Dyke, Howard Morton) took over for the execrable revival, *The Munsters Today* (ITV 1990–).

CAST *Herman Munster* Fred Gwynne *Lily Munster* Yvonne DeCarlo *Grandpa Munster* Al Lewis *Edward Wolfgang 'Eddie' Munster* Butch Patrick *Marilyn Munster* Beverly Owen/Pat Priest /*cr* Joe Connelly, Bob Mosher /*pr* Joe Connelly, Bob Mosher /*dr* inc Jack Marquette, Harry Larrecq, Lawence Dobkin, Charles Rondeau, Joseph Pevney, Earl Bellamy /*wr* Joe Connelly, Bob Mosher, James Allardice, Richard Baer / *mus* Jack Marshall /*MCA:Universal* (USA) /70 x 25m bw /US tx CBS 1964–6.

Fred Gwynne and Yvonne DeCarlo starred in spoof horror show *The Munsters.* Gwynne spent an hour and a half each shooting day having his face painted green – although the show was shot in black and white.

The Muppet Show
Comedy. ITV 1976–81

Fixtures on US TV (including ➢*Sesame Street*) for over a decade, Jim Henson's bizarre half marionette, half glove puppet (hence their name) creatures only received a programme of their own because of British impressario, Lew Grade. Each episode of the resultant zestful mayhem that was *The Muppet Show* featured a human guest star who was mock humiliated as he or she became caught in the frantic efforts of the Muppets – argumentative Miss Piggy, Kermit the Frog, The Great Gonzo, Animal, aged hecklers Statler and Waldorf, Fozzie Bear and all – to put on a variety performance. A worldwide success, the series spun off five feature films (*The Muppet Movie, The Great Muppet Caper, The Muppets Take Manhattan, Muppet Christmas Carol* and *Muppet's Treasure Island*). On the tide of muppetmania, Henson launched *Fraggle Rock* (ITV, 1984–9), a puppet show about strange beings called Fraggles who lived on a remote stretch of southern coast near the Captain's (Fulton Mackay from ➢*Porridge*) lighthouse.

Although Jim Henson died in 1990, the muppets were revived in *Muppets Tonight!* (BBC1, 1996–), an update of the old format which saw the featured creatures doing their putting-on-a-show routine for K-MUP TV. A troupe of new characters were added, of whom the dreadlocked Clifford ('your homey made of foamey'), poor man's Sinatra, Johnny Fiama, and a line of dancing cheeses shone out.

CAST *Kermit the Frog/Waldorf* Jim Henson *Miss Piggy Lee/Sam the Eagle/Fozzie Bear* Frank Oz *Gonzo* Dave Groelz *Statler/Scooter* Richard Hunt *Rizzo the Rat* Steve Whitmire *Pops/Sgt Floyd* Jerry Nelson /*cr* Jim Henson, Frank Oz /*exec pr* David Lazer /*pr* Jack Burns, Jim Henson /*wr* Jim Henson, Jack Burns, Marc London, Jerry Juhl /*ATV: Henson Associates: Central TV* (UK) /130 x 25m col /US tx Syndicated 1976–81.

Murder Bag
Crime. ITV 1957–9

Took its title from the black briefcase full of forensic equipment toted to the scene of crime by Detective Superintendent Lockhart. Transmitted live, the authentic looking procedurals of *Murder Bag* were popular enough to earn the snuff-sniffing Lockhart a promotion to *Crime Sheet* (Associated-Rediffusion, 1959) and then ➢*No Hiding Place.*

Bald-headed former-Shakespearean actor Daniel Benzali headed the cast of *Murder One*, the first law drama to follow a single case for an entire season.

CAST *Det. Supt Tom Lockhart* Raymond Francis /*cr* Glyn Davies /*pr* Barry Baker /*Associated Rediffusion* (UK) /55 x 30m bw.

Murder Most Horrid

Comedy. BBC2 1991–

Whodunnit spoofs, one per week, always starring Dawn French (in her first solo project). It won Comedy Awards, although at times the excellent casts (Hugh Laurie, Nigel Havers, Jane Asher, Jim Broadbent et al.) had to stuggle with clankingly heavy handed scripts. The best of the narratives, however, had a perverted, inescapable logic which drove them to their daffy denoument. A linking thread was provided by the character Hattie Harbottle (French) who introduced the episodes in the manner of Edward Lusgarten crossed with Miss Marple. Made by TalkBack, the production company owned by Mel Smith and Griff Rhys Jones (➢*Alas Smith and Jones*, ➢*Not the Nine O'Clock News*).

CAST Dawn French /*cr* Dawn French /*exec pr* Peter Fincham, Jon Plowman /*pr* Sophie Clarke-Jervoise, Jon Plowman /*dr* inc Bob Spiers, James Hendrie, Dewi Humphreys, Ferdinand Fairfax /*wr* inc Steven Moffat, Ian Hislop & Nick Newman, Graham & Jez Alborough, Paul Smith, Anthony Horowitz /*TalkBack* (UK) /12+ x 30m col.

Murder One

Crime. Sky Movies/Sky1 1996–

Unprecedented legal drama serial, the first to follow a single case for an entire season (23 episodes). Claimed by creator Steve Bochco (➢*Hill Street Blues*, ➢*LA Law* ➢*NYPD Blue*) to be his easiest ever sale to a network, it featured bald-headed legal eagle Theodore Hoffman, the defence attorney in the trial for murder and rape of Hollywood star Neil Avedon (the victim was a 15-year-old girl). Did he do it, or was it the work of devilish businessman Richard Cross? Whodunnitry was complimented by unusually effective characterization, masterful performances (especially by former RSC actor Benzali as Hoffman and Tucci as Cross), and a shadowy visual style suggestive not only of mystery but of moral depths. In the USA, scheduled against NBC's mighty ➢*ER* and in the aftermath of the O.J. Simpson trial, its viewers dwindled, but in Britain it achieved a loyal following, viewers forcing BBC2 (which carried it several weeks behind satellite channel, Sky1) to rescind a planned postponement because of the Olympiad. A second series followed, although with Anthony LaPaglia's James Wyler replacing Benzali's Hoffman (judged a miss with US viewerdom) as lead lawyer and a new format of three consecutive trials.

CAST *Theodore Hoffman* Daniel Benzali *Justine Appleton* Mary McCormack *Chris Docknovich* Michael Hayden *Lisa Gillespie* Grace Phillips *Arnold Spivak* J.C. MacKenzie *Richard Cross* Stanley Tucci *Neil Avedon* Jason Gedrick *James Wyler* Anthony LaPaglia *Miriam Grasso* Barbara Bosson /*cr* Steven Bochco, Charles H. Elgee, Channing Gibson /*exec pr* Steven Bochco, Charles J. Elgee /*pr* inc Joe Ann Fogle, Ann Donahue / *dr* Charles Haid, Nancy Sevoca, Adam Nimoy, Michael Fresco /*wr* inc Charles H. Elgee, Steven Bochco, Charles D. Holland, Gay Walch /*mus* Mike Post /*Steven Bochco Productions: Twentieth Century-Fox TV* (USA) /32 x 60m col /US tx ABC 1995–.

Murder, She Wrote

Crime. ITV 1985–

Popular American mystery series, unmistakably a stateside steal of Agatha Christie's ➢*Miss Marple.* British-born actress Angela Lansbury (who had even played Marple in the 1980 movie *The Mirror Crack'd*) starred as silver-haired Jessica Fletcher, a best-selling authoress of detective stories who was never short of inspiration since her relatives and friends were murdered, or framed for same, at quite a prodigious rate, even in her quiet home town of Cabot Cove, Maine, a sort of St Mary Mead by the sea. Since in one sort of TV crime show the cops are hopeless plods (in *MSW* it was Sheriff Amos, played by Tom Bosley from ➢*Happy Days*, later to graduate to a tec show of his own in ➢*Father Dowling Investigates*), Fletcher was obliged to use her amateur sleuthing skills to find whodunnit. In *Murder, She Wrote – The Movie* she even saved the sun-tanned hide of Hawaiian private dick ➢*Magnum PI.*

The plots were merely cryptic puzzles made televisual, entirely bereft of moral or intellectual substance. But briskly done. And Lansbury's pleasure in her character was winningly evident.

CAST *Jessica Fletcher* Angela Lansbury *Sheriff Amos Tupper* Tom Bosley *Dr Seth Hazlitt* William Windom *Sheriff Mort Metzger* Ron Masak *Grady Fletcher* Michael Horton /*cr* Peter S. Fischer, Richard Levinson, William Link /*exec pr* Peter S. Fischer /*pr* inc Robert F. O'Neill, Robert E. Swanson /*dr* Alexander Singer, Alan Cooke, Allen Resisner, Walter Graumann, Philip Leacock, John Astin, Ed Abroms, Hy Averback, Bernard McEveety, Charles Dubin, Bob Williams, Corey Allen, E.W. Swackhamer, John Llewellyn Moxey, Peter Crane, Seymour Robbie, Philip Leacock, Chuck Bowman / *Universal TV* (USA) /264 x 60m col /US tx CBS 1984–96.

Murphy Brown

Comedy. Sky1 1992–

Sitcom starring Candice Bergen (daughter of Oscar-winning ventriloquist Edgar Bergen, and formerly best known for the anti-Western Western movie *Soldier Blue*) as TV news reporter Murphy Brown. Crafted and honed in ➢*The Mary Tyler Moore Show* manner (with which it has obvious similarities), the series was influential enough for Vice President Dan 'Potatoe' Quayle to infamously cite the unmarried but pregnant Brown as symbolizing the collapse in American family values which caused the LA riots. The TV industry, at least, considered Bergen's performance good enough to bestow a clutch of Emmys upon her person.

CAST *Murphy Brown* Candice Bergen *Eldin* Robert Pastorelli /*exec pr* Diane English, Joel Shukovsky /*dr* inc Barnet Kellman, Lee Shailat, Peter Bonerz, Bill Bixby, Lee Zlotoff, Peter Baldwin, Burt Brinckerhoff /*wr* inc Diane English /*Shulovsky-English Prods: Warner Bros TV* (USA) /247 x 30m col /US tx CBS 1989–98.

My Favourite Martian

Comedy. ITV 1963–4

The progenitor of a long line of the alien-in-the-home sitcoms. En route to the office, Los Angeles *Sun* journalist Tim O'Hara (Bill Bixby, in the first of many starring small-screen roles) sees a space ship crash and befriends its occupant, a professor of anthropology from Mars. Taken home to O'Hara's apartment, Uncle Martin, the human-looking alien (who had retractable antennae), caused sticky plot situations galore for his human host, thanks to the mischievous use of his powers of levitation, telepathy and invisibility. Light (if heart-warming), humorous fare, the show entered the top 10 of the US Nielsens on the back of its own novelty, eventually spinning off a 16-episode animated version, *My Favourite Martians* (Filmation, 1973–5).

Ray Walston, the actor who played 'Uncle Martin', was previously best known for his role as Luther Billis in the film version of *South Pacific.*

CAST *Uncle Martin* Ray Walston *Tim O'Hara* Bill Bixby *Lorelei Brown* Pamela Britton *Angela Brown* Ann Marshall / *cr* John L. Greene / *pr* Jack Chertok / *dr* inc Alan Rafkin, Sheldon Leonard / *mus* George Greeley / *A Jack Chertok Production* (USA) /107 x 30m bw:col /US tx CBS 1963–6.

My Friend Flicka

Children's. ITV 1957

A boy-and-his-horse adventure show of ➢*The Adventures of Champion* type, though filmed through a mite more obviously saccharine-coated lens. Set on a Montana ranch (the Goose Bar) at the turn of the 20th-century, it was based on the book by Mary O'Hara and the 1943 film with Roddy McDowall. One of the first children's series to be made in colour, *MFF* starred Johnny Washbrook as 11-year-old Ken McLaughlin, and a black stallion called Wahama as 'Flicka' (from the Swedish for Little Girl).

CAST *Ken McLaughlin* Johnny Washbrook *Nell McLaughlin* Anita Louise *Rob McLaughlin* Gene Evans / *exec pr* Buddy Adler / *pr* Alan A. Armor, Sam White, Peter Packer, Herman Schlom / *Twentieth Century-Fox TV* (USA) /39 x 26m bw:col /US tx CBS 1956–9, ABC 1959–63.

My Mother and the Car

Comedy. ITV 1965

Starred Jerry Van Dyke (brother of Dick) as Dave Crabtree, a lawyer who buys a 1928 Porter car, only to find that it is the machinating reincarnation of his domineering mother. To his embarrassment, she is also taste-challenged and requests leopard-print seat covers.

A quarter of a century ago it was hailed as offbeat; by a modern audience it is more likely to be viewed as offbeam trash. Producer Rod Amateau continued his comedic interest in automobiles with ➢*The Dukes of Hazzard.*

CAST *Dave Crabtree* Jerry Van Dyke *Mother: The Car* (voice) Ann Sothern *Barbara Crabtree* Maggie Pierce *Randy Crabtree* Randy Whipple *Cindy Crabtree* Cynthia Eilbacher *Bernard Manzini* Avery Schreiber / *pr* Rod Amateau / *wr* inc Lila Garrett, Bernie Kahn / *United Artists: Cottage Industries: NBC* (USA) /26 x 30m col.

Mystery and Imagination

Drama. ITV 1966–70

Nightmare tales of crime and the supernatural, adapted from the library of Gothic classics. Those presented included *Dracula* (*dr* Patrick Dromgoole, with Denholm Elliott as the Transylvanian Count), *Frankenstein* (*dr* Voytek), R.L. Stevenson's *The Body Snatcher*, and Poe's *The Fall of the House of Usher*. The episodes were narrated by David Buck, who appeared in the guise of Victorian adventurer Richard Beckett.

Spine-chillingly scripted and shot. Only to be viewed with the lights on.

CAST *Richard Beckett* David Buck / *cr* Jonathan Alwyn, Terence Feely / *pr* Jonathan Alwyn, Reginald Collins / *dr* inc Voytek, Alan Cooke, Patrick Dromgoole / *wr* inc Robert Muller, Vincent Tilsley, John Russell Taylor / *ABC TV: Thames TV* (UK) /16 x 50–65m, 6 x 90m col.

My Two Dads

Comedy. C4 1990–1

Another post-nuclear-family sitcom. Here two single men jointly inherit a daughter (12-year-old Nicole) when it cannot be determined which of them was the father. The compromises of the starch-shirted financial advisor, Michael Taylor, and bohemian artist, Joey Harris, forced to share a flat as well as to co-parent, provided the consistent giggles. The theme was written and performed by star Greg Evigan.

CAST *Michael Taylor* Paul Reiser *Joey Harris* Greg Evigan *Nicole Bradford* Staci Keanan *Judge Wilbur* Florence Stanley / *pr* Michael Jacobs, Danielle Alexander / *dr* Andrew D. Weyman, Andrew Cardiff, John Tracy, John L. Lobue, Florence Stanley, Peter Baldwin / *mus* Greg Evigan (theme) / *Michael Jacobs Prods: Tri Star* (USA) /61 x 30m col /US tx NBC 1988–90.

My Wife Next Door

Comedy. BBC1 1972

On his divorce, George Bassett decides to move out of London, buying No. 1 Copse Cottage near Stoke Poges; by stupendous coincidence, he finds that No. 2 is occupied by his ex-wife, Suzi.

If you could believe it, it was pleasant enough, and the charmingly likeable performances of John Alderton (➢*Emergency – Ward 10*, ➢*Please*

Sir!) and Hannah Gordon (➢*Telford's Change*, ➢*Upstairs, Downstairs*) helped. By Brian Clemens and Richard Waring, *MYND* won a Royal Television Society Award.

CAST *George Bassett* John Alderton *Suzi Bassett* Hannah Gordon /*cr* Brian Clemens, Richard Waring / *pr* Graeme Muir /*wr* Richard Waring /*mus* Dennis Wilson /*BBC TV* (UK) /13 x 30m col.

Naked City

Crime. ITV 1962–3

Hyper-realistic police procedural, based on Mark Hellinger's 1948 movie. *Naked City* had many famous leading players – principally John McIntire from ➢*Wagon Train* – but the real star of the show was the vast metropolitan city which formed its backdrop: New York, New York. Against atmospheric locales from downtown Manhattan to Statten Island, veteran cop Muldoon taught new boy Halloran the means of catching the city's assorted villainry. Unlike Jack Webb's ➢*Dragnet*, *Naked City* did not pretend that police officers were angels in blue clothing, but recognized them as fallible human beings, sometimes no better than the crooks. After a 16-month break, occasioned by McIntire's departure, the series returned in a 55m format with Lieutenant Mike Parker as the old hand and Adam Flint as the novice. It made a point of bizarre episode titles (e.g. 'Today the Man Who Kills Ants is Coming') and gave screen breaks to a clutch of the not-yet-famous: Dustin Hoffman, Robert Redford and Peter Falk. The pay-off line, intoned by the narrator, has passed into legend: 'There are eight million stories in the Naked City. This has been one of them.'

CAST *Det. Lt Dan Muldoon* John McIntire *Det. Jim Halloran* James Franciscus *Lt Mike Parker* Horace McMahon *Det. Adam Flint* Paul Burke *Libby* Nancy Malone /*cr* Sterling Silliphant /*exec pr* Herbert B. Leonard /*pr* Charles Russell /*dr* inc Buzz Kulik, Stuart Rosenberg, William Conrad, Laslo Benedek, Tay Garnett, Paul Wendkos, Walter Grauman, Robert Ellis Miller /*wr* inc Sterling Silliphant, Herbert B. Leonard, Gene Roddenberry /*mus* Nelson Riddle, Billy May, Milton Raskin (theme) /*Shelle Productions: Screen Gems: Columbia Pictures TV* (USA) /39 x 23m, 99 x 55m bw /US tx ABC 1958–62.

Naked Video

Comedy. BBC2 1986–91

Rapid-fire comic sketch show from BBC Scotland, indiscriminate in aim. It found hits in John Sparke's IQ-challenged Welsh poet invention, Shadwell, and Gregor Fisher's Baldy Man and ➢*Rab C. Nesbitt* characters. Also among the ensemble cast was Helen Lederer. Based on the radio series *Naked Radio*. Cultish.

CAST Gregor Fisher, John Sparkes, Helen Lederer, Tony Roper, Ron Bain, Andy Gray, Elaine C. Smith, Louise Beattie, Jonathan Watson /*pr* Colin Gilbert, Philip Differ /*BBC TV* (UK) /32 x 30m col

Nancy Astor

Drama. BBC2 1982

Biopic of Nancy Astor (née Langhorne), from her youthful days as a Southern belle to her 20s sojourn in the House of Commons as Britain's first female MP. Mildly watchable, not very historical.

CAST *Nancy Astor (née Langhorne)* Lisa Harrow *Robert Gould Shaw* Pierce Brosnan *Waldorf Astor* James Fox *Nanaire Langhorne* Sylvia Sims *Phyllis Brand* Lise Hilboldt *Chillie Langhorne* Dan O'Herlihy *Lord Revelstoke* Julian Glover /*pr* Philip Hinchcliffe /*dr* Richard Stroud /*wr* Derek Marlowe /*BBC TV: Time Life Prods* (UK: USA) /9 x 55m col.

Nearest and Dearest

Comedy. ITV 1968–72

On the death of their father, two ageing (and mutually loathing) siblings inherit the family's Lancashire-based Pledges Pickle factory. And produce 'saucy' double-entendres and heavily vinegared insults ('big girl's blouse') by the lorry load.

Energetically vulgar Northern sitcom, perfectly suited to the music-hall styles of Jimmy Jewell and Hylda Baker. A cinema version appeared in 1972, and the Americans tried the recipe in *Thicker Than Water* (ABC, 1973).

CAST *Nellie Pledge* Hylda Baker *Eli Pledge* Jimmy Jewel *Walter* Edward Malin *Lily* Madge Hindle *Stan* Joe Gladwin /*cr* Vince Powell & Harry Driver /*pr* inc Peter Eckersley, Bill Podmore /*dr* inc Bill Podmore, June Howson /*wr* inc Vince Powell & Harry Driver, John Stevenson, Tom Breannad & Roy Bottomley / *mus* Derek Hilton /*Granada TV* (UK) /47 x 25m col.

Neighbours

Melodrama. BBC1 1986–

The early history of the Australian mega-melodrama was suitably soaplike in its improbablility; it was the brainchild of Reg Watson (who learned his sudster craft in Britain as the first producer of ➢*Crossroads*). Set in Ramsey Street, Melbourne, a distinct fictional echo of the Brisbane road of his childhood, and intended as light TV relief by Watson (who had already given the viewing world *Sons and Daughters*, *The Young Doctors*, ➢*Prisoner: Cell Block H*), *Neighbours* was launched on Australia's Seven Network as stern-faced drama; it lasted 171 episodes before being axed. At the persuasive behest of Grundy's Ian Holmes, Channel Ten then bought it and injected it with humour and 'yoof' appeal, including the bronzed, good-looking shapes of Jason Donovan and Kylie Minogue. It caught on, but only after a massive publicity campaign. (To restore their lost soap honour, Seven created ➢*Home and Away*.) Among those watching the new, super-improved *Neighbours* was a BBC buyer scouring the markets for a cheap filler. Screened in Britain, the serial all but disappeared into the daytime schedule until schoolgirl Alison Grade complained to her father that she and her friends were forced to miss the lunchtime episodes in term time. So her father, who happened to be Michael Grade, the then Controller of BBC1, arranged for repeats to be screened at 5.35 p.m. Within months, *Neighbours* was challenging ➢*EastEnders* and ➢*Coronation Street* at the top of the ratings.

Initially the leading families of Ramsey Street were the Ramsey-Mitchell-Bishops and the Robinsons. Madge Bishop (née Ramsey) was the matriarch of the former clan, barmaid at the Waterhole and mother to Charlene (Minogue) and Henry (Craig MacLachlan, who subsequently moved to *Home and Away* and ➢*Bugs*). Later, Madge married fuddy-duddy Harold Bishop (Ian Smith, formerly associate producer on *Prisoner: Cell Block H*). Heading the discernibly middle-class Robinsons was the ever-understanding Helen Daniels (*Prisoner: Cell Block H*), mother-in-law to Jim and grandmother of Paul, the JR-like owner of the Lassiters Hotel complex. Paul Robinson's business affairs and turbulent marriages (including to an identical twin, Christina Alessi) were frequent providers of storylines. As the episodes progressed, the Willis and Allessi families took over the spotlight, only to be suceeded in turn by the Starks and the Kennedys and the Martins.

The fictional populace of Ramsey Street changed, but the *Neighbours* formula remained the same: a cast stuffed with teen-dream characters, an apparently free and easy surfing lifestyle, endlessly sunny blue skies, some near comic characters (most famously Joe Mangel and his gossipy mother) and a pacy beat. The serial also boasted Bogota levels of mortality, but such tragedies were quickly forgotten, the deceased replaced by a never-heard-of-before-long-lost-relative. As if to underscore *Neighbours*' debt to the *Crossroads* style of utter unlikelihood, its droning theme tune was also by Tony Hatch. Also of musical note is that *Neighbours*, sold to 50 countries around the world, launched the pop careers of Kylie Minogue, Jason Donovan (whose father played Ramsey Street's Doug Willis), Craig MacLachlan and the Blakeney sisters.

CAST *Madge Bishop* Anne Charleston *Helen Daniels* Anne Haddy *Jim Robinson* Alan Dale *Charlene Robinson* Kylie Minogue *Scott Robinson* Darius Perkins /Jason Donovan *Henry Ramsey* Craig MacLachlan *Paul Robinson* Stefan Dennis *Joe Mangel* Mark Little *Mrs Mangel* Vivean Gray *Shane Ramsey* Peter O'Brien *Mike Young* Guy Pearce *Des Clarke* Paul Keane *Gail Robinson* Fiona Corke *Kerry Bishop* Lynda Hartley *Caroline Alessi* Gillian Blakeney *Christina Alessi* Gayle Blakeney *Harold Bishop* Ian Smith *Todd Landers* Kristian Schmid *Doug Willis* Terence Donovan *Pam Willis* Sue Jones *Cody Willis* Amelia Frid/Peta Brady *Annalise Hartman* Kimberley Davies *Brad Willis* Scott Michaelson *Billy Kennedy* Jesse Spencer *Karl Kennedy* Alan Fletcher *Susan Kennedy* Jackie Woodburne *Philip Martin* Ian Rawlings /*cr* Reg Watson /*exec pr* Marie Trevor, Don Battye /*pr* inc Sue Masters, Philip East, Margaret Slarke /*dr* inc Chris Adshead, Judith John-Story, Nicholas Bufalo /*wr* inc Christine Madefferi, Betty Zuin, Geoffrey Truman /*mus* Tony Hatch (theme music), Jackie Trent (theme lyrics) /*Grundy Television Productions* (Aus) /3000+ x 25m col.

Nero Wolfe

Crime. ITV 1983

Televersions of Rex Stout's stories featuring his orchid-loving sedentary NY amateur 'tec.

More fatman-detective work for William Conrad (➢*Cannon*). Easy watching, sometimes to the point of somnipathy.

CAST *Nero Wolfe* William Conrad *Archie Goodwin* Lee Horsley *Saul Panzer* George Wyner /*exec pr* Ivan Goff, Ben Roberts /*dr* inc Michael O'Herlihy, Ron Satlof / *Paramount TV* (USA) 13 x 60m col /US tx NBC 1981.

Never Mind the Quality, Feel the Width

Comedy. ITV 1967–71

Cheerfully low-brow sitcom about two East End tailors, Jewish jacket-maker Manny Cohen and Irish trouser-maker Patrick Kelly. The humour exploited their stereotyped differences in religion and ethnicity, with Rabbi Levy and Father Ryan officiating. Derived from a 1967 Vince Powell and Harry Driver piece for ➢*Armchair Theatre*, the series was first made by ABC but when it lost its franchise in 1968, Thames took over the production honours.

CAST *Emmanuel 'Manny' Cohen* John Bluthal *Patrick Michael Kevin Aloysius Brendan Kelly* Joe Lynch *Father Ryan* Eamon Kelly *Rabbi Levy* Cyril Shaps /*cr* Vince Powell & Harry Driver /*pr* Ronnie Baxter, Stuart Allen /*dr* inc Ronnie Baxter /*ABC TV:Thames TV* (UK) / 39 x 30m col.

Never the Twain

Comedy. ITV 1981–91

Johnnie Mortimer sitcom about two antiques dealers, Simon Peel (Donald Sinden) and Oliver Smallbridge (Windsor Davies from ➢*It Ain't Half Hot, Mum*), who couldn't end their feud even when their Romeo and Juliet offspring fell in love. Overacted farce which lasted way past its sell-by date. Former ➢*The Avengers* gal Honor Blackman played the rivals' disputed fancy, Veronica Barton.

CAST *Simon Peel* Donald Sinden *Oliver Smallbridge* Windsor Davies *David Peel* Robin Kermode *Lyn Smallbridge* Julia Watson *Aunt Eleanor* Zara Nutley *Veronica Barton* Honor Blackman *Ringo (shop assistant)* Derek Deadman /*cr* Johnnie Mortimer /*pr* Peter Frazer-Jones, Anthony Parker /*dr* inc Robert Reed, Douglas Argent /*wr* Johnnie Mortimer, Dick Hills, John Kane, Vince Powell /*Thames TV* (UK) /69 x 30m col.

Neverwhere

Sci-fi. BBC2 1996

Urban fantasy in which credulous City broker Richard Mayhew encounters a strange girl (Door) and is persuaded into secret, subterranean London, where he must combat two hired assassins.

A live-action graphic novel, it had the stuff beloved of aficionados – mock medievalism, arcane language, cute heroine, comic baddies, easily recognizable archetypes – which is exactly the stuff others found teenage and predictable. Based on an idea by award-winning writer Neil Gaiman and comedian Lenny Henry.

CAST *Richard Mayhew* Gary Bakewell *Door* Laura Fraser *Mr Croup* Hywel Bennett *Mr Vandemar* Clive Russell /*cr* Neil Gaiman, Lenny Henry /*pr* Clive Brill / *dr* Dewi Humphrey /*wr* Neil Gaiman /*Crucial Films* (UK) /6 x 30m col.

The New Adventures of Batman

Children's. BBC1 1977–8

The Caped Crusader and Boy Wonder in more bat-tastic Zap! Kerpow! encounters with the devilish villains of Gotham City, this time in animated form. They were joined in their fight for good by Batgirl and mascot Bat-Mite. Voicing the dynamic duo were ➢*Batman* originals Adam West and Burt Ward.

CAST (voices) *Batman* Adam West *Robin* Burt Ward *Batgirl* Melendy Britt *Bat-Mite* Lennie Weinrib /*pr* Norm Prescott, Lou Scheimer /*Filmation* (USA) / 16 x 25m col /US tx CBS 1977–8.

The New Adventures of Charlie Chan

Crime. ITV 1957–8

Earl Derr Bigger's oriental, proverb-spouting detective transferred to London (from Honolulu) to pursue complex cases, with the help of eager pup 'Number One Son'.

Stagey and embarrassing drivel. Although J. Carrol Naish was not the first Caucasian to be yellowed up for the role of Chan (being preceded by, among others, Warner Oland and Sydney

Toler in the movies), by the 50s the device was becoming transparently racist. It did not help that Naish himself appeared so ill-at-ease in the role. A pre-➢*Maigret* Rupert Davies appeared as the Yard's Inspector Duff.

A kiddie cartoon version of the Chan adventures, *The Amazing Chan and the Chan Clan*, was released in 1972 by Hanna–Barbera, with Keye Luke (Master Po in ➢*Kung Fu*) as the voice of Chan.

CAST *Charlie Chan* J. Carrol Naish *Barry Chan* James Hong *Insp. Duff* Rupert Davies *Insp. Marlowe* Hugh Williams /*exec pr* Leon Fromkess /*pr* Sidney Marshall, Rudolph Flothow /*ITC* (UK) /39 x 30m bw /US tx Syndicated 1957.

The New Adventures of Flash Gordon

Children's. BBC1 1983

Flash! Saviour of the Universe... Animated version of Alex Raymond's sci-fi epic (originally brought to the screen by actor Buster Crabbe in the 30s movie serials) following the exploits of pilot Flash Gordon, Dale Arden and Dr Zarkov as they fearlessly battle evil Ming the Merciless of planet Mongo. Made in the USA as a 16 x 30m series, it was transmitted in the UK as 23 x 20m one.

CAST (voices) *Flash Gordon* Bob Ridgely *Ming the Merciless/Dr Zarkov* Alan Oppenheimer *Dale* Diane Pershing /*Filmation: King Features* (USA) /16 x 30m col /US tx NBC 1979–80.

The New Adventures of Superman

Sci-fi. BBC1 1994–/Sky1 1996–

Is it a bird? Is it a plane? No, it's a postmodernist reading of *Action Comic*'s spandexed hero, who first flew onto TV in the kidult, visibly-wired ➢*The Adventures of Superman.* Initially, Deborah Joy LeVine's production played it straight, but a makeover in season two reduced the acrobatics and upped the comedy and, especially, the romance between Superman (Dean Cain, previously Brenda's boyfriend in ➢*Beverly Hills 90210*) and *Daily Planet* reporter Lois Lane. The ratings boomed and thereafter *The New Adventures of Superman* viewed like ➢*Moonlighting* in Metropolis. Naturally, the course of true love did not run smooth; villainous billionaire Lex Luthor courted Lois almost unto the altar, while Clark Kent (Superman's human alter ego) was pursued by *Planet* man-eater, Cat Grant, just as he himself flirted with DA Mayson Drake. Eventually, however, Superman and Lois tied the knot as Mr and Mrs Kent. De-mything the Superman legend (one less-than-awestruck Metropolis inhabitant declared Superman to be 'a freak in a blue suit') into an ironical, camp, romantic comedy lit up Saturday evenings for 10 million BBC viewers, making *The New Adventures of Superman* one of the most popular US imports since the heady days of the ➢*The A-Team* (15 million watchers at peak).

CAST *Clark Kent/Superman* Dean Cain *Lois Lane* Teri Hatcher *Perry White* Lane Smith *Lex Luthor* John Shea *Jimmy Olsen* Michael Landes/Justin Whalin *Catherine 'Cat' Grant* Tracy Scoggins *Mayson Drake* Farrah Forke /*cr* Deborah Joy LeVine /*exec pr* Deborah Joy LeVine, David Jacobs, Robert Singer /*dr* inc Daniel Attias, Robert Butler, Alan J. Levi /*wr* inc Deborah Joy LeVine, Dan Levine, Chris Ruppenthal, Thania St John /*mus* Jay Gruska /*sfx* John Sheele /*Roundelay: December 3rd Productions: Warner Bros* (USA) / 1 x 120m, 85+ x 60m col.

The Newcomers

Drama. BBC1 1965–9

Twice-weekly soap following the fortunes and feelings of the London Cooper family on their removal to the fictitious rural village of Angelton (Haverhill in real life). They endured numerous humdrum melodramas – usually based on the difficulties of understanding the bumpkin locals and adapting to life on a modern housing development – until the Robertson clan took over the new family-on-the-estate mantle. Dreary. Judy Geeson (soon to be a star of the movies, and sister of ➢*Bless This House*'s Sally), Alan Browning (➢*Coronation Street*) and Wendy Richard were to be found amongst the cast.

CAST *Ellis Cooper* Alan Browning *Vivienne Cooper* Maggie Fitzgibbon *Philip Cooper* Jeremy Bulloch *Maria Cooper* Judy Geeson *Lance Cooper* Raymond Hunt *Grannie* Gladys Henson *Joyce Harker* Wendy Richard *Hugh Robertson* Jack Watling *Olivia Robertson* Mary Kenton *Julie Robertson* Deborah Watling *Adrian Robertson* Paul Bartlett *Michael Robertson* Robert Bartlett /*cr* Colin Morris /*pr* Verity Lambert, Morris Barry, Ronald Travers, Bill Sellars /*dr* inc Ronald Wilson, Philip Dale /*wr* inc Barry Letts /*BBC TV* (UK) / 430 x 30m bw.

New Faces

Light Entertainment. ITV 1973–8/1986–8

Talent show for starry-eyed artistes who had never appeared on TV before. The true entertainment for the viewer at home was less the performance of the hopefuls than the frequently cruel comments of the four experts (especially pop producer Mickie Most) who sat in judgement. Among the acts which went onto showbiz success were Victoria Wood, Jim Davidson, Lenny Henry and Les Dennis. A 1986 resurrection of the show was hosted by Marti Caine, herself a former *New Faces* winner.

CAST Derek Hobson, Nicky Martin, Marti Caine /*pr* Les Cocks, Albert Stevenson, Richard Holloway /*dr* inc Paul Stewart Laing, John Pullen /*mus* The Johnny Patrick Orchestra, The Harry Rabinowitz Orchestra / *ATV: Central* (UK) /approx 190 x 50m col.

New Scotland Yard

Crime. ITV 1972–4

Moderately popular (reaching 11 in the ratings) police series about a pair of ultra-dedicated NSY detectives, Kingdom and Ward. Made with the best of intentions – to show coppering 'how it really is' – but ever so gloomily. For a final series, the partnership was replaced by DCS Clay and DS Dexter (played by Clive Francis, scion of ➢*No Hiding Place*'s Raymond).

CAST *DCS Kingdom* John Woodvine *DS Ward* John Carlisle *DCS Clay* Michael Turner *DS Dexter* Clive Francis /*exec pr* Rex Firkin /*pr* Jack Williams /*dr* inc Cyril Coke, Derrick Goodwin /*wr* inc P.J. Hammond, Stuart Douglass /*LWT* (UK) /45 x 60m col.

The New Statesman

Comedy. ITV 1987–92

Knockabout political satire starring Rik Mayall as Alan Beresford B'Stard, a connivingly amoral far-right Tory MP (Haltemprice constituency) who jackbooted over all in pursuit of money, power and sex. Michael Troughton played his wimpish assistant Piers Fletcher-Dervish and Marsha Fitzalan his aristo bi-sexual wife Sarah. The fourth season saw B'Stard, after a spell in a Russian gulag (courtesy of a revengeful Sarah), transfer his attentions to Europe, becoming the MEP for a lucrative corner of Saxony. A funnily frightening portrait of the Essex-wing of Thatcherism. From the reliable firm of Marks and Gran.

CAST *Alan Beresford B'Stard* Rik Mayall *Sarah B'Stard* Marsha Fitzalan *Piers Fletcher-Dervish* Michael Troughton *Crippen* Nick Stringer *Roland Gidleigh-Park* Charles Gray *Sidney Bliss* Peter Sallis *Sir Greville* Terence Alexander /*cr* Laurence Marks, Maurice Gran / *exec pr* Michael Pilsworth, John Bartlett /*pr* David Reynolds, Tony Charles, Andrew Benson, Bernard McKenna /*dr* Grame Harper, Geoffrey Sax /*wr* Laurence Marks & Maurice Gran /*mus* Modest Moussorgsky 'Pictures at an Exhibition' theme /*Alomo for Yorkshire TV* (UK) /27 x 30m, 1 x 78m col.

Nice Time

Comedy. ITV 1968–9

Lived up to its title, and more, with off-the-wall sketches concocted to satisfy viewers' requests for re-enactments of fave moments from funny movies. Initially shown in the Granada region only, it was eventually networked, thus providing Kenny Everett with his TV break and propelling Germaine Greer (then a barely known University of Warwick lecturer) forward into national prominence. The producer was a certain John Birt, later Director General of the BBC.

CAST (presenters) Kenny Everett, Germaine Greer, Jonathan Routh /*pr* John Birt, Mike Murphy /*Granada TV* (UK) /26 x 30m col.

Night Gallery

Horror. BBC2 1970/ITV 1972–3

Tales of the occult and supernatural, presented by Rod Serling (➢*The Twilight Zone*) from an art gallery where he invited the viewer to gaze upon a painting that contained a suitably chilling scene from the forthcoming flick. Before and behind camera talent was exceptional (Steven Spielberg was on the directors' roster), but the changes to its format (it went from three playlets per hour episode, to single half-hour stories) weakened any overall coherence as a show.

CAST (narrator) Rod Serling /*cr* Rod Serling /*pr* Jack Laird /*dr* inc Steven Spielberg, Jeannot Swarc, Leonard Nimoy, John Badham /*wr* inc Rod Serling /*A Jack Laird Production: Universal TV* (USA) /98 x 60:30m col /US tx NBC 1970–3.

Nightingales

Comedy. C4 1990–2

Surreal twin-set (office rest-room, toilets) sitcom about a trio of security guards who whiled away the stationary dark hours in fantasies, squabbles and constant arm-flapping refrains of 'Nobody here but us chickens'. Their bizarrities were often interrupted by a visitor, most often Eric the Werewolf, but also including – on Christmas Eve – a pregnant Mary who, after signing a contract agreeing she was not an allegory, gave birth to a goldfish and a roomful of consumer goods. A TV *Waiting for Godot*, brilliantly acted (by David Threlfall, Robert Lindsay and James ➢'*Z Cars*' Ellis), and to be counted among the most adventurous sitcoms of the 90s, it was an acquired taste but, once aquired, addictive.

CAST *Carter* Robert Lindsay *Bell* David Threlfall *Sarge* James Ellis /*cr* Paul Makin /*pr* Esta Charkham, Laurie Greenwood, Rosie Bunting /*dr* Tony Dow /*wr* Paul Makin /*mus* Clever Music /*Alomo* (UK) /13 x 30m col.

1990

Drama. BBC2 1977–8

Thriller from 1977 set in a future Britain overrun by bureaucracy and under the draconian rule of the Public Control Department. Edward Woodward as journalist Jim Kyle led the resistance.

Sub-Orwellian, certainly, but not without a certain frisson, since the bad guys in William Greatorex's gloomy vision were but real VAT men, tax men, and all ranks of petty official men writ large and populous.

CAST *Jim Kyle* Edward Woodward *Herbert Skardon* Robert Lang *Dave Brett* Tony Doyle *Faceless* Paul Hardwick *Delly Lomas* Barbara Kellerman *Dan Mellor* John Savident /*cr* William Greatorex /*pr* Prudence Fitzgerald /*dr* inc Alan Gibson, David Sullivan Proudfoot /*wr* inc William Greatorex, Edmund Ward, Jim Hawkins /*BBC TV* (UK) /16 x 55m col.

No Bananas

Drama. BBC1 1996

➢*A Family at War*, but doubled. To the siren sounds of WWII, the upper-class Hamiltons and prole-ish Slaters are forcibly united by marriage when Mary Hamilton is 'put in the family way' by Harry Slater. Join-the-old-chestnuts drama, satisfactory as a Sunday evening couch-out. And Stephanie Beacham played the bitch with her usual gravel-scrunching, fur-flung-over-the-shoulder élan.

CAST *Harry Slater* Dominic Rowan *Thomas Slater* Tom Bell *Ellen Slater* Linda Bassett *Grandma* Edna Dore *Mary Hamilton* Rachel Power *Arthur Hamilton* Michael Elwyn *Dorothea Grant* Stephanie Beacham *Edward Grant* Michael Byrne *Evelyn Hamilton* Alison Steadman *Kaye Bentley* Rachel Pickup /*cr* Ginnie Hole / *pr* Peter Norris /*dr* Alan Dossor, Roger Bamford, Moira Armstrong, Robert Tronson /*wr* Ginnie Hole, Lisa Evans, Sam Snape, Stan Hey, Brian Thompson / *mus* John Altman /*BBC TV* (UK) /10 x 50m col.

Noel's House Party

Light Entertainment. BBC1 1991–

Live Saturday evening show hosted by Noel Edmonds (in the slot previously warmed by his *The Late, Late Breakfast Show* and *Noel Edmond's Saturday Road Show*) from a mock manor house in the fictitious village of – nudge, nudge – Crinkley Bottom. Here, ring-master Edmonds, mouth permanently set on grin and shirt on glare, encouraged celebrities and hapless punters to perform pranks and sillinesses for the delectation of the whooping studio audience. Some of the favourite items were NTV (hidden cameras in viewers' homes), Grab-a-Grand (celebs catching money in a wind-machine for charity), Wait Till I Get You Home (precocious brats telling tales on their parents), My Little Friend (tots conversing with 'talking' household objects), the Gotcha Oscars (a celebrity conned into doing something embarrassing on film) and a gunge tank which poured psychedelic slurry over guests. A later addition was a pink plastic dummy with yellow spots called Mr Blobby. Depending on your point of view, *House Party* was either 50 minutes of frolicking fun or the absolute proof of the decline of the Western world.

CAST (presenter) Noel Edmonds /*exec pr* Michael Leggo /*pr* Michael Leggo, Jonathan Beazley, Guy Freeman /*BBC TV* (UK) /approx. 70 x 50m col.

Noggin the Nog
Children's. BBC 1959–1965/BBC1 1982

'Listen and I will tell you more of the saga of Noggin the Nog...'

Revered adventures (in serial form) of a brave Norse prince, beginning with his voyage to the Land of the Midnight Sun to fetch Eskimo princess Nooka to be his bride. Other prominent characters were Olaf the Lofty, the magical talking bird Graculus, strongman Thor Nogson, Noggin's son Prince Knut, and Noggin's scene-stealingly evil uncle, Nogbad. After ➢*Ivor the Engine*, it was the second animated product from the Smallfilms partnership of Pete Firmin and Oliver Postgate. Two colour episodes appeared in 1982, a remake of 'Noggin and the Ice Dragon' and the all new 'Noggin and the Pie'.

CAST (narrators) Oliver Postgate, Ronnie Stevens /*cr* Pete Firmin /*pr* Oliver Postgate /*mus* Vernon Elliott / *Smallfilms* (UK) /approx 40 x 10m bw:col.

No Hiding Place
Crime. ITV 1959–67

More villain-chasing adventures for ace Scotland Yard detective DCS Lockhart, previously met in ➢*Murder Bag* and *Crime Sheet*. Efficient and popular (topping the ratings several times), it spun off Lockhart's young sidekick Baxter to *Echo Four Two*; amongst those who eventually replaced him as the sleuth's right hand was DS Russell, played by pre-➢*Coronation Street* Johnny Briggs. Most episodes were transmitted live.

CAST *DCS Tom Lockhart* Raymond Francis *DS Harry Baxter* Eric Lander *DS Russell* Johnny Briggs *DS Gregg* Sean Caffrey *DS Perryman* Michael McStay /*pr* Ray Dicks, Jonathan Goodman, Richard Matthews, Peter Willes, Geoffrey Hughes, Michael Currer-Briggs, Ian Fordyce /*dr* inc Marc Miller, Christoper Hodson, Richard Gilbert /*wr* inc George Baxt, John Kaiser, Jack Trevor Story, Nicholas Jones /*Associated Rediffusion* (UK) /236 x 60m bw.

No – Honestly
Comedy. ITV 1974–5

Starred husband-and-wife team of John Alderton (from ➢*Please Sir!*) and Pauline Collins (later *Shirley Valentine*) in a domestic sitcom where they played the newly wedded Danbys. He was a patient thespian, she was the dippy, book-writing (tales of 'Ollie the Otter') daughter of a peer. Episodes were wrapped around with Burns and Allenesque direct addresses to camera. The same idea, with the cast changed to Donal Donnelly and Liza Goddard became *Yes – Honestly* (ITV, 1976–7).

CAST *Charles 'CD' Danby* John Alderton *Clara Danby* Pauline Collins *Lord Burrell* James Barwick /*cr* Terence Brady, Charlotte Bingham /*pr* Humphrey Barclay /*dr* Bill Turner, David Askey /*wr* Terence Brady, Charlotte Bingham /*mus* Lyndsey De Paul (theme) /*LWT* (UK) /13 x 30m col.

No Problem!
Comedy. C4 1983–5

Home-alone comedy show featuring the Powell kids of Willesden, London, whose parents returned to Jamaica for an extended visit.

C4's first original sitcom which, almost ridiculously true to the station's liberal reputation, was written by two black writers, Farukh Dhondy and Mustapha Matura, for an all-black cast. Raucously exuberant. But likeable.

CAST *Sensimilia* Judith Jacob *Bellamy* Victor Romero Evans *Beast* Malcolm Frederick *Toshiba* Chris Tummings *Terri* Shope Shodeinde *Angel* Janet Kay *Susannah* Sarah Lam /*cr* Mustapha Matura, Farukh Dhondy /*pr* Charlie Hanson, Mickey Dolenz /*wr* Mustapha Matura, Farukh Dhondy /*LWT* (UK) / 22 x 30m col.

North and South
Drama. ITV 1986

Sprawling historical drama adapted from John Jakes' equally sprawling novel, concerning the entwined lives and romances of two families – the Hazards from the North, the Mains from the South – in the years before the Civil War. It launched the career of Patrick Swayze as a muscular but tender himbo, and proved useful cv material for Jonathan Frakes (later ➢*Star Trek: TNG*) and Kirstie Alley. The star-studded guest list was headed by Robert Mitchum, Gene Kelly and Elizabeth Taylor. A five-part sequel, *North and South, Book II* followed the fortunes of the Mains and Hazards during the years of war and wrath. The melodrama continued unabated in 1994's *North and South, Book III*.

CAST *Orry Main* Patrick Swayze *George Hazard* James Read *Justin LaMotte* David Carradine *Madeline Fabray LaMotte* Lesley-Anne Down *Virgilia Hazard Grady* Kirstie Alley *Isobel Hazard* Mary Crosby *Stanley Hazard* Jonathan Frakes *Jefferson Davis* Lloyd Bridges *Mrs Neal* Olivia de Havilland *Rose Sinclair* Linda Evans *Miles Colbert* James Stewart *Congressman Sam Greene* David Ogden Stiers *Maude Hazard* Inge Swenson /*pr* David Wolper /*dr* Richard Heffron /*wr* John Jakes /*Touchstone: Columbia* (USA) /6 x 120m col /US tx ABC 1985.

Northern Exposure

Drama. C4 1991–6

The comi-tragic attempts of confirmed New Yorker, Joel Fleischmann, to come to terms with the odd-ball inhabitants and check-shirt lifestyle of the remote arctic town of Cicely.

Half-baked Alaska. A fanatically-followed series, frequently likened to David Lynch's excercise in smalltown weirdness, ➢*Twin Peaks*, but altogether of lighter, quirkier spirit; indeed, Cicely, unlike Lynch's timber town, was almost idyllically free of evils – social, religious or psychological – being not so much a place as a New Age state of mind.

In addition to the Jewish Fleischmann, the other prominent townsfolk were token baddie Maurice Minnifield, an ex-NASA astronaut whose dream was to pave Cicely with Burger Kings; 18-year-old film-obsessed American Indian Ed Chigliak (IQ: 180); Chris Stevens, the resident DJ on KBHR radio, whose patter was smattered with cosmic thoughts, Jung, and Walt Whitman; Ruth-Anne, an OAP store owner; Holling Vincoeur, owner of The Brick Diner, and his young blonde girlfriend, Shelly Tambo; Marilyn Whirlwind, Fleischmann's mystical Native American receptionist; Maggie O'Connell, the local air pilot, who had a love–hate relationship with Fleischmann (she was also his landlady); cordon-bleu backwoodsman Adam and his hypochondriac wife Eve; Chris Stevens' Afro-American half-brother (with whom he is telepathically linked), Bernard; and a moose called Mort who liked to wander mainstreet.

Filmed in the town of Roslyn, Washington (about 1,000 miles from Alaska), and made by the team behind ➢*St Elsewhere.*

Wonderful.

CAST *Dr Joel Fleischmann* Rob Morrow *Maggie O'Connell* Janine Turner *Ed Chigliak* Darren E. Burrows *Chris Stevens* John Corbett *Maurice Minnifield* Barry Corbin *Marilyn Whirlwind* Elaine Miles *Holling Vincoeur* John Cullum *Shelly Tambo* Cynthia Geary *Ruth-Anne* Peg Phillips /*cr* Joshua Brand, John Falsey /*exec pr* John Falsey, Andrew Schneider, Rob Thompson /*pr* inc Cheryl Bloch, Diane Frolov /*dr* inc Bill D'Elia, Tom Moore, Eric Laneuville, Daniel Attias, David Carson, Charles Braverman /*wr* inc Dennis Koenig, Diane Frolov, Jeff Melvoin, Martin Sage /*mus* David Schwartz /*Falsey-Austin Street: Finegun-Pinchuk: Cine Nevada: Universal TV* (UK) / 110+ x 60m col / US tx CBS 1990–.

Not in Front of the Children

Comedy. BBC1 1967–70

Domestic comedy by Richard Waring, starring Wendy Craig as the matriarch-referee of the disputatious Corner family. Derived from a 1967 ➢*Comedy Playhouse* piece entitled 'House in a Tree', it blue-printed the scatty, middle-class housewife persona Craig would take to Waring's *And Mother Makes Three/Five* (as Sally Harrison; Thames TV, 1971–6) and Carla Lane's ➢*Butterflies.*

CAST *Jennifer Corner* Wendy Craig *Henry Corner* Paul Daneman/Ronald Hines *Trudi* Roberta Tovey/Verina Greenlaw *Robin* Hugo Keith-Johnston *Amanda* Jill Riddick /*cr* Richard Waring /*pr* Graeme Muir /*wr* Richard Waring /*BBC TV* (UK) /35 x 30m col.

Not Only… But Also…

Comedy. BBC2 1965–6/1970–3

Revue-style show with *Beyond the Fringers* Peter Cook and Dudley Moore. Originally scheduled as a one-off episode, it achieved instant cult status (and thus a full series) because its absurdist skits – the Leaping Nuns of St Beryl, the 'Good v Evil' cricket match, and a Gerry Anderson puppet pastiche entitled 'Superthunderstingcar' come to mind – captured the incipient psychedelic unreality of the 60s age. But also because of the pure brilliance of Cook and Moore's timeless Pete and Dud 'Dagenham' routine, in which a pair of cloth-capped proletarians began by philosophizing on life's mundanity and ended up in the sublimely fantastic ('Tap, tap, tap at the bloody window pane. I looked out – you know who it was? Bloody Greta Garbo.') A treasure for all TV time. The closing song 'Goodbye-ee' even made the Top 20 in 1965.

Guests included Spike Milligan, Peter Sellars, Barry Humphries and John Lennon, the latter once appearing as the commissionaire of a gents' lavatory.

CAST Peter Cook, Dudley Moore /*cr* Peter Cook, Dudley Moore /*pr* Joe McGrath, Dick Clement, John Street, James Gilbert /*wr* Peter Cook, Dudley Moore, John Law, Robert Fuest /*BBC TV* (UK) /14 x 45m, 7 x 30m, 2 x 50m bw:col.

Not the Nine O'Clock News

Comedy. BBC2 1979–82

Favourite satirical and topical sketch show from the twilight of the 70s. Conducted at a clip of 1.25m each, the skits were rooted in a vulgar reality recognizable to almost all 'yoof' (unlike the twee oldster humour of the then dominant ➢*The Two Ronnies* type) and wonderfully offensive; everyone from Margaret Thatcher to Angela Rippon to Abba was unceremoniously done over, with a gag about a squashed hedgehog causing apoplexy amongst the responsible classes. New Romanticism was holed in 'Nice Video, Shame About the Song' and ➢*Monty Python* in a sketch about a humble carpenter who thought he was the new Messiah, John Cleese. The most obviously punk-influenced comedy show to be broadcast on UK TV, the series launched the careers of Rowan Atkinson, Griff Rhys Jones, Mel Smith and Pamela Stephenson (although Stephenson, the wife of Billy Connolly, eventually departed showbiz to work as a psychiatrist in LA). The writers did well, too. Richard Curtis went on to ➢*Blackadder* and ➢*The Vicar Of Dibley*, and scripted *Four Weddings and a Funeral*; Andy Hamilton and Guy Jenkin begat ➢*Drop the Dead Donkey*, and David Renwick spawned ➢*One Foot in the Grave.*

CAST Mel Smith, Griff Rhys Jones (from second series), Pamela Stephenson, Rowan Atkinson, Chris Langham (first series only) /*cr* John Lloyd /*pr* John Lloyd, Sean Hardie /*wr* inc Mel Smith, Rowan Atkinson, Griff Rhys Jones, Arnold Brown, John Lloyd, Guy Jenkin, Andy Hamilton, Richard Curtis, Nigel Planer, Peter Richardson, Peter Brewis, Colin Bostock-Smith, Philip Pope /*BBC TV* (UK) /28 x 30m col.

Nurses

Comedy. C4 1992–3

American hospital comedy, from the pen of ➢*Soap* and ➢*The Golden Girls* creator Susan Harris. Less *Carry On Doctor* than a charactercom set in the fixed confines of the workplace, it featured a ward of ill-matched Miami nurses – caustic divorcee Sandy, Vietnam vet Greg, sympathetic Annie, culturally bemused Mexican Gina and phobic Julie – who injected sharp one-liners whilst changing the bedpans. Quipped Sandy to a Ku Klux Klan member admitted for treatment: 'We keep all our sheets here numbered ... just in case you were thinking of wearing one home.' Good fun. Unfortunately enervated by the disease common to US sitcoms: sentimentalitis.

CAST *Sandy* Stephanie Hodge *Annie* Arnetia Waker *Greg* Jeff Altman *Julie* Mary Jo Keenan *Gina* Ada Maris *Dr Kaplan* Kenneth David Gilman *Paco* Carlos Lacamara *Jack* David Rasche /*cr* Susan Harris /*dr* inc Terry Hughes, Andy Cardiff, Peter D. Beyt, Bob Berlinger /*Witt-Thomas-Harrisk* (USA) /67 x 30m col.

NYPD Blue

Crime. C4 1994–

A police procedural out of the ➢*Dragnet*/➢*Naked City* school of New York verité, created by small-screen wunderkind Steven Bochco (➢*Hill Street Blues*, ➢*LA Law*, ➢*Cop Rock*, ➢*Doogie Howser, MD*, ➢*Hooperman*, *Civil Wars*), along with sometime Yale professor of English Literature David Milch (➢*Hill Street Blues*, *Beverly Hills Buntz*). Veteran producer/director Gregory Hoblit, winner of 10 Emmys, completed the *NYPD Blue* creative partnership. Though ostensibly bleaker than Bochco's other law-based shows, it contained a large – and agreeable – degree of schmaltz, dwelling on the emotional and private lives of its caring cop characters, making it a sort of ➢*Thirtysomething* with handcuffs. The principal protagonists were sensitive ginger-haired Detective John Kelly, who earned his detective shield aged 28 (and at the cost of his marriage to attorney Laura), and his long-term partner, the brusque, ex-alcoholic and permanently sweating Detective Andy Sipowicz (played by Vietnam vet Dennis Franz, previously *Hill Street Blues*, *Beverly Hills Buntz*). Storylines weaved romance, comradeship or competition in the precinct with moral-cum-social-based storylines like wife battering, racism on the streets or AIDS victims in the tenements.

Also accorded a starring part was the camera work, tense, jerky and hand-held, which fully allowed the viewer to feel the pressure of policing in the 15th Precinct. Authenticity was only added to by the half-lighting and ear-straining sound. The series received a record-breaking 26 Emmy nominations at the end of its first season (winning six: Lead Actor for Franz, Writing, Directing, Editing, Art Direction, Casting). In series two a new member was introduced into the precinct, Detective Bobby Simone, played by Jimmy Smits (Victor Sifuentes in *LA Law*, but whose first police series was actually the pilot of ➢*Miami Vice*, where he played Don Johnson's sidekick), who took over as Sipowicz's partner when Kelly's character was ruthlessly written out of the story (Caruso, to studio ire, had quit for Hollywood). Surprisingly, the new pairing was as watchable and nuanced as the old, an antagonistic start (Simone telling Sipowicz to 'kiss my French–Portuguese ass') giving way to a working compromise. The other squadroom regulars were: Kelly's amour, Mob-linked Officer Janice Licalsi; streetwise young Detective James Martinez (Nicholas Turturro, brother of John Turturro, star of *Barton Fink*), who increasingly took over some of John Kelly's caring, sharing mantle; the by-the-book precinct commander, Lieutenant Arthur Fancy (James McDaniel, previously *Malcolm X*); self-destructive Greg Medavoy (Gordon Clapp, co-star of the cult film *Return of the Secaucus Seven*); the voluptuous but sensitive clerk Donna Abandando; and rising Assistant DA Sylvia Costas, who eventually became Mrs Sipowicz. In a 1998 90-minute special ('Hearts and Souls') Simone died after a cardiac arrest, leaving Danny Sorenson as the new boy on the precinct. Those sharing the directing honours included Donna Deitch from the movie *Desert Hearts* and actress Kathy Bates (*Misery*).

CAST *Det. John Kelly* David Caruso *Det. Andy Sipowicz* Dennis Franz *Lt Arthur Fancy* James McDaniel *Laura Kelly* Sherry Stringfield *James Martinez* Nicholas Turturro *Det. Bobby Simone* Jimmy Smits *Det. Greg Meadavoy* Gordon Clapp *Asst DA Sylvia Costas* Sharon Lawrence *Donna Abandando* Gail O'Grady *Det. Danny Sorenson* Rick Schroder / *cr* Steven Bochco, David Milch /*pr* Steven Bochco, David Milch, Gregory Hoblit /*dr* inc Gregory Hoblit, Daniel Sachheim, Donna Deitch, Mark Tinker, Elodie Keene, Michael M. Robin /*wr* inc Steven Bochco, David Milch, Burt Amus, Ann Biderman /*mus* Mike Post / *Steven Bochco Productions* (USA) /117 x 50m col / US tx ABC 1993–.

The Odd Couple
Comedy. ITV 1971

A compulsively tidy photographer, Felix Unger, shares a NY apartment with a slobbish sportswriter, Oscar Madison.

Sitcomized extrusion of Neil Simon's Broadway hit play, which managed a successful chemistry between its principals and some wry writing. Bound, however, to suffer comparison with the 1968 movie version starring Jack Lemmon and Walter Matthau. Penny Marshall, sister of producer Garry K. Marshall, and later ➢*Laverne & Shirley* appeared as Myrna Turner, Oscar's secretary. A version with two black stars (Ron Glass and Demond Wilson) was screened in the USA as *The New Odd Couple* in 1982–3.

CAST *Felix Unger* Tony Randall *Oscar Madison* Jack Klugman *Off. Murray Grechner* Al Molinaro /*pr* Garry K. Marshall, Jerry Belson, Harvey Miller, Sheldon Keller /*dr* inc Jerry Paris, Jay Sandrich /*Paramount TV* (USA) /100 x 25m col /US tx ABC 1970–5.

The Odd Man
Crime. ITV 1962–3

An early example of the 60s tendency towards offbeat thrillers, this serial from Edward Boyd (who would later create ➢*The Corridor People*) followed the interplay between five characters – Detective Sergeant Swift, Chief Inspector Gordon, part time PI Steve Gardiner, his wife Judy, and her murderer, South – as they became enmeshed in crime and intrigue. During the second season of the darkly Hitchcockian narrative Inspector Rose entered the affair, to be eventually spun off (with an increasing lightness of being) to *It's Dark Outside* (ITV, 1964–5, 16 x 60m bw, and a cast which included a yet-to-be-discovered Oliver Reed and a No. 1 song in Jackie Trent's 'Where Are You Now?' theme) and *Mr Rose* (ITV, 1968, 25 x 60m col). Quite weird and almost wonderful.

CAST *Steve Gardiner* Edwin Richfield *Judy Gardiner* Sarah Lawson *Chief Insp. Gordon* Moultrie Kelsall *DS Swift* Keith Barron *South* Christopher Guinee *Chief Insp. Rose* William Mervyn /*cr* Edward Boyd /*pr* Stuart Latham /*wr* inc Edward Boyd /*Granada TV* (UK) / 24 x 60m bw.

Oh Brother!
Comedy. BBC1 1968–70

Starred Derek Nimmo as the bumbling Brother Dominic of Mountacres Priory. The character, promoted up the clerical career ladder for a sequel, *Oh Father!* (BBC1, 1971, 7 x 30m), was essentially a resurrection of Nimmo's bashful, plum-voiced Noote from ➢*All Gas and Gaiters*. Gently watchable, though.

CAST *Brother Dominic* Derek Nimmo *Father Anselm* Felix Aylmer *Master of the Novices* Colin Gordon /*cr* David Climie, Austin Steele /*pr* Duncan Wood, Harold Snoad, Johnny Downes /*wr* David Climie, Austin Steele /*BBC TV* (UK) /19 x 30m col.

Oh, Doctor Beeching!
Comedy. BBC1 1996–

Relentlessly unfunny sitcom from David Croft about a rural railway of the (still) steam-age 60s threatened with closure. A rip-off of Ealing's 1952 *Titfield Thunderbolt* it economically recycled Paul Shane, Su Pollard and Jeffrey Holland, who had all served (in much the same roles) in Croft's earlier ➢*Hi-de-Hi!* and ➢*You Rang? M'Lord?*.

CAST *Jack Skinner* Paul Shane *Ethel Schumann* Su Pollard *Cecil Parkin* Jeffrey Holland *May Skinner* Julia Deakin *Harry Lambert* Stephen Lewis /*cr* David Croft / *pr* David Croft /*dr* Roy Gould /*wr* David Croft, Richard Spendlove /*BBC TV* (UK) /9 x 30m col.

Oh No! It's Selwyn Froggitt

Comedy. ITV 1976–7

Misadventures of a cheerily incompetent handyman with the Public Works Department of the (fictitious) Yorkshire town of Scarsdale, who also served as secretary of the archetypal local Working Men's Club and Institute. Froggitt's catchphrase was a thumbs-up 'Magic'.

Memorable character (created by Alan Plater, energetically acted by Bill Maynard), but his antics often ran to an irritating stupidity. A sequel, *Selwyn* (ITV, 1978), saw Froggitt become the Entertainments Officer for the Paradise Valley holiday camp on the Yorkshire coast.

CAST *Selwyn Froggitt* Bill Maynard *Maurice* Robert Keegan *Clive* Richard Davies *Ray* Ray Mort *Jack* Bill Dean *Mrs Froggitt (mother)* Megs Jenkins */cr* Alan Plater / *pr* Ronnie Baxter */wr* inc Alan Plater, H.V. Kershaw, Bernie Sharp */Yorkshire TV* (UK) /18 x 25m col.

The Onedin Line

Drama. BBC1 1971–80

The salty saga of James Onedin, a 19th-century Liverpool ship's master with a vaulting ambition to own a fleet of sailing vessels. His first step was to form a partnership with the owner, Webster, of the neglected three-masted schooner, the *Charlotte Rhodes* (episodes opened with a stirring shot of the boat under full sail, to the music of Aram Khachaturian's *Spartacus*), an arrangement cemented by Onedin's marriage to Webster's daughter, Anne. A wine contract in his pocket, the gruff Onedin began his ruthless empire-building. Anne, however, died in childbirth and in the lonely years that followed, Onedin relied for support on the faithful, whiskered Captain Baines. Meanwhile, Onedin's sister Elizabeth married shipowner Albert Fraser, inheriting a line of her own on his untimely death. To complete the jealous Onedin's misery, he lost his fortune in a rash South American venture and his second wife, Letty, died of lergy... By the end of the series, Onedin had married yet again, this time, to the Spaniard Margarita Juarez. Part of the BBC's enduring fascination with matters nautical (➢*Triangle*, ➢*Howard's Way*), *The Onedin's Line*'s astute mélange of briny action, boudoir, boardroom and costume drama made it the virtual quintessence of 70s Sunday evening melodrama. The location sequences were filmed off Charlestown and Dartmouth in Devon. Allegedly Marshal Tito of Yugoslavia's favourite programme.

CAST *James Onedin* Peter Gilmore *Robert Onedin* Brian Rawlinson *Elizabeth Frasier (née Onedin)* Jessica Benton *Anne Onedin (née Webster)* Anne Stallybrass *Baines* Howard Lang *Margarita Juarez* Roberta Iger */cr* Cyril Abraham */pr* Peter Graham Scott */dr* inc Pennant Roberts, David Sullivan Proudfoot, Jonathan Alwyn, David Cunliffe */wr* inc Cyril Abraham, Ian Kennedy Martin, Elaine Morgan, Ian Curteis */mus* Aram Khachaturian */BBC TV* (UK) /91 x 50m col.

One Foot in the Grave

Comedy. BBC1 1990–7

David Renwick's acidly amusing OAP sitcom featuring the misadventures of splenetic Victor Meldrew (former mortuary assistant Richard Wilson, ➢*Only When I Laugh*) as he sought to understand the illogical behaviour of household appliances and everybody else. Prime among those enduring the seething Meldrew's diatribes and accidents were his pillar-of-patience wife Margaret (Annette Crosbie), and, from 1992, when the Meldrews moved to a modern housing estate in Bournemouth, next-door neighbours Patrick (Angus Deayton) and bus-driving Pippa. Unusually reluctant to stay within the usual confines of British situation comedy, *One Foot* also broached pathos, even surrealism, yet always remained credible due to Renwick's highly controlled writing and characterization. Arguably the best, and certainly the most popular, BBC sitcom of the early 90s, it sold to America, where its sharp-edged humour was left on the sanitized cutting-room floor of the new (Bill) ➢*Cosby Show*. 'I don't believe it', as Meldrew might have said.

CAST *Victor Meldrew* Richard Wilson *Margaret Meldrew* Annette Crosbie *Mrs Warboys* Doreen Mantle *Patrick* Angus Deayton *Pippa* Janine Duvitski *Nick Swainey* Owen Brenman */cr* David Renwick */pr* Susan Belbin */dr* Susan Belbin */wr* David Renwick */mus* Eric Idle (theme) */BBC TV* (UK) /28 x 30, 1 x 90m, 1 x 60m col.

199 Park Lane

Melodrama. BBC1 1965

Voyeuristic 'lives of the rich and glossy' serial – something like ➢*Coronation Street* for the upmarket crowd – set in the luxury London apartment block of the title. Though created by old screenwriting hand William Fairchild, it was demolished after a scant nine weeks.

CAST Derek Bond, Edwin Richfield, Isabel Dean, Brenda Kaye, Philip Bond /*cr* William Fairchild /*pr* Morris Barry /*wr* William Fairchild /*BBC TV* (UK) / 18 x 30m bw.

Only Fools and Horses

Comedy. BBC1 1981– 96

Uproariously brilliant John Sullivan sitcom which took its title from from the cockney saying 'only fools and horses work' (also an episode title in Sullivan's earlier ➢*Citizen Smith*), and depicted the wide-boy antics and delusions-of-imminent-wealth of Sarf London's Derek 'Del Boy' Trotter (immortally performed by David Jason). Assisting him in the family firm – which flogged iffy goods – was naive younger brother 'Plonker' Rodney (Nicholas Lyndhurst), the proud possessor of two GCSEs, and Grandad (later replaced, on actor Lennard Pearce's death, by Buster Merryfield's Uncle Albert). A clapped-out yellow Robin Reliant with the legend 'Trotter's Independent Trading Company' on the side served as the delivery vehicle for the dodgy gear which Brut-swathed, gold-splashed Del stored in their council flat (No. 368) in high-rise Mandela House, Peckham. Also seen were a coterie of credibly bizarre friends and associates, most of whom like Del (favourite drink: Drambuie and grapefruit juice) – were habitués of the Nag's Head: brain-fused road-sweeper Trigger (Roger Lloyd Pack ➢*The Vicar of Dibley* and father of Emily Lloyd); barman Mike; gangster-like businessman Boycie and his good-time-gal wife Marlene, and nervy lorry driver Denzil. Although Sullivan had originally intended the sitcom to be about 'three men of different generations, all without a woman in their lives', by the early 90s Rodney had married the middle-class Cassandra and Del Boy had fallen in love with former stripogram/ actress Raquel, who bore him 'The Son of Del', Damian. Although 1991 saw the last full series of *Only Fools and Horses*, it continued in Christmas specials (which, like ➢*The Morecombe and Wise Show* of yore, became the turkey and cranberry sauce of Yuletide TV) until a 'final' three-parter in 1996 saw Del and Rodney walk off into the sunset after finding a watch worth £6 million in their garage. A record 24.35 million viewers tuned in.

CAST *Derek 'Del Boy' Trotter* David Jason *Rodney Trotter* Nicholas Lyndhurst *Grandad Trotter* Lennard Pearce *Uncle Albert* Buster Merryfield *Cassandra Trotter (née Parry)* Gwyneth Strong *Raquel* Tessa Peake-Jones *Boycie* John Challis *Marlene* Sue Holderness *Mike Fisher* Kenneth MacDonald *Trigger* Roger Lloyd Pack *Denzil* Paul Barber *Mickey Pearce* Patrick Murray *Roy Slater* Jim Broadbent /*cr* John Sullivan /*pr* Ray Butt, Gareth Gwenlan /*dr* inc Ray Butt, Gareth Gwenlan, Susan Belbin, Mandie Fletcher, Martin Shardlow /*wr* John Sullivan /*BBC TV* (UK) / 33 x 30m, 13 x 50m, 3 x 60m col.

Only When I Laugh

Comedy. ITV 1979–83

Medical mirth with a bickering trio of long-term hospital patients, gentlemanly hyphochondriac Glover, loud-mouthed lorry driver Figgis and naive Binns. Fairly obvious situations (the fight for the bed under the window, tormenting new arrivals with bloody tales of quackery, the inadequacies of hospital radio) but, performed by a cast of distinction, it achieved chart-topping ratings.

CAST *Archie Glover* Peter Bowles *Norman Binns* Christopher Strauli *Roy Figgis* James Bolam *Dr Gordon Thorpe* Richard Wilson *Staff Nurse Gupte* Derrick Branche *Matron* Brenda Cowling *Cook* Pamela Cundell /*cr* Eric Chappell /*pr* Vernon Lawrence /*wr* Eric Chappell /*Yorkshire TV* (UK) /41 x 25m col.

On the Buses

Comedy. ITV 1970–5

Like Wolfe and Chesney's earlier show, ➢*The Rag Trade,* a workplace sitcom of cheerfully lowbrow humour. Commissioned by the then Head of Comedy for LWT, Frank Muir, it starred ex-music hall turn Reg Varney (*The Rag Trade, Beggar Thy Neighbour*), as chirpy bus driver Stan Butler, and Bob Grant as his lothario conductor pal, Jack; together they were the Luxton Bus Company's least efficient employees, the bane of the life of Stephen Lewis's black-hearted Inspector Blake (catchphrase: 'I'll get you Butler!'/'I 'ate you Butler!'). At home, Stan lived with his domineering mother, plain sister Olive (former stripper Anna Karen, later Peg Mitchell's sister in ➢*EastEnders)* and idle brother-in-law, Arthur. A bus depot in Wood Green, London, provided the exteriors. Three movies based on the show were released in the cinema (the first, *On The Buses,* being the highest earning British film of 1971) and the format sold to America as *Lotsa Luck.*

CAST *Stan Butler* Reg Varney *Jack* Bon Grant *Insp. Blake ('Blakey')* Stephen Lewis *Mum* Cicely

Reg Varney (third from left) and the cast of the gorblimey workplace sitcom *On the Buses.* The show rode to the top of the British ratings in 1970, 1971 and 1972.

Courtneidge/Doris Hare *Olive* Anna Karen *Arthur* Michael Robbins /*cr* Ronald Wolfe & Ronald Chesney /*pr* Stuart Allen /*dr* Stuart Allen /*wr* Ronald Wolfe & Ronald Chesney /*London Weekend Television* (UK) / 70 x 25m col.

Open All Hours

Comedy. BBC2 1976–85

Roy Clarke (➢*Last of the Summer Wine*, ➢*Keeping Up Appearances*) sitcom set in a Yorkshire corner shop, which opened as a 1974 ➢*Comedy Playhouse* and received its first run on BBC2, where it picked up only modest custom. A repeat on BBC1 in 1979, however, took it to the very pinnacle of the ratings. Ronnie Barker starred as the stammering, scrooge-like shopkeeper Arkwright who, in-between meanly counting his money, bullied his daydreaming assistant, nephew Granville (David Jason), and lusted after big-bosomed, Morris Minor-driving, Nurse Gladys Emmanuel. Seaside-postcard laughs, always overly dependent on Barker's performance as Arkwright. Luckily, he was never s-s-s-hort of brilliant.

CAST *Arkwright* Ronnie Barker *Granville* David Jason *Nurse Gladys Emmanuel* Lynda Baron *Mrs Featherstone* Stephanie Cole /*cr* Roy Clarke /*pr* Sydney Lotterby /*dr* inc Sydney Lotterby /*wr* Roy Clarke /*mus* Max Harris / *BBC TV* (UK) /25 x 30m col.

Opportunity Knocks!

Light Entertainment. ITV 1956–78/BBC1 1987–90

Long-running talent show, begun on Radio Luxembourg, in which the genial steel-haired host Hughie Greene ('And I mean that most sincerely folks…') easily overshadowed the aspiring acts. So did his 'clapometer' gimmick whereby the studio audience selected their favourite turn of the week by applauding, the highest score on the instrument equalling victory; the official winner, though, was drearily selected by the viewers at home sending in their votes on postcards. In a technological update for the BBC1 revival, *Bob [Monkhouse] Says 'Opportunity Knocks!'* (1987–90), telephone polling replaced the postal vote. Freddie Starr, Frank Carson, Paper Lace, Little and Large, Tom O'Connor, muscle-man Tony Holland, Mary Hopkin and Bonnie Langford were among the awesome entertainers upon whom the *OK!* viewers bestowed their favours. For the final season of the BBC version, Les Dawson – himself an *OK!* winner – presented.

CAST (presenters) Hughie Greene, Bob Monkhouse, Les Dawson /*pr* Peter Dulay, Milo Lewis, Robert Fleming, Royston Mayoh, Keith Beckett, Stewart Morris /*dr* inc Stuart Hall, Milo Lewis, Ronnie Baxter, Royston Mayoh /*ABC: Thames* (UK) /approx. 500 x 50m bw:col.

Oranges Are Not the Only Fruit

Drama. BBC2 1990

Adapted by Jeanette Winterson from her own novel, *Oranges Are Not the Only Fruit* related the sour-taste story of a young adopted Lancashire girl, Jess (played as a teenager by Charlotte Coleman, later *Four Weddings and Funeral*), in sapphic rebellion against the religious fanaticism of her Pentecostal mother.

Unusual material and of unusually heavy weight, the vivid production repaid the faith of the BBC (Kidron had never directed a TV drama before, Giles had never produced one) with almost universal acclaim.

CAST *Jess* Emily Aston/Charlotte Coleman *Mother* Geraldine McEwan *Pastor Finch* Kenneth Cranham *Melanie* Cathryn Bradshaw *Miss Jewsbury* Celia Imrie *Mrs Green* Freda Dowie *May* Elizabeth Spriggs *Elsie* Margery Withers /*cr* Jeanette Winterson /*pr* Phillipa Giles /*dr* Beeban Kidron /*wr* Jeanette Winterson /*BBC TV* (UK) /3 x 55m col.

Origami

Children's. ITV 1968–71

A godsend for those with shares in paper companies, *Origami* presented the ancient Japanese art of making models of everything under the rising sun from pieces of 10-inch-square paper. It was hosted by world-expert Robert Harbin, and directed by Jess Yates (father of Paula), also the presenter of *Stars on Sunday.*

CAST (presenter) Robert Harbin /*dr* Jess Yates /*Yorkshire TV* (UK) /approx. 32 x 25m col.

O.S.S.

Spy. ITV 1957–8

World War II espionager, its tales of cloak-and-dagger derring-do in occupied Europe taken from the filing cabinets of America's Office of Strategic Studies (the forerunner of the CIA). Shot in ill-met-by-moonlightish monochrome, it starred Ron Randell as OSS Captain Frank Hawthorne and Robert Gallico as his trusty Sgt O'Brien. Co-produced by Colonel Wiliam Eliscu, an ex-OSS staff officer.

CAST *Capt Frank Hawthorne* Ron Randell *The Chief* Lionel Murton *Sgt O'Brien* Robert Gallico /*pr* William Eliscu /*dr* inc Robert Siodmak /Buckeye: ITC (UK / USA) /26 x 25m bw.

OTT

Light Entertainment. ITV 1982

Late night and live version of ➢*Tiswas* for adults, intended by Chris Tarrant to send viewers to bed with a 'smile on their faces and perhaps a few mucky thoughts'. Alas, the studio slapsticking was grimly crude and, while custard-covered nubiles may have provided a rise in testostorone levels, it was so blatantly sexist that Central was forced to deliver the axe. Tarrant, Alexei Sayle, Lenny Henry and Helen Atkinson-Wood all emerged from the critical wreckage of *OTT* (standing, appositely, for 'Over The Top') amazingly unscathed.

CAST inc Chris Tarrant, Alexei Sayle, Lenny Henry, Helen Atkinson Wood /*cr* Chris Tarrant, Howard Imber, Peter Harris /*pr* inc Chris Tarrant /*Central TV* (UK) /12 x 60m col.

Our Friends in the North

Drama. BBC2 1996

Peter Flannery's state-of-the-nation epic, begun as a 1982 play for the RSC, which followed the fortunes of four Tyneside friends – Nicky (Chris Eccleston, *Let Him Have It,* ➢*Cracker*), Tosker, Mary and Geordie – from youthful optimistic 1964 to sceptical, middle-aged 1995. En route, *Our Friends* visited all the crucial moments and trends of modern British history (with a contentious cynicism that caused nervous BBC lawyers to suggest that the serial was set in a fictional country called Albion), but was always at its most riveting when dealing with the personal, particularly Nicky's relationship with his father, an ex-Jarrow marcher who had Alzheimers (the performance of an acting lifetime by Peter Vaughan). The quibbles (glitches in accent, tendency to mark the decades by hairstyles, occasional socialist navel-gazing, potholes in plot) were minor, the Monday evening satisfaction major.

CAST *Nicky Hutchinson* Christopher Eccleston *Geordie Peacock* Daniel Craig *Tosker Cox* Mark Strong *Mary Soulsby* Gina McKee *Felix Hutchinson* Peter Vaughan *Florrie Hutchinson* Freda Dowie *Austin Donahue* Alun Armstrong *Bennie Barrett* Malcolm McDowell *Claudia Seabrook* Saskia Wickham /*cr* Peter Flannery /*pr* Charles Pattinson /*dr* Pedr James /*wr* Peter Flannery /*BBC TV* 9 x c70m col.

Our House

Comedy. ITV 1960–1

Raucous farce about nine comic caricature allsorts who pool their money to buy a dilapidated mansion. Any resemblance to *Carry On* cinema – beyond the presence of Charles Hawtrey, Bernard Bresslaw, Hattie Jacques and Joan Sims – was not accidental; it was created by Norman Hudis, the pen behind many of the earliest *CO* films.

CAST *Georgina Ruddy* Hattie Jacques *Simon Willow* Charles Hawtrey *Daisy Burke* Joan Sims *Captain Iliffe* Frank Pettingell *Mrs Iliffe* Ina de la Haye *Stephen Hatton* Trader Faulkner *Marcia Hatton* Leigh Madison *Gordon Brent* Norman Rossington *Herbert Keene* Frederick Peisley *William Singer* Bernard Bresslaw *Henrietta* Hylda Baker /*cr* Norman Hudis /*pr* Ernest Maxin /*wr* Norman Hudis, Bob Block, Brad Ashton /*ABC TV* (UK) /13 x 55m, 7 x 45m bw

Our Man at Saint Mark's

Comedy. ITV 1963–5

Quaintly funny incidents in the everyday life of an English country vicar (Felgate parish).

It could hardly fail with Leslie Phillips (followed by Donald Sinden) in the be-cassocked lead role, and didn't, reaching No. 3 in the ratings. Joan Hickson (➢*Miss Marple*) supported as the housekeeper and Harry Fowler as the ex-crook turned sexton. A 1966 sequel, *Our Man from St Marks*, followed Sinden's character (now an archdeacon) into the hallowed ground of the local cathedral.

CAST *Rev. Andrew Parker* Leslie Phillips *Rev. Stephen Young* Donald Sinden *Mrs Peace* Joan Hickson *Anne Gibson* Anne Lawson *Harry Yo Yo* Harry Fowler /*cr* James Kelly, Peter Miller /*pr* Eric Maschwitz /*dr* inc Christopher Hodson, Richard Doubleday /*wr* James Kelly, Peter Miller /*Associated-Rediffusion* (UK) / approx 33 x 30m bw.

Out

Crime. ITV 1978

On his release from prison, bone-hard bank-robber Frank Ross (an awesomely excellent Tom Bell) obsessively and murderously searches for the informer who snitched on him.

Superb revenge thriller, which took the viewer on a pacy but morally uncomfortable tour of a bleak London gangland where the cops and the robbers were but different sides of the same bent coin.

CAST *Frank Ross* Tom Bell *Rimmer* Robert Walker *Anne Ross* Lynne Farleigh *Cimmie* Katharine Schofield *Chris Cottle* Brian Croucher *DI Bryce* Norman Rodway / *exec pr* Johnny Goodman /*pr* Barry Hanson /*dr* Jim Goddard /*wr* Trevor Preston /*Thames TV: Euston Films* (UK) /6 x 60m col.

Out of the Blue

Crime. BBC1 1995–

Grubbily realistic British police detective show, transparently modelled (especially in the camera-work and taboo subjects department) on American cousins ➢*NYPD Blue* and ➢*Homicide – Life on the Street*. But pretty watchable for all that, with the squad of detectives at Yorkshire's Brazen Gate police station morassed in highly believable personal problems. Relief from its own morose *weltanschaung* was offered by nice touches of black humour.

CAST *DI Eric Temple* John Duttine *DS Jim 'Lew' Llewyn* David Morrissey *DC Marty Brazil* Neil Dudgeon *DC Warren Allen* Darrell D'Silva *DS Rebecca Bennett* Orla Brady *DC Bruce Hannaford* Lennie James *DC Ron Ludlow* Peter Wright *DC Tony Bromley* Andy Rashleigh *Franky Drinkall* John Hannah /*pr* Laura Mackie /*dr* inc Julian Farino, Keith Boak /*wr* inc Peter Bowker, Bill Gallagher /*BBC TV* (UK) /12 x 50m col.

Out of the Unknown

Sci-fi. BBC2 1965–71

A sci-fi anthology made by talent (the likes of J.B. Priestly and Terry Nation in the script department, Philip Saville in the director's chair) and largely sourced from classic authors (John Wyndham, Isaac Asimov, Malcolm Bradbury *et al*). Britain's answer to ➢*The Twilight Zone*. It was initially overseen by Irene Shubik, who had previously been the script editor on ➢*Out of This World*, but the third and fourth seasons were given to Alan Bromly who took the series so far to the edge of sci-fi that it transmuted into the genre of the supernatural. Ridley Scott worked on the series as a designer.

cr Irene Shubik /*pr* Irene Shubik, Alan Bromly /*dr* inc Peter Potter, George Spenton-Foster, Peter Sasdy, Peter Duguid, Philip Saville, Rudolph Cartier /*wr* inc Terry Nation, Ian Curteis, Leon Griffiths, Stanley Miller, Troy Kennedy Martin, J.B. Priestly, Clive Exton, Julian Bond, Nigel Kneale /*mus* Norman Kay (theme) /*BBC TV* (UK) /12 x 50m, 37 x 60m bw:col.

Out of This World

Sci-fi. ITV 1962

Seminal – indeed, the original – British sci-fi anthology, developed by ➢*Armchair Theatre's* Irene Shubik (who acted as story editor) and drawing most of its playlets from the works of the masters, Asimov and Philip K. Dick included. Boris Karloff introduced. Clearly onto a TV winner, Shubik replicated the experiment with ➢*Out of the Unknown*, but this time for the BBC.

CAST (host) Boris Karloff /*cr* Irene Shubik /*pr* Leonard White /*dr* inc Jonathan Alwyn, Peter Hammond, Guy Verney /*wr* inc Terry Nation, Leon Griffiths, Julian Bond, Clive Exton /*ABC TV* (UK) /13 x 60m bw.

Outside Edge

Comedy. ITV 1994–6

One of ITV's few quality sitcoms of the 90s. Derived from the stage piece by Richard Harris (a Mike Leigh on uppers), *Outside Edge* explored the perennial British themes of sex and class through the antics of Brent Park Cricket Club, in particular the anally retentive middle-class captain, Roger, and his mousey wife, Mim, and the lusty commoners, Kevin and Maggie. Sufficiently self-confident to eschew a laughter track, the series won – among other prizes – a British Comedy Award, with Brenda Blethyn picking up a best actress gong.

CAST *Roger Dervish* Robert Daws *Mirium Dervish* Brenda Blethyn *Dennis Broadley* Denis Lill *Kevin Costello* Timothy Spall *Maggie Costello* Josie Lawrence *Bob Willis* Michael Jayston /*cr* Richard Harris /*pr* Paula Burdon /*dr* Nick Hurran /*wr* Richard Harris /*Central TV* (UK) /22 x 30m col.

The Outer Limits

Sci-fi. ITV 1964

'There is nothing wrong with your television set. Do not attempt to adjust the picture ... we will control the vertical. We will control the horizontal... You are about to experience the awe and mystery which reaches from the inner mind to the Outer Limits.'

Classic sci-fi anthology. Stylishly overseen by producer Joseph Stefano (who had written the screenplay for Hitchcock's *Psycho*), *TOL* was hall-marked by a shadowy *film noir* shooting style and the Buggest-Eyed Monsters yet to creep over a TV studio. (Sample: parasite molluscs which attached themselves to human spinal cords all the better to dominate their hosts in 'The Invisibles', the queen bee in humanoid form in 'Z-z-z-z'). Yet, *TOL* had serious as well as super-scary designs, frequently probing at the nature of humanity and the role of science. Death-voiced narrator Vic Perrin was the sole regular cast member, aside from William O. Douglas Jr, the man behind many of the alien masks. Writers included future Oscar-winner Robert Towne and Harlan Ellison (whose segments included the Hugo winner, 'Soldier'). Only the habit of closing episodes with a moral homily struck a bum note. (Although *TOL* episodes were first screened in Britain by Granada in 1964, not until BBC2 transmitted the series in 1980–1 was it networked.)

Inevitably, *TOL* did not escape the TV nostalgia boom of the 90s. An American-made production from Trilogy Entertainment/Atlantic Films revived the show with widely varied results, buttressing episodes with such big-name guest stars as Leonard 'Spock' Nimoy and Lloyd and Beau Bridges.

CAST (narrator) Vic Perrin /*cr* Leslie Stevens /*exec pr* Leslie Stevens /*pr* Joseph Stefano, Ben Brady /*dr* inc Leslie Stevens, Gerd Oswald, Alan Crosland Jr, Laslo Benedek, John Brahm, Charles Haas /*wr* inc Leslie Stevens, Joseph Stefano, Meyer Dolinsky, Robert Towne, John Mantley, Jerry Sohl, Harlan Ellison, Robert C. Dennis /*mus* Dominic Frontiere, Harry Lubin /*Daystar-Villa di Stefano: United Artists TV* (USA) /49 x 60m bw /US tx ABC 1963–5.

P

Pacific Blue

Crime. Sky1 1996–

Eco-friendly mix of ➢*CHiPS* with ➢*Baywatch*, in which an elite squad of beach police patrolled Santa Monica on ... bikes. Inevitably, there was a certain amount of unintentional Keystone comedy in the sight of pumping-kneed cycle cops chasing baddies in Ferraris, though few adolescent males – with a screen full of bikini babes and thumping rock soundtrack before them – found a hand to file a complaint. Yet *PacBlue* was also less mindless than its precursors, and even betrayed wit on occassion.

CAST *Lt Anthony Palermo* Rick Rossovich *Off. T.C. Calaway* Jim Davidson *Off. Chris Kelly* Darlene Vogel *Off. Victor Del Toro* Marcos Ferraez *Off. Cory McNamara* Paula Trickey /*cr* Bill Nuss /*exec pr* Bill Nuss, Gary Nardino /*dr* inc Mickey Dolenz /*North Hall Productions* (USA) /57+ x 60m col /US tx USA TV 1996–

Paddington Bear

Children's. BBC1 1981

Michael Bond's stories, featuring the child-like talking bear adopted by the Browns of London after being found at Paddington Station, transferred to TV via a meld of stop-action animation and cut-out background figures. The version for US screens came with an introduction by Oscar-winner Joel Gray.

CAST (voices) *narrator and all characters* Michael Hordern /*Film Fair* (UK) /5 x 30m col /US tx PBS 1981.

Pallas

Comedy. C4 1991

Spoof on the British Royal Family which overlaid rare archive footage of the Windsors with ➢*Spitting Image*-type voices and humour. Rejigged, the various pieces came together to tell the story of how the Queen, tiring of life on the throne, decided to select a successor through a giant allcomers ➢*It's A Knockout* competition. The storyteller was Richard E. Grant.

Madly amusing and faintly seditious, although the thrill of the technique had already been stolen by ➢*The Staggering Stories of Ferdinand de Bargos.*

CAST (voices) *Charles/Philip* Jon Glover *Andrew / Major Ron/Lancelot (the horse)* Enn Reiter *The Queen / Diana/Sarah* Kate Robbins *Storyteller* Richard E. Grant; also Jim Broadbent, Joanna Brookes, Roger Blake /*pr* Geoff Atkinson /*wr* Charlie Bell, Eric Pilkington /*Noel Gay Television* (UK) /10 x 5m bw:col.

The Pallisers

Drama. BBC1 1974

➢*The Forsyte Saga* imitation (complete with actress Susan Hampshire, here as flighty Lady Glencora) about a 19th-century aristocratic family with political ambitions and scandalous lives. Adapted by Simon Raven from the Palliser novels of one-time Liberal candidate Anthony Trollope, it failed to fly artistic heights despite fine production (on a modest £50,000 budget) from Martin Lisemore.

CAST *Lady Glencora Palliser (née McCluskie)* Susan Hampshire *Plantagenet Palliser* Philip Latham *Duke of Omnium* Roland Culver *Countess Midlothian* Fabia Drake *Laura Kennedy* Anna Massey *Lord Fawn* Derek Jacobi *The Earl of Silverbridge* Anthony Andrews *Lady Mabel Grex* Anna Carteret *Burgo Fitzgerald* Barry Justice /*cr* Martin Lisemore /*pr* Martin Lisemore /*dr* Hugh David, Ronald Wilson /*wr* Simon Raven /*mus* Herbert Chappell, Wilfred Josephs /*BBC TV* (UK) / 26 x 50m col /US tx 1975.

Paradise

Western. BBC1 1991–2

Passably good-looking horse opera, part of the revival of the genre initiated by ➢*Lonesome Dove.* It starred Lee Horsley as gunfighter Ethan Cord of the ironically named mining town of Paradise, whose footloose ways are ended when he inherits his sister's orphaned family. This soapish element aside, the action quotient remained high since Cord was still required to pack a six, sometimes for money, sometimes for Right. Episodes were stacked with veteran Western guest stars, which made spot-the-old-timer-oater-star a pleasing pastime for *cognoscenti.* Also screened as *Guns of Paradise.*

CAST *Ethan Allen Cord* Lee Horsley *Amelia Lawson* Sigrid Thornton *Claire Carroll* Jenny Beck *Joseph Carroll* Matthew Newmark *Ben Carroll* Brian Lando *George Carroll* Michael Patrick Carter *Scotty McBride (bartender)* Mark Dryden *Tiny* John Bloom *Dakota* John Teresky *Deputy Charlie* James Crittenden /*dr* inc Cliff Bole, Robert Scheerer, Nick Havinga, David Jacobs, Michael Caffey, Russ Mayberry, Peter Crane, Kate Tilley, Harry Harris /*Roundlay: Lorimar* (USA) /56 x 60m col /US tx CBS 1988–91.

The Paradise Club

Crime. BBC1 1989–90

Gangland crime caper starring Leslie Grantham ('Dirty Den' from ➢*EastEnders*) and Don Henderson (*Bulman*) as two differing brothers – one an upwardly mobile villain, the other a defrocked Catholic priest – who inherit a seedy East End dance hall on the death of their mother, the local Mrs Big.

The partnership between the Kane Brothers was an enjoyable one; shame about the credulity-stretching underworld storylines.

CAST *Danny Kane* Leslie Grantham *Frank Kane* Don Henderson *DI Campbell* Kitty Aldridge *Carol Kane* Barbara Wilshere /*cr* Murray Smith /*pr* Selwyn Roberts / *wr* Murray Smith /*Zenith* (UK) /20 x 50m col.

Para Handy – Master Mariner

Comedy. BBC 1959–60

Popular BBC Scotland comedy series, from the 1905 *Glasgow Evening News* sketches by Neil Munro (under the pseudonym Hugh Foulis). The stories followed roguish Captain Peter 'Para Handy' McFarlane and the thirsty swabs of the small cargo boat *The Vital Spark* as they plied their slightly shady trade along the charmingly clichéd coast of western Scotland. Five years after the end of the series, a ➢*Comedy Playhouse* revival 'The Vital Spark' launched Para Handy and his salt dogs on a sequel, *The Vital Spark* (1966–7), itself hauled from the depths for a valedictory six episodes in 1974. The timeless quaintness of Munro's material was only proved in 1994 when a new cast, led by Gregor Fisher (➢*Naked Video*, ➢*Rab C. Nesbitt*) as McFarlane, took to the airwaves in *The Tales of Para Handy*, with the setting updated to the 1930s.

CAST *Para Handy McFarlane* Duncan Macrae *Macphail* John Grieve *Sunny Jim* Angus Lennie *Dougie* Roddy McMillan /*pr* Pharic McLaren /*wr* Duncan Ross / *BBC TV* (UK) /16 x 30m bw.

Pardon the Expression

Comedy. ITV 1965–6

Spin-off from ➢*Coronation Street* (the only one to date) in which Arthur Lowe's pompous teetotaller Leonard Swindley became the assistant manager of the local branch of Dobson and Hawk chainstore. Naturally, such a prestigious posting only increased his comic self-importance. When the series was concluded with the dismissal of Swindley and store manager Hunt, the twosome reunited to become (improbably enough) ghost-hunters in *Turn Out the Lights.* It was transmitted in 1967, a year before Lowe donned khaki – and TV immortality – as Captain Mainwaring in ➢*Dad's Army.*

CAST *Leonard Swindley* Arthur Lowe *Ernest Parbold* Paul Dawkins *Walter Hunt* Robert Dorning *Mrs Edgely (canteen manageress)* Betty Driver /*pr* Harry Driver, Derek Granger, H.V. Kershaw /*dr* inc Michael Cox, Walter Butler /*wr* inc Harry Driver, Christopher Bond, Vince Powell, Jack Rosenthal /*Granada* (UK) /39 x 30m bw.

Paris

Crime. ITV 1980–81

Steven Bochco's first cop series (preceeding ➢*Hill Street Blues* by two years) and also the first US weekly series to star a black actor. This was James Earl Jones, who played Woody Paris, detective head of the LAPD's elite Metro Squad and part-time criminology professor at UCLA. Even excusing the sometimes Beta-level scripts, Jones' personal charisma and likeably thoughtful character should have made for a long run; that *Paris* lasted only 13 episodes suggested that white America was not yet ready for an Afro-American in a leading weekly part.

CAST *Woodrow 'Woody' Paris* James Earl Jones *Barbara Paris* Lee Chamberlain *Willie Miller* Mike Warren *Deputy Chief Jerome Bench* Hank Garrett *Stacey Erickson* Cecilia Hart *Ernie Villas* Frank Ramirez /*cr* Steven Bochco /*exec pr* Steven Bochco / *pr* Gregory Hoblit, Edward De Blasio /*dr* inc Georg Stanford Brown, Arnold Laven, Jackie Cooper, Jack Starrett /*wr* inc Steven Bochco, Edward De Blasio, Burton Armus /*MTM* (USA) /13 x 60m col /US tx CBS 1979–80.

Parker Lewis Can't Lose

Comedy. BSkyB 1992–

Initially slated as a carbon copy of *Ferris Bueller's Day Off* (the movie and the TV series), this US sitcom chronicling the machinations and misadventures of ice-cool, rule-avoiding Santo Domingo High School student Parker Lewis actually had a style all of its own. Made with a single camera, full of unusual angles and special video effects, it erred towards a 'toon-like' bizarrity which ensured youth cult status. Adults liked it, too. Lewis' motto was, 'Not a problem'. From 1993 the show went out as plain *Parker Lewis.*

CAST *Parker Lewis* Corin 'Corky' Nemec *Ms Musso* Melanie Chartoff *Mikey Randall* William Jayne *Jerry Steiner* Troy Slatten *Annie Sloan* Jennifer Guthrie /*exec pr* Clyde Philips /*pr* Lon Diamond, Russell Marcus, Robert Lloyd Lewis /*dr* inc Andy Tennant, Rob Bowman, Tucker Gates /*Clyde Phillips Productions: Columbia Pictures TV* (USA) /60+ x 30m col /US tx *Fox TV* 1990–.

The Partridge Family

Comedy. BBC1 1971–4

In which a suburban widowed mom, Shirley Partridge, joins her kids' band as a singer – and, hey presto, they become a big hit. Embarking in a painted school bus, the Partridge family duly tour the USA making music and having squeaky-clean sitcom fun.

Though Shirley Jones was ostensibly the star, her real-life stepson David Cassidy – who played the eldest Partridge son, Keith – fast emerged as the headline act and became, for a brief rocket-glare while, the biggest teen idol on the globe.

For the record, the Partridge Family line up was: Shirley Partridge, 16-year-old Keith, 15-year-old Laurie, 10-year-old Danny, 7-year-old Chris, 5-year-old Tracy, and dog Simone. Among their chart hits were the 60s covers, 'Breaking Up Is Hard To Do' and 'Walking in the Rain'.

Jodie Foster received one of her earliest screen roles as the character Julie Lawrence.

A 1974 animated spin-off from Hanna–Barbera, *Partridge Family: 2200 AD*, posited the phenomenon of widow Partridge (her forename changed to Connie) leading the clan band on a rock'n'roll tour of the planets. 'Come on, get happy!'

CAST *Shirley Partridge* Shirley Jones *Keith Partridge* David Cassidy *Laurie Partridge* Susan Dey *Danny Partridge* Danny Bonaduce *Christopher Patridge* Jeremy Gelbwaks/Brian Forster *Tracy Patridge* Suzanne Crough *Reuben Kinkaid (manager)* Dave Madden /*cr* Bernard Slade /*exec pr* Bob Claver /*pr* Bob Claver, Mel Swope, William S. Bickley, Michael Warren /*mus* inc Hugh Montenegro /*Screen Gems* (USA) /96 x 25m col / US tx ABC 1970–4.

Party of Five

Drama. C4 1996–

Much revered American soap about the trials of the Salinger children as they grow up without parents. If too heavy on the introspective head-examining dialogue of the ➢*Thirtysomething* variety, there was no denying its emotional punchiness and fine ensemble acting. A Golden Globe, among other honours, resulted.

CAST *Charlie Salinger* Matthew Fox *Claudia Salinger* Lacey Chabert *Bailey Salinger* Scott Wolf *Julia Salinger* Neve Campbell *Owen Salinger* Taylor & Brandon Porter *Kirsten* Paula Devicq *Will* Scott Grimes /*Columbia TV* (USA) /100 x 60m col /US tx CBS 1995–.

Pathfinders
Sci-fi. ITV 1960–1

Early British space show (produced by Sydney Newman, later co-creator of ➢*Doctor Who*) for the family Sunday evening gather-round-the-glowing-tube. It followed the continuing adventures in the near galaxy – begun with *Target Luna* – of the Wedgwood family, headed by rocket scientist pop, Professor Wedgwood. The three stories issued under the *Pathfinders* umbrella were, *Pathfinders in Space*, *Pathfinders to Mars* and *Pathfinders to Venus*.

Pathfinders was also the title of a Thames TV drama documentary about the target-finding force of the RAF during WWII (1972–3, 13 x 60m col).

CAST *Prof. Wedgwood* Peter Williams *Conway Henderson* Gerald Flood *Geoffrey Wedgwood* Stewart Guidotti *Prof. Mary Meadows* Pamela Barney *Harcourt Brown* George Coulouris *Jimmy Wedgwood* Richard Dean /*pr* Sydney Newman /*dr* Guy Verney, Reginald Collin /*wr* Malcolm Hulke, Eric Paice /*ABC TV* (UK) / 21 x 30m bw.

Paul Temple
Crime. BBC1 1969–71

Adventures in criminal-catching of an urbane Chelsea thriller writer and his wife. Entirely adequate dashing detective series (and one of the first homegrown TV products to be made in colour) from the prolific British inkslinger Francis Durbridge, who first sent Temple a-sleuthing in the 1938 radio serial, *Send for Paul Temple*.

CAST *Paul Temple* Francis Matthews *Steve Temple* Ros Drinkwater /*cr* Francis Durbridge /*pr* Alan Bromly, Peter Bryant, Derrick Sherwin /*wr* inc Francis Durbridge, Victor Canning /*BBC TV:Taurus* (UK) / 46 x 50m col.

Peak Practice
Melodrama. ITV 1993–

Soapy GP drama set in bucolic Cardale in the Peak District. Initially the melodrama – not unlike ➢*All Creatures Great and Small* but with lumbar pains and NHS fundholding issues replacing swine fever – centred on African returnee Dr Jack Kerruish (Kevin Whately, ➢*Auf Wiedersehen, Pet*, ➢*Inspector Morse*), who joined the struggling practice (The Beeches) of Beth Glover (Amanda Burton, ➢*Brookside*) and Will Preston. Though frequently at professional odds with Glover, Kerruish nonetheless married her in-between patronizing casework among Derbyshire folk peculiarly prone to disease. By the fourth season Whately and Burton had quit for other projects, the cast-haemorrhage filled by dashing, ➢*ER*-like young bloods Saskia Wickham (grandaughter of Van Heusen's chairman, previously *Clarissa*, and topless in the Danish 'film' *The Prince of Jutland*), Gary Mavers and Adrian Lukis. A large syringe of pure slush which addicted over 12.5 million viewers.

CAST *Dr Jack Kerruish* Kevin Whately *Dr Beth Glover* Amanda Burton *Dr Will Preston* Simon Shepherd *Dr Andrew Attwood* Gary Mavers *Dr David Shearer* Adrian Lukis *Dr Erica Matthews* Saskia Wickham *Dr Joanna Graham* Haydn Gwynne /*cr* Lucy Gannon /*exec pr* Jonathan Powell /*pr* Tony Virgo, Michele Buck *dr* Kate Webster, Shelagh McLeod /*dr* Alan Grint, Nigel Cole, Tony Garner, Anthony J. Quinn /*wr* inc Tony Etchells /*Carlton TV* (UK) /35+ x 60m col, 1 x 90m.

Pennies From Heaven
Drama. BBC1 1978

Dennis Potter's innovative (actors miming to popular songs of the 20s and 30s) tale of an itinerant songsheet salesman, Arthur Parker, escaping his suburban marriage by temporary – and doomed – dalliance with a generous schoolteacher, Eileen. Overlong, yet also inspirationally scripted, acted – with Bob Hoskins magnificent – and directed. A film version starring Steve Martin (why?) and Bernadette Peters was released by MGM in 1981.

CAST *Arthur Parker* Bob Hoskins *Eileen* Cheryl Campbell *Joan Parker* Gemma Craven *The Accordian Man* Kenneth Colley *Tom* Hywel Bennett /*cr* Dennis Potter /*pr* Kenith Trodd /*dr* Piers Haggard /*wr* Dennis Potter /*BBC TV* (UK) /6 x 75m col.

Perfect Scoundrels
Comedy. ITV 1990–2

Two conmen perform confidence tricks on the shady deserving.

Undemandingly amusing sitcom, devised by actors Peter Bowles and Bryan Murray (who had previously teamed together on ➢*The Irish RM*) as a vehicle for their own employment, with them playing true to type (Bowles suave, Murray a rough diamond). Ray Connolly, most famous for screenwriting the rock movies *That'll Be The Day* and *Stardust*, scripted. A British *The Sting*? Not quite.

CAST *Guy Buchanan* Peter Bowles *Harry Cassidy* Bryan Murray /*cr* Peter Bowles, Bryan Murray /*exec pr* Graham Benson /*pr* Tim Aspinall, Terence Williams, Tony Virgo /*wr* Ray Connolly /*TVS* (UK) /16 x 60m col.

The Perils of Penelope Pitstop
Children's. BBC1 1970

In which dastardly Sylvester Sneekly (aka 'The Hooded Claw') tried to prevent delicious Penelope Pitstop (formerly of ➢*The Wacky Races*) from winning car-race competitions via every dirty trick in the book. And then some.

Cartoon lampoon of *The Perils of Pauline*, aimed at small kids but mostly enjoyed by world-weary sophisticates of around 16.

CAST (voices) *narrator* Gary Owens *Penelope Pitstop* Janet Waldo *Sylvester Sneekly* Paul Lynde /*Hanna–Barbera* (USA) /17 x 22m col /US tx CBS 1969–71.

Perry Mason
Crime. BBC1 1961–7

Hugely successful crime series based on Earl Stanley Gardner's stories (which began with the 1933 *The Case of the Velvet Claws*) featuring crime-solving Los Angeles lawyer Perry Mason; it ran for nine years on US network CBS (before going into continuous syndication) and made a star of former Hollywood heavy and Parisian café singer Raymond Burr (later ➢*Ironside*). Undoubtedly part of its appeal lay in its reassuringly unchanging construction: every episode began with Lieutenant Tragg and DA Ham Burger building a watertight case, the accused turning to Mason, who would then investigate with the devoted help of secretary Della Steet and PI Paul Drake, before concluding in a courtroom trial where a crucial witness would yield under Mason's dogged questioning or be undone by a last minute piece of evidence rushed in by Drake – at which Mason's wrongly accused client would walk free.

CBS attempted to revive the series in 1973 as *The New Adventures of Perry Mason*, with Monte Markham leading an entirely new cast. It flopped, but a 1985 NBC reunion movie, *Perry Mason Returns* with Burr and Barbara Hale (the other regular cast members had gone to the great studio in the sky; their replacements included Hale's son William Katt as Drake and ➢*M*A*S*H*'s David Ogden Stiers as the new DA, Michael Reston) led to a season of feature-length episodes.

CAST *Perry Mason* Raymond Burr *Della Street* Barbara Hale *Paul Drake* William Hopper *Hamilton Burger* William Talman *Lt. Arthur Tragg* Ray Collins *Steve Drumm* Richard Anderson *Terence Clay* Dan Tobin /*exec pr* Gail Patrick Johnson, Arthur Marks / *pr* Art Seid, Sam White, Ben Brady /*dr* inc Richard Donner, Ted Post, Andrew V. McLaglen /*mus* Richard Shores, Fred Steiner /*Paisano Productions* (USA) / 270 x 60m bw, 1 x 60m col /US tx CBS 1957–66.

The Persuaders!
Crime. ITV 1971–2

Trans-Atlantic crime caper from Sir Lew Grade, featuring two bored rich boys – self-made millionaire New Yorker Danny Wilde (Tony Curtis), and toffish Brit Lord Brett Sinclair (Roger Moore) – blackmailed by a retired judge into becoming international sleuths. And thus they wandered 26 jet-set episodes, bickering, buddying, thwacking villains and – above all – chasing girls, girls, girls.

Camp 70s nonsense. But stylish camp 70s nonsense, from John '007' Barry's 'dum dum di dum dum' theme, to the stars' cool clothes (Curtis' brown leather bomber jacket, his habit of wearing driving gloves around the house, Moore's self-designed safari suits), via the big-haired guest starlettes (Anouska Hempel, Susan George, Joan Collins) that come-hithered through every episode. All this, and directors such as Val Guest (*When Dinosaurs Ruled the Earth*, *The Quatermass Experiment*) and Basil Dearden (*The Blue Lamp*) too.

Curiously enough, the one market in which *The Persuaders!* failed to sell was the one it was intended for, the USA, where ABC cancelled after just 24 episodes. It did enormous business elsewhere, however, and still runs as a staple of European networks, holding up, unflagging, well against the course of TV time.

Tony Curtis and Roger Moore were *The Persuaders!*, Sir Lew Grade's barely disguised attempt to follow up the trans-Atlantic success of *The Saint*.

CAST *Lord Brett Sinclair* Roger Moore *Danny Wilde* Tony Curtis *Judge Fulton* Laurence Naismith /*cr* Robert S. Baker /*pr* Robert S. Baker, Terry Nation, Johnny Goodman /*dr* Basil Dearden, Roy Ward Baker, Roger Moore, Val Guest, Leslie Norman, Peter Hunt, Gerald Mayer, Sidney Hayers, Peter Medak /*wr* inc Terry Nation, Brian Clemens, John Kruse, Michael Pertwee, Tony Williamson, Donald James, Tony Barwick, Harry H. Junkin /*mus* John Barry (theme), Ken Thorne /*A Tribune Production* (UK) /24 x 60m col /US tx ABC 1971–2.

Peter Gunn

Crime ITV 1960–1

Jazz-driven crime show starring Craig Stevens as Peter Gunn, a smooth PI with a brush hair-do who worked out of a conspicuously well-appointed office at 351 Ellis Park Road, LA. For kicks, Gunn hung around a nite spot called Mother's, where his main squeeze was the resident chanteuse.

Likeable, sharply-dressed stuff, which not only spawned a rash of moody imitators (including *Pete Kelly's Blues* and ➢*Johnny Staccato*, a 1967 film version and a hit record in Mancini's theme), but also propelled the career of its creator-producer Blake Edwards onto the Hollywood fast-track, including the helming of the Pink Panther cycle. (He returned, however, to the small set in 1991 as the exec producer of the sitcom *Julie*, starring his wife Julie Andrews). Among the directors clocking in for work was Robert Altman.

CAST *Peter Gunn* Craig Stevens *Edie Hart* Lola Albright *Lt Jacoby* Herschel Bernadi *'Mother'* Hope Emerson/Minerva Urecal /*cr* Blake Edwards /*pr* Blake Edwards /*dr* inc Blake Edwards, Robert Altman, Gene Reynolds, Lamont Johnson /*mus* Henry Mancini / *A Spartan Production* (USA) /110 x 30m bw /US tx NBC 1958–61.

Petrocelli

Crime. BBC1 1978–9

In which the underrated Barry Newman reprised his 1970 film role in *The Lawyer*, the Italian-American Anthony Petrocelli here giving up the big city to practise law in the southwestern town of San Remo. Usually, Petrocelli performed his services *gratis*, leaving his wife and himself in trailer-living penury. Cowhand Pete Ritter was hired on as investigator.

Amiable crime show, moral hearted and intelligent. It notched up a respectable 21.7 million viewers at its 1979 British peak.

CAST *Anthony Petrocelli* Barry Newman *Maggie Petrocelli* Susan Howard *Pete Ritter* Albert Salmi *Lt Ponce* David Huddleston /*cr* Sindey J. Furie, Harold Buchman, E. Jack Newman /*pr* Thomas L. Miller, Edward J. Milkis /*dr* inc Bernard McEveety, Richard Donner, Paul Stanley, Jerry London, James Sheldon, Irving Moore /*Miller-Mikis: Paramount TV* (USA) / 46 x 60m col /US tx NBC 1974–6.

Peyton Place

Melodrama. ITV 1965–70

Based on Grace Metalious's best-selling novel (which had already done service as a 1957 Hollywood film with Lana Turner), *Peyton Place* was America's first prime-time soap opera. Set in the New England town of the title, its principal (indeed, almost sole) theme was illicit sexual liaison. Such controversially steamy stuff sent *PP* to the top of the ratings, with screen newcomers Mia Farrow and Ryan O'Neal the main beneficiaries of the adulation. Farrow was Allison Mackenzie, the bastard daughter of bookstore owner Constance Mackenzie, and O'Neal played her rich-boy suitor, Rodney Harrington. Linking the shenanigan stories was the personage of Dr Michael Rossi, whose work took him into every home and relationship.

In 1965 *PP* was imported to Britain by ITV (who paid £30,000 for the privilege). This was not without its irony, since *PP* the TV series had been inspired by the success of ➢*Coronation Street.* Yet *PP* proved much shorter-lived, its production-line method of (eventually) thrice-weekly instalments resulting in laughable telematic standards and a plot so impenetrable that new viewers switched on only to switch off. Ratings fell, the axe descended – just as Dr Rossi was brought up on a murder charge. (Unsatisfied Dutch viewers flew the cast out to Holland to film a happy ending.) A 1972 daytime revival, *Return to Peyton Place*, with but two of the original cast (Frank Ferguson and Patricia Morrow), failed to find an audience, as did 1985's *Peyton Place: The Next Generation*, which introduced Mackenzie's never-heard-of-before daughter to the seething proceedings.

CAST *Constance Mackenzie* Dorothy Malone *Allison Mackenzie* Mia Farrow *Dr Michael Rossi* Ed Nelson *Matthew Swain* Werner Anderson *Rodney Harrington* Ryan O'Neal *Leslie Harrington* Paul Langton *Eli Carson* Frank Ferguson *Rita Jacks* Pat Morrow *Steven Cord* James Douglas *Elliott Carson* Tim O'Connor *Norman Harrington* Chris Connelly *Betty Anderson* Barbara Perkins /*cr* Paul Monash /*exec pr* Paul Monash / *pr* Everett Chambers /*mus* Franz Waxman /*Twentieth Century-Fox TV* (USA) /514 x 30m /US tx ABC 1964–9.

Philip Marlowe

Crime. BBC 1960

Raymond Chandler's fictional Los Angeles sleuth played in gentlemanly style by Philip Carey. More softboiled than hardboiled, the concept never clicked for an audience raised on Bogart's world-weary interpretation of Marlowe in *The Big Sleep.* Marlowe reappeared in several future forms, including a 1983 five-part Home Box Office cable mini-series, *Philip Marlowe – Private Eye*, with Powers Boothe.

The immoral – and immortal – Sergeant Bilko in *The Phil Silvers Show.* The role won Silvers three Emmys.

CAST *Philip Marlowe* Philip Carey /*pr* Glen Wang / *ABC* (USA) /26 x 30m bw /US tx ABC 1959–60.

The Phil Silvers Show

Comedy. BBC1 1957–61

Although signed to an MGM film contract in 1940, Jewish New York actor Phil Silvers (born Philip Silversmith) found his lasting fame in television as the star of *The Phil Silvers Show* (aka *You'll Never Get Rich*). This won him three Emmys for his perfect portrayal of Master Sergeant Ernie Bilko of Fort Baxter, Kansas, a 'Machiavellian clown in uniform' forever chasing get-rich-quick schemes and scamming everyone within a 1,000-mile radius (even his own unfortunate Motor Pool subordinates in times of desperation). Fast-talker Bilko was, above all, the master of implausible flattery ('Hello Miss – the Colonel didn't tell me his daughter was visiting – why! It's *Mrs* Hall...') and the elaborate excuse, these guaranteed to extract him from periodic possible undoings. Modelled closely by creator Hiken on congenital gambler Silvers himself, the indestructible Bilko was also a modern incarnation of the clever servant character from Ancient Greek theatre (with Hall as the dumb master). There was strong support from the cast – headed by Ford's Hall, and Gosfield's Doberman, the 'slob of the century' – and sharp satirizing of army life, but it was Silvers' show in fact and name, his oxygen-consuming performance frequently leaving the rest to gasp 'But Sarge...!' Arguably the greatest sitcom act of all TV time.

Almost inevitably, the Bilko character overshadowed eveything Silvers did thereafter on the small screen (factory sitcom *The New Phil Silvers Show*, *Just Polly and Me*, the spoof *The Slowest Gun in the West*, and *Summer in New York*) and on the big (*A Funny Thing Happened on the Way to the Forum*, *Carry On... Follow that Camel*). There were homages to *The Phil Silvers Show* in the form of Hanna–Barbera's animated ➢*Boss Cat* and an unsatisfactory 1996 movie with Steve Martin as *Bilko* (Silvers died in 1985, after years of clinical depression), which was viewed like endless foreplay.

CAST *M/Sgt Ernie Bilko* Phil Silvers *Cpl Rocco Barbella* Harvey Lembeck *Pte Sam Fender* Herbie Faye *Col John T. Hall* Paul Ford *Pte Duane Doberman* Maurice Gosfield *Sgt Rupert Ritzik* Joe E. Ross *Cpl Henshaw* Allan Melvin *Pte Dino Paparelli* Billy Sands *Nell Hall* Hope Sansberry *Sgt Joan Hogan* Elizabeth Fraser /*cr* Nat Hiken /*pr* Nat Hiken, Al De Caprio, Edward J. Montagne /*dr* Nat Hiken, Al De Caprio /*wr* inc Nat Hiken, Neil Simon, Arnie Rosen, Leonard Stern /*mus* John Strauss /*CBS* (USA) /138 x 30m bw / US tx CBS 1955–9.

Picket Fences
Crime. Sky1 1995–7

The anti-➢*Twin Peaks* of US TV, set in a small town (Rome, Wisconsin) where everything was humdrummingly normal. Reliable Tom Skerritt (previously the co-star of the movie *M*A*S*H* and Evan Drake in ➢*Cheers*) starred as the shining-badged local sheriff, Jimmy Brock, whose wife Jill was the town physician. If a patented Capraesque *It's a Wonderful Life* factor was part of its charm, it also managed, under the executive eye of David Kelley (➢*LA Law*, *Chicago Hope*, husband of Michelle Pfeiffer), a dramaturgy decent enough to win an Emmy Award. There were thespian Emmys for Tom Skerritt and Kathy Baker, too.

CAST *Sheriff Jimmy Brock* Tom Skerritt *Dr Jill Brock* Kathy Baker Maxine Stewart Lauren Holly *Kenny Lacos* Costas Mandylor /*exec pr* David E. Kelley /*dr* inc Kris Tabori, Dan Lerner, Lou Antonio, Michael Pressman, Tom Moore, Joan Tewkesbury /*CBS Television* (USA) /1 x 120m, 86 x 60m col /US tx NBC 1995–7.

Picture Book
Children's. BBC 1955–63

Was the Monday edition of ➢*Watch with Mother*, with Patricia Driscoll 'turning the pages' to introduce items ranging from stories (read by Charles E. Stidwell) to puppet adventures (Bizzy Lizzy, the Jolly Jack Tars) through to make-your-own simple toys. When Driscoll departed for Sherwood Forest and ➢*The Adventures of Robin Hood*, her seat was taken by Vera McKechnie. A classic from the 50s Golden Age of Toddler TV.

CAST (presenters) Patrica Driscoll, Vera McKechnie /*pr* Freda Lingstrom, David Boisseau /*BBC TV* (UK) / approx. 560 x 30m bw.

Pie in the Sky
Crime. BBC1 1994–

Soft-crime Sunday evening entertainment out of the same jolly TV territory as ➢*Lovejoy*, starring Richard Griffiths as a disillusioned detective plod who prefers cooking up dishes in his Middletown Pie in the Sky restaurant (speciality: traditional English food) to apprehending villains as per the demands of ACC Freddy Fisher. The fly in the show's soup was that the ample, benignly countenanced Griffiths never convinced as a policeman. Created by Andrew Payne, whose partner, the cookery writer Lindsey Bareham, served as culinary consultant.

CAST *Henry Crabbe* Richard Griffiths *Margaret Crabbe* Maggie Steed *ACC Freddie Fisher* Malcolm Sinclair *WPC/Sgt Sophia Cambridge* Bella Enahoro *Steve Turner (co-chef)* Joe Duttine *Linda (waitress)* Alison McKenna *John (waiter)* Ashley Russell *Nicola (waitress)* Samatha Janus *Gary (sous-chef)* Matthew Lamont *Sally* Marsha Thomason *DS Lorna Purvis* Abigail Thaw /*cr* Andrew Payne /*pr* Jacky Stoller, Chrissy Skins, David Wimbury /*dr* inc Jim Hill, Paul Harrison /*wr* inc Andrew Payne, Robert Jones / *WitzEnd: Nicework* (UK) /18+ x 50m col.

Pingu

Children's. BBC1 1989

Stop-action animated antics of an innocently mischievous baby penguin who lived on the ice cap with his mother and father and friend, seal.

dr Otmar Guttman /*Tricksfilmstudio* (Nor) /26 x 5m col.

Pingwings

Children's. ITV 1965

Early Smallfilms animation featuring a knitted family of penguin-like creatures who lived in a barn at Berrydown Farm, where they waddled charmingly to an endless refrain of 'pingwing, pingwing'. A dispatch from a bygone Britain of charming innocence.

cr Oliver Postgate, Peter Firmin /*Smallfilms* (UK) / 12 x 10m bw.

The Pink Panther Show

Children's. BBC1 1970–1

Filler cartoon series featuring the mute feline from the title sequence of Blake Edwards' *Pink Panther* films. Usually, in the UK transmissions, the misadventures of the disaster-prone 'one and only/Truly original panther, Pink Panther/From head to toe' bookended those of Clouseau carbon-copy, The Inspector. The famous 'durumm, durumm' theme was by Henry Mancini. The programme was the first of numerous other packages featuring the stoic cat, including *The New Pink Panther Show* (DePatie-Freleng, 1971–6) and *Pink Panther and Sons* (DePatie-Freleng: Hanna–Barbera, 1984–5).

CAST (voice) *The Inspector* Pat Harrington Jr plus Rich Little, Joan Gerber, Larry Storch, Paul Frees, Mark Skor /*exec pr* David DePatie, Fritz Freleng /*dr* Gerry Chiniquy, Fritz Freleng /*mus* Henry Mancini (theme) /*DePatie-Freleng* (USA) /approx. 32 x 30m col / US tx NBC 1969–71.

Pinky and Perky

Children's. BBC 1957–68 /ITV 1969–72

Were twin porcine puppets (Pinky wore red, Perky blue and a hat) who sang songs – often cover versions of pop hits – at 78 r.p.m. and generally hammed it up at the fictitious PPC TV station with their stringed stooges. These included: Ambrose Cat, singing bird band The Beakles (geddit?), Horace Hare, Conchita the Cow, and Bertie the baby elephant. At the height of their fame Pinky and Perky received more fan mail than The Beatles, and so great was their influence perceived to be that the BBC decided to shelve a mildly controversial 1966 skit, 'You Too Can Be a Prime Minister', until after that year's General Election. Public outcry forced its reinstatement. Two years later, possibly in swinish revenge, Pinky and Perky (theme song: 'We belong together') trotted over to ITV. They were the creation of Czech immigrants Jan and Vlasta Dalibor.

CAST (presenters) Jimmy Thompson, John Slater, Roger Moffat, Brian Burdon, Fred Emney /*cr* Jan & Vlasta Dalibor /*pr* inc Trevor Hill, Stan Parkinson / *wr* inc Margaret Potter, Don Nichols /*mus* Norman Newell & Philip Green (theme) /*BBC TV: Thames TV* (UK) /approx. 220 x 30m bw:col.

Pipkins

Children's. ITV 1974–81

Pre-school glove-puppet show, set in the shop of the title, featuring artistic Hartley Hare (manipulated by Nigel Plaskitt from the immortal Vicks Sinex advertisement with the stuffy-nosed Malcolm), Pig, and Topov the Monkey.

CAST *Johnny (presenter)* Wayne Laryea *Hartley Hare /Narrator/Tortoise* Nigel Plaskitt *Topov/Pig/Octavia* Lorain Bertorelli/Elizabeth Lindsay /*cr* Susan Pleat, David Cregan /*pr* Michael Jeans /*dr* Michael Jeans /*wr* inc Susan Pleat, David Cregan, Gail Renard, Denis Bond /*mus* Chris Hazell /*ATV Network Productions* (UK) /approx. 200 x 30m col.

The Plane Makers

Melodrama. ITV 1963–5

Soapish serial following the turbulent relations between labour and capital at fictitious Scott Furlong aviation factory. After two seasons it dropped the unsexy workplace grime to focus on the ruthless scheming of boss Sir John Wilder and became *The Power Game* – a change virtually dictated by Patrick Wymark's imposing, camera-seducing turn as the executive boardroom baron. The ratings-topping *Power Game* continued until Patrick Wymark's death in 1969, by which time Wilder had powered his way through both merchant banking and the diplomatic service.

CAST *Sir John Wilder* Patrick Wymark *Pamela Wilder* Barbara Murray/Ann Firbank *Don Henderson* Jack Watling /*cr* Wilfred Greatorex /*pr* Rex Firkin /*dr* inc Eric Price, John Cooper, Geoffrey Nethercott /*wr* inc Wilfred Greatorex, Edmund Ward, Raymond Bowers / *ATV* (UK) /26 x 50m bw.

Planet of the Apes

Sci-fi. ITV 1974–5

The TV franchise of Franklin Schaffer's 1967 movie of the same title, itself based on the allegorical novel by Pierre Boulle.

The plot: spacemen Virdon and Burke pass through a timewarp and land back on Earth in the year AD 3085 – to find a topsy-turvey society where the apes rule and human beings are just the unpaid help. An inquisitive young chimp called Galen – Roddy McDowall reprising his film role – helps the astronauts avoid the militaristic, human hating gorillas of chief Urko (Mark Lennard, also Sarek, Spock's father in ➢*Star Trek*).

While something of the philosophical subtlety of the film and its outlandish look was maintained, too many of the telescripts went to churn-'em-out writers. The result: a semi-primitive actioner with repetitive storylines, which pleased few, among them the executives of America's CBS network who accordingly cancelled in mid-run, leaving the plight of Virdon and Burke unresolved.

A cartoon series, *Return to the Planet of the Apes,* was made in 1975 by David DePatie and Fritz Freleng. Shortly afterwards, the episodes of *Planet of the Apes* were pasted up into a series of 120-minute TVMs which air occasionally in the off-peak hours.

CAST *Virdon* Ron Harper *Burke* James Naughton *Galen* Roddy McDowall *Urko* Mark Lennard *Zauis* Booth Colman /*exec pr* Herbert Hirschman /*pr* Stan Hough /*dr* inc Don Weiss, Arnold Laven, Ralph Senensky, Jack Starrett, Alf Kjellan, John Meredyth Lucas /*wr* inc S. Bar-David, Robert Hamner, Edward J. Lasko, Barry Oringer, Walter Black /*mus* Lalo Schifrin / *Twentieth Century-Fox TV* (USA) /15 x 50m col /US tx CBS 1974.

Play Away

Children's. BBC2 1971–84

Long-running Saturday afternoon version of ➢*Play School* for grown-up sophisticates (i.e. five- to seven-year-olds) and with a bigger laughs register. Such consummate toddlertime presenters as Brian Cant, Floella Benjamin, Derek Griffiths and Tony Robinson led the studio-based antics, with Jonathan Cohen and the Play Away Band providing the musical accompaniment. Amazing but true: Jeremy Irons made his TV debut on the show and Anita Dobson (➢*EastEnders*) was selected as a *PA* presenter over Patricia Hodge. It also spun off *Fast Forward, Think of a Number* and *Think Again.*

CAST (presenters) inc Brian Cant, Toni Arthur, Derek Griffiths, Julie Stevens, Lionel Morton, Floella Benjamin, Tony Robinson, Anita Dobson /*pr* Ann Reay, Cynthia Felgate, John Smith, Anne Gobey, Jeremy Swann /*mus* Lionel Morton (theme); Jonathan Cohen /*BBC TV* (UK) /approx. 500 x 23:30m col.

Play for Today

Drama. BBC1 1970–84

Essentially ➢ *The Wednesday Play* moved to a Thursday (then Tuesday) transmission slot. Like its forebear, it proved the major Corporation outlet for new scripwriting talent. From its hallowed frames came forth such classics as Mike Leigh's excruciating suburban tragi-comedy 'Abigail's Party' (1977), Jim Allen's politically committed 'The Rank and File' (1971, directed by Ken Loach), Jack Rosenthal's 'Bar Mitzvah Boy' (1976), Alan Gibson and Jeremy Paul's time-travel tale 'The Flipside of Dominick Hyde' (1980) and sequel 'Another Flip for Dominick' (1982), and, perhaps the consummate TV play by the consummate TV playwright, Dennis Potter's nostalgic 'Blue Remembered Hills' (1979, with its then original conceit of putting adult actors into children's clothing). Also like its predecessor, *PFT* was no stranger to infamy: Potter's 'Brimstone and Treacle' was banned for its scenes of devil-rape and Roy Minton's 'Scum' for its graphic violence (both pieces would eventually be transmitted, over a decade later, after impetus from cinematic versions). Less contentiously, *PFT* also provided the first appearance in court of John Mortimer's irascible Rumpole (1975) (➢*Rumpole of the Bailey*).

pr inc Richard Eyre, Chris Cherry, Irene Shubik /*dr* inc Ken Loach, Lindsay Anderson, Mike Leigh, Richard Eyre, Roland Joffe, Philip Saville /*wr* inc Jim Allen, John Osborne, David Storey, Adrian Mitchell, John Mortimer, Mike Leigh, Dennis Potter, Jack Rosenthal, Jeremy Paul and Alan Gibson /*BBC TV* (UK) / 60 x 60:95m col.

Play School

Children's. BBC2 1964–88

Ready to play? What's the day? A daily TV 'nursery school' for tots, the first programme to be transmitted on BBC2's opening, and ending 24 years later, its songs, games and stories presented along the way by the likes of Brian Cant, Floella Benjamin, Eric Thompson (➢*The Magic Roundabout*) and Johnny Ball. But much more celebrated than these mere humans were Jemima, Big Ted, Humpty, Little Ted and Hamble (replaced by black doll Poppy in the mid 80s), while the round, arched and square windows, and tuneful clock (once stopped by a trade-union demarcation dispute) are the stuff of tele-lore.

CAST (presenters) inc Virginia Stride, Gordon Rollings, Johnny Ball, Brian Cant, Toni Arthur, Floella Benjamin, Miranda Connell, Brian Croucher, Wally Whyton, Eric Thompson, Lionel Morton, Derrick Griffiths, Pyllida Law, Julie Stevens, Terrance Holland / *cr* Joy Whitby /*pr* inc Joy Whitby, Sue Peto, Ann Reay, Michael Grafton-Robinson, Christine Hewitt /*BBC TV* (UK) /approx 4000 x 30m bw:col.

Please Sir!

Comedy. ITV 1968–9

Actor John Alderton, in his first starring role since ➢*Emergency – Ward 10*, was the teacher attempting to tame 5C, a class of delinquents at inner-city Fenn Street School. By 1970 (with most of the class clearly well past school finishing age) they joined the adult world of work in *The Fenn Street Gang*. Inspired by the 1967 movie *To Sir With Love*, the show was formatted in the USA as ➢*Welcome Back Cotter*, launching one John Travolta into the celebrity firmament. The novice writing team behind *Please Sir!*, John Esmonde and Bob Larbey, were themselves destined for greatness, creating a string of British TV classics: ➢*Get Some In*, ➢*The Good Life*, ➢*Ever Decreasing Circles* and *As Time Goes By*.

CAST *Bernard 'Privet' Hedges* John Alderton *Price* Richard Davies *Doris Ewell* Joan Sanderson *Potter* Deryck Guyler *Smith* Erik Chitty *Eric Duffy* Peter Cleall *Frankie Abbott* David Barry *Maureen Bullock* Liz Gebhardt *Peter Craven* Malcolm McFee *Denis Dunstable* Peter Denyer *Sharon Eversleigh* Penny Spencer /*cr* John Esmonde & Bob Larbey /*pr* Mark Stuart /*dr* Mark Stuart /*wr* John Esmonde & Bob Larbey /*London Weekend TV* (UK) /40 x 25m col.

Pobol Y Cwm

Melodrama. BBC1/S4C 1973–

Long-running Welsh-language sudster set in the fictional village of Cwmderi. Initially a ponderous geriatric weekly, it was overhauled in the late 80s into a daily 20-minute serial which, if not exactly hot, was at least decently warm (sample storyline: formerly prim, Chapel-going headmistress Beth begins an adulterous relationship with a toyboy). Almost uniquely, episodes were recorded on the day of transmission. Networked in 1992, it foundered on the English-speaking Brit's dislike of subtitles.

Roughly translated, *Pobol Y Cwm* means 'An Everyday Tale of Valley Folk'. Among the cast was veteran Welsh actress Rachel Thomas, co-star (with Paul Robeson) of the proletarian classic movie *The Proud Valley*.

CAST *Reg* Huw Ceredig *Megan* Lisabeth Miles *Dil* Haydn Edwards *Clem* Glan Davies *Meic Pierce* Gareth Lewis *Derek* Hywel Emrys *Dic Deryn* Ifan Huw Dafydd *Sgt James* Ieuean Rhys *Beth* Eirlys Britton *Hywel Llywelyn* Andrew Teilo *Barry* Geraint Morgan *Bella* Rachel Thomas *Mrs McGurk* Iola Gregory /*pr* inc Robin Rollinson, Glenda Jones /*wr* inc William Jones / *BBC TV* (UK) /500 x 30m, approx. 2500 x 20m bw:col.

Pogle's Wood

Children's. BBC1 1966–7

If you went down to the woods in the late 60s you would have been sure to bump into Mr and Mrs Pogle ('Wife'), son Pippin and pet squirrel Tog, a family of puppets who lived at the base of a tree. And next to a magic bean plant. Athough the

Pogles spoke with thick hick accents, they were clearly intended to be educators, for their miniature adventures frequently uncovered the marvels of nature.

Originally called *The Pogles* (featuring a witch, who was promptly sent on her broomstick by the BBC who thought she might scare the tiny viewers), the series was transmitted as part of ➢*Watch with Mother*. It was by Postgate and Firmin's Smallfilms, and innovatively intercut film footage of pastoral scenes between the puppetry.

CAST (voices) Olwen Griffiths, Steve Woodman, Oliver Postgate /*cr* Oliver Postgate /*wr* Oliver Postgate / *mus* Vernon Elliott /*sfx* Peter Firmin (puppetry) / *Smallfilms* (UK) /13 x 15m bw.

Poldark

Melodrama. BBC1 1976–7

Arriving home to brooding 18th-century Cornwall after service fighting the Americans in their War of Independence, squire Ross Poldark (Robin Ellis, *The Good Soldier*, ➢*Play for Today*'s 'Blue Remembered Hills') found his estate run down, his copper mines about to be sold and the love of his life (so far) Elizabeth, about to plight her troth to cousin Francis. Over the following 28 episodes, the pony-tailed, tight-britched Poldark fought for his birthright, fought the perfidious French, and fought the corrupt control of scheming George Warleggan (Ralph Bates) over local politics. Between the flint-eyed derring-do, Poldark tried to resolve his feelings for old flame Elizabeth, and his passion for urchin servant girl Demelza (Angharad Rees).

Demelza won.

At its peak, this Sunday evening bodice-ripper, based on the novels by Winston Graham, attracted 12 million viewers. A 1996 feature-length sequel from HTV earned sulks from the Poldark (or Pol-darrrrrk, as it is irresistibly pronounced) Appreciation Society for desecration, since it jettisoned Ellis and Rees in favour of a new cast (John Bowe as Ross, Mel Martin as Demelza, Kelly Reilly as their daughter Clowance) and an update in time to 1810. This notwithstanding, it was reasurr-rrringly the same old tosh of tossing seas, family feuds and heaving bosoms.

CAST *Ross Poldark* Robin Ellis *Demelza* Angharad Rees *Elizabeth* Jill Townsend *George Warleggan* Ralph Bates *Francis Poldark* Clive Francis *Caroline* Judy Geeson *Rev. Ossie Whitworth* Christopher Biggins /*pr* Tony Coburn, Richard Beynon, Morris Barry /*dr* Paul Annett, Kenneth Ives, Christopher Barry, Philip Dudley, Roger Jenkins /*wr* Paul Wheeler, Peter Draper, Jack Pulman, Alexander Baron, John Wiles, Martin Worth /*London Films: BBC TV* (UK) /29 x 50m col.

Police Squad!

Comedy. ITV 1982

Spoof police show from the makers of *Airplane!*, with that film's star, Leslie Nielsen, as fearless Frank Drebin. Nielsen effortlessly satirized his previous straight-cop ventures, ➢*The Protectors* and the *The New Breed*, playing it deadpan amidst a deluge of sight gags (giant policeman Al was only ever seen from the neck down), non sequiturs and literalisms; when Drebin requested a colleague to 'Cover me!', the officer did so – with a coat. In his fight to keep the streets clean, Drebin had the help of forensic scientist Ted Olson (who had an unhealthy interest in young children) and stoolie shoeshine Johnny, who could give information on any subject – for a price. 'Tonight's guest star' was inevitably killed off within seconds of the opening credits. US network ABC cancelled after six programmes, reportedly because the show required too much concentration from the viewer, though it went on to become the basis for the successful *The Naked Gun* ('From the files of Police Squad') cinema cycle.

CAST *Det. Frank Drebin* Leslie Nielsen *Ed Hocken* Alan North *Ted Olson* Ed Williams *Al* John Wardell *Johnny* William Duell /*cr* Jim Abrahams, David Zucker, Jerry Zucker /*pr* Bob Weiss /*dr* Jerry Zucker, Reza S. Badiyi, Paul Krasny, Joe Dante, Georg Stanford Brown /*wr* inc Jim Abrahams, Jerry Zucker, David Zucker, Tino Insana, Robert Wuhl, Nancy Steen / *mus* Ira Newborn /*Paramount TV* (USA) /6x 30m col / US tx ABC 1982.

Police Story

Crime. ITV 1974–80

American anthology series realistically portraying police work. Joseph Wambaugh, a former LAPD detective turned best-selling crime novelist, devised the concept and served as consultant and authenticity monitor. The series, which had no recurring stars, spun off *Joe Forrester* from its episode 'The Return of Joe Forrester' (with Lloyd Bridges) and ➢*Police Woman* (with Angie Dickinson) from 'The Gamble'.

cr Joseph Wambaugh /*exec pr* David Gerber, Stanley Kallis /*pr* Christopher Morgan, Liam O'Brien /*dr* inc John Badham, William A. Graham, James Darren, Gary Nelson /*Columbia Pictures TV* (USA) /86 x 60m, 8 x 120m col /US tx NBC 1973–80.

Police Surgeon

Crime. ITV 1960

Short-lived tape series featuring a young police surgeon unable to resist turning 'tec on his Bayswater cases. As feeble as it sounds. Significant only for being the indirect basis for ➢*The Avengers*, since Ian Hendry carried on his white coat and magnifying glass routine (as the renamed Dr David Keel) into that show's opening episodes.

Police Surgeon was also the title for a series (52 x 30m col., CIV Production, USA, 1971–4) starring Sam Groom as Dr Simon Locke, intermittently screened on ITV.

CAST *Dr Geoffrey Brent* Ian Hendry *Inspector Landon* John Warwick /*pr* Julian Bond, Leonard White /*ABC TV* (UK) /12 x 30m bw.

Police Woman

Crime. ITV 1975–9

Hit US crime show which derived from 'The Gamble' episode of ex-cop Joseph Wambaugh's anthology ➢*Police Story*. Angie Dickinson (aka Angeline Brown, also ➢*Men into Space, Cassie*) starred as LAPD vice-detective Sergeant Pepper Anderson, a character who revolutionarily broke the male preserve of small-screen copdom but also set the tone for the 'jiggle TV' of ➢*Charlie's Angels* and its clones. Thus, Anderson's cases invariably required her to spend as much time undercover in scanty attire (strip clubs were a favourite story setting) as they did toting a gun or sleuthing clues. Her team colleagues were Detective Styles and (black) Detective Royster, with Lieutenant Bill Crowley handing out the assignments. ➢*The Man from UNCLE*'s Robert Vaughn was among those sharing the directing chores.

CAST *Sgt Suzanne 'Pepper' Anderson* Angie Dickinson *Lt Bill Crowley* Earl Holliman *Det. Joe Styles* Ed Bernard *Det. Pete Royster* Charles Dierkop *Cheryl (Pepper's sister)* Nichole Kallis /*cr* Robert Collins /*exec pr* David Gerber /*pr* Douglas Benton, Edward DeBlasio /*dr* inc Robert Collins, Robert Vaughn, Corey Allen, Alvin Ganzer /*wr* inc Robert Collins /*mus* Morton Stevens /*Columbia Pictures TV* (USA) / 91 x 60m col /US tx NBC 1974–81.

The Politician's Wife

Drama. C4 1995

Three-parter from Paul Milne about a fragrant Tory wife whose minister husband (Trevor Eve, ➢*Shoestring*, husband of Gold Blend's Sharon Maughan) is caught dallying with an ex-call girl.

Juliet Stevenson impressed particularly as the betrayed Flora Matlock, and as a revenge tragedy it had enough icy bite (and twilight Tory government topicality) to bring a BAFTA and an Emmy back between its teeth... And yet there was something about Flora Matlock's politicking that edged the whole unbelievably and uncomfortably close to the thriller genre.

CAST *Flora Matlock* Juliet Stevenson *Duncan Matlock* Trevor Eve *Jennifer Caird* Minnie Driver *Sir Donald Frazier* Ian Bannen /*cr* Paul Milne /*pr* Jenny Edwards, Jeanna Polley, Neal Weisman /*dr* Graham Theakston / *wr* Paul Milne /*Granada TV* (UK) /3 x 75m col.

Porridge

Comedy. BBC1 1974–7

'Norman Stanley Fletcher ... you are an habitual criminal who accepts arrest as an occupational hazard and presumably accepts imprisonment in the same casual manner...'

So intoned the judge over the opening credits of Dick Clement's and Ian La Frenais' sitcom about an old Muswell Hill lag sentenced to a five-year term at HM Slade Prison in darkest Cumbria. There, the sly, quick-quipping Fletcher (Ronnie Barker) shared a cell with naive Birmingham offender Godber (Richard Beckinsale, ➢*Rising Damp*, ➢*The Lovers*), and generally rang comic rings around the warders – notably strutting Scottish, Hitlerian Mr Mackay – whilst earning the awestruck admiration of fellow cons 'Bunny' Warren, brain-dead Blanco (David Jason), gay cook Lukewarm and 'Black Jock' McLaren. A half-hour stacked with brilliant performances, droll repartee and sparklingly funny moments which cleverly steered clear of sentimentality (note the presence in the wings of such criminal heavies as Peter Vaughan's Harry Grout). Derived from a play, 'Prisoner and Escort', seen on Barker's 1973 anthology for BBC2, *Seven of One*. A sequel, ➢*Going Straight*, followed Fletcher's fortunes on release. Black Lion-Witzend released a cinema version, *Porridge*, with the TV cast, in 1979.

CAST *Norman Fletcher* Ronnie Barker *Lennie Godber* Richard Beckinsale *Mr Barrowclough* Brian Wilde *Mr Mackay* Fulton Mackay *McLaren* Tony Osoba *Harry Grout* Peter Vaughan *Lukewarm* Christopher Biggins *Warren* Sam Kelly *Blanco* David Jason *Ingrid Fletcher* Patricia Brake *Harris* Ronald Lacey /*cr* Dick Clement & Ian La Frenais /*pr* Sydney Lotterby /*dr* Lotterby / *wr* Dick Clement & Ian La Frenais /*BBC TV* (UK) / 19 x 30, 2 x 40:45m col.

Porterhouse Blue
Comedy. C4 1987

Dramatization by Malcolm Bradbury of Tom Sharpe's satirical novel about a shambolic and fossilized Cambridge college wrenched into the 20th century by a new Master, Sir Godber Evans. Not the least of his reforms was the dismissal, after 45 years' service, of irascible head porter Skullion (the *de facto* ruler of fictitious Porterhouse), who led the Old Guard resistance. Replete with good writing, memorable scenes (including the launch of a thousand inflated condoms) and, in David Jason's portrayal of Skullion, BAFTA-winning acting. Other garlands included an International Best Drama Emmy.

CAST *Skullion* David Jason *Sir Godber Evans, College Master* Ian Richardson *The Dean* Paul Rogers *Sir Cathcart* Charles Gray *Cornelius Carrington* Griff Rhys Jones *Lady Mary* Barbara Jefford *Lionel Zipser* John Sessions *The Bursar* Harold Innocent *Professor Siblington* Willoughby Goddard /*pr* Brian Eastman / *dr* Robert Knights /*wr* Malcolm Bradbury /*Picture Partnership Production* (UK) /4 x 60m col.

Postman Pat
Children's. BBC1 1981

The toddlers' favourite. Cartoon high-drama on the rural rounds of the jolly ginger-haired postman from Greendale (who could fail to remember the time a tractor blocked the lane, obliging Pat to drive the van – registration, PAT 1 – the long way round?) accompanied by 'his black and white cat', Jess. Though a scant 12 episodes and four specials were originally made, the Corporation's generous policy of endlessly repeating them ensured that many children (and their parents) knew the scripts to word perfection. In 1997 Pat returned for 13 brand spanking new adventures, which also introduced his wife, Sara, and son, Julian.

CAST (narrator/voices) Ken Barrie /*cr* John Cunliffe / *pr* Ivor Wood /*mus* Bryan Daly /*BBC: Woodlands Animation* (UK) /25 x 15m, 4 x 30m col.

Potter
Comedy. 1979–83

Roy Clarke's restless retirement sitcom featuring Redvers Potter (Arthur Lowe), an intolerant OAP busybody who had reluctantly handed over the reins of the family firm, Potter's Mints. Though it smacked of a piece made to suit Lowe's pompous screen persona, it had enough legs to survive his death in 1982, when Robin Bailey took over the role. John Barron (➢*The Fall and Rise of Reginald Perrin*) continued as Potter's eccentric vicar friend, and Noel Dyson (from ➢*Father Dear Father*) as Potter's standard-TV-issue understanding wife.

CAST *Redvers Potter* Arthur Lowe/Robin Bailey *Aileen Potter* Noel Dyson *Vicar* John Barron *'Tolly' Tolliver* John Warner /*cr* Roy Clarke /*pr* Peter Whitemore, Bernard Thompson /*wr* Roy Clarke /*mus* Ronnie Hazlehurst /*BBC TV* (UK) /20 x 30m col.

Press Gang
Children's. ITV 1990–2

Ace school-newspaper drama, based in the offices of *Junior Gazette* at Norbridge High. Of the same teatime realistic stripe (episodes covered drug abuse, teenage suicide, local political corruption and incest) as ➢*Grange Hill*, *Press Gang* also traded old-fashioned romance (between Julia Sawalha's editor, Lynda, and Dexter Fletcher's American reporter, Spike) and distinctly Americanesque ensemble scenes between attractive, fast-talking and quick-witted characters. For its third series, *Junior Gazette* went independent (the editorial staff had left school) and computer terminals replaced the manual typewriters, while the fourth and fifth series developed a ➢*Moonlighting*-ish taste for post-modernist parody. The series was created by Glasgow headmaster Bill Moffat, and written by son Steven (later ➢*Joking Apart*, *Chalk*). There were just awards from BAFTA and the Royal

Television Society, while Julia Sawalha and Dexter Fletcher (previously Al Pacino's son in *Revolution*) went on to adult things.

CAST *Lynda Day* Julia Sawalha *Spike Thomson* Dexter Fletcher *Kenny Phillips* Lee Ross *Sarah Jackson* Kelda Holmes *Colin Matthews* Paul Reynolds *Frazz Davies* Mmoloki Chrystie *Sam Black* Gabrielle Anwar *Lucy Benjamin* Julie Craig /*cr* Bill Moffat /*pr* Sandra C. Hastie / *dr* Bob Spiers, Gerry O'Hara, Bill Ward, Bren Simpson, Lorne Magory, John Hall /*wr* Steven Moffat /*Richmond Film and TV: Central TV* (UK) /33 x 30m col.

The Pretender

Spy adventure. Sky1 1996–

At the age of four Jarod, a child with an IQ off the scale, was seized from his parents by a secret institute, based in Blue Cove, Delaware, known as The Centre. There, under the auspices of Dr Sydney Green, Jarod – along with other, similar children – was raised ('coaxed') to be a Pretender, someone who has the intelligence and chameleon-like ability to assume the personalities of other people. On discovering that The Centre was using his abilities for evil (organizing military coups, manipulating financial markets) and tiring of his prison-like existence, Jarod fled, determined to use his life for good. Each week he assumed the occupation of someone new and in need (a surgeon exposing medical malpractice, a tanker captain stopping toxic dumping), all the while searching for his allegedly dead parents. Only problem was, The Centre wanted him back. Alive if possible, dead if necessary.

Entirely unoriginal suspense show (derivative of ➢*VR5*, ➢*Quantum Leap*, among others), but professionally executed, with taut-wire tension. Directors included Anson Williams, better known as 'Potsie' in ➢*Happy Days.*

CAST *Jarod* Michael T. Weiss *Dr Sydney Green* Patrick Bauchau *Miss Parker* Andrea Parker *Young Jared* Ryan Merriman *Young Miss Parker* Ashley Peldon /*cr* Craig W. Van Sickle, Steven Long Mitchell /*exec pr* Craig W. Van Sickle, Steven Long Mitchell /*pr* Marianne Canepa, Kimberley Costello, Harvey Frand, Tim Iacotano /*dr* inc Rick Wallace, Michael Zinberg, Anson Williams, James Whitmore Jr, Ian Toynton /*wr* inc Steven Long Mitchell, Craig W. Van Sickle, Tommy Thompson, Juan Carlos Coto, Chris Ruppenthal /*mus* inc Ray Velton Bunch, John Debney /*NBC Studios: Mitchell /Van Sickle Productions: 20 Century-Fox Television: MTM Entertainment* (USA) /18+ x 50m col /US tx NBC 1996–.

The Price is Right

Light Entertainment. ITV 1984–8

Game show based on a vintage (1956) American format. Leslie ➢*'Crackerjack'* Crowther invited sterling-eyed studio contestants to 'come on down!' (at which news they became strangely hysterical) and guess the retail price of consumer objects. The contestant with the closest guestimate won. It topped the ratings in 1984.

CAST (host) Leslie Crowther /*pr* William G. Stewart /*dr* inc Paul Harrison, Mike Holgate, Richard Bradley / *Talbot: Central TV: Goodson–Todman Prods* (UK) / approx. 60 x 30m col.

Pride and Prejudice

Drama. BBC1 1995

Continued the generally unsatisfactory run of adaptations of Jane Austen's satirical novel of Georgian manners and marriage (viz a 1940 Hollywood epic by Aldous Huxley which the starring Olivier hated, and TV versions from the BBC in 1958, 1967 and 1980, the latter adroitly scripted by Fay Weldon but studio-bound). Andrew Davies' intrepretation was clumsily obvious and over-long, and the production was turned out with the lavish – £1 million an hour – inauthentic chocolate box, Olde English-look beloved of American co-financiers. Nevertheless, a huge success. Plaudits went especially to Colin Firth's (*Another Country*, *Nostromo*, *Fever Pitch*) tight-breeches-wearing portrayal of Darcy, a Mills & Boon romantic hero made televisual flesh, and Jennifer Ehle's intelligently polysemic Elizabeth. Something like TV Austenmania followed, with versions of *Persuasion* (BBC1 1995, a modernistic view by director Roger Michell), *Jane Austen's Emma* (ITV 1997) and *Sense and Sensibility* (1997).

CAST *Mr Darcy* Colin Firth *Elizabeth Bennet* Jennifer Ehle *Mrs Bennet* Alison Steadman *Mr Bennet* Benjamin Whitrow *Kitty Bennet* Polly Maberly *Jane Bennet* Susannah Harker *Lydia Bennet* Julia Sawalha *Mary Bennet* Lucy Briers *Miss Bingley* Anna Chancellor *Mr Bingley* Crispin Bonham-Carter /*pr* Sue Birtwistle /*dr* Simon Langton /*wr* Andrew Davies / *BBC TV: Arts & Entertainment* (UK/USA) /6 x 55m col.

The Prime of Miss Jean Brodie

Drama. ITV 1978

Engaging adaptation of Muriel Spark's novel about a 30s Edinburgh schoolteacher, Jean Brodie (a luminescent turn by Geraldine McEwan, ➢*Oranges Are Not the Only Fruit*), with avant-garde ideas on the education of young gals. The producer was Richard Bates, son of 'Darling Buds' author, H.E. Adaptor Jay Presson Allen had also written the screenplay for 20th Century-Fox's cinema version of *Jean Brodie* (1968), with Maggie Steed in the title role.

CAST *Jean Brodie* Geraldine McEwan /*pr* Richard Bates /*wr* Jay Presson Allen /*Scottish TV* (UK) / 7 x 50m col.

Prime Suspect

Crime ITV 1991–

Relentlessly gripping thriller cycle from Lynda La Plante focusing on the shackles of sexism that bound the career of ambitious Metropolitan CID officer DCI Jane Tennison as she pursued high-profile crimes, beginning with a serial prostitute murderer in 1991's two-parter, *Prime Suspect.* Such was its success that the chain-smoking, not-so-gentle-touch Tennison was back in *PS 2* a year later (macabre buried corpse in a racially antagonized black backstreet), while *PS 3* saw her transferred from Southampton Row to Soho's vice squad and a case of paedophilia. *PS 4* saw a change of format to a series of three 120m films (*The Lost Child, Inner Circles, The Scent of Darkness*), their common link being that they more fully explored the way professional women – the emblematic Tennison – mis(use) power as well as experience it. For *PS 5* Tennison (based on real-life policewoman DCI Jackie Malton) was demoted to Manchester where the confession by a 12-year-old boy to the murder of a small-time drug-dealer opened up a dizzying vista of police corruption. Much of the series' continuing success was down to actress Helen Mirren (born Ilyena Mironoff, daughter of a Tsarist colonel), recognized not least by a 1996 Best Female Actress Emmy.

CAST inc *DCI/DS Jane Tennison* Helen Mirren *DS Bill Ottley* Tom Bell (1, 3) *DCS Mike Kernan* John Benfield (1, 2, 4) *DI Muddyman* Jack Ellis (1, 2, 4) *DI Richard Haskons* Richard Hawley (1, 2, 4) /*cr* Lynda La Plante /*pr* Don Leaver, Paul Marcus, Brian Park, Lynn Horsford /*dr* inc Christopher Menaul, John Strickland, David Drury, Sarah Pia, John Madden, Philip Davis / *wr* inc Lynda La Plante, Allan Cubitt, Eric Deacon, Guy Hibbert, Guy Andrews, Paul Billing /*Granada TV* (UK) 2 x 120m, 2 x 120m, 3 x 120m, 2 x 110m, 2 x 120m col /US tx WSG Boston 1995.

The Prisoner

Spy. ITV 1967–8

A British spy resigns abruptly from his job, drives to his flat in a Lotus 7 (reg: KAR 120C), packs a suitcase – but, before he can close the lid, is gassed by a man dressed as an undertaker. Later, the spy wakes in his room; outside the window, however, is not London but 'The Village', a sort of Shangri-La from Hell. There, the anonymous authorities use techniques from brainwashing to hallucinogenic drugs to discover why the spy – who, like the other inmates, is now known by a number, in his case, Six – quit his ministry job. He refuses to tell the rulers' representative, Number Two (a succession of different people), while at the same time trying to escape the colony and discover the identity of Number One, the supreme controller.

Such was the premise of Patrick McGoohan's absurdist espionage series, *The Prisoner*, probably the cultiest and most analysed show in British TV history. The series grew out of McGoohan's dissatisfaction with his hit actioner ➢*Danger Man*, but also owed debts to it. To an extent (disputed), *The Prisoner* was developed by *Danger Man*'s script editor George Markstein (seen as the ministry man behind the desk in *The Prisoner*'s opening credits), who had served with British Intelligence and allegedly known of an isolation camp for spies 'who knew too much'. Certainly, such an institution had figured in the *Danger Man* episode 'Colony Three'. Markstein also insisted that Number Six was *Danger Man*'s John Drake in a new lease of TV life (McGoohan was adamant that he was not). Less controversially, it was on location for *Danger Man* that McGoohan first stumbled on Portmeirion, Sir Clough Wiliams-Ellis' Italianate folly in North Wales which would form the setting for *The Prisoner.* To make The Village even more bizarre on screen, McGoohan decked out the cast with piped blazers and installed tannoys and surveillance equipment. The soundtrack included snatches of nursery rhymes.

The inevitable question about *The Prisoner*, which McGoohan intended to be an 'allegorical conundrum' (his production company was called

Everyman, in clear reference to the morality plays of the Middle Ages), is what did it mean? Its main theme was certainly that of individual freedom, with Number Six refusing to be 'pushed, filed, stamped, indexed, briefed, debriefed or numbered' and proclaiming 'I am not a number! I am a free man!' A host of sub-themes whirled around, but the opaque series never pursued them to the end because Sir Lew Grade refused to bankroll it further than 17 episodes (out of a planned 36), either because it was over budget or because its drug references were proving too controversial. The show ended with a hastily written episode of legendary enigma: Number Six caught the elusive Number One, pulled off his mask to reveal the face of an ape and then the face of Number Six himself. (A subtle clue to Number One's identity had been revealed in nearly every episode in a piece of dialogue by which Six asked 'Who is Number One?', to which Two stonewalled 'You are, Number Six'.) Outraged viewers complained to ITV about obfuscation, but the message was simple enough: we are our own prisoners. Be seeing you.

CAST *Number Six* Patrick McGoohan *The Butler* Angelo Muscat *Number Two* Colin Gordon/Clifford Evans/Mary Morris/John Sharpe/Peter Wyngarde / Guy Doleman/Leo McKern /*cr* Patrick McGoohan, George Markstein /*exec pr* Patrick McGoohan /*pr* David Tomblin /*dr* inc Patrick McGoohan, David Tomblin, Don Chaffey /*wr* George Markstein, Patrick McGoohan, David Tomblin, Vincent Tilsley, Anthony Skene, Gerald Kelsey, Roger Parkes, Michael Cramoy, Lewis Greifer, Roger Woddis, Terence Feely /*mus* Ron Grainer /*An Everyman Films Production* (UK) / 17 x 60m col /US tx CBS 1968.

Prisoner: Cell Block H

Melodrama. ITV 1989–1993

Australian jail-house schlock. Low-budget, late-night melodrama set in fictitious Wentworth Detention Centre, Melbourne, where the women inmates pursued TV violence and sensationalism with heady abandon. The first brutal handful of scripts alone featured a stabbing (fatal), a suicide, a hanging and an assault with a hot iron. Leading prisoners were tattooed lesbian biker Franky Doyle (serving a nine-year sentence for armed robbery), dual killer Bea Smith, multiple-poisoner Lizzie Birdsworth and spouse-stabbing school mistress Karen Travers. The jailors were scarcely less colourful, with sadistic warder Joan 'The Freak' Ferguson, head 'screw' Vera 'Vinegar Tits' Bennett, and Meg Morris (pack-raped by inmates) in the front uniformed rank. The creator was Reg Watson (later ➢*Neighbours*), who had honed his tacky sudster skills on ➢*Crossroads*.

Screened simply as *Prisoner* in Australia (the title was elongated for the American and British markets to avoid confusion with McGoohan's ➢*The Prisoner*), the series gathered a devoted worldwide audience, much of it sapphic, with a two-hour special, *The Franky Doyle Story*, made from edited-down episodes, reputed to be the most VCR-copied telemovie of all time. (Britain came late to the 'Blockie' phenomenon, it being screened there almost a decade after its Australian transmission began.) A male equivalent from Grundy TV, *Punishment* (1981–2), despite harbouring the talents of a young Mel Gibson, flopped.

CAST *Frieda 'Franky' Doyle* Carol Burns *Karen Travers* Peita Toppano *Bea Smith* Val Lehman *Marilyn Ann Mason* Margaret Laurence *Lynnette Warner* Kerry Armstrong *Doreen Anderson* Colette Mann *Lizzie Birdsworth* Sheila Florance *Jeannie 'Mum' Brooks* Mary Ward *Meg Jackson (née Morris)* Elspeth Ballantyne *Governor Erica Davidson* Patsy King *Warder Vera Bennett* Fiona Spence *Warder Joan Ferguson* Maggie Kirpatrick *Jim Fletcher* Gerard Maguire *Dr Greg Miller* Barry Quinn /*cr* Reg Watson /*exec pr* Reg Watson, Godfrey Philip /*pr* Ian Bradley, Philip East, John McRae, Sue Masters, Marie Trevor /*dr* inc Graeme Arthur, Rod Hardy /*wr* inc Reg Watson, Marie Trevor, Ian Bradley, Michael Brindley, Denise Morgan /*mus* Allan Caswell (theme) /*O-Ten: Grundy TV* (Aus) /692 x 60m col.

Private Schulz

Comedy. BBC2 1981

Underrated WWII black comedy from Jack Pulman starring a pre-➢*Boon* Michael Elphick as a cowardly fraudster recruited by SS Counter Espionage, for whom he dreamed up the bizarre plan of flooding Blighty's wartime economy with dud £5 banknotes. Also seen was Billie Whitelaw thesping it up nicely as a Marlene Dietrich clone, and Ian Richardson (➢*House of Cards*) as Schulz's crazed-eyed commander.

CAST *Pte Schulz* Michael Elphick *Major Neuheim* Ian Richardson *Bertha Freyer* Billie Whitelaw /*pr* Philip Hinchcliffe /*dr* Robert Chetwyn /*wr* Jack Pullman / *BBC TV* (UK) /6 x 50m col.

The Professionals

Crime. ITV 1977–83

Crypto-fascism or clever spoof on hardboiled actioners? The jury is still out on Brian ➢'*The Avengers*' Clemens' 70s hit, *The Professionals*, although the weight of evidence suggests the former. Ex-SAS soldier Bodie and ex-East End cop Doyle were action-men members of Criminal Intelligence 5 (CI5), an elite anti-terrorist police unit headed by the gruff, limping George 'The Cow' Cowley. Episodes consisted mainly of Cowley barking orders (not very convincingly, since for most contemporary TV watchers he was still Hudson the butler from ➢*Upstairs, Downstairs*), much tyre-screeching in Doyle's Ford Capri, followed by bouts of bullets. Public outcry forced a toning down of violence (two explosions per story only) and the pulling of the episode 'The Klansman', but the most damning indictment of *The Professionals* was that its own principals disliked it. Actor Martin Shaw (later *The Chief*, *Rhodes*), in a belated display of taste, dismissed his character Doyle as a 'violent puppet' and forbade repeats until 1992. Occasionally defended for its lack of swearing (Mary Whitehouse's Viewers and Listeners Association) and prophetic suggestion that the Intelligence Service would evolve into police-type work (former con-turned-pundit, John McVicar, bless his Sociology Made Simple), the show has been remorselessly lampooned by many, Keith Allen's *The Bullshitters* prime among them.

A rare moment of calm for door kicking, car chasing cops Bodie (middle) and Doyle (front) in *The Professionals*. Much criticised for its violence, moral guardian Mary Whitehouse meanwhile applauded the show for its lack of swearing.

CAST *William Bodie* Lewis Collins *Ray Doyle* Martin Shaw *George Cowley* Gordon Jackson /*cr* Brian Clemens /*exec pr* Brian Clemens, Albert Fennell /*dr* inc Douglas Camfield, Charles Crichton, Peter Medak, Pennant Roberts, Tom Clegg, Gerry O'Hara /*wr* Brian Clemens, Dennis Spooner, Ted Childs, Tony Barwick, Christopher Wickling, Roger Marshall /*mus* Laurie Johnson /*Avengers Mark I: LWT* (UK) /57 x 60m col.

The Protectors

Crime. ITV 1972–4

The Protectors: a worldwide, freelance crime-fighting team who hired out to whichever government, business or individual could afford them. American Harry Rule (Robert Vaughn, ➢*The Man From UNCLE*), Contessa di Contini (Nyree Dawn Porter, Irene in ➢*The Forsyte Saga*) and Frenchman Paul Buchet were the top agents.

Sub-Bond, mid-Atlantic schlock from ITC, with the, by now, de rigueur exotic locales, sleek cars, sleek women (Rule's karate-chopping au pair, Suki, woof woof), and buttressing by named guest stars. Mildly watchable. Gerry ➢'*Thunderbirds*' Anderson co-produced.

CAST *Harry Rule* Robert Vaughn *Contessa di Contini* Nyree Dawn Porter *Paul Buchet* Tony Anholt *Suki* Yasuko Nazagumi *Chino* Anthony Chinn /*cr* Lew Grade /*pr* Gerry Anderson, Reg Hill /*dr* inc Don Chaffey, Robert Vaughn, Charles Crichton, Michael Lindsay-Hogg, Don Leaver, Roy Ward Baker /*wr* inc Brian Clemens, Ralph Smart, Tony Barwick, Dennis Spooner, Terry Nation, John Kruse, Trevor Preston, Terence Feely, Sylvia Anderson, Anthony Terpiloff, Shane Rimmer, Robert Banks Stewart /*mus* John Cameron, Mitch Murray & Peter Callender ('Avenues and Alleyways' theme), Tony Christie (theme vocals) /*Group Three: ITC* (UK) /52 x 30m col /US tx Syndicated 1972.

Public Eye

Crime. ITV 1965–75

Featured private investigator Frank Marker, the prototype British TV seedy gumshoe (➢*Hazell*, ➢*Shoestring* and *Sharman* being his screen heirs), in lone, raincoated investigations of believably petty crimes. Blackmail, missing persons, thefts and divorce work were his staple. Initially, Marker (played by the suitably gaunt, bruised-looking Alfred Burke, ➢*The Borgias*) worked in London, but later transferred his business to Birmingham and Brighton. The 1968 episode 'Cross that Palm When we Come to It' found him imprisoned for possession of stolen jewellery.

CAST *Frank Marker* Alfred Burke *DI Firbank* Ray Smith *Ron Gash* Peter Childs *Helen Mortimer* Pauline Delany /*cr* Roger Marshall, Anthony Marriott /*exec pr* Lloyd Shirley, Robert Love /*pr* inc Robert Love, Richard Bates, Don Leaver, John Bryce, Kim Mills, Michael Chapman /*dr* inc Don Leaver, Kim Jonathan Alwyn, Guy Verney, Quentin Lawrence, Patrick Dromgoole, Douglas Camfield, Bill Bain /*wr* inc Roger Marshall, Robert Holmes, Julian Bond, Jack Trevor Story, Brian Finch, Richard Harris, Robert Banks Stewart /*mus* Robert Earley /*ABC: Thames TV* (UK) / 28 x 60m bw, 59 x 60m col.

The Pursuers

Crime. ITV 1961–2

➢*The Adventures of Rin Tin Tin* meets ➢*Fabian of the Yard.* Sometime Hollywood actor Louis Hayward starred as Scotland Yard DI Steve Bollinger who plodded the streets of London with his trusty canine, Ivan (a German shepherd dog), by his side. Edit-room tinkering notwithstanding, it was deficient in all departments and was put out if its – and the audience's – misery after 39 episodes.

CAST *DI Steve Bollinger* Louis Hayward *DS Steve Wall* Gaylord Cavallaro /*exec pr* Donald Hyde /*Crestview: ABC TV* (UK) /39 x 30m bw.

QB VII
Drama. BBC1 1975

Adaptation of Leon Uris' novel about an American author who accuses a Jewish doctor (Adam Kelno) of assisting medical crimes at a Nazi death camp. The doctor sues for libel.

Coined by Uris from his own experience – he had been taken to court in Britain by one Dr Wladislaw Dering for a derogatory reference in his tome *Exodus* – it was windily directed and scripted and mindfully ignored the complexities of history. Its importance lies in its format: transmitted in two chunks of 110m, it was one of the foundations of the erroneously termed 'mini-series'.

CAST inc Ben Gazzara, Anthony Hopkins, Leslie Caron, Lee Remick, Jack Hawkins /*pr* Douglas S. Cramer /*dr* Tom Gries /*wr* Edward Anhalt /*Douglas S. Cramer Co: Screen Gems* (USA) /2 x 110m col /US tx ABC 1974.

Quantum Leap
Sci-fi. BBC2 1990–4

Time-travel drama featuring Dr Sam Beckett as a scientist whose flawed experiment with a Quantum Leap accelerator doomed him to visit the bodies and lives of assorted 20th-century people (usually ordinary Joes and Josephines, but including Elvis Presley and Lee Harvey Oswald). Unlike previous time-journey heroes, Beckett was able, even required, to interfere in history to improve a person's lot. He was aided by rumpled guardian-angel hologram Al Calavicci (Dean Stockwell from *Paris Texas* and *Blue Velvet*), invisible to everyone but Sam, small children, pets and blondes. Nostalgically rummaging the more optimistic (and music-soundtrack friendly) decades, especially the 50s to 70s, it achieved trans-Atlantic cult status.

The show, created and produced by Don P. Bellisario (➢*Airwolf* amd ➢*Magnum PI*) ended with a disquieting last episode, 'Mirror Image', in which Sam materialized on the day of his birth and pontificated on his destiny with a Pennsylvania bartender whom he believed to be God.

CAST *Dr Sam Beckett* Scott Bakula *Al Calavicci ('The Observer')* Dean Stockwell /*cr* Don P. Bellisario /*pr* Don P. Bellisario, Deborah Pratt, Chris Ruppenthal, Tommy Thompson, John Hill, Harker Wade, Michael Zinberg, Charles Johnson /*dr* inc David Hemmings, Scott Bakula, Aaron Lipstadt, Alan J. Levi, Mark Sobel /*wr* inc Don P. Bellisario, Deborah Arakelian, Richard C. Okie /*mus* Velton Ray Brunch /*Bellisarius Productions* (USA) /2 x 90m, 95 x 50m col /US tx NBC 1989–93.

Quatermass
Sci-fi. BBC 1953–9

The foundation of British telefantasy. In 1953 the BBC spent its entire adult-drama budget (£250) on commissioning a script from Nigel Kneale, winner of the 1950 Somerset Maugham Prize for Literature. Their return was *The Quatermass Experiment*, an eerie and sensational story (6 x 30m bw) about a professional scientist of that name whose experimental spaceship returns to Earth with its sole occupant (Victor Caroon, played by Duncan Lamont) contaminated by an alien virus which subsequently transmutes him into a 100-foot vegetable. The serial, which played succinctly on contemporary fears about space travel, held the new TV nation agog.

But the success of *Quatermass* was due to more than Kneale's script; its production and direction – it was transmitted live – by Rudolph Cartier was pioneeringly brilliant, dispensing with the stagey theatricality of existing small-screen drama. In one of the first examples of special effects on TV, Caroon's alien look was achieved by covering a leather glove with bits of foliage and using a blown-up still of Westminster Abbey as background.

In *Quatermass II* (1955, 6 x 30m bw) Kneale and Cartier collaborated on a story in which Bernard Quatermass (now played by John Robinson) accidentally discovered a Martian plan to take over the world by infiltrating human minds. Eventually, Quatermass was able to prevent the invasion, although the upper classes proved particularly susceptible to the Martians' manoeuvres (a veiled criticism by Kneale of the British Establishment's past flirtations with fascism). The special effects were markedly superior, thanks to the recent creation of a BBC Visual Effects Department, headed by Bernard Wilkie and John Kine.

A third *Quatermass* serial from the team of Kneale and Cartier, *Quatermass and the Pit* (1958–9), was a cabalistic tale of the excavation of an ancient alien insect capsule in Knightsbridge, London, with Quatermass (Andre Morell) battling to prevent the reawakened influence of the Martians on the human race. A tense narrative, superbly filmed in chilling monochrome by A.A. Englander, was atmosphere-laden, with darkly weird noises from the fledgling BBC Radiophonic Workshop.

All three serials were later filmed by Hammer for theatrical release. In 1979 Kneale belatedly revived *Quatermass* for a Euston Films/Thames TV serial with Sir John Mills as the good professor.

CAST *Professor Bernard Quatermass* Reginald Tate (1953)/John Robinson (1955)/Andre Morell (1958–9) / *cr* Nigel Kneale /*pr* Rudolph Cartier /*dr* Rudolph Cartier /*wr* Nigel Kneale /*sfx* inc Bernard Wilkie, Jack Kine /*mus* inc Trevor Duncan /*BBC TV* (UK).

Queenie's Castle

Comedy. ITV 1970–2

Starred former starlet Diana Dors (aka the carefully pronounced Diana Fluck) as an iron-willed proletarian matriarch who ruled her family with the rough tongue of a fake Yorkshire brogue. They all lived unhappily in a block of council flats called The Buckingham, hence the royal title.

As bad as it sounds. Keith Waterhouse co-wrote, and future ➢*Coronation Street* star Lynne Perrie played the nosy neighbour. Dors later headed another Yorkshire TV sitcom, *All Our Yesterdays* (1973).

CAST *Queenie Shepherd* Diana Dors *Douglas Shepherd* Barrie Rutter *Bunny Shepherd* Brian Marshall *Raymond Shepherd* Freddie Fletcher *Jack* Tony Caunter *Mrs Petty* Lynne Perrie /*cr* Keith Waterhouse & Willis Hall /*pr* Graham Evans, Ian Davidson /*Yorkshire TV* (UK) /18 x 30m col.

The Quest

Western. BBC1 1976–7

Two reunited brothers roam the Wild West of the 1880s on the trail of their sister, abducted by the Cheyenne a decade before.

A lower-case *The Searchers.* Pretty photography, not-so-pretty violence. Developed from a 1976 TVM (100m produced by David Gerber) of the same title.

CAST *Morgan Beaudine ('Two Persons')* Kurt Russell *Quentin Beaudine* Tim Matheson /*cr* Tracy Keenan Wynn /*pr* Mark Rodgers, James H. Brown /*David Gerber Productions* (USA) /15 x 52m col /US tx NBC 1976.

Quick Draw McGraw

Children's. BBC 1960

Was a dense-headed horse saddled with the job of keeping the law out West. His Mexican sidekick, Deputy Baba Looey, could only close his eyes helplessly as McGraw trotted happily into catastrophe episode in and episode out.

Hugely successful – and enjoyable – cartoon from Hanna-Barbera, their second exclusively for the kiddie TV market (after ➢*The Huckleberry Hound Show*). Also featured in the package were cat and mouse *Snooper and Blabber* and canine father and son *Augie Doggie and Doggie Daddy.*

CAST *Quick Draw McGraw/Baba Looey/Injun Joe / Snooper/Blabber/Augie Doggie* Daws Butler *Sagebrush Sal* Julie Bennett *Doggie Daddy* Doug Young /*Hanna-Barbera* (USA) /135 x 30m col /US tx Syndicated 1959–62.

Quiller

Spy. BBC1 1975

Espionager based on Adam Hall's (aka Elleston Trevor) pulp 60s novel about a code-named fixer who worked for a deep-basement government agency, 'The Bureau'. Formula product, competently made.

CAST *Quiller* Michael Jayston, plus Sinead Cusack, Moray Watson /*pr* Peter Graham Scott /*BBC TV* (UK) / 13 x 50m col.

Quincy

Drama. ITV 1977–85

Dr R. Quincy was a widowed medical examiner with the Los Angeles County Coroner's Office. Stemming from the US *Mystery Movie* anthology, the series – known in the USA as *Quincy, ME* – began as a cops'n'robbers caper, with raucous-voiced Quincy essentially a pathologist who amateur-sleuthed, before subtly shifting genre so that all conundrums medical were put under his gruff crusading microscope. (Later episodes involved the medical examiner in problems of autistic children, an outbreak of botulism at a football game, and drug abuse.) Popular for his role in ➢*The Odd Couple*, Jack Klugman overcame this almost indelible viewer association to create a TV character even more beloved the globe over than Oscar Madison. Among the supporting cast were Robert Ito as the necessary sidekick assistant and Val Bisolglio as Quincy's boat-living friend Danny, the restaurateur owner of Danny's Place.

CAST *Quincy ME* Jack Klugman *Sam Fujiyama* Robert Ito *Danny Tovo* Val Bisoglio *Lt Frank Monahan* Garry Walberg *Lee Potter* Lynette Mettey *Dr Robert J. Asten* John S. Ragin /*cr* Glen A. Larson, Lou Shaw /*exec pr* Glen A. Larson /*pr* Lou Shaw, Peter Thompson, Michael Star, Robert F. O'Neil /*dr* inc E.W. Swackhamer, Paul Krasny, Ron Satlof, Daniel Petrie, Michael Vejar, Rod Holcomb /*wr* inc Jack Klugman /*Glen A. Larson Productions* (USA) / 5 x 120m, 143 x 60m col.

R

R3

Sci-fi. BBC1 1964–5

Set in Research Centre Number Three (thus *R3*), an invented agency belonging to HM Government, a low-key sci-fi series with the stated design 'to go beyond the laboratory door and into the daily background of a scientist's life'. Sir Michael Gerrard (John Robinson, ➢*Quatermass*) led the men and women in the white coats. Like ➢*Doomwatch* a decade later, it made a virtue of dramatizing contemporary scientific issues. A second season moved the camera to R3's elite unit, Consultancy Service, where the deputy was Dr Richard Franklin, played by a young Oliver Reed. Ridley Scott was among the series' set designers.

CAST *Sir Michael Gerrard* John Robinson *Dr May Howard* Elizabeth Sellars *Dr George Fratton* Moultrie Kelsall *Dr Jack Morton* Simon Lack *Tom Collis* Derek Benfield *Philip Boult* Michael Hawkins *Dr Richard Franklin* Oliver Reed /*cr* N.J. Crisp /*pr* Andrew Osborn, John Robins /*dr* inc Terence Williams, Moira Armstrong, Bill Hays /*wr* inc N.J. Crisp, Elaine Morgan, Bill MacIlwraith, Donald Bull, Julian Bond, Arden Winch /*mus* Ken Thorne /*BBC TV* (UK) / 26 x 50m bw.

Rab C. Nesbitt

Comedy. BBC2 1990–3

The string-vested Glasgow street philosopher made his debut in ➢*Naked Video* sketches before spinning off into a series (via a 1989 one-off, *Rab C. Nesbitt's Seasonal Greet*) which took the British sitcom into the unusual realm of grotesquerie.

Operating on a perptually full tank of alcohol, Nesbitt (a touching injured-warrior performance by Gregor Fisher, ➢*Para Handy – Master Mariner*) ranted in foul-mouthed Scots on life and (especially) the Establishment, in-between raucous squabbles with wife Mary and revolting kids Burney (Eric Cullen, d. 1996) and Gash. At least they were united in killing the rats – a frying pan being the weapon of choice – which infested their tenement kitchen. Also seen was Nesbitt's lugubrious drinking partner, Jamesie. Painfully, perceptively funny.

CAST *Rab C. Nesbitt* Gregor Fisher *Mary Nesbitt* Elaine C. Smith *Jamesie Cotter* Tony Roper *Gash Nesbitt* Andrew Fairlie *Burney Nesbitt* Eric Cullen / *pr* Colin Gilbert /*dr* Colin Gilbert /*wr* Ian Pattison / *BBC TV* (UK) /18 x 30m col.

The Racing Game

Crime. ITV 1979–80

Thriller series based on the stories of ex-royal jockey Dick Francis. On being semi-crippled in an accident, steeplechase jockey Sid Halley turns private investigator of crimes on the seamy side of the racing world. Since the doping/gambling fix/ horseknapping etc. was committed by villains straight from Baddies-R-Us, a solution was usually reached.

CAST *Sid Halley* Mike Gwilym *Chico Barnes* Mick Ford /*exec pr* David Cunliffe /*pr* Jacky Stoller /*wr* Trevor Preston, Terence Feely, Evan Jones, Leon Griffiths /*mus* Mike Moran /*Yorkshire TV* (UK) / 6 x 60m col /US tx WGBH Boston 1980–1.

Raffles

Crime. ITV 1977

E.W. Hornung's popular gentleman thief made his entrance in the 1899 novel *Raffles, The Amateur Cracksman*, progressing to the stage, Hollywood, and eventually, in 1975, TV. Anthony Valentine (➢*Colditz*) starred as the romantic hero, Christopher Strauli as his loyal chum (and ex-fag) Bunny, in both the 78m pilot, *Raffles – The Amateur Cracksman* (*dr* and *pr* Christopher Hodson), and the series – sourced mostly from Hornung's short yarns – which followed.

CAST *Raffles* Anthony Valentine *Bunny Manners* Christopher Strauli /*exec pr* David Cunliffe /*pr* Jacky Stoller /*dr* inc James Goddard /*wr* Philip Mackie / *Yorkshire TV* (UK) /13 x 50m col.

Rag, Tag and Bobtail

Children's. BBC 1953–5

The ever-so-tiny adventures of three animals who lived in an English wood: Rag the hedgehog, Tag the mouse and Bobtail the rabbit, all glove-puppets manipulated by the hands of Sam and Elizabeth Williams. Aired as the Thursday edition of ➢*Watch with Mother*, with each episode repeated no less than 30 times until the final showing in 1965. A classic.

CAST (narrators) Charles E. Stidwill, David Enders, James Urquhart /*pr* Freda Lingstrom, David Boisseau / *wr* Louise Cochrane /*BBC TV* (UK) /24 x 10m bw.

The Rag Trade

Comedy. BBC 1961–3

The East End workshop of Fenner Fashions was the setting for Wolfe and Chesney's situation comedy of workplace strife, much loved but clearly indebted to the cinema hit *I'm All Right Jack*. Militant machinist shop steward Paddy (Miriam Karlin, later the Paul A. Mendelson series *So Haunt Me*) led the work-shy women workers, with an ever-ready cry of 'Everybody Out!' (it became a national catchphrase), against the unscrupulous schemes of boss Mr Fenner. A not-inaccurate picture of shop-floor-life in the early 60s, it was assisted by an astral cast of heavenly configuration (in addition to Karlin, Reg Varney, Sheila Hancock, Peter Jones, Barbara Windsor) drawn from the West End. For a crudely misplaced revival by LWT (1977–8, 26 x 30m), only Karlin and Jones assumed their old roles; among the new faces on the factory-floor were Christopher Beeny, Anna Karen (➢*On the Buses*) and Gillian Taylforth (➢*EastEnders*).

CAST *Paddy* Miriam Karlin *Mr Fenner* Peter Jones *Reg* Reg Varney *Carole* Sheila Hancock *Little Lil* Esma Cannon *Judy* Barbara Windsor *Shirley* Wanda Wentham /*cr* Ronald Wolfe & Ronald Chesney /*pr* Dennis Main Wilson /*wr* Ronald Wolfe & Ronald Chesney /*BBC TV* (UK) /35 x 30m bw.

Rainbow

Children's. ITV 1971–92

Pre-schoolers show. Intended to be worthy, with three puppet characters – Zippy, pink hippo George, and Bungle the bear – as pretend kids in need of some education, stories and songs; alas, the threesome and their successive human stooges – David Cook and Geoffrey Hayes (formerly DC Scatliff in ➢*Z Cars*) – were so cornily, cuddily innocent that the only lesson generations of sophisticated toddlers learnt was the laughability of camp. After Thames lost its franchise in 1992, the show was revived as *Rainbow Days* in 1994.

CAST (presenters) David Cook, Geoffrey Hayes / *exec pr* Charles Warren, Alan Horrox /*pr* inc Pamela Lansdale, Vic Hughes, Lesley Burgess, Sheila Kinany, Paul Cole /*mus* inc Rod Burton, Matthew Corbett, Freddy Marks, Roger Walker /*Thames: HTV: Tetra* (UK) /approx. 1000 x 20m col.

Randall and Hopkirk (Deceased)

Crime. ITV 1969–70

'There's something different about this pair of private eyes ... one of them is dead'

Thus was trailed *Randall and Hopkirk (Deceased)*, a fantasy-comedy-crime oddballer in which PI Hopkirk (Kenneth Cope, previously: Sonny Jim in ➢*Coronation Street*; ➢*That Was The Week That Was*; the villain who shot Jack Warner in a 1956 ➢*Dixon of Dock Green*) returned from the dead to assist his partner as an immaculately white-suited spectre. Poor production values (in the first three episodes Hopkirk's toupee was back to front) were more than papered over by the ghostly gimmick and witty scripts. A regular fixture in rerun heaven. Known in the USA as *My Partner the Ghost*.

CAST *Jeff Randall* Mike Pratt *Marty Hopkirk* Kenneth Cope *Jean Hopkirk* Annette Andre /*cr* Dennis Spooner, Monty Berman /*pr* Monty Berman /*dr* Cyril Frankel, Ray Austin, Paul Dickson, Leslie Norman, Jeremy Summers, Roy Ward Baker, Robert Tronson /*wr* inc Ralph Smart, Mike Pratt & Ian Wilson, Tony Williamson, Gerald Kelsey /*ITC* (UK) /26 x 60m col / US tx Syndicated 1973.

The Range Rider
Western. BBC 1955

Featured muscular ex-stuntman Jock Mahoney as a mysterious buckskinned fighter for good (on a horse, of course, with a name, Lucky) on the American frontier of the 1860s. One-note plots and non-stop hard ridin' action, both introduced by the famed 'Home on the Range' theme, equalled 50s kiddie audience popularity.

CAST *The Range Rider* Jock Mahoney *Dick West* Dick Jones /*exec pr* Armand Schaefer /*pr* Louis Gray /*Flying A Prods* (USA) /76 x 25m bw /US tx Syndicated 1951–2.

Rawhide
Western. ITV 1961–6

'Rollin', rollin', rollin'...'

Like ➢*Wagon Train*, *Rawhide* was an oater on the move, a trans-West episodic odyssey. It featured events in the lives of a team on a meandering cattle drive from San Antonio, Texas, to Sedalia, Kansas, during the rugged 1860s. Most prominent of the trail crew were boss Gil Favor, ramrod second-in-command Rowdy Yates (Clint Eastwood in the role that brought him to the attention of spaghetti-Western director Sergio Leone, and hence astral luminescence), cantankerous cook Wishbone, scout Pete Nolan (country singer Sheb Wooley), and hands, Mushy, Quince and Simon Blake (Raymond St Jacques, aka James Arthur Johnson, the first black actor to appear regularly in a Western TV series). Contrary to myth, the crew did finish their original drive, but only to embark upon others, the constant travelling allowing people (i.e. guest stars) met along the way to tell their troubled tale.

Based on material from drover George Dutfield's 1866 diary, the series was developed for TV by Charles Marquis Warren (➢*The Virginian*) under the original title of *Cattle Drive*. Theme music and lyrics were by the Academy Award-winning (*High Noon*, 1952) firm of Dimitri Tiomkin and Ned Washington.

CAST *Gil Favor* Eric Fleming *Rowdy Yates* Clint Eastwood *Pete Nolan* Sheb Wooley *Wishbone* Paul Brinegar *Jim Quince* Steve Raines *Harkness 'Mushy' Musgrove* James Murdock *Hey Soos Patines* Robert Carbal *Joe Scarlett* Rocky Shahan *Simon Blake* Raymond St Jacques *Jed Colby* John Ireland /*cr* Charles Marquis Warren /*exec pr* Charles Marquis Warren / *pr* Vincent M. Fennelly, Bruce Geller, Bernard L. Kowalski, Endre Bohem /*dr* inc Charles Marquis Warren, Tay Garnett, Jack Arnold, Christian Nyby, Ted Post, Harry Harris, Andrew V. McLaglen, Gene L. Coon /*wr* inc Charles Marquis Warren, Clair Huffaker, Al Ward, Bernard Girard /*mus* Ned Washington & Dimitri Tiomkin (theme), Frankie Laine (theme vocals) /*CBS TV* (USA) /217 x 52m bw /US tx CBS 1959–66.

Rebecca
Drama. BBC1 1979

Daphne du Maurier's 1938 romantic classic about the naive second wife of a brooding Cornish landowner was first televised in a stage-bound 1947 BBC version (with Michael Hordern as Maxim De Winter). Thirty years later, the Corporation revisited Manderley Hall for a sepia-toned makeover with the late Jeremy Brett and Anna Massey leading the cast as brutal De Winter and menacing Mrs Danvers. Joanna David's pageboy hairstyle even set a fashion trend. Its intelligence was immediately signalled by the famous opener – 'Last night I dreamed I went to Manderley again...' – being spoken in conversation rather than delivered as a narratorly announcement.

The obsession of 90s TV programmers with period pieces meant that another *Rebecca* was a near-certainty, and thus it came to pass that Carlton filmed a 2 x 120m adaptation in 1997, with a cast including Charles Dance, Diana Rigg, Faye Dunaway and Geraldine James. Emilia Fox, coincidentally the daughter of Joanna David (and Edward Fox), played the new Mrs De Winter struggling against the images and memories of the first Rebecca. And yet all these pale in comparison with Hitchcock's 1940 spellbinding cinema classic, with Laurence Olivier and Joan Fontaine – heavenly configuration – in David O. Selznick's production.

CAST *Maxim De Winter* Jeremy Brett *Mrs De Winter* Joanna David *Mrs Danvers* Anna Massey *Favell* Julian Holloway /*pr* Richard Beynon /*dr* Simon Langton /*wr* Hugh Whitemore /*BBC TV* (UK) /3 x 50m col.

Record Breakers

Children's. BBC1 1972–

Juvenile TV version of the *Guinness Book of Records* (whose founders, Norris and Ross McWhirter, appeared in the early episodes), with most of the record-breaking antics taking place in the studio. Host for over 20 years, until his death in 1994, was the energetic Roy Castle (himself the holder of tap-dancing and parascending records, and singer of the 'You Need Dedication' theme), but the most intriguing presenter was Ron Reagan Jr, son of the US President, who reported on the tallest, smallest, greatest, etc., for a season Stateside.

CAST (presenters) inc Roy Castle, Ross McWhirter, Norris McWhirter, Cheryl Baker, Ron Reagan Jr, Kriss Akabusi, Mark Curry /*pr* Alan Russell, Eric Rowan, Greg Childs /*BBC TV* (UK) /approx. 500 x 30m col.

Redcap

Crime. ITV 1964–6

Starred John Thaw as Sergeant John Mann, a uniformed military policeman – 'redcap' in Army slang – as the Special Investigation Branch pursuing serious transgressions (murder, desertion, rape, etc.) by British troops from Cyprus to Borneo.

Studio-bound, though laudably original, ABC series which minted Thaw's persona as a grim faced detective.

CAST *Sgt John Mann* John Thaw /*cr* Jack Bell /*pr* John Bryce /*ABC Weekend Network Prod* (UK) /26 x 60m bw.

Red Dwarf

Sci-fi. BBC2 1988–

Space-age sitcom which originated as a Radio 4 *Son of Cliché* sketch before transferring to TV. In this incarnation, anti-hero slob Dave Lister was the sole survivor of a radiation leak aboard mining vessel *Red Dwarf*. Brought out of a three-million-year-long 'stasis' by ship's computer Holly, he was given company in the form of pompous hologram Rimmer (Chris Barrie, ➢*The Brittas Empire*, ➢*Spitting Image*). Also aboard was Cat, a narcissistic Little Richard-type dude who had evolved, in the hold, from Lister's pet feline. When Lister mislaid *Red Dwarf*, the intergalactic Young Ones were obliged to fly around in shuttle craft, *Starbug*. As with ➢*The Young Ones*, the humour – with its stream of curry and socks jokes, and 'smeg' expletives – was schoolboyishly scatological. Storylines, meanwhile, were sometimes suspiciously familiar (strange how writers Grant and Naylor had, in episode 'Backwards', the same time-reverse idea as expressed in *Counterclock World* by the sci-fi writer Philip K. Dick). Yet the show's chirpy enthusiasm was difficult to resist. It was also more serious than it initially appeared; Rimmer was a parody of Thatcher Man, and two of the shows from season four, 'Dimension Jump' and 'Meltdown', were held back by the BBC at the time of the Gulf conflict because of their anti-war content.

On its first voyages along the airwaves Red Dwarf bumped the bottom of the ratings (though it scored high in Audience Appreciation); the great lift upwards came with the more recognizable sci-fi situations and increase in production values of series three, which coincided with comedian Hattie Hayridge replacing Norman Lovett as Holly and the introduction of subservient android Kryten. In 1994 the show was awarded an International Emmy. After a break of three years (largely caused by co-creator Rob Grant jumping ship, and actor Craig Charles being tried – and cleared – of rape), the show was revived from TV stasis in 1997 to become BBC2's longest-running sitcom. In the interval, addicted fans had made it the Corporation's most popular series on video. Actress Chloe Annett (ex-➢*Byker Grove*) replaced ex-Altered Images singer Claire Grogan as recurring character Kochanski, Lister's unrequited (and initially hologrammic) love interest.

CAST *Dave Lister* Craig Charles *Arnold Rimmer* Chris Barrie *Cat* Danny John-Jules *Kryten* David Ross /Robert Llewellyn *Holly* Norman Lovett/Hattie Hayridge *Kochanski* Claire Grogan/Chloe Annett /*cr* Rob Grant & Doug Naylor /*pr* Ed Bye, Rob Grant, Doug Naylor, Hilary Bevan Jones /*dr* Ed Bye, Juliet May, Rob Grant, Doug Naylor /*wr* inc Rob Grant, Doug Naylor, Paul Alexander, James Hendries /*mus* Howard Goodall (theme) /*BBC TV: A Paul Jackson Production: Grant Naylor Productions* (UK) /42 x 30m col.

Reilly – Ace of Spies

Adventure. ITV 1983

Ripping-yarn adventures of Sidney Reilly, a British spy in early Bolshevik Russia. Derived (if colourfully) from the Robin Bruce Lockhart biography, expensively produced and tautly written by Troy Kennedy Martin. Worth catching, if only to see Kenneth Cranham as Lenin.

CAST *Sidney Reilly* Sam Neill *Bruce Lockhart* Ian Charleson *Margaret Reilly (née Thomas)* Jeananne Crowley *Fothergill* Peter Egan *Cummings* Norman Rodway *Dzerzhinsky* Tom Bell *Lenin* Kenneth Cranham *Basil Zaharov* Leo McKern *Insp. Tsientsin* David Suchet *Stalin* David Burke /*exec pr* Verity Lambert /*pr* Chris Burt /*dr* Jim Goddard, Martin Campbell /*wr* Troy Kennedy Martin /*Thames TV: Euston Films* (UK) /1 x 75m, 11 x 60m col.

Remington Steele

Crime. BBC1 1983–4/C4 1986–7

When LA private eye Laura Holt (Stephanie Zimbalist, daughter of ➢*77 Sunset Strip*'s Efrem) has trouble attracting clients because of her sex, she creates a fictitious male boss, Remington Steele. Lo, shortly afterwards a mysterious handsome stranger turns up claiming to be Remington Steele. Holt (somewhat improbably) makes him a partner, and together they cleverly solve cases, in-between flirting and reparteeing wittily.

Generally watchable, lighter-than-air detective comedy (if you closed your senses to the penchant for excruciatingly unfunny episode title puns, e.g. 'Thou Shalt Not Steele') though producer Glenn Gordon Caron somewhat improved the formula with ➢*Moonlighting*. The hint of substance underneath – the problems of a woman professional in a man's world – never came through. Its legacy, of course, was to make famous Pierce Brosnan, who eventually succeeded to the shoes of the big screen's 007.

CAST *Laura Holt* Stephanie Zimbalist *Remington Steele* Pierce Brosnan *Mildred Krebs* Doris Roberts *Bernice Foxe* Janet DeMay *Murphy Michaels* James Read /*cr* Michael Gleason, Robert Butler /*exec pr* Michael Gleason /*pr* Glenn Gordon Caron, Gareth Davies, Lee Zlotoff /*dr* inc Robert Butler, Seymour Robbie, Nick Havinga, Burt Brinckerhoff, Kevin Connor, Peter Medak, Don Weis /*wr* inc Michael Gleason, Lee Zlotoff, Glenn Gordon Caron, Jeff Melvoin, Susan Baskin /*mus* Henry Mancini, Richard Lewis Warren /*An MTM Production* (USA) /72 x 60m col /US tx NBC 1982–7.

Ren & Stimpy

Children's. Sky1 1991–

Launched on US cable TV kids' channel Nickleodeon as part of its promotion of original creator-based animations, ➢*Ren & Stimpy* featured the irritable, nuclear-fried chihuahua (with cod-Pancho voice, sample: 'You Eeee-diot') and stupid fat cat of those names, together with an avalanche of knowing lateral jokes, surreal graphics and gross-out violence. And bodily functions. In one memorable, but not untypical, example the pair escaped from a dog pound after Stimpy sicked up furballs to stick on Ren to disguise him as a poodle. The show also bit the hand that fed it and viciously satirized junior TV, seen best in its spoof toy advertisments.

Educationalists issued dire warnings, but what the heck, it made great TV – for adults. Understanding that *R&S* was lost on youth, most channels which took the show also screened it at an hour which saved the over-sevens having to arise disgustingly early. Flattery came in the form of imitations from other TV companies, including Disney's *Schnooky and Meetums* and Hanna-Barbera's *Two Stupid Dogs*.

It was too good to last. Eventually, Nickelodeon dispensed with creator Kricfalusi's services (either because of his inability to meet deadlines, or because the product, especially the obviously homo-erotic relationship between Ren & Stimpy, was proving too controversial) and lesser men and women took the cartoon's helm.

CAST (voices) *Ren Hoek* John Kricfalusi (aka John K) / Bob Camp *Stimpson J 'Stimpy' Cat* Billy West /*cr* John Kricfalusi /*exec pr* Vanessa Coffey /*pr* John Kricfalusi, Bob Camp, Jim Smith, Jim Ballentine, Frank Sapperstein /*dr* inc John Kricfalusi, Bob Camp, Vincent Waller, Greg Vanzo /*wr* inc John Kricfalusi, Bob Camp, Vincent Waller, Jim Smith, Will McRobb, Bill Wray, Jim Gomez, Elinor Blake, Richard Purcel / *Spumco: Carbunkle* (USA) /40 x 25m col /US tx Nickelodeon 1991–.

Revelations

Melodrama. ITV 1994–

Outrageously kitsch late-night soap following the shenanigans of Anglican Bishop Edward Rattigan and his lust/drug/alcohol/dark secrets-sodden family. Surreally wooden (in the ➢*Crossroads* manner), strangely devoid of background music, cultishly compulsive, it debuted in ITV regions before satellite screening by Sky1.

CAST *Bishop Edward Rattigan* Paul Shelley *Jessica Rattigan* Judy Loe *Gabriel Rattigan* Stephen Mapes *Mary Beckett* Carole Nimmons *Mark* Matthew Radford /*pr* Anthony Wood /*dr* inc Kay Patrick /*wr* inc Russell T. Davies /*Granada: Central: Carlton* (UK) / 42+ x 30m col.

Rhoda

Comedy. BBC2 1974–80

The character of Rhoda first appeared as the overweight, over-anxious neighbour on ➢*The Mary Tyler Moore Show* before being slimmed down, made more obviously Jewish, and given an occupation as a window dresser and a series of her own. She was also relocated to New York, where she initially lived with her parents, Ida and Martin, before moving in with her dowdy sister Brenda (played by Julie Kavner, later the voice of Marge in ➢*The Simpsons*). A marriage to Joe Gerard, owner of the New York Wrecking Company, fell quickly asunder, largely because the scriptwriters decided that the abrasive but vulnerable Rhoda (an Emmy-winning portrayal by Valerie Harper) worked comically best as a neurotic single gal. In Britain the show was first aired in BBC2's 'Yankee Treble' slot in autumn 1974.

CAST *Rhoda Morgenstern Gerard* Valerie Harper *Brenda Morgenstern* Julie Kavner *Ida Morgenstern* Nancy Walker *Martin Morgenstern* Harold J. Gould *Joe Gerard* David Groh *Gary Levy* Ron Silver *Carlton, the doorman* (voice) Lorenzo Music /*cr* James L. Brooks, Allan Burns /*exec pr* James L. Brooks, Allan Burns /*pr* Lorenzo Music, David Davis, Charlotte Brown /*dr* inc James Burrows, Charlotte Brown, Bob Claver, Howard Storm, Alan Rafkin, Joan Darling /*mus* Billy Godenburg /*MTM* (USA) /110 x 25m col /US tx CBS 1974–8.

Richard Strauss (right) and Nick Nolte were *Rich Man, Poor Man*, a star-studded mega-hit which caused a 70s spate of mini-series based on block-buster novels.

Richard the Lionheart

Adventure. ITV 1962–3.

On learning of the death of his father, good King Richard returns from the chain-mailed Crusades to prevent bad Prince John from usurping the throne of England.

Middling period swashbuckler, from the time when TV executives thought of little else.

CAST *Prince /King Richard* Dermot Welsh *Prince John* Trader Faulkner *Blondel* Ian Gregory *Sir Gilbert* Robin Hunter *Lady Berengaria* Sheila Whittington /*pr* Edward J. Danziger, Harry Lee Danziger /*Danziger Productions* (UK) /39 x 25m bw.

Rich Man, Poor Man

Melodrama. ITV 1976

Adapted from Irwin Shaw's 1970 blockbuster, the fabulous saga of the Jordache boys as they escaped from their stifling American small town at the end of WWII, to 1965 by which time Rudy had become a successful politician and Tom (a then-unknown Nick Nolte) a trouble-hungry boxer. Julie Prescott was the love of both brothers' life (though seduced on a lazy afternoon by daiquiri-plying Teddy Boylan). A star-spangled parade of actors trooped the 12 episodes as rivals, buddies and romantic entanglements. In its time it was a TV spectacle and caused a rush of novel-sourced mini-series plus two sequels, *Rich Man, Poor Man – Book II* (1976–7) and *Beggar Man, Thief* (1978, which introduced the Jordache's previously unmentioned sister, Gretchen).

CAST *Rudy Jordache* Peter Strauss *Tom Jordache* Nick Nolte *Axel Jordache* Ed Asner *Mary Jordache* Dorothy McGuire *Julie Prescott/Abbott/Jordache* Susan Blakely *Duncan Calderwood* Ray Milland *Willie Abbott* Bill Bixby *Teddy Boylan* Robert Reed *Teresa Sanjoro* Talia Shire *Joey Quayles* George Maharis /*exec pr* Harve Bennett /*pr* Jon Epstein /*dr* David Greene, Boris Sagal / *wr* Dean Reisner /*mus* Alex North /*Universal TV* (USA) /12 x 60m col /US tx ABC 1976.

Riders

Melodrama. ITV 1993

Wink, wink, double-entendre title for jolly super Jilly Cooper's adaptation of her own bonkbuster about shagging amongst the horsey set. The story, such as it was, concerned the equestrian rivalry between caddish upper-class Rupert Campbell-Black and swarthy lower-class Jake Lovell. Mostly, though, the camera stayed voyeuristically in bed.

There were criticisms that the characters were hollow and their lines cringingly awful ('...you have such marvellous hair. It's the colour of drenched fox') which rather missed *Riders*' singular credit: it was an almost documentary-like record of the braying classes at play.

CAST *Rupert Campbell-Black* Marcus Gilbert *Jake Lovell* Michael Praed /*dr* Gabriel Beaumont /*Anglia* (UK) /4 x 60m col.

Rides

Drama. BBC1 1992–3

A rare BBC excursion into feminist drama, focusing on a women-only minicab firm in Dalston, London. Head of the firm was disillusioned, fortysomething, ex-soldier, Patricia Jenner (Jill Baker), with an ex-teacher (Louise Jameson, ➢*Doctor Who*), a pushy freelance journo, daffy 'resting' actress and an Irish hardnut with troublesome kids among her human-flotsam crew. Underneath the heavy-handed pushes of the viewers' nose into women's troubles and society's difficulties, was an appealing, Carla Lane-esque humour and warmth. Worth the fare. Dreamed up by actress-writer-director Carole Hayman.

CAST Jill Baker, Louise Jameson, Katherine Schlesinger, Erica Grant, Lynda Steadman, Trevor Byfield /*cr* Carole Hayman /*pr* Frances Heasman /*dr* Andrew Morgan, Diana Patrick /*wr* Carole Hayman / *Warner Sisters* (UK) /12 x 50m col.

The Riff Raff Element

Comedy. BBC1 1993–4

Debbie Horsfield (➢*Making Out*) drama which moved the proletarian Belcher clan into the servants' quarters of the aristo Tundish family for an offbeat comedy of the classes. Adulterous pregnancy and murder were among the blackly funny consequences of some strange liaisons and allegiances at crumbling Tundish Hall. Critically acclaimed, largely unwatched

CAST *Ambassador Roger Tundish* Ronald Pickup *Joanna Tundish* Celia Imrie *Mortimer Tundish* Richard Hope *Boyd Tundish* Nicholas Farrell *Carmen Belcher* Jayne Ashbourne *Declan Belcher* Cal Macaninch *Petula Belcher* Mossie Smith *Acky Belcher* Trevor Peacock *Alister* Greg Wise *Vincent* George Costigan /*cr* Debbie Horsfield /*pr* Liz Trubridge /*wr* Debbie Horsfield / *BBC TV* (UK) /12 x 50m col.

The Rifleman

Western. BBC 1959–63

The sagebrush saga of widowed homesteader Lucas McCain (hard-faced former baseball pro Chuck Connors, later ➢*Branded*) as he tried to make a living off his ranch and a man out of his boy, Mark (Johnny Crawford, brother of ➢*Laramie*'s Bobby Crawford). The setting was North Fork, New Mexico, the marshal of which was incapable of dealing with the local desperadoes and was thus obliged to call on the services of Lucas McCain and his modified, fast-firing .40–44 Winchester rifle. Initially popular, the series began to slip in its third season, not least because the rifleman's somewhat righteous tone grated too long on the viewers' sensibilities.

Developed from a 1958 episode ('The Sharpshooter') of *Dick Powell's Zane Grey Theatre*, this intermittently exciting show was the creation of the legendary movie director, Sam Peckinpah (though not of the same deeply textured quality as his other gift to TV, *The Westerner*), who also helmed many of the early – and better – *Rifleman* episodes. Michael Ansara's Indian lawman character, Sam Buckhart, was spun off into another successful oater show, *Law of the Plainsman.*

CAST *Lucas McCain* Chuck Connors *Mark McCain* Johnny Crawford *Marshal Micah* Paul Fix /*cr* Sam Peckinpah /*pr* Sam Peckinpah, Jules Levy, Arnold Laven, Arthur Gardner /*dr* inc Sam Peckinpah /*mus* Hershel Burke Gilbert /*Four Star: Sussex Productions* (USA) /168 x 25m col /US tx ABC 1958–63.

Ripcord

Adventure. BBC1 1964–5

Action-filled series featuring clean-cut Ted McKeever and Jim Buckley, the all sky-diving, crime-fighting proprietors of Ripcord Inc.

Pure corn, strangely bewitching to 60s children.

CAST *Ted McKeever* Larry Pennell *Jim Buckley* Ken Curtis *Chick Lambert* Paul Comi *Charlie Kern* Shug Fisher /*exec pr* Ivan Tors /*pr* Maurice Unger, Leon Benson /*United Artists* (USA) /76 x 25m bw.

Ripping Yarns

Comedy. BBC2 1977–9

Hilariously irreverent parodies of Victorian Edwardian *Boy's Own* literature from ex-*Monty Pythons*, (➢*Monty Python's Flying Circus*) Michael Palin and Terry Jones. A 1976 one-off, *Tompkinson's Schooldays* (BBC2), inaugurated the series, which presented such exhuberant dottiness as stiff-upper-lipped heroes (British, of course, what?) crossing the Andes by frog and escaping from the frightfully secure Stalag Luft 112B. And no matter the milieu, the period detail was spot on. Awarded a BAFTA for light entertainment.

CAST Michael Palin /*pr* Alan J.W. Bell /*dr* Terry Hughes, Alan J.W. Bell, Jim Franklin /*wr* Michael Palin, Terry Jones /*BBC TV* (UK) /9 x 30m col.

Rising Damp

Comedy. ITV 1974–8

Originally a stage show called *Banana Box*, Eric Chappell's masterly series about a sneering, conniving landlord, Rigsby, and his seedy boarding house was one of ITV's few quality comedy hits in the 70s. Almost as obnoxious – and immortal – a character as the elder Steptoe or Alf Garnett, the arms-folded, tongue-flicking, 'My-y-y God'-uttering Rigsby (dressed always in sleeveless cardigan) lusted ceaselessly after his one female boarder, spinster Miss Ruth Jones, and endlessly battled with his two male boarders, effete medical student Alan, and scion of an African chief Philip. Rigsby's snide manner was perfectly evidenced in the first episode when the fashionably barneted Alan defended himself saying, 'Jesus had long hair.' 'Yes,' replied Rigsby, 'but I bet he never had a hairdryer.' The series was compelling, not only for such one-liners, but also for its acting – especially former insurance salesman Rossiter's awesome comic timing – and its pure distillation of the experience of life in 'rented digs'.

Of the TV cast only Richard Beckinsale (➢*The Lovers*, ➢*Porridge*) did not appear in the original stage play. A film version was released in 1980 by ITC /Black Lion.

CAST *Rigsby* Leonard Rossiter *Philip* Don Warrington *Alan* Richard Beckinsale *Miss Jones* Frances de la Tour *Spooner* Derek Newark *Brenda* Gay Rose /*cr* Eric Chappell /*pr* inc Vernon Lawrence /*dr* Vernon Lawrence, Ronnie Baxter, Len Lurcuck, Ian MacNaughton /*wr* Eric Chappell /*Yorkshire TV* (UK) /28 x 30m col.

The Rivals of Sherlock Holmes

Crime. ITV 1971–3

Gaslight crime anthology featuring Sherlock Holmes' contemporaries. Such 'tecs as R. Austin Freeman's Dr Thorndyke, Ernest Bramah's blind Max Carrados, E. Phillip Oppenheim's Laxworthy, Palle Rosenkrantz's Danish policeman Holst (portrayed by John Thaw), and William Le Queux's William Drew (Derek Jacobi) were presented, usually dependably, in suitably Victorian atmosphere-drenched self-contained cases. Based on the collection of stories compiled by Sir Hugh Greene, sometime Director General of the BBC.

exec pr Lloyd Shirley, Kim Mills /*pr* Robert Love, Jonathan Alwyn, Reginald Collin /*mus* Bob Sharples / *Thames TV* (UK) /26 x 60m col.

The River

Comedy. BBC1 1988

Popster David Essex starred as Davey Jackson, a cockney wideboy (regulation sitcom chirpy issue) who fancied the quiet life as a canal lock-keeper at Chumley-on-the-Water. A brief encounter with broken-propellered Scots bargee Sarah MacDonald led to love in Jackson's rustic cottage, despite the worst efforts of his frowning Marxist Aunt. Also seen was the local Colonel Blimp, Jackson's assistant Tom, and Jim, the supine landlord of The Ferret. To no great surprise, a second season was not commissioned.

CAST *Davey Jackson* David Essex *Sarah MacDonald* Kate Murphy *Aunt Betty* Vilma Hollingberry *Col. Danvers* David Ryall *Tom Pike* Shaun Scott /*cr* Michael Aitkin /*pr* Susan Belbin /*wr* Michael Aitkin /*mus* David Essex (theme) /*BBC TV* (UK) /6 x 30m col.

Riverboat

Western. ITV 1960

Wild West adventure series set aboard a cargo sternwheeler, *The Enterprise*, plying its trade along the Missippi–Ohio rivers during the 1840s. The captain-owner was former rum-runner and soldier Grey Holden (Darren McGavin, later ➢*Kolchak: The Night Stalker*), who won the boat in a poker game. All the romance and dangers of the river life were played on in this something-different Western, heralded by Elmer Bernstein's magnificent score. Burt Reynolds – in his career break – took the wheel as orphan pilot Ben Frazer for most of the first season, to be replaced as co-lead by Noah Beery (➢*Circus Boy*, ➢*The Rockford Files*) thereafter.

CAST *Grey Holden* Darren McGavin *Ben Frazer* Burt Reynolds *Bill Blake* Noah Beery Jr *Travis* William D. Gordon /*pr* Jules Bricken /*mus* Elmer Bernstein / *Meladre Company* (USA) /44 x 52m col /US tx NBC 1960–1.

Riviera Police

Crime. ITV 1965

Four police detectives on the sun-scorched Côte d'Azur *chattez up les femmes sur la plage* in-between *cherchez les villains.*

The clunker title was a fair clue to a contrivedly glamorous product (from the British Associated-Rediffusion company), ineptly executed. One hundred per cent lead.

CAST *Lt Col. Sorel* Frank Lieberman *Insp. Le Grand* Brian Spink *Supt Adam Hunter* Geoffrey Frederick *Supt Bernie Johnson* Noel Trevarthen /*pr* Jordan Lawrence /*mus* Laurie Johnson /*Associated-Rediffusion* (UK) /13 x 60m bw.

Robin of Sherwood

Adventure. ITV 1984–6

Inspired longbow-and-magic version of the Greenwood legend from Richard Carpenter (➢*Catweazle*) and HTV's golden age of adventure TV. On the destruction of his home by Norman soldiers, a revengful 12th-century Robin of Loxley (Michael Praed) is endowed by an incarnation of Herne the Hunter with Albion, one of the seven swords of Wayland. Thus equipped, Robin dons a disguise to become 'Robin in the Hood', joined in his heroic Saxon fray against the Norman oppressor by Maid Marion and the usual stalwarts, plus the Carpenter-created deadly Saracen, Nasir. A far arrow-shot from the usual Merry Men light-actioner (epitomized by the Errol Flynn *Adventures of Robin Hood*, 1938), the series plunged through two seasons of pagan-drenched atmosphere, intriguing characters (none more so than Ray Winstone's psychopathic Will Scarlet and Nickolas Grace's delightfully politicking Sheriff of Nottingham) and clean-limbed action until Robin met a hero's death on a lone hilltop in 'The Greatest Enemy'. His rebel spirit, however, was resurrected in the body of Robert of Huntington (played by Jason Connery, son of Sean) who led the outlaw-band for a series of valedictory romping through the green-leaved beauty of Sherwood Forest. Clannad supplied the BAFTA-winning soundtrack.

CAST *Robin of Loxley* Michael Praed *Will Scarlet* Ray Winstone *Little John* Clive Mantle *Maid Marion* Judi Trott *Much* Peter Llewellyn-Williams *Friar Tuck* Phil Rose *Nasir* Mark Ryan *Sheriff of Nottingham* Nickolas

Grace *Guy of Gisburne* Robert Addie *Gulnar* Richard O'Brien *Baron Simon de Belleme* Anthony Valentine *Sir Richard of Leafad* George Baker *Robert of Huntington* Jason Connery /*cr* Richard Carpenter /*exec pr* Patrick Dromgoole /*pr* Paul Knight, Esta Charkham /*dr* inc James Allen, Ben Bolt, Dennis Abbey, Alex Kirby /*wr* inc Richard Carpenter, Anthony Horowitz /*mus* Clannad (theme) /*HTV: Goldcrest* (UK) /2 x 100m, 22 x 50m col.

Robin's Nest

Comedy. ITV 1977–81

Spin-off from ➢*Man About the House* in which Robin Tripp qualifies as a chef, moves into a Notting Hill pad with air-hostess girlfriend Vicky Nicholls (Tessa Wyatt, ex-wife of Radio 1 DJ Tony Blackburn) and opens the eponymous bistro. To hinder him comically in this endeavour are one-armed washer-upper Albert Riddle and Vicky's interfering father, James. Predictable, thus easily digestible, Mortimer and Cooke sitcom which topped the ratings in 1978.

CAST *Robin Tripp* Richard O'Sullivan *Vicky Nicholls* Tessa Wyatt *James Nicholls* Tony Britton *Marion Nicholls* Honor Blackman/Barbara Murray *Albert Riddle* David Kelly *Gertrude* Peggy Aitchison /*cr* Johnnie Mortimer & Brian Cooke /*pr* Peter Frazer-Jones /*wr* inc Johnnie Mortimer & Brian Cooke, George Layton, Adele Rose /*Thames TV* (UK) /36 x 30m col.

Robocop

Sci-fi. Sky1 1995

Short-lived spin-off from the 1987 Paul Verhoeven film of the same title. Followed cyborg cop Murphy on his futuristic Detroit beat, with Detective Lisa Madigan as the sidekick and orphan Gadget as the old TV reliable, the cute kid. An amiable vein of pop satire was evident through the predictable, formulaic action stories.

CAST *Murphy* Richard Eden *Det. Lisa Madigan* Yvette Nipar *Gadget* Sarah Campbell /*exec pr* Stephen Downing /*pr* J. Miles Dale /*Skyvision Entertainment: Rysher Entertainment* (USA) /1 x 120m, 22 x 50m col / US tx Syndicated 1994.

Rock Follies

Drama. ITV 1976

The pop life: it's different for girls. Such was the premise of Howard Schuman's 70s musical drama about a three-girl rock group, The Little Ladies, gigging the pub–club circuit with glitzy dreams (shown in fantasy sequences derived by the American Schumann from the Busby Berkeley 30s extravaganzas) of making it big. Meanwhile, they suffered rip-off managers, bankers, publishers and A & R men. Original music was by guitarist Andy Mackay of Roxy Music. It won a 1977 BAFTA for Best Drama Series, earned a sequel, *Rock Follies of 77* (with the addition of Beth Porter as American agent Kitty Schreiber to the cast), but became somewhat tarnished when three actresses, who sang together as Rock Bottom, brought a £500,000 plagiarism suit.

CAST *Anna Ward* Charlotte Cornwell *Nancy 'Q' Cunard de Longchamps* Rula Lenska *Devonia 'Dee' Rhoades* Julie Covington *Derek Huggin (manager)* Emlyn Price /*cr* Howard Schuman /*exec pr* Verity Lambert /*pr* Andrew Brown /*dr* Brian Farnham, Jon Schofield /*wr* Howard Schuman /*mus* Andy Mackay, Howard Schuman (lyrics) /*Thames TV* (UK) /6 x 60m col.

The Rockford Files

Crime. BBC1 1975–82

Chandleresque TV private-eye show featuring James Garner (James Baumgarner, winner of two Purple Hearts in the Korean War) as Jim Rockford, only and eponymous operative of LA's Rockford Detective Agency. From a beachfront trailer (where the answerphone famously played over the opening of every *File*, 'This is Jim Rockford. At the tone, leave your name and message. I'll get back to you.'). Rockford set forth in his Gold Pontiac Firebird on the $200-a-day-plus-expenses cases, usually fallen into by accident. Despite an aversion to violence (he kept his gun in a biscuit barrel) and the LAPD (he had once been wrongly imprisoned in San Quentin), nearly every episode involved him being beaten to a pulp by enormous heavies or landing in jail-type schtuck from which he needed to be rescued by attorney girlfriend Beth Davenport. Not infrequently, Rockford was led astray by former cellmate Angel Martin, a half-baked petty criminal (Stuart Margolin in double Emmy-winning stuff); the PI's other less-than-upright

James Garner (right) as the conniving anti-hero of PI show *The Rockford Files*. Eventually Garner was forced to quit the role, having severely damaged his legs doing six seasons of his own stuntwork.

acquaintances included disbarred lawyer John Cooper and tough guy Gandy Fitch (Isaac 'Shaft' Hayes). Rockford's retired truck-driving father 'Rocky' (veteran character actor Noah Beery Jr, ➢*Circus Boy*) constantly badgered his boy to taken up a safer line of work. Yet, it is often forgotten that Rockford was a good detective, even if he employed conniving means (he carried a portable press in his car to print fake ID cards) as much as ratiocinative ones.

Superbly acted by Garner – as confirmed by a 1977 Lead Actor Emmy – with more than a nod to his earlier role as ➢*Maverick* (likewise created by Roy Huggins), atmospherically filmed in cynical washed-out colour and with literate teleplays, it is to be counted as one of the finest TV crime shows ever made. A final-season appearance by Tom Selleck as irritatingly perfect private eye Lance White led to a worthy heir in ➢*Magnum PI*.

CAST *Jim Rockford* James Garner *Joseph 'Rocky' Rockford* Noah Beery Jr *Sgt Dennis Becker* Joe Santos *Beth Davenport* Gretchen Corbett *Evelyn 'Angel' Martin* Stuart Margolin *John Cooper* Bo Hopkins *Gandy Fitch* Isaac Hayes /*cr* Roy Huggins, Stephen J. Cannell /*exec pr* Stephen J. Cannell, Meta Rosenberg / *pr* Juanita Bartlett, David Chase, Charles Floyd Johnson, Lane Slate /*dr* inc Stephen J. Cannell, James Garner, Stuart Margolin, Corey Allen, Lou Antonio, Dana Elcar, James Coburn, Winrich Kolbe, Jeannot Swarc, Russ Mayberry, Bruce Kessler, William Wiard, Joseph Pevney, Reza S. Badiyi /*wr* inc Stephen J. Cannell, John Thomas James (aka Huggins), Juanita Bartlett, Robert Hamner, Edward J. Lasko /*Roy Huggins-Public Arts: Cherokee Productions: Universal TV* (USA) /114 x 60m col /US tx NBC 1974–80.

Rocky and Bullwinkle

Children's. Nickelodeon 1996

Classic toon of America's yesteryear, featuring flying squirrel Rocky and his dim-witted moose friend, Bullwinkle, in a serialized spoof spy-chase of evil nemesis Boris Badenov and his assistant, Natasha Fatale. Narrated in thunderous hyperbole by William Conrad (later ➢*Cannon*), loaded with cultural in-jokes (Boris Badenov was a name-play on Moussorgsky's operatic hero, Boris Gudunov) and droll barbs about the Eisenhower Cold War/Hot Consumerism era, it became only the second animation to be networked in the USA (after ➢*The Flintstones*). Developed from Jay Ward's earlier show, *Crusader Rabbit*, it aired in

Cicely Tyson as Binta in *Roots*, an epic about slavery which gathered nearly half the American nation around the TV set for its concluding episode.

expanded form as *The Bullwinkle Show* from 1961, later rerunning as *The Rocky and Bullwinkle Show*. Other animated segments seen in the package were *Fractured Fairytales, Aesop and Son, Peabody Improbable History, Dudley Do-Right* (a wacky Mountie of much hygiene but no brain in is attempted apprehensions of villianous Snidley Whiplash) and *Mr Know It All.*

CAST (voices) *narrator* William Conrad *Rocky / Natasha Fatale* June Foray *Bullwinkle Moose/Dudley Do-Right* Bill Scott *Boris Badenov* Paul Frees *Aesop /Aesop Narrator* Charles Ruggles *Aesop Jr* Daws Butler *narrator Fractured Fairy Tales* Edward Everett Horton / *cr* Jay Ward /*pr* Jay Ward, Bill Scott /*dr* inc Bill Hurtz, Ted Parmalee, Lew Keller, Pete Burness /*wr* inc Al Burns, Chris Hayward, Lloyd Turner /*mus* Fred Steiner, George Steiner, Frank Comstock, Dennis Farnon /*Jay Ward Productions: Producers Associates of Television* (USA) /approx. 183 x 30m col /US tx ABC 1959–1961, NBC 1961–4.

Roobarb and Custard

Children's. BBC1 1974

Inspired animation from Oscar-winner Bob Godfrey featuring a green dog, Roobarb, and a bright pink cat, Custard, in a relationship of never-ending rivalry. Drawn in low-budget magic-marker on paper (instead of the traditional acetate cell method) it birthed a distinctive wobbly visual style, much copied since. Johnny Hawksworth, of the Ted Heath band, composed and performed the perfectly complimentary twangy guitar music.

CAST (narrator) Richard Briers /*cr* Grange Caveley /*pr* Bob Godfrey /*dr* Bob Godfrey /*wr* Grange Caveley / *mus* Johnny Hawksworth /*Bob Godfrey's Movie Emporium* (UK) /30 x 5m col.

Roots

Drama. BBC1 1977

Landmark TV mini-series, based on Alex Haley's novel *Roots*, chronicling the history of a black family: it began with the birth of Kunta Kinte (LeVar Burton, later beamed up to ➢*Star Trek TNG*) in 1700s Gambia, through his capture by slavers and shipment to America; then on via the story of his daughter Kizzy (raped by a white plantation owner) and her son, Chicken George, to end with Kunta Kinte's grandson, Tom Harvey, and the emancipation of the slaves in post-Civil War USA. In America 85 per cent of TV households tuned in, a phenomenon all the more remarkable for the fact that the scripts were average, the direction of jobbing sort (though this at least avoided pretension) and, as a version of history, it was dubiously sensational. Yet its epic subject matter also touched the guilty heart of American society and gave it a mass catharsis via the tube. And even in the longeurs, there was always another famous face to spot, none more intriguing than O.J. Simpson lamming it through the African bush.

A 14-hour sequel, *Roots: The Next Generation* (1979), continued the chronicle of Kunte Kinte's descendants, from Reconstruction to modern times, with James Earl Jones playing author Alex Haley himself.

CAST *Kunte Kinte (slave name: 'Toby')* LeVar Burton /John Amos *Chicken George Moore* Ben Vereen *Fiddler* Louis Gossett Jr *Binta* Cicely Tyson *Kizzy* Leslie Uggams *Capt. Davies* Edward Asner *John Reynolds* Lorne Greene *Tom Moore* Chuck Connors *Evan Brent* Lloyd Bridges *Sam Bennett* Richard Roundtree *Tom Harvey* Georg Stanford Brown *Irene Harvey* Lynne Moody *Ames* Vic Morrow *Dr William Reynolds* Robert Reed *Kadi Touray* O.J. Simpson *Nyo Boto* Maya Angelou *Sir Ian Russell* Ian McShane /*exec pr* David L. Wolper /*pr* Stan Margulies /*dr* Marvin Chomsky, David Greene, Gilbert Moses, John Erman /*wr* William Blinn, Ernest Kinoy, James Lee, Max Cohen / *mus* Quincy Jones, Gerald Fried /*David L. Wolper Productions* (USA) /4 x 120m, 4 x 60m col /US tx ABC 1977.

Roots

Comedy. ATV 1981

Sitcom about a Jewish dentist who decides to throw over his career to become an artist. As enjoyable as an extraction without anaesthetic, and a rare failure for Marks and Gran. Lesley Joseph (later ➢*Birds of a Feather*) played the counterpoint reliable sister.

CAST *Melvin Solomons* Allan Corduner *Harry Solomons* Stanley Meadows *Nettie Solomons* Joy Shelton *Melanie Goldblatt* Lesley Joseph /*cr* Laurence Marks & Maurice Gran /*pr* Keith Farthing /*wr* Laurence Marks & Maurice Gran /*ATV* (UK) / 6 x 30m col.

Roseanne

Comedy. C4 1989–97

Blue-collar comedy about a caustic and corpulent mother, Roseanne Conner, set in the Illinois town of Lanford. The rest of the clan were: equally large husband Dan (John Goodman, destined to become a movie star), variously a dry-waller and motocycle repairer; small son DJ; cynical Darlene; and precocious boy-mad Becky. Jackie was Roseanne's frequently seen sister. A rare instant success, the series was created by Jewish waitress-turned-comic Roseanne Barr and developed from her irreverent stand-up routine about family life. (Barr recycled her waitress past with a show storyline in which Roseanne co-ran a diner, The Lunch Box.) Aside from the regular cast, those appearing in *Roseanne* (which grossed $91 million per annum at peak) have included Shelley Winters as Roseanne's grandmother, Mary; Estelle Parsons as Roseanne's mother, Bev; Barr's on–off husband Tom Arnold (subsequently star of the lead-ballasted *The Jackie Thomas Show*) as neighbour Arnie and Sandra Bernhard as bisexual friend, Nancy. Mariel Hemingway appeared as a lesbian stripper, whose much-hyped sapphic kiss with Roseanne caused a minor moral controversy. Despite a famously relentless turnover of writers, the show deteriorated in later seasons, as Roseanne remodelled her character (and herself, courtesy of the surgeon's blade) into something distinctly glamorous. The show bowed out with an unlikely and unappealing storyline in which the Conners won the state lottery.

CAST *Roseanne Conner* Roseanne Barr *Dan Conner* John Goodman *Darlene Conner* Sara Gilbert *David Jacob 'DJ' Conner* Michael Fishman *Becky Conner* Lecy Goranson/Sara Chalke *Jackie Harris* Laurie Metcalf *Crystal Conner (née Anderson)* Natalie West *Ed Conner* Ned Beatty *David Healey (Darlene's boyfriend)* Johnny Galecki *Mark Healey (Becky's husband)* Glenn Quinn *Arnie Thomas* Tom Arnold *Nancy Bartlett* Sandra Bernhard *Booker* George Clooney /*cr* Matt Williams / *exec pr* Marcy Carsey, Tom Werner, Roseanne Barr, Tom Arnold /*dr* inc Gail Mancuso, John Whitesell, Ellen Falcon, Andrew D. Weyman, Jeff Margolis / *Carsey-Werner Productions* (USA) /221 x 25m col / US tx ABC 1988–97.

Rosie

Comedy. BBC1 1975–81

First transmitted as *The Growing Pains of PC Penrose*, this whimsical sitcom by whimsical sitcom-maestro Roy Clarke focused on the mishaps of naive probationer constable Penrose (nicknamed Rosie, to his embarrassment). The setting was (largely) the northern town of Raven's Bay; here Rosie was dominated by mother Millie, Aunt Ida, and girlfriend Gillian. Headstrong police partner PC Wilmot was his boon male companion. Actor Paul Greenwood (later ➢*Spender*) co-wrote and sang the theme song.

CAST *PC Michael 'Rosie' Penrose* Paul Greenwood *Sgt Flagg* Bryan Pringle *PC Wilmot* Tony Haygarth *Millie Penrose* Avril Elgar/Patricia Kneale *Auntie Ida* Lorraine Peters *Gillian Chislehurst* Frankie Jordan *Uncle Norman* Allan Surtees *WPC Whatmough* Penny Leatherbarrow *Merv* Robert Gillespie /John Cater /*cr* Roy Clarke /*pr* Douglas Argent, Bernard Thompson / *BBC TV* (UK) /34 x 30m col.

Rowan and Martin's Laugh-In

Comedy. BBC2 1968–71

Running wild variety show, hugely influential in America (although already anticipated in the UK by ➢*That Was the Week That Was*). Hosted by nightclub comedians Dan Rowan and Dick Martin, *Laugh-In* formed a madcap hour of stand-up gags, music, satirical skits (the best remembered of them being the talent-show send-up, the 'Flying Fickle Finger of Fate') and clownery from a revolving repertory company of players (Lily Tomlin and Goldie Hawn among them). Catchphrases zipped out by the episode: 'sock it to me' (at which Judy Carne got drenched), 'here come de judge', and 'verrry interrresting, but stupid' (Arte Johnson's German soldier). For three years it ruled the airwaves, its enthusiasm and daringness seeming to catch the liberated mood of the late 60s. Even President Nixon dropped in. A cynical 1977 NBC revival, however, was almost universally divellicated. 'Look that up in your Funk and Wagnalls.'

CAST inc Dan Rowan, Dick Martin, Ruth Buzzi, Gary Owens, Goldie Hawn, Judy Carne, Lily Tomlin, Arte Johnson, Larry Hovis, Pigmeat Markham, Alan Sues, Jud Strunk, Dave Madden /*pr* George Slatter, Paul W. Keyes, Ed Friendly, Carolyn Raskin /*Romart inc* (USA) / 150 x 50m col /US tx NBC 1967–72.

The Roy Rogers Show

Western. ITV 1955–7

Modern Western for the kiddie crowd in which the singing cowboy played himself in a straight-arrow fight for truth and justice. Other regulars at crusade HQ, the Double R Bar Ranch in Paradise Valley, were Roger's wonder horse Trigger, his wife Dale Evans, her horse Buttermilk, bumbling pardner Pat Grady (who drove a Jeep, Nellybelle) and dog Bullet. Episodes frequently involved abandoned children, to whom Rogers and Evans then became paragon surrogate parents.

Which was a prime case of art following life. Western fashion-plate Rogers (born Leonard Franklin Slye) and Dale Evans were the parents of five adopted children of assorted ethnic backgrounds, and received countless awards for their humanitarian work with juveniles.

CAST Roy Rogers, Dale Evans, Pat Grady, The Sons of the Pioneers /*cr* Roy Rogers /*pr* Roy Rogers, Jack Lacey, Bob Henry, Leslie H. Martinson /*dr* inc Leslie H. Martinson /*mus* Dale Evans ('Happy Trails To You' theme lyrics), Roy Rogers, The Sons of the Pioneers / *Roy Rogers Productions: Frontier Productions* (USA) / 100 x 26m bw /US tx CBS 1952–7.

Rugrats

Children's. Nickelodeon 1996–

Toon depicting life and adults as seen through the eyes of a gang of 'rugrats' (American slang for children). Led by Tommy Pickles, these were beastly cousin Angelica, best friend Chuckie, pet dog Spike, and twins Phil and Lil. Cute cartoon, slyly script-sharp on adult foibles. Christine Cavanagh (the voice of cinema porker *Babe*) throated for Chuckie, while David Doyle, Bosley in ➢*Charlie's Angels*, did the same for Grandpa. Rejecting the services of 'Composers-R-Us', the 'toon used music by Mark of punk band Devo.

CAST (voices) *Tommy* E.G. Daily *Angelica* Cheryl Chase *Phil /Lil* Kathy Souci *Chuckie* Christine Cavanagh *Grandpa* David Doyle /*dr* inc Jim Duffy, Howard E. Baker, Rich Bugental /*Klasky Csupo: Nickelodeon* (USA) /93+ x 2:15m col /US tx Nickelodeon 1995–.

Rumpole of the Bailey

Drama. ITV 1975–92

John Mortimer's eccentric lawyerly creation, Horace Rumpole, first appeared in a 1975 BBC ➢*Play for Today*, before taking up regular casework at Thames TV when the Corporation shillied over the commissioning of a follow-up series. (This proved to be a long and profitable relationship between Rumpole and Thames: in 1991 *Rumpole* became the first British TV series to be sponsored.) A suitably Dickensian performance by Leo McKern as the bibulous, *Oxford Book of English Verse*-quoting Rumpole, defence scourge of the courtroom (but henpecked by his wife, the original 'she who must be obeyed'), was the topping on barrister–playwright Mortimer's assured, often richly ironic and socially caustic, scripts. Though Mortimer retired Rumpole on several occasions, the devious old campaigner returned intermittently for nearly two decades to prick the consciences and pomposity of his peers.

CAST *Horace Rumpole* Leo McKern *Claude Erskine-Brown* Julian Curry *Phyllida Erskine-Brown (née Trant)* Patricia Hodge *Guthrie Featherstone* Peter Bowles *George Frobisher* Moray Watson *Samuel Ballard* Peter Blythe *Marigold Featherstone* Joanna Van Gyseghem *Hilda Rumpole* Peggy Thorpe Bates/Marion Mathie *Nick Rumpole* David Yelland *Liz Probert* Samantha Bond /Abigail McKern /*cr* John Mortimer /*exec pr* Lloyd Shirley /*pr* Irene Shubik, Jacqueline Davies /*dr* Roger Bamford, John Gorries, Herbet Wise, Robert Tronson /*wr* John Mortimer /*Thames TV* (UK) / 46 x 60m, 2 x 120m col.

The Ruth Rendell Mysteries

Crime. ITV 1987–

Ruth Rendell's bucolic Inspector Wexford (florid-faced TV veteran, George Baker) of Kingsmarkham was first introduced to TV in the 1987 'Wolf to the Slaughter', beginning a two-decade procession of sedate whodunnits which, if never quite ➢*Inspector Morse*, adequately filled their Sunday evening time slot. In his persistent inquiries into the gruesome murders which periodically gripped the southern market town, the hick-talking but quick-witted Wexford was aided by a detective helpmate, widower DI Mike Burden (appropriately named in view of his grieving air; and even when he later married history teacher Jenny the manner scarcely lightened). Wexford's spouse, Dora, was played by Louie Ramsay, Baker's wife in real life. Dramatized from Rendell's Wexford novels and stories (or at least until these ran out; Baker was one of those who contributed some of the all-new stories), the series – confusingly – changed into a general Rendell anthology in the mid-90s; it was not until 1996, after a three-year absence, that the Shakespeare-quoting Wexford recommenced his TV investigations with the 'Simisola' case.

CAST *DCI Reg Wexford* George Baker *DI Mike Burden* Christopher Ravenscroft *Dora Wexford* Louise Ramsay *Jenny Burden (née Ireland)* Diane Keen *Jean Burden* Ann Penfold *Sgt Barry Vine* Sean Pertwee *DS Martin* Ken Kitson /*exec pr* Graham Benson /*pr* John Davies, Neil Zeiger /*dr* inc Don Leaver, Mary McMurray, Sandy Johnson, Herbert Wise /*wr* inc Clive Exton, Geoffrey Case, Trevor Preston, George Baker /*mus* Brian Bennett /*TVS: Meridian* (UK) /45 x 60m, 2 x 90m, 2 x 120m col /US tx Arts & Entertainment 1990–.

Rutland Weekend Television

Comedy. BBC2 1975–6

Eric Idle's follow-up to ➢*Monty Python's Flying Circus* cast him as the programme controller of fictional Rutland Weekend Television, based in England's smallest county. From there essayed forth sub-*Python* parodies of TV – and one solid gold masterpiece in the 1978 one-off sequel *The Rutles* (BBC2, 65m). This presented the spoof documentary history of the 'pre-Fab four', Dirk, Nasty, Stig and Barry, intercutting the interviews with real rock faces (Mick Jagger and Ron Wood among them) with footage of the Rutles performing such classics as 'WC Fields Forever' and 'Goose-Step Mama'.

CAST Eric Idle, Neil Innes, David Battley, Henry Woolf, Gwen Taylor /*pr* Ian Keill /*wr* Eric Idle /*mus* Neil Innes /*BBC TV* (UK) /12 x 30m col.

Saber of London

Crime. ITV 1959–61

The continuing cases of monochrome British peeper ➢*Mark Saber*, though with a different team of underlings. So typecast was Donald Gray by the Saber role, that other screen parts eluded him thereafter, leaving him to work in radio and commercials until his death in 1978.

CAST *Mark Saber* Donald Gray *Bob Page* Robert Arden *Peter Paulson* Neil McCallum *Eddie Wells* Jerry Thorne *Insp. Parker* Colin Tapley /*pr* Edward & Harry Lee Danziger /*Danzigers* (USA) /83 x 30m bw /US tx NBC 1957–60.

The Saint

Crime. ITV 1962–9

'...a roaring adventurer who loves a fight ... a dashing daredevil, imperturbable, debonair, preposterously handsome, a pirate or a philanthropist as the occasion demands.'

Thus novelist Leslie Charteris defined his most famous creation, Simon Templar, aka 'The Saint' because of his initials but also his penchant for helping those (especially modern-day damsels) in distress. Initially, Charteris himself tried to develop the character for TV (with David Niven in the lead role), but the project only came to small-screen fruition under the guidance of Lew Grade, the man with the golden trans-Atlantic touch.

Initially, Patrick McGoohan (➢*Danger Man*, ➢*The Prisoner*) was offered the title part, but he turned it down (The Saint womanized too much for his taste), so the part went to former cardigan model Roger Moore, already familiar to audiences in both the UK and USA for ➢*Ivanhoe* and ➢*Maverick*. It was a good choice; Roger Moore played The Saint with memorable dry style, perfect coiffeur and a quizzical arch to the eyebrow. The episodes themselves were entertaining action capers, with plenty of fist-slamming action (excellently choreographed) in exotic locales (Paris, Rome, Nassau, etc.) against blackmailers, thieves and murderers, this interrupted by dalliance with the episode's adorning beauty. (Those draping themselves over Templar's torso included Jane Asher, Honor Blackman, Kate O'Mara – no less than four times – and Julie Christie.) Apart from The Saint, the only other regular character was Chief Inspector Teal, invariably referred to by Templar in dismissive tones 'as Scotland Yard's finest'. While in Britain, Templar drove a yellow Volvo P1800 (reg: ST 1), much admired by 60s audiences.

In 1966 filming of *The Saint* switched to colour; the consequence was an obvious tightening of the budget in the props department. The show, however, continued its triumphant commericial progress; some estimates have put its earnings as high as £370 million. (Since Moore owns the rights to the colour segments, this makes him a man of some wealth.)

A 1978 remake starred Ian Ogilvy as the suave crusader. Though competently made, it sacrificed the archness of the Moore version for a straight product which never grabbed.

CAST *Simon Templar* Roger Moore *Chief Insp. Teal* Ivor Dean /*cr* Robert S. Baker, Monty Norman /*pr* Robert S. Baker, Monty Norman /*dr* inc Peter Yates, Roger Moore, Roy Baker, Freddie Francis /*wr* inc Terry Nation, John Kruse, Harry H. Junkin, Norman Borisoff /*mus* Edwin Astley /*ATV: New World: Bamore: ITC* (UK) /71 x 60m bw:col /US tx NBC 1967–9.

St Elsewhere

Drama. C4 1983–9

Realistic medical drama, set in the battered Boston teaching hospital of St Eligius (nicknamed 'St Elsewhere', since it was the dump for the city's poor patients) with a staff of compassionate muddlers. These were headed by Chief of Services Dr Donald Westphall, heart surgeon Mark Craig,

Set in a downtown Boston hospital, grittily realistic medical drama *St Elsewhere* came from the same production company as *Hill Street Blues*.

Dr Bob Caldwell (a tottyholic who contracted HIV) and black doctor Philip Chandler (played by a pre-Hollywood Denzel Washington). When the hospital was taken over by a private company, Ecumenia, the financial pressures grew, and Westphall showed the new executive officer his naked arse and quit. A truly magnificent small-screen moment. Much influenced in its pace, style and intertwined plotting by ➢*Hill Street Blues* (also from MTM), *St Elsewhere* also upped the humour, subtly parodying other shows and films, even adding some injections of absolute comic bizarrity, including a pathologist who liked to bonk in the morgue. The ratings were dire, but the show lasted for six years because those who loved it, loved it – and tended to be from the ad peoples' favourite AB1 category. In the final episode, St Eligius was seen to be a model inside a snowglobe held by Westphall's autistic son, implying that the whole thing had been a dream.

CAST *Dr Donald Westphall* Ed Flanders *Dr Mark Craig* William Daniels *Dr Bob Caldwell* Mark Harmon *Dr Philip Chandler* Denzel Washington *Dr Daniel Auschlander* Norman Lloyd *Dr Victor Ehrlich* Ed Begley Jr *Dr Wayne Fiscus* Howie Mandel *Dr Ben Samuels* David Birney *Nurse Helen Rosenthal* Christina Pickles *Dr Jack Morrison* David Morse *Luther Hawkins* Eric Laneuville *Dr Annie Cavanero* Cynthia Sykes *Dr Peter White* Terence Knox *Dr Hugh Beale* G.W. Bailey *Nurse Daniels* Ellen Bry /*cr* Joshua Brand, John Falsey / *exec pr* Bruce Paltrow /*dr* inc Bruce Paltrow, Mark Tinker, Thomas Carter, Eric Laneuville, Tim Matheson / *wr* inc Joshua Brand, John Falsey, Tom Fontana, Mark Tinker, John Tinker /*mus* Dave Grusin /*MTM* (USA) /137 x 60m col /US tx NBC 1982–8.

Sale of the Century

Light Entertainment. ITV 1971–83

Game show in which host Nicholas Parsons (a former film actor and straight man to Eric Barker and Arthur Haynes) asked contestants £1, £3, or £5 general-knowledge questions, the lucre gained allowing them to buy tempting bargain-price goods. The claim of the title, however, was weekly undermined by the opening announcement, 'From Norwich…' Enormously popular (21.2 million viewers at peak), the show prompted numerous *Celebrity Sale of the Century* charity specials. Here, as in the episodes proper, the announcer was John Benson and most prizes bigger than a Magimix came draped in a half-clad Carole or Debbie. Though ridiculed for his unctuous-style, Parsons proved his own best lampooner with a late 80s quizmaster skit, *The Alphabet Quiz*, for ITV's *Night Network*.

CAST (host) Nicholas Parsons /*pr* Peter Joy, Bill Perry /*dr* Joy, Perry /*Anglia TV* (UK) /approx. 230 x 30m col.

Sam
Drama. ITV 1973–5

Charted the saga of Sam Wilson, from fatherless boy in the grim 30s Yorkshire mining village of Skellerton, through escape to the sea and marriage to Sarah, to reflective middle age as an engineering manager in the Hillman Minx 1950s.

Obviously ambitious serial, with Sam (played in adulthood by a pre-➢*Taggart* Mark McManus) an exemplar for his generation and class, which also managed enormous popularity. Something of a watcher's chore towards the dwindling end, however,

CAST *Sam Wilson* Kevin Moreton/Mark McManus *Toby Wilson (grandfather)* Frank Mills *Jack Barraclough (grandfather)* Michael Godliffe *Polly Barraclough (grandmother)* Maggie Jones *George Barraclough* Ray Smith *Sarah Wilson (née Corby)* Jennifer Hilary /*cr* John Finch /*pr* Michael Cox /*dr* inc Les Chatfield /*wr* John Finch /*Granada TV* (UK) / 39 x 60m col.

Samson and Delilah
Drama. Sky 1 1996

Part of *The Bible* series, the first complete screen adaptation of the Old Testament. Nic Roeg, on the slum from movieland, directed a stellar line-up, headed by the pouting Liz Hurley (as the pouting Delilah), nearly all of them miscast – none more so that Dennis Hooper as the introspective Philistine soldier, General Tariq. Opulently produced, with sheaves of costume gold, but even in the lavish-stakes it paled against Cecil B. DeMille's gargantuan 1949 film version with Victor Mature as the hirsute Samson and Hedy Lamarr as his beautiful betrayer.

CAST *Samson* Eric Thal *Delilah* Elizabeth Hurley *General Tariq* Dennis Hopper *Caceriere* Keith Allen *Re Hamun* Michael Gambon /*exec pr* Gerald Rafshoon /*pr* Eleonora Andreatta, Heinrich Krauss, Luca Bernabei, Lorenzo Minoli /*dr* Nicolas Roeg /*wr* Alan Scott /*mus* Marco Frisina, Ennio Morricone /*Turner Pictures (USA) /BetaFilm Gmbh (France) /Lube Production (Germany) /Lux Vide (Italy)* /2 x 120m col / US tx Fox TV 1996.

The Sandbaggers
Spy. ITV 1978–80

Espionage drama featuring the strong-arm activities of a British Special Intelligence Force (SIF) unit, headed by Neil Burnside. Praiseworthily, measuredly realistic – it was conceived and written by a former spy, Ian Mackintosh – but distractingly under-produced. More distracting still were Burnside's several changes of head. Of the several actors to play the part, Marsden continued the aloof, laconic mode, as Inspector Dalgliesh in Anglia's P.D. James series (1983–).

CAST *Neil Burnside* Roy Marsden/Richard Vernon / Dennis Burgess *Laura Dickens* Diane Keen *Willie Caine* Ray Lonnen *Sir Geoffrey Wellingham* Alan MacNaughtan *Mike Wallace* Michael Cashman /*cr* Ian Mackintosh /*exec pr* David Cunliffe /*pr* Michael Ferguson /*wr* Ian Mackintosh /*Yorkshire TV* (UK) / 19 x 60m col.

Sapphire and Steel
Sci-fi. ITV 1979–82

'All irregularities will be handled by the forces controlling each dimension...'

Hypnotic, low-key telefantasy from P.J. Hammond featuring two enigmatic agents whose job – preceded by *sotto voce* discussion – was to repair ruptures in time. 'Adventure One' set the menacing tone which enveloped the short-lived series (it became a victim of ATV's loss of franchise), when nursery rhymes spoken in a farmhouse caused the fourth dimension to rip into the present and steal two children. Joanna Lumley (ex-➢*The New Avengers*) starred as the supersensory Sapphire, David McCallum (ex-➢*The Man from UNCLE*) as the tough, unemotional Steel.

CAST *Sapphire* Joanna Lumley *Steel* David McCallum *Silver* David Collings /*cr* P.J. Hammond /*pr* Shaun O'Riordan /*dr* Shaun O'Riordan, David Foster /*wr* P.J. Hammond, Don Houghton, Anthony Read /*mus* Cyril Ornadel /*ATV Network Production* (UK) /34 x 30m col.

Saracen

Crime. ITV 1989

Saracen Systems was a private security firm which sold its bodyguard services (usually the pecs-and-Uzi team of Tom Duffy and David Barber) to VIPs around the strife-ridden globe. Co-created by the ever-busy Chris Kelly (*World in Action* narrator, presenter of *Wish You Were Here...?*, host of *Food and Drink* and producer of ➢*Soldier, Soldier*).

CAST *Tom Duffy* Patrick James Clarke *David Barber* Christian Burgess /*cr* Ted Childs, Chris Kelly /*pr* Deirdre Keir, Patrick Harbinson /*dr* inc Ian Knox /*wr* inc John Foster /*Central TV* (UK) /6 x 60m col.

Saturday Live/Friday Night Live

Light Entertainment. C4 1985–8

Revue-style series for upcoming comedians, based on the American model *Saturday Night Live*. After a problematic start involving items too dubious for an early evening audience and rotation of guest presenters (including, unbelievably, Michael Barrymore), the show was shifted to a 10 p.m. time-slot and Ben Elton (the 'smug git in the shiny suit') hired as permanent host. In-between anti-Thatcher PC-rants, he introduced a selection of alternative comics destined for glittering careers: Jo Brand ('The Sea Monster'), Julian Clary and Craig Charles among them. Yet, in selective memory, at least, the entire showcase was stolen by Harry Enfield, whose Greek kebab-shop-owner character ('Hello, matey peeps') was only eclipsed by his turbo-driving, wads-of-money-waving plasterer, Loadsamoney – probably the most telling caricature of Essex Man during the 80s. When Loadsamoney became appropriated by the selfsame Essex Man, Enfield introduced 'Buggarallmoney' as a balance, before killing off the character entirely. Despite its topicality, *Saturday Live* (the programme being retitled *Friday Night Live* for its change in transmission day) stands up to re-viewing remarkably well.

CAST (presenters) Ben Elton, also including Michael Barrymore, Tracey Ullman, Lenny Henry /*cr* Paul Jackson /*pr* Geoff Posner, Geoff Perkins /*Thames TV* (UK) /approx. 32 x 60m col.

Savannah

Melodrama. ITV 1996–7

Sultry southern melodrama from Aaron Spelling, the king of hi-gloss tack. Set in the Georgia town of the title, where virginal rich girl Reese considered her housekeeper's daughter, Peyton, a best friend – but, since this was Spellingworld, white-trash Peyton was actually having an affair with Reese's fiancé, lawyer Travis Paterson. This self-same lawyer, meanwhile, had divested Reese's other best friend, Lane, (a future drink and drug addict) of her bank account. At which entirely unconnected point, supercon white-trash Tom Massick wooed Reese's rich Pa. Complications and intrigue ensued, with larceny and murder the satisfyingly absurd consequence, committed between much activity in the sack. And elsewhere. 'I've never done it on a roulette table before,' drawled one babe. Morally deficient, lushly made, completely compulsive. A soap with belles on.

CAST *Reese Burton* Shannon Sturges *Lane McKenzie* Robyn Lively *Peyton Richards* Jamie Luner *Travis Peterson* George Eads *Dean Collins* David Gail *Tom Massick* Paul Satterfield *Veronica Koslowsky* Beth Toussaint *Edward Burton* Ray Wise /*cr* Constance M. Burge /*exec pr* Aaron Spelling, E. Duke Vincent, James Stanley, Diane Messina Stanley /*pr* James T. Davis /*dr* inc Richard Lang, Mark Jean, Les Sheldon /*wr* inc Constance M. Burge, Diane Messina Stanley, James Stanley /*mus* Christopher Stone (theme), Gary Stevan Scott /*Spelling Television Inc* (USA) /1 x 120m, 32 x 60m col /US tx WB Network 1996–7.

Scarecrow and Mrs King

Spy. ITV 1984

A housewife (divorced) becomes the sidekick of a US spook (male), the twosome going on to perform cloak-and-dagger missions for the US government.

The old 'innocent-person-caught-in-the-spy-game' trick, borrowed from ➢*The Man From UNCLE*. Boxleitner later moved on to ➢*Babylon 5*. Star Jackson (ex-➢*Charlie's Angels*) was among those sharing the directing duties.

CAST *Amanda King* Kate Jackson *Lee Stetson (code name: 'Scarecrow')* Bruce Boxleitner /*pr* inc Bill McCutchen /*dr* inc Harry Harris, James Frawley, Bernard McEveety, Christian I. Nyby II, Ivan Dixon, Rich Kolbe, Russ Mayberry, Michael Vejar, Kate Jackson /*Universal TV* (USA) /89 x 60m col / US tx CBS 1983–7.

The Scarlet Pimpernel

Adventure. ITV 1955–6

'They seek him here, they seek him there...'

An apparent fop, Sir Percy Blakeney, dons rapier and disguises by the valise-full to help the poor persecuted aristocrats of 18th-century Revolutionary France as the daring Scarlet Pimpernel.

Tolerable costumer, based on Baroness Orczy's famous tale. The star, Goring, had already played the Blakeney/Pimpernel part for a 1949 radio production.

CAST *Sir Percy Blakeney/The Scarlet Pimpernel* Marius Goring *Sir Andrew Ffoulkes* Patrick Troughton *Chauvelin* Stanley Van Veers *Lord Richard Hastings* Anthony Newlands /*pr* Dennis Vance, David Macdonald, Marius Goring /*Towers of London: ITP* (UK) /39 x 30m bw /US tx Syndicated 1956.

Scooby-Doo, Where are You?

Children's. BBC1 1970–2.

Took its title from a line in the Frank Sinatra song 'Strangers in the Night' ('scooby-dooby-doo'), and chronicled the adventures of a gang of teenage detectives – and eponymous cowardly Great Dane – who roamed the countryside in their Mystery Machine van in search of supernatural phenomena.

A Hanna-Barbera cartoon which, in the brothers-in-panicking-arms relationship between Scooby (voiced by Don Messick) and unkempt human Shaggy (Casey Kasem), found comedic gold, prompting a bonanza of spin-offs. Between 1972 and 1974 *The New Scooby-Doo Comedy Movies* appeared, to be followed by *The Scooby-Doo/Dynomutt Hour* (1976–7), *Scooby's All-Star Laff-A-Lympics* (1979–80), *Scooby and Scrappy-Doo* (1979–80) – which introduced Scooby's feisty little nephew (battle cry: 'Puppy Power!') – and then *The Scooby and Scrappy-Doo/Puppy Hour* (1982–3) and *Scooby's Mystery Funhouse* (1985–6). 'Wurrrrr.'

CAST (voices) *Scooby-Doo* Don Messick *Shaggy* Casey Kasem *Freddy* Frank Welker *Velma* Nicole Jaffe *Daphne* Heather North /*cr* Ken Spears, Joe Ruby /*pr* Joseph Barbera, William Hanna /*dr* Oscar Dufau, George Gordon, Charles A. Nichols, Ray Patterson, Carl Urbano /*wr* Ken Spears, Carl Urbano /*Hanna-Barbera* (UK) /72 x 30m col /US tx ABC 1969–72.

Screen Test

Children's. BBC1 1970–84

Quizzed school teams on their observational powers after running clips from famous movies before their eyes. A regular fixture was the Young Film Makers Competition, which encouraged wannabe directors to experiment behind the camera.

CAST (presenters) Michael Rodd, Brian Trueman, Mark Curry /*pr* John Buttery, Tony Harrison, David Brown /*BBC TV* (UK) /approx. 160 x 30m col.

Scully

Children's. C4 1984

Alan Bleasdale comedy chronicling the adolescent misadventures of a streetwise Liverpudlian teen with dreams of turning soccer pro. A half-hour packed with colourful scenes and characters, among them Franny Scully's railway-obsessed brother Henry (rock star Elvis Costello), friend Mad Dog (Mark McGann), lust-object Joanna (Cathy Tyson, later ➢*Band of Gold*) and piña-colada supping Gran (Jean Boht from ➢*Bread*). Footballer Kenny Dalglish guested. Adapted by Bleasdale from his own novels and first presented on TV as a 1978 ➢*Play for Today*, 'Scully's New Year's Eve'.

CAST *Franny Scully* Andrew Schofield *Henry Scully* Elvis Costello *Arthur Scully* Jimmy Gallagher *Mrs Scully* Val Lilley *Mr Scully* Joey Kaye *Gran* Jean Boht *Mooey* Ray Kingsley *Mad Dog* Mark McGann *Joanna* Cathy Tyson *Snotty Dog* Richard Burke /*cr* Alan Bleasdale /*pr* Steve Morrison /*dr* Les Chatfield /*wr* Alan Bleasdale /*mus* Elvis Costello ('Painting the Town Red' theme) /6 x 30m, 1 x 60m col.

Sea Hunt

Children's. ITV 1958–60

Mike Nelson, a former US Navy frogman and owner of *The Argonaut*, hires himself out as a global underwater troubleshooter. And finds himself in metaphorical deep waters, usually only escaping by the skin of his wetsuit.

Clean-limbed action adventure show from Ivan Tors (who returned to the wet stuff with ➢*Flipper*), with excellent submarine scenes and a personable lead in Lloyd Bridges. His sons, Beau and Jeff, occasionally guested in the kid parts.

A revised version appeared in 1987, with Ron Ely – the former ➢*Tarzan* – as Nelson.

CAST *Mike Nelson* Lloyd Bridges /*pr* Ivan Tors, Leon Benson, John Florea /*dr* inc Leon Benson, John Florea / *mus* Ray Llewellyn (theme) /*Ziv TV* (USA) /155 x 25m bw /US tx Syndicated 1957–60.

SeaQuest DSV

Sci-fi. ITV 1993–6

Hi-tec ➢*Voyage to the Bottom of the Sea* for a 90s eco-aware audience. The crew of a 1000-foot supersub, *SeaQuest* Deep Submergence Vehicle, led by Roy Scheider (entering the sea again, just when he thought it might be safe after besting *Jaws*), patrols the deep on behalf of the United Earth/Oceans Organization. The opening season was strongly 'space faction' and green-oriented, which caused a choppy critical reception. Nervous executives insisted on more Bug-Eyed Monsters and fantasy – to the displeasure of Scheider (and many hardcore fans) who dismissed it as 'childish trash'. It arose from the schlocky abyss for a cyberpunkish third season, but with Michael Ironside replacing Scheider on the bridge of *SeaQuest Mk II* (the original having been used to plug a magma fissure to stop a catastrophic earthquake) and the loss of the scene-stealing CGI/animatronic-generated dolphin, Darwin 9 (too costly). The action was updated to 2032. Made by Steven Spielberg's Amblin company, created by ➢*Alien Nation*'s Rockne O'Bannon.

CAST *Capt. Nathan Bridger* Roy Schneider *Capt. Oliver Hudson* Michael Ironside *Lt Cmdr Katherine Hitchcock* Stacy Haiduk *Lucas Wolenczak* Jonathan Brandis *Dr Kristin Westphalen* Stephanie Beacham *Cmdr Jonathan Ford* Don Franklin *Lt Tim O'Neill* Ted Raimi *Dagwood* Peter (son of Dom) DeLuise /*cr* Rockne S. O'Bannon /*exec pr* Steven Spielberg, Rockne S. O'Bannon, David J. Burke, Tommy Thompson, Patrick Hasburgh /*dr* inc Bryan Spicer, Bill Norton, Les Sheldon, John T. Kretchmer /*wr* inc Rockne S. O'Bannon, Tommy Thompson, Patrick Hasburgh, David Kemper, Hans Tobeason, David J. Burke, John J. Sakmar /*Amblin Television: Universal TV* (USA) / 1 x 90m, 58 x 60m col /US tx NBC 1993–.

Secret Army

Drama. BBC1 1977–9

Tense, ambience-heavy escapades of the Belgian Resistance during WWII as they smuggled Allied airmen back to Britain. Albert Foiret (Bernard Hepton), proprietor of Brussels' restaurant La Candide, and Lisa Colbert (Jan Francis, before she found comedy) headed the Lifeline cell, while Sturmbahnfuhrer Kessler (later spun off to a series of his own, ➢*Kessler*), the archetypal cold-eyed Gestapo boss, was their chief adversary. Admittedly edge-of-the-seat serial entertainment (with spell-setting theme music in Django Reinhardt's 'Nuages'), its continual po-facedness, however, lay it open to ridicule – which duly came in the cruelly exact spoof ➢*'Allo, 'Allo.*

CAST *Albert Foiret* Bernard Hepton *Lisa Colbert* Jan Francis *Sturmbahnfuhrer Kessler* Clifford Rose *Monique Duchamps* Angela Richards *Flt Lt John Curtis* Christopher Neame *Brandt* Michael Culver *Paul Vecors* Ralph Bates *Max Brocard* Stephen Yardley /*cr* Gerard Glaister, William Greatorex /*pr* Gerard Glaister /*dr* inc Tristan De Vere Cole, Viktor Ritelis, Kenneth Ives /*wr* inc Gerard Glaister, Allan Prior, Paul Annett, Simon Masters, N.J. Crisp, Willis Hall, John Brason /*mus* Django Reinhardt (theme) /*BBC TV: BRT* (UK /Bel) / 48 x 55m col.

The Secret Diary of Adrian Mole, Aged 13¾

Comedy. ITV 1985

Sue Townsend adapted her own best-selling novel into this delightful six-parter charting the angst-ridden (spots, the existence or otherwise of God, lust for Pandora) adolescence of schoolboy Adrian Mole. A sequel, transmitted as *The Growing Pains of Adrian Mole* (Thames 1987), saw pop singer Lulu replace Julie Walters as Mole's divorced Mum. Beryl Reid played Grandma in both shows.

CAST *Adrian Mole* Gian Sammarco *Pauline Mole (mother)* Julie Walters *George Mole (father)* Stephen Moore *Grandma Mole* Beryl Reid *Bert Baxter* Bill Fraser *Pandora* Lindsey Stagg /*cr* Sue Townsend /*exec pr* Lloyd Shirley /*pr* Peter Sasdy /*wr* Sue Townsend / *Thames TV* (UK) /6 x 30m col.

Secret Service

Children's. ITV 1969

Sublimely bizarre Gerry ➢'*Thunderbirds*' Anderson show which blended live action and supermarionation to relate the spy-adventures of Father Stanley Unwin, a parish priest who was also a top undercover agent with BISHOP (British Intelligence Service Headquarters Operation Priest). At the call of duty, Unwin shrank the gardener Yokel Matthew (also an agent) into a briefcase with the aid of a 'minimizer', before setting off in his Model T. Ford, Gabriel. On revealing the baddies, Unwin sprayed them with gobbledygook, whilst special regimold thrifty fool Matthew tinkered with arcane electrical circuitry to save the world from assassinations/explosions/hijackings/kidnappings (delete as necessary). Mission accomplished, Father Unwin returned to his peaceful parish to exploit the moral lesson of his case in his Sunday sermon as the end credits rolled to the burblings of the Mike Sams Singers.

The series was never networked by ITV, and Lew Grade, aghast at the £20,000 per episode cost, limited the run to 13. Anderson, meanwhile, made the transition to full live action with ➢*UFO*.

CAST *Father Unwin* Stanley Unwin *Yokel Matthew* (voice) Keith Alexander *Agent Matthew* (voice) Gary Files *Mrs Appleby, the housekeeper* (voice) Sylvia Anderson *The Bishop* (voice) Jeremy Wilkin /*cr* Gerry & Sylvia Anderson /*exec pr* Reg Hill /*pr* David Lane /*dr* inc Alan Perry Leo Eaton, Ian Spurrier, Ian Anderson /*wr* inc Gerry & Sylvia Anderson, Donald James, Tony Barwick, Shane Rimmer /*mus* Barry Gray, The Mike Sams Singers /*sfx* Derek Meddings /*Century 21: ITC; ATV* (UK) /13 x 30m col.

Seinfeld

Comedy. BBC2 1993–8

The American sitcom sensation of the mid-90s. Though reminiscent of ➢*Rhoda* (the NY apartment set, the open house to a group of loser friends) and ➢*The Dick Van Dyke Show* (the comedian-lead playing himself), *Seinfeld* consciously re-drew the boundaries of the sitcom. It featured the nerdy, toothsome, white-sneakered stand-up comic Jerry Seinfeld (small-screen debut: playing a gag-writer in ➢*Benson*) pontificating on the absurd minutiae of life with 'schlubs' luckless George, former girlfriend Elaine

Zen and the art of sitcom; Jerry (centre) and fellow schlubs in *Seinfeld.* When the star cancelled the hit show, a desperate NBC network offered Seinfeld a reputed $5 million per episode to continue. He refused.

and shock-haired neighbour Kramer. There were no plots, canned laughter, or moral pieties ('No Hugs, No Lessons' was the production mantra). That this tricksy act of dramatizing everyday life – obsessively observed – could last 30 minutes let alone should entertain 30 million American per espisode was due to precision-tuned scripts and a flurry of set-piece jokes that cunningly linked into a whole. Zen and the art of sitcom maintenance. Much imitated since, but never bettered.

CAST *Jerry* Jerry Seinfeld *Elaine* Julia Louise-Dreyfus *George* Jason Alexander *Kramer* Michael Richards /*cr* Jerry Seinfeld, Larry David /*dr* inc Tom Cherones, David Steinberg, Jason Alexander, Joshua White /*wr* inc Jerry Seinfeld, David King /*Castle Rock Entertainment* (USA) /150 x 30m col /US tx NBC 1990–98

A Sense of Guilt

Drama. BBC1 1990

Another darkly tangled tale of sex and betrayal from Andrea Newman (➢*Bouquet of Barbed Wire*). Trevor Eve starred as amoral author Felix Cramer, whose seduction of his friend's stepdaughter tore all their worlds apart.

CAST *Felix Cramer* Trevor Eve *Elizabeth Cramer* Morag Hood *Sally Hinde* Rudi Davies *Richard Murray* Jim Carter *Helen Irving* Lisa Harrow /*cr* Andrea Newman /*pr* Simon Passmore /*wr* Andrea Newman / *BBC TV* (UK) /6 x 60m col.

Sergeant Cork

Crime. ITV 1963–8

Long-running series dreamed up by Ted Willis (➢*Dixon of Dock Green*) featuring a Victorian CID sergeant whose modernistic desire for scientific detection was frowned on by his cobwebbed colleagues.

It suffered from a lack of convincing peasouper atmosphere and never dwelled quite long enough on the seamy underside of late 19th-century London. William Gaunt, who played Cork's eager sidekick, was later seconded to the ultimate in avant-garde crime-busting, ➢*The Champions.*

CAST *Sgt Cork* John Barrie *Sgt Marriott* William Gaunt *Supt Nelson* John Richmond *Det. Bird* Arnold Diamond *Supt Rodway* Charles Morgan /*cr* Ted Willis / *pr* Jack Williams /*dr* inc Quentin Lawrence /*wr* inc Ted Willis /*ATV Network* (UK) /65 x 60m bw.

Sergeant Preston of the Yukon

Crime. ITV 1959–61

Thundering tales of crime-catching in the frozen gold-rushed wastes of 1890s Canada, with Sergeant Preston of the Royal North-west Mounted Police and his husky sidekick, Yukon King. Naturally, they always got their bad man.

Efficient juvenile actioner, with plenty of one-note plots and simplistic moral homilies, as per creators Trendle and Striker's previous goods, ➢*The Lone Ranger* and ➢*The Green Hornet.* Like those, *Sergeant Preston* had debuted on radio.

CAST *Sgt William Preston* Richard Simmons /*cr* George W. Trendle, Fran Striker /*pr* Tom R. Curtis, Charles E. Skinner /*mus* Emil Von Reznick ('Donna Diana Overture' theme) /*Wrather Films* (USA) / 78 x 30m bw /US tx Syndicated 1955.

Serpico

Crime. BBC1 1977

A loner cop, Frank Serpico (badge number: 21049), has an undercover mission to clean NY's 22nd Precinct of corruption.

Briefly-lived crime series, which trod slightly different ground to the 1973 film starring Al Pacino, downplaying corruption in the NYPD itself in favour of more acceptable prime-time villainry. Both movie and TV series were based on the story (as written by Peter Maas) of a real-life police crusader by the title name.

CAST *Frank Serpico* David Birney *Lt Tom Sullivan* Tom Atkins /*exec pr* Emmett G. Labery /*pr* Don Ingalls / *dr* inc Art Fisher, Reza Badiyi, David Moessinger, Michael Caffey, Robert Collins, Robert Markowitz / *mus* Robert Dransin, Elmer Bernstein /*Paramount TV* (USA) /15 x 60m col /US tx NBC 1976–8.

Sesame Street

Children's. ITV 1971–86/C4 1987–

Under the helmswomanship of Joan Ganz Cooney and her non-profit-making Children's Television Workshop, *Sesame Street* celebratedly applied advertising techniques to pre-school education. Set in a garbage-lined Harlem alleyway, it was especially aimed at ethnic/deprived children and ensured their attention by dazzling rapid-fire items (songs, animations, sketches, games, film inserts, but nothing longer than 30 seconds) with the day's essential lesson – a number and a letter – endlessly repeated. On hand to help with the basics of spelling and arithmetic were a cast of friendly Muppets (Jim Henson's marionette-puppets, previously seen on *Sam and Friends*, later to graduate to their own hit spin-off, ➢*The Muppet Show*): Big Bird, Oscar the Grouch, Grover, Elmo, Snuffleupagus among them. Guest stars (usually from the movies) abounded. Over the years, the cast of kid and adult actors who populated Sesame Street changed considerably (the death of Will Lee, who played sweetshop keeper Mr Hooper, in 1984 was marked by an *SS* special) and the show broadened its remit to include social and environmental issues. The producer was David Connell, formerly with the American tiny TV series *Captain Kangaroo* (1955–84), a show hosted for much of its run by Bill Cosby.

CAST *Bob* Bob McGrath *Susan* Loretta Long *Gordon* Roscoe Orman/Matt Robinson *David* Northern J. Callaway *Mr Hooper* Will Lee *Gina* Alison Bartlett *Linda* Linda Bove *Luis* Emilio Delgado *Maria* Sonia Manzano *Uncle Wally* Bill McCutcheon *Lillian* Lillias White *Kermit/Bert* (voice) Jim Henson *Big Bird/Cookie Monster/Oscar the Grouch/Miss Piggy* (voice) Frank Oz /*cr* Joan Ganz Cooney /*exec pr* David D. Connell, Jon Stone, Al Hyslop /*Children's Television Workshop* (USA) /3200+ x 60m col /US tx PBS 1969–.

Seven Deadly Sins

Drama. ITV 1966

Septet of self-contained plays, one per vice, by assorted scribes (including Joe Orton). The cute trick was that the identity of the sin was not revealed until the roll of the final credits. Associated–Rediffusion followed up with *The Seven Deadly Virtues* (ITV 1967), where the virtues had a murderous habit of going awry.

pr Peter Wiles /*dr* inc Peter Moffat /*wr* inc Alun Falconer, Joe Orton, Anthony Skene /*Rediffusion* (UK) /7 x 50m bw.

77 Sunset Strip

Crime. ITV 1958–64

Prototype glam PI show, created by Roy Huggins (➢*Maverick*, ➢*The Rockford Files*), featuring a firm of Hollywood detectives who were smart in both senses – brains and dress. Efrem Zimbalist Jr (son of violinist Sr, and opera star Alma Gluck, father of ➢*Remington Steele*'s Stephanie) starred as cultured Stu Bailey, Ivy League Ph.D. and former OSS officer. Roger Smith played his partner, Jeff Spencer, a former government spook. However, it was Edd Byrnes as the jive-talking teenage car attendant 'Kookie', at next-door Dino's restaurant who stole the show; his fan mail reached 10,000 letters a week and Warners issued a 'Kookie Speak' glossary (e.g. 'let's exitville' for leave, 'piling up the Zs' for sleeping). Byrnes even had a hit record with 'Kookie, Kookie, Lend Me Your Comb', sung with ➢*Hawaiian Eye*'s Connie Stevens. Meanwhile, the copycat record deals of Zimbalist and Smith bombed. Unsurprisingly, Byrnes/Kookie was promoted to a partnership in the 77 Sunset Strip agency, though by 1963 the series had, anyway, outworn its novelty welcome. Drastic changes were wrought in an effort to lift declining ratings, with Jack Webb (➢*Dragnet*) brought in as executive producer and William Conrad (later to find on-screen fame as ➢*Cannon*) as principal director. In a change of format, Zimbalist's character became a freelance investigator travelling the globe on a no-expense spared budget. It didn't help and the show was closed in 1964, a pack of imitations snapping at its heels.

77 Sunset Strip was developed for the small screen by two pilot TVMs – *Anything for Money* (1957) and *Girl on the Run* (1958).

CAST *Stu Bailey* Efrem Zimbalist Jr *Jeff Spencer* Roger Smith *Gerald Lloyd Kookson III ('Kookie')* Edd Byrnes *Roscoe (racetrack tout)* Louis Quinn *Suzanne Farbrey (switchboard operator)* Jacqueline Beer *J.R. Hale* Robert Logan /*cr* Roy Huggins /*exec pr* William T. Orr, Jack Webb /*pr* Howie Horwitz, William Conrad, Fenton Earnshaw, Harry Tatelman, Joel Rogosin /*dr* inc Richard L. Bare, William Conrad, Leslie H. Martinson, George Waggner, Andre De Toth /*mus* Mack David, Jerry Livingston /*Warner Bros* (USA) /205 x 60m bw /US tx ABC 1958–64.

Sexton Blake

Children's. ITV 1968–71

Routine, somewhat sanitized, mysteries featuring Hal Meredith's *Boy's Own* detective hero. The setting was the 1920s, with the cigar-smoking Blake (who, like Holmes, lived in Baker Street) tooling about London in a Rolls nicknamed 'The Grey Panther'. He was standardly accompanied by bloodhound Pedro and assistant Tinker. The BBC filmed a Blake series, *Sexton Blake and the Demon God* in 1978, though to no greater merit.

CAST *Sexton Blake* Laurence Payne *Edward 'Tinker' Clark* Roger Foss *Mrs Bardell (housekeeper)* Dorothea Phillips *Insp. Cutts* Ernest Clark *Insp. Van Steen* Leonard Sachs /*pr* Ronald Marriott /*Associated–Rediffusion: Thames TV* (UK) /28 x 30m col.

Shaft
Crime. ITV 1974–5

'Who is the man who fights for his brother man? Shaft!'

Richard Roundtree (later ➢*Roots*) reprised his cinema role as Afro-American PI John Shaft in this rare TV venture into blaxploitation. To make the product more palatable to white taste, however, network bosses emasculated Shaft's trigger-happy violence, nigger-with-attitude cool and sex-machine exploits. They even gave him a Caucasian buddy, NYPD Lieutenant Al Rossi. All that remained of the film was Roundtree's muscular walk and Isaac Hayes's Oscar-winning theme song. In the US it rotated as part of *The New CBS Tuesday Night Movie.* Based on Ernest Tidyman's 1970 novel, *Shaft.*

CAST *John Shaft* Richard Roundtree *Lt Al Rossi* Ed Barth /*exec pr* Allan Balter /*pr* William Reed Woodfield / *dr* Ivan Dixon, Nicholas Colasanto, John Llewellyn Moxey, Alexander Singer, Harry Harris, Allen Reisner, Lawrence Dobkin, Lee Philips /*wr* William Reed Woodfield, Allan Balter, Ellis Marcus, Ken Kolb /*mus* Isaac Hayes ('Shaft' theme), Johnny Pate /*MGM TV* (USA) /7 x 90m col /US tx CBS 1973–4.

Sharpe
Drama. ITV 1993–7

Splendid historical hokum featuring promoted-from-the-ranks Major Richard Sharpe of the South Essex as he derring-doed his way through the Napoleonic Wars, pausing only for sojourns in my lady's chamber and the besting of some sherry-drinking (i.e. nancy boy) British snob. Painterly filmed on location, mainly in the Crimea and Turkey, with a budget that allowed for convincing battles and sets it made for rare epic TV. So convincing, meanwhile, was Sean Bean's (*Clarissa, Lady Chatterley's Lover*) empathy with the title character that it convinced source novelist Bernard Cornwell to pen further Sharpe novels.

CAST *Major Richard Sharpe* Sean Bean *Harper* Daragh O'Malley *Havercamp* Norman Rossington *Lady Jane* Caroline Langrishe *Jane Sharpe (wife)* Abigail Cruttenden *Wellington* Hugh Fraser /*exec pr* Muir Sutherland /*pr* Malcolm Craddock /*dr* inc Tom Clegg /*wr* inc Charles Wood, Eoghan Harris /*Celtic: Picture Palace: Carlton* (UK) /12 x 120m col.

Shelley
Comedy. ITV 1979–88/1992

Sitcom starring Hywell Bennett as a lazy, unemployed cynic (shades of ➢*Hancock's Half Hour*) with a Ph.D. and a gift for sarcastic one-liners, frequently at the expense of DHSS bureaucracy and the building society. Sharing his bedsit at Pangloss Road, North London (prop: Mrs H) was pregnant girlfriend Fran, whom he eventually married. During season two he was obliged to take a job (as a copywriter), but was inevitably sacked. By this time, the series had soared up the weekly ratings to No. 2. The third season ended with Shelley once more in employment (at the Foreign Office); at this point creator Peter Tilbury quit the show to develop *It Takes a Worried Man*, leaving others (including future ➢*Drop the Dead Donkey* writers Hamilton and Jenkin) to write a last season which saw Shelley, having been sacked by both the FO and Fran, leave for America. After five years, Shelley came back to Britain in *The Return of Shelley* (1988–92, 26 x 30m col), to direct his ire at yuppies; this continued through a 1992 season of episodes transmitted under the title *Shelley.* For these, Shelley lived in a community of OAPs.

At its best – which was the first three seasons – it captured a mood of national disenchantment, with Bennett's petulant characterization spot-on. It trailed off, however, into repetition and caricature.

CAST *James Shelley* Hywell Bennett *Frances Smith* Belinda Sinclair *Mrs Edna Hawkins* Josephine Tewson *Isobel Shelley* Sylivia Kay *Gordon Smith* Frederick Jaeger *Desmond (the doorman)* Garfield Morgan /*cr* Peter Tilbury /*pr* Anthony Parker /*dr* Anthony Parker / *wr* Peter Tilbury, Barry Pilton, Guy Jenkin, Andy Hamilton /*Thames TV* (UK) /33 x 30m col.

Sherlock Holmes
Crime. BBC 1965

The adventures of the pipe-smoking Victorian detective were first filmed (for live transmission) by the BBC in 1951, in a version most notable for the future endeavours of its cast: Alan Wheatley (Holmes) went onto the villainy as the Sheriff of Nottingham in ➢*The Adventures of Robin Hood*, Raymond Francis (Watson) starred in ➢*No Hiding Place* and, two decades later, Bill Owen (Lestrade) tipped up as Compo in ➢*Last of the Summer Wine.* Returning to Conan Doyle's bookshelves once more in 1964, the BBC produced a one-off (*The Speckled Band*) for the ➢*Detective* anthology, following this up with a safely, safely series version, with some levity in an almost comically bumbling Watson. It pleased, and the BBC thought there was enough footage in the incompetent Watson idea to commission a second series in 1968, billed as *Sir Arthur Conan Doyle's Sherlock Holmes.* For this ratings' topping outing, Douglas Wilmer was replaced as Holmes by Hammer star Peter Cushing. Yet none of these Corporation versions was remotely faithful to Conan Doyle's dark portrait of Holmes as a half-mad, cocaine-snorting genius, and viewers had to wait until Jeremy Brett in ➢*The Adventures of Sherlock Holmes* for a definitive, unsanitized, version.

CAST *Sherlock Holmes* Douglas Wilmer *Dr Watson* Nigel Stock *Insp. Lestrade* Peter Madden /*pr* David Goddard, William Sterling /*dr* inc Shaun Sutton, Bill Bain, Graham Evans /*wr* inc Anthony Read, Vincent Tilsley /*BBC TV* (UK) /28 x 50bw.

Shine on Harvey Moon

Comedy. ITV 1982–5/1995–

Post-war-blues comedy drama featuring RAF stores clerk Harvey Moon (Kenneth Cranham), who returns to native Hackney on demob to find his house destroyed, himself a cuckold (several times over) and his 17-year-old daughter Maggie (Linda Robson, ➢*Birds of a Feather*) 'stepping out' with his former best friend, Lou Lewis (Nigel Planer, ➢*The Young Ones*). Episodes – initially 30 minutes, then promoted to an expansive 60 minutes – related Moon's efforts, in a nostalgically (though not unfaithfully) pictured austerity society, to build his life anew, notably the dating of son Stanley's headmistress and his election as a Labour councillor. Eventually Harvey and wife Rita reconciled, though dicily. In 1995, after a 10-year absence (not least because Marks and Gran had been engaged in another period comedy, ➢*Goodnight Sweetheart*) the show was revived with an updated setting of 1953. Nicky Henson replaced Cranham in the title role.

CAST *Harvey Moon* Kenneth Cranham/Nicky Henson *Rita Moon* Maggie Steed *Maggie Moon* Linda Robson *Nan* Elizabeth Spriggs *Lou Lewis* Nigel Planer *Stanley* Lee Whitlock *Veronica* Pauline Quirke *Eric Gottlieb* Leonard Fenton *Noah* Colin Salmon /*cr* Laurence Marks & Maurice Gran /*pr* Tony Charles, Allan McKeown /*dr* Baz Taylor /*Central TV* (UK) /12 x 30m, 23 x 60m col.

Shoestring

Crime. BBC1 1979–80

'Private ear' detective series featuring Eddie Shoestring, a low-key gumshoe who solved the cases of listeners to England's Radio West. In the dishevelled, Cortina estate-driving Shoestring, Trevor Eve found a genuine creation and a breakthrough career role. Michael Medwin from ➢*The Army Game* played the station boss, and Liz Crowther (daughter of Leslie ➢*Crackerjack* Crowther) the receptionist. The episode 'The Farmer Had a Wife' marked one of the very first screen appearances (if fleeting) of Daniel Day Lewis, cast as a DJ. Devised by Robert Banks Stewart, later to dream up ➢*Bergerac.*

CAST *Eddie Shoestring* Trevor Eve *Don Satchley* Michael Medwin *Erica Bayliss* Doran Godwin *Sonia* Liz Crowther /*cr* Robert Banks Stewart /*pr* Robert Banks Stewart /*dr* inc Paul Ciapessoni, Douglas Camfield, Mike Vardy /*wr* inc Robert Banks Stewart, Terence Feely, John Kruse /*mus* George Fenton /*BBC TV* (UK) / 21 x 50m col.

Shogun

Adventure. BBC1 1982

Mini-series (reputedly, at $22 million plus, the most expensive ever) ever-so-languidly chronicling the fortunes of a 17th-century British sailor, John Blackthorne (Richard Chamberlain, previously ➢*Dr Kildare*), shipwrecked on the coast of Japan. After capture and cultural acclimatization (taking the name Anjin-san, lusting after Lady Mariko) he pursued the prize of becoming the first western-born top-grade Samurai warrior – a Shogun. Adapted from James Clavell's forest-razing novel, itself based on the true story of mariner Will Evans, and filmed on pretty locations in Japan with numerous star Nipponese actors, including Toshiro Mifune.

CAST *John Blackthorne* Richard Chamberlain *Lady Toda Buntaro-Mariko* Yoko Shimada *Lord Toranaga* Toshiro Mifune *Friar Domingo* Michael Hordern *Vasco Rodriguez* John Rhys-Davies /*cr* James Clavell /*exec pr* James Clavell /*dr* Jerry London /*wr* Eric Bercovici /*mus* Maurice Jarre /*Paramount TV* (USA) /6 x 96m col /US tx NBC 1990.

Shooting Stars

Light Entertainment. BBC2 1996–

Post-modern quiz show in which 'top comic duo' Vic Reeves and Bob Mortimer asked completely pointless questions of baffled celebrity teams.

Painfully funny stuff. The inane bizarrity of Reeves and Mortimer (➢*Vic Reeves' Big Night Out, The Smell of Reeves and Mortimer*) was perfectly counterpointed by the team captains, glum '50s throwback' Mark Lamarr (*The Word*) and Ulrika Jonsson (sometime TV weathergirl, ➢*Gladiators* and 1992's Rear of the Year). Dressed-as-a-baby George Dawes was the man with the scores, and the winners (arbitrarily decided) went home with such worthwhile prizes as a Bob Hoskins mask. Developed as part of Reeves and Mortimer's £2 million deal with the Corporation. 'Ulrika-ka-ka-ka-ka...'

CAST (presenters) Vic Reeves, Bob Mortimer, Mark Lamarr, Ulrika Jonsson /*pr* Alan Marke /*dr* Mark Mylod /*BBC TV* (UK) /42+ x 30m col.

A Show Called Fred

Comedy. ITV 1956

Derived ultimately from radio's *The Goons*, via Peter Sellars' 1956 Idiot Weekly, *Price 2d* (in which his act as the editor of a Victorian rag interspersed sketches) to present a novel half-hour of off-the-studio-wall skitsy prankery and surrealism. Example: a theatre audience watches the stage curtain open – to reveal an audience looking at them. Sellers and Spike Milligan led the team, which carried on the zanery in *Son of Fred* (1956). The director of both was Dick Lester, later to helm The Beatles' films.

CAST Peter Sellars, Spike Milligan, Kenneth Connor, Valentine Dyall, Graham Stark, Patti Lewis, Max Geldray /*dr* Dick Lester /*wr* inc Spike Milligan, John Antrobus, Dave Freeman /*Associated-Rediffusion* (UK) /6 x 30m bw.

The Simpsons

Comedy. Sky1 1990–

'Ay Carumba!'

Animated events in the life of a dysfunctional blue-collar American family which became the first 'toon since ➢*The Flintstones* to become a prime-time hit. The immediate Simpsons clan (who had just four digits per hand and yellow skin, and hailed from average-town Springfield) were: bonehead Homer, who worked at the local nuclear power plant: his wife Marge (voiced by Julie Kavner, ➢*Rhoda*), a devoted reader of *Mom* magazine and possessor of an enormous blue beehive; 10-year-old son Bart (an anagram of brat), a spiky-haired underachiever; Lisa, the saxophone-playing daughter, the resident intellectual; Maggie, the baby, crawling everywhere with a perpetual pacifier in her mouth. Dreamed up by 'Life in Hell' cartoonist Matt Groening, *The Simpsons* debuted as inserts on ➢*The Tracey Ullman Show*, but was quickly developed into a series of its own by Fox TV (and comedy deity James L. Brooks) to become one of the phenomena of all TV time (celebrities queued for guest voice spots, a *Simpson*'s appearance being the *ne plus ultra* of the 90s; Elizabeth Taylor provided Maggie's first word). Initially, the show centred on Bart and showered witty though irrelevant gags, but then subtly shifted centre to food-mad Homer (who once sold his soul to the devil for a single doughnut), deepened characterization and, quite brilliantly, began to lampoon everything from movies to politics – though within the confines of the episode's narrative. Of course, at core, *The Simpsons* was a subversion of the domestic sitcom – and the idea of the all-American nuclear family itself. The imperfections of the Simpsons, as Fox's own research revealed, endeared them to viewers because they were, simply, 'a family like us'. Not all approved. The morally-rigid American right campaigned against the show and US President George Bush himself declared 'We need a nation closer to the Waltons than the Simpsons.' In Britain, the Simpsons were first seen on satellite TV after the BBC, having bought *The Tracey Ullman Show*, decided that the little yellow people from Springfield were not funny – and cut them out. Doh!

CAST (voices) *Homer Simpson* Dan Castellaneta *Marge Simpson* Julie Kavner *Bartholomew 'Bart' Simpson* Yeardley Smith *Lisa Simpson* Nancy Cartwright *Mr Burns/Principal Skinner/Ned Flanders / Smithers/Otto the bus driver* Harry Shearer *Moe/Chief Wiggum* Hank Azaria /*cr* Matt Groening /*exec pr* James L. Brooks, Matt Groening, Sam Simon, Al Jean, Mike Reiss, Josh Weinstein /*pr* inc Jon Vitti, David Silverman /*dr* inc David Silverman, Rich Moore, Jim Reardon /*wr* inc John Swartzwelder, Conan O'Brien /*mus* Danny Elfman (theme), Alf Clausen /*Gracie Films: 20th Century Fox TV* (USA) /200 x 30m col /US tx Fox TV 1989–.

The Singing Detective
Drama. BBC1 1986

Dennis Potter's extraordinary musical drama featuring Philip Marlow (Michael Gambon), a pulp writer bed-ridden in a London hospital. As he endured treatment for psoriatic arthritis (the illness from which Potter himself suffered), Marlow fantasized a feverish, surreal mix of scenes from his thrillers, his childhood and the ward around him, laced with paranoia over the plan (imagined or not) of his wife and her lover to steal the film rights to a Marlow novel. An unrepeatable box of scripted tricks, gloriously produced. TV art at its highest expression.

CAST *Philip E. Marlow* Michael Gambon *Nurse Mills / Carlotta* Joanne Whalley *Mrs Beth Marlow/Lili* Alison Steadman *Mark Binney/Mark Finney/Raymond Binney* Patrick Malahide *Philip Marlow (as boy)* Lyndon Davies *Mr Marlow* Jim Carter *Nicola Marlow* Janet Suzman /*cr* Dennis Potter /*pr* Kenith Trodd, John Harris /*dr* Jon Amiel /*wr* Dennis Potter /*BBC TV* (UK) / 6 x 60:80m col /US tx PBS 1988.

The Singing Ringing Tree
Children's. BBC1 1964

Much loved fairy tale in which a prince hunted for a magic tree to give to a petulant princess. Made in East Germany, it was screened under the *Tales from Europe* umbrella.

CAST (narrator) Antony Bilbow *Prince* Charles-Hans Vogt *Princess* Christel Bodenstein /*dr* Francesco Stefani / *wr* (English version) Peggy Miller /*DEFA* (E Ger) / 3 x 25m bw.

Sir Francis Drake
Adventure. ITV 1961–2

Seafaring actioner, launched in the wake of ➢*The Buccaneers*, charting the adventures of Queen Elizabeth's favourite salt dog aboard *The Golden Hind*. Acceptable sail-and-sword fare, some episodes were later spliced together as TVMs for the American market. Of note to star-spotters are Drake's brother (a pre-➢*Some Mothers Do 'Ave 'Em* Michael Crawford) and his swarthy Spanish nemesis, Mendoza (Roger Delgado, later The Master in ➢*Doctor Who*).

CAST *Sir Francis Drake* Terence Morgan *Queen Elizabeth* Jean Kent *John Drake* Michael Crawford *Mendoza* Roger Delgado *Trevelyan* Patrick McLoughlin / *pr* Anthony Bushell /*ABC: ATV* (UK) /26 x 25m bw / US tx NBC 1962 (as *The Adventures of Sir Francis Drake*).

The Six Million Dollar Man
Sci-fi. ITV 1974–8

A pop-culture phenomenon of the 70s, based on Martin Caidin's novel, *Cyborg*, and developed for TV via a Howard Rodman- and Steven Bochco-authored movie. When NASA astronaut Steven Austin (Lee Majors, late of ➢*The Big Valley*, ➢*The Men from Shiloh*) loses both legs, one arm and an eye during a test flight, he is refurbished by scientist Rudy Wells with atomic replacements. Thus bionically equipped, Austin repays his $6 million debt to Internal Revenue by taking up employment with Oscar Goldman's Office of Strategic Studies (a CIA lookalike), serially besting the enemies of the US of A. These were usually Lombroso criminal stereotypes, or cunning spies, but included such sci-fi adversaries as the run-amok 'seven million dollar man' (Monte Markham) and Bigfoot (actually an alien robot played by the ➢*The Addams Family*'s Ted 'Lurch' Cassidy). Major's girlfriend (later wife), Farrah Fawcett guest-starred in the segments 'The Rescue of Atlanta One', 'Nightmare in the Sky' and 'The Golden Pharaoh'. While the opening credit's dialogue ('Gentlemen. We have the technology – we can rebuild him...') and generous use of slow-mo were widely parodied, the series topped ratings around the world. A spin-off, ➢*The Bionic Woman*, also did good business. Not until 1978 was the 60 m.p.h. SMDM unplugged, primarily because comic-strip-hero films, led by ➢*The Adventures of Superman*, had made his budget-challenged TV stunts seem distinctly substandard. That said, the SMDM did not escape the revival craze of the 80s/90s, with a spree of TVMs: *Return of the Bionic Couple* (1987), *Bionic Showdown* (1989) and *Bionic Ever After* (1994). There was even a Hollywood makeover, *The Six Million Dollar Man* (1996).

CAST *Col Steve Austin* Lee Majors *Oscar Goldman* Richard Anderson *Dr Rudy Wells* Alan Oppenheimer / Martin E. Brooks /*cr* Harve Bennett /*exec pr* Harve Bennett, Glen A. Larson, Allan Balter, Kenneth Johnson /*dr* inc Glen A. Larson, Edwards Abrams, Reza Badiyi, Arnold Laven, Cliff Bole, Richard Irving, Jeannot Swarc /*wr* inc Glen A. Larson, Kenneth

Johnson, D.C. Fontana, Mark Frost, Alan Levi, Henri Simoun /*mus* Oliver Nelson, Dusty Springfield (theme vocal) /*Universal TV* (USA) /1 x 85m, 102 x 60m col / US tx ABC 1973–8.

The Six Wives of Henry VIII

Drama. BBC2 1970

Award-winning historical drama, essentially a sequence of six self-contained biopic plays (one for each of the eponymous fat Tudor king's wives). Intelligent scripts and lavishly accurate production were capped by powerful thespian performances, especially by Keith Michell (later Captain Beaky) as a decaricatured, complex Henry. And it contained just the right amount of regal sex and violence. During its initial run on BBC2 it set new audience records, and subsequently sold to over 75 countries. ➢*Elizabeth R* was essentially a sequel.

CAST *Henry VIII* Keith Michell *Narrator* Anthony Quayle *Catherine of Aragon* Annette Crosbie *Anne Boleyn* Dorothy Tutin *Jane Seymour* Anne Stallybrass *Anne of Cleves* Elvi Hale *Catherine Howard* Angela Pleasance *Katherine Parr* Rosalie Crutchley *Duke of Norfolk* Patrick Troughton *Thomas Cranmer* Bernard Hepton /*cr* Maurice Cowan /*pr* Ronald Travers /*wr* inc Rosemary Ann Sisson, Jean Morris, Beverly Cross / *BBC TV* (UK) /6 x 90m col /US tx CBS 1971.

Skippy

Children's. ITV 1967–9

Classic Australian adventure series featuring a smart kangaroo, pet of Sonny, the scion of Waratah National Park ranger Matt.

Lots of outdoor action in stunning landscapes, an alluring lead animal (who alerted his human sidekick to the weekly crime/accident with a memorable 'tut-tutting'), all led in by a jaunty, cockles-of-the-hearts-warming theme as the roo bounced through the scrub towards his young friend: 'Skippy, Skippy, Skippy, the bush kangaroo…' Liza Goddard made her TV debut as Clancy Merrick, a young girlfriend of the all-male Hammond family.

After an interval of 26 years, the marsupial character bounced back on to the TV screens in *The Adventures of Skippy*. Here Sonny (now played by Andrew Clarke from *Anzacs*) had followed his father's boots into park rangering, and the kangaroo was the pet of his twin children Lou and Jerry.

CAST *Sonny Hammond* Garry Parkhurst *Matt Hammond* Ed Devereaux *Mark Hammond* Ken James *Clarissa 'Clancy' Merrick* Liza Goddard /*exec pr* John McCallum, Bud Austin /*pr* Lee Robinson, Dennis Hill / *dr* inc Max Varnel, Eric Fullilove /*wr* Ross Napier, Ed Devereaux /*mus* Eric Jupp /*Norfolk International* (Aus) / 91 x 25m col /US tx Syndicated 1969.

Sky

Children's. ITV 1976

Was a young blue-eyed being from another dimension who became stranded on Earth. With the help of three West Country kids, he sought to return before the forces of Mother Nature – disturbed by his alien presence – annihilated him. Above-average telefantasy.

CAST *Sky* Mark Harrison *Arby Vennor* Stuart Lock *Jane Vennor* Cherrald Butterfield *Roy Briggs* Richard Speight /*cr* Bob Baker, Dave Martin /*exec pr* Patrick Dromgoole /*pr* Leonard White /*dr* Derek Clarke /wr Bob Baker, Dave Martin /*HTV* (UK) 7 x 30m col.

Sledge Hammer!

Comedy. ITV 1987–8

Enthusiastic parody of the tough-guy detective genre, featuring square-jawed, brain-free DI Hammer ('Trust me, I know what I'm doing.'). The cases – which included a classic story of a multiple killer of Elvis Presley impersonators – were usually solved by Hammer's blonde female sidekick, Detective Doreau, the macho man himself being too busy caressing his .44 Magnum ('Gun', as he cooingly called it) or shooting off the same at any 'lowlife' he took a right-wing prejudice to.

Inconsequential. But fun.

CAST *DI Sledge Hammer* David Rasche *Det. Dori Doreau* Anne-Marie Martin /*cr* Alan Spencer /*exec pr* Alan Spencer, Robert Lovenheime /*dr* inc Bill Bixby, Thomas Schlamme, Jackie Cooper, Martha Coolidge, Reza Badiyi, Seymour Robbie, Charles Braverman, Charles Dubin /*wr* inc Chris Ruppenthal, Al Jean and Mike Reiss /*A New World International Production* (USA) /41 x 30m col /US tx ABC 1986–88.

Sliders
Sci-fi. Sky1 1996–

Whilst tinkering in his basement, whizz-kid physics student Quinn Mallory (a slimmed-down Jerry O'Connell from *Stand By Me*) creates a 'sliding' device that enables him, plus archetypal manipulative professor Arturo, hacker Wells, and an innocent passer-by, soul musician Rembrandt Brown, to jaunt through alternative (parallel) versions of Earth's history.

Shameless pillage by John Landis of ➢*The Time Tunnel* (itself more than a nod to 50s show *You Are There*), uncertain of its target audience and cliché-foolish (scenarios included a *Red Dawn* occupation of the USA by the USSR with Oliver North as US President). But intriguing fun. From time to time.

CAST *Quinn Mallory* Jerry O'Connell *Prof. Maximilian Arturo* John Rhys-Davies *Wade Welles* Sabrina Lloyd *Rembrandt 'Crying Man' Brown* Cleavant Derricks /*cr* Robert K. Weiss, Tracy Torme /*exec pr* John Landis, Leslie Belzberg /*dr* Jefrey Levy /*St Clare Entertainment* (USA) /70+ x 60m col /US tx Fox TV 1995–.

Soap
Comedy. ITV 1978–82

Sitcom satirizing US daytime soaps, which courted controversy with its absurdist, nonsensical plots ('Confused? You will be!') of adultery, transvestism, homosexuality and impotence. Featured were two sisters and their families, residents of Dunns River, Connecticut. The dim Jessica Tate was married to super-rich (and super-unfaithful) stockbroker Chester, and those living under her mansion roof included her father, who believed that WWII was still in full swing. Her sardonic black butler was later spun off to his own hit show, ➢*Benson*. Poorer in money, but not in ill-fortune, was Mary Campbell, married to blue-collar second husband Burt, who had some difficulty in relating to gay stepson Jodie (Billy Crystal) and racketeer stepson Danny. Yet such prosaic problems were put in perspective when Burt's own lothario son, Peter (Robert Urich, later ➢*Spenser: For Hire*), was murdered (with Jessica Tate convicted, but the true culprit, Chester, later confessing), and Burt himself cloned by aliens. Meanwhile, Corinne Tate's baby turned out to be the spawn of the devil (literally), which required a quick exorcism, and Jessica had a steamy entanglement with a South American revolutionary, 'El Puerco'. Having redrawn the boundaries of the sitcom, creator Susan Harris went on to move them again with ➢*The Golden Girls*, a sitcom about ageing women. Her husband, Paul Junger Witt, was *Soap*'s executive producer.

CAST *Jessica Tate* Katherine Helmond *Chester Tate* Robert Mandan *Corrine Tate* Diane Canova *Eunice Tate* Jennifer Salt *Billy Tate* Jimmy Baio *Benson* Robert Guillaume *The Major* Arthur Peterson *Mary Dallas Campbell* Cathryn Damon *Burt Campbell* Richard Mulligan *Jodie Campbell* Billy Crystal *Danny Campbell* Ted Wass *Peter Campbell* Robert Urich *Father Timothy Flotsky* Sal Viscuso *Dutch* Donnelly Rhodes *Det. Donahue* John Byner *Carlos 'El Puerco' Valdez* Gregory Sierra /*cr* Susan Harris /*exec pr* Tony Thomas, Paul Junger Witt /*pr* Susan Harris /*dr* inc Jay Sandrich, J.J. Lobue /*wr* inc Susan Harris /*Witt: Thomas: Harris* (USA) /93 x 30m col /US tx ABC 1977–93.

Softly, Softly
Crime. BBC1 1966–76

Successful (top 10) spin-off from ➢*Z Cars*, which relocated detectives Barlow and Watt to the fictitious West Country town of Wyvern. In 1970 the title was changed to the cumbersome *Softly, Softly – Task Force*, with Barlow promoted to Head of Thamesford Constabulary CID's Task Force, Watt acompanying him as his soft-cop alter ego. After brief service there, Stratford John's perennially popular bull-headed Detective Chief Superintendent character was seconded to the Home Office in *Barlow at Large* (BBC1 1971–5, 30 x 50m, the latter seasons shortened in title to *Barlow*). Meanwhile, the *Softly, Softly* cast plodded on until 1976, always with quality scripts, but also with a disconcerting black hole in the screen where Barlow had once loomed. Realizing the waste of one of the British small screen's great double acts, BBC teamed Barlow and Watt in a 1973 investigation of the real-life Jack the Ripper case, the format being continued in *Second Verdict* (BBC1 1976), in which the duo put the magnifying glass on six true-crime mysteries of yesteryear.

CAST *DCS Charlie Barlow* Stratford Johns *DCI John Watt* Frank Windsor *DI Harry Hawkins* Norman Bowler *Sgt Evans* David Lloyd Meredith *PC Henry Snow* Terence Rigby *DCI Lewis* Garfield Morgan *DC Stone* Alexis Kanner /*pr* David E. Rose, Leonard Lewis, Geraint Morris /*dr* inc Philip Dudley, Vere Lorrimer / *wr* inc Alan Plater, Elwyn Jones, Robert Jones /*BBC TV* (UK) /264 x 60m bw:col.

Soldier, Soldier

Drama. ITV 1991–

Followed a long parade of army dramas (*The Regiment, Spearhead,* etc.), though was more successful than any of its predecessors. Invented by ex-military policewoman Lucy Gannon (who went on to create ➢*Peak Practice, Bramwell, Insiders*) it related events in the 'ordinary' life of the soldiers and officers of B Company, the King's Own Fusiliers Infantry Regiment, on duty at home and abroad. With its chirpy squaddism – exemplified in the near comedic double act between Lance Corporal Garvey (Jerome Flynn) and Fusilier Tucker (Robson Green) – it was more Lad's Army than Dad's Army. If this was to public taste, much more so were the large doses of soapiness Gannon introduced into the story, usually through the strong line-up of women characters who inhabited the world of the KOF as wives, girlfriends and WRACs. The show's occasional forays into the combat zone, however, were woefully unconvincing (not least because, as one *Soldier, Soldier* actor pointed out, he and his fellows were 'lardcakes'). The show survived a haemorrhage of lead characters, including Flynn (formerly ➢*London's Burning*) and Green (formerly ➢*Casualty*) – who went on to a £50 million career covering pop classics, plus heading, individually or together, *Reckless, Ain't Misbehavin'* and so forth – though with the ratings somewhat dented.

CAST *Major Tom Cadman* David Haig *Laura Cadman* Cathryn Harrison *Lance Cpl/Cpl/Sgt Paddy Garvey* Jerome Flynn *Fuslier/Lance Cpl Dave Tucker* Robson Green *Cpl Nancy Garvey (née Thorpe)* Holly Aird *Donna Tucker* Rosie Rowell *Cpl/Sgt Tony Wilton* Gary Love *Lt Jeremy Forsythe* Bea Nealon *Lance Cpl Steve Evans* Shaun Dingwell /*cr* Lucy Gannon /*pr* Chris Kelly, Christopher Neame, Ann Tricklebank /*dr* inc Tony Garner, Michael Brayshaw, Paul Brown, Patrick Lau, Douglas Mackinnon, Graham More, Catherine Morshead /*wr* inc Lucy Gannon, Peter Barwood, James Clare, Ann Brown /*Central TV* (UK) /70+ x 60m col.

Solo

Comedy. BBC1 1981–2

Carla Lane-scripted sitcom in which 30-year-old Gemma Palmer decided to get a new life (kicking her job, kicking out her two-timing boyfriend, Danny) and go – solo. Something of the same woman-home-alone premise was behind Lane's ➢*The Mistress* (also starring Felicity Kendal) three years later.

CAST *Gemma Palmer* Felicity Kendal *Danny* Stephen Moore *Mrs Palmer* Elspet Gray /*cr* Carla Lane /*pr* Gareth Gwenlan /*wr* Carla Lane /*BBC TV* (UK) / 13 x 30m col.

Some Mothers Do 'Ave 'Em

Comedy. BBC1 1973–8

'Ohh Betty…'

Misadventures of an accident-prone genial simpleton in a beret and mac. Throughout every DIY disaster, anti-social malapropism and loss of employment, his understanding wife supported.

A throwback to the slapstick style of the silent film era, with a camp, nervous-twitching characterization by Michael Crawford that proved the laugh of the land. The stunts, all performed by Crawford himself (his previous service in swashbuckler ➢*Sir Francis Drake* presumably standing him in good stead) were truly, breath-suckingly excellent. Twenty million tuned in.

CAST *Frank Spencer* Michael Crawford *Betty Spencer* Michele Dotrice /*cr* Raymond Allen, Michael Crawford /*pr* Michael Mills /*wr* Raymond Allen / *BBC TV* (UK) /19 x 30m, 3 x 50m col.

The Sooty Show

Children's. BBC 1955–67/ITV 1968–93

The little prankster glove-puppet teddy bear with the sooty ears and nose (and Harry Corbett's hand inside him) made his TV debut in a 1952 episode of *Talent Night,* graduating to his own show – via *Saturday Special* – in 1955. Two years later Sweep the dog joined the team, followed by Sooty's panda girlfriend Soo in 1964 (despite BBC fear that their relationship was 'introducing sex into children's TV'). In 1967 Sooty was axed from the BBC schedule, but then crossed over to Thames TV to continue his assaults on Corbett with water/flour/eggs/hammer unabated. When Corbett retired from the fray, his son Matthew stepped in as puppeteer-presenter, the show being retitled *Sooty & Co* when Granada purchased it on Thames' loss of franchise in 1992. This lasted until 1997, when Sooty and gang (together with Sooty's favourite props, the water-pistol and the wand) were sold for £1.4 million. A spin-off series, *Sooty's Amazing Adventures*, however, continued the antics in animated form.

CAST (presenters) Harry Corbett, Matthew Corbett / *pr* inc Daphne Shadwell / *BBC: Thames TV* (UK) / approx. 400 x 25m bw:col.

Sorry

Comedy. BBC1 1981–8

Ronnie Corbett starred in this suburban sitcom about a 40-year-old librarian, Timothy Lumsden, still living at home and attached by umbilical cord to his domineering *mater.* Aggravatingly successful (topping the ratings in 1981), thanks to a cast, especially the sheepish Corbett, acting at the top of their caricatures.

It was not the first time that the vertically challenged Corbett played a mummy's boy: the series *Now Look Here!*, by Graham Chapman and Barry Cryer, in which he starred between 1971–3, had much the same premise.

CAST *Timothy Lumsden* Ronnie Corbett *Mrs Lumsden* Barbara Lott *Mr Lumsden* William Moore *Frank* Roy Holder / *cr* Ian Davidson, Peter Vincent / *pr* David Askey / *BBC TV* (UK) / 43 x 30m col.

South Park

Comedy. Sky1 1998–

Animation featuring a quartet of snot-nosed brats from snowy South Park, Colorado, which became the US TV and cultural phenomenon of 1997. The foursome were: Waspy Stan, the permanently hooded and regularly killed Kenny ('Omigod, they've killed Kenny'), fiendish fat boy Eric Cartman, and confused Jew, Kyle. Dubbed 'Peanuts on acid' – by virtue of its elemental art style as much as its bizarrity – the 'toon was decked in unashamedly parent-unfriendly language ('dildo', 'pigfucker') which ensured a late-night scheduling berth on most networks (though this did little to stop the show becoming a crossdown hit to the playground crowd). The initial episode, 'Cartman Gets an Anal Probe', in which a midnight encounter with aliens left Cartman with an 80-foot radio telescope up his butt, set the scatological and surreal tone for everything that followed. There was a memorable gallery of supporting characters in schoolteacher Mr Garrison (with his hand puppet, Mr Hat), Isaac Hayes' soul-man school caterer and football coach ('Hold the ball like you're holding yo woman'), and goody-goody Wendy Testaburger. Originating out of a five-minute video Yuletide card, 'The Spirit of Christmas', commissioned from twenty-something animators Matt Stone and Trey Parker by Fox executive Brian Graden, *South Park* spun off $30 million in merchandizing in its first season alone, and a posse of Hollywood faces came calling for bit parts to prove their hipness. Among the chosen were Tom Wopat (➢*Dukes of Hazzard*, ➢*Cybill*), Jonathan Katz and Jay Leno. ➢*ER*'s George Clooney got to play the gay dog, Sparky. Woof.

CAST (voices) *Stan Marsh/Eric Cartman/Mr Garrison / Officer Barbrady* Trey Parker *Kyle Broslofski/Kenny McCormick/Pip* Matt Stone *Chef* Isaac Hayes *The Mayor/Sheila Broslofski/Cartman's mother/Wendy Testaburger* Shannen Cassidy *Ike Broslofski* Jesse Howell / *cr* Matt Stone, Trey Parker / *exec pr* Brian Graden, Matt Stone, Trey Parker / *pr* Anne Garefino / *dr* Trey Parker, Matt Stone / *wr* Trey Parker, Matt Stone, Dan Sterling / *cr* Matt Stone, Trey Parker / *exec pr* Brian Graden, Matt Stone, Trey Parker / *pr* Philip Stark / *mus* inc Les Claypool, Alan Berry, Matt Stone / *Comedy Partners: Celluloid Studios* (USA) / 24+ x 30m col / US tx Comedy Central 1997–.

South Riding

Drama. ITV 1974

Stan Barstow's adaptation of Winifred Holtby's novel about a progressive headmistress in a mythical Yorkshire town in depressed, class-ridden 1932. Judged by BAFTA to be the best drama of 1994, helped by an able cast.

CAST *Sarah Burton (headmistress)* Dorothy Tutin *Robert Carne* Nigel Davenport *Mrs Beddows* Hermione Baddeley / *pr* James Ormerod / *dr* Alistair Reid / *wr* Stan Barstow / *Yorkshire TV* (UK) / 13 x 60m col.

Space

Drama. ITV 1987

A stupendously produced mini-series 'faction-alizing' America's space effort. An undemanding attention-occupier, it was the TV equivalent of a good read. Which is exactly what it was derived from, namely James Michener's epic book of the same title.

CAST *Norman Grant* James Garner *Elinor Grant* Susan Anspach *Randy Clagett* Beau Bridges *Stanley Mott* Bruce Dern *Rachel Mott* Melinda Dillon *John Pope* Harry Hamlin *Dieter Kolff* Michael York /*exec pr* Dick Berg /*pr* Martin Manulis /*dr* Lee Philips, Joseph Sargent /*wr* Dick Berg, Sterling Silliphant /*Dick Berg: Stonehenge: Paramount Network* (USA) /7 x 60:180m col /US tx CBS 1987.

Space: Above and Beyond
Sci-fi. Sky1 1996

Top Gun in space. In AD 2063 a group of novice (and good-looking) starfighter pilots from the Marine's Corps 58th Squadron is all that stands between Earth and an alien invasion.

High-grade CGI (Computer Generated Image) combat scenes; save for that, a parade of expensive ($2 million per episode) clichés raided from cinema's war and space-opera archives. Created, in so far as it was original, by ex-➢*The X-Files* executive producers and writers, Glen Morgan and James Wong.

CAST *Nathan West* Morgan Weisser *Shane Vansen* Kristen Cloke *Vanessa Damphousse* Lanei Chapman *Paul Wang* Joel Dan La Fuente *McQueen* James Morrison /*cr* Glen Morgan, James Wong /*exec pr* Glen Morgan, James Wong /*dr* inc David Nutter, Felix Alcala, Rick Kolbe, Michael Katleman /*wr* Glen Morgan, James Wong, Steve Zito, Marylyn Osbourne / *Fox TV: Hard Eight* (USA) /1 x 120m, 13 x 60m col /US tx Fox TV 1995.

Space: 1999
Sci-fi. ITV 1975–8

When a nuclear dump on the dark side of the moon explodes, Moonbase Alpha and its crew of 311 are sent spinning into the galaxy for close encounters with Bug-Eyed Monsters, comic gas clouds and alien civilizations.

Gerry Anderson's second live action show (after ➢*UFO*), intended as a British ➢*Star Trek* (it even used *Trek* producer Fred Freiberger). Curiously, it lacked the optimism of Anderson's animations (and *Trek* itself), resulting in depressing storylines where no brotherhood was ever possible between the Alpha inmates and beings from visited planets, only suspicion and war. Worse still was the mumbling stiffness of the cast (especially husband-and-wife team Martin Landau and Barbara Bain, previously, ➢*Mission: Impossible*, as leads Commander Koenig and Medical Officer Russell), were more wooden than Anderson's famed puppets on a string. Only Catherine Schell's exotic alien Maya, the sfx and models shone out of the dark tedium and the almost bottomless budget. A galaxy-sized turkey.

CAST *Cmdr John Koenig* Martin Landau *Dr Helena Russell* Barbara Bain *Alan Carter* Nick Tate *Prof. Victor Bergman* Barry Morse *Maya* Catherine Schell *Tony Verdeschi* Tony Anholt /*cr* Gerry & Sylvia Anderson /*exec pr* Gerry Anderson /*pr* Sylvia Anderson, Fred Freiberger /*dr* inc Lee Katzin, Peter Medak, Charles Crichton, Tom Clegg, David Tomblin /*wr* inc Johnny Byrne, Anthony Terpiloff, Tony Barwick, Charles Woodgrove (aka Freiberger), Terrance Dicks, Michael Winder /*mus* Barry Gray, Derek Wadsworth /*sfx* Brian Johnson, Martin Bower /*ITC: RAI* (UK) /It) /48 x 60m col /US tx Syndicated 1975–8.

Space Patrol
Children's. ITV 1963–4

Trailed the peace-keeping adventures of space craft Galasphere 347 in the year 2100, as she and those who served aboard her (Earthman Captain Larry Dart, Venusian Slim, Martian Husky) patrolled the galaxy.

Endearing puppet show from Roberta Leigh – who had previously scribed the stories for Gerry Anderson's first stringed shows, *Twizzle* and ➢*Torchy* – inexplicably neglected.

CAST (voices) *Capt. Larry Dart* Dick Vosburgh *Husky / Slim/Prof. O'Brien Haggerty* Ronnie Stevens *Cassiopea O'Brien Haggerty Gabblerdictum* Libby Morris /*cr* Roberta Leigh /*pr* Roberta Leigh, Arthur Provis /*dr* Frank Goulding /*wr* Roberta Leigh /*sfx* Bill Palmer, Bert Walker, Brian Stevens /*National Interest Picture Prod: Wonderama Productions Ltd* (UK) /39 x 30m bw / US tx Syndicated 1964.

Space Precinct
Sci-fi. Sky1 1995–

In the 21st century NY cop Patrick Brogan (Ted Shackelford from ➢*Knot's Landing*) is transferred to Demeter City on planet Altor. Although assisted by human officers Jane Castle (beautiful) and Jack Haldane (boorish), most of the inhabitants are alien Creons and Tarns. And hostile.

Risible live-action drama from Gerry ➢'*Thunderbirds*' Anderson, with the aliens, all purple heads and saucer eyes, apparently refugees from ➢*The Muppets*. Plots and characterization both slight. The special effects, which must have swallowed a huge chunk of the $36 million budget, were occasionally stupendous, however. Directors numbered John Glen from the *Bond* movie cycle.

The original pilot, *Space Police*, was shot in 1987. With jokes like, 'Raise your hands! All of them!' this was clearly targetted at kids. The series aimed up the age range at teens and adults, but never quite left childish things behind it.

CAST *Lt Patrick Brogan* Ted Shackelford *Off. Jack Haldane* Rob Youngblood *Off. Jane Castle* Simone Bendix *Sally Brogan* Nancy Paul *Podly* Jerome Willis *Orrin* Richard James *Took* Mary Woodvine *Fredo* David Quilter /*cr* Gerry Anderson /*exec pr* Tom Gutteridge /*dr* inc John Glen, Sidney Hayers, Piers Haggard /*sfx* Richard Gregory (animatronics) / *Mentorn Films: Gerry Anderson Prod: Grove Television Enterprises* (UK /USA) /24 x 60m /US tx 1994.

Special Branch

Spy. ITV 1969–74

Videotape espionage series featuring the cloak and fist activities of Scotland Yard's security department. Nods in the direction of modern mores and fashion (the coppers wore flares and sideburns, this being the late 60s), together with regular slammings of thick-ear action, took it to the top of the ratings by 1970. At the end of the second season, production was handed over to fledgling Euston Films (for shooting on film), and the cast was overhauled for a critical – and popular – golden age. Pock-marked cockney actor George Sewell (later ➢*UFO*, ➢*The Detectives*) muscled and brusqued brilliantly as SB head DCI Alan Craven, with Patrick Mower (later ➢*Target*) brought in as the smoothio ladies' man, and Paul Eddington (➢*The Good Life*, ➢*Yes, Minister*) cast as civil servant Strand.

CAST *Insp. Jordan* Derren Nesbitt *Supt Eden* Wensley Pithey *Det. Supt Inman* Fulton Mackay *DCI Alan Craven* George Sewell *DCI Haggerty* Patrick Mower *Strand* Paul Eddington /*exec pr* Lloyd Shirley, George Taylor /*pr* Reginald Collin, Robert Love, Geoffrey Gilbert, Ted Childs /*dr* inc Dennis Vance, Mike Vardy, William G. Stewart, Voytek, Peter Duguid, Guy Verney, Tom Clegg, William Brayne, Douglas Camfield / *wr* inc George Markstein, Trevor Preston, P.J. Hammond, Ian Kennedy Martin, Adele Rose /*mus* Robert Earley /*Thames TV: Euston Films* (UK) / 52 x 60m col.

Spender

Crime. BBC1 1991–3

Streetwise 90s police show starring Geordie actor Jimmy Nail (previously Oz in ➢*Auf Wiedersehen, Pet*). Episodes followed the undercover detective – transferred back to Newcastle by a Met unhappy at his impolitic attitude – through a drab Tynescape in search of crims from corrupt industrialists to drug traffickers, the story powered along by a rock soundtrack reminiscent of US cop series ➢*Miami Vice*. In addition to playing the title role, Nail also co-created the show (with Ian La Frenais) and contributed teleplays.

CAST *Spender* Jimmy Nail *Stick* Sammy Johnson *Frances Spender (ex-wife)* Denise Welch *Supt Yelland* Paul Greenwood *DCS Gillespie* Peter Guiness *DS Dan Boyd* Berwick Kaler /*cr* Jimmy Nail, Ian La Frenais / *pr* Martin McKeand, Paul Raphael /*BBC TV* (UK) / 22 x 55m col.

Spenser: For Hire

Crime. BBC1 1989–93

PI series, set in Boston, featuring Robert Urich as the eponymous modern day Galahad-with-a-gun. He was aided in his principled quests by psychologist girlfriend Susan, while his black, Magnum-carrying associate, Hawk (Avery Brooks, later ➢*Star Trek: DS9*) earned a short-lived spin-off, *A Man Called Hawk*.

Curiously soft-sell version of Robert B. Parker's novels, almost entirely lacking their Chandleresque wise-cracking wit and tough-guy violence, though watchable enough on its own middle-of-the-road terms.

CAST *Spenser* Robert Urich *Susan Silverman* Barbara Stock *Hawk* Avery Brooks *Ada Rita Fiori* Carolyn McCormick *Lt Martin Quirk* Richard Jaeckel /*exec pr* John Wilder /*pr* William Robert Yates, Dick Gallegy, Robert Hamilton /*dr* inc John Wilder, William Wiard, Sutton Roley, Virgil W. Vogel, Don Chaffey, Richard Colla /*John Wilder Prod: Warner Bros* (USA) /66 x 60m col /US tx ABC 1985–8.

Created by the carefully pronounced Fluck and Law, the satirical puppet show *Spitting Image* broke new TV ground by parodying the Royal Family, previously comedic untouchables.

Spider-Man
Children's. ITV 1969–70

'Spider-Man, Spider-Man/Does whatever a spider can.../Spins a web any size/Catches thieves just like flies...'

Animated crime-buster based on Stan Lee's *Marvel* comic-strip about a High School student, Peter Parker, who is bitten by a radioactive spider. On discovering his resultant arachnoid abilities (the climbing of walls/ceilings, the spinning of webs), Parker takes a job with the *Daily Bugle*, kits himself out in a latex disguise, and super-heroically trounces such venomous villains as The Sorcerer, Blotto and Scorpion.

After a gap of more than a decade, the webbed-wonder returned to TV in 1981 in *Spider-Man and His Amazing Friends* (these being teenagers Iceman and Firestar), a distinctly light-hearted interpretation from Marvel Productions. By this time the airwaves had become choc-a-bloc with arachnoid cartoon heroism, since DePatie-Freleng's *Spider-Woman* (voiced by Joan Van Ark, 1979–80) was also on the crawl for criminals.

CAST (voice) *Peter Parker/Spider-Man* Bernard Cowan/Paul Sols /*exec pr* Robert L. Lawrence, Ralph Bakshi /*Grantray-Lawrence: Krantz: Marvel Comics* (USA) /55 x 30m col /US tx ABC 1967–9.

Spin City
Comedy. C4 1997–

Hit American sitcom starring the tiny, boyish Michael J. Fox (actually, Michael Andrew Fox) as deputy mayor of New York, a job less to do with governing than rescuing his inept boss from gaffes (e.g. saving the last dance at the ball for his mistress). Likeable and brisk, it re-teamed Fox with Gary David Goldberg, the producer who had launched him to stardom with ➢*Family Ties.* Perhaps its best joke was the most obscure for British audiences: an ironic cameo by former Clinton aide George Stephanopolous, the diminuitive spin doctor whose metaphorical clothes Fox borrowed for the show.

CAST *Michael Flaherty* Michael J. Fox *Mayor Randall Winston* Barry Bostwick *Ashley* Carla Gugino *Stuart* Alan Ruck *Paul* Richard Kind *Nikki* Connie Britton *Carter* Michael Boatman /*cr* Gary David Goldberg, Bill

Lawrence /*exec pr* Gary David Goldberg, Michael J. Fox /*pr* Walter Barnett /*dr* inc Lee Shallat Chemel / *wr* inc Michelle Nader, Amy Cohen, Richard Childs, Michael Craven /*mus* Shelly Parker /*UBU: Dreamworks* (USA) /59 x 30m col /US tx NBC 1996–.

Spitting Image

Comedy. ITV 1984–96

The latex puppets of the carefully pronounced Fluck and Law debuted in 1984, immediately winning *Spitting Image* a reputation for cruelly accurate satire. Yet, at best, the topical scripts (from, among others, Ian Hislop) were variable; the show's true turn-on was its irreverence. It mercilessly lampooned the Royal Family (previously virtual comedic untouchables), picturing the Queen Mother as an alcohol-guzzling horse-racing afficionado, plus all politicians of any rank and party. Towards the end, as the show broadened its remit ever more to include popsters, media-folk, thespians and a jive-talking pontiff, it lost direction and shambled around like a toothless dog. But, from the 80s, a dozen classical skits, images and songs remain, among them: Liberal leader David Steel living in David Owen's pocket (which produced a popular misconception that the former was physically smaller than the latter; a testament to the show's influence); the search for President Reagan's brain; the *Sun* journalist pigs; a fascistic Margaret Thatcher singing 'Tomorrow Belongs to Us' in a 1987 election special; and Philip Pope's anti-Apartheid ditty, 'I've never met a nice South African'.

CAST (voices) inc Steve Nallon, Chris Barrie, Steve Coogan, Harry Enfield, Jan Ravens, Pamela Stephenson, Rory Bremner, Harry Enfield, John Sessions /*cr* Peter Fluck & Roger Law /*pr* Jon Blair, John Lloyd, Geoffrey Perkins, Bill Dare, David Tyler /*dr* inc Bob Cousins, Peter Harris /*wr* inc Ian Hislop, Nick Newman, Rob Grant, Doug Naylor, Geoff Atkinson, James Hendrie, Steven Punt /*Central TV: Spitting Image Productions* (UK) /122 x 30, 2 x 60m col.

Split Ends

Comedy. ITV 1989

Sitcom vehicle for ➢*EastEnder* Anita Dobson, which cast her as the owner of a hairdressing salon dithering between two romances. As comic cuts went, it was the short, quick and mediocre equivalent of the pudding basin.

CAST *Cath* Anita Dobson *Clint* Harry Ditson *David* Peter Blake /*pr* James Maw /*dr* Alan J.W. Bell /*wr* Len Richmond /*Granada* (UK) /6 x 30m col.

Spyder's Web

Comedy. ITV 1972

Spoofy cloak-and-dagger series featuring 'The Web', an ultra-secret government agency dedicated to unmasking spies in plots elaborately packed with red herrings. Roy Clarke (➢*Last of the Summer Wine*, ➢*Keeping Up Appearances*) was writer-in-chief.

CAST *Wallis Ackroyd* Veronica Carlson *Charlotte 'Lottie' Dean* Patricia Cutts *Clive Hawksworth* Anthony Ainley *Albert Mason* Roger Lloyd Pack /*cr* Richard Harris /*pr* Dennis Vance /*dr* inc James Gatward /*wr* inc Richard Harris, Roy Clarke /*ATV* (UK) /13 x 60m col.

The Squirrels

Comedy. ITV 1975–7

Jovially undemanding mishaps (sample: a month's supply of crisps goes AWOL from the canteen) amongst the bickering accounts staff at International Rentals, a TV hire company. Those contributing scripts included a young Phil Redmond and former ➢*Randall and Hopkirk (Deceased)* star, Kenneth Cope. The series stemmed from a 1974 one-off play, and proved its worth when creator Eric Chappell economically recycled it in 1991 as *Fiddlers Three*.

CAST *Mr Fletcher* Bernard Hepton *Rex* Ken Jones *Harry* Alan David *Susan* Patsy Rowlands *Burke* Ellis Jones *Carol* Karin McCarthy /*cr* Eric Chappell /*pr* Shaun O'Riordan /*wr* Eric Chappell, Kenneth Cope, Alan Hackney, Richard Harris /*ATV* (UK) /38 x 30m col.

The Staggering Stories of Ferdinand de Bargos

Comedy. BBC2 1991

Inspired re-dubbing and re-editing of old documentary footage to tell a new – and surreally funny – tale. Took its title from the Spanish eccentric who refused to use but six letters of the alphabet in conversation.

CAST (voices) inc Enn Reitel, Kate Robbins /*pr* Kim Fuller, Geoff Atkinson /*wr* Kim Fuller, Geoff Atkinson / *BBC TV* (UK) /6 x 20m bw:col.

Star Cops
Sci-fi. BBC2 1987

In 2027 an irascible career policeman is assigned – against his will – to command the amateurish International Space Police Force, with the job of maintaining law and order among the space stations which ring Earth.

A thinking person's sci-fi/cop hybrid from Chris Boucher, previously script editor on ➢*Blake's 7*, refreshingly free from Bug-Eyed Monsters, with solidly interesting stories and characters (corpulent chauvinist Colin Devis, with his immortal line: 'Fancy a quick game of Hide the Sausage' comes to mind). But, bedevilled by a non-discernible budget, behind-the-scenes disharmony, a dreary theme from Justin Haywood (of the Moody Blues) and Tony Visconti and poor scheduling, it failed to take.

CAST *Nathan Spring* David Calder *David Theroux* Erick Ray Evans *Pal Kenzy* Linda Newton *Colin Devis* Trevor Cooper *Alexander Krivenko* Jonathan Adams *Anna Shoun* Sayo Inaba /*cr* Chris Boucher /*pr* Evgeny Gridneff /*dr* Christopher Blake, Graeme Harper /*wr* Chris Boucher, Philip Martin, John Collee /*mus* Justin Haywood & Tony Visconti ('It Won't Be Easy' theme) / *sfx* Robin Lobb (video) /*BBC TV* (UK) /9 x 55m col.

Star Maidens
Sci-fi. ITV 1976

Two male servants, Adam and Shem, escape role-reversal planet Mendusa for the chauvinistic delights of Earth. Their mistress, Supreme Councillor Fulvia, goes in pursuit; unable to capture the runaways, she takes a brace of Earthling hostages.

Anglo–German production, intended to be a spoof, but few caught the joke, with the dominatrix aspect coming over more as sex-manual fetishism than stellar fantasy. Actor Gareth Thomas went once more on the lam from a predatory female in ➢*Blake's 7*.

CAST *Adam* Pierre Brice *Shem* Gareth Thomas *Fulvia* Judy Geeson *The President* Dawn Addams /*cr* Eric Paice /*pr* James Gatward /*dr* James Gatward, Wolfgang Stoch, Freddie Francis, Hans Heinrich /*wr* Eric Paice, John Lucarotti, Ian Stuart Black /*Portman: Scottish and Global Television Enterprises: Jost Graf von Hardenburg & Co: Werbing-in-Rundfunk* (UK /Ger) /13 x 30m col / US tx Syndicated 1977.

Stars in Their Eyes
Light Entertainment. ITV 1990

Kitsch, strictly amateur version of ➢*New Faces* crossed with *Who Do You Do?* Members of the Great British public impersonated their favourite musical stars with the help of the Ray Monk Orchestra. Leslie ➢'*Crackerjack*' Crowther, and later Matthew Kelly, compèred in camp style.

CAST (hosts) Leslie Crowther, Matthew Kelly /*exec pr* Dianne Nelmes /*pr* Jane Macnaught /*dr* inc Robert Khodadad /*Granada* (UK) /32 x 30m col.

Starsky and Hutch
Crime. BBC1 1976–81

'Freeze!'

Prototype squealing-tyres cop show. It starred David Soul (originally Solberg, and later crooner of the immortal hit 'Don't Give Up on Us Baby') as soft-spoken, yoga-loving undercover cop Ken Hutchinson, with Paul Michael Glaser as his cardigan-wearing, junk-food eating partner, Dave Starsky. Together they sped around an unidentified American city (but presumed to be LA) in a red 1974 Ford Torino with white speed stripes, on a mission to put lowlifes behind bars. Easily burlesqued for its car chases and 'buddyism', *Starsky and Hutch* contained – for its time – some grittily real storylines (the BBC refused to broadcast an episode, 'The Fix', about drugs) and settings. It was also one of the first cop shows to introduce major (though not always positive) black characters: jive-talking superfly-snitch Huggy Bear (played by Antonio Fargas, who later sent up the role which made him immortal in *I'm Gonna Git You Sucka!*) and boss Captain Dobey. In the UK, where the series reached the pinnacle of the ratings, police chief Kenneth Oxford complained that the example of *Starksy and Hutch* caused police officers to begin 'driving like bloody maniacs'. Michael Mann, later to create ➢*Miami Vice* and forge a career as a Hollywood director, was to be found toiling in the script department.

'Freeze!' David Soul (right) and Paul Michael Glaser in the squealing-tyres cop show *Starsky and Hutch*. British police chiefs complained that the show influenced their officers into 'driving like maniacs'.

CAST *Det. Dave Starsky* Paul Michael Glaser *Det. Ken Hutchinson* David Soul *Huggy Bear* Antonio Fargas *Capt. Harold Dobey* Bernie Hamilton /*cr* William Blinn /*exec pr* Aaron Spelling, Leonard Goldberg /*pr* Joseph T. Naar /*dr* inc Earl Bellamy, Georg Stanford Brown, Fernados Lamas, David Soul, Paul Michael Glaser, Dick Moder, Barry Shear, Sutton Roley /*wr* inc William Blinn, Michael Mann, Anthony Yerkovich, Rick Edelstein, Marshall Kauffman /*Spelling Goldberg* (USA) /88 x 60m col /US tx ABC 1975–9.

Star Trek

Sci-fi. BBC1 1969–70

It might now be one of the most successful TV shows of all time, but *Star Trek* almost never got made: the original pilot ('The Cage', featuring Jeffrey Hunter from Western classic *The Searchers*) was dismissed by American network NBC as 'too cerebral'. An unprecedented second pilot was made and a series went ahead – but never upwards in the ratings. Only a campaign by fans (not yet 'Trekkies') and such sci-fi writers as Poul Anderson ensured a third season. It was not until the repeats of the 70s that *Star Trek* become a viewer phenomenon and a multi-million-pound industry.

The series was the creation of Gene Roddenberry, a former WWII pilot turned TV scribe. For years he had been head writer on oater ➢*Have Gun, Will Travel* and consciously designed *Star Trek* as a galactic horse-opera ('Space: The Final Frontier...') and borrowed its journeying, episodic format from ➢*Wagon Train*. Indeed, *ST*'s original title was *Wagon Train to the Stars*.

The new 'pioneers' of *ST* were noble Captain James Tiberius Kirk (played by Canadian actor William Shatner, Hunter having left the project after the pilot) and the 432 officers and crew of the *USS Enterprise*, principal amongst them: pointy eared half-Vulcan, half-human first officer Mr Spock; black communications officer Lieutenant Uhura (Nichelle Nichols, a former singer with Duke Ellington); Chief Engineer Montgomery 'Scotty' Scott; southern gentlemen ship's doctor Leonard 'Bones' McCoy; and helmsman Mr Sulu. At the start of the second season, another member was added to the bridge – Russian Mr Chekov.

Famously propelled by a split infinitive, the *Enterprise* – a 190,000-ton Constellation class cruiser belonging to the United Federation of Planets – went forth on a five-year mission to seek

'Highly illogical, Captain.' Leonard Nimoy as pointy-eared Vulcan Mr Spock in *Star Trek.* Created by former LA cop Gene Roddenberry, the show was based on the TV oater *Wagon Train.*

out new life forms and new civilizations. The most notorious of the aliens who attacked the ship along the way were the Klingons and the Romulans. The special effects were cheap but ingenious: the transporter effect of dissolving /reassembling atoms was achieved by throwing aluminium dust into a beam of light.

Although equipped with many fine stories (by, among others, Harlan Ellison, Richard Matheson and D.C. Fontana), the appeal of the show – the first adult space drama since the US ➢*Space Patrol* of the 50s – came to rest on the relationship between Kirk-Spock-McCoy and the show's extraordinary optimism about the future. Humankind's potential tolerance was nowhere better seen than in Kirk's refusal to kill the Gorn after the duel in 'Arena', while the racial harmony aboard the *Enterprise* suggested the United Nations in space. Many segments were allegories of earthly problems: Vietnam was tackled in 'A Private Little War', totalitarianism in 'Patterns of Force'.

It should, though, be pointed out that women did not fare well aboard *ST*. Uhura was little more than an intergalactic receptionist, while no less than 17 women died for the love of Kirk. Sexism was exacerbated by Jerry Finnerman's soft-focus photography of women subjects (including Nurse Christine Chapel, played by Roddenberry's wife, Majel Barrett).

Since the boom of Trek mania in the 70s there have been an animated *Star Trek* (US 1973, 17 x 30m) and six *ST* motion pictures. In 1987 a full-scale revival of the TV *Trek* began with ➢*Star Trek: The Next Generation.*

The catchlines of the original were: 'He's dead, Jim.' (McCoy); 'Kirk to Enterprise.'; 'We need more power!'; 'Ahead, Mr Sulu, warp factor...' (Kirk); 'She'll not take much more Captain.' ('Scotty'); 'Highly illogical, Captain.' (Spock'); 'Beam me up, Scotty' (Kirk).

CAST *Capt. James T. Kirk* William Shatner *Mr Spock* Leonard Nimoy *Dr Leonard 'Bones' McCoy* DeForest Kelly *Mr Sulu* George Takei *Lt Uhura* Nichelle Nichols *Montgomery 'Scotty' Scott* James Doohan *Yeoman Janice Rand* Grace Lee Whitney *Ensign Pavel Chekov* Walter Koenig *Nurse Christine Chapel* Majel Barrett /*cr* Gene Roddenberry /*exec pr* Gene Roddenberry /*pr* Gene Roddenberry, Gene L. Coon, John Meredyth Lucas, Fred Freiberger /*dr* inc Marc Daniels, Lawrence Dobkin, James Goldstone, Leo Penn, Vincent McEveety, Joseph Sargent, Herscel Daughterty, Marvin Chomsky /*wr* inc Gene Roddenberry, Gene L. Coon, D.C. Fontana, John D.F. Black, Richard Matheson, Stephen Kandel, Shari Lewis, Harlan Ellison, Don Mankiewicz, Rick Vollaerts /*sfx* Jim Rugg, William Ware Theiss (costumes) /*mus* Alexander Courage, Gerald Fried, George Duning /*Desilu: Norway: Paramount* (USA) /79 x 50m col /US tx NBC 1966–9.

Star Trek: Deep Space Nine
Sci-fi. Sky1 1993–

If the original ➢*Star Trek* was a sci-fi take on ➢*Wagon Train,* the third owed something to oaters ➢*The Rifleman* and ➢*Gunsmoke.* The eponymous desolate space station, reluctantly commanded by Benjamin Sisko (former theatre professor Avery Brooks, ex-➢*Spenser: For Hire*), was located at the back end of the universe orbiting the planet Bajor. A 360-degree promenade on *DS9* – only recently freed from Cardassian rule – was a 26th-century version of Dodge's main drag. Like *The Rifleman,* Sisko was a lone father trying to bring up a son (Jake) on the far frontier.

The show was no sooner launched than it ran into a meteoric shower of criticism. Denuded of the questing format of the earlier *Treks, DS9* was insipid, even soap-opera-ish. Creators Michael Piller and ex-Paramount VP Rick Berman also had a darker vision than trekmaster Roddenberry (who died in 1991, playing no part in *DS9*'s execution). Squabbles and sins among the crew – principally Sisko, shape-shifting security chief Odo (Rene Auberjonois from ➢*Benson*), domestically troubled chief operations officer Miles O'Brien and the virulently patriotic Bajoran first officer, Major Nerys – were endemic. (Science officer Jadzia Dax had little need to spat with others, being a member of the joined species Trill, thus was mainly a mollusc inside her delectable human host.) During the second and third seasons, Paramount (successfully) revamped the show, introducing a new warship, the *Defiant*, and a new enemy, the Dominion. There was also a new assignment to *DS9*'s crew list, Klingon Starfleet Officer Worf from *TNG*, an event marked by a 120m special, complete with *Star Wars*-like space battle.

CAST *Cmdr/Capt. Benjamin Sisko* Avery Brooks *Lt Worf* Michael Dorn *Odo* Rene Auberjonois *Major Kira Nerys* Nana Visitor *Lt Jadzia Dax* Terry Farrell *Chief Operations Officer Miles O'Brien* Colm Meaney *Dr Julian Bashir* Siddig El Fadil *Jake Sisko* Cirroc Lofton *Quark* Armin Shimerman *Vedek Winn* Louise Fletcher *Lt Ezri* Nicole deBoer /*cr* Rick Berman, Michael Piller /*exec pr* Rick Berman, Michael Piller, Ira Steven Behr / *pr* Rene Echevarria, Ronald D. Moore, Robert Hewitt Wolfe /*dr* inc David Livingstone, James L. Conway, Alexander Singer, Winrich Kolbe, Jonathan Frakes, Avery Brooks, Reza Badiyi /*wr* inc Rick Berman, Michael Piller, Ira Steven Behr, Joe Menosky, Jim Trombetta, Kathryn Powers, Sam Rolfe, D.C. Fontana, Jeri Taylor, Ronald D. Wolfe /*mus* Jerry Goldsmith (theme) /*sfx* Glenn Neufeld, Gary Hutzel /*Paramount* (USA) /2 x 120m, 149 x 60m col /US tx 1993–.

Star Trek: The Next Generation

Sci-fi. BBC2 1990–2/Sky1 1992–5

These then were the new voyages of USS *Enterprise*. Set 78 years after the original mission, the sequel featured an upgraded ship (Galaxy Class) and a new crew on the bridge. The captain was reserved Jean-Luc Picard (British Shakesperian actor Patrick Stewart), less inclined to heroic action than his predecessor, and a man who often allowed the off-board crises to be dealt with by Commander William Riker ('No. 1'), the closest in *TNG* to Kirk in looks and persona (hence the phonetic similarity of the surnames). Other prominent ship's officers were the empathetic half-Betzoid counsellor, Deanna Troi: Lieutenant Commander Data, a whey-faced android; Lieutenant Worf, the Klingon security officer (the Federation now having achieved peace with his race): Lieutenant Commander Geordi LaForge (played by LeVar Burton from ➢*Roots*), the blind helmsman who saw with the aid of VISOR glasses; Chief Medical Officer Beverly Crusher and her son, Ensign Wesley; and Transporter Chief Miles O'Brien (Colm Meaney, ex-➢*Z Cars*). Hollywood actress Whoopi Goldberg played Guinan, the bartender of the *Enterprise*'s Ten Forward lounge. The new bad guys of the Universe were the Ferengi, the lizard-necked Cardassians and the cybernetic Borg.

The initial involvement of *Star Trek*'s creator, Gene Roddenberry, ensured that *TNG* was as concerned to make moral points as the original. (It was also noticeable that Roddenberry had taken complaints about *Star Trek*'s sexism on board, and that the 1,000 crew members of the new *Enterprise* featured several women in leading positions.) Yet *TNG* lacked warmth and charm, and Roddenberry's liberalism was out of kilter with the designer sets. The cast was less interesting, the humour rare, save for Guinan's trick on Worf that prune juice was a 'warrior's drink'. Yet, taken on its own terms, *TNG* was enjoyable entertainment, with exemplary special effects. It became the highest-rated non-network programme shown in the US. On its back, Paramount launched two more *Trek* TV series, as well as sending the *TNG* cast to the movies.

CAST *Capt. Jean-Luc Picard* Patrick Stewart *Cmdr William T. Riker* Jonathan Frakes *Lt Geordi LaForge* LeVar Burton *Lt Tasha Yar* Denise Colby *Lt Worf* Michael Dorn *Lt Cmdr Data* Brent Spiner *Dr Beverly Crusher* Gates McFadden *Counsellor Deanna Troi* Marina Sirtis *Ensign Wesley Crusher* Wil Wheaton *Dr Katherine 'Kate' Pulaski* Diane Muldaur *Guinan* Whoopi Goldberg *Transporter Chief Miles O'Brien* Colm Meaney *Ensign Ro Laren* Michelle Forbes /*cr* Gene Roddenberry /*exec pr* Gene Roddenberry, Rick Berman, Michael Piller, Jeri Taylor /*pr* inc Ronald D. Moore, Ira Steven Behr, Brannan Braga, Joe Menosky, Wendy Neuss, David Livingston /*dr* inc Chip Chalmers, Jonathan Frakes, Robert Weimer, Patrick Stewart, Winrich Kolbe, Adam Nimoy, Corey Allen, LeVar Burton /*wr* inc Gene Roddenberry, Sam Rolfe, D.C. Fontana, Rene Echevarria /*mus* Jerry Goldsmith & Alexander Courage (theme) /*sfx* inc Robert Legato, Ron Moore, David Stipes /*Paramount TV* (USA) / 42 x 90m, 174 x 50m col /US tx Syndicated 1987–94.

Star Trek: Voyager

Sci-fi. Sky1 1996–

No sooner had ➢*Star Trek: Deep Space Nine* been manufactured in the Paramount yards, than the dilithium crystals of the *Trek* franchise were powered up to produce a fourth TV series, *Star Trek: Voyager*. Set in the 24th century, it featured a Federation ship, USS *Voyager* (complete with an advanced drive system that allowed it to exceed the warp speed limit), blown 70,000 light years into an unchartered region of Delta Quadrant by a mysterious energy wave. The task of the crew, a 200-strong mix of Federation personnel and previously rescued Maquis freedom-fighters, was to find their way home. Thus *Voyager* incorporated the same journey theme as the original *Trek*, but with a notable inversion: *Star Trek* was the televisual metaphor of JFK's expansionist 60s USA; *Voyager* was the small-screen reflection of the USA in isolationist, end-of-the-century mood. But the most obvious variation from classic *Trek* was that the captain's chair on *Voyager* was occupied by a XX chromosome, Kathryn Janeway.

Initially cast for the part was Academy Award nominee Genevieve Bujold but (apparently unprepared for the rigours of Paramount conveyor-belt TV) she resigned two days into filming. Iowa-born actress Kate Mulgrew (previously *Mrs Columbo/Kate Columbo* and Sam Malone's love interest in a sequence of ➢*Cheers* episodes) then took over the show's helm (beating, among others, former ➢*Bionic Woman* Lindsey Wagner and Patsy Kensit to the job) with a feisty interpretation of Janeway that dubbed the character 'the granddaughter Kirk never knew he had'. Certainly she was by far the most original of the *Voyager* crew, as they ploughed their way through storylines borrowed heavily from James T. Kirk's own endeavours.

CAST *Capt. Kathryn Janeway* Kate Mulgrew *First Off. Chakotay* Robert Beltran *Lt Tom Paris* Robert Duncan McNeil *Tactical/Security Off. Tuvok* Tim Russ *Ops /Communications Off. Harry Kim* Garrett Wang *Chief Engineer* Roxann Biggs-Dawson *Neelix* Ethan Phillips *Kes* Jennifer Lien *Doctor* Robert Picardo /*cr* Rick Berman, Michael Piller, Jeri Taylor /*dr* inc Winrich Kolbe, Kim Friedman, Les Landau, LeVar Burton, Jonathan Frakes, Robert Scheerer /*wr* inc Michael Piller, Jeri Taylor, Brannon Braga, Jim Trombetta, Bill Dial /*mus* Jerry Goldsmith (theme) /*sfx* Dan Curry, David Stipes, Ron B. Moore /*Paramount* (USA) / 10 x 60m col /US tx UPN 1995–.

Stephen King's Golden Years

Horror. C4 1993

An elderly janitor, Harlan Williams (Keith Szarabajka from ➢*The Equalizer*), is contaminated by a mysterious explosion at a secret US laboratory. Although given a clean bill of health by the doctors, his wife begins to notice subtle changes ... and the government suddenly becomes menacingly interested.

Creeper-serial from legendary horror author Stephen King – his first direct-for-TV product.

CAST *Harlan Williams* Keith Szarabajka *Gina Williams* Frances Sternhagen *Dr Richard Todhunter* Bill Raymond /*pr* Mitchell Galin, Peter R. McIntosh / *Laurel-King* (USA) /7 x 60m col /US tx 1992.

Steptoe and Son

Comedy. BBC1 1964–73

Created by ➢*Hancock's Half Hour* scriptwriters Ray Galton and Alan Simpson, this situation comedy about a malicious rag-and-bone man and his frustrated son, premiered as a one-off play, 'The Offer', in the BBC's fertile ➢*Comedy Playhouse* slot. From the outset the show broke most of the rules of TV comedy, filled as it was with pathos (even tragedy) rather than laughs. The central characters were the tattered-mitten-wearing father Albert ('you dirty old man'), and his 38-year-old son Harold ('you great lummox'). It was Harold's dream to better himself, and to this end he listened to classical music in the cluttered sitting room while reading Shaw's *Everybody's Political What's What*. Yet every time the aspirant Harold tried to escape the yard, his petty, conniving father blackmailed him back ('Harold ... I think I'm having an 'art attack, Harold...') into staying. The ties of blood were simply too strong to escape. And beneath the bickering and hate there was love and mutual need. 'He's not a bad boy,' Albert tells the old burglar (played by Leonard Rossiter) who hides out with them in 'Desperate Hours', with real pride on his face. If the humour of the show was dark, it struck a chord with many and it topped the ratings in 1964, helped by the sterling acting of Dublin-born Bramble and method thespian Harry H. Corbett. The series spawned two feature films, *Steptoe and Son* (1972) and *Steptoe and Son Ride Again* (1973), and was remade in America as *Sanford and Son* (with a black cast of Redd Fox and Desmond Wilson). Sweden's version, meanwhile, was called *Albert og Herbert*, Portugal's, *Camilio et Fihlio.*

CAST *Albert Steptoe* Wilfred Bramble *Harold Steptoe* Harry H. Corbett /*cr* Ray Galton, Alan Simpson /*pr* Duncan Wood, David Croft, John Howard Davies, Douglas Argent /*dr* inc Douglas Argent /*wr* Ray Galton, Alan Simpson /*mus* Ron Grainger /*BBC TV* (UK) /40 x 30m bw:col.

Steven Spielberg's Amazing Stories

Fantasy. BBC1 1992–3

Marked Steven Spielberg's return to the medium that launched him (via a segment on Rod Serling's ➢*Night Gallery*), overseeing an anthology of telefantasy made at fabulous cost ($1 million per 30-minute episode). For turns in the director's chair, he brought with him from Hollywood Clint Eastwood, Martin Scorsese, Robert Zemeckis, Joe Dante and Danny DeVito. Big-named actors lured over included Harvey Keitel, Charlie Sheen, Kevin Costner, Kiefer Sutherland, Dom DeLuise, Patrick Swayze and Carrie Fisher. (There was also English rocker Adam Ant.) A paucity of good scripts, however, made for an uneven, superficial product that never satisfied, leaving the industry whispering that it was TV's '*Heaven's Gate*'. Most escaped the wreckage, including Spielberg's Amblin Company. So did his producers, Joshua Brand and John Falsey, who went on to create cult shows ➢*St Elsewhere* and ➢*Northern Exposure.*

CAST inc Harvey Keitel, Kevin Costner, Carrie Fisher /*cr* Steven Spielberg, Joshua Brand, John Falsey /*exec pr* Steven Spielberg /*pr* Joshua Brand & John Falsey /*dr* inc Steven Spielberg, Clint Eastwood, Martin Scorsese, Burt Reynolds, Phil Joanou, Joan Darling, Thomas Carter, Paul Bartel, Danny DeVito, Joe Dante, Robert Zemeckis, Paul Michael Glaser, Tobe Hopper /*wr* inc Joshua Brand & John Falsey, Steven Spielberg, Earl Pomerantz, Mick Garris, Richard Matheson, Rockne S. O'Bannon, Anne Spielberg /*mus* John Williams (theme) /*Amblin Entertainment: Universal* (USA) / 43 x 30m, 2 x 60m col /US tx 1985.

Stingray

Children's. ITV 1964–5

Submarine supermarionation from Gerry Anderson (➢*Twizzle*, ➢*Torchy*, ➢*Four Feather Falls*, ➢*Supercar*, ➢*Fireball XL5*, ➢*Thunderbirds*, etc.), and the first British series to be filmed in colour, although originally broadcast in black and white. It featured the intrepid 21st-century heroes of the World Aquanaut Security Patrol (WASP), principally: Troy Tempest, captain of the atomic sub *Stingray* (equipped with 16 sting missiles and the agility of a dolphin); his hydrophones sidekick, George Sheridan; and unofficial crew member enchanting, greenhaired Marina, daughter of Emperor Aphony of Pacifica. Pulling the crew's strings at WASP's Marineville HQ was hovering, paraplegic Commander Shore and his brunette bombshell assistant Atlanta (voiced by Lois Maxwell, the Miss Moneypenny of the James Bond 007 films). Meanwhile, the principal series' badguy was the hegemonic green-skinned Titan, overlord of Titanica, whose evil underwater deeds were carried out by the fearsome Aquaphibians in their Terror Fish. Bungling Agent X20 was Titan's man on land. Inventively made – *Stingray*'s undersea movements were achieved by filming a model of the sub through a thin aquarium full of guppies – and full of narrative suspense, the series also drew a crossover adult audience with its neat tongue-in-cheekness, as highlighted by the unrequited love triangle of the closing credit sequence where Atlanta soapily swooned over handsome Troy who mooned over Marina.

CAST (voices) *Troy Tempest* Don Mason *Phones /Agent X20* Robert Easton *Atlanta* Lois Maxwell *Cmdr Shore/Titan/Sub-Lt Fisher* Ray Barrett /*cr* Gerry & Sylvia Anderson /*pr* Gerry Anderson /*dr* Alan Pattillo, John Kelly, Desmond Saunders, David Elliott /*wr* Gerry & Sylvia Anderson, Alan Fennell, Dennis Spooner /*mus* Barry Gray /*sfx* Derek Meddings /*AP Films: ATV: ITC* (UK) /39 x 30m col /US tx Syndicated 1965.

The Storyteller

Children's. C4 1988

Delightful anthology of European folk tales, filmed with a mix of live actors and Jim Henson's fanciful muppets, and a complementary dash of magical sfx. John Hurt played the gnomic Storyteller, a master yarner, accompanied during his fireside commentary by his intelligent dog.

CAST *Storyteller* John Hurt *Storyteller's dog (voice)* Brian Henson /*pr* Duncan Kenworthy /*dr* Jim Henson, Steve Barron, Jon Amiel, Charles Sturridge, Paul Weiland, Peter Smith /*wr* inc Anthony Minghella / *mus* Rachel Portman /*TVS: Jim Henson* (UK /USA) / 9 x 30m col.

Strangers
Crime. ITV 1978–82

Continued the undercover detective career of glove-wearing Sergeant Bulman (Don Henderson) from ➢*The XYY Man*, though with a disciplinary transfer 'up North' to Manchester's C23 unit. Bulman, however, returned to London in the third season as part of the peripatetic 'Inner City Squad' under the command of DCS Lambie (Mark McManus in a virtual try-out for ➢*Taggart*). After five seasons *Bulman*, by now a DCI, quit the force, but only to turn up in solo-series *Bulman* (ITV 1985–7, 20 x 30m col) where his plans for a retirement mending clocks on Shanghai Road were interrupted by the arrival of Lucy McGinty (Siobhan Redmond, later ➢*Between the Lines*), who persuaded him to become a PI. By this time the appeal of the Bulman character – his odd mix of hard-case jazz-lover and hamster-owner – had palled.

CAST *DCS/DCI George Bulman* Don Henderson *DC Derek Willis* Denis Blanch *WDC Linda Doran* Frances Tomelty *WDC Vanessa Bennett* Fiona Mollison *DS David Singer* John Ronane *DCI Rainbow* David Hargreaves *DCS Jack Lambie* Mark McManus /*cr* Murray Smith, Richard Everitt /*pr* Richard Everitt /*dr* inc William Brayne /*wr* inc Murray Smith, Edward Boyd /*mus* Mike Moran /*Granada TV* (UK) /32 x 60m col.

The Strange World of Gurney Slade
Drama. ITV 1960.

The title did not lie. Singer-actor Anthony Newley played a man with a clinically overactive imagination who wandered a bizarre landscape talking to trees, stones, dogs and, in one episode, dancing with a girl who stepped out of a vacuum cleaner poster.

A curiosity.

CAST *Gurney Slade* Anthony Newley /*pr* Alan Tarrant /*wr* Sid Green, Dick Hills /*mus* Max Harris /*ATV* (UK) / 6 x 30m bw.

The Streets of San Francisco
Crime. ITV 1973–80

Quinn Martin cop show, based on the novel *Orphan, Poor Orphan* by Carolyn Weston. As Oscar-winning actor Karl Malden once pointed out, '*The Streets of San Francisco* had three stars – Mike Douglas, me and San Francisco.' Filmed on location with much panache, *Streets* used hilly 'Frisco in the same way that ➢*Naked City* had used New York. The city was more than a backdrop: it was a character, moody and dangerous beneath its urbane charm. Milieu, plus fine scripts, added together with delightful acting from the bulbous-nosed Malden (born Mladen Sekulovich) as the old cop and Michael 'son of Kirk' Douglas as the young college-grad cop, equalled a classic 70s crime series. It also launched Douglas to celebrity, the actor quitting in 1975 (Richard Hatch, as DI Dan Robbins, took over as Malden's human co-star) for the Hollywood screen, via a stint as producer on *One Flew Over the Cuckoo's Nest.*

CAST *Det. Lt Mike Stone* Karl Malden *DI Steve Keller* Michael Douglas *DI Dan Robbins* Richard Hatch *Lt Lessing* Lee Harris /*cr* Quinn Martin /*exec pr* Quinn Martin /*pr* John Wilder, Cliff Gould, William Yates /*dr* inc Walter Grauman, William Hale, Virgil W. Vogel, Theodore J. Flicker /*mus* Pat William (theme), John Elizade, Robert Prince /*Quinn Martin Prod: Warner Bros* (USA) /120 x 60m col /US tx ABC 1972–80.

Strike It Lucky
Light Entertainment. ITV 1987–

Game show hosted by Michael Barrymore – former hairdresser to the stars (Shirley Bassey included) and the warm-up man for ➢*Are You Being Served?* – in which couples answered general-knowledge questions in the hope of advancing up an arch of steps equipped with TV monitors; when struck, the screen of the monitors revealed either a prize or a punitive 'hotspot'. All this was accompanied by Barrymore's manic, sub-Cleese physical comedy and painless mockery of the contestants. The show survived the revelation of the host's homosexuality, to continue as *Michael Barrymore's Strike It Rich.*

CAST (presenter) Michael Barrymore /*exec pr* Robert Louis /*pr* Maurice Leonard /*dr* inc Brian Penders, John Birkin, Paul Kirrage, Russell Norman /*Thames TV* (UK) /120+ x 30m col.

The Sullivans

Melodrama. ITV 1977–82

Epic saga following the fortunes of a middle-class Melbourne family through WWII and beyond, their lives also touching those of immigrant Jewish neighbours the Kauffmans. Inspired by ➢*A Family At War* and ➢*The Waltons*, the above-average (and sometimes lachrymose) serial was the first Australian sudster to be screened in Britain, bought in by ITV as a lunchtime replacement for ➢*Emmerdale Farm* when it was promoted to peak time. The period nature of *The Sullivans* made it a practically timeless TV commodity, to be aired repeatedly the globe over.

CAST *David Sullivan (father)* Paul Cronin *Grace Sullivan (mother)* Lorraine Bayly *John Sullivan* Andrew McFarlane *Tom Sullivan* Steven Tandy *Kitty Sullivan* Susan Hannaford *Terry Sullivan* Richard Morgan *Anna Kaufman* Ingrid Mason *Otte Kaufman* Macella Burgoyne *Hans Kaufman* Leon Lissek *Carla* Kylie Minogue /*cr* Jack blair, Ian Jones /*Crawford* (Aus) / 1115 x 30m col.

Sunnyside Farm

Comedy. BBC2 1997–

Cast Phil Daniels (*Quadrophenia*, and a 90s cult personality thanks to his 'Parklife' crooning with Blur) to yobbish type as a weasly, lewd farmer, co-owner with his retarded brother of the decrepit smallholding of the title. Full of sniggering innuendo and Trumptonesque characterization, suggestive of a deliberate ironic statement about the contemporary sitcom, with its filthy set a crying reference to the golden age of ➢*Steptoe and Son*. Then again, it might have been a steaming pile of manure.

CAST *Ray Sunnyside* Phil Daniels *Ken Sunnyside* Mark Addy *Ezekiel Letchworth* Michael Kitchen *Wendy* Beth Goddard /*pr* Spencer Campbell /*dr* Andy De Emmony /*wr* Richard Preddy & Gary Howe /*BBC TV* (UK) /6 x 30m col.

Supercar

Children's. ITV 1961–2

Adventures (by land, air, sea and space) of a futuristic all-terrain rocket car and its fearless test pilot, Mike Mercury. At Nevada desert HQ, inventors Professor Popkiss and Dr Beaker, and 10-year-old Jimmy (plus talking monkey, Mitch) provided back-up. Masterspy was the arch-enemy, Zarin his bungling accomplice.

Gerry Anderson's first 'supermarionation' series, with a cast of advanced 18-inch-high puppets with internal machinery (triggered by control wires) that 'realistically' moved their eyes and lips. Staggeringly successful (selling to 40 countries), the series prompted a run of supermarionation sci-fi shows: ➢*Fireball XL5*, ➢*Stingray*, ➢*Thunderbirds* and ➢*Captain Scarlet and the Mysterons*.

CAST (voices) *Mike Mercury* Graydon Gould *Dr Beaker / Mitch/Zarin* David Graham *Prof. Popkiss/Masterspy* George Murcell *Jimmy* Sylvia Anderson /*cr* Gerry Anderson, Reg Hill /*pr* Gerry & Sylvia Anderson /*dr* David Elliott, Alan Pattillo, Desmond Saunders, Bill Harris /*wr* Reg Hill, Gerry & Sylvia Anderson, Hugh & Martin Woodhouse /*mus* Barry Gray /*AP Films: ATV: ITC* (UK) /39 x 30m bw /US tx Syndicated 1962.

Supergran

Children's. ITV 1985–7

Jenny McDade adapted Forrest Wilson's books about an old lady accidentally struck by a ray from a magic beam machine; the superpowers she consequently acquired enabled her to defend the good folk of Chisleton from villainous Scunner Campbell (Iain Cutherbertson). Lively nonsense, with a memory-catching effect in Supergran's Heath Robinson Fly Cycle. Billy Connolly co-wrote the theme music.

CAST *Granny Smith ('Supergran')* Gudrun Ure *Scunner Campbell* Iain Cutherbertson *Inventor Black* Bill Shine /*pr* Keith Richardson /*dr* Anthony Simmons / *wr* Jenny McDade /*mus* Billy Connolly & Phil Coulter /*Tyne Tees* (UK) /26 x 30m col.

The Survivors

Sci-fi. BBC1 1975–7

This series from Terry Nation (former writer on ➢*Doctor Who*, ➢*Blake's 7* and ex-gag scripter for Tony Hancock) is something of an underrated treasure. The nightmarish premise, effected in the opening episode, was that an Oriental scientist had dropped a deadly virus which wiped out 95 per cent of the Earth's population.

Subsequent episodes followed the fortunes of a small British group of survivors – principally Abby Grant, Greg Preston, architect Charles Vaughan and

Jenny Richards – as they tried to build new communities and reinvent skills in an island plunged back almost to a technological and social Year Zero. Executed with intelligence and *froideur* (by a production team largely drawn from another series with optimism on hold, ➢*Doomwatch*), particularly in its early seasons, it was also notable for being a sci-fi serial with a woman (Abby) lead character.

CAST *Abby Grant* Carolyn Seymour *Jenny Richards* Lucy Fleming *Greg Preston* Ian McCulloch *Tom Price* Talfryn Thomas *Charles Vaughan* Denis Lil *Pet* Lorna Lewis *Hubert* John Abineri /*cr* Terry Nation /*pr* Terence Dudley /*dr* inc Pennant Roberts, Gerald Blake, Tristan de Vere Cole, George Spenton Foster, Terence Dudley / *wr* inc Terry Nation, Terence Dudley, M.K. Jeeves (aka Clive Exton), Roger Parkes, Roger Marshall, Don Shaw / *mus* Anthony Isaac /*BBC TV* (UK) /38 x 50m col.

Sutherland's Law

Drama. BBC1 1973–6

Starred Iain Cuthbertson (ex-➢*Budgie*) as the procurator fiscal – in Scottish law an investigative advocate – of a Highland fishing town. Played to its strengths – Cuthbertson's dour charisma, the picturesque setting – and the episodes passed effortlessly. Derived from a 1972 *Drama Playhouse.*

CAST *John Sutherland* Iain Cuthbertson *Alex Duthie* Gareth Thomas *Sgt McKechnie* Don McKillop *Christine Russell* Maev Alexander *Helen Matheson* Virginia Stark /*cr* Lindsay Galloway /*pr* Neil McCallum, Frank Cox /*BBC TV* (UK) /24 x 30m col.

S.W.A.T.

Crime. ITV 1976

Derived from an episode of *The Rookies* and followed the bullet-spraying exploits of an elite Californian Special Weapons and Tactics squad. Judged the most violent crime show on prime-time US TV, it was cancelled after 34 episodes. Steve Forrest (formerly ➢*The Baron*) and Robert Urich (➢*Soap*, ➢*Spenser: For Hire*) headed the dismissed cast.

CAST *Lt Dan Harrelson* Steve Forrest *Off. Jim Street* Robert Urich *Sgt David Kay* Rod Perry *Off. Dominic Luca* Mark Shera *Off. T.J. McCabe* James Coleman /*cr* Robert Hamner /*exec pr* Aaron Spelling, Leonard Goldberg /*mus* Barry De Vorzon /*Spelling Goldberg: ABC* (USA) /34 x 60m col /US tx ABC 1975–6.

The Sweeney

Crime. ITV 1975–82

'Get yer trousers on – yer nicked...'

Developed from a 1974 pilot, *Regan*, aired as part of ➢*Armchair Theatre*, Euston's landmark police series eschewed the cosiness of the paradigmatic ➢*Dixon of Dock Green* in favour of hard-edged realism and visceral action. Notably, its portrait of New Scotland Yard's detectives was far from flattering: the series' chief characters, DI Jack Regan (John Thaw, ➢*Redcap*), and his young sidekick, George Carter (Dennis Waterman, ➢*Just William*), routinely ignored the rule book, hit suspects, associated with villains, and swore and drank to excess. In one episode, Jack Regan burgled the office of CI Haskins – the man with the unenviable job of commanding the surly Regan – in search of his disciplinary report. At the end of the run Regan, his morale eroded (notably by a wrongful arrest for corruption), quit the force.

Made on a shoestring budget of £40,000 per episode, *The Sweeney* – the title derived from 'Sweeney Tod', cockney slang for the NSY's Flying Squad – was shot on film, with slammings of muscular action and squealings of car chases (usually in an E-type Jag). This, however, was perfectly complimented by witty writing and the matey chemistry between Regan and Carter, which was so successful that the producers killed off Carter's wife (Stephanie Turner, later ➢*Juliet Bravo*) to enable him to spend more time with his kipper-tie-wearing (and divorced) guvnor.

Though there was contemporary criticism of *The Sweeney*'s violence allotment, in retrospect the series has a curious innocence under its bruiser façade. The villains apprehended were almost without exception professional 'blaggers' of banks and security vans. Bad boys, certainly, but not serial psychopathic murderers.

A large guest cast list was headed by John Hurt, George Cole (thus acting with Waterman several years before ➢*Minder*), Diana Dors, and Morecombe and Wise ('The Hearts and Minds' episode). There were two spin-off theatrical releases: *Sweeney!* (1976) and *Sweeney 2* (1978).

CAST *DI Jack Regan* John Thaw *DS George Carter* Dennis Waterman *CI Frank Haskins* Garfield Morgan / *cr* Ian Kennedy Martin /*pr* Ted Childs /*dr* inc Chris Burt, Murray Smith, Chris Menaul, Terry Green, Tom Clegg, Jim Goddard, Douglas Camfield, Mike Vardy, Viktor Ritelis /*wr* inc Ian Kennedy Martin, Troy

'Get yer trousers on – yer nicked!' Dennis Waterman (left) and John Thaw, stars of *The Sweeney*. The landmark police series was developed from an *Armchair Theatre* presentation.

Kennedy Martin, Richard Harris, Roger Marshall, Robert Banks Stewart, Tony Hoare, P.J. Hammond / *mus* Harry South / *Euston Films: Thames TV* (UK) / 52 x 60m col.

Sweet Valley High

Children's. Nickelodeon 1995–

Teen drama, set in a permanently sunny Californian town and its lesson-free, dating-mandatory High School. Principal characters were twins Jessica and Elizabeth Wakefield (played by the Daniel sisters, previously stars of Wrigley chewing-gum advertisements). Unlike ➢*Beverly Hills 90210*, *SVH* assiduously avoided social issues, in empty-headed favour of romantic revenge (the plot staple) and sweet-16 crushes (typical *SVH* dialogue: 'Who *is* that guy? I've not seen him in school before.') Adapted from the mega-selling novels of Francine Pascal (who served as co-executive producer), and made by Saban Entertainment, the world's largest independent purveyor of kiddie entertainment.

CAST *Jessica Wakefield* Britanny Daniel *Elizabeth Wakefield* Cynthia Daniel *Patty Gilbert* Amarilis *Todd Wilkins* Ryan James Bittle/Jeremy Garrett *Bruce Patman* Brock Burnett *Enid Rollins* Amy Danles *Lila Fowler* Bridget Flanery *Winston Egbert* Michael Perl *Manny Lopez* Harley Rodriguez / *exec pr* Lance H. Robbins, Haim Saban, Francine Pascal / *pr* David Garber, William G. Dunn Jr, Ronnie Hadar / *dr* inc Harvey Frost, Douglas Barr, David Winning / *Teen Drama Prods: Saban Entertainment Inc* (USA) / 90+ x 30m col /US tx 1994–.

Sword of Freedom

Adventure. ITV 1958–60

US actor Edmund Purdom buckled his swash through 39 episodes of this costume actioner set in Renaissance Florence, where his Marco del Monte artist character led freedom's battle against the corrupt de Medici and their political henchman, Machiavelli. The Italian Robin Hood was aided in his noble task by his model, Angelica, (Adrienne Corri), and gentle-giant friend, Sandro.

Moderately enjoyable time-filler. Those contributing scripts included blacklisted (for alleged pro-Communism) American writer Ring Lardner Jr.

CAST *Marco del Monte* Edmund Purdom *Angelica* Adrienne Corri *Sandro* Rowland Bartrop *Machiavelli* Kenenth Hyde *Duke de Medici* Martin Benson *Francesa de Medici* Monica Stevenson /*exec pr* Hannah Weinstein /*pr* Sidney Cole /*wr* inc Ring Lardner Jr, Ian McLellan Hunter /*Weinstein Prods: Sapphire Films* (UK) /39 x 30m bw /US tx Syndicated 1957.

Sykes

Comedy. BBC 1960–5/BBC1 1971–9

Much-loved sitcom in which the ever-seeking-to-better-himself Sykes and his twin sister Hattie (Hattie Jacques, wife of John Le Mesurier) shared a house at 24 Sebastopol Terrace, Suburbia. Initially, the weekly plots were prompted by the arrival of new gadgets or goods, the episode being transmitted as 'Sykes and a...' (with 'Sykes and a Plank' being expanded into a classic Monsieur Hulot-like silent comedy film of that title in 1967), but later seasons settled down into more standard domestic crises. Usually to be found on plot-periphery was Mr Brown, the belittling neighbour, and pompous local PC, Corky (Deryck Guyler, ➢*Please Sir!*).

CAST *Eric* Eric Sykes *Hattie* Hattie Jacques *Corky* Deryck Guyler *Mr Brown* Richard Wattis /*cr* Eric Sykes / *pr* inc Dennis Main Wilson, Sydney Lotterby, Philip Barker, Roger Race /*wr* Eric Sykes, Johnny Speight / *BBC TV* (UK) /78 x 30m bw:col.

Taggart
Crime. ITV 1983–

Starred Mark McManus (➢*Sam*, ➢*Strangers*) as a bolshy working-class police detective in an ultra-urban Glasgow. Production values in the early seasons were low, but Taggart's anti-hero (the character was first seen in a 1983 STV three-parter, *Killer*) and Glenn Chandler's dryly complex plots achieved massive viewing figures (up to 18.3 million for one of the numerous specials). When McManus died prematurely in 1994, the series continued with Taggart's middle-class sidekick DI Jardine and sassy DC Reid leading the investigations. *Taggart* without Taggart worked better than it ought, largely because McManus' jaded anti-hero performance had left an indelible impression on the screen. By implication, he still seemed to be there, back at the station in Northern Division glumly issuing orders and pronouncements.

CAST *DCI Jim Taggart* Mark McManus *DS/DI Mike Jardine* James MacPherson *WDC/WDS Jackie Reid* Blythe Duff *DS Peter Livingstone* Neil Duncan *Jean Taggart* Harriet Buchan *Alison Taggart* Geraldine Alexander *Supt McVitie* Iain Anders *DC Stuart Fraser* Colin McGredie *Dr Andrews* Robert Robertson /*cr* Glenn Chandler /*exec pr* Robert Love /*pr* inc Murray Ferguson /*dr* inc Haldane Duncan, Peter Barber-Fleming, Laurence Moody, Marcus D.F. White /*wr* inc Glenn Chandler, Julian Jones, Stuart Hepburn /*mus* Mike Moran /*STV* (UK) /63+ x 60m, 4 x 90m col.

Take the High Road
Melodrama. ITV 1980–

Sudster serial about rural life in the many-acred Scottish estate of Glendarroch. When Elizabeth Cunningham, the owner of the estate (which included a bustling village), was killed in a car accident, new lairds in the English form of Sir John and Lady Margaret Ross-Gifford moved into Glendarroch House, to tight-lipped native disapproval. From 1995 onwards it was broadcast as *High Road*, a small concession to soap-opera modernity; otherwise, it continued through the afternoons as soporifically as ever.

CAST *Elizabeth Cunningham* Edith MacArthur *Fiona Cunningham* Caroline Ashley *Brian Blair* Kenneth Watson *Isabel Blair/Morgan* Eileen McCallum *Jimmy Blair* Jimmy Chisholm *Derek Andeos* David Blair *Obediah Murdoch* Robert Trotter *Dave Sneddon* Derek Lord *Sheila Lamont/Ramsey* Lesley Fitz-Simons *Sir John Ross-Gifford* Michael Browning *Lady Margaret Ross-Gifford* Jan Waters /*cr* Don Houghton /*pr* Clarke Tait, Frank Cox, John G. Temple /*dr* inc Clarke Tait / *Scottish TV* (UK) /400+ x 30m col.

Take Three Girls
Comedy. BBC1 1969–71

Sitcom about a trio of swinging girls (originally cellist Victoria, actress Kate and cockney art student Avril) in London SW3. Episodes tended to dwell on individuals, giving it a disconcerting anthology feel. But the basic format of single girls flat-sharing has since been inflicted on audiences by, *inter alia*, ➢*The Liverbirds*, ➢*Girls on Top* and even a *Take Three Girls* reunion special, *Take Three Women*, screened in 1982.

CAST *Victoria* Liza Goddard *Avril* Angela Down *Kate* Susan Jameson *Mr Edgecombe* David Langton *Lulie* Barra Grant *Jenny* Carolyn Seymour /*cr* Gerard Savory / *pr* Michael Hayes /*dr* inc Tristan De Vere Cole, Mark Cullingham /*wr* inc Terence Brady & Charlotte Bingham /*BBC TV* (UK) /18 x 50m col.

Take Your Pick
Light Entertainment. ITV 1955–68/1992–

Long-running game show, hosted by 'Your Quiz Inquisitor', New Zealander Michael Miles. Contestants were eliminated by a 'Yes/No' inter-lude where they had to respond (without hesitation) to quick-fire questions without using the words 'yes' and 'no'. Offenders were 'gonged out' by assistant Alec Dane. The survivors would then select a numbered key to a mystery box, at which Miles would offer increasing temptations of cash – if they answered three more general-knowledge questions – in return for the key. A delirious audience shouted conflicting advice, 'take the money', 'open the box'. The box, when opened, could contain anything from a prune to a car. Bob Danvers-Walker was the announcer, Harold Smart the man on the organ. On the conclusion of *Take Your Pick* (which derived originally from Radio Luxembourg), Miles returned to the TV screen with another game-of-chance show, *Wheel of Fortune*, while *Take Your Pick* itself was resurrected by an ideas-starved Thames in 1992. This time round Des O'Connor was the japester. Among his assistants were ex-➢*Neighbours* twins, Gayle and Gillian Blakeley.

CAST (presenters) Michael Miles, Des O'Connor /*dr* inc Audrey Starrett /*Associated-Rediffusion: Arlington: Thames* (UK) /approx. 300 x 30m bw:col.

Tales from the Crypt

Horror. Sky1 1995–

Supernatural anthology hosted by the flesh-decaying 'The Cryptkeeper', based on the cult 50s comic book. Executive producers – and Hollywood directors – Walter Hill, Richard Donner and Robert Zemeckis helmed segments, as did Arnold Schwarzenegger, Tobe Hooper (of *Poltergeist*), Michael J. Fox, Stephen Hopkins (*Nightmare on Elm Street 5*) and Tom Hanks.

exec pr Walter Hill, Richard Donner, Robert Zemeckis, David Giler, Joel Silver /*Metromedia* (USA) /40 x 30m col /US tx HBO 1980–.

Tales of Mystery

Drama. ITV 1961–3

Suspense anthology based on the stories of dark-minded spook-writer Algernon Blackwood. It was introduced by John Laurie (*Whisky Galore*), taking the guise of Blackwood, in the hammy, doom-voiced style he would take to ➢*Dad's Army*.

CAST *Algernon Blackwood* John Laurie /*exec pr* John Frankau /*pr* Peter Graham Scott /*dr* inc John Frankanau, Jonathan Alywyn /*wr* inc Philip Broadley, Kenneth Hyde /*Associated-Rediffusion* (UK) /29 x 30m bw.

Tales of the River Bank

Children's. BBC 1960–4

Canadian series which ingeniously used real animals to relate the furrysome adventures of Hammy Hamster, Roderick Rat, and their friends. Narrated by Johnny Morris (➢*Animal Magic, The Hot Chestnut Man*), the films were shot at twice normal speed (so that the creatures' movements appeared slower, thus friendlier, on broadcast), and delightfully captured Hammy and crew transporting themselves around in miniature planes and cars, as well as dwelling in furnished homes. Transmitted in Britain as part of ➢*Watch with Mother*, the series was repeated until 1971 on the BBC. A second tranche of 26 episodes was produced in the 70s, with a sequel, *Further Tales of the Riverbank*, airing on C4 in 1993.

CAST (narrator) Johnny Morris /*pr-dr-wr* Dave Ellison, Paul Sutherland /*Dave Ellison: Ray Billings* (Can) /52 x 30m bw:col.

Tales of the Unexpected

Drama. ITV 1980–88

Began as 1979's *Roald Dahl's Tales of the Unexpected*, being a collection of sting-in-the-tail suspense yarns drawn from the author's own *oeuvre*. The shorter-titled show continued in the same sardonic mode, although with teleplays by others, including such masters of crime as Ruth Rendell, Julian Symons and Stanley Ellin. Smart performances (Derek Jacobi, John Gielgud, Rachel Kempson and Joan Collins figure prominently in the memory) gave added bite. The sinister 'Carousel' theme music was by Ron Grainer.

CAST inc Derek Jacobi, John Gielgud, Rachel Kempson, Joan Collins /*cr* Roald Dahl /*exec pr* Sir John Woolf /*pr* John Rosenberg /*dr* inc Michael Tuchner, Alistair Reid, Herbert Wise, Alan Gibson /*wr* Roald Dahl, Ruth Rendell, Bill Pronzini, Stanley Ellin, Julian Symons, Edward D. Hoch /*mus* Ron Grainer ('Carousel' theme) /*Anglia TV* (UK) /72 x 25m col / US tx Syndicated 1979.

Tales of Wells Fargo

Western. BBC 1959–61

Jim Hardie was a strong but silent troubleshooter for transport company Wells Fargo in the 1860s, his job being to protect the company's gold and passengers from no-good outlaws. Originally aired in *Schlitz Playhouse of Stars* in 1956, the show was expanded in 1961 to a 60-minute format, and storylines began to include Hardie's adventures as a rancher in San Francisco. Jack Nicholson appeared in one of his first screen roles in the 1961 episode, 'The Washburn Girl'.

CAST *Jim Hardie* Dale Robertson *Beau McCloud* Jack Ging *Jeb Gaine* William Demarest *Ovie* Virginia Christine /*cr* Frank Gruber /*pr* Earle Lyon, Nat Holt / *dr* inc Earl Bellamy, William Whitney /*wr* inc Frank Gruber, Frank Bonham, William R. Cox /*mus* Stanley Wilson /*MCA: Universal: Overland: Juggernaut* (USA) / 167 x 25m, 34 x 60m bw /US tx 1957–61.

Target

Crime. BBC1 1977–8

The door-kicking, pistol-in-the-face cases of Superintendent Steve Hackett (Patrick Mower, ➢*Special Branch*), a detective with a crime squad working the South Coast ports.

Intended as the BBC's ➢*The Sweeney*, it mistook violence for realism, with the result that a squall of protests cut short the first season and toned down the second. Even so, it continued to confuse over-dramatic seriousness for police professionalism and a third season was not commissioned.

CAST *DS Steve Hackett* Patrick Mower *DCS Tate* Philip Madoc *DS Louise Colbert* Vivien Heilbron /*pr* Philip Hinchcliffe /*dr* inc Douglas Camfield /*mus* Dudley Simpson /*BBC TV* (UK) /22 x 50m col.

Tarzan

Adventure. ITV 1967–9

TV version of Edgar Rice Burrough's classic yarn about the abandoned blue-blooded English boy raised by an ape to be King of the Jungle. Ron Ely was muscularly convincing in the lead (although the famous jungle yell had to be dubbed by former film Tarzan, Johnny Weissmuller) and there were enough thrilling jungle fights (with animals and men) to keep small noses glued to the screen. A strong vein of sentiment in Ely's interpretation was also evident, Tarzan being the fatherly protector of Cheetah the chimp and Jai the orphan. There was no Jane, a sexual connotation being deemed unsuitable. Guest stars included Diana Ross and The Supremes (as nuns in the episode 'The Convert').

More TV Tarzans followed in Ely's bare footsteps. A cartoon *Tarzan: Lord of the Jungle* (Filmation) appeared in 1976–8, to be succeeded by another animation, *Tarzan and the Super 7* (Filmation) in 1978, and an environmental live-action *Tarzan* in 1991. This latter version, which featured Wolf Larsen in the loin-clothed role, contained a cameo by Ely himself.

CAST *Tarzan* Ron Ely *Jai* Manuel Padilla Jr *Jason Flood* Alan Caillou *Rao* Rockne Tarkington *Tall Boy* Stewart Raffill /*exec pr* Sydney Weintraub /*pr* Jon Epstein, Maurice Unger /*dr* inc Robert Day, Lawrence Dobkin, R.G. Springsteen, William Witney, William Wiard /*wr* Carey Wilbur, Don Brinkley, George S. Slavin, Richard & Esther Shapiro, Richard Landau, Sam Roeca, Robert Sabaroff /*mus* Nelson Riddle / *Banner Productions* (USA) /58 x 60m col /US tx NBC 1966–8.

Taxi!

Comedy. BBC 1963–4

Another TV vehicle for Sid James, this time as a London cabbie with a penchant for sticking his nose into other people's business.

A bemusing mix of sitcom and worthy drama (the creator was Ted Willis, also ➢*Dixon of Dock Green*), it failed to pick up enough passengers to warrant a third season. Bill Owen (later ➢*Last of the Summer Wine*) and Ray Brooks (➢*Big Deal*) were amongst the drivers.

CAST *Sid Stone* Sid James *Fred Cuddell* Bill Owen *Terry Mills* Ray Brooks *Madeleine* Vanda Godsell /*cr* Ted Willis /*pr* Michael Mills, Harry Carlisle, Douglas Moodie /*dr* inc Douglas Argent /*wr* Jack Rosenthal, Harry Driver /*BBC TV* (UK) /21 x 45m bw.

Taxi

Comedy. BBC1 1978–83

US sitcom following the frustrations and aspirations of the staff of New York's Sunshine Cab Company. The principal characters – most of whom were deluded part-timers hoping to use the garage as a way-station on the road to better things – were philosophizing Alex, Latka the barely English-speaking mechanic, spaced-out ex-hippie Reverend Jim (a shock-haired Christopher Lloyd), bit-actor Bobby, boxer Tony, and Elaine, an art-gallery assistant. Louie DePalma (a memorably malevolent Danny DeVito) was the dwarfish, slimeball dispatcher, who sat in his cage giving orders. It won three consecutive Emmys for Outstanding Comedy Series, but when ratings (never huge anyway) began to drop, network ABC unceremoniously dumped it. NBC tried a revival, but to no avail. Popular taste was changing, and the show's sympathy for the misfit underdog just did not fit Reaganite times. Guest actors included Rhea Perlman (who married DeVito on set during a lunchbreak) and Ted Danson, who did a turn as an egotistical hairdresser; both went on to star in ➢*Cheers*, the next work of *Taxi* producers Les and Glen Charles.

CAST *Alex Rieger* Judd Hirsch *Louie DePalma* Danny DeVito *Elaine Nardo* Marilu Henner *Bobby Wheeler* Jeff Conaway *Jim Caldwell Ignatowski* Christopher Lloyd *Tony Banta* Tony Danza *Latka Gravas* Andy Kaufman *Simka Dahblitz Gravas* Carol Kane /*cr* James L. Brooks, Stan Daniels, David Davis, Ed Weinberger /*exec pr* James L. Brooks, Stan Daniels, David Davis, Ed Weinberger /*pr* Glen Charles, Les Charles /*dr* inc James Burrows, Danny DeVito, Noam Pitlik, Harvey Miller /*wr* inc James L. Brooks, Stan Daniels, David Davis, Ed Weinberger, Earl Pomerantz, Sam Simon / *mus* Bob James /*John Charles Walters Productions* (USA) /113 x 30m col /US tx ABC /NBC 1978–83.

Taz-Mania
Children's. ITV 1991–

Warner Bros' cartoon teenage Tasmanian Devil first appeared in their *Looney Tunes* anthology before whirling off, after a mere six appearances, to his own off-the-wall show. Here he waited on tables at ramshackle antipodean Hotel Tasmania, chaotically ate everything in sight, and lived – with the rest of The Devil clan – in a cave tastefully furnished in Danish Modern. Splendid second-row characters (con-dog Didgeri Dingo, narcissistic Buddy Boar, egotistical dunderhead Bushwacker Bob) and zippy stories made for a fun 30 minutes. Those providing the voice work included Dan Castellaneta (➢*The Simpsons*), John Astin (➢*The Addams Family*) and Jim Cummings, double Emmy-winner for his vocalizing of Winnie the Pooh.

CAST (voices) *Taz/Buddy Boar/Wendel T. Wolf / Bushwacker Bob* Jim Cummings *Mr Thickly* Dan Castellaneta *Molly Devil* Kellie Martin *Bull Gator* John Astin *Hugh Devil/Daniel Platypus/Bush Rat* Maurice LaMarche *Jean Devil* Miriam Flynn *Jake Devil* Debi Derryberry *Dog/Didgeri Dingo/Francis X. Bushland / Ax /Timothy Platypus* Rob Paulsen *Matilda /Constance Koala* Rosalyn Landor /*exec pr* Tom Ruegger, Jean MacCurdy /*pr* Art Art Vitello /*dr* inc Vitello, Doug McCarthy, Keith Baxter /*wr* inc Bill Kopp, Mark Saraceni /*mus* Richard Stone /*Warner Bros* (USA) / 28 x 30m col /US tx Fox TV 1991–.

Teenage Health Freak
Comedy. C4 1992–3

Sex, diaries and videotape. Energetic, clever comedy about an angsty teenager, Peter Payne, in lust with a schoolgirl and with a habit of using his camcorder for confessionals. Adapted by Daniel Peacock (➢*The Comic Strip Presents...*), who played Payne's alcoholic pest-controller father, from the the book *Diary of a Teenage Health Freak* by Aidan Macfarlane and Anne McPherson.

CAST *Peter Payne* Alex Langdon *Amanda Jeffs* Liza Walker *Mr Payne* Daniel Peacock *Mrs Peacock* Tilly Vosburgh *The Headmaster* Tony Robinson *Miss Blazeby* Jenny Lecoat /*pr* Adrian Bate /*dr* Metin Husey, Peter Cattaneo /*wr* Daniel Peacock /*Limelight: ISIS* (UK) /12 x 30m col.

Teenage Mutant Hero Turtles
Children's. BSkyB 1988–95

Four pet-store turtles – Donatello, Raphael, Michaelangelo and Leonardo – accidentally fall into the NY sewer system, where they are contaminated by 'Mutogen'. As a result, they begin to walk upright, talk and fight a fearless crusade for justice (primarily against the evil Shredder, voiced by James Avery from ➢*Fresh Prince of Bel Air*), being aided in this endeavour by copious quantities of pizza.

The *Teenage Mutant Ninja Turtles* may go down in TV history as one of the most profitable jokes of all time. They were conceived in 1983 as a napkin doodle by Kevin Eastman and Peter Laird as a parody of the Japanese samurai-type heroes then occupying comic strips. A *Turtle* comic book followed, with the characters picked up by Group W for a TV animated mini-series in 1987 (*dr* Yoshikatsu Kasai) and succeeded in turn by two hit live-action cinema features, *Teenage Mutant Ninja Turtles* (1990) and *Teenage Mutant Ninja Turtles II: The Secret of the Ooze* (1991). In Britain concerns about the Turtles' use of 'Ninja' fighting techniques resulted in both the series and movies being retitled *Teenage Mutant Hero Turtles.*

CAST (voices) *Donatello* Barry Gordon *Leonardo* Can Clarke *Michaelangelo* Townsend Coleman *Raphael* Rob Paulsen *April* Ranae Jacobs *Shredder* James Avery *Splinter* Peter Renady /*cr* Kevin Eastman, Peter Laird / *pr* inc Fred Wolf, Walt Kubiak /*dr* inc Fred Wolf /*wr* inc Michael Reaves, Brynne Stephens, J. Larry Carroll / *Murakami Wolf Swenson Inc: Group W Productions* (USA) /89 x 30m col /US tx Syndicated 1988–95.

TekWar

Sci-fi. Sky2 1996

In 2045 an ex-cop, Jake Cardigan (Greg Evigan from ➢*My Two Dads*), joins the Cosmos Detective Agency where he is employed to hunt down traffickers of Tek, an addictive virtual-reality programme. Efficient futuristic actioner, based on the *Tek* novels of ex-➢*Star Trek* actor William Shatner (who hammed it up in the series as Cosmos boss, Bascom) and preceded by a slew of *Tek* TVMs.

CAST *Jake Cardigan* Greg Evigan *Walter H. Bascom* William Shatner *Sid Gomez* Eugene Clark *Beth Kittridge* Toni Higginson *Sam Houston* Maria del Mar *Nika* Natalie Radford /*cr* William Shatner /*pr* Stephen Roloff /*dr* inc Allan Kroeker /*wr* Marc Scott Zicree /*Atlantic Films* (USA) /18 x 60m col /US tx USA Network 1995.

Telegoons

Comedy. BBC 1963–4

Puppet version of radio's *The Goon Show.* It mostly used archive scripts (though there was a tad of new material), with the *Goon* regulars providing the voices of Neddy Seagoon and crew.

CAST (voices) *Major Dennis Bloodnok /Henry Crun /Bluebottle/Hercules Grytpype-Thynne* Peter Sellars *Eccles/Minnie Bannister/Count Moriarty* Spike Milligan *Neddy Seagoon* Harry Secombe /*pr* Tony Young /*wr* Spike Milligan, Larry Stephens, Eric Sykes /*BBC TV: Grosvenor Films* (UK) /25 x 15m bw.

Teletubbies

Children's. BBC2 1997–

'Eh-oh.' Toddlers' TV show concerning five alien-like beings – Dipsy, Po, Laa Laa and Tinky Winky – who live in a surreal land (complete with baby sun, Noo Noo the vacuum cleaner, weird flowers) where they communicate in nonsensical burblings, eat Tubby toast and custard, and watch TV on their tummy screens.

Although intended to be of educational value for pre-school tots, there was controversy over the characters' inarticulate – and repetitive – warblings, with vehement claims by parents that the show diminished, rather than encouraged, the speech abilities of their offspring. More scandal followed when the actor who played Tinky Winky, David Thompson, was discovered to be a nude dancer. Several countries refused to buy the show, but what the BBC lost in foreign sales it gained in a surprise market at home: students. A merchandizing bonanza ensued, and a Teletubbies record reached No. 1 in the music charts. The show was dreamed up by Anne Wood, formerly the creator of TV AM's Roland Rat, whose production company Ragdoll also produced *Rosie and Jim* and *Tots TV.* The set for Tubbyland, for those who care, was a field in Warwickshire, while the voice cast included Sandra Dickinson (➢*The Hitchhiker's Guide to the Galaxy*) and Rudolph Walker (formerly ➢*Love Thy Neighbour*). Time for tubby bye-bye.

CAST (voices) *Tinky Winky* Dave Thompson *Laa Laa* Sandra Dickinson *Po* Pui Fan Lee *Dipsy* Rudoph Walker /*cr* Anne Wood /*wr* Andy Davenport /*Ragdoll: BBC TV* (UK) /60 x 25m col /US tx PBS 1998–.

Telford's Change

Melodrama. BBC1 1979.

Short-run serial about a high-achieving bank official, Mark Telford, who decided to downshift to a provincial manager's job. His London-loving wife, with her sights on a showbiz career, refused to go. Episodes followed the resultant strain on their marriage.

Its very provincialism gave it an air of believability, enforced by Barkworth's just-so performance as Telford. A soap of class (middle), a niche the Corporation made its own during the 70s.

CAST *Mark Telford* Peter Barkworth *Sylvia Telford* Hannah Gordon *Tim Hart* Keith Barron /*pr* Mark Shivas /*dr* Barry Davis /*wr* Brian Clark /*BBC TV* (UK) / 10 x 50m col.

Tenafly

Crime. ITV 1974

Cases of Harry Tenafly, a black PI working for High Tower Investigations Inc. in Los Angeles.

Despite the blaxploitation title, a self-consciously unsensational crimer (Tenafly was happily married), which failed to woo audiences because of its lack of sensations. Aired in the USA as part of NBC's *Wednesday Mystery Movie* package.

CAST *Harry Tenafly* James McEachin *Ruth Tenafly* Lillian Lehman *Herb Tenafly* Paul Jackson *Lt Sam Church* David Huddleston /*cr* Richard Levinson, William Link /*exec pr* Richard Levinson, William Link / *pr* Jon Epstein /*dr* Richard A. Colla, Robert Day, Bernard Kowalski, Jud Taylor, Gene Levitt /*wr* Richard Levinson, William Link /*Universal TV* (USA) /5 x 90m col /US tx NBC 1973–4.

Tenko

Drama. BBC1 1981–4

Taking its title from the Japanese for roll-call, Lavinia Warner's drama told (with boils-and-all realism) of the suffering of a group of expatriate British and Dutch women imprisoned after the fall of Singapore in 1942. Filmed in Singapore and Dorset (the camp scenes). Leading characters were upper-class camp leader, Marion Jefferson; crusty Dr Beatrice Mason (Stephanie Cole, ➢*Waiting for God*); Rose Millar (Stephanie Beacham, divested of her usual sex-bitch image); suffragette Joss Holbrook; and tragic Dorothy Bennett, who turned to prostitution with the camp guards. During seasons two and three the *Tenko* women endured a forced march through the jungle to a new camp and a direct hit during an allied attack. Those who survived the war were reunited for an incongruous one-off murder mystery, set in 1950, entitled *Tenko Reunion* (1985).

CAST *Marion Jefferson* Ann Bell *Rose Millar* Stephanie Beacham *Sister Ulrica* Patricia Lawrence *Kate Norris* Claire Oberman *Nellie Keene* Jeananne Crowley *Dr Beatrice Mason* Stephanie Cole *Christina Campbell* Emily Bolton *Major Yamauchi* Burt Kwouk *Mrs Van Meyer* Elizabeth Chambers *Dorothy Bennett* Veronica Roberts *Sally Markham* Joanna Hole *Joss Holbrook* Jean Anderson *Verna Johnson* Rosemary Martin *Miss Hasan* Josephine Welcome /*cr* Lavinia Warner /*pr* Ken Riddington, Vere Lorrimer /*dr* inc Pennant Roberts, David Askey, David Tucker /*wr* Jill Hyen, Anne Valery, Paul Wheeler /*mus* James Harpham /*BBC TV* (UK) / 30 x 55m, 1 x 110m col.

Tenspeed and Brown Shoe

Crime. ITV 1981

Or what Jeff Goldblum did before fame descended. Here he played a demure LA stockbroker (thus 'a brown shoe' or square) who teamed up with a street-wise con artist (Ben Vereen, from ➢*Roots*) to form an unlikely PI agency. So unlikely, indeed, that they only lasted for 11 episodes, despite some slick actioneering.

CAST *E.L. 'Tenspeed' Turner* Ben Vereen *Lionel 'Brown Shoe' Whitney* Jeff Goldblum /*cr* Stephen J. Cannell /*pr* Stephen J. Cannell, Alex Beaton, Chuck Bowman, Juanita Bartlett /*dr* inc Stephen J. Cannell, Rod Holcomb, Harry Winer /*mus* Mike Post & Pete Carpenter /*Paramount* (USA) /1 x 96m, 10 x 60m col / US tx ABC 1980.

Terrahawks

Children's. ITV 1983–6

In 2020 Earth is threatened with invasion – this time by Zelda, queen of Guk and her ugly minion hordes. Only the elite combat unit Terrahawks, led by Dr Tiger Ninestein and operating from Hawknest in South America, can save the planet.

Drearily familiar Gerry Anderson format, though with a new line of ultra-sophisticated puppets (this being 14 years on from ➢*Secret Service*). These were stringless wonders packed with internal electronics, an advance which Anderson dubbed 'Supermacromation'. Among the cast was Windsor Davies, playing Sergeant Major Zero in a virtual voice reprise of his camp turn in ➢*It Ain't Half Hot, Mum.*

CAST (voices) *Zelda/Mary Falconer* Denise Bryer *Sgt Major Zero* Windsor Davies *Dr Ninestein/Hiro/Johnson* Jeremy Hitchin *Kate Kestrel/Cy-Star* Anne Ridler *Hudson/Space Sgt 101/Yung-Star* Ben Stevens /*cr* Gerry Anderson /*pr* Gerry Anderson, Christopher Burr /*wr* inc Tony Barwick /*mus* Richard Harvey /*sfx* Stephen Begg /*Anderson Burr: LWT* (UK) /39 x 30m col.

Terry and June
Comedy. BBC1 1979–87

'Surburban sitcom of marital ups and downs' (as it was po-facedly billed) set in Purley, Surrey, with Terry Scott and June Whitfield as the Medfords. The series was a virtual TV synonym for comfortable middle-class niceness; the crises out of which Terry and June made dramas included visits from Terry's boss, looking after a friend's dog, and Terry's misunderstanding about his wife's 'infidelity'. Throughout, Terry (played to overgrown-schoolboy perfection by Scott) blustered, and English-rose June smiled knowingly. Although not described as such, it was a sequel to ➢*Happy Ever After*, minus the mynah.

CAST *Terry* Terry Scott *June* June Whitfield /*cr* John Kane /*pr* Peter Whitmore, John B. Hobbs, Robin Nash / *dr* inc Peter Whitmore, David Taylor /*wr* inc John Kane, Colin Bostock-Smith, Jon Watkins /*BBC TV* (UK) /65 x 30m col.

Testament of Youth
Drama. BBC1 1979

Adaptation of the autobiography of Vera Brittain (mother of ex Labour/SDP MP Shirley Williams) charting her life as a young woman and nurse during the maelstrom of WW1. Snatches of archive film resonated with Elaine Morgan's scripts and Geoffrey Burgon's score to produce a compelling, evocative, even emotional TV experience. Four BAFTAs were bestowed upon it.

CAST *Vera Brittain* Cheryl Campbell *Roland Leighton* Peter Woodward /*pr* Jonathan Powell /*dr* Moira Armstrong /*wr* Elaine Morgan /*mus* Geoffrey Burgon / *BBC TV* (UK) /5 x 50m col.

That Was the Week That Was
Comedy. BBC TV 1962–3

Or *TW3* as it came to be abbreviated, grew out of the English political satire boom of the early 60s (witness: the founding of Peter Cook's Establishment Club and *Private Eye*), a movement rocket-fuelled by the Profumo scandal. *TW3* took the new satire to TV, with a team of presenters – led by David Frost – who gleefully, skillfully, filleted and ridiculed the week's nonsense and pomposities in sketches, reports and songs (trilled by Millicent Martin). John Cleese, Dennis Potter and Keith Waterhouse were amongst the boys toiling in the writing room. The ratings were tall, the influence broad, although an American version, also with Frost, never took off.

CAST (presenters) David Frost, William Rushton, Kenenth Cope, Lance Percival, David Kernan, Al Mancini, Bernard Levin, Millicent Martin, Timothy Birdsall, John Wells, John Bird, Eleanor Bron, Roy Hudd /*cr* Ned Sherrin /*pr* Ned Sherrin /*dr* Ned Sherrin / *wr* inc cast, Malcolm Bradbury, John Cleese, Anthony Jay, Gerald Kaufman, Dennis Potter, Jack Rosenthal, Peter Tinniswood, Keith Waterhouse, Christopher Booker, David Nobbs /*BBC TV* (UK) /36 x 50m, 1 x 150m, 1 x 100m bw /US tx NBC 1964.

Then Churchill Said To Me
Comedy. UK Gold 1993

Frankie Howerd's last sitcom, to all humorous intents and purposes a transfer of his ➢*Up Pompeii!* persona into WWII khaki (he played a bungler in Churchill's underground London bunker). It was banned on its scheduled 1982 transmission because of sensitivity over the Falklands/Malvinas War, to gather dust in the BBC vaults for 11 years until screened by satellite channel, UK Gold. Howerd (born Francis Howard) died a year before its eventual airing.

CAST *Pte Percy Potts* Frankie Howerd /*wr* Maurice Sellar, Lou Jones /*BBC TV* (UK) /6 x 30m col.

Thick as Thieves
Comedy. ITV 1974

Half-remembered sitcom from Dick Clement and Ian La Frenais (➢*The Likely Lads*). It featured a small-time crook, Dobbs (Bob Hoskins), coming out of prison to find his best friend and fellow 'leave it aht' villain Stan (John Thaw), shacked up with his wife. The resulting *ménage-à-trois* provided most of the frequent laughs. When LWT inexplicably let the series go, Clement and La Frenais modified it for the BBC, but by then Thaw had moved on to ➢*The Sweeney* and Bob Hoskins was in the process of becoming a removal man in the adult literacy series *On the Move*. Nothing daunted, the writers tinkered with Dobbs' wide-boyish character, returned him to prison, and so created ➢*Porridge*.

CAST *Dobbs* Bob Hoskins *Stan* John Thaw *Annie* Pat Ashton *Tommy Hollister* Trevor Peacock /*cr* Dick Clement & Ian La Frenais /*pr* Derrick Goodwin / *dr* Derrick Goodwin /*wr* Dick Clement & Ian La Frenais /*LWT* (UK) /8 x 30m col.

The Thin Blue Line
Comedy. BBC1 1995–7

Ben Elton-created sitcom (which re-teamed him with ➢*Blackadder* star Rowan Atkinson) set in a police station populated by half-witted caricatures (effeminate moron, senile black PC etc.) and mostly composed of half-witted inanities. The remainder of the script was seemingly reject material from *Blackadder* ('Don't snivel like a Frenchman who's caught his baguette in his bicycle spokes.'). Anything more heavy handed would surely have broken Elton's writing arm. Yet, it oozed an old-fashioned good-heartedness, which put some in mind of ➢*Dad's Army* (underscored by the fact that both shows were ensemble pieces about 'bumblers'), and secured 12 million-plus viewers. And a 1996 Best New Comedy Award. The setting was the fictitious town of Gasforth.

CAST *Insp. Fowler* Rowan Atkinson *DI Grim* David Haig *WPC Habib* Mina Anwar *PC Goody* James Dreyfus *DC Boyle* Mark Addy *Sgt Hawkins* Serena Evans *PC Gladstone* Rudolph Walker /*cr* Ben Elton / *pr* Ben Elton & Geoffrey Perkins /*dr* John Birkin / *wr* Ben Elton /*Tiger Aspect Productions* (UK) / 14 x 30m col.

The Thin Man
Crime. BBC 1957–8

A sophisticated NY husband and wife (plus dog, Asta) sleuth cases in-between reparteeing wittily.

Suffered in comparison to the *Thin Man* movie cycle (starring William Powell and Myrna Loy, and likewise based on the stories of Dashiell Hammett), being their inferior in plotting, pace and banter. However, the format of a comedy-mystery with married 'tecs would come back to the small screen again and again, not least with ➢*Hart to Hart* and ➢*McMillan and Wife.*

CAST *Nick Charles* Peter Lawford *Nora Charles* Phyllis Kirk /*pr* Samuel Marx, Edmund Beloin /*MGM* (USA) /78 x 25m bw /US tx NBC 1957–8.

The Third Man
Crime. BBC 1959–64

Bore next to no relation to Graham Greene's book or, indeed, Carol Reed's 1949 version of it (starring Orson Welles) for cinema. Instead it resurrected black marketeer Harry Lime from the sewers of post-war Vienna and turned him into a suave amateur sleuth. He also happened to be a millionaire, the money made from an entirely proper import-export business. If you could suspend incredulity, the cases were smooth affairs. An Anglo–American production, *The Third Man* featured Jonathan Harris (later ➢*Lost In Space*) as Lime's factotum and Rupert Davies (later ➢*Maigret*) as his contact at the Yard.

CAST *Harry Lime* Michael Rennie *Bradford Webster* Jonathan Harris *Arthur Shillings* Rupert Davies /*exec pr* Vernon Burns /*pr* Felix Jackson, Irving Asher /*dr* inc Robert M. Leeds /*wr* inc R.K. Palmer /*mus* Anton Karas (theme) /*BBC TV: British Lion Film Corp: National Telefilm Associates of America* (UK:USA) / 77 x 30m bw /US tx Syndicated 1960.

3rd Rock from the Sun
Sci-fi. BBC2 1996–

Starred movie-actor John Lithgow (*Terms of Endearment, The World According to Garp*) as the leader of a team of aliens whose mission was to explore life on the Universe's most unimportant planet: Earth ('the 3rd rock from the Sun'). To avoid detection, they took on human shape, with Lithgow's alien High Commander assuming the relatively unproblematic form of Dick Solomon, an Ohio university professor. Alas, the rest of the squad were not so lucky: his male military expert became Solomon's sexy, statuesque sister, Sally; the oldster intelligence expert became Solomon's teenage son, Tommy; and then there was oddball Harry (the ship had a spare seat) who became Solomon's brother. Splendidly clueless as to human etiquette and entirely lacking in the usual human inhibitions, the aliens turned everyday situations into wry-but-outrageously funny 'fish out of water' comedy. And, as mandatory in the aliens-on-earth comedy sub-genre (see ➢*My Favourite Martian*, ➢*Mork and Mindy*, ➢*Alf*), the show pointed up the absurdities (and hypocrisies) of human behaviour. The show garnered numerous awards, including two consecutive comedy actor Emmys for Lithgow, and a comedy actress Emmy for Jane Curtin, who played Dr

'Er, um, maybe we should talk about this.' Hope Steadman (Mel Harris), Nancy Weston (Patricia Wettig) and Michael Steadman (Ken Olin) in the angst-ridden yuppie melodrama *Thirtysomething*. In real life, Wettig was married to Olin.

Mary Albright, Solomon's university colleague and on-off affair (on when she found his quirks amusing, off when they were embarrassing). Written with considerable brio, *3rd Rock* became NBC's biggest comedy hit after ➢*Seinfeld*. The show was created by former *Saturday Night Live* writers Bonnie Turner and Terry Turner.

CAST *Dick Solomon* John Lithgow *Sally Solomon* Kristen Johnston *Tommy Solomon* Joseph Gordon-Levitt *Harry Solomon* French Stewart *Dr Mary Albright* Jane Curtin *Nina* Simbi Khali *Mrs Dubcek* Elmarie Wendel /*cr* Bonnie Turner, Terry Turner /*exec pr* Marcy Carsey, Tom Werner, Caryn Mandabach, Bonnie Turner, Terry Turner, Bill Martin, Mike Schiff / *pr* Patrick Kienlen, Bob Kushell, Christine Zander /*dr* Bob Berlinger, James Burrows, Terry Hughes /*wr* inc Bonnie Turner, Terry Turner, Bill Martin, Mike Schiff / *mus* Ben Vaughn /*The Carsey-Werner Co: YBYL Productions* (USA) /78 x 30m col /US tx NBC 1996–.

Thirtysomething

Drama. C4 1989–92

'Er, um, maybe we should talk about this...'

Addictive yuppie (melo)drama about a group of angst-ridden Philadelphians. These were, principally: ad-writer Michael Steadman and wife Hope Murdoch Steadman, a Princeton over-achiever now bringing up baby; Elliot Weston, business partner of Michael, and his wife Nancy, a former 60s flower child; Melissa, Michael's want-it-all photographer cousin; Ellyn, Hope's worried single friend; and Gary, Michael's best buddy, an easy-going Assistant Classics Professor. Major storylines concerned Elliot and Nancy's separation (they reconciled) and Nancy's subsequent diagnosis of cancer; the bankruptcy of Michael and Elliot's business, and their employment by the cynical Miles Drentell; and the death, in 1991, of Gary (played by Peter Horton, sometime husband of Michelle Pfeiffer, and later director of movie *The Cure*). Famed for its mumblingly realistic dialogue, endless self-therapy and liberalism (a scene with two men in bed cost the network $1.5 million in cancelled advertising), the show was created by East Coast Jewish writers Marshall Herskowitz (a friend of Woody Allen's) and Ed Zwick. They had both come up scribing scripts for Aaron Spelling's soap *Family* (1976–80).

CAST *Michael Steadman* Ken Olin *Hope Murdoch Steadman* Mel Harris *Janey Steadman* Brittany and Lacey Craven *Elliot Weston* Timothy Busfield *Nancy Weston* Patricia Wettig *Ethan Weston* Luke Rossi *Brittany Weston* Jordana 'Bink' Draper *Melissa Steadman* Melanie Mayron *Professor Gary Shepherd* Peter Horton *Ellyn Warren* Polly Draper *Miles Drentell* David Clennon /*cr* Marshall Herskowitz, Ed Zwick / *pr* Marshall Herskowitz, Ed Zwick, Paul Haggis /*dr* Marshall Herskowitz, Ken Olin, Peter Horton, Timothy Busfield, Scott Winnant, Steve Robman, John Pasquin /*wr* inc Marshall Herskowitz, Ed Zwick / *Bedford Falls: MGM* (USA) /85 x 60m col /US tx ABC 1987–91.

This Life

Melodrama. BBC2 1996–8

Twentysomething middle-class British soap about a group of house-sharing young lawyers – mostly sorted for Es, whizz, sex, swearing and envy at Porsche-drivings thirtysomethings, rather than the tiresome burden of legal work. Tailor-made for the elusive 16–24 viewerdom, it tried for the stark, catchy visuals of *NYPD Blue*, but failed. But a major cult anyway.

CAST *Miles Andrews* Jack Davenport *Milly Nassim* Amita Dhiri *Edgar 'Egg' Cook* Andrew Lincoln *Anna Forbes* Daniela Nardini *Ferdy* Ramon Tikaram *Hooperman* Geoffrey Bateman *Kira* Luisa Bradshaw-White *O'Donnell* David Mallinson *Paul* Paul Medford *Nicki* Juliet Cowan *Jo* Steve John Shepherd *Graham* Cyril Nri *Kelly* Sacha Craise *Rachel* Natasha Little /*cr* Michael Jackson, Tony Garnett, Amy Jenkins /*exec pr* Tony Garnett /*pr* Jane Fallon /*dr* inc Audrey Cooke, Nigel Douglas /*wr* inc Jenkins /*BBC TV* (UK) / 11 x 45m col.

Thomas the Tank Engine and Friends

Children's. ITV 1984–92

The character of Thomas the Tank Engine was created by the Rev W. Awdry (d. 1997) in 1944 as a means of entertaining his three-year-old son who was suffering from measles. After a spectacular career in publishing, Thomas and his puffer-train pals were filmed for TV (as models) by the Britt Allcroft Group, with dry narration by ex-Beatle Ringo Starr (later Michael Angelis from ➢*The Liver Birds*, ➢*The Boys from the Blackstuff*). Although a hit with tiny tots in 43 countries, they were disliked by Awdry himself, who urged childen not to watch them, citing as his reason 'their lamentable gross ignorance' about railway practices. He was bemused by the Americans who insisted, in the cause of political correctness, in calling the Fat Controller by his proper name of Sir Topham Hat. Meanwhile, the Britt Allcroft Group, which owned the screen and merchandizing rights to the Thomas stories, made pre-tax profits of around £2 million per annum.

CAST (narrators) Ringo Starr, Michael Angelis /*exec pr* Britt Allcroft /*dr* David Mitton /*wr* Britt Allcroft, David Mitton /*Britt Allcroft Group: Clearwater Films: Central TV* (UK) /60+ x 10:15m col /US tx Syndicated 1992.

The Thorn Birds

Melodrama. BBC1 1984

Carmen Culler's five-part adaptation of Colleen McCullough's doorstop about a handsome Catholic priest, Ralph de Bricassart (former ➢*Dr Kildare*, Richard Chamberlain), enticed into a forbidden affair in the Australian outback by beautiful sheepfarmer's daughter Meggie Cleary. Their illigitimate son, Dane, also entered the church. Hugely successful fluff.

CAST *Father Ralph de Bricassart* Richard Chamberlain *Meggie Cleary* Sydney Penny/Rachel Ward *Mary Carson* Barbara Stanwyck *Archbishop Contini-Verchese* Christopher Plummer *Luke O'Neill* Bryan Brown *Fiona 'Fee' Cleary* Jean Simmons *Anne Mueller* Piper Laurie /*pr* David L. Wolper, Stan Margulies /*dr* Daryl Duke /*wr* Carmen Culver / *ABC* (USA) /5 x 75:90m col.

Three of a Kind

Comedy. BBC1 1981–3

Originally a 1967 revue series to advertise the talents of Lulu, Mike Yarwood and Ray Fell; in the early 80s Paul Jackson (➢*The Young Ones*) clamped electrodes to *TOAK*'s head, and it arose again as a showcase, this time for Lenny Henry, Tracey Ullman and David Copperfield (not the American magician). Widely acclaimed, it did much for the TV careers of Henry and Ullman (Copperfield went to the cabaret circuit), not to mention those in the gag'n'sketch-writing backroom, among them Ian Hislop, Rob Grant and Doug Naylor.

CAST (presenters) Tracey Ullman, Lenny Henry, David Copperfield /*pr* Paul Jackson /*wr* inc Ian Hislop, Rob Grant, Doug Naylor, Mike Radford /*BBC TV* (UK) / 12 x 30m col.

3-2-1

Light Entertainment. ITV 1978–87

Long-running game show hosted by comedian Ted Rogers, with the help of hostesses known as 'The Gentle Secs' and a small parade of comedians, celebrities and dancers. Three pairs of couples competed (through eliminator rounds of questions, some presented in cryptic sketches) for the star prize of a car. The booby was a metal dustbin, representing the show's mascot, Dusty Bin. Based on the Spanish show *Uno, Dos, Tres.*

CAST (presenter) Ted Rogers /*pr* Derek Burrell-Davies, Mike Goddard, Ian Bolt, Graham Wetherell, Terry Heneberry /*dr* inc Ian Bolt, David Millard, Paddy Russell, Don Clayton /*YTV* (UK) /180 x 60m col.

Thunderbirds

Children's. ITV 1965–6

'5, 4, 3, 2, 1 – Thunderbirds are go!'

Superior Gerry Anderson 'supermarionation' featuring the 21st-century's International Rescue organization. Run by millionaire Jeff Tracy from his secret South Pacific island HQ, the life-saver missions of IR were undertaken, in super tech vehicular hardware, by his quintet of sons (all named after real-life US astronauts): Scott (in Thunderbird 1, a 70,000 m.p.h. rocket); Virgil (Thunderbird 2, a giant green carrier); Alan (Thunderbird 3, an orange spaceship; Gordon (Thunderbird 4, a yellow submarine); and John (Thunderbird 5, a space satellite). Maintaining the fleet were boffin designer Brains and female electronics expert Tin Tin, with Tin Tin's father acting as Jeff's butler, Kryano. But the two puppets who stole the show were IR's London agent, the blonde-bouffanted Lady Penelope Creighton-Ward (one of the few puppets ever to smoke on TV), and her 'cor-blimey' East End butler, Parker. (He also got to drive – 'Yus, m'lady' – around in her pink six-wheeled Rolls Royce, complete with machine-gun located behind the radiator and FAB 1 number plate.) Despite the allure of the fantastic craft, John Read's marvellously mobile camera work, edge-of-the-seat stories and a grade A nemesis in The Hood, the show's phenomenal and enduring success was largely an accident. When Lew Grade, head of ITV, saw the rushes, he declared 'This is too damned good for half an hour', and instructed Anderson to increase the length of episodes to 50 minutes. Anderson did so by inserting cheap padding dialogue – which allowed the puppets to develop distinct personalities. This, together with Anderson's perennial optimism over the future, sealed *Thunderbirds*' crossover appeal to adults. There were two movie spin-offs: *Thunderbirds Are Go*, 1966, and *Thunderbird Six.* A repeat of the series in 1991 achieved stratospheric ratings.

FAB.

CAST (voices) *Jeff Tracy* Peter Dyneley *Scott* Shane Rimmer *Virgil* David Holliday *Alan* Matt Zimmermann *Gordon/Brains/Parker/Kryano* David Graham *John/The Hood* Ray Barrett *Tin Tin* Christine Finn *Lady Penelope Creighton-Ward* Sylvia Anderson /*cr* Gerry & Sylvia Anderson /*pr* Gerry Anderson /*dr* inc Alan Pattillo, Desmond Saunders, David Elliott /*wr* inc Gerry & Sylvia Anderson, Alan Pattillo, Alan Fennell, Dennis Spooner, Tony Barwick /*AP Films: ATV: ITC* (UK) /32 x 60m col /US tx Syndicated 1968.

Thundercats

Children's. BBC1 1987

Cartoon sorcery featuring a septet of muscular felines – Wilykat, Wilykit, Lion-O, Panthro, Tygra, Cheetara and Snarf from a lost world, waging a never-ending battle against evil, principally Mumm-Ra and his mutants. A mystical 'Sword of Omens' gave Lion-O a useful edge over the competition. Based on the toys and cult stuff amongst junior-league viewers.

CASt (voices) Robert McFadden, Larry Kenney, Earl Hammond, Peter Newman, Lynne Lipton, Gerrianne Raphael, Earle Hyman /*pr* Jules Bass, Arthur Rankin Jr /*Rankin Bass* (USA) /1 x 60m, 1 x 120m, 32 x 20m col /US tx Syndicated 1985.

Till Death Us Do Part

Comedy. BBC1 1966–74

The monstrous caricature of an East End working-class Tory that was Alf Garnett (ex-radio Luxembourg DJ, Warren Mitchell), West Ham supporter and hater of 'yer coons', first appeared

A former Radio-Luxembourg DJ, Warren Mitchell (born Warren Misell) found TV stardom as legendary East End bigot Alf Garnett in *Till Death Us Do Part.*

in a 1965 BBC ➢*Comedy Playhouse.* There, the family was known as the Ramseys and Gretchen Franklin (later ➢*EastEnders*) played the 'silly old moo', otherwise known as disdainful wife Else. In translation to a regular series, the cast stabilized as Mitchell, Dandy Nichols as Else, Una Stubbs as daughter Rita, and Anthony Booth (father of Cherie, wife of Labour PM Tony Blair) as son-in-law Mike, the 'randy scouse git'. To Alf's eternal ire, Mike had longish hair (occasioning the epithet 'Shirley Temple') and was a Trotskyist, a reader of the *Keep Left* newspaper. Week after week, docker Alf treated his family to rants on whatever subject happened to catch his fancy, delivering the diatribes from the armchair below the flying ducks and the picture of 'yer Majesty' in the sitting room of their house in Wapping High Street. Particular targets were blacks, the permissive society and Edward Heath (for going to a grammar school, not a proper Tory-training ground like Eton, and for taking Great Britain into the Common Market). The series attracted numerous complaints – not least from moral guardian Mary Whitehouse, who once counted 78 'blaadys' in one episode – and from those who failed to see that Garnett was an ironic portrait. Mitchell's performance was a tour de force; perfect in every word and physical gesture, although the rest of the cast were crucial as foils. A 1985 sequel, *In Sickness and Health*, in which, of the originals, only Mitchell appeared regularly, was mediocre in comparison. The fact that a Conservative government was in power (one, moreover, in ideological tune with Garnett) made Alf's outrages difficult to pull off with plausibility. The format of *Till Death* sold to the USA as ➢*All in the Family*, with Garnett translated into Archie Bunker, another sitcom colossus.

CAST *Alf Garnett* Warren Mitchell *Else* Dandy Nichols *Rita* Una Stubbs *Mike* Anthony (Tony) Booth / *cr* Johnny Speight /*pr* Dennis Main Wilson, David Croft /*dr* Douglas Argent, Colin Strong /*wr* Johnny Speight /*BBC TV* (UK) /50 x 30m bw:col.

Timeslip

Sci-fi. ITV 1970–1

Telefantasy for juveniles, featuring two kids – Liz Skinner and Simon Randall – who discover an invisible time barrier which allows them to travel to their own past and future. Self-consciously educational (episode 1 was introduced by then ITN science correspondent Peter Fairley), the show explored such themes as climatic change and the dangers inherent in scientific 'progress' – but usually with a high sense of adventure. And a good dollop of horror; the episode in which a woman character took a faulty dose of longevity drug HA57, and aged 100 years in a wink, kept a generation awake at night. Denis Quilley, something of a minor star in 70s time-travel TV here menaced as government scientist Commander Traynor.

CAST *Simon Randall* Spencer Banks *Liz Skinner* Cheryl Burfield *Frank Skinner* Derek Benfield *Jean Skinner* Iris Russell *Cmdr Traynor* Denis Quilley /*cr* Ruth Boswell, James Boswell /*pr* John Cooper /*dr* John Cooper, Peter Jeffries, Ron Francis, Dave Foster /*wr* Bruce Stewart, Victor Pemberton /*ATV Midlands* (UK) / 26 x 30m col.

The Time Tunnel

Sci-fi. BBC 1968 /ITV 1970

Two American scientists, Tony Newman and Doug Phillips, invent a time tunnel and get trapped in the fourth dimension when a US senator insists on a premature demonstration.

Cult sci-fi show from Irwin Allen, the Caesar Augustus of cheapskate hokum. It used stock footage of old Fox movies for the dangerous historical settings (the Wild West, sinking of the Titanic, the Trojan War) into which Newman and Philips dropped every week – with nary a hair out of place – although for futuristic episodes, Mr Allen prudently reused the sets from his ➤ *Lost in Space.* Still, the swirling 'time tunnel' vortex, which seemed to reach into the back of the set, was a visual gem, and the cast was eminently watchable (Colbert, Darren and former Miss America, Lee Meriwether, would all be sent travelling on their careers by the show). A TVM revival in 1976, however, failed to lead into a new series.

CAST *Dr Tony Newman* James Darren *Dr Doug Phillips* Robert Colbert *Dr Ann MacGregor* Lee Meriwether /*cr* Irwin Allen /*exec pr* Irwin Allen /*dr* inc Irwin Allen, Harry Harris, Sobey Martin, William Hale, Herschel Daugherty /*wr* inc Robert Hamner, Carey Wilbur, Harold Jack Bloom, Allan Balter /*mus* John Williams /*sfx* L.B. Abbott /*Fox TV* (USA) / 30 x 50m col /US tx ABC 1966–7.

Standing before the pop-art vortex that transported them to the hot-spots of history, James Darren (front) and Robert Colbert (second from front) starred in *The Time Tunnel.* In an effort to cut costs, the show plundered stock footage of old Fox movies.

Tinker, Tailor, Soldier, Spy

Spy. BBC2 1979

Superlative espionage serial tracking the painstaking efforts of retired spy George Smiley (Alec Guinness, in appropriately weary form) to unearth a double agent in the British Secret Service. Adapted from John le Carré's novel, it was succeeded by *Smiley's People* (BBC2 1982, co-scripted by le Carré). The spy-master returned once again to the screen – though this time played by Denholm Elliott – in *A Murder of Quality* (Thames TV: Portobello 1991; screenplay by le Carré).

CAST *George Smiley* Alec Guinness *Percy Alleline* Michael Aldridge *Ricki Tarr* Hywel Bennett *Toby Esterhase* Bernard Hepton *Bill Haydon* Ian Richardson *Peter Guillam* Michael Jayston *Connie Sachs* Beryl Reid *Roy Bland* Terence Rigby /*pr* Jonathan Powell /*dr* John Irvin /*wr* Arthur Hopcraft /*mus* Geoffrey Burgon ('The Nunc Dimittis' theme) /*BBC TV* (UK) /7 x 50m col.

Tiswas

Children's. ITV 1974–82

Anarchic live TV show, presented from ATV/ Central's Birmingham studio, which revolutionized staid Saturday morning kiddie TV with its orgy of Phantom Flan-flinging, comedy, sketches, cartoons, pop interviews, and water-drenchings of the hapless ones trapped in 'The Cage'. The main hosts were Chris Tarrant, Sally James (big cleavage, which stretched her Tiswas T-shirt into illegal shape), Trevor East, Bob Carolgees (plus punk dog, Spit) and former Scaffold member, John Gorman, with Lenny Henry and Frank Carson amongst the studio pranksters. The title was an acronym for Today Is Saturday Wear A Smile. An adult version, ➢*OTT*, bombed unceremoniously (not least because it was superfluous; the most ardent of *Tiswas*'s five million viewers were anyway the teen–twenty crowd, who could catch all the subliminal risqué jokes). The show spawned a top 26 hit in 1980, 'The Bucket of Water Song'. For the record, the words of the first verse are: 'This is a song we lovers of water sing/We can't go wrong, we're happy as a king/We beat the drums as we march along/We clash the cymbals and beat the gong/We sing out strong The Bucket of Water Song...'

CAST (presenters) inc Chris Tarrant, Sally James, Trevor East, John Gorman, Bob Carolgees, Clive Webb / *pr* inc Chris Tarrant, Peter Harris, Glyn Edwards / *ATV: Central* (UK) /150+ x 120m col.

T.J. Hooker

Crime. ITV 1983–5

A veteran street cop helps out the rookies of the Academy Precinct of the LCPD.

T.J. Hooker was a show not so much produced as committed – like a crime. Ex-➢*Star Trek* actor, William Shatner was notably kitted out in a toupee which constantly engaged the laughter cords. Meanwhile, the stories were heavy-handed moralistic affairs. Even a cameo from Leonard Nimoy only served to divert the mind upwards to the USS *Enterprise*. Unlikely that Aaron Spelling puts this at the top of his cv.

CAST *Sgt T.J. Hooker* William Shatner *Off. Stacy Sheridan* Heather Locklear *Off. Jim Corrigan* James Darren *Off. Vince Romano* Adrian Zmed *Capt. Sheridan* Richard Herd /*cr* Rick Husky /*exec pr* Aaron Spelling, Leonard Goldberg /*dr* inc Cliff Bole, Charles Picerni, Corey Allen, Don Chaffey, Don Weis, Michael Caffey, William Shatner /*Spelling-Goldberg: Columbia* (USA) /78 x 60m col /US tx ABC:CBS 1982–7.

Toma

Crime. ITV 1984

Like ➢*Serpico*, an undercover detective series based on the maverick exploits of a real cop, here Dave Toma of the Newark, New Jersey, PD. (The real Toma guested in every episode, and served as consultant.) Although a ratings success, the show closed after one season because actor Musante found the production schedule a grinding chore; ABC imported a new star, Robert Blake, tweaked the format, and issued ➢*Baretta* in its place.

CAST *Det. Dave Toma* Tony Musante *Insp. Spooner* Simon Oakland *Patty Toma* Susan Strasberg /*cr* Edward Hume /*exec pr* Roy Huggins, Jo Swerling Jr /*pr* Stephen J. Cannell /*dr* inc Nicholas Colasanto, Richard Bennett, Charles S. Dubin, Marc Daniels, Jeannot Swarc /*wr* inc Stephen J. Cannell, Edward Hume, Juanita Bartlett, John Thomas James (aka Huggins), Dave Toma, Tony Musante, Gerald DiPego /*Roy Huggins-Public Arts: Universal TV* (USA) /22 x 60m, 1 x 90m col /US tx ABC 1973–4.

Tombstone Territory

Western. ITV 1957

Set in the eponymous Arizonan mining town, where Sheriff Clay Hollister and *Epitaph* editor Claybourne tamed the local man-for-breakfast lawless. Moderate oater from Ziv-TV, with some episodes based loosely on reports from the real life *Tombstone Epitaph*.

CAST *Sheriff Clay Hollister* Pat Conway *Harris Claybourne* Richard Eastham /*pr* Andy White, Frank Pittman /*Ziv-TV* (USA) /91 x 26m bw /US tx ABC 1957–9.

The Tomorrow People

Sci-fi. ITV 1973–9

'Let's Jaunt, TIM!'

A group of precocious teenagers, having reached the next stage of evolution to become Homo Superior (so acquiring the powers of telekinesis and teleporting, and the right to wear digital watches), pacifistically protect planet Earth on behalf of the Galactic Federation. Their base was a disused tunnel of London Underground, which housed a talking biotronic computer, TIM.

Neatly contrived piece of juvenile telefantasy, which developed a fanatical teen following despite tinfoil sets. Creator Roger Price allegedly dreamed up the idea after talks with Dr Christopher Evans, author of psychic tome *The Mind in Chains*, and rocker David Bowie. Intended as ITV's answer to ➢*Doctor Who*, the show ironically provided the screen debut for future Time Lord, Peter Davison. He appeared in the 1975 offering 'A Man for Emily' as Elmer, an alien in silver briefs. (Davison met his future wife, Sandra Dickinson, on the set of this episode.) In 1992 American cable company Nickelodeon revived the show, casting former ➢*Neighbours* star Kristian Schmid as the new lead Homo Superior.

CAST *John* Nicholas Young *Stephen* Peter Vaughan-Clarke *Elizabeth* Elizabeth Adare *Carol* Sammie Winmill *Kenny* Stephen Salsmon *Tyso* Dean Lawrence *Mike Bell* Mike Holloway *Hsui Tai* Misako Koba *Voice of TIM* Philip Gilbert /*cr* Roger Price /*pr* Roger Price, Ruth Boswell, Vic Hughes /*dr* inc Roger Price, Paul Bernard, Stan Woodward, Leon Thau /*wr* Roger Price, Brian Finch, Jon Watkins /*mus* Dudley Simpson / *Thames TV* (UK) /68 x 30m col.

The Top Secret Life of Edgar Briggs

Comedy. ITV 1974

Starred David Jason as Briggs, an incompetent inadvertently made assistant to the Commander of the SIS (Special Intelligence Service). There, he caused slapstick spy mayhem in the manner already mined by ➢*Get Smart*'s Maxwell Smart.

CAST *Edgar Briggs* David Jason *The Commander* Noel Coleman *Buxton* Michael Stainton *Jennifer Briggs* Barbara Angell /*cr* Bernard McKenna, Richard Laing / *pr* Humphrey Barclay /*dr* Bryan Izzard /*wr* Bernard McKenna, Richard Laing /*LWT* (UK) /13 x 30m col.

Torchy

Children's. ITV 1960

The be-stringed adventures of 'the Battery Boy', sent by rocket to Topsy Turvy Land, a fantasy world inhabited by such discarded toys as Pop-Pom the poodle, Squish the Space Boy and Sparky the baby dragon. On his periodic returns to Earth, Torchy found himself in the company of rude girl Bossy Boots.

Created by Roberta Leigh and directed by Gerry Anderson (the duo having already made ➢*Twizzle*), with puppetry by Christine Glanville.

CAST (voices) Olwyn Griffiths, Kenneth Connor, Jill Raymond, Patricia Somerset /*cr* Roberta Leigh /*pr* Gerry Anderson, Arthur Provis /*dr* Gerry Anderson, Vivian Milroy /*wr* Roberta Leigh /*mus* Roberta Leigh / *AP Films: Associated-Rediffusion* (UK) /26 x 15m bw.

To the Manor Born

Comedy. BBC1 1979–81

Popular sitcom (it topped the ratings for three consecutive seasons) built around the British comedic perennial: class. Penelope Keith starred as snobbish Audrey fforbes-Hamilton whose widowed penury obliged her to sell her 400 year old country pile, Grantleigh Manor in Cricket St. Thomas, to *nouveau riche* grocer, Richard DeVere (Peter Bowles). Moving into the gatehouse, she then endured a love–hate relationship with the gaffing DeVere until love triumphed and she moved back into Grantleigh as Mrs DV. Throughout, Audrey's friend Marjory was an absolute brick. Originally intended for radio, the series finally aired on its intended medium in 1997, with Keith Barron as DeVere.

CAST *Audrey fforbes-Hamilton* Penelope Keith *Richard DeVere* Peter Bowles *Mrs Polouvicka (DeVere's mother)* Daphne Heard *Marjory Frobisher* Angela Thorne *Brabinger (the butler)* John Rudling /*cr* Peter Spence /*pr* Gareth Gwenlan /*wr* Peter Spence, Christopher Bond /*mus* Ronnie Hazlehurst /*BBC TV* (UK) /21 x 30m col.

A Touch of Frost

Crime. ITV 1992–

David Jason overcame the accumulated type-casting of comic roles to play – with success – the part of downbeat DI Jack Frost in YTV's adaptations of R.D. Wingfield's stories. Set in fictional Denton, the cases of the bacon sandwich-loving irascible 'tec enjoyed calibre writers (Malcolm Bradbury penned the first sheaf) and a strong supporting cast, but it was Jason – in a virtual masterclass of acting, drawing out every nuance of character of a plausibly real copper – that drew 16 million-plus viewers to the 'on' button on Sunday evenings.

CAST *DI Jack Frost* David Jason *Supt Mullett* Bruce Alexander *DS Toolan* John Lyons *DS Barnard* Matt Bardock *DC Ernie Trigg* Arthur White *DCI Peters* Nigel Harrison /*exec pr* David Reynolds, Richard Bates, Philip Burley /*pr* inc Martyn Auty /*dr* inc David Reynolds, Paul Seed, Graham Theakston, Sandy Johnson /*wr* inc Malcolm Bradbury, Michael Russell, Sian Orrells /*YTV* (UK) /20 x 120m col.

Tour of Duty

Drama. ITV 1989

Not quite the ➢*Combat* of the Vietnam War, but close. A gruellingly realistic drama about life in an infantry outfit ('Bravo Company') in Nam in 1967, which caught its tragedy, its terror and the pure, distilled adrenalin of battle. The theme music was the Rolling Stones' 'Paint it Black'. Terence Knox took the lead role as avuncular Sergeant Zeke Anderson, whose duties consisted of protecting his charges from their own self-destructiveness and the idiocy of their superiors, as well as from the 'gooks' themselves.

CAST *Sgt Zeke Anderson* Terence Knox *Lt Myron Goldman* Stephen Caffrey *Pte 'Doc' Randy Matsuda* Steve Akahoshi *Cpl Danny Percell* Tony Becker *Pte Alberto Ruiz* Ramon Franco *Pte Scott Baker* Eric Bruskotter *Pte Marvin Johnson* Stan Foster *Pfc Thomas 'Pop' Scarlet* Lee Majors /*pr* Zev Braun, Bill Norton /*dr* inc Bill Duke, Aaron Lipstadt, Charles Correll, Steve Dubin, James L. Conway, Ed Scherin /*Zev Braun Productions* (USA) /32 x 60m col /US tx CBS 1987–90.

The Tracey Ullman Show

Comedy. BBC2 1988

Originally a chorus dancer for Les Dawson (a job from which she was sacked after forgetting to attire herself in underwear one performance), Tracey Ullman first came to notice in ➢*Three of a Kind*. Stints on *A Kick Up the Eighties* and ➢*Girls on Top* followed, before she headed to Hollywood and her own sketch/playlet series, *The Tracey Ullman Show* (created by James L. Brooks). Much taken by Ullman's talent for characterization (e.g. yuppie Sara Downey, Tina the postal worker, anthropologist Ceci Beckwith) and mimicry, the Americans awarded a 1990 Emmy, although when the series was sold to the UK the material seemed weak, and Ullman and supporting cast (including Julie Kavner and Dan Castellaneta) underused.

Not the least important aspect of the series was that it aired between the playlets short animations about a dysfunctional yellow family that became ➢*The Simpsons*; Ullman later tried to sue for a share of the *Simpsons* gross profits, but to no avail.

CAST Tracey Ullman, Julie Kavner, Dan Castellaneta, Joe Malone, Sam McMurray, Anna Levine /*cr* James L. Brooks /*exec pr* James L. Brooks, Heide Perlman, Ken Estin, Jerry Belson, Sam Simon /*Twentieth-Century Fox TV: Gracies Films* (USA) /52 x 30m col /US tx Fox 1987–90.

Traffik

Drama. C4 1989

Award-winning drama (BAFTAs and an International Emmy) about the international opium trade. It traced a triangle of menace between the poppy fields of Pakistan, importation into Germany, and the anti-drug efforts of a politician in Britain. Intensely told, atmosphere-drenched.

CAST *Jack Lithgow* Bill Patterson *Caroline Lithgow* Julia Ormond *Fazal* Jamal Shah *Helen* Lindsey Duncan /*pr* Brian Eastman /*dr* Alistair Reid /*wr* Simon Moore /*Picture Partnership* (UK) /1 x 120m, 5 x 60m col.

Trainer

Drama. BBC1 1991–2

Dreary drama about an up and coming horse-racing trainer, Mike Hardy of Arkenfield Stables, seeking to succeed in the Sport of Kings. Poorly cast (David McCallum as gambler John Grey and Mark Greenstreet as the lead were both eminently resistible). It failed to include enough of the 'shagging-in-the-shires' factor that made Jilly Copper's equine serial ➢*Riders* so compulsive. The theme song was performed by Cliff Richard.

CAST *Mike Hardy* Mark Greenstreet *John Grey* David McCallum *Rachel Ware* Susannah York *James Brant* Nigel Davenport *Joe Hogan* Des McAleer *Alex Farrell* Claire Oberman / *cr* Gerald Glaister / *pr* Gerald Glaister / *mus* Mike Reid (theme), Cliff Richard (theme vocal) / *BBC TV* (UK) /20 x 50m col.

Treasure Hunt

Light Entertainment. ITV 1982–9

Exhausting game show in which two studio-bound contestants shouted instructions to a heliborne 'runner' out in the countryside, in the hope that discovered – and correctly answered – cryptic clues would lead them to £1,000. Accompanying Anneka Rice, the runner, was a fast-footed camera team, who mostly lingered the lens on Rice's posterior. When Rice (aka Annie Rice) moved on to the charity-benefitting *Challenge Anneka*, her place was taken by former tennis player Annabel Croft (also *Interceptor*). Throughout, ex-newscaster Kenneth Kendall maintained gravitas and studio order.

CAST (presenters) Anneka Rice, Annabel Croft, Kenneth Kendall, Wincey Willis / *cr* Ann Meo / *pr* Malcolm Heyworth, Peter Holmans, Angela Breheny / *dr* Chris Gage, Mike Hand Bowman / *Chatsworth TV* (UK) /88 x 45m col.

Triangle

Melodrama. BBC1 1981–3

The definitively awful soap opera, so bad that it was mesmeric. The geometric shape of the title was the route taken (exotic Felixstowe to Gothenburg to Rotterdam) by a ferry boat. Episodes pursued the business and sexual affairs of the crew as they sailed the North Sea. (Lead actress Kate O'Mara's purpose as show totty was made bare in the opening episode, in which she appeared semi-naked.) At the time the series was hailed as a breakthrough in drama production, because new lightweight cameras allowed all filming to be done on location on the ferry *Tor Scandinavia*. Unfortunately, the production crew (headed by Bill Sellars, ➢*The Brothers*) overlooked the small fact that the North Sea is amongst the roughest in the world; as a result, the actors constantly had the green pallor of sea sickness, while the light balance inside the cabins was so uneven that the porthole curtains had to be kept permanently closed. The result was gloomy claustrophobia, and the series sank out of the schedules at the end of the third season.

Kate O'Mara as Katherine Laker in the ferry-boat soap *Triangle*. Arguably the definitively awful melodrama, the show sunk after two seasons.

CAST *Katherine Laker* Kate O'Mara *John Anderson* Michael Craig *Matt Taylor* Larry Lamb *Wally James* Nigel Stock *Charles Woodhouse* Paul Jericho *David West* George Baker *Sarah Hallam* Penelope Horner / *cr* Bill Sellars / *pr* Bill Sellars / *dr* inc Marc Miller, Terence Dudley / *wr* inc Luanshya Greer, Ben Steed, David Hopkins / *mus* Johnny Pearson / *BBC TV* (UK) / 79 x 25m col.

The Tripods

Sci-fi. BBC1 1982–5

Kid-vid sci-fi adventure. Adapted by Alick Rowe from John Christopher's novels, it featured two teenage cousins, Will and Henry Parker, who joined the struggle to free 2029 Earth from the rule of bug-eyed monsters from Trion (mode of transport: giant laser-firing Tripods). Poor ratings and reviews caused the £1 million show to be ignominiously cancelled in mid-run. Unfortunate, since a handful of duff season-one scripts aside, it was commendable stuff, with above-average acting and sfx.

CAST *Will Parker* John Shackley *Henry Parker* Jim Baker *Beanpole (Jean Paul)* Ceri Seel *Fritz* Robin Hayter *Master 468* John Woodvine /*cr* John Christopher /*pr* Richard Bates /*dr* Graham Theakston, Christopher Barry, Bob Blagden /*wr* Alick Rowe, Christopher Penfold /*mus* Ken Freeman /*sfx* Robin Lobb, Steven Drewett, Kevin Molly, Steve Bowman, Simon Taylor, Michael Kelt /*BBC TV* (UK) /22 x 30m col.

The Troubleshooters

Drama. BBC1 1965–72

Began as *Mogul*, a studio-bound soap about the oil industry set in the boardroom of the Mogul International company but, as attention shifted to the glamorous fixers in the fields, changed its spots to *The Troubleshooters*. In this drama–adventure format, with strong use of exotic location filming, it sent principal troubleshooters Thornton (Australian actor Ray Barrett) and Stewart (Robert Hardy) on an almost consistently exciting around-the-world cycle of fires on rigs, oil rushes, geopolitical turmoil and industry intrigue. Those sitting in the director's chair included tyro Ridley Scott.

CAST *Brian Stead* Geoffrey Keen *Willy Izzard* Philip Latham *Peter Thornton* Ray Barrett *Alec Stewart* Robert Hardy /*cr* John Elliott /*pr* Peter Graham Scott, Anthony Read /*dr* inc Terence Dudley, Moira Armstrong, Viktor Ritelis, Alan Gibson, Ridley Scott / *wr* inc John Elliott, James Mitchell, Roy Clarke, Ian Kennedy Martin /*BBC TV* (UK) /136 x 50m bw:col.

Trumpton

Children's. BBC1 1967

'This is the clock, the Trumpton clock, telling the time, never too quickly, never too slowly...'

These words, which stuck in the memory of every 60s child, introduced each episode of Gordon Murray's puppet sequel to ➢*Camberwick Green.* Set in Trumpton, the county capital of Trumptonshire, it principally told of moustachioed Captain Flack and his intrepid firemen – 'Hugh, Pugh, Barney McGrew, Cuthbert, Dibble and Grubb' – and their latest minor emergency (cat rescuing being a favourite). Other characters included the verbose Miss Lovelace and the Town Clerk, Mr Troop. Although, to the accompaniment of tiny tears, *Trumpton* ended after 13 episodes, the greater drama of Trumptonshire continued in ➢*Chigley.*

CAST (narrator) Brian Cant /*cr* Gordon Murray / *wr* Gordon Murray, Alison Prince /*BBC TV* (UK) / 13 x 15m col.

Tutti Frutti

Drama. BBC1 1987

Not to be confused with the German game show of the same name in which buxom models shed an item of clothing for every point won. John Byrne's *Tutti Frutti* was the tale of ageing Scottish rockers, The Majestics, whose lead singer, Big Jazza McGlone (Robbie Coltrane), was killed in a car crash, to be replaced by his lookalike brother Danny (Coltrane) on the band's eventful silver jubilee tour. Scripts and performances sparkled, and it established Coltrane and co-star Emma Thompson, previously comic acts, as serious thespian players. (Thompson appeared, to acclaim, in ➢*Fortunes of War* later the same year.) Byrne followed up with ➢*Your Cheatin' Heart.*

CAST *Big Jazza McGlone/Danny McGlone* Robbie Coltrane *Suzi Kettles* Emma Thompson *Eddie Clockerty* Richard Wilson *Vincent Driver* Maurice Roeves *Bomba MacAteer* Stuart McGugan *Fud O'Donnell* Jake Darcy *Dennis Sproul* Ron Donachie /*cr* John Byrne /*pr* Andy Park /*dr* Tony Smith /*wr* John Byrne /*mus* Zoot Money /*BBC TV* (UK) /6 x 60m col.

The Twilight Zone

Sci-fi. ITV 1963

'There is a fifth dimension beyond those known to man. It is a dimension vast as space and timeless as infinity... This is the dimension of imagination. It is an area we call... The Twilight Zone.'

Cult fantasy anthology, created by Purple Heart-winning paratrooper Rod Serling, who remained the main creative mover and shaker through the show's run, writing the majority of the stories. His somewhat whimsical style, however, was complemented by the darker work of Charles Beaumont and the structured, suspenseful pieces of Richard Matheson (most famous as the writer of *Duel*). Perennial themes were time slips,

The classic fantasy anthology *The Twilight Zone* was created by Rod Serling, a butcher's son from New York. Serling also narrated and wrote over half the 156 episodes.

Faustian pacts, dopplegangers and machines with wills of their own. Don Siegel, Ida Lupino and Richard Donner led the director's list, while those appearing in front of the *TZ* camera included Robert Redford, Burt Reynolds, Dennis Hopper, William Shatner and Leonard Nimoy. In 1983 *The Twilight Zone – The Movie* saw old *TZ* scripts re-worked and re-shot by Steven Spielberg, Joe Dante, John Landis and George Miller (whose version of Matheson's *Nightmare at 20,000 Feet* was by far the best of the new offerings). Two years later, a new *TZ* series began on TV. While, generally, it lacked the allegorical nature of the original, together with its cohesive identity, it provided reasonable entertainment.

CAST (narrator) Rod Serling /*cr* Rod Serling /*exec pr* Rod Serling /*pr* Buck Houghton, Herbert Hirschman, William Froug, Bert Granet /*dr* inc Robert Stevens, John Brahm, Douglas Heyes, Lamont Johnson, Richard L. Bare, Jacques Tourneur, Richard Donner, Don Siegel, Ida Lupino /*wr* inc Rod Serling, Charles Beaumont, Richard Matheson, Earl Hamner Jr, Ray Bradbury /*mus* Bernard Herrmann, Marius Constant, Jerry Goldsmith /*Cayuga Prod* (USA) /138 x 30m, 18 x 60m bw.

Twin Peaks

Crime. BBC2 1990–1

An eerie and bizarre murder mystery set in the verdant American Pacific Northwest, which became an obsession in America and Britain in 1990. The mastermind behind the project was avant-garde film-maker David '*Blue Velvet*' Lynch, the show continuing his fascination with the dark life behind the white picket fences of smalltown Ameria.

The TV series, co-developed with ➢*Hill Street Blues* stalwart Mark Frost and set in the lumber town of the title, hinged around the question: 'Who killed Laura Palmer?', Laura being a beautiful high-school student. The main investigator was an obsessive FBI agent, Dale Cooper, prone to ecstasy when drinking coffee and eating cherry pie and whose detecting methods included Tibetan myticism, dreams and ESP. (It was an open secret that Cooper was a Lynch self-portrait.) Gradually, Cooper's search for the murderer revealed that Palmer was not the innocent she seemed, and that Twin Peaks was a mired pool of drugs, adultery, avarice, pornography and satanism (some of these evils were explored through sub-plots) beneath its postcard image. The finger of suspicion pointed at most of the inhabitants before it was revealed that the culprit was Palmer's own father, possessed by the demonic 'Killer Bob'.

There was an almost surreal, dream-like mood to the show, especially in the segments helmed by Lynch, enhanced by the famously weird minor characters and touches: the Log Lady, who lovingly ported a piece of lumber with her wherever she went; Cooper's delivery of his own narrative into a micro-recorder for unseen secretary Diane; and the fish in the percolator at the Diner. Cooper's one-liners, 'This is where pies go when they die' and 'Damn fine coffee – and hot' (actually a steal from Deputy Chester in ➢*Gunsmoke*), became virtual mantras amongst TV watchers.

The large cast featured two of Lynch's stock movie actors, Kyle MacLachlan and Jack Nance (*Eraserhead*); Lynch himself appeared occasionally as FBI Chief Cole. The series also introduced a gallery of new faces, including Sherilynn Fenn (who later starred in Jennifer Lynch's *Boxing Helena*). David Duchovny, later of ➢*The X-Files*, played a transvestite FBI agent.

Although ratings dipped dramatically towards the end of the opening season (largely because of lightweight, directionless scripts), the show staggered through to its conclusion, even spinning off a movie, *Fire Walk With Me*, in 1992. It left a heavy imprint on such subsequent off-beat TV shows as ➢*Northern Exposure* and ➢*Eerie Indiana.*

CAST *Agent Dale Cooper* Kyle MacLachlan *Sheriff Harry S. Truman* Michael Ontkean *Leland Palmer* Ray Wise *Audrey Horne* Sherilynn Fenn *James Hurley* James Marshall *Jocelyn 'Josie' Packard* Joan Chen *Laura Palmer/Madelaine Ferguson* Sheryl Lee *Donna Hayward* Lara Flynn Boyle *Catherine Martell* Piper Laurie *Peter Martell* Jack Nance *Benjamin Horne* Richard Beymer *Shelly Johnson* Mädchen Amick *Leo Johnson* Eric Da Re /*cr* David Lynch, Mark Frost /*exec pr* David Lynch, Mark Frost /*pr* Hayley Payton /*dr* David Lynch, Duwayne Dunhamn, Diane Keaton, Tina Rathbone /*wr* inc David Lynch, Mark Frost /*mus* Angelo Badalamenti /*Lynch-Frost Prod: Spelling Entertainment* (USA) /2 x 120m, 28 x 60m col /US tx ABC 1990–1.

2 Point 4 Children

Comedy. BBC1 1991–8

Popular sitcom about a cash-short working family, the Porters of East Chiswick, headed by caterer mum Bill, and heating engineer dad Ben. The kids were brats. Dubbed originally the 'British ➢*Roseanne*', it increasingly erred towards fantasy, though never to a degree likely to stimulate the audience. On the contrary, the show's strength was its utter, comfortable tepidness, with every joke telegraphed ten minutes ahead. A further boon was that most of the gags were familiar from other shows: viz the lottery ticket left in the jeans which go in to the washing machine; the meeting of two grandmas, one of whom is German – don't mention the War, Basil!…

CAST *Bill Porter* Belinda Lang *Ben Porter* Gary Olsen *Jenny Porter* Clare Woodgate/Clare Buckfield *David Porter* John Pickard *Rona* Julia Hills *Bette* Liz Smith /*cr* Andrew Marshall /*pr* Richard Boden /*dr* inc Richard Boden, Nick Wood /*wr* Andrew Marshall, Paul Alexander, Paul Smith /*BBC TV* (UK) /49 x 30m, 1 x 50m col.

The Two Ronnies

Comedy. BBC1/2 1971–86

Ronnie Barker and Ronnie Corbett (who had first worked together on ➢*The Frost Report*), together in a sketch and gag show of unchanging format: mock news items, some skits, a transvestite musical number, song from a MOR chanteuse, Corbett in a sit-down monologue, and the tag-out line, 'It's goodnight from me, and it's goodnight from him.'

Some fun on the comic postcard level, mostly from the Barker routines where he masticated the English-language into glorious innuendoes and malapropisms whilst retaining the straight-faced persona of a bank manager or some sort of suit. The spoof serials – Spike Milligan's *The Phantom Raspberry Blower of Old London Town*, and the Charley Farley and Piggy Malone PI investigations – also scored.

CAST Ronnie Barker, Ronnie Corbett /*exec pr* James Gilbert, Michael Hurll /*pr* inc Peter Whitmore, Paul Jackson, Marcus Plantin /*dr* inc Marcus Mortimer /*wr* inc Gerald Wiley (aka Barker), John Cleese, Spike Milligan, Graham Chapman, David Nobbs, Michael Palin, Terry Jones, John Sullivan /*BBC TV* (UK) / 68 x 30m, 4 x 60m col.

UFO

Sci-fi. ITV 1970–1

1980. Aliens in spinning UFOs raid Earth to secure body parts to maintain their sterile race. Against them is pitched secret outfit SHADO (Supreme Headquarters Alien Defence Organization) led by Ed Straker from a base under London's Harlington-Straker Film Studios.

Pretty damn good Anderson live-action show (their first) for adults, edge-of-the-seat-exciting and with an impressive array of hardware (tank-like SHADOmobiles, a submarine/aircraft called *Skydiver* and the Space Intruder Detector early-warning system). Only the acting and costumes (70s glam-rock stuff, most memorably bedecking the purple-wigged babes who staffed Moonbase) flunked. ITV stations, with the Andersons pigeon holed as kiddie entertainers, were uncertain how to promote it, eventually consigning *UFO* to graveyard slots; one episode 'The Long Sleep', was held back because of an LSD sequence. Season two, ironically, was cancelled to produce the markedly inferior ➢*Space 1999.*

And wasn't that...? *Avant garde* actor and writer Steven Berkoff played a SHADO astronaut, Shane Rimmer (the man behind the voice of ➢*Thunderbirds* Scott Tracy) guested in 'Identified', Gabrielle Drake (➢*The Brothers*, ➢*Crossroads*) took the role of a Moonbase operative, as did Ayshea Brough (➢*Lift Off*) and Anouska Hempel, whose later work included a whip-wielding plantation mistress in the Russ Meyer exploitation flic, *Slaves* (1973).

CAST *Cmdr Ed Straker* Ed Bishop *Col. Alec Freeman* George Sewell *Col. Paul Foster* Michael Billington *Capt. Peter Karlin* Peter Gordeno *Joan Harrington* Antonia Ellis *Col. Virginia Lake* Wanda Ventham *General Henderson* Grant Taylor /*cr* Gerry & Sylvia Anderson, Reg Hill /*exec pr* Gerry Anderson /*pr* Reg Hill /*dr* inc Gerry Anderson, David Lane, Alan Perry, David Tomblin, Cyril Frankel /*wr* inc Gerry & Sylvia Anderson, David Tomblin, Tony Barwick, Alan Pattillo, Terence Feely /*mus* Barry Gray /*sfx* Derek Meddings /*Century 21 Pictures Ltd* (UK) /26 x 60m col /US tx Syndicated 1972.

Undermind

Sci-fi. ITV 1965

ETs brainwash ordinary human types (through use of high-pitched radio signals) into performing subversive acts against society.

Alien-invasion thriller of obvious influences, but pleasantly understated execution. The dreamer-upper was Robert Banks Stewart, later the deviser of ➢*Shoestring* and ➢*Bergerac.*

CAST *Drew Heriot* Jeremy Wilkin *Anne Heriot* Rosemary Nicols *Prof. Val Randolph* Denis Quilley / *cr* Robert Banks Stewart /*pr* Michael Chapman /*dr* inc Bill Bain, Peter Potter, Laurence Bourne, Patrick Dromgoole, Raymond Menmuir /*wr* inc Robert Banks Stewart, John Kruse, Robert Holmes /*ABC* (UK) / 11 x 60m bw.

United!

Melodrama. BBC1 1965–7

Unlikely BBC soap – one of its periodic attempts to tackle the dominance of ITV's ➢*Coronation Street* – following the boardroom and on-field trials of struggling fictional second division soccer club, Brentwich United. Crushingly dull and near-guaranteed to alienate the main viewer-base of soaps (women), the serial itself was relegated after two seasons, despite the employment of Jimmy Hill as 'technical adviser' and cameo performer. Ronald Allen (➢*Compact*, ➢*Crossroads*) played the club's second manager, Mark Wilson.

CAST *Gerry Barford (manager)* David Lodge *Jimmy Stokes* George Layton *Jack Birkett* Bryan Marshall *Kenny Craig* Stephen Yardley *Horace Martin* Harold Goodwin *Mark Wilson (manager)* Ronald Allen /*cr* Brian Hayles /*pr* Bernard Hepton, David Conroy, John

McRae, Anthony Cornish /*BBC TV* (UK) /147 x 30m bw.

University Challenge

Light Entertainment. ITV 1962–87 /BBC2 1994

'Your starter for ten...'

Student challenge quiz with eggheady questions, based on US show *College Bowl.* The original question-master was the energetic Bamber Gascoigne, replaced by Jeremy Paxman for the BBC2 knock-out-style revival. Most other elements remained constant throughout the years however – the contestants 'read' their subjects, the team mascots were embarrassingly uncool rip-offs of Sebastian's teddy in ➢*Brideshead Revisited* or a natural scientist's idea of a jape, and the nerd who never answered correctly sat on the end.

CAST (presenters) Bamber Gascoigne, Jeremy Paxman / *cr* Don Reid /*pr* Barrie Heads, Patricia Owtram, Douglas Terry, Peter Mullings, Kieran Roberts (BBC) / *dr* inc Peter Mullings /*Granada: BBC TV* (UK) / 560 x 30m bw:col.

The Untouchables

Crime. ITV 1966–9

A band of incorruptible Chicago G-Men, led by Eliot Ness, hunt down gangsters during Prohibition.

Classic Quinn Martin action-drama, piloted as a *Desilu Playhouse* two-parter, 'The Scarface Mob', brilliantly made, with a deserved reputation as 'the weekly bloodbath', and reeking of period 20s/30s authenticity. Columnist Walter Winchell provided the staccato voice-over commentary.

CAST *Narrator* Walter Winchell *Eliot Ness* Robert Stack *Agent Martin Flaherty* Jerry Paris *Agent William Longfellow* Abel Fernandez *Agent Enrico Rossi* Nick Georgiade *Agent Cam Allison* Anthony George *Agent Lee Hobson* Paul Picerni *Agent Rossmann* Steve London *Frank Nitti* Bruce Gordon /*exec pr* Quinn Martin, Jerry Thorpe, Leonard Freeman /*pr* Howard Hoffman, Alan A. Armer, Alvin Cooperman, Lloyd Richards, Fred Freiberger, Charles Russell /*dr* inc Walter Grauman, Howard Koch, Tay Garnett, Stuart Rosenberg /*mus* Wilbur Hatch, Nelson Riddle /*Desilu: Langford* (USA) /117 x 60m bw /US tx ABC 1959–63.

Robert Stack (sitting right) as G-man Eliot Ness in crimebuster classic *The Untouchables*, one of the most violent shows ever made. Critics dubbed it 'the weekly bloodbath.'

The Upper Hand

Comedy. ITV 1990–6

Terminally cosy role-reversal sitcom, a British version of America's *Who's the Boss?*

On suffering injury as a professional soccer player, Charlie Burrows takes up a position as resident housekeeper to ambitious ad executive (with the firm of Blake and Hunter), Caroline Wheatley. An on-off love affair follows for six long seasons, before the toothsome twosome marry. No visible humour beyond the concept of a male home-help and a sex-crazed OAP (the character Laura West, mother of Wheatley) played by Honor Blackman of ➢*The Avengers* fame.

CAST *Caroline Wheatley* Diana Weston *Charlie Burrows* Joe McGann *Laura West* Honor Blackman *Joanna Burrows* Kellie Bright *Tom Wheatley* William Puttock *Michael Wheatley* Nicky Henson /*exec pr* Paul Spencer /*pr* Christopher Walker /*dr* inc Martin Dennis, Martin Shardlow, Michael Owen Morris /

The servants are revolting. Dreamed up by resting actresses Jean Marsh (right) and Eileen Atkins, period soap *Upstairs, Downstairs* was one of the most successful shows of all time, viewed by over 300 million people in 50 countries.

wr inc Martin Cohan, Blake Hunter, Danny Kallis, Phil Doran /*Central TV: Carlton* (UK) /95 x 30m col.

Up Pompeii!

Comedy. BBC1/BBC2 1969–72.

Ancient-Roman costume romp, featuring Frankie Howerd as the irrepressible Lurcio, slave to the philandering senator Ludicrus Sextus. It exploded Vesuvius-like with bad taste, bawdy *double entendres* (which, legend has it, even caused Howerd to 'blink a bit') and daft characters (Senna the Soothsayer, Sextus' effete son, Nausius). Asides to camera enabled Howerd to re-use much of his wink-wink stand-up routines and drum into the memory the catchphrases 'titter ye not missus' and 'nay, nay, thrice nay'.

Crude. But brilliant. Derived loosely from the farce *A Funny Thing Happened on the Way to the Forum* (and beyond that from the plays of Plautus), *Up Pompeii!* was sequelized in 1973 as *Whoops Baghdad!*, with the action transferred to Persia and Howerd adopting the role of Ali Oopla. The jokes remained the same. There was also an *Up Pompeii!* film, a 1975 special and a 1991 TV one-off update, *Up Pompeii's Missus* (LWT), with Lurcio now a free man, the manager of Bacchus's Vino Bar.

CAST *Lurcio* Frankie Howerd *Senna* Jeanne Mockford *Plautus* Walter Horsburgh/William Rushton *Ammonia* Elizabeth Larner *Ludicrus* Max Adrian /Wallis Eaton *Ambrosia* Lynda Baron *Erotica* Georgina Moon *Nausius* Kerry Gardner *Flavia* Mollie Sugden *Odius* John Junkin /*cr* Talbot Rothwell /*pr* Michael Mills, David Croft, Sidney Lotterby /*wr* Talbot Rothwell & Sid Colin /*mus* Alan Braden /*BBC TV* (UK) /14 x 30m col.

Upstairs, Downstairs

Drama. ITV 1971–5

Soapy Edwardian period drama, tracing the fortunes of the aristo Bellamy family and, especially, those who served them 'below stairs' at 165 Eaton Place, London. Conceived by resting actresses Jean Marsh (who would play *UD*'s housemaid Rose) and Eileen Atkins, it became one of the most profitable and popular British series of all time, helped by faultless casting (especially Gordon Jackson as dour Scottish butler Hudson and Pauline Collins as pert maid Sarah) and handsome production. A huge success in American network PBS's 'Masterpiece Theatre' slot, it was bestowed with five Emmys; a Yankee imitation in the shape of CBS's *Beacon Hill* followed. Another copy was the spoofish ➢*You Rang, M'Lord?* – which, funnily enough, must have viewed much like Marsh and Atkins' (later, creators of ➢*The House of Eliott*) initial shaping of *UD*: a comedy called *Beyond the Green Baize Door*.

CAST *Hudson (butler)* Gordon Jackson *Mrs Bridges (cook)* Angela Baddeley *Edward* Christopher Beeny *Sarah* Pauline Collins *Rose* Jean Marsh *Lord Richard Bellamy* David Langton *Lady Marjorie Bellamy* Rachel Gurney *Hazel Bellamy* Meg Wynn Owen *Virginia Hamilton* Hannah Gordon *Capt. James Bellamy* Simon Williams *Georgina Worsley* Lesley-Anne Down *Elizabeth* Nicola Pagett /*cr* Jean Marsh, Eileen Atkins / *pr* John Hawkesworth /*dr* inc Bill Bain, Cyril Coke, Raymond Menmuir, James Ormerod /*wr* inc John Hawkesworth, Fay Weldon, Elizabeth Jane Howard, Charlotte Bingham, Rosemary Anne Sisson, Anthony Skene /*mus* Alexander Faris /*LWT* (UK) /68 x 50m col / US tx PBS 1974–7.

Up the Elephant and Round the Castle

Comedy. ITV 1983–5

Starred cheeky-cockney-chappie comedian Jim 'Nick! Nick!' Davidson (*Give Us a Break*) as cheeky-cockney-chappie Jim London, a first-time home-owner, on his inheritance from Aunt Mimi of 17 Railway Terrace, in London's Elephant and Castle manor. Nearly 15 million tuned in. A sequel, *Home James* (Thames 1987–90) followed London's career as chauffeur to the millionaire owner of an electronics factory (played by George Sewell from ➢*Special Branch*).

CAST *Jim London* Jim Davidson *Arnold* Christopher Ellison *Mum* Rosalind Knight *Dad* John Bardon *Councillor Arnold Moggs* Nicholas Day /*pr* Anthony Parker /*wr* Spike Mullins, Tony Hoare, Jim Eldridge, Colin Bostock-Smith /*Thames TV* (UK) /23 x 30m col.

Up the Workers

Comedy. ITV 1974–6

Not too-bad a version of the old TV chestnut of 'trouble up factory 'twixt workers and bosses'. Here, the setting was the Midland's company of Cocker's Components Ltd. Based on an idea by Lance Percival, who played the firm's luckless labour relations officer, Bernard Peck.

CAST *Dicky Bligh* Henry McGee *Sid Stubbins* Norman Bird *Bernard Peck* Lance Percival *Sir Henry Carmichael* Ivor Dean *Bert Hamflitt* Dudley Sutton *Sir Charles* Charles Lloyd Pack /*cr* Lance Percival /*pr* John Scholz-Conway, Alan Tarrant /*wr* Tom Brennand, Roy Bottomley /*ATV* (UK) /12 x 30m col.

V (the mini-series)

Sci-fi. ITV 1984

Blockbuster space-opera about an invasion of Earth by aliens (reptiles underneath their humanoid exterior) from planet Sirius. No sooner disembarked from their 31 five-mile wide spaceships, than the 'Visitors' launched a totalitarian state – and secretly began rounding up Earthlings to eat back home. At which, scientist Julie Parrish, mercenary Ham Tyler and alien fifth columnist Willie (Robert Englund from *Nightmare on Elm Street*) launched a Resistance movement in LA, taking the old 'V for Victory' sign of the WWII Allies as their symbol.

V was, of course, a thinly veiled parable about the rise of Nazism in the 30s. Taking no chances on the intelligence or culture of their viewers, however, the producers got a Jewish character to spell out the similarities between the invasion in *V* and the rise of Adolf Hitler. It might not have been sophisticated but it was fast-moving and resplendent with special effects and elaborate sets. Not to mention the novelty of left-wing prime-time heroes and some deliciously vile moments capped by the charismatic Visitor leader Diana 'eating' a live rat. Although the aliens were defeated in *V: The Final Battle,* they came back for another invasion – and thus a full series of 19 episodes. Here the Nazi parallel was dropped, and *V: The Series* was a routine actioner.

CAST *Diana* Jane Badler *Julie Parrish* Faye Grant *Mike Donovan* Marc Singer *Robert Maxwell* Michael Durrell *Robin Maxwell* Blair Tefkin *Willie* Robert Englund *Ham Tyler* Michael Ironside *Martin* Frank Ashmore /*cr* Kenneth Johnson /*exec pr* Kenneth Johnson /*pr* Chuck Bowman /*dr* Kenneth Johnson /*wr* Kenneth Johnson /*mus* Joe Harnell /*Kenneth Johnson: Warner Bros* (USA) /5 x 110m col /US tx NBC 1984.

Van Der Valk

Crime. ITV 1972–91

Languid cases of a moody blond Amsterdam CID detective, based on the cycle of novels begun by Nicholas Freeling in 1962. Eminently watchable, if only for the unusual setting. Jack Trombey's (aka Jan Stoeckhart) 'Eye Level' theme was a No. 1 UK hit in 1973. A 90s revival, in a 120m format, failed to take.

CAST *Piet Van Der Valk* Barry Foster *Arlette* Susan Travers/Joanna Dunham/Meg Davies *Samson* Nigel Stock/Ronald Hines *Wim* Richard Huw /*exec pr* Lloyd Shirley, George Taylor, Brian Walcroft /*pr* Michael Chapman, Robert Love, Geoffrey Gilbert, Chris Burt /*dr* inc Douglas Camfield, Mike Vardy, Anthony Simmons /*wr* inc Arden Winch, Philip Broadley /*Thames TV: Euston Films: Elmgate* (UK) /25 x 60m, 4 x 120m col.

Vegas

Crime. ITV 1978–81

PI show featuring Robert Urich (to don gumshoes again in ➢*Spenser: For Hire*) as Vegas-based 'tec Dan Tanna.

Lively hardboiler, with a sure-hit setting in the cashpots and fleshpots of the Arizonan capital. Creator Michael Mann continued his career in crime TV with ➢*Miami Vice* and ➢*Crime Story.*

CAST *Dan Tanna* Robert Urich *Beatrice Travis* Phyllis Davis *Angie Turner* Judy Landers *Bobby Borso ('Binzer')* Bart Braverman *Eli Two Leaf* Will Sampson *Lt David Nelson* Greg Morris *Philip Roth* Tony Curtis /*cr* Michael Mann /*exec pr* Aaron Spelling, Douglas S. Cramer /*pr* Alan Godfrey, E. Duke Vincent /*mus* Dominic Frontiere /*Spelling-Cramer* (USA) /1 x 74m, 67 x 60m col /US tx ABC 1978–81.

Vendetta

Crime. BBC1 1966–8

Underworld investigations of Mafia-hunter, Danny Scipio.

Contrived BBC effort at an international crimer, filmed on location in Malta (whatever the global setting) and not helped by the casting of accent-slipping Brit actors as Johnny foreigner. At least the Corporation's budget stretched to the hiring of a genuine Italian actor, Stelio Candelli, as Scipio.

CAST *Danny Scipio* Stelio Candelli *Angelo James* Neil McCallum *Mike Hammond* Kieron Moore /*cr* Brian Degas, Tudor Gates /*pr* Anthony Coburn, William Slater /*BBC TV* (UK) /35 x 50m bw.

A Very British Coup

Drama. C4 1988

Followed the destabilizing of an elected Left-wing British Government by shadowy forces from the Right. Alan Plater adapted it from the novel by Chris Mullin (a former *Tribune* editor), with Ray McAnally in BAFTA-winning form as working-class Labour PM, Harry Perkins.

CAST *Harry Perkins* Ray McAnally *Sir Percy Browne* Alan MacNaughton *Fison* Philip Madoc /*pr* Ann Skinner, Sally Hibbin /*dr* Mick Jackson /*wr* Alan Plater / *Skreba* (UK) /3 x 60m col.

A Very Peculiar Practice

Comedy. BBC1 1986–8

Andrew Davies' (*Marmalade Atkins*, TV adaptor *sans pareil*) series about a young GP, Stephen Daker, who joins the health clinic of the fictitious Lowlands University. As well as detailing the misadventures of Daker and his blackly funny colleagues – radical feminist Rose Marie, amoral Thatcherite Bob, alcoholic head of practice Jock – Andrew Davies' scripts took a savage satirical swipe at modern academia. By the second season, the University had been taken over by an American company interested only in asset-stripping and weapons-technology research. A 1992 one-off *Screen One* (BBC1 95m) followed Daker's sojourn in Poland following his marriage to Lowland's Polish art historian, Grete Grotowska.

CAST *Dr Stephen Daker* Peter Davison *Dr Bob Buzzard* David Troghton *Dr Jock McCannon* Graham Crowden *Dr Rose Marie* Barbara Flynn *Grete Grotowska* Joanna Kanska *Jack B. Daniels* Michael J. Shannon /*cr* Andrew Davies /*pr* Ken Riddington / *dr* David Tucker /*wr* Andrew Davies /*BBC TV* (UK) / 15 x 60m col.

The Vicar of Dibley

Comedy. BBC1 1994–

'You were expecting a bloke with a beard, a Bible and bad breath, you've got a babe with a bob cut and a magnificent bosom...'

Richard Curtis (*Four Weddings and a Funeral*, ➢*Blackadder*, ➢*Mr Bean*) sitcom casting the generously proportioned Dawn French in a crusade against sexism and snobbery in a village not quite ready for a distaff parson.

Topicality of the subject matter aside, a conventional, cosy British character comedy, redolent of ➢*Dad's Army*, and none the worse for it.

CAST *Geraldine 'Gerry' Granger* Dawn French *David Horton* Gary Waldhorn *Hugo Horton* James Fleet *Frank Pickle* John Bluthal *Owen Newitt* Roger Lloyd Pack *Jim Trott* Trevor Peacock *Letitia Cropley* Liz Smith *Alice Tinker* Emma Chambers /*cr* Richard Curtis / *pr* Jon Plowman, Sue Vertue /*dr* Dewi Humphreys, Gareth Carrivick, John Howard Davies /*wr* Richard Curtis, Paul Mayhew Archer, Kit Hesketh-Harvey / *BBC TV* (UK) /12 x 30m, 2 x 60m col.

Vic Reeves Big Night Out

Comedy. C4 1990–3

Almost undefinable – though 'a Northern Dadaist variety show' might get close – entertainment, featuring velvet-suited Vic Reeves (born Jim Moir) and ex-solicitor sidekick Bob Mortimer. Developed from a stage show, *Big Night*'s novel characters (Les, Wavy Davy, Graham Lister, the Slitherer – the latter Paul Whitehouse in his TV debut) and cultural parodying (Novelty Island, the Wheel of Justice) ensured cult status with *Viz*-readers home from the pub. If thoroughly pointless, it was also totally funny, if you were atuned or intoxicated enough; catchphrases 'What's on the end of the stick, Vic?' and 'You wouldn't let it lie!' became playground favourites. The nonsense continued in *The Smell of Reeves and Mortimer* and the more accesible gameshow ➢*Shooting Stars*.

CAST Vic Reeves, Bob Mortimer /*exec pr* Alan Marke, Robert Jones /*pr* Peter Orton /*dr* Peter Orton /*wr* Vic Reeves, Bob Mortimer /*Channel X* (UK) /28 x 30m col.

Victoria Wood – As Seen on TV

BBC2 1985–6

Monologue and sketch showcase for former ➢*New Faces* winner and *That's Life* topical songster, Victoria Wood. A formidable repertory cast – Julie Walters, Patricia Routledge, Maureen Lipman and Celia Imrie among them – helped wring the laughs, with weekly highlights being the shaky-set ➢*Crossroads*-spoof 'Acorn Antiques' and couch diva send-up, Margery and Joan. Wood's other TV offerings included a transfer to BBC1 with *Victoria Wood* (1989, 6 x 30m), a series of playlets – emphatically not sitcoms – on familiar domestic subjects (daytime TV, health farms), again with the aid of Walters and Imrie. A 1995 BBC1 show, *Victoria Wood – Live in Your Own Home*, reverted to the format of *As Seen*, though with a perceptible change of material to include politics. Yet most everything drama-based by Wood palled in comparison with those occasions when she gave *An Audience with Victoria Wood*, entertaining celebrities with only a piano and a stool to hand.

CAST Victoria Wood, Celia Imrie, Julie Walters, Patricia Routledge, Maureen Lipman, Duncan Preston, Susie Blake /*pr* Geoff Posner /*dr* Geoff Posner /*wr* Victoria Wood /*BBC TV* (UK) /12 x 30m col.

The Virginian

Western. BBC1 1965–72

TV sagebrush saga, the first at 90 minutes, based on Owen Wister's seminal 1902 novel of the same title. Although thrice filmed by Hollywood, including a 1929 attempt that kick-started the career of Gary Cooper, Charles Maquis Warren's version remains branded in the forefront of memory, thanks to James Drury's laconic performance as the eponymous mysterious foreman of Shiloh Ranch, Wyoming. Inspirational photography, a directors' list that included Sam Fuller, a fine support cast in Clu Gulager, Lee J. Cobb and Doug McClure, and calibre weekly guest cameos from the likes of George C. Scott and a rising Robert Redford all helped. A sequel, ➢*The Men From Shiloh*, upped the saddle-soap element (with the ranch hands forming a quasi-extended family) and brought forward the tamin'-of-the West narrative by a decade to the 1890s.

Home on the range – James Drury (centre) starred as the mysterious ranch foreman in *The Virginian*, the first 90-minute TV Western.

CAST *The Virginian* James Drury *Trampas* Doug McClure *Emmett Ryker* Clu Gulager *Judge Henry Garth* Lee J. Cobb *Steve* Gary Clarke *Belden* L.Q. Jones *John Grainger* Charles Bickford *Clay Grainger* John McIntire /*cr* Charles Maquis Warren /*exec pr* inc Charles Maquis Warren, Roy Huggins, Leslie Stevens /*pr* inc Howard Christie, Glen A. Larson /*dr* inc Sam Fuller, Ida Lupino, Andrew McLaglen, Burt Kennedy, Gene L. Coon, John Florea, William Witney, Jeannot Swarc /*wr* inc Glen A. Larson, Sam Fuller, Roland Kibbe, William R. Cox /*mus* Percy Faith (theme), David Shire, Bernard Herrmann /*Universal: Revue Productions* (USA) /208 x 90m col /US tx NBC 1962–70.

Virgin of the Secret Service

Spy. ITV 1968

Featured Captain Robert Virgin, dashing defender of 1907 Britain against her perditious enemies – chiefly, dastardly Hunnish spies, Karl von Brauner and Klaus Striebeck.

Cape-and-sabre show, with a giant measure of spoofery – both of the TV/cinema spy craze of the 60s, and the *Boy's Own* tales on which deviser Ted Willis (➢*Dixon of Dock Green*) was brought up.

CAST *Capt. Robert Virgin* Clinton Greyn *Mrs Virginia Cortez* Veronica Strong *Doublett (batman)* John Cater *Karl von Brauner* Alexander Dore *Klaus Striebeck* Peter Swannick *Col. Shaw-Camberley* Noel Coleman /*cr* Ted Willis /*pr* Josephine Douglas /*ATV* (UK) /13 x 60m col.

Vision On

Children's. BBC1 1964–76

'Unfortunately we can't return any paintings, but a prize is given for each one shown...'

Juvenile educational programme for deaf viewers – and those with hearing, if they cared for it – which succeeded the patronizing *For Deaf Children*. Hosted throughout by signing Pat Keysell, joined early on by artist Tony Hart and later by Sylvester ➢'*Doctor Who*' McCoy; regular items were the 'The Gallery' of viewers' art works and sketches, and the escapades of pipe-men Phil O'Pat and Pat O'Phil. With the end of *Vision On*, Hart moved on to the general kiddie art programmes *Take Hart*, which in 1977 introduced the world to animated plasticine creature Morph, and *Hartbeat*.

CAST (presenters) Pat Keysell, Tony Hart, Sylvester McCoy, Professor Wilf Lunn, Larry Parker, Ben Benison, David Cleveland /*pr* Ursula Eason, Leonard Chase, Patrick Dowling /*dr* inc Patrick Dowling / *BBC TV* (UK) /260 x 30m bw:col.

Voyage to the Bottom of the Sea

Sci-fi. ITV 1964–6

TV spin-off from Irwin Allen's 1961 blockbuster movie of the same title, following the undersea patrols of atomic sub *Seaview*. Ostensibly an instrument of the Nelson Institute of Marine Research, the *Seaview* was, naturally, a secret weapon dedicated to preserving the world from bad guys and bad aliens. After a quality start – due, in large part, to the re-use of the movie's expensive props – the show plummeted to the depths of trash; after season two's horror-show gimmicks and season three's weirdities ('The Plant Man'), season four was reduced to attacking the crew with toys bought from a kiddie shop. The crew's inability to remember that the villain *always* hid in the air-conditioning beggared belief. Allen continued his 60s TV endeavours with ➢*Lost in Space*, ➢*The Time Tunnel* and ➢*Land of the Giants*.

CAST *Admiral Harriman Nelson* Richard Basehart *Cmdr Lee Crane* David Hedison *Lt Cmdr Chip Morton* Robert Dowdell *CPO Curley Jones* Henry Kulky *Chief Sharkey* Terry Becker *Stu Riley* Allan Hunt *Kowalsky* Del Monroe *Patterson* Paul Trinka *Sparks* Arch Whiting /*cr* Irwin Allen /*exec pr* Irwin Allen /*dr* inc Irwin Allen, Sobey Martin, Gerald Oswald, Tom Gries, John Brahm, Alan Crosland, Harry Harris /*wr* inc Irwin Allen, Harlan Ellison, Richard Landau, Allan Balter, Shimon Wincelberg, Allan Caillou /*mus* Lionel Newman /*Irwin Allen: Twentieth Century-Fox TV* (USA) /110 x 50m bw:col /US tx ABC 1964–8.

VR5

Sci-fi. Sky1 1995

Short-run cyberpunk drama. Former ➢*Fame* actress Lori Singer starred as nerdy but beautiful hacker Sydney Bloom who accidentally discovered that she can enter people's minds through her telephone-linked Virtual Reality system – a talent quickly employed by shadowy government organization The Committee. Woven into the plot was the strange disappearance of Bloom's father (➢*The Man from UNCLE*'s David McCallum) and the comatose state of her mother (Oscar-winner Louise Fletcher).

CAST *Sydney Bloom* Lori Singer *Joseph Bloom* David McCallum *Nora Bloom* Louise Fletcher *Professor Morgan* Michael Easton *Oliver Sampson* Anthony Head /*cr* Thania St John, Michael Katleman, Geoffrey Hemwell, Jeannine Renshaw, Adam Cherry /*exec pr* John Sacret Young /*dr* inc D.J. Caruso, Rob Bowman, Steve Dubin, Michael Katleman, Deborah Reinisch /*wr* inc Thania St John, John Sacret Young /*mus* John C. Frizell /*Samoset Production: Rysher Entertainment* (UK) /12 x 60m col /US tx Fox TV 1994.

The Wacky Races
Children's. BBC1 1969–70

Eccentric race-car drivers and their equally weird vehicular contraptions enter cross-country competitions with the aim of winning the title 'The World's Wackiest Racer'. Their attempts to do so are threatened by the machinations of villainous Dick Dastardly – and sniggering canine sidekick, Muttley – in The Mean Machine.

Hanna–Barbera cartoon, loosely based on the Lemmon–Curtis feature *The Great Race*, which marked a new, more anarchic phase of the company's output, with less technically complex animation. Enjoyable for all that, and a big enough hit to carry two spin-offs on its back: ➢*The Perils of Penelope Pitstop* and ➢*Dastardly and Muttley in their Flying Machines.*

The Wacky Races contestants were, in addition to Dastardly and Muttley: The Slag Brothers in the Bouldermobile; The Gruesome Twosome in the Creepy Coupé; Professor Pat Pending in the Convert-A-Car; Red Max in the Crimson Haybailer; 'glamour girl' Penelope Pitstop in The Compact Pussycat; Sarge and Meekly in the Army Surplus Special; The Ant Hill Mob in the Roaring Plenty; Luke and Blubber in the Arkansas Chugga-Bug; Peter Perfect in the Varoom Roadster; and Rufus Ruffcut and Sawtooth in The Buzz Wagon.

CAST (voices) *Dick Dastardly* Paul Winchell *Muttley* Don Messick *Penelope Pitstop* Janet Waldo *Red Max /Rufus Ruffcut/Rock and Gravel/Peter Perfect/The Ant Hill Mob* Daws Butler *Luke and Blubber Bear/The General* John Stephenson *Narrator* Dave Wilcock /*cr* William Hanna, Joseph Barbera /*pr* William Hanna, Joseph Barbera /*dr* Iawo Takamoto /*Hanna-Barbara* (USA) /52 x 25m col /US tx CBS 1968–70.

Wagon Train
Western. ITV/BBC 1958–64

Sprawling oater epic, the story of pioneers trekking their way West in conestogas (covered wagons) in the 1860s. Initially, the wagon train was led by Ward Bond as Major Seth Adams, with Robert Horton as scout McCullough. After five seasons, however, Horton quit for the movies (only to return to TV horse-operas in ➢*A Man Called Shenandoah*) and was replaced by ➢*Laramie* star Robert Fuller as Cooper Smith. When Bond died of a heart attack on location in Texas on 5 November 1960, John McIntire (later ➢*The Virginian*) took over the reins as wagon master Chris Hale. The show had a distinctive episodic format (copied by ➢*Star Trek*, among others) whereby the wagon train picked up new recruits – all with a problem or tale in tow – or wandered into dramatic situations each week. For these, *Wagon Train* writers raided everything from stock Western clichés (warpathing Indians) to British literary classics – *Pride and Prejudice* appeared as 'The Steel Family Story'.

Production values were high, with the entire cast and crew occasionally moved out of the confines of the studio for such panoramic locations as Monument Valley. Another large chunk of budget went on the weekly guest stars: Barbara Stanwyck, Henry Fonda, Mickey Rooney, Ronald Reagan and Joseph Cotton were among those who appeared during *Wagon Train*'s nine-year saga. Dennis Hopper and Clint Eastwood earned early acting spurs on the show, while future blockbuster producer Aaron Spelling was a principal writer.

Based loosely on John Ford's 1950 film *Wagon Master* (in which the gruff Ward Bond had also appeared), the series was perhaps the closest TV has come to that director's democratic, poetic vision of the American West. Ford himself directed the *Wagon Train* episode 'The Colter Craven Story', in which his lead stock actor John Wayne appeared in an uncredited cameo as General Sherman – his only dramatic appearance in a TV show.

Among the most successful small-screen Westerns ever made, *Wagon Train* dominated the ratings on both sides of the Atlantic on its initial release. In 1962 series episodes were expanded to 75m and shot in colour. But *Wagon Train* was part of a black and white age, and the new-fangled colour simply didn't suit. Thankfully, classic Bond–Horton episodes are regularly repeated on networks everywhere, sometimes under the title *Major Adams* and *Major Adams, Trailmaster.*

'Wagon Train, Keep on rolling…'

CAST *Major Seth Adams* Ward Bond *Flint McCullough* Robert Horton *Chris Hale* John McIntire *Bill Hawks* Terry Wilson *Charlie Wooster* Frank McGrath *Duke Shannon* Scott Miller *Cooper Smith* Robert Fuller *Barnaby West* Michael Burns /*cr* Bert Glennon /*exec pr* Howard Christie /*pr* Richard Lewis, Richard Irving /*dr* Allen H. Miner, Virgil Vogel, John Ford, Tay Garnett, William Whitney, Jerry Hopper, Joseph Pevney, Herschel Daughtery, Earl Bellamy /*wr* inc Aaron Spelling, Gene L. Coon, Thomas Thompson, D.B. Newton /*mus* David Buttolph (theme) /*Universal: MCA: Revue* (USA) /252 x 52m bw, 32 x 90m col /US tx NBC 1957–65.

Waiting for God

Comedy. BBC1 1990–4

Retirement-home sitcom in which two geriatrics, former photo-journalist Diana Trent and eccentric accountant Tom Ballard, rebel against the lethargy of their fellow inmates and the dodgy schemes of the Bayview's manager, Harvey.

A splendid half-hour of tragi-comedy, at best, blackly reminiscent of Mike Leigh.

CAST *Diana* Stephanie Cole *Tom* Graham Crowden *Harvey Bains* Daniel Hill *Jane* Janine Duvitski *Marion* Sandra Payne *Geoffrey* Andrew Tourell /*cr* Michael Aitkens /*pr* Gareth Gwenlan /*dr* Gareth Gwenlan /*wr* Michael Aitkens /*BBC TV* (UK) /47 x 30m col.

Wait Till Your Father Gets Home

Children's. BBC1 1973

Animated sitcom featuring the generation-gap laughs of old-fashioned father, Harry Boyle (president of the Boyle Restaurant Supply Company), and his with-it 70s kids.

Wildly funny, clearly indebted to ➢*All in the Family*, and though broadcast in a children's slot almost certainly wasted on anyone below the age of puberty. Tom Bosley carried on playing the American suburban pop in ➢*Happy Days.*

CAST (voices) *Harry Boyle* Tom Bosley *Irma Boyle (wife)* Joan Gerber *Alice Boyle* Kristina Holland *Chet Boyle* David Hayward *Jamie Boyle* Jackie Hayler *Ralph* Jack Burns /*Hanna–Barbera* (USA) /48 x 30m col /US tx Syndicated 1972–4.

Walker, Texas Ranger

Crime. Sky1 1993–

Was Cordell Walker, a Vietnam vet turned lone modern-day Texas Ranger. Sprawling all-action series, a TV excuse to feature the hardcase talents of Hollywood veteran Chuck 'MIA' Norris.

CAST *Cordell Walker* Chuck Norris *C.D. Parker* Noble Willingham *Prosecutor Alex Cahill* Sheree J. Wilson *James 'Jimmy' Trivette* Clarence Gilyard /*exec pr* Rick Applebaum /*dr* inc Eric Norris, Joe Coppoletta, Tony Mordente /*CBS* (USA) /32+ x 60m col /US tx CBS 1993–.

The Waltons

Drama. BBC1 1974–81

Schmaltzy saga about a barefoot-but-happy hick family which operated a sawmill in the Blue Ridge Mountains of Virginia during the depressed 30s. The uplifting events were seen through the perpetually moist eyes of oldest son John Boy, who in the 1977 season achieved his American dream of becoming a writer and moving to New York. The rest of the clan back on Walton's Mountain, meanwhile, nearly drowned in weepiness: Grandma became ill, Grandpa died and Walton *mère*, Olivia, contracted TB (triple Emmy-winning actress Michael Learned wanted out of the series). At the series' end, by which time the Waltons had been through WWII, *père* John Walton sold the mill to son Ben and moved to Arizona to be with Olivia during her convalescence.

Based on the autobiographical novel by narrator Earl Hamner Jr, the wholesome, heart-winning series – an Outstanding Drama Emmy in 1973 – piloted as a TV movie, *The Homecoming.* (A rather more rugged cinema version of Hamner's tome, *Spencer's Mountain,* had been released in 1967, starring Henry Fonda.) Although *The Waltons* finished production in 1981, it spawned three made-for-TV movie sequels: *A Day For Thanks on Walton's Mountain,*

Mother's Day on Walton's Mountain, and *Wedding on Walton's Mountain.*

CAST *Narrator* Earl Hamner Jr *John Walton* Ralph Waite *Olivia Walton* Michael Learned *John Boy Walton* Richard Thomas/Robert Wightman *Mary Ellen Walton* Judy Norton-Taylor *James Robert 'Jim-Bob' Walton* David W. Harper *Elizabeth Walton* Kaimi Cotler *Jason Walton* Jon Walmsley *Erin Walton* Mary Elizabeth McDonough *Ben Walton* Eric Scott *Grandpa Zeb Walton* Will Geer *Grandma Esther Walton* Ellen Corby *Ike Godsey* Joe Conley *Corabeth Godsey* Ronnie Claire Edwards *Dr Curtis Willard* Tom Bowyer/Scott Hylands *Arlington Westcott 'Jonesy' Jones* Richard Gilliland / *cr* Earl Hamner Jr / *exec pr* Earl Hamner Jr, Lee Rich / *pr* Robert L. Jacks, Andy White / *dr* inc Fielder Cook, Harry Harris, Philip Leacock, Richard Benedict / *wr* inc Colly Cibber, Rod Peterson, Claire Whitaker, Earl Hamner Jr / *mus* Jerry Goldsmith / *Lorimar* (USA) / 220 x 50m col / US tx CBS 1972–81.

Wanted: Dead or Alive

Western. ITV 1985

The series which made Steve McQueen a star, and virtually set the mould for his loner screen image. He played Josh Randall, a bounty hunter in the 1870s West who pursued those with a price on their head armed with a 'Mare's Leg', a sawn-off carbine used like a pistol. Developed from a segment entitled 'Bounty' in the *Trackdown* series, *Wanted* was computer colourized in the 80s for US syndication.

CAST *Josh Randall* Steve McQueen *Jason Nichols* Wright King / *exec pr* John Robinson / *pr* Harry Harris, Ed Adamson, Vincent M. Fennelly / *dr* inc Thomas Carr, R.G. Springsteen, Richard Donner / *mus* Rudy Schrager (theme song) / *Four Star: Malcolm Enterprises* (USA) / 94 x 26m bw / US tx CBS 1958–61.

War of the Worlds

Sci-fi. ITV 1991–2

After their apparent defeat in the 1953 movie, the Martians revive and cunningly take over human bodies, all the better to achieve their aim of dominating Earth.

Moderately pleasing combination of ➢*Quatermass III* and ➢*The Invaders*, with at least one good idea: according to the episode 'Eye for an Eye', the infamous 1938 Orson Welles radio version of H.G. Wells' seminal story was a cover up for a real alien attack. Jared Martin from 70s show *The Fantastic Journey* played *Homo sapiens'* best hope, Dr Harrison Blackwood.

CAST *Dr Harrison Blackwood* Jared Martin *Norton Drake* Philip Akin *Suzanne McCullough* Lynda Mason Green *Lt Col. Paul Ironside* Richard Chaves *Maltzor* Denis Forest / *cr* Greg Strangis / *exec pr* Greg Strangis, Sam Strangis, Frank Mancuso Jr / *pr* Jonathan Hackett / *dr* inc George Bloomfield, Winrich Kolbe, William Fruet / *wr* inc Greg Strangis, Herb Wright, Tom Lazarus, D.C. Fontana / *mus* Billy Thorpe, Larry Brown / *Triumph Entertainment: Universal: Ten Four* (USA) / 1 x 120m, 42 x 60m col / US tx Syndicated 1988–90.

Washington: Behind Closed Doors

Drama. BBC1 1977–8

Thinly (very) veiled version of Watergate, sprawlingly adapted from John Erlichman's *The Company.*

CAST *President Richard Monkton* Jason Robards *Frank Flaherty* Robert Vaughan *Sally Whalen* Stephanie Powers *William Martin* Cliff Robertson *Linda Martin* Lois Nettleton *Esker Anderson* Andy Griffith / *cr* David W. Rintels / *exec pr* Stanley Kallis / *pr* Norman Powell / *dr* Gary Nelson / *wr* David W. Rintels, Eric Bercovici / *Paramount TV* (USA) / 6 x 120m col / US tx ABC 1977.

Watch with Mother

Children's. BBC/BBC1 1950–80

It succeeded *For the Children* as the BBC's pre-school series, though it was suffused with the same dreamy, laudable objective of bonding *mater* and offspring in the act of viewing, to usher in a Golden Age of Daytime Tiny TV. By the mid-50s the weekly line-up had become the classic: ➢*Picture Book* on Monday; ➢*Andy Pandy* on Tuesday; ➢*The Flowerpot Men* on Wednesday; ➢*Rag, Tag and Bobtail* (rural adventures of a hedgehog, a mouse and a rabbit, as narrated by Charles E. Stidwell) on Thursday; and ➢*The Woodentops* on Friday. These were made and repeated until the mid 60s. Subsequent occupants of the *WWM* 1.30 p.m. slot included the ➢*Camberwick Green* trilogy, ➢*Pogle's Wood, Mary, Mungo and Midge, Joe* (an animation about a boy whose father ran a café near a lorry park), *Bizzy Lizzy*, ➢*The Herbs, Fingerbobs, Barnaby, Mister Men*, ➢*Mr Benn*, and ➢*Bagpuss*. From

1980, with baby as likely to be watching TV with a childminder as with a parent, the programming slot was changed to the politically unproblematic *See-Saw*.

cr Fred Lingstrom / *BBC TV* (UK) /approx. 3000 x 15m bw:col.

Waterfront Beat
Crime. BBC1 1990–1

Police drama set in London's Inner City and Waterfront Division.

Created and written by Phil Redmond (➢*Grange Hill*, ➢*Brookside*), but too low-key to last. The use of real actors' names for characters (Don Henderson, Ronnie Barker) also smacked of an author being too clever for his, and the audience's, own good.

CAST *Det. Chief Supt Don Henderson* John Ashton *Supt Peter Fallows* Rupert Frazer *Det. Supt Frank Matthews* Geoffrey Leesley *PC Ronnie Barker* Brian McCardie *WDS Jackie Byrnes* Eve Bland *WDC Jane Long* Helena Little / *cr* Phil Redmond / *pr* Phil Redmond / *wr* Phil Redmond / *New Media Age* (UK) / 16 x 50m col.

The Water Margin
Adventure. BBC2 1976–8

Sword and magic version of the 13th-century Chinese epic by Shih Nai-an, relating the tale of 108 reborn knights who fight tyranny from their base in the marshlands of the Lian Shan Po. Lin Chung was their charismatic leader. David Weir adapted the Japanese scripts (English voices came from, among others, Bert Kwouk and Miriam Margoyles) with appropriate high theatricality, and followed up the samurai TV success with ➢*Monkey*.

CAST *Lin Chung* Atsuo Nakamura *Kao Chia* Kei Sato *Wu Sung* Hajine Hana *Hu San-niang* Sanae Tschida *Hsiao Lan* Yoshiyo Matuso (English voices: Michael McClain, Miriam Margoyles, Peter Marinker, Elizabeth Proud, Sean Lynch, Trevor Martin, Bert Kwouk) / *dr* Toshio Masuda, Michael Bakewell (English dubbing) / *wr* David Weir (English adaptation) / *mus* Masaru Sato / *NTV Toyko* (Jap) /30+ x 45m col.

Wayne's World
Comedy. BBC2 1992

The excellent! adventures of two Heavy Metal teens, smart-arse Wayne (British comedian Mike Myers) and gimpy Garth, as they present a cable programme from a mid-American basement, with guest star interviews, 'slut court', indulges in pubescent fantasy (like an in-bed with a fetishistically dressed Madonna – schwing!) and omnipresent air-guitar playing.

Mirth quotient? Maximum. For nerds. Originally screened as vignettes in the American *Saturday Night Live*, *Wayne's World* spun off a 1992 $100-million grossing movie (directed by Penelope Spheeris), while its idiosyncratic language briefly entered the Zeitgeist. Echoes of *WW* down the 90s were to be found in shows as diverse as ➢*Beavis and Butt-Head* and the British DIY TV series, *The Adam and Joe Show*, presented from a Brixton bedsit.

CAST *Wayne Campbell* Mike Myers *Garth Angar* Dana Carvey / *NBC Entertainment* (USA) /8 x 10m col / US tx NBC 1988–94.

Weavers Green
Melodrama. ITV 1966

Short-lived twice-weekly sudster based around a rural vet's practice. Shot on mobile VTR equipment, one of the first to be so.

CAST inc Maurice Kaufmann, Grant Taylor, Megs Jenkins, Eric Flynn, Susan Field / *cr* Peter Lambda / *pr* John Jacobs / *wr* Peter & Betty Lambda / *Anglia TV* (UK) /49 x 30m bw.

The Wednesday Play
Drama. BBC1 1964–70

The BBC's school for scandalously left-wing 60s TV drama, modelled after ATV's socio-realist anthology experiment ➢*Armchair Theatre*, which it quickly eclipsed. For whatever reasons – the generous use of filmstock, a fairly free editorial hand – *TWP* become the key means by which the Angry Young Men of British theatre reached a mass audience. And how enraged they were! Jim Allen contributed an excoriating piece on casual labour in the building trade, 'The Lump' (1965), while Nell Dunn's 'Up the Junction' (also 1965) became a cause célèbre for its scenes of backstreet abortion. The following year saw Jeremy Sandford's 1966 'Cathy Come Home', about a homeless London couple (played by Carol White and Ray Brooks, directed by Ken Loach in the documentary style he would patent), which has a claim to being the most influential piece of TV of the decade. Other writers attracted to the *TWP* opportunity were Dennis Potter – 'The Confidence Course', the cynical exploration of parliamentary politics that was 'Vote, Vote, Vote for Nigel Barton', and 'Stand Up, Nigel Barton' – along with David Mercer, James Hanley, Peter Nichols and Michael Frayn. So pervasive was the influence of this relatively small band of revolutionary political writers (and their behind-the-camera co-thinkers, like Tony Garnett and Waris Hussein) that the fact that *TWP* also staged European classics and domestic tragedies is all but forgotten. When the day of transmission was changed, *TWP* became ➢*Play for Today*, the same show of single plays in all but name.

pr inc Irene Shubik, James McTaggart, Peter Luke, Kenith Trodd, Tony Garnett /*dr* inc Tony Garnett, Kenneth Loach, Philip Saville, Jack Gold, Rudolph Cartier, Waris Hussein, Gil Calder, Ronald Eyre /*wr* inc Jim Allen, Jeremy Sandford, Nell Dunn, David Mercer, Dennis Potter, Nigel Kneale /*BBC TV* (UK) / 60 x 60m bw:col.

Welcome Back Kotter

Comedy. ITV 1981

A Jewish teacher, Gabe Kotter (played by co-creator Gabriel Kaplan), at Brooklyn's Buchanan High School has comic problems keeping his class misfits – known as 'The Sweat-hogs' – under control.

Americanized ➢*Please Sir!* Palatable enough. The part of star 'Sweat-hog', Vinnie Barabrino, sprang a certain John Travolta into the arms of fame.

CAST *Gabe Kotter* Gabriel Kaplan *Vinnie Barbarino* John Travolta *Mr Woodman* John Sylvester White *Julie Kotter* Marcia Strassman *Arnold Horshak* Ron Palillo *Freddie 'Boom Boom' Washington* Lawrence Milton-Jacobs /*cr* Gabe Kaplan, Peter Myserson /*pr* David Wolper, James Komack /*mus* John B. Sebastian / *The Komack Co: Wolper Productions* (USA) /95 x 30m / US tx ABC 1975–9.

Whack-O!

Comedy. BBC 1956–60/BBC1 1971–2

Popular 50s sitcom starring comedian Jimmy Edwards DFC as the crafty, cane-swishing headmaster of Chiselbury public school (motto: 'They Shall Not Pass'). A cinema version, entitled *Bottoms Up!*, appeared in 1960 (also written by Frank Muir and Denis Norden), followed by a radio adaptation in 1971 and a TV revival a decade later.

CAST *Prof. Jimmy Edwards* Jimmy Edwards *Mr Pettigrew* Arthur Howard /Julian Orchard *F.D. Price Whittaker* Kenneth Cope *R.P. Trench* Peter Glaze *S.A. Smallpiece* Norman Bird *Matron* Barbara Archer / Charlotte Mitchell *Mr Halliforth* Edwin Apps /Peter Greene (1971) /*cr* Denis Norden, Frank Muir /*pr* Douglas Moodie, Eric Fawcett, Douglas Argent (1971) / *wr* Denis Norden, Frank Muir /*BBC TV* (UK) / 53 x 30 bw:col.

What's My Line?

Light Entertainment. BBC1 1951–63/BBC2 1973–4/ITV 1984–90

Four celebrity panellists try to guess, from a contestant's mime, his or her line of work. Extraordinarily popular show, devised in the USA, where it ran for a quarter of a century, by Goodson and Todman, the kings of quiz.

CAST (hosts) Eamonn Andrews, David Jacobs, Penelope Keith, Angela Rippon /*cr* Mark Goodson, Bill Todman /*pr* T. Leslie Jackson, Dicky Leeman, Harry Carlisle, John Warrington, Richard Evans, Ernest Maxin, Maurice Leonard /*BBC TV: Thames* (UK) /approx. 400 x 30m bw:col.

When the Boat Comes In

Drama. BBC1 1976–7/1981

James Mitchell's 20s compulsive Tyneside saga following the likely-lad progress of Jack Ford (James Bolam) from demob at the end of WW1, through shipyard trade unionism, to attempted capitalism. At the end of the third season Ford left for the USA, to return (on the run from the FBI) for redemption: participation in the Jarrow March and the Spanish Civil War. The stick-in-the-memory theme ('you shall have a little fishy on a little dishy') was a reworking, by David Fanshawe, of a traditional northeast nursery rhyme.

CAST *Jack Ford* James Bolam *Jessie Seaton* Susan Jameson *Tom Seaton* John Nightingale *Billy Seaton* Edward Wilson *Dolly* Madelaine Newton *Lady Caroline* Isla Blair /*cr* James Mitchell /*pr* Leonard Lewis, Andrew Osborn, David Maloney /*wr* James Mitchell /*BBC TV* (UK) /51 x 50m col.

Whiplash

Western. ITV 1960–1

In the lawless 1850s an American establishes Australia's first stagecoach line, Cobb & Co.

Down-under Western, suprisingly good. Actor Peter Graves later resurfaced as ➢*Mission: Impossible*'s Jim Phelps.

CAST *Christopher Cobb* Peter Graves *Dan* Anthony Wickert /*ATV* (UK) 34 x 25m bw.

Whirligig

Children's. BBC 1950–6

Fortnightly Saturday afternoon variety show for the short-trousered crowd (the first such), presented by puppeteer Humphrey Lestocq ('Goody goody gumdrops') and his wooden assistant, Mr Turnip. Over the seasons the bill included the pioneering British sci-fi serial *Stranger from Space*, the animated *The Adventures of Hank* (a carefree cowboy and his hoss), conjuring with Geoffrey Robinson, Steve Race on the piano, ➢*The Sooty Show* with Harry Corbett and, in his TV debut, Rolf Harris with Willoughby, a drawing board with a life of its own. Among the writers were Peter Ling and Hazel Adair, later to create ➢*Crossroads*.

CAST (presenter) Humphrey Lestocq /*cr* Cecil Madden /*BBC TV* (UK) /approx. 110 x 60m bw.

Whirlybirds

Adventure. BBC 1958–62

Half-hour juvenile show with the (then new) conceit of two pilots operating a rent-a-chopper company, Whirlybird Service of Longwood Field, California. They were hired for crime-busting, daredevil rescues – in fact, anything that required airborne stunt action. Extremely popular in its day, with a directors' rota that included Robert Altman.

CAST *Chuck Martin* Ken Tobey *Pete 'PT' Moore* Craig Hill /*pr* N. Gayle Gitterman /*dr* inc Robert Altman /*Desilu* (USA) /111 x 25m bw /US tx CBS 1954–8.

Who Dares Wins

Comedy. C4 1984–8

Sketch show. It recalled ➢*Not the Nine O'Clock News* in its brashness (signified both by the comic use of the SAS motto as title and Tony Robinson's bum-naked appearances) and was less tied to topicality and politics than its alternative-comedy peers. A sequence of skits featuring two zoo pandas, variously plotting their escape (under the alias of a Belgian dentist) and abusing Japanese tourists, remains solid gold. All the cast went on to other things (even if it was only ➢*2 Point 4 Children* in the case of Julia Hills) and from the show evolved influential TV independent company Hat Trick.

CAST Tony Robinson, Julia Hills, Rory McGrath, Philip Pope, Jimmy Mulville /*wr* Rory McGrath, Philip Pope, Jimmy Mulville, Tony Robinson, Julia Hills /*Holmes* (UK) /24 x 30m col.

Whoops! Apocalypse

Comedy. ITV 1982

Black comedy about the globe plunging into WWIII thanks to the machinations and miscalculations of US President Johnny Cyclops (a lobotomized ex-actor from Omaha), Premier Dubienkin of the USSR and British PM Kevin Pork.

Had something of the appeal of *Dr Strangelove* about it and, in its day, was too possible for comfort.

CAST *President Johnny Cyclops* Barry Morse *Premier Dubienkin* Richard Griffiths *Kevin Pork* Peter Jones *The Deacon (US Security Advisor)* John Barron *Commissar Solzhenitsyn* Alexei Sayle *Foreign Secretary* Geoffrey Palmer *Lacrobat* John Cleese *Jay Garrick* Ed Bishop /*cr* Andrew Marshall, David Renwick /*pr* Humphrey Barclay /*dr* John Reardon /*wr* Andrew Marshall, David Renwick /*mus* Nigel Hess /*LWT* (UK) / 6 x 30m col.

Whose Line Is It Anyway?
Comedy. C4 1988–

Half-hour show of improvised comedy based on studio audience suggestions, these perfomed by alternating alternative comic stalwarts under the sceptical eye of chairperson, ex-barrister Clive Anderson (*Clive Anderson Talks Back*, *Clive Anderson All Talk*). Not the first impro TV show – that honour went to BBC2's *Impromptu* way back in 1964 – but enduringly popular and a BAFTA winner in 1991. Several of the perfomers went on to additonal TV things: Josie Lawrence in *Josie*; stone-face Paul Merton in *Paul Merton – The Series* and ➢*Have I Got News For You*; Mike McShane in *S & M* and *The Big One* (with *Whose Line* regular Sandy Toksvig); and the ever-busy Tony Slattery in *S & M* and *The Music Game*.

CAST inc Clive Anderson (chair), John Sessions, Paul Merton, Josie Lawrence, Greg Proops, Mike McShane, Tony Slattery, Ryan Stiles, Arthur Smith, Sandy Toksvig, Steve Frost, Jonathan Pryce /*cr* Dan Patterson & Mark Leveson /*exec pr* Denise O'Donoghue /*pr* Dan Patterson /*dr* Chris Bould, John F.D. Northover, Dan Patterson /*mus* Richard Vranch (piano accompaniment) /*Hat Trick Productions* (UK) / 120+ x 30m col.

Widows
Crime. ITV 1983

Tough-gal drama from Lynda La Plante about four women who stage the armed robbery of a security van in a subway, using the plan devised by their late spouses. Although this passed off successfully (with the villainesses flying down to Rio, money stashed in suitcases at the denoument) in a 1985 sequel, *Widows II*, lead felon, Dolly Rawlins discovered that her late husband was not actually dead – and wanted his share of the cash. A decade later *She's Out* followed Rawlins' life on release from prison, a new gang of cohorts around her and assorted unsavoury types trying to discover her hidden loot.

CAST *Dolly Rawlins* Ann Mitchell *Linda Perelli* Maureen O'Farrell *Bella O'Reilly* Eve Mottley *Shirley Miller* Fiona Hendley *DI Resnick* David Calder /*cr* Lynda La Plante /*exec pr* Verity Lambert, Linda Agran, Johnny Goodman /*pr* Linda Agran /*dr* Ian Toynton / *wr* Lynda La Plante /*Thames TV: Euston Films* (UK) / 6 x 60m col.

The Wilde Alliance
Crime. ITV 1978

Ho-hum attempt to make an anglicized ➢*The Thin Man*. Former ➢*The Main Chance* star John Stride played novelist-sleuth Rupert Wilde, who sallied forth from his Yorkshire mansion to solve comedy whodunnits in the company of comely spouse Amy. The material stretched to 13 episodes. Barely.

CAST *Rupert Wilde* John Stride *Amy Wilde* Julia Foster *Christopher Bridgewater* John Lee /*exec pr* David Cunliffe /*pr* Ian Mackinstosh /*dr* inc Marc Miller / *Yorkshire TV* (UK) /13 x 60m col.

Wild Palms
Sci-fi. BBC2 1993

VR mini-epic from Hollywood helmsman Oliver Stone (his first foray onto the small screen), standing as a dystopian vision of a future TV-dominated society. Set in a forbidding, fascistic Los Angeles of 2007, it starred James Belushi (brother of *The Blues Brothers*' John) as yuppie Harry Wyckoff, seduced into an executive job at the Channel 3 network where he is to produce a new holographic TV show, *Church Windows*. Soon, however, Wyckoff begins to understand that he is a mere pawn in the scheme of the messianic cult, The Fathers (led by C3's owner, Senator Anton Kreutzer), to take power via the influence of 3D TV and a mind-altering drug, Mimezine. *Wild Palms* itself, with its hallucinogenic images (a rhino in a swimming pool), baroque sets and paranoid labyrinthine plot, was dubbed 'the sort of television you have to have a drug problem to enjoy.'

Comparison with the other early 90s exercise in left-field weird TV, ➢*Twin Peaks*, was inevitable but unrewarding. A fine ensemble cast included Bebe Neuwirth (➢*Cheers*), Brad Douriff and an awesomely bewitching Angie Dickinson as the murderous grandmother, Josie Ito. Based on Bruce Wagner's comic strip of the same title.

CAST *Harry Wyckoff* James Belushi *Grace Wyckoff* Dana Delany *Senator Anton Kreutzer* Robert Loggia *Eli Levitt* David Warner *Josie Ito* Angie Dickinson *Tabba Schwartzkopf* Bebe Neuwirth *Chickie Levitt* Brad Douriff /*cr* Bruce Wagner /*exec pr* Oliver Stone /*pr* Michael Rauch /*dr* Peter Hewitt, Keith Gordon, Kathryn Bigelow, Phil Joanou /*mus* Ryuichi Sakamoto / *Ixtlan: Greengrass* (USA) /1 x 90m, 4 x 50m col /US tx Fox TV 1993.

The Wild, Wild West

Sci-fi. ITV 1968

Take an Old West setting, a dash of sci-fi gadgetry, a pinch of James Bond and a large measure of camp humour and, hey presto, you have *The Wild, Wild West*, a bizarre but wholly original TV show.

In the 1870s, so the premise went, the Wild Frontier of America was menaced by megalomaniac supervillains armed with such fantastic devices as A-bombs and submarines (all with Victorian Gothic cladding). To protect the USA, President Ulysses S. Grant despatched top secret agents James T. West (macho swashbuckler) and Artemus Gordon (inventor and master of disguise) aboard a luxury train which served as their mobile HQ. A periodic panic about TV violence brought cancellation of the show in 1969, though a subsequent thawing in the moral climate saw TVM revivals in 1979 with *The Wild, Wild West Revisited* and in 1980 with *More Wild, Wild West*, both alas without dwarf actor Michael Dunn (a suicide in 1973) who played the series' memorable mad scientist superfoe, Dr Miguelito Loveless. Something of *TWWW*'s fantasy-Western concept later surfaced in US show *The Adventures of Brisco County Jr* (*Boan: Cuse: Warner Bros* 1993–4, starring Bruce Campbell), in which the eponymous lawman tracks an outlaw across 1890s California, eventually revealed as a traveller from another dimension in search of a mysterious Orb which grants genie-like powers to its possessor.

CAST *James T. West* Robert Conrad *Artemus Gordon* Ross Martin *Dr Miguelito Loveless* Michael Dunn *Jeremy Pike* Charles Aidman *Tennyson* Charles Davis /*cr* Michael Garrison /*exec pr* Michael Garrison /*pr* Gene L. Coon, Paul Playdon, Fred Freiberger, Collier Young, Bruce Lansbury, John Mantley /*dr* inc Paul Wendkos, Irving J. Moore, Jesse Hibbs, Richard Sarafian, MArvin Chomsky, Alvin Ganzer /*wr* inc Gene L. Coon, Stephen Kandel, Edward J. Lasko /*mus* Richard Shores, Morton Stevens, Richard Markowitz / *Garrison: Lansbury: CBS* (USA) /104 x 60m bw:col / US tx 1965–9.

The Wind in the Willows

Children's. ITV 1984–8

Delightful animated musical version of Kenneth Grahame's classic 1908 tale of the adventures of Mole, Rat, Toad and Badger, spun off from a 90-minute feature made in 1983 (with Ian Carmichael as Rat). TV again returned to Grahame's Edwardian countryside with a 1995 animation voiced by Rik Mayall (Toad), Alan Bennett (Mole, naturally), Michael Palin (Rat) and Michael Gambon (Badger). A seamless 1996 sequel, *The Willows in Winter*, written by William Horwood, saw the furry friends in watery trouble with Mole swept away by the icy river.

CAST (voices) *Mole* Richard Pearson *Rat* Peter Sallis *Toad* David Jason *Badger* Michael Hordern /*pr* Mark Hall, Brian Cosgrove /*Cosgrove-Hall* (UK) /16 x 30m col.

The Winds of War

Drama. ITV 1983

Enormously long adaptation of Herman Wouk's doorstop in which US naval attaché Captain Victor 'Pug' Henry wanders Europe in 1939–41 as the, er, winds of WWII begin to envelop the USA and soapish problems turmoil his own family.

Pretty much panned on its release, it wasn't in truth so terrible, but the American ABC publicity department made the elementary mistake of a hype that could not be reached. Robert Mitchum was physically magnetic, and what the hell he delivered his lines as though speaking into a tannoy. A bigger (at 29 hours) and even costlier 1989–90 sequel, *War and Remembrance*, followed Henry and his clan's fortunes in WWII, from 1941–5 (with the help of 44,000 other actors). Unfortunately here the ➢*'Allo, 'Allo* factor kicked in, with Anglo-American actors reduced to ever-sillier foreign accents. The exception was John Gielgud as a Theresienstadt concentration camp elder, who opted for Shakespearean quavers.

CAST *Capt. Victor 'Pug' Henry* Robert Mitchum *Byron Henry* Jan-Michael Vincent *Warren Henry* Ben Murphy *Rhoda Henry* Polly Bergen *Madeline Henry* Lisa Eilbacher *Natalie Jastrow* Ali MacGraw *Berel Jastrow* Topol *Palmer 'Fred' Kirby* Peter Graves *Pamela Tudsbury* Victoria Tennant /*pr* Dan Curtis /*dr* Dan Curtis /*wr* Herman Wouk /*ABC* (USA) /1 x 240m, 7 x 120m col /US tx ABC 1983.

Wings
Drama. BBC1 1977–8

Adventures of three Royal Flying Corps pilots over the Western Front during WWI.

Never in the field of war drama has so little been made of so much. A sequence of clichés (not least the eventual acceptance of the prole-ish Alan Farmer by his gentlemanly comrades), stuck together with some – admittedly good – flying scenes.

CAST *Sgt/Lt Alan Farmer* Tim Woodward *Lt Charles Gaylion* Michael Cochrane *Capt. Triggers* Nicholas Jones *Lt Richard Bravington* David Troughton *Harry Farmer* John Hallam *Molly Farmer* Anne Kristen /*cr* Barry Thomas /*pr* Peter Cregeen /*mus* Alexander Faris / *BBC TV* (UK) /25 x 50m col.

Within These Walls
Drama. ITV 1973–8

Former British cinema 'bad girl' Googie Withers (aka Georgette Withers, wife of Australian TV producer John McCallum) starred in her debut small-screen series as Faye Boswell, liberalizing governor of fictitious Stone Park in this slice of everyday life in a women's prison. Depressing, with support acting of solid teak, it was only ever a moderate success, despite a subsequent reputation as one of the classics of 70s TV. Withers herself quit after two seasons (to be replaced as top billing by, successively, Katharine Blake and Sarah Lawson) and the show's enduring legacy might well prove to be its part in inspiring infamous sudster ➢*Prisoner: Cell Block H.*

CAST *Faye Boswell* Googie Withers *Helen Forrester* Katharine Blake *Susan Marshall* Sarah Lawson *Charles Radley* Jerome Willis *Chief Officer Mrs Armitage* Mona Bruce *Dr Mayes* Denis Hawthorne *Miss Clarke* Beth Harris /*exec pr* Rex Firkin /*pr* Jack Williamson /*dr* inc Philip Casson, Bill Bain /*wr* inc P.J. Hammond /*LWT* (UK) /44 x 60m col.

The Wombles
Children's. BBC1 1973

Furry, velvet-nosed creatures who lived in a burrow under Wimbledon Common, from which they ventured forth to collect and recycle human rubbish ('Making good use of the things that we find/Things that the everyday folks leave behind'). Invented by novelist Elizabeth Beresford, the Wombles – Great Uncle Bulgaria, Orinoco, Wellington, Bungo, Tomsk, Madame Cholet, Miss Adelaide and eccentric inventor Tobermory – had their adventures narrated for TV by a whimsical Bernard Cribbins; animation was by Ivor Wood. Mike Batt contributed the wombling theme, which became a chart hit in 1974; it was followed by such vinyl masterpieces as 'Remember You're A Womble', 'Wombling Merry Christmas' and 'Let's Womble to the Party Tonight'. A feature film, *Wombling Free* (*dr* Lionel Jeffries) was released by Ian Shand Productions-Rank in 1977.

Over a decade later *The Wombles* were dug up by ITV for a repeat run, the interest generating a 1991 half-hour special, *The Wandering Wombles*, in which the furrysome conservationists found that even the gardens of Buckingham Palace contained discarded trash.

CAST (narrator) Bernard Cribbins /*cr* Elizabeth Beresford /*dr* Ivor Wood /*wr* Elizabeth Beresford /*mus* Mike Batt (theme) /*Filmfair* (UK) /60 x 5m col.

The Wonder Years
Comedy. C4 1989–95

Sitcom about growing up in suburban America between 1968 and 1973, as seen through the eyes of teen Kevin Arnold (an effortlessly excellent Fred Savage) and narrated by the hindsight voice of his adult self (Daniel Stern). Use of news clips and music from the age of Flower Power and Vietnam upped the nostalgia though, in general, the show avoided cultural wallowing in favour of domestic drollery (sometimes poignant), concentrating on Arnold's relations with his siblings, parents and friends.

CAST *Kevin Arnold* Fred Savage/Daniel Stern (voice only) *Wayne Arnold* Jason Hervey *Jack Arnold (Dad)* Dan Lauria *Norma Arnold (Mom)* Alley Mills *Karen Arnold* Olivia D'Abo *Paul Pfeiffeer* Josh Saviano *Winnie Cooper* Danica McKellar /*cr* Neal Marlens, Carol Black /*exec pr* Bob Brush /*pr* Neal Marlens, Carol Black, Michael Dinner /*dr* inc Neal Marlens, Carol Black, Michael Dinner, Peter Baldwin, Steve Miner, Thomas Schlamme /*wr* inc Neal Marlens & Carol Black /*mus* Joe Cocker ('With a Little Help From My Friends' theme) /*New World International* (USA) / 115+ x 30m col /US tx ABC 1988–93.

Wonder Woman

Sci-fi. BBC1 1978–80/Sky1 1992

The superheroine from Paradise Island, 'lost' land of a band of Amazonians with amazing powers thanks to their discovery of magic mineral Feminum, first made her appearance in Charles Moulton's 1941 *bande dessinée*. She ventured into series TV (after two pilots) with the floating *The New Original Wonder Woman* in 1976 for American network ABC, with statuesque former Miss America Lynda Carter in the star-spangled bodice. With the offer of a regular berth, the show moved to CBS in 1977 as *The New Adventures of Wonder Woman*, for which the action was updated from WWII to the 70s. This gave Wonder Woman plenty of opportunity to make gutsy women's lib speeches (in one scene a woman declared 'I'll rely on myself, not a man'; 'Don't forget that,' WW replied approvingly) as she fought terrorists and other subversives for the undercover organization Inter-Agency Defense Command (IADC). Although the producers intended an all-action format, a certain ➢*Batman*-esque camp happily seeped in around the edges. Future Hollywood star Debra Winger received her career break in 1976 as *WW*'s younger sister, Drusilla, the Wonder Girl. In Britain the second US series (*The New Adventures*) was broadcast first, with debut series not receiving an airing until the early 90s by Sky1.

CAST *Wonder Woman/Diana Prince* Lynda Carter *Major Steve Trevor/Steve Trevor Jr* Lyle Waggoner *Gen. Phillip Blankenship* Richard Eastman *Queen Mother* Carolyn Jones *Wonder Girl/Drusilla* Debra Winger /*cr* Stanley Ralph Ross /*pr* Wilfred Baumes, John G. Stevens, Bruce Lansbury, Charles B. Fitzsimons /*dr* inc Alan Crosland, Seymour Robbie, Michael Caffey /*wr* inc Stephen Kandel, Alan Brennert /*mus* Charles Fox / *Warner Bros* (USA) /1 x 120m, 13 x 60m col (*TNOWW*); 1 x 80m, 45 x 45m col (*TNAWW*).

The Woodentops

Children's. BBC 1955–8

For 15 minutes every Friday *The Woodentops* filled the final segment of ➢*Watch with Mother*, relating the cosy adventures of the farming Woodentop family: Mummy, Daddy, Baby Woodentop, twins Willie and Jenny, plus Mrs Scrubit the char, Sam the farmhand, Buttercup the cow and, of course, the scene-stealing Spotty Dog, 'the biggest spotty dog you ever did see.' All came with wires clearly attached, pulled by Audrey Atterbury and Molly Gibson. The original series lasted only three years, but repeats kept *The Woodentops* on the air until 1973.

CAST (voices) Peter Hawkins, Eileen Brown, Josephina Ray /*cr* Freda Lingstrom, Maria Bird /*wr* Maria Bird /*mus* Maria Bird /*BBC TV* (UK) /approx. 160 x 15m bw.

The Worker

Comedy. ITV 1965–70

Starred comedian Charlie Drake (aka Charles Springall) as an incompetent unable to hold down a job, to the volcanic frustrations of the clerks of Weybridge Labour Exchange. Especially Henry McGee's Mr 'Poo' (Pugh).

Those who liked Charlie Drake loved it. Of whom, apparently the nation was awash, for the show was revived in 1969, and again in 1978 as part of LWT's *Bruce Forsyth's Big Night*.

Everyone else looked on askance.

CAST *Charlie* Charlie Drake *Mr Whittaker* Percy Herbert *Mr Pugh* Henry McGee /*pr* Alan Tarrant, Shaun O'Riordan /*dr* Shaun O'Riordan, Paul Annett / *wr* Lew Scharz, Charlie Drake /*ATV* (UK) /24 x 30m bw:col.

Worzel Gummidge

Children's. ITV 1979–81

Barbara Euphan Todd's famous talking scarecrow character from children's fiction was first televized in 1953 in the BBC's *Worzel Gummidge Turns Detective*. Over a quarter of a century on, Southern TV revived the calamity-attracting turnip-headed resident of Ten Acre Field, Scatterbrook Farm, for a series of popular kiddie comedies, energetically acted by Time Lord Jon Pertwee as Gummidge and Una Stubbs as his skittle-doll girlfriend. Also on the cast list were Barbara Windsor, Lorraine Chase and a youthful Charlotte Coleman (one day to emerge as a star of *Four Weddings and a Funeral*). Keith Waterhouse and Willis Hall penned the scripts. A New Zealand-produced sequel, *Worzel Gummidge Down Under*, screened on C4 1987–9, also starred Pertwee and Stubbs.

CAST *Worzel Gummidge* Jon Pertwee *Aunt Sally* Una Stubbs *Saucy Nancy* Barbara Windsor *Dolly Clothes-Peg* Lorraine Chase *John Peters* Jeremy Austin *Sue Peters* Charlotte Coleman *The Crowman* Geoffrey Blaydon /*cr* Barbara Euphan Todd /*pr* James Hill / *dr* James Hill /*wr* Keith Waterhouse & Willis Hall / *Southern TV* (UK) /52 x 30m, 1 x 60m col.

WRKP in Cincinnati

Comedy. ITV 1981–2

Set in a small – and ailing – Cincinnati radio station, *WRKP* focused on the lives of its staff, principally: modernizing programme controller Andy Travis; incompetent station manager Arthur Carlson; nerdy reporter Les Nessman; jive-talking jock Dr Johnny Fever; laid-back black DJ, Venus Flytrap; and sexy blonde secretary, Jennifer Marlowe.

Imagine ➢*The Mary Tyler Moore Show* set in the world of small-time rock wireless and you have it. Strange to relate, *WRKP* came from Moore's own *MTM* company.

Amusing time-passer, even if it wasn't original. A syndicated version, with three of the original characters (Nessman, Tarlek, Arthur Carlson) took to the American airwaves anew in 1991.

CAST *Arthur Carlson ('Big Guy')* Gordon Jump *Andy Travis* Gary Sandy *Johnny Caravella ('Dr Johnny Fever')* Howard Hesseman *Gordon Sims ('Venus Flytrap')* Tim Reid *Les Nessman* Richard Sanders *Herb Tarlek* Frank Bonner *Jennifer Marlowe* Loni Anderson *Mama Carlson* Sylvia Sydney /Carol Bruce /*cr* Hugh Wilson /*pr* Hugh Wilson /*dr* inc Jay Sandrich, Michael Zinberg, Asaad Kelada, Frank Bonner /*mus* Tom Wells /*MTM* (USA) /48 x 30m col /US tx CBS 1978–82.

Xena: Warrior Princess
Adventure. Sky2 1996–/C5 1997–

Sword-and-myth show, spun-off from ➢*Hercules: The Legendary Journeys*, in which warrior princess Xena (New Zealand actor and former miner, Lucy Lawless) renounces her bad-girl ways to quest after wicked warlords, man-eating centaurs and the like. Her sidekick is the sharp-tongued runaway, Gabrielle.

Verdict? About as much fun as one can have with a screen dominatrix. Created by horror film maestros Sam Raimi and Rob Tapert.

CAST *Xena* Lucy Lawless *Gabrielle* Renee O'Connor / *cr* Sam Raimi, Robert Tapert /*exec pr* Sam Raimi, Robert Tapert /*pr* R.J. Stewart /*Renaissance Pictures* (USA) /22+ x 60m col /US tx Syndicated 1995–.

The X-Files
Sci-fi. Sky1 1994–

'The truth is out there...'

Supernatural drama series about a pair of charismatic FBI agents, Mulder (former soft-porn actor David Duchovny, ➢*Twin Peaks*) and Dana Scully (Gillian Anderson) who investigated unexplained phenonema. The creation of former surfing writer Chris Carter, the show debuted to little fanfare, but grew into a world-wide cult, prospering through its freaky-deaky subject matter (which purported to be real: 'inspired by actual documented accounts'), air of post-Watergate government conspiracy, seductively easy filming style and mysterious characters (Deep Throat, Cigarette-Smoking Man) – not to mention a hefty helping of old-fashioned sexual tension. If dramatic quality was high, it was not consistently so. The factory-like demands of TV resulted in a tendency to narrative cannibalism and cliché. A segment entitled 'Firewalker' was a reworking of 'Ice', itself derived from John Carpenter's cinematic chiller *The Thing*. The episode 'Dod Kalm', in which Mulder and Scully suffered rapid ageing aboard a latterday *Marie Celeste*, was commissioned largely because the producers wanted to get their money's worth from the ship used in 'Colony' and 'End Game'. (Reasons of economy also caused the programme to be shot in Vancouver.) Meanwhile, the agents' endless lighting-up of eerie corners with their flashlights verged on the mirthful, as did their habitual stone-facedness. Still, *The X-Files* hit the Zeitgeist of the anti-rational, UFO-loving 90s more than any other TV show. It aired in countries as diverse as China (as *X-Dang An*) and Norway (*Salaiset Kansiot*). There was a splash of sad British look-alikes, among them ➢*Neverwhere* and *Bliss*.

The truth is out there ... Scully and Mulder in *The X-Files*, a show inspired by the 70s cult series *Kolchak: The Night Stalker*.

CAST *Fox Mulder* David Duchovny *Dana Scully* Gillian Anderson *Deep Throat* Jerry Hardin *Assistant Director Skinner* Mitch Pileggi *Cigarette-Smoking Man* William B. Davis /*cr* Chris Carter /*exec pr* Chris Carter, James Wong, Glen Morgan, R.W. Goodwin /*pr* Howard Gordon, Alex Gansa /*dr* inc Robert Mandel, Daniel Sackheim, Rob Bowman, Michael Katleman / *wr* inc Chris Carter, Glen Morgan, James Wong, Chris Ruppenthal, Chris Brancanto, Scott Kauffer /*mus* Mark Snow /*Ten Thirteen: 20th Century Television* (USA) /120+ x 50m col /US tx Fox TV 1993–.

The X-Men

Children's. Sky1 1993–

Kiddietime sci-fi animation, based on the 60s Marvel strip by Stan Lee and Jack Kirby.

The X-Men (the 'X' referring, suprise, surprise, to their X-tra capabilities) were a band of mutants who, under mentor Professor Charles Xavier, fought the dark forces of villainy which threatened to engulf humanity. A tendency on behalf of the X-men to personal angst gave the show a dimension beyond the usual cartoon conveyor-belt product, whilst the narrative thread that had an ungrateful humanity persecuting the X-Men for their mutancy was a positively perverse pleasure. Initially Cyclops, Storm, Rogue and Co debuted on *Spiderman and His Amazing Friends*; on being given their own show, they became a rocket-powered 90s success. Made by schlock supremos Saban, with Stan Lee himself as executive producer.

CAST (voices) Cedric Smith, Norm Spencer, Catherine Disher, Alison Sealy-Smith, Lenore Zann, Chris Potter, Cal Dodd, Alyson Court, George Buza / *exec pr* Stan Lee, Joe Calamari /*pr* Scott Thomas, Larry Houston /*mus* Shuki Levy, Kussa Mahci /*GRAZ Entertainment: Saban International Services* (USA) / 60 x 30m col /US tx Fox TV 1992–.

The XYY Man

Spy. ITV 1976–7

Was William 'Spider' Scott, a cat-burglar with a genetic defect (an extra Y chromosome, which allegedly inclined him to crime), who was recruited for dodgy jobs by MI5. Tense, persuasive thriller, adapted from Kenneth Royce's novel, which carried on the character of Scott's dogged nemesis, DS George Kitchener Bulman (Don Henderson, late of *Warship*) into ➢*Strangers*.

CAST *William 'Spider' Scott* Stephen Yardley *Fairfax (MI5 liaison)* Mark Dignam *DS George Bulman* Don Henderson *DC Derek Wills* Dennis Blanch *Maggie Parsons* Vivienne McKee /*cr* Richard Everitt /*pr* Richard Everitt /*dr* inc Ken Grieves /*wr* inc Murray Smith, Eddie Boyd, Ivor Marshall /*Granada TV* (UK) / 13 x 60m col.

Y

Yellowthread Street

Crime. ITV 1990

Followed the Triad-busting cases of a group of Royal Hong Kong Police Force detectives, based in the colony's Yellowthread precinct.

Try-something-different YTV crime show which never took, despite the exotic setting and sometimes lavish production. A clearly uncomfortable cast (seemingly selected for looks rather than screen gravitas) and throw-away plots did not help.

CAST *CI Alex Vale* Ray Lonnen *Det. Kelly Lang* Catherine Neilson *Det. C.J. Brady* Mark McGann *Det. Eddie Pak* Tzi Ma *Det. Jackie Wu* Doreen Chan *Det. Peter Marenta* Robert Taylor *Det. Nick Eden* Bruce Payne /*exec pr* Keith Richardson /*pr* Ranald Graham / *mus* Roger Bellon /*Yorkshire TV* (UK) /13 x 60m col.

Yes, Minister

Comedy. BBC2 1980–2

Satirical comedy featuring the Rt. Hon. James Hacker, (Paul Eddington, ➢*The Good Life*, d. 1995) the newly appointed Minister for Administrative Affairs whose idealistic schemes were always undone by his double-talking, all-powerful civil servant, Sir Humphrey Appleby, the Mephistopheles of Whitehall. The erudite, finely detailed scripts from Jonathan Lynn and Anthony Jay (who had seen inside the wormy can of British parliamentary politics during a spell on *Tonight*), with their elaborate dialogue exchanges, attracted praise from public and industry alike. Even politicians, though depicted as supine idiots in the control of the bureaucracy, liked it; such was the admiration of the then PM, Margaret Thatcher, that she enacted a scene with actor Paul Eddington at the National Viewers and Listeners Association Awards in 1984. Presumably this close encounter gave Lynn and Jay ideas, for by 1986 Jim Hacker had been elevated to the premiership in *Yes, Prime Minister* (1986–8, 16 x 30m). Accompanying him to Number 10 was Sir Humphrey (Nigel Hawthorne) promoted to Cabinet Secretary; also returning was put-upon Private Secretary Bernard Woolley (Derek Fowlds, late of ➢*The Basil Brush Show*). The new show lost one of the central comic principles of the old – Hacker's inbuilt fear of damaging his prospects for advancement – but continued to provide a half-hour of hilarity way above the norm of the British 80s sitcom.

CAST *Rt. Hon. James Hacker* Paul Eddington *Sir Humphrey Appleby* Nigel Hawthorne *Bernard Wolley* Derek Fowlds /*cr* Anthony Jay, Jonathan Lynn /*pr* Stuart Allen, Sydney Lotterby, Peter Whitmore /*wr* Anthony Jay, Jonathan Lynn /*BBC TV* (UK) /1 x 45m, 21 x 30m col /US tx The Entertainment Channel 1982.

Yogi Bear

Children's. ITV 1960–4

'Smarter than the average bear…'

A genial bear and his shy sidekick purloin 'pic-a-nic' baskets from vacationers to the Jellystone National Park. Much to the ire of perpetual adversary Ranger John Smith.

Hugely successful Hanna-Barbera cartoon, spun off from a segment in ➢*The Huckleberry Hound Show*, with the bears supported in their 30 minutes of madcappery by individual episodes featuring accident-prone lion *Snagglepuss* and dwarf duck *Yakky Doodle*. A number of shows and specials featuring Yogi Bear (named after NY Yankees pitcher Yogi Berra) followed, among them Hanna-Barbera's first full-length feature, *Hey There It's Yogi Bear* (1964) and *Yogi's Gang* (1973). In 1988 Yogi and Boo were revived for an all-new series for first-run syndication in the USA.

CAST (voices) *Yogi Bear/Snagglepuss* Daws Butler *Boo Boo/Ranger John Smith* Don Messick *Cindy Bear* Julie Bennett *Yakky Doodle* Jimmy Weldon *Chopper* Vance

Colvig /*cr* William Hanna, Joseph Barbera /*pr* William Hanna, Joseph Barbera /*wr* Warren Foster, Mike Maltese /*Hanna-Barbera* (USA) /123 x 25m col / US tx Syndicated 1958–62.

You Must be Joking!

Children's. ITV 1975–6

Something like a junior ➢*That Was The Week That Was*, two years of gags and skits, written and performed by teenagers from a children's theatre. Jim Bowen (later ➢*Bullseye*) was the token adult host; also presenting was 16-year-old Pauline Quirke (her future ➢*Birds of a Feather* partner, Linda Robson, was an occasional performer) whilst 14-year-old Gary Kemp supplied some of the music. He later tipped up in New Romantic band Spandau Ballet.

Not to be confused with the 80s BBC panel show of the same title, minus the exclamation mark.

CAST (presenters) inc Jim Bowen, Pauline Quirke / *Thames TV* (UK) /16 x 30m col.

The Young and the Restless

Melodrama. UK Living 1994–

Long-running American daytime soap, set in the fictional midwest metropolis of Genoa. It revolutionized the genre by foregrounding storylines geared towards younger audiences and by its constant breaking of taboo TV subjects: date rape, AIDs, bulimia, crack babies, alcoholism, all had their 60 minutes of infamy. David Hasselhoff (➢*Knight Rider*, ➢*Baywatch*) was amongst its cast of thousands.

cr William J. Bell, Lee Philip Bell /*exec pr* inc William J. Bell, Edward Scott /*pr* David Shaughnessy /*dr* inc Frank Pacelli, Randy Robbins, Heather Hill, Mike Denney /*wr* inc William J. Bell, Lee Philip Bell, Kay Alden, Jerry Birn, Jack Smith /*Columbia Tristar* (USA) / 700+ x 30m, 1200 x 60m col /US tx CBS 1973–.

The Young Ones

Comedy. BBC2 1982–4

Innovative and surreal sitcom which grew out of the 'alternative comedy' movement of the early 80s. Set in a squalid student household (complete with a pair of speaking rats) it followed the antics – in so as far as they made sense – of a quartet of cartoon caricatures: trendy Rick, lentil-loving hippy Neil, ultra-violent punk Vivyan and the paranoid wide-boy, Mike. Together, the eternal students kicked hell out of each other – and the dominant ideology. Loosely structured, episodes also found time for guest bands during an interval, and menaces from the landlord, Jerzy Balowski (Alexei Sayle). The title derived from 'The Young Ones' song by Rik's hero, Cliff Richard. Mayall and Edmondson continued the infantile, anarchic humour of *The Young Ones* in ➢*Bottom*, and ➢*Filthy Rich and Catflap*, while Planer moved on to the more mainstream products of ➢*King and Castle, Bonjour La Classe.* ➢*Shine On Harvey Moon, Nigel Craig*, and ➢*The Magic Roundabout.* Also sprung to success by the show was writer Ben Elton, and a helping hand was given to the myriad future stars who passed through in comic cameos: Paul Merton, Dawn French, Stephen Fry, Hugh Laurie, Emma Thompson, Robbie Coltrane, Norman Pace, Gareth Hale, Lenny Henry and Jennifer Saunders among them.

CAST *Rick* Rik Mayall *Vivyan* Adrian Edmondson *Mike* Christopher Ryan *Neil* Nigel Planer /*pr* Paul Jackson /*wr* Rik Mayall, Ben Elton, Lise Meyer (plus Alexei Sayle) /*mus* Peter Brewis /*BBC TV* (UK) / 12 x 35m col.

You Rang, M'Lord?

Comedy. BBC1 1988–93

Croft and Perry spoof of ➢*Upstairs, Downstairs*, set in the Edwardian London household of the nice but dim Lord Meldrum; the servants were led by the swindling Alf Stokes (Paul Shane from ➢*Hi-De-Hi!*).

Effective enough to last for five years, but then so was the plague. It was disconcerting, to say the least, that half the cast seemed to be still in role from previous Croft and Perry sitcoms (Donald Hewlett's Meldrum was his ➢*It Ain't Half Hot, Mum*'s Colonel Reynolds in mufti) and most of the jokes were conspicuous by their absence. There was, though, a narrative surprise at the last, when the Meldrum family became impoverished – their Union Jack Rubber plantation was eaten by beetles – and were obliged to sell up.

CAST *Alf Stokes* Paul Shane *Lord George Meldrum* Donald Hewlett *James Twelvetrees* Jeffrey Holland *Ivy Teesdale* Su Pollard *Hon. Teddy Meldrum* Michael

Knowles *Mrs Lipton* Brenda Cowling *Poppy Meldrum* Susie Brann *Cissy Meldrum* Catherine Rabett *Lady Lavender Meldrum* Mavis Pugh *The Honourable Teddy Meldrum* Michael Knowles *PC Wilson* Bill Pertwee *Henry* Perry Benson *Mabel* Barbara New *Sir Ralph Shawcross* John Horsley *Lady Agatha Shawcross* Angela Scoular /*cr* Jimmy Perry, David Croft /*pr* David Croft / *wr* David Croft, Jimmy Perry /*mus* Bob Monkhouse, Paul Shane (theme vocals) /*BBC TV* (UK) /1 x 60m, 25 x 50m col.

Your Cheatin' Heart

Drama. BBC1 1990

John Byrne's follow up to ➢*Tutti Frutti* was a six-part musical shenanigan in which waitress Cissie Crouch (Tilda Swinton) employed restaurant journalist McClusky (John Gordon Sinclair) to prove the drugs-charge innocence of her Country & Western-singing husband, Dorwood.

Which made for a delicious, can-swigging caricature of the C&W scene and the Glasgow underworld – but it took four episodes at least for Sassenach ears to be able to decipher the broad brogue. The music was also less well integrated than in *TF*.

CAST *Cissie Crouch* Tilda Swinton *Dorwood Crouch* Kevin McMonagle *Frank McClusky* John Gordon Sinclair /*cr* John Byrne /*pr* Peter Broughan /*dr* Michael Whyte /*wr* John Byrne /*BBC TV* (UK) /6 x 50m col.

Z Cars

Crime. BBC1 1962–78

Seminal drama series, dreamed up by writer Troy Kennedy Martin when he was bed-bound during a bout of mumps. To pass the time Martin listened to police radio, which caused him to realize that the cosy staple of British crime-time TV, ➢*Dixon of Dock Green*, was out of date.

Developed with the help of documentarists Elwyn Jones and Robert Barr, the resultant *Z Cars* was set in the docklands of Liverpool (Kirby became the overspill estate new town for the series) and depicted in gritty urban detail the professional lives of a squad of panda-car drivers. Controversially, these policemen were depicted as fallible humans; in episode one, heralded by the flute-and-drum theme 'Johnny Todd', a frustrated PC Steele was seen beating his wife, and PC Lynch asking for the result of a horse race. The Police Federation, among others, complained (even though much of the subject material was supplied by former officers), but within two months the series was attracting an audience of 14 million. James Ellis, Colin Welland, Brian Blessed and Leonard Rossiter became household names, and two other early stars, Stratford Johns and Frank Windsor, were given their own series, ➢*Softly, Softly*. *Z Cars* lasted until 1978 when, in turn, it began to look dated against such tyre-squealing, door-kicking shows as ➢*The Sweeney*.

CAST *DI Charlie Barlow* Stratford Johns *PC Jock Weir* Joseph Brady *PC/DC Bert Lynch* James Ellis *PC Bob Steele* Jeremy Kemp *PC Sweet* Terence Edmond *PC David Graham* Colin Welland *DS John Watt* Frank Windsor *PC 'Fancy' Smith* Brian Blessed *DI Bamber* Leonard Rossiter *DI Witty* John Woodvine *DI Todd* Joss Ackland *PC Owen Culshaw* David Daker *PC Alec May* Stephen Yardley *DI Brogan* George Sewell *WPC Bayliss* Alison Steadman /*cr* Troy Kennedy Martin /*pr* David E. Rose, Richard Beynon, Ronald Travers, Ron Craddock /*dr* inc John McGrath, Ken Loach, Shaun Sutton, Terence Dudley /*wr* inc Troy Kennedy Martin, Alan Plater, Allan Prior, Elwyn Jones /*mus* Johnny Keating ('Johnny Todd' theme) /*BBC TV* (UK) / 667 x 25:50m bw:col.

Zero One

Crime. BBC1 1962–5

Followed the smartly-made cases of airline detective Alan Garnett, chief London operative with the International Air Security Board (call sign: 'Zero One'). It was co produced by MGM but, er, crashed in the USA where sponsors shied away from its narrative matter of sky-jacks, trafficking and sabotage.

CAST *Alan Garnett* Nigel Patrick *Maya (secretary)* Katya Douglas *Jimmy Delaney* Bill Smith /*pr* Lawence P. Bachmann /*BBC: MGM* (UK /USA) /39 x 25m bw / US tx Syndicated 1964.

Zig and Zag's Dirty Deeds

Children's. C4 1996–

The fuzzy-felt puppets – aliens from Planet Zog – first landed on Ireland RTE's show *Den TV*, then switched to C4's morning flagship *The Big Breakfast*, before finally going it alone in *Zig And Zag's Dirty Deeds*. Here the vindictive, neon-toned twosome performed 'mission impossibles' for filthy lucre on behalf of celeb clients: Chris Evans hired them to stage a musical 'Gingerella', boy band Upside Down hired their services to wreck the career of rivals BoyZone … it was like *Challenge Anneka*, but without the laughs. Scatological and imcomprehensible, not worth wasting time on. Unless you were eight and under, or found 'poo' a funny word.

pr Simon Wright /*dr* Angelo Abela /*Working Title* / 6+ x 30m col.

The Zoo Gang

Crime. ITV 1974

Thirty years after the end of WWII a crack French Resistance cell – the Zoo Gang – reassembles to track down a Nazi war criminal. The job done, the four – Tommy Devon, Stephen Halliday, Alec Marlowe and Manouche Roget – set about cleaning up common-or-garden crime on the Côte d'Azur.

Star-bright, script-dull adaptation of Paul Gallico's novel. The theme music was by Paul and Linda McCartney.

CAST *Tommy Devon (codename: Elephant)* John Mills *Manouche Roget (Leopard)* Lili Palmer *Alec Marlowe (Tiger)* Barry Morse *Stephen Halliday (Fox)* Brian Keith *Lt Georges Roget* Michael Petrovitch /*pr* Herbert Hirschman /*mus* Paul & Linda McCartney (theme) / *ATV: ITC* (UK) /6 x 60m col /US tx NBC 1975.

Zoo Time

Children's. ITV 1956–68

Educational and entertaining weekly series about animal behaviour, standardly presented by Dr Desmond Morris (and Congo the artistic chimp, one of whose paintings was once bought by Picasso...) from the den at London Zoo. For the last seasons the location switched to Chester Zoo, with Chris Kelly introducing. The show set a trend for wildlife programming for children, which continued through *Animal Story* (1960–2 also with Desmond Morris), *A to Zoo* (1960–1) and *Breakthrough* (1961), to reach its classic expression in Johnny Morris's ➢*Animal Magic.*

CAST (presenters) Desmond Morris, Jimmy Hanley, Harry Watt, Chris Kelly /*pr* Milton Shulman, Derek Twist, David Warwick, Peter Mullings /*Granada TV* (UK) /331 x 30m bw.

Zorro

Western. ITV 1958–60

Zorro, masked swordsman of Old California, first appeared in a 1919 short story 'The Curse of the Capistrano' by Johnston McCulley, and was the hero of several motion pictures (played by, among others, Tyrone Power and Douglas Fairbanks Sr) before Walt Disney sent him to defend the poor oppressed peons on the small screen. Accompanying Zorro (whose *alter ego* was foppish aristo Don Diego de la Vega) was mute sidekick Bernado and their respective steeds Phantom and Tornado. One-note plots, plenty of dashing action, an easily recognizable comic-baddie in hapless Sergeant Garcia and thoughly bad-baddie in Captain Monastario, made for a splendid Western actioner for kids. The theme ('Zorro – the fox so cunning and free/ Zorro – make the sign of the Z!') was recorded by Henry Calvin (Sgt Garcia) and was later a hit for the Chordettes.

Two cinema features were made from episodes, *Zorro the Avenger* and *The Sign of Zorro*, both released in 1958. In 1983 a Walt Disney sequel appeared, *Zorro and Son*, but this played it for laughs rather than thrills, the premise being that the masked crusader (Henry Darrow, ➢*The High Chaparral*, ➢*Harry O*) was now too aged to swing from the chandeliers. A more traditional interpretation was offered by a new *Zorro* series aired in the USA in 1990, with Duncan Regehr as Zorro and Efrem Zimbalist Jr (➢*77 Sunset Strip*) as his father, Don Alejandro.

CAST *Don Diego de la Vega ('Zorro')* Guy Williams *Bernardo* Gene Sheldon *Sgt Garcia* Henry Calvin *Capt. Monastario* Britt Lomond *Anna Maria Verdugo* Jolene Brand *Don Alejandro* George J. Lewis /*cr* Walt Disney / *exec pr* Walt Disney /*pr* William H. Anderson /*dr* inc Norman Foster, Hollingsworth Morse, William Whitney /*mus* George Burns (theme), William Lauar / *Walt Disney Productions* (USA) /70 x 26m bw /US tx ABC 1957–9.